Human Behavior and the Social Environment

HUMAN BEHAVIOR AND THE SOCIAL ENVIRONMENT

Models, Metaphors, and Maps for Applying
Theoretical Perspectives to Practice

James A. Forte
Salisbury University

THOMSON

BROOKS/COLE

Australia • Brazil • Canada • Mexico • Singapore • Spain
United Kingdom • United States

THOMSON

✦

BROOKS/COLE

Human Behavior and the Social Environment: Models, Metaphors, and Maps
for Applying Theoretical Perspectives to Practice
James A. Forte

Acquisitions Editor: Dan Alpert
Assistant Editor: Alma Dea Michelena
Editorial Assistant: Ann Lee Richards
Technology Project Manager: Julie Aguilar
Marketing Manager: Meghan McCullough
Senior Marketing Communications Manager: Tami Strang
Project Manager, Editorial Production: Marti Paul
Creative Director: Rob Hugel
Art Director: Vernon Boes
Print Buyer: Judy Inouye

Permissions Editor: Roberta Broyer
Production Service: Melanie Field, Strawberry Field Publishing
Photo Researcher: Eric Schrader
Copy Editor: Margaret C. Tropp
Cover Designer: Paula Goldstein
Cover Image: Jacey/Getty Images
Cover Printer: Thomson West
Compositor: Interactive Composition Corporation
Printer: Thomson West

Printed in the United States of America
1 2 3 4 5 6 7 10 09 08 07 06

Library of Congress Control Number: 2006924108

ISBN 0-495-00659-9

Thomson Higher Education
10 Davis Drive
Belmont, CA 94002-3098
USA

For more information about our products, contact us at:
Thomson Learning Academic Resource Center
1-800-423-0563
For permission to use material from this text or product,
submit a request online at
http://www.thomsonrights.com.
Any additional questions about permissions can be
submitted by e-mail to
thomsonrights@thomson.com.

To Eileen

Contents

PART II | MODELS, METAPHORS, AND MAPS APPLIED

CHAPTER 4 **Applied Ecological Theory**   117

CHAPTER 5   **Applied Systems Theory**   164

CHAPTER 10   **Applied Symbolic Interactionism**   369

CHAPTER 13 Applied Critical Theory 496

LIST OF TABLES

LIST OF FIGURES

FOREWORD

Dr. James Forte has written a critically important book for the profession. It is a work that represents a prodigious output of time and energy, and for this he is to be strongly commended. It is a scholarly work of high relevance for students, teachers, and practitioners. It is a volume that stresses the complex topic of a dialogical approach to theoretical pluralism, a much sought for hallmark of current practice.

It is a positive, enthusiastic volume that shows pride in the profession, but a pride tempered with the humbling reality of coming to terms with a vastly expanding body of what we know and what we do not know. This reality puts us assuredly in the family of the senior professions that also have similar challenges of diversity and interprofessional opportunity.

Clearly he is a teacher. Throughout the volume he keeps students in mind, as demonstrated by the consistent and thorough way each chapter is designed with useful sections, subheadings, and challenging questions. However, although not stated, there is an implication and understanding of a reality of which all of us as practitioners in the human services are continuously aware. We are to be students the rest of our lives. In this way the volume is of import to us all, at all levels and in all settings. It will be of particular use to colleagues long out of school who were educated from a unitheory base but who have learned that one can no longer retain this position. Rather, it is critical to develop a broad and diverse theory base.

He shows a welcomed and comprehensive understanding of the term *theory* and of its many dimensions. This leads to an understanding of the various ways in which theories relate to practice, an area where I believe we have sometimes been naively simplistic and thus have underserved our students.

Near the end of the book Dr. Forte tells us that he once worked with his cousin as a carpenter's helper and from this experience learned about the importance of tools and their differential utility. This theme of the importance of a multitude of tools for practice is reflected throughout the chapters. Of particular note is his position that theory is a tool and that our challenge in today's practice is how to come to terms with the rich plurality of theories that drive our profession. We need to incorporate their power into our practice, thus expanding our set of tools.

Throughout he comes to the task from the basis of the big picture of our body of knowledge. In this regard an important and unifying theme is that the very nature of our profession, unlike many others, demands a vast and diverse body of knowledge. Our practice requires that we look broadly at virtually all professions for concepts that aid us in the understanding of our clients and their realities, in order to develop strategies for responsible intervention.

His material, built upon a solid basis of ecological thinking, is very well organized and richly referenced. From this common base and his strong conviction of the utility of eco-maps, Dr. Forte takes the reader through a series of ten theoretical positions each of which is analyzed from a common and integrated framework. I was pleased to note that one of the ten that he selected, from the many others that could have been included, was role theory. I mention this because I have always believed it was an important theory that came into prominence only for a short time and for some unknown reason quickly faded from the scene. However, this presentation underscores the richness of this theory and of its continuing utility and importance for today's practice.

A particularly important component of the presentation of each theory is the inclusion in each chapter of a rich yet compact three or four biographies of the important figureheads in the development of the theory, including in each instance some of our own professional family. I believe this component of the book will be of particular interest to students. It should help them in the development of a strong positive self-image as they see how we can comfortably take our place with stars from other disciplines. It shows that not only have we received from others but we have contributed much in the development of theory.

He rightly warns us against the futility of interfamilial intertheoretical rivalries and turf wars, cognizant that such rivalries have marked virtually all disciplines. Such rivalries have inhibited the advancement of knowledge both within and between discipline boundaries.

From the perspective of this volume's utility as a course text, Dr. Forte has added a cluster of Learning Activities at the end of each chapter. These will be of use both to students and to teachers. His use of the first person and his style of speaking directly to the reader will be appreciated by beginning students. Although he does not address directly the question of student level for which he views this work to be principally directed, it appears from the early pages to be designed for students new to the profession. However, I suggest that, although not stated, it will be useful to students at all levels.

In seeking to develop a text for students new to the profession, I suggest that Dr. Forte underestimates the extent to which much of his material will also be of great utility to all levels of practice and in particular to doctoral students. One of the realities as the profession advances is the place of the doctorate and its growing importance and prevalence. With the rapid expansion of our body of knowledge both in quantity and complexity and the depth of analysis required to incorporate and develop knowledge, more and more of our colleagues are and will be seeking doctoral studies. In fact, with the reality of interprofessional knowledge exchange and the demands for sophisticated research in all fields, undoubtedly the doctorate in social work in the not too distant future is to become the required degree for professional qualification.

We need to be proud of our theoretical development over the last hundred years. We need to continue to advance our knowledge and practice bases in quality, sophistication, interconnectedness, and enhanced applicability. Dr. Forte has made a major and significant contribution to this process. We congratulate him and wish him well.

Francis J. Turner
Professor Emeritus
Wilfrid Laurier University

PREFACE

Cybernetics, niche, deoxyribonucleic acid, schemas, catharsis, unconditioned stimulus, sociality, salience hierarchy, externalities, praxis—these are concepts.

In rapidly changing social environments, morphogenetic social systems are more likely to attain desired goals than morphostatic social systems. Members of low-status groups are more often labeled deviant by official organizations than members of high-status groups. Maintaining a position of aesthetic distance during the working through of the emotional response cycle is associated with adaptive grief management. The total change of entropy in an open system can be represented by the equation $d_S = d_eS + d_iS$. These are propositions.

Blending the family systems perspective with a family development framework generates the following interrelated predictions about male members of National Guard families. Family system change reverberates; therefore, family life cycle stages will be correlated with similar changes at the personal, dyad, and family system levels. There will be a curvilinear relationship between family stages and men's reported personal happiness. There will be a curvilinear relationship between family stages and men's reported marital satisfaction. There will be a curvilinear relationship between family stages and men's reported perception of family cohesion. This is a theory stated in testable form.

Let's pause a minute and try to make sense. A language is composed of words, sentences, and paragraphs. Theories are composed of concepts, propositions, and statements about the logical relationship of its set of concepts. Theories are the languages that scientists and applied scientists (social workers, for example) use to communicate with one another and to solve intellectual and practical problems. Theories can be very difficult to understand.

I suspect that when you read the first three paragraphs of this preface, you felt as though you were in ancient Greece, distant Mongolia, or a colony of alien Klingons. What do these theoretical words, sentences, and paragraphs mean? The language of theory presented in Human Behavior and the Social Environment (HBSE) classrooms and in HBSE textbooks often seems foreign and incomprehensible to social work students. In this book, I will enact the role of translator and help you learn how to read and listen to odd-sounding theoretical words, sentences, and paragraphs.

Translation is the process of transforming an incomprehensible statement or text into clear and familiar language. At the turn of the 20th century, Chicago was a city of many languages. Some of the first social workers at Hull House served as language and cultural translators for Russian, German, Italian, Greek, Irish, and Polish immigrants to that great city. By the turn of the 21st century, professional practice has become a world of many theoretical languages, akin to multiethnic and multiracial Chicago nearly a century ago, reminiscent of the biblical story of the Tower of Babel. Social workers must learn to speak the languages of clients, allies from other professions, and knowledge developers in other disciplines.

Part One of this book will introduce you to a new way of understanding theories and theorizing and to a set of tools for translating theoretical languages. Chapter 1 describes a dialogical approach to scientific knowledge building and problem solving. I report also on the many languages spoken by social workers and our professional allies, and I identify the theorizing competencies for advancement toward multilingual social work.

Theory translation can be within a theory or across theories. Within-theory translation transforms the subtle or complex ideas of a theory into clearer and simpler ideas and displays. Cross-theory translation transforms the words of one theoretical language into the words of a different theoretical language. Chapter 2 introduces three within-theory translation devices. I show how social workers can use exemplary models, root metaphors, and theoretical models to better understand theoretical languages. I also provide my own model for connecting theory to practice and a set of practical suggestions for learning new theoretical languages. Chapter 3 introduces three more translation tools. Theoretical mapping facilitates within-theory translation by transforming a theory into its basic building blocks and into simple diagrams. Ecosystems mapping facilitates cross-theory translation by transforming foreign theoretical languages into the social work language of ecosystems. Universal social work standards facilitate cross-theory translation and appraisal by evaluating how well different theoretical languages conform to our profession's scientific, value, and ethical preferences.

In Part Two, I demonstrate how to use these translation tools to understand ten theoretical languages, and how to translate these theoretical languages into the ecosystems terminology common to social workers. Chapters 4 and 5 translate the two major theoretical components of the primary social work language, the ecosystems paradigm: ecological theory and systems theory.

Chapters 6 through 9 translate theories that social workers often use with micro-size systems, especially the individual person. Chapter 6 summarizes my translation of applied biology. Chapter 7 interprets applied cognitive psychology for social work use. Chapters 8 and 9 make sense of applied psychodynamic ego psychology and applied behaviorism, respectively.

Chapters 10 (applied symbolic interactionism) and 11 (applied social role theory) translate theoretical languages often used for social work practice with medium-size social systems: the group, the family, and the network.

Chapter 12 translates applied economic theory, and Chapter 13 translates applied critical theory. These theoretical languages provide direction to practitioners helping systems of all sizes, but they have special value for practice with larger systems such as organizations, communities, and governments.

To ease your work in learning these ten new languages, Chapters 4 through 13 are all organized in the same way. Each chapter will cover:

- Related dialects and schools of thought
- Exemplary role models (useful theorists and scholarly social work practitioners)
- Root theoretical metaphors for the social environment, the person, and the social worker
- Core assumptions, including theoretical perspectives on human development
- A theory-specific eco-map
- Translation of the theoretical language into the ecosystems language of total environment, systems, connections, resources, resource flow, change, diversity, and ideal conditions
- A critical appraisal, using social work's universal standards
- A theory-specific model for practice
- Learning activities

In Part Three, Chapter 14, I introduce the idea of theoretical integration, the purposeful blending of theoretical languages as needed for different professional tasks. A set of tables comparing the ten theoretical frameworks by conceptual model, root metaphor, theoretical map, and ecosystem map is provided to facilitate the cross-theory translation essential to theoretical integration.

Professional social work education will prepare you in many ways. Your practice courses prepare you to help community members solve problems and realize their aspirations. Your policy courses prepare you to analyze current policy and to advocate for better policies. Your research courses prepare you to collect and make sense of data. For what do your courses in human behavior and the social environment prepare you? Many social work educators assume that the purpose of these courses is for students to learn and remember the knowledge base of the profession.

In this book, *Human Behavior and the Social Environment: Models, Metaphors, and Maps for Applying Theoretical Perspectives to Practice,* I make a different assumption. I suggest that your human behavior courses should prepare you for theorizing. This includes theory knowledge but also theory comprehension, theory analysis, theory synthesis, theory evaluation, and most important, theory application (practical theorizing) and theory communication. Theorizing proficiency will enrich your research, your policy work, and your practice. Therefore, I will introduce you to essential theoretical knowledge (as do other HBSE textbooks), but I will also share with you a set of translation tools—models, metaphors, and maps—that can prepare you for an exciting and effective social work career in a multitheory world. Join with me and let's enlarge your professional toolkit so that you can bring many methods, many roles, many skills, and *many theories* to your work as a generalist social worker.

ACKNOWLEDGMENTS

I thank the theorists who have served as my role models. David Franks, a great symbolic interactionist, shared his love for theorizing and applying theories whenever we were together, even on the racquetball court. Francis Turner, the great social work theory popularizer, demonstrated the value of a multitheory approach. Hans Falck, group worker and social work theorist with few peers, taught me much about membership and metatheorizing. My social work students at Christopher Newport University were immensely helpful. In five years of Human Behavior and the Social Environment classes, they listened, responded, and reacted (generally with enthusiasm) to my pilot eco-map lectures and learning activities on theories and theorizing. I am indebted to the members of the Baccalaureate Program Director's (BPD) Human Behavior and the Social Environment Topic Group. Wayne Evens, Carol Brownstein-Evans, and Mary Rawlings have consistently offered me their insight, teaching experience, and support. I thank the following reviewers for their careful and extensive reflections on earlier eco-maps for this book, for their encouragement, and for their gently phrased criticisms: Carol Brownstein-Evans, SUNY Brockport; Wayne C. Evens, Bradley University; Mindy Murphy, University of Kentucky Hospital; and Adelle Sanders, Governors State University. I am appreciative of the wise counsel, the technical expertise, the enthusiastic support, and the vision of innovative textbook writing provided to me by Lisa Gebo, my Thomson Brooks/Cole editor. I also gratefully recognize Melanie Field, Peggy Tropp, Alma Dea Michelena, and the other book production specialists who helped convert my manuscript into its final form. Dean Dennis Patanizek and Chairperson Marvin Tossey at Salisbury University have encouraged my work, sponsored my trial runs at many conferences, and provided a forum for sharing my writing with colleagues.

Thanks.

About the Author

James A. Forte is Associate Professor at the Department of Social Work, Salisbury University, Salisbury, Maryland. He is the author of *Theories for Practice: Symbolic Interactionist Translations* and many articles on the application of theory in areas such as homelessness, domestic violence, bereavement, volunteer service, web-based advocacy, and multicultural practice. He has a special interest in symbolic interactionism and has written on the history of partnerships between interactionists and social workers, on interactionist metatheory, and on applied symbolic interactionism (a chapter in the *Handbook of Symbolic Interactionism*). His interests include the use of social and behavioral theories; the history of collaboration among pragmatists, interactionists, and social workers; and constructionist models of personal and public problem solving. He was recipient of the Outstanding Virginia Social Work Educator Award, Virginia Social Work Education Consortium, October 14, 1994. He received the President's Award for Outstanding Teaching at Christopher Newport University in 1996.

An Introduction to Theory and Practical Theorizing

1

INTRODUCTION

Remember the old fairy tale about Little Red Riding Hood. One day, this young village girl puts on a red cape and hood, accepts some cake from her mother, and sets off to see her sick grandmother. In the woods, she tells a friendly wolf about her plans for a visit. The wolf arrives first and eats the grandmother. Then, the wolf disguises himself in bed with a nightcap and sheets. Little Red Riding Hood arrives and asks her grandma why her arms, and her legs, and her ears, and her eyes, and her teeth are so big. The wolf answers the last question with "the better to eat you with," jumps out of bed, and swallows Little Red Riding Hood. Later, a hunter hears the wolf's snores, enters the house, and realizes that the wolf might have devoured the old woman. The hunter takes a knife and slices open the wolf's belly. Little Red Riding Hood and her grandmother come out safe and whole. Little Red Riding Hood vows never again to venture into the woods without her mother's permission.

Let's imagine that this story, like many fairy tales, tells us something about social life, perhaps about child abuse. Several different theoretical interpretations of the story's meaning have been offered (Gardner, 2000). Some of the first psychoanalysts argued that this is a story about a girl's premature sexuality. They used the terminology of psychoanalytic theory in their explanation. The girl experiences conflicted impulses. She desires both to have sex with her father (the wolf) and to follow the dictates of her conscience (the mother). The hunter's opening of the wolf's womb represents the pregnancy and the birth that will follow the girl's loss of virginity.

Later, some psychoanalysts called Neo-Freudians offered a variation on this interpretation. They used a revised psychodynamic vocabulary. The red cape symbolizes a girl's menstrual blood. Little Red Riding Hood is maturing and seeking an opportunity to act on her sexual impulses. But Little Red Riding Hood is like the female patients who struggle with a psychological disorder. She is frigid and hates men. The ridiculing of the wolf by clothing it in granny's outfit and the final murder of the wolf, the Neo-Freudians said, symbolizes the female's triumph over males. Contemporary psychoanalysts, by the way, would use a different theoretical language. They would offer interpretations of this fairy tale that show sensitivity to Little Red's concerns about coping with real-life challenges and that highlight the need to support her threatened ego.

Here is one last interpretation. Feminists think that the story tells us about the prevalence of rape and violence in a sexist community. Little Red Riding Hood does not suffer from unconscious desires for sex and danger. She does, however, have the strength and intelligence to fight off predators. A feminist interpreter might also change the story's ending. Our female heroine refuses to be exploited or oppressed. In the new version, Ms. Hood immediately recognizes the wolf. The girl confronts the impostor, takes a pepper spray can out of her pocket, and temporarily blinds her assailant.

Social workers can learn some important lessons from my discussion of this story about Little Red Riding Hood. Theorists talk about and explain the predicaments faced by our clients in many different ways. Each theoretical perspective or language uses a distinctive vocabulary and offers a particular approach to assessment (free association to identify repressed impulses versus social criticism of the pervasive negative effects of female inequality, for instance). Each theoretical perspective recommends a distinctive action strategy for improving the situation (lengthy psychoanalysis versus collective social action), and each offers a theoretically based characterization of the worker role (passive or active, expert or partner, detached or involved). A professional team serving the Hood family, for instance, would include members with different theoretical vocabularies, different understandings of the client's problems and of the best solutions, and different conceptualizations of the ideal design of the worker–client relationship. Today, social workers provide services in a multitheory practice world, and we need to be familiar with the perspectives and languages of many different theoretical communities.

THEORIZING AND GENERALIST SOCIAL WORK

Thank you for deciding to become a social worker. You are joining a group of professionals dedicated to understanding and helping members of various sized social organizations. Social workers apply knowledge to enhance the quality of social membership and to ameliorate social problems. Social workers also try to change membership organizations so that they will be more just, democratic, and caring. However, many unsolved public problems and serious community needs remain. The money and other resources available for social work are very limited. Your energy, intelligence, and commitment can make a difference.

The job of the contemporary social worker is very complicated. Social workers are **generalists** who work to help community members realize their membership potentials in many different ways. Social workers as generalists learn how to enact many roles: the roles of advocate, counselor, teacher, researcher, administrator, policy analyst, and mediator (Baker, 1976; Kirst-Ashman & Hull, 2001; Miley, O'Melia, & DuBois, 2001). Generalist practitioners can help individuals, families, groups, communities, organizations, social movements, societies, and international associations (Johnson & Yanca, 2001; Kirst-Ashman & Hull, 2001; Locke, 1998; Miley et al., 2001). Generalists possess multiple skills: skills for micro-, mezzo-, and macro-level practice (Kirst-Ashman & Hull, 2001). Generalists are prepared to help people in very different settings: rural, urban, or suburban (Derezotes, 2000). Social work generalists learn to help people at every stage of the life course. We appreciate the multidimensionality of the human experience, and we try to respond to each client as a whole person with physical, psychological, social, economic, and spiritual concerns. Social work generalists work in many fields, for various formal and informal organizations, and on interdisciplinary teams with all sorts of short-term and permanent partners. Social work generalists develop the sensitivity and competencies necessary for effective work with people from varied cultural and social membership groups.

Social work generalists are resourceful, versatile, adaptive, and multi-talented. Generalists may differ in the particular configuration of knowledge, skills, and attitudes that each brings to the practice setting. However, generalists are united as social workers and share a **common base:** the profession's mission, value preferences, and ethical guidelines; a mastery of the planned change process and problem-solving skills; and a commitment to social justice and to a strengths perspective (Johnson & Yanca, 2001; Landon, 1995). We are like a big and complicated democratic society. We differ in many ways, yet we are united by our core social work identity and our commitment to work together for personal and social betterment.

The common base includes a commitment to use knowledge to guide our professional activity. A social worker learns to become a generalist in approaching scientific knowledge, too (Kirst-Ashman & Hull, 1999). The Council on Social Work Education, for example, requires educators to teach you to "use theoretical frameworks supported by empirical evidence to understand individual development and behavior across the life span and the interactions among individuals and between individuals and families, groups, organizations, and communities" (2001, p. 6).

The profession's toolbox includes a set of tools of special importance called theories. **Theories** are ways of organizing or structuring knowledge for use by practitioners. Theories enable us to understand and improve membership behavior and conditions. Social work generalists should learn about many different theories and then select from their professional toolboxes (collections of theories), so that they have the best tool for each social work job. Some social workers even become advanced generalists or specialists. Such training prepares the social worker for masterful use of complex theories as tools for working on extremely intricate and challenging membership problems. Social work educators, researchers, and practitioners have created many theory-based tools that can help you become a great generalist social worker or a specialized expert.

Because the social work job is so complex, social workers often borrow and adapt theoretical tools developed by experts in other disciplines. Practitioners also work with members of other occupational groups, such as psychiatrists, physicians, nurses, realtors, priests and ministers, teachers, bankers, corporate executives, accountants, police officers, judges, and lawyers. These partners in practice generally speak theoretical languages different from those used by social workers. This primer is for novice generalists, social workers learning to use theories for practice. It will make it possible for you to use many different theories and theory-based tools, and to communicate effectively with those from other professions and disciplines.

During a professional career, many social workers supplement their generalist training with preparation for a professional **specialization.** You might eventually specialize in a particular field of practice such as correctional social work, or a social problem area such as addictions, or a method such as family counseling (Landon, 1995). Social workers can specialize also in theorizing and become expert in using multiple theoretical language and practice models

(Derezotes, 2000, p xi; Schatz, Jenkins, & Sheafor, 1990; Tolson, Reid, & Garvin, 1994). I believe that this book will be useful also to specialists-in-training.

A DIALOGICAL APPROACH TO THEORETICAL KNOWLEDGE

In this section, I will introduce you to my theory about theories and theoretical knowledge. This **metatheory** is the philosophical foundation for the approach to *Human Behavior and the Social Environment* used in this book. The prefix *meta* means "about" or "beyond" (Zhao, 2001). A theory's subject matter is something in the physical and social environment—for example, the problems experienced by children with insecure attachments. A metatheory goes beyond a theory. A metatheory's subject matter is the structure of the theory or the process of theorizing. Metatheorizing is the systematic study of the knowledge base of a discipline or profession (Ritzer, 1991).

To start our discussion of the dialogical metatheory, let's assume that science, scientific knowledge, and the scientific method are critical to contemporary social work practice (Reid, 2001).

SCIENCE IS A LANGUAGE

A language is "a system of symbols that expresses and shares meaning" (Bloom, Wood, & Chambon, 1991, p. 530). Science is a language, but it is a language that is different in many ways from everyday English. Scientists communicate by using complex symbol systems, including natural language, diagrams, graphs, figures, gestures, and sometimes mathematics (Sarukkai, 2002). Scientists talk, write, and draw on blackboards to communicate their ideas (Duncker, 2001). Scientific articles and books summarize these ideas in words and images, and the publications of scientists often use multiple communication devices including sentences, statistics, and visual displays to represent research processes, empirical findings, and theories. Theories are a major part of the language system that scientists and applied scientists use for scientific problem solving (Fararo, 1989).

SCIENTIFIC PROBLEM SOLVING IS A CONVERSATION

The knowledge-building enterprise of science can be compared to a conversation among diverse speakers (Gergen, 1982). Brown (1992) comments on this dialogical approach: "like all of human experience, science is a conversation that takes place over time in which accounts of what is, what has occurred and what is true of the past and present are negotiated through symbolic interaction" (p. 227). Scientists are participants in problem-solving conversations. From this perspective, "the theorist is fundamentally a source of linguistic activity" (Gergen, 1982, p. 95).

Like pluralistic communities characterized by a diversity of languages (take a walking tour of lower Manhattan in New York City, for example, and you will hear English, Spanish, Chinese, and numerous other languages), science is characterized by **theoretical pluralism** (Duncker, 2001). Universities and other academic settings, scientific conferences, and human service arenas where scientific knowledge is applied include members aligned with various disciplines and professions. Each discipline and profession speaks a distinctive theoretical language and develops a unique culture. The languages of theoretical communities overlap to some extent. Behavioral and social exchange theorists make similar assumptions and share some terminology. Applied scientists all share "science" as a reference point. However, clear and identifiable differences are apparent in the ways that members of each language community interpret and talk about human behavior and the social environment.

Each theoretical tradition within science has a distinctive language with its own central metaphors, core concepts, categories, typical sentences, implicit rules of grammar, pronunciations, dialects, and preferred displays. Speakers of different theoretical languages most frequently interact in networks of like-speaking scholars, researchers, and practitioners (Watson, 1985). Novices learn a language of scientific theory by association with full members of their disciplinary or theoretical community (Gergen, 1982). Membership in a particular practice association or scientific network (ego-psychological clinical social workers or behaviorally oriented correction workers, for instance) includes the obligation to use the "right" language (Wagner-Pacific & Bershady, 1993). Members of different professional groups speak different scientific languages and have some difficulty communicating across theory-based language communities (King & Fawcett, 1997). I will show later that the total universe of theoretical languages is expanding rapidly.

The social work profession, like the world of science, is also characterized by the use of multiple languages (Bloom et al., 1991). In the United States, most social workers speak the basic or native language, English. Social workers must also learn and respond to the lay languages of their clients. Social workers use the empirical language of scientific research. The profession has transformed its ideals into a distinctive language of values and ethical guidelines. Social workers develop jargon specific to their field of practice or professional specialty, such as the many technical terms that I used when working in the criminal justice system. The abstract language of theory serves as an important tool for social workers. Like scientists, social workers must learn to speak diverse languages and to translate from one kind of language to another as part of their professional training.

A DIALOGICAL APPROACH TO SCIENCE

The development and use of scientific knowledge involve dialogue and debate. Unfortunately, not all discourse among scientists or applied scientists is positive. Sometimes, the more powerful speakers talk loudest and prevail despite the weak merits of their position (Payne, 1997). At other times, social scientists and practitioners may misunderstand or ignore the contributions of their predecessors or their colleagues (Maines, Bridger, & Ulmer, 1996). Some theory creators and users communicate like gangsters (Scheff, 1995). They align themselves with a "school of thought" and seek career advancement by constantly signaling loyalty to their theoretical group by using its specialized jargon and by provoking turf wars with other theorizers. Some scientists prefer a monologue to two-way exchanges. Scientific conversation may be characterized not by dialogue but by hostile and competitive interaction, verbal attacks, and nonrecognition of or indifference to those showing enemy colors. Many scientists and scientific practitioners only like to converse with like-minded members of the same theoretical traditions, disciplines, and research networks. Theoretical strangers are avoided.

The public problems addressed by scientists and social workers have a complexity, chronicity, and cost that necessitate high-quality and convivial conversations (Deegan, 1989). Practical necessity justifies trespassing across linguistic boundaries and requires the facilitation of cross-theory conversations (Zlotnik et al., 1999). I advocate in this book, therefore, for a **dialogical approach** to knowledge building and scientific problem solving. Theoretical or scientific dialogue has several important features (Camic & Joas, 2004; Safran & Messer, 1997). During a dialogue, participants listen carefully to each other and try to understand the assumptions, perspectives, and models of those who speak other theoretical languages. Participants learn from contact with members who use different vocabularies and hold different viewpoints. In dialogue, participants test their theoretical convictions through open-minded communication with others, and participants value mutual criticism. Scientific dialogue welcomes many voices. All persons with a stake in the scientific or practical problem can speak and will be listened to in a respectful manner. Dialogical conversations aim for better problem solving and improved science.

Social workers apply scientific knowledge to ameliorate social problems and to enhance the quality of social membership. Social workers can use the dialogical approach and learn to speak with partners from many different disciplines, even when these partners talk in "foreign" tongues (Zlotnik et al., 1999). Zlotnik and her social work colleagues reported, for example, on a collaborative project that applied science to solve public problems. Interdisciplinary teams shared their knowledge and then advocated for child-focused, family-centered public policies for the economically marginalized in the neighborhoods of South Central Los Angeles. Disciplinary partners brought different theoretical perspectives to these collaborative problem-solving efforts. The effective social workers on this team were multilingual.

COMPONENTS OF THE DIALOGICAL APPROACH

My communication approach to theorizing draws upon the intellectual traditions of pragmatism and symbolic interactionism. Five concepts are useful in characterizing the ideal knowledge-based and dialogical practice community

(Mead, 1934): the universe of discourse, communication capacities, the larger self, the pragmatic test of truth, and the working hypothesis.

Successful community life—whether in a neighborhood of different ethnic or racial groups or among a set of human service professionals—requires the development of a **universe of discourse,** or standardized and common language (Weigert & Gecas, 1995). This is a set of significant symbols or shared meanings that allow members with different backgrounds to understand each other and to work together. Through much of Europe, for instance, people speak English as well as their native language. The use of English as a common language for cross-cultural interaction enables interactants to complete the business at hand without sacrificing the distinctive cultural viewpoint embedded in their own languages. A friend of mine is an engineer. He works on teams with various cultural backgrounds, but they all use the language of engineering science and thus can cooperate on very demanding projects. This idea of a common discourse system or language can be applied to the challenge of learning multiple theoretical frameworks.

Much social work practice occurs in settings where participants speak different theoretical languages. These settings are like the trading zones created by two nations that share a border. Trading zones are places where envoys from each nation meet to barter and trade their special goods (Sarukkai, 2002). In these trading zones, interactants must begin to learn their counterparts' language or, more commonly, to create new words and devices for communicating. The common language is like a creole, a communication system originating from contact between two different speech communities. Even when trading agents hold totally different viewpoints, the interlanguage makes cooperation and exchange possible (Duncker, 2001). Social workers have developed the ecosystems perspective as a common language to facilitate communication between social workers about a wide range of activities "so that knowledge and information about practice can accumulate systematically" (Specht, 1977, p. 34). In the ten theory chapters in this book, I will demonstrate the value of ecosystems terminology as a theoretical universe of discourse, or common language.

Second, professional socialization for participation in a diverse community of scientists or practitioners entails the progressive enhancement of **communication capacities** related to perspective-taking skill and inclination (Schwalbe, 1988b). Perspective taking is similar to the social work concepts of empathy and "tuning in." It entails grasping a given situation as perceived, conceptualized, and communicated by another person. An engagement with diverse others (or with multiple theories) can increase students' perspective-taking propensity, the motivation to understand the social world as theorized by those different from them. Engagement with diverse others can also expand students' perspective-taking powers: perspective-taking depth, the capacity to grasp the central assumptions, images, ideas, and models used in a theoretical language; perspective-taking accuracy, the capacity to decode correctly the language of particular theories of interest; and perspective-taking range, the capacity to identify, understand, and use a variety of theoretical traditions to

FIGURE I.I
MULTIPLE
PERSPECTIVES
AND SOCIAL
WORK
PRACTICE

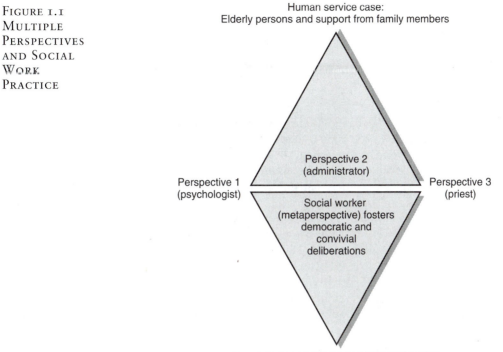

Human service case:
Elderly persons and support from family members

Perspective 2
(administrator)

Perspective 1
(psychologist)

Perspective 3
(priest)

Social worker
(metaperspective) fosters
democratic and
convivial
deliberations

Convergence on inquiry and intervention plan

guide professional action. After developing perspective-taking skills and dispositions, team members from different educational backgrounds will be motivated and able to view a practice challenge from each other's viewpoint, even when members are speaking different theoretical languages.

Teams that listen to and understand multiple descriptions of ways to deal with challenges related to person–environment transactions are often more successful than teams that listen to one perspective (Barker, 2000). Figure 1.1 illustrates how a social worker might consider the perspectives of multiple others before helping to formulate an assessment and intervention plan for an elderly client. Each of the theory chapters in this book will take this dialogical approach to practice and offer a different perspective on a practice problem. In each theory-based chapter, I will discuss also how we might listen to and learn from that perspective as it guides the planned change process.

Third, ideal communities have many members with "**larger selves**" and few with "narrow selves" (Mead, 1929/1964). Using the imagery of size, Mead suggests that people can expand or shrink the self depending on their attitude toward incorporating the perspectives of diverse others. Social workers with narrow selves restrict their interaction to a few like-minded others, or they communicate in shallow ways with people who are different. They resist any threats to established ways of thinking, and they do not grow as professionals. Social workers who desire to enlarge their selves engage in dialogue with diverse others and import the voices of adherents to many theoretical perspectives into their personalities. Consequent reflection on such outer and inner dialogues sharpens their intelligence, increases their tolerance, expands their range of identifications, promotes their sense of commonality with those who are different, and deepens their sensitivity to the many forms of human suffering. Later in the chapter, I will identify several different stances toward theories and theorizing. The atheoretical, the theoretical monists, the proselytizers, and the dilettantes fail to develop their professional selves through theoretical dialogue. The theoretical internationalists are committed to enlarging their professional selves.

Fourth, the dialogical approach is **pragmatic.** Knowledge should serve practical ends and be useful for the community and its members. This philosophy of pragmatism demands that social work teachers and practitioners evaluate and choose theories based on how well the theories address pressing challenges, not because the theories have the most powerful spokespersons, or they bring the greatest status, or they make the most sophisticated use of mathematical models, or because they use complicated and important-sounding terms. The best theories are the most useful theories. Useful theories increase the number and quality of insights into membership problems, and they help practitioners improve clients' everyday membership experiences. The focus of this book will be on useful knowledge: applied science and applied theory.

Finally, the dialogical approach to knowledge building and problem solving proposes a scientific and **experimentalist stance.** Communities of practitioners who talk to each other about theory application and use theory to solve client problems need to record the effectiveness of their theory tests. This means that we continually generate theoretical "working-hypotheses" (Mead, 1899/1968), reasonable and provisional conjectures about strategies for interdisciplinary teamwork and for helping projects. And we continually subject these theoretical conjectures to evaluation. Ineffective theories must be improved or abandoned. Each theory-based chapter will include a summary of the critical responses to the theory and a discussion of its strengths, limitations, and practical effectiveness.

THEORY TRANSLATOR: A NEW SOCIAL WORK ROLE

Settlement workers used a dialogical approach to increase their understanding of and empathic identification with the poor (Forte, 2002a). These workers lived in the neighborhoods of their clients and discovered the problems of the community by becoming "an understanding part of it" (Mead, 1907–1908, p. 3). Over time, the language and meanings held central by the immigrants and other struggling neighbors became intelligible to the social workers. Settlement workers learned to translate American society to the help-seeking members of Hull House. Some even became language instructors and taught English (Addams, 1910/1990). Successful instruction helped members make sense of the bewildering experiences of urban Chicago. Successful language translation made work in factories possible, and decreased the likelihood of starvation and early death. Addams (1895/2002) reported, for instance, on a first meeting between Russian Jews who were trained tailors and the American-Irish girls who were moving into this industry without training and for lower wages. She noted "they were separated by strong racial differences, by language, by nationality, by religion, by mode of life, by every possible social distinction." Addams added, however, that "the interpreter stood between the two sides of the room" (p. 51) and worked hard to help the two groups realize their economic and social interdependence.

Social workers like Addams and Jesse Taft developed useful translation techniques (Deegan, 1992). These workers created the method of "communication by current event." Immigrants were taught to participate in debates about local problems and news stories. Discussion leaders supported the expression of distinctive national and cultural perspectives, yet encouraged members to develop a shared consciousness about major issues. Settlement workers also experimented with "communication by art." Different groups in multicultural Chicago were helped to use theater, textiles, music, and folklore to communicate about cherished symbols and meanings to other Chicagoans. "Communication by public gathering" invited diverse neighbors to participate in religious celebrations, festivals, and holiday rituals. People from different generations, cultures, and neighborhoods learned the traditions of those who spoke other languages. These programs helped participants create a sense of shared community based on the acknowledgment of differences and commonalities. Hull House became "an information and interpretation bureau" that "acts between various institutions of the city and the people for whom these institutions were erected" (Addams, 1910/1990, p. 99).

Community building also required that social workers at the settlement houses render the immigrant's meaning understandable to the local, middle-class citizens who had been ignorant or hostile. Such translations were necessary to defend members, to engage neighbors in solving public problems, to obtain support for legislation, and to announce the accomplishments of Hull House programs. Jane Addams was a premier interpreter. She translated the members' experience to academic audiences. She contributed to social studies about poor and immigrant neighborhoods enriched by the sympathetic contributions of neighborhood residents. These collaborative reports served as translations of alien languages and cultures that made unintelligible issues and experiences intelligible to the English-speaking political and academic leaders and other members of the regional community.

Translation for practice purposes is important. Social workers have also developed strategies for translating research (Allen-Meares, Hudgins, Engberg, & Lessnau, 2005; Hudgins & Allen-Meares, 2000). Borrowed from medical scientists, translation research is "the practice of translating basic science data or discoveries from the laboratory bench into clinical applications aimed at treating various diseases" (p. 2). Translation research builds a bridge connecting the professional arenas (and different languages) of practitioners and researchers. Research translators can help practitioners and community members who see no use for social work research findings. The translator works to make empirical studies accessible and applicable by creating simple and short summaries, for instance. The translator also works as a member of collaborative teams of researchers, theorists, direct service practitioners, and policy makers and shows how empirical information can contribute to public problem-solving activities.

THE NEED FOR THEORY TRANSLATION

Theory translation is necessary for a variety of reasons. Theories are often stated in obscure and unclear ways (Burr, 1973). Theorists use very abstract and general terms that are hard to apply to the particulars of situations faced by social workers. Some theorists use ill-defined terms (Lazarus & Messer, 1991). Some use well-defined terms in unusual ways. Some use very specialized terms that are quite unlike words from natural languages.

Theory translation is necessary because so many theoretical languages are useful to social workers, and because the major theoretical languages are alive and changing continually. New terms are constantly added, and outdated terms dropped (Specht, 1977). Theory translation is necessary because there are so many theories, and because explanations are tailored to and used in so many different social contexts, including team meetings, sessions with clients, and discussions with family members (Turner, 1980). No one social worker can master the vocabularies of all these languages. Most professional training is in only one language or in a very limited number of theoretical languages. Translators who specialize in particular languages can help.

Translation is necessary but difficult because some theoretical language communities are isolated from others. Opportunities for refining meanings based on cross-theory conversations are limited. Work teams are often composed of professional members who speak different theoretical languages and have limited contact with each other. Helping groups are composed of social workers who speak a professional language and clients who speak their everyday language. Work teams and helping groups are prone to communication breakdowns. Attention to translation issues is very important (Kuhn, 1970). Cooperation with team members and clients is prone to misunderstanding, noncomprehension, and belated understanding. The esoteric and idiosyncratic parts of the different scientific, professional, and layperson languages cannot be brought together easily. Language differences usually indicate underlying cultural differences. A translation between theoretical languages is not a simple matter because it takes extra effort to translate both the words and the cultural particularities of diverse language users (Duncker, 2001).

Social work has a special need for theory translators. Our profession "may be the multilingual profession par excellence because it deals with many dialects of lay language, borrows heavily from many basic sciences, uses research findings and methods from a variety of disciplines, is involved in value considerations from diverse points of view, and has chaotic and uncontrolled jargon" (Bloom et al., 1991, p. 530). Coady and Lehmann (2001b) concur, and they "support the long-range goal of translating theories into ordinary English in order to further demystification and to facilitate cross-theory dialogue" (p. 415).

THE ROLE OF THEORY TRANSLATOR

Bloom (1975) views translation as central to social work problem solving: "the major task of using theories from the literature is to find them . . . to know how to understand them, and, finally, to translate them into direct strategy statements" (p. 162). **Translation** is the act of translating from one language into another, rendering meanings intelligible across languages (Forte, 2002a). A translator is a person who specializes in providing equivalent terms in a target language for the terms in a source language (Sarukkai, 2002). Theory translators are "people who are in touch with the best in theory and research, who can translate this into effective programs, and who can evaluate these programs. Translators are thus social scientists who have a commitment to theory-and-research-based action for people" (Egan, 1979, p. 15). Translators are specialists who take on the tasks of familiarizing themselves with the vast classic and contemporary theoretical literature, translating diverse theoretical languages into the common ecosystems language, and disseminating translation dictionaries among practice educators and practitioners. These theory interpreters are the tour guides who aid novice scholarly practitioners as they travel to new theoretical locations (Forte, 2001).

The following discussion identifies the role behaviors associated with the job of theory translator. The translator works to identify the terms and phrases that may be clear within one language group but cause difficulties when members of different language communities are interacting (Kuhn, 1970). The translator aids participants in work teams and helping groups as they try to take each other's perspective and understand what the other is trying to say. The translator can help participants learn the basics of each other's language. The translator can convert the theoretical language of one subgroup into the terms of the other group. The translator can help participants develop a common and shared vocabulary. The translator can also help the participants in a multitheory dialogue begin to learn the craft of translation so that they can undertake efforts on their own to clarify misunderstandings.

The translator translates complex theoretical languages for use by individual practitioners (Burr, 1973). The translator translates theoretical languages and professional jargon into plain English for the sake of clients. The translator translates scientific languages into language understandable by the general public so that the knowledge and skills developed by social workers can be shared with a wide audience (Egan, 1979). I will enact the role of translator in this book.

Scientific translation is of several types (Sarukkai, 2002). In translation within one language system, the translator uses different and simpler words, phrases, or other symbols to communicate the meanings of one language. Each of my theory chapters will provide a translation of the theoretical language into everyday language, and into simple metaphors, models, and maps. Translation across two language traditions is the translation from one language to another language. A social worker learns to think, feel, and act in line with the profession's native or natural language but needs to assimilate a variety of other theoretical languages (Wierzbicka, 1997). In each theory chapter, I will try to convert the foreign language of the theory into the more natural social work language of the ecosystems paradigm.

LEVELS OF THEORETICAL LANGUAGE

A theory is a language, and languages are made up of words. Words are abstractions (Chafetz, 1978). The word *dog* is not the same as the wet, smelly, cocker spaniel that you are petting. Theoretical languages are formalized at different levels of abstraction. When identifying the varied approaches to social work theorizing, we might imagine a range from the most abstract and encompassing level to the most concrete and specific level; from the most complex organization of abstract ideas, a paradigm, to the least complex organization, hunches about observations stated in simple terms (Rule, 1997). Let's begin the process of translation, then, by identifying the different levels of theoretical language.

PARADIGM

Social workers do not completely agree on the definition of the concept *paradigm*. The concept has many different definitions (Ritzer, 1975). Kuhn (1970) defines a paradigm as a coherent collection of beliefs and theories, or a worldview that has become accepted unquestionably and established as truth. It helps to think of theory in terms of its scope or ambitiousness. A **paradigm** has the greatest scope. It is a particular way of viewing the world shared by members of a community, a shared and coherent tradition (Kuhn, 1970). Marshall (1994) defines scientific paradigm as a "consensus across the relevant scientific community about the theoretical and methodological rules to be followed, the instruments to be used, the problems to be investigated, and the standards by which research is judged" (p. 376). A paradigm might be compared fruitfully to the culture of a language community. Cultural members agree about the sacred symbols and images of the community. Members of a disciplinary or professional community agree that the paradigm offers the best image of the community's focal subject matter.

Paradigms differentiate one community from another. The paradigms identified by social scientists that divide communities, for example, include the prescientific paradigm (the cultural belief systems and patterns of Australian aborigines, for instance); the positivistic paradigm, an approach that guides many social work researchers who report on statistical findings from their "objective" studies; and the interpretive or postpositivistic paradigm, the approach of some scientists and practitioners who use words to characterize the "subjective" aspect of a client subculture (Reid, 2001). Most social workers are familiar with the ecosystems paradigm. This is a core part of our professional culture. Colleagues from different disciplines, such as economics or theology, or professional backgrounds, such as attorneys or architects, use paradigms very different from the ecosystems paradigm accepted by many social workers.

Ritzer (1975), an expert on sociological paradigms, asserts that contemporary science is best characterized as a multiparadigm science. Different paradigms compete for influence, and the supporters of the competing paradigms repeatedly question and challenge each other's allegiance. These paradigm battles, he adds, cause many problems. Scientists and practitioners may act according to a paradigm without realizing that they have made a choice and without considering the strengths of alternative paradigms. Adherents of a paradigm lose the ability to question their basic assumptions and detect unusual patterns or deviations from expectations. Paradigm supporters often exaggerate the explanatory power and usefulness of their paradigm. Adherents to a paradigm frequently criticize their rivals for not using the preferred paradigm to guide research, practice, and theory building. Because of this bias, they fail to understand why the rival did what he or she did and what the rival learned.

Ritzer (1975) concludes that a scientific community needs paradigm bridgers. These are theory users who can respect and make use of multiple paradigms, and who can attempt to show the possibilities for communication between those aligned with different paradigms. The concept of paradigm bridger is similar to my notion of theory translator. To write this book, I have tried to use my communication capacities to take the perspective of the advocates of each major theoretical language that I studied, and I will attempt to enact the role of a theory bridger for you, the reader.

THEORETICAL LANGUAGE OR TRADITION

A **theoretical tradition,** or "school of thought," refers to a group of scholars and practitioners who are united by their recognition of a special leader or founder. In linguistic theory, a school of thought could be compared to a speech community, a group of people who share a language and a set of rules for using the language (Romaine, 2000).

The theoretical tradition often began in a particular ecological setting— Chicago, the University of Chicago, and Hull House for the symbolic interactionist tradition. Members of a theoretical tradition make a commitment to a particular way of understanding social life, conducting scientific inquiry, and talking about theorizing. Adherents to a theoretical tradition generally regard their framework as a comprehensive organization of knowledge.

Let me elaborate on the idea that symbolic interactionism is a theoretical tradition. The tradition's origin is linked historically to George Herbert Mead and Jane Addams. It flourished at the School of Sociology in Chicago during the first half of the 20th century. It gives central importance to humans as symbol makers and symbol users. It uses a language full of concepts describing communication and interaction, and it endorses a participant-observation approach to scientific inquiry.

The institutions aligned with the school of thought are like language laboratories where students learn the tradition's language and how to use it. Schools of thought develop a teaching network with varied vehicles of communication to spread the language. The vehicles include universities, journals, websites, training centers and workshops, and discussion groups.

Theoretical traditions are sometimes called theoretical frameworks, theoretical perspectives, or theoretical orientations. When a theoretical language, or a collection of ideas associated with the theoretical language, are used to sensitize or orient social work practitioners to important aspects of reality, it is often referred to as a **theoretical perspective** (Skidmore, 1979). Here, we are using the theory for its general suggestions and explanations about a practice challenge. We might take the symbolic interactionist perspective on a family dispute and give priority to communication successes and failures, or we might shift to a structural functionalist perspective and think of the family dispute in terms of its function for the whole system.

Some theoretical traditions, such as psychoanalysis, even include subschools or variations on the themes of the overall framework. Schools of thought splinter into such subschools. Plural communication systems coexist within the comprehensive theoretical language. They are like the wings of a massive building where members develop their own lingo (Fararo, 1989). The idea of subschools is comparable also to the regional and social dialects or sublanguages found in a large speech community. English-speaking Americans, for example, vary by region in pronunciation, grammar, and vocabulary (Romaine, 2000). Interactionists have identified a Chicago School, an Iowa School, and a Berkeley School. Members of the various schools all understand the base language of interactionism, but members of these competing schools sound slightly different; they emphasize different theoretical concepts and different theorizing rules. Culturally competent social workers develop awareness of their clients' dialects. Theorizing competence requires awareness of the major dialects of each theoretical tradition. Each theory chapter in this book will identify variations on the chapter's major school of thought.

THEORIES

In everyday language, *theory* refers to a belief, an insight, or a hunch about something in the world. We might develop a theory about why a friend is angry or why the boss doesn't promote us. Scientific theory is somewhat different. Here are a few orienting definitions: A theory is a "systematic set of ideas which provides explanation and which also must be generalizable" (Thompson, 2000, p. 24). A theory is a set of "plausible relationships proposed among concepts and sets of concepts" (Strauss & Corbin, 1994, p. 279). Rule (1997) defines theories as "statements of contingency that hold across some variety of contexts" (p. 204).

Theories are the important explanatory stories developed by members of a scientific language community. A theory is a guide to the unknown that can help the theory user explore and gain a grip on parts of the world that would otherwise seem random and unknowable. A theory is a tool for coping with the social relationships, processes, and structures prevalent in our environment. We might hear or read about a theory at various developmental points, from the complete and carefully refined theory to the incomplete or partial theory requiring further refinement.

GRAND OR GENERAL THEORIES   A few theorists—Talcott Parsons, for example—have attempted to create grand and complete theories, a theory about everything (Rule, 1997). Instead of trying to understand a particular kind of society or a dimension of human experience, the theorist builds a framework for understanding social life in all its permutations. General theories, Burr (1973) explains, "have great scope and high informative value, and they are not specifically tied to any social context" (p. 280). Grand theories are often very complex, and they are stated at a very general level of abstraction (Tomey, 1998).

THEORIES IN A TOPIC AREA   These theories are more modest than a theoretical tradition or grand theory. They organize knowledge about a particular topic. Symbolic interactionists, for instance, have theorized extensively about topics such as socialization, reference groups, and face-to-face interaction. Theorists construct topic area theories to solve practical puzzles or theoretical problems (Skidmore, 1979). Social workers might use such theories when they try to understand a particular set of client challenges, such as those related to the biopsychosocial development of adolescents in a low-income neighborhood or to recent increases in a region's violent crimes.

MIDDLE-RANGE THEORIES   These theories are also modest in scope rather than grand. A middle-range theory organizes a set of concepts and propositions in a way that enhances our understanding of a specific aspect of the social world. Middle-range theories lend themselves to empirical testing. Edwin Sutherland and his successors, for example, advanced a differential association theory of delinquent behavior (Matsueda, 1988). This mid-range theory explains a youth's decision to engage in antisocial conduct. Sutherland theorized that a person's associates powerfully influence his attitudes and behavior. Adolescents who begin to interact frequently with those who consider carjacking, shoplifting, and mugging as acceptable activities soon define these behaviors in the same way. Youth who associate with models of prosocial, responsible thinking and behaving tend to refrain from delinquent conduct. Burr (1973) notes that middle-range theories are less context-free and less generalizable than general theories.

PRACTICE THEORIES   Another use of the term *theory* refers to the practice theories developed and tested by social work specialists. These theories are also called *practice models* or *models of practice*. Instead of organizing knowledge about human behavior in the social and physical environment, these theories organize knowledge about the social work helping method. Payne (2002b) asserts that practice models "seek to explain in organized ways how social workers may usefully act, using their knowledge about the social world in which they operate" (p. 123).

Practice wisdom is an individual and informal theory developed by a practitioner as a conceptualization of what she is doing and why she is doing it (Bloom, 1975). A practice theory is different from practice wisdom because practice wisdom includes mostly ideas about professional practice that have not been rigorously tested (Specht, 1977).

Practice theories are also different from basic social and behavioral theories. Practice theories provide knowledge about how to use those social and behavioral theories, whereas social and behavioral theories provide knowledge about phenomena (Fook, 2002). Good practice theory systematizes directives and offers guides for action that are empirically supported (Specht, 1977). Such a theory might include concepts, principles, and guidelines for all phases of the planned change process. Practitioners use practice theory to direct their assessment, intervention, and evaluation activities. The task-centered practice theory, for instance, assumes that social workers and clients face pressures limiting the length of time that can be given to the helping process. Concepts such as time limits, target problems, task, task identification, and task strategies are defined and organized into a systematic problem-focused model of helping action. William Reid (1992) and others have extensively used and tested this approach to practice.

THEORIES BY SYSTEM SIZE   Social workers often characterize theories in terms of their primary focus. **Micro theories** focus on small-size social systems, such as individuals and couples. **Mezzo theories** focus on intermediate-size social systems, such as support networks and extended families, and **macro theories** focus on larger-size social systems, including organizations, communities, and societies. However, be aware that many theories transcend this categorization scheme and provide theoretical understanding of social systems of various sizes.

INFORMAL OR EVERYDAY THEORIES   Informal or everyday theories are like the native languages that speakers use for daily communication. People are continually theorizing and interpreting information in terms of their casual and untested theories (Skidmore, 1979). We may speculate about why traffic is backed up or what has triggered a bout of grumpiness from a family member. These theories help us understand how things work (Shoemaker, Tankard, & Lasorsa, 2004). When many people believe in the same theory, we may refer to it as common knowledge or common sense. Unlike the scientific theories included in theoretical traditions, people do not test and continually revise their informal, everyday theories. Therefore, this kind of theorizing is less careful, less comprehensive, and less useful than the formal theorizing necessary to create theoretical traditions, middle-range theories, and practice theories.

EMPIRICAL GENERALIZATION

At the lower level of this continuum of theoretical scope is **empirical generalization.** Empirical generalizations are statements of uniformity among a group of events (Bloom, 1975). They describe social patterns that have been documented as occurring widely. They may be observed across different social situations or different historical periods, for example. Have you ever noticed that you seem to understand your professor very well, but he has little understanding of you? You are not alone. Much evidence supports the empirical generalization that power and status differences, especially as related to social markers of gender, race, ethnicity, class, and bureaucratic position, affect empathy and role-taking processes in face-to-face social situations. Specifically, persons in positions of relative powerlessness are more likely to take the perspective of or empathize with those in positions of power than the other way around. Thus, women tend to empathize more than their male husbands and partners. Minority group members generally understand the desires and intentions of majority group members better than the majority members understand them. Low-level employees exert themselves to take the perspective of their employers, but employers are often blind to the troubles of their workers. Students try hard to figure out their professors, whereas professors spend less time imagining their students' concerns and attitudes. This is an important and useful generalization about social life.

OBSERVATIONS

Finally, the foundational elements of theorizing are observations. Here, the social work theorizer is close to the empirical world, recording sensory impressions obtained through sight, sound, touch, smell, or taste. In this book, I will report on theoretical positions and statements at all levels of theoretical abstraction.

WHAT THEORETICAL LANGUAGES DO SOCIAL WORKERS SPEAK?

Social work practice settings and schools of social work are characterized by diversity and difference. Social workers often collaborate, as indicated earlier, on interdisciplinary teams with members of different disciplines, professions, or theoretical traditions. A **discipline** is "an established field of social sciences knowledge" (Bentz & Shapiro, 1998, p. 82) recognized as such within academic institutions and in society. Social workers collaborate with partners from economics, philosophy, anthropology, psychology, political science, biology, and many other disciplines. A **profession** is the umbrella term for an association "covering both discipline and practice that fosters status and respect by establishing entrance examinations, practice standards, and codes of ethics to assure quality and protect the public" (Perlstadt, 1998, p. 268). Professional groups participating in human services endeavors include business, education, nursing, law, and social work. I have already introduced the concept of theoretical tradition. Social workers may collaborate with those who use behavioral, cognitive, psychoanalytic, family systems, and many other theoretical approaches.

Interdisciplinary teams, then, include members from different backgrounds (Smelser, 2004). The team members often conceptualize their work by using different languages or theoretical orientations. A **theoretical orientation** is, for the practitioner, a "structure of explicit theories, concepts, principles, procedures, and processes of operation concerning some domain of practice" (Siporin, 1989, p. 476). Arenas for practice include adherents to numerous different theoretical traditions and schools of thought, each defined by a unique set of intellectual commitments and its own research agenda (Colomy & Brown, 1995; Ritzer & Smart, 2001). When engaging in helping work, practitioners might turn selectively to various theory specialists and benefit from their collective experience and wisdom. Because social work educators and practitioners work in organizations that include partners from varied disciplinary, professional, and theoretical allegiances, effective practice requires that we learn to communicate and cooperate with people who talk, assess, and intervene in many different ways.

In the following sections, I report on the theoretical orientations taught by social work educators, the theoretical preferences of social workers, and the theoretical preferences of human service professionals who work with social workers. I document my earlier assertion that social workers usually practice in a multitheory practice universe. This review of the research on theory use is also a way of characterizing the practice world and helping you become familiar with the names and types of theories available to the social work profession.

THEORETICAL ORIENTATIONS TAUGHT BY SOCIAL WORKERS

Table 1.1 lists the major theoretical approaches that are taught by social work educators. To develop this table, I reviewed the table of contents of 18 social work textbooks published in the last 40 years and added each chapter title to the list. As Table 1.1 shows, more than 40 different approaches have been recommended as part of the social work theoretical knowledge base.

Textbooks that survey various theoretical perspectives on human behavior and the social environment are valuable resources that can help you become a great generalist practitioner. However, a few brief observations about this collection of books are in order. Social work textbook writers mix terms for theory at various levels of scope. The summary list includes theoretical traditions or schools of thought, variations within a tradition, middle-range theories, and practice theories. Some writers organize chapters around approaches that combine two or more theoretical frameworks. Textbooks include theoretical approaches that are widely known, such as objects relation

Afrocentric theory	Humanistic/person-centered theory
Attachment theory	Existential theory
Behavioral theory	Phenomenological approach
Behavioral modification approach	Life stage theory
Social learning theory	Postmodern perspective
Body-oriented approaches	Problem-solving theory
Bioenergetic analysis	Task-centered approach
Evolutionary biology	Psychoanalytic perspective
Genetics	Ego psychology theory
Sociobiology	Erikson's life stages model
Cognitive theory	Object relations theory
Cognitive-behavioral perspective	Self psychology
Piaget's cognitive development model	Transactional analysis
Rational emotive therapy	Psychosocial theory
Crisis theory	Social constructionism
Conflict/emancipatory theories	Social exchange theory
Critical theory	Social role theory
Materialist framework	Spiritually based approaches
Marxist perspective	Transpersonal theory
Neo-Marxist approaches	Symbolic interactionism
Eclectic approach	Dramaturgical perspective
Ecological perspective	Labeling theory
Ecosystems perspective	Systems approach
The life model	Family systems theory
Feminist perspective	General systems theory
	Social systems theory
	Structural functionalism

theory and the life model, but also less familiar approaches, such as bio-energetic analysis and the phenomenological approach. The list includes practice models with long histories, such as the task-centered approach, and newer ways to organize knowledge for practice, such as Afrocentric theory.

THEORIES PREFERRED BY SOCIAL WORKERS

Table 1.2 provides a different way of characterizing the practice universe. This table presents a survey of surveys. I collected all the research studies I could

TABLE 1.2 | RANK ORDER OF THEORETICAL ORIENTATIONS PREFERRED BY SOCIAL WORKERS

	Brooks (n = 234)	Cocozelli (n = 171)	Gibbs (n = 187)	Jayaratne (n = 437)	Jensen (n = 107)	Mackey (n = 415)	Saltman (n = 195)	Tolman* (n = 54)	Overall PTS/RANK	
Psychodynamic	1	1	–	1	2	1	4	–	38	1
Systems	2	2	2	–	3	2	1	–	36	2
Behavioral	5	–	–	5	3 tied	–	6	–	13	3
Cognitive-Behavioral	–	–	–	–	–	3	.	1	11	4
Eclectic	3	–	–	–	1	–	–	–	11	4
Neo-Freudian	–	–	–	4	–	–	2	–	10	5
Other	4	–	–	–	4	–	–	–	8	6
Psychosocial	–	4	–	–	–	5	–	–	7	7
Ecosystems	–	–	1	–	–	–	–	–	7	7
Psychoeducational	–	–	–	–	–	–	–	2	6	8
Reality Therapy	–	–	–	2	–	–	–	–	6	8
Existential	–	–	–	–	–	3	–	–	5	9
Humanistic	–	–	–	3	–	–	–	–	5	9
Problem-Solving	–	3	–	–	–	–	–	–	5	9
Developmental	–	–	3	–	–	–	–	–	5	9
Self-Help	–	–	–	–	–	–	–	3	5	9
Sociocultural	–	–	–	–	–	4	–	–	4	10
Cognitive	–	–	–	–	–	–	5	–	3	11
Ecological	–	–	–	–	–	–	7	–	1	12

Rank in each study was converted to points: Rank 1 = 7 points, Rank 2 = 6 points, Rank 3 = 5 points, Rank 4 = 4 points, Rank 5 = 3 points, Rank 6 = 2 points, Rank 7 = 1 point, Not Ranked = 0 points. Total Points were added and then each framework was given an overall rank based on the total number of points received.

*Theoretical orientations identified as primary in group work research studies; theoretical orientations with less than three respondents were not included.

find that investigated the topic "theoretical orientations used by social workers." Then, I recorded the importance by rank of each theoretical framework in each study. Finally, I summarized these scores and calculated an overall rank for each orientation. The resulting table might be compared to a composite list of the favorite baseball players of all time or of the most loved rock songs of the 1980s or 1990s.

Social workers conducted studies of theoretical preferences from 1980 to 1994. The following information about the studies included in Table 1.2 may help you understand how researchers decide which theories are preferred by practitioners and educators.

Some researchers have asked practitioners about their preferences. Saltman and Greene (1993) used a systematic random sample method to obtain information from members of the National Association of Social Workers. In their study, they reported on 225 practitioners who responded and gave opinions about the "school of thought that most influenced their current social work practice" (p. 95). Jayaratne (1980–1981) surveyed 1037 clinical social workers listed in *NASW Register of Clinical Social Workers*. Results were based on 437 who considered themselves "eclectic" and identified the theoretical approach "most used." Mackey, Burek, and Charkoudian (1987) also used the NASW register; they questioned 415 practitioners selected at random with representation from all the states in the United States. Practitioners responded to a question about "human behavior theories that were most influential in organizing their approaches to practice" (p. 371). Jensen, Bergin, and Greaves (1990) reported on four sets of questionnaires sent to therapists with various professional occupations. The 107 social workers who responded were members of the National Association of Social Workers (Clinical) and each reported on "his or her orientation in psychotherapy (p. 125). Cocozelli (1987) used a purposive sample of practice settings that employ social workers in a midwestern metropolitan area. His study included 202 master's- and doctoral-level respondents, 187 of whom reported on the theorist most influential in shaping their approach to practice. Cocozelli and a research associate matched the theorists with theoretical schools.

Social work researchers have also checked on the theoretical preferences of educators. Gibbs (1986) surveyed 191 representatives of accredited undergraduate social work programs and asked about the "conceptual framework" that these teachers used. Brooks (1986) queried educators indirectly by studying the curriculums of 66 graduate schools along with 481 courses listed in their catalogs. Specifically, Brooks identified the "major theoretical focus" associated with catalog descriptions for Human Behavior and the Social Environment courses.

Researchers have investigated the theoretical orientations preferred by other social work researchers. Tolman and Molidor (1994) did not use a survey but a content analysis method. They examined 54 articles from eight different social work journals. Each article reported on a group work outcome study that referenced a theoretical perspective.

And the winners are . . . Here are some highlights of my analysis: The theoretical orientations ranked first and second—psychodynamic and systems, respectively—received almost the same number of votes. Two other theoretical frameworks, the psychosocial approach and the ecosystems approach, were also tied in popularity. Overall, analysis of this set of studies indicates that social work practitioners and educators have created a practice community with many different theoretical orientations.

Let me share a few other observations. Our list includes 17 perspectives and the choices "eclectic" and "other." Researchers, however, do not use a common classification scheme for describing theoretical orientations or for asking respondents about their preferences. The titles for the various theoretical orientations sometimes overlap. Some perspectives—psychodynamic and cognitive-behavioral, for example—would have received even more votes if combined with the related approaches of Neo-Freudian and psychosocial or cognitive and behavioral, respectively. Researchers did not include "antitheoretical" or "no theory" as a choice, so some respondents may have selected a theoretical preference even if their preference was not to use any theory. No study included data from social workers outside the United States, so comparisons in theoretical preferences across societies are not possible.

What about orientations with a small number of users? This set of studies searched for the most popular theoretical languages, not for the total spectrum including perspectives with a small but devoted following. Prochaska and Norcross (1999), experts on systems of psychotherapy, estimated that there are more than 400 different theoretical approaches to therapy. My summary of studies underestimates the total number of theories used by social workers.

What theoretical languages will be popular in the future? My survey of surveys cannot answer that question. Prochaska and Norcross' study (1999) can. They reported on a Delphi poll of 75 experts on practice theories. These observers predicted a growth in popularity of systems and family systems, eclectic, cognitive, psychobiological, and behavioral approaches. The experts predicted that humanistic and person-centered, existential, and psychodynamic approaches were likely to decrease in popularity.

Many additional questions about theory use cannot be answered by this set of studies. What factors influence a social worker's choice of theoretical orientation? Can we identify changes in the theoretical preferences of social workers over the past five decades? Do certain types of agencies tend to use certain types of theoretical frameworks? Do correctional agencies regularly adopt behavioral frameworks, for example? Do certain types of practitioners prefer some theories to others? Do women prefer feminist approaches and African Americans prefer Afrocentric and conflict perspectives? Unfortunately, no study of preferences has appeared in more than a decade; the most recent study was published in 1994. Therefore, this characterization of social work is probably dated. What are contemporary theoretical preferences? Perhaps you may help answer some of these research questions later in your career.

Theories Preferred by Various Professionals

Table 1.3 summarizes the research literature on the theoretical and professional affiliations of potential partners to social work practitioners. This survey of surveys also informs us about the practice world that social work novices enter. My summary of this literature will be briefer than the summary of social work studies.

These researchers conducted their studies from 1980 to 1998. Dankoski, Penn, Carlson, and Hecker (1998) surveyed 109 members of the American Association of Marriage and Family Therapy attending the organization's 1995 national conference. Study participants responded to a question about the theoretical orientation(s) that guided their work. Delshadi (1998) asked 153 experienced psychologists from all levels of professional education to respond to a mailed survey on their orientation to therapy. These respondents worked in hospitals, research therapy centers, and private practice settings. Jensen, Bergin, and Greaves (1990) reported on four surveys; their survey of social workers has already been discussed. These researchers also received mailed questionnaires from 122 psychologists, members of the Clinical Psychology division of the American Psychological Association; 121 family therapists, members of the American Association of Marriage and Family Therapists; and 73 psychiatrists, members of the American Psychiatric Association. All respondents reviewed a list of 13 possible theoretical orientations to practice and then identified their preferred orientation. Larson (1980) conducted a national survey of 339 psychotherapists—159 psychologists, 53 psychiatrists, 63 social workers, and 64 counselors. The representatives of the four professional groups were obtained by sampling the major associations and networks of therapists—for example, the Society for Psychoanalytic Psychology. Sammons and Gravitz (1990) reported on survey results from a study of 68 practicing psychologists, randomly selected from the National Register of Health Service Providers in Psychology. Each participant selected his or her theoretical orientation from a list of frameworks popular in the discipline. Sanderson and Ellis (1992) were interested in the theoretical preferences of sociologists. They randomly sampled members of the American Sociological Association, using the group's biographical directory; the majority (95%) worked in colleges or universities. The respondents reviewed a list of theoretical perspectives and selected their primary perspective from the list.

What have we learned from this set of studies on theoretical orientations, and how do social workers differ from other human service professionals? Psychologists, psychiatrists, family therapists, and other professionals, like social workers, operate in a diverse and multitheory practice world. This set included 29 different theoretical orientations, a much larger number than in the social work set. Analysis of these studies shows that the eclectic approach is ranked first. The psychodynamic and systems approaches are ranked in the top five. A similar pattern of preferences for these two frameworks appeared in the social work set of studies.

TABLE 1.3 | RANK ORDER OF THEORETICAL ORIENTATIONS PREFERRED BY VARIOUS PROFESSIONALS

	Dankoski	Delshadi	Jensen	Jensen	Jensen	Larson	Sammons	Sanderson	Overall PTS	RANK
Eclecticism	–	5	1	1	1	1	2	–	73	1
Psychodynamic	10	2	2	3	2	4	–	–	61	2
Systems	12	–	5	2	3	–	5	–	43	3
Behavioral	–	6	3	–	–	3	4	–	40	4
Cognitive-Behavioral	5	1	–	–	–	–	3	–	33	5
Humanistic	–	4	–	–	–	–	–	2	22	6
Other	–	3	–	–	–	–	–	6	21	7
Gestalt	–	–	–	–	–	–	1	–	13	8
Strategic	4	–	–	–	–	–	–	–	13	8
Conflict Theory	–	–	–	–	–	–	–	1	13	8
Family Structural	2	–	–	–	–	–	–	–	12	9
Transactional	–	–	–	–	–	2	–	–	12	9
Transgenerational	3	–	–	–	–	–	–	–	11	10
Symbolic Interactionism	–	–	–	–	–	–	–	3	11	10
Cognitive	–	–	4	–	–	–	–	–	10	11
Structuralism	–	–	–	–	–	–	–	4	10	11
Feminist	6	–	–	–	–	–	–	–	8	12
Marxism	–	–	–	–	–	–	–	7	7	13
Social Constructionist	7	–	–	–	–	–	–	–	7	13

TABLE 1.3 | (Continued)

	Dankoski	Delshadi	Jensen	Jensen	Jensen	Jensen	Larson	Sammons	Sanderson	Overall PTS/RANK
Emotion-Focused	8	–	–	–	–	–	–	–	–	6 14
Weberianism	–	–	–	–	–	–	–	–	8	6 14
Phenomenology	–	–	–	–	–	–	–	–	9	5 15
Symbolic Experiential	9	–	–	–	–	–	–	–	–	5 15
Exchange/Rational Choice	–	–	–	–	–	–	–	–	10	4 16
Sociobiology	–	–	–	–	–	–	–	–	11	3 17
Solution-Focused	1	–	–	–	–	–	–	–	–	3 17
Systemic, Milan	11	–	–	–	–	–	–	–	–	3 15
Atheoretical	–	–	–	–	–	–	–	–	12	2 18
Evolutionism	–	–	–	–	–	–	–	–	13	1 19
	n = 109	n = 153	n = 122	n = 121	n = 73		n = 339	n = 68	n = 162	

Rank in each study was converted to points: Rank 1 = 13 points, Rank 2 = 12 points, Rank 3 = 11 points, Rank 4 = 10 points, Rank 5 = 9 points, Rank 6 = 8 points, Rank 7 = 7 points, Rank 8 = 6 points, Rank 9 = 5 points, Rank 10 = 4 points, Rank 11 = 3 points, Rank 12 = 2 points, Rank 13 = 1 point. Not Ranked = 0 points. Total Points were added and then each framework was given an overall rank based on the total number of points received.

*Theoretical orientations with less than three respondents were not included.

Some frameworks that do not yet appear on social work lists were important to other professionals, including the feminist approach (rank 12) and the social constructionist approach (rank 13). Several of the sociologists' preferences, such as Weberianism, evolutionism, and sociobiology, are rarely referred to by social workers. Nor do they appear in the textbooks used by social work educators. Perhaps we do not use these perspectives because the models for applying them have only been sketchily developed. Or perhaps other professionals have the resources and support necessary to explore newer frameworks, whereas social work programs and agencies do not. Six surveys gave respondents the option of "eclectic," and one study included the choice "atheoretical." Comparing this set of research studies with those shown in Table 1.2 also suggests that some other theoretical languages preferred by practitioners and social scientists (symbolic interactionism, exchange/rational choice, and Marxism, for example) are not identified by social work respondents as familiar, preferred, influential, or relevant theoretical orientations.

Let's summarize the major point. The contemporary practice scene seems like the work at the Tower of Babel. This story tells about a building project in biblical times. The construction team was so ambitious that they aimed for the heavens. God reacted to their excessive pride by splitting the builders' language into thousands of different languages. The tower builders were no longer able to work together effectively, and the project was halted. Analysis of this set of studies demonstrates that many social work practitioners will need to learn about varied theoretical orientations. When a group of social workers cooperate on a project or are employed by the same agency, it is likely that they will have some theoretical differences. When social workers collaborate with allies from other disciplines and professions, it is likely that many of these allies will differ in their preferred theoretical orientations. Social workers who participate on professional teams with members from other theoretical traditions can enhance their power, status, and effectiveness on the team by understanding the theoretical perspectives of these diverse partners. They can better help rebuild clients' lives. Human service professionals should not aim as high as the biblical builders. However, the modern Tower of Babel problem must be overcome if we are to work together and solve client problems and public problems.

THE VALUE OF MULTITHEORY PRACTICE

In this chapter, I have repeatedly suggested that social workers will benefit from learning how to speak multiple theoretical languages. Social work has a mandate to serve people, a mandate that is very complex. One theory cannot provide all the necessary knowledge. New theoretical languages are broadening our understanding of the human condition, especially the plight of vulnerable populations, the importance of human resilience and strengths, and the power of social structures to constrain human action. One of the first and premier advocates for multitheory use, Francis Turner, argued that "the challenge for the field is to differentially draw from the spectrum of practice theories we are privileged to have and put together a profile of intervention that best suits the situations of various vulnerable individuals, dyads, families, groups, and communities" (Turner, 1999, p. 30). In this section, I will elaborate on the argument for learning multiple theoretical languages.

The social worker who speaks multiple theoretical languages can help his or her clients better than the no-language or one-language social worker. A multitheory orientation provides a more comprehensive and detailed depiction of the many aspects of the client-concern-context configuration (Greene, 1999). This improves client assessment work. Theoretical multilingualism increases worker effectiveness because the worker can select from among a variety of theoretical frameworks and practice theories those that provide the deepest understanding and those that work best in the particular situation (Rosen, 1988b). The practitioner conversant in many theoretical languages can avoid the ones that have been shown to cause harm to clients (Turner, 1999). More theoretical choices for the worker means more possibilities for understanding and generating ameliorative action (Payne, 1997) and a greater likelihood of a maximal positive impact based on the differential use of theories (Turner, 1996a). Multitheory users, in short, are likely to provide better service to their clients (Reid, 1998).

The social worker committed to learning multiple theoretical languages advances his or her personal and professional growth. The effort to appreciate the multiple realities or perspectives captured by different theoretical languages increases our intellectual flexibility while reducing the noncritical thinking associated with personal bias, insularity, and excessive certainty (Greene & Ephross, 1991). The development of capacities for multitheory practice stimulates our creativity as we learn to synthesize or integrate different theoretical ideas (Greene & Ephross, 1991). Multitheory training is personally and professionally rewarding because we learn more about the character and components of the theoretical framework(s) that we prefer (Camic & Joas, 2004), especially as we contrast our favorites with other perspectives.

The multitheory practitioner will also improve in verbal and written communication abilities (Payne, 2002b). The practitioner can use formal theoretical languages with peers to clarify and organize his or her ideas about how to help. The practitioner can also communicate better, both in writing and orally, with judges, administrators, family members of a client, and colleagues from other disciplines because the practitioner can use the audience members' preferred language and can translate scientific terminology into a language that these people understand. Multilingual practitioners can use the appropriate theoretical languages to explain their practice choices at case conferences and in supervisory meetings with helpers from other theoretical backgrounds.

The social worker committed to learning multiple theoretical languages can better contribute to helping teams. The multitheory social worker continually expands his or her breadth of disciplinary knowledge, and thus can provide more perspectives on a greater range of the social situations and human troubles and challenges that social workers face (Hardiker & Barker, 1988). Multitheory professionals have knowledge of many theoretical resources for their helping projects (Camic & Joas, 2004) and can make sense of the core assumptions, root metaphors, concepts, and middle-range theories used by other team members when conceptualizing cases. The multitheory stance increases the quality of interaction among team members with different theoretical, professional, and disciplinary allegiances. Members learn a sense of humility about their theoretical knowledge and become wary of those with a sense of absolute certainty. Members show respect for those who speak different theoretical languages. The multitheory team can better divide labor and avoid wasteful duplication by going with each member's theoretical strengths. Team members will develop an appreciation for and make use of social workers' distinctive contributions as theory borrowers and translators.

The social work profession will become stronger and more effective as the number of multitheory social work theory users increases. Our profession's knowledge base will expand (Turner, 1999). Energy and time spent on fights and rivalries among theoretical subgroups within the profession will lessen. Boundaries between theory-based associations and professional groups will become more permeable, increasing the opportunity for cross-theory dialogues and resource development that will benefit practitioners (Turner, 1999). Perhaps social work's connections to the larger public will improve, too, when we learn how to use both theoretical and nontheoretical languages purposefully.

THEORIZING

Theoretical activity can be divided into product and process (White, 2005). Many Human Behavior and the Social Environment (HBSE) textbooks introduce you to a variety of theories and to much important social work knowledge. These are important products of theorizing, and I will review the products of ten theoretical traditions in this book. However, **theorizing** is also a process, the act of creating a theoretical product. My primary emphasis will be teaching HBSE as the process of theorizing. In your research classes, you learn how to use the scientific research process. In your policy classes, you learn how to analyze policy. In your practice classes, you learn how to use the planned change process with different-size social systems. I propose to present scientific social work both as product, a "written-down set of statements" (Shoemaker et al., 2004, p. 148), and as the process of theorizing.

Everyday theorizing is the act of creating an idea or set of ideas based on different types of experiences (Fook, 2002). We theorize to understand and make sense of social life. We theorize when our forward movement toward goals is stopped. We theorize daily by asking and answering questions: why does this occur, how does this work, what are the relevant processes, where is this most likely to happen, what begins this pattern and what ends the pattern?

Scientific theorizing is a mental process by which theorists systematically relate general explanatory statements to suggest new hypotheses for empirical testing. Within the traditional scientific paradigm, theorizing "is the process of scientists acquiring explanations about why certain variations occur and why they do not . . . [a matter of] learning the circumstances under which variation in variables brings about variations in other variables in a way that acquires multiple levels of generality" (Burr, 1973, p. 23).

Let's not restrict ourselves to a positivistic definition. Practical theorizing, such as the theorizing of reflective social workers, is the attempt to explain processes and dynamics through which conditions in the community change and different desired outcomes can be generated (Powers, 2004). Meleis (1997) nicely summarizes the activities of theorizing to include "the processes of analysis of situations, events, and actions that include reflection, connection with other ideas, interpretation, generating meaning, abstracting, comparing, contrasting, and/or utilizing theories to explain situations or guide actions" (p. 36).

METATHEORIZING

In research, a study is the investigation of a pattern in the empirical world. A metastudy or metasynthesis is a second-order study, the study of a set of studies (Finfgeld, 2003). **Metatheorizing** is a new kind of social work activity similar to the synthesizing work of researchers. It involves theorizing about theories and about theorizing. Metatheorists focus on the fundamental problems of scientific thinking, such as how theorists might best conceptualize the tension between human choice and social constraint or subjective interpretations and objective reality. Metatheorizing requires "reflexivity," self-examination and self-monitoring of the profession's theoretical development by the profession's members (Zhao, 2001). When social work theory experts study and classify theories by system-size focus (micro, mezzo, or macro) or by primary dimension of human functioning (biological, psychological, social, or spiritual), they are using the process of metatheorizing. Ritzer (1991a), a sociologist, urged metatheorists to study "theories, theorists, and communities of theorists" (p. 6) and to deepen their "understanding of the full range of [sociological] theories" (p. 303). He called this activity "metatheorizing for understanding." Ritzer, however, did not relate metatheorizing to the concerns of practitioners, nor did he identify the specific ways that metatheorizing might increase practice effectiveness. I will expand Ritzer's idea of metatheorizing to include "metatheorizing for application."

Metatheorizing can result in the creation of a metatheory, a theory about theories. Metatheories are at a higher level of abstraction than behavioral theories or theories of client problems (Fitzpatrick, 1997). A metatheory might present a statement "about what counts as knowledge [knowledge includes theory], which knowledge structures are important, and how to structure knowledge within the discipline" (Kramer, 1997, p. 51). I would add that a metatheory might also stake out a position on the collaborative and communication processes necessary to knowledge creation and use. Early in this chapter, for example, I introduced my metatheory and explained the scientific enterprise as a continually developing conversation among problem solvers.

Novice theory users cannot be expected to engage in the process of metatheorizing or to create metatheoretical products. However, I will teach theorizing by using several metatheoretical tools that I have developed. So, it may be helpful that you are now familiar with the concepts of metatheory and metatheorizing.

SPECIFIC USES OF THEORETICAL LANGUAGES

Each theoretical tradition has an associated language with its own vocabulary, its rules of grammar and pronunciation, and its particular networks of native-speaking scholars, researchers, and practitioners. Human services are offered in many different settings or fields of practice. These settings are almost like different countries; a particular theoretical language may be spoken in each. Correctional workers, for instance, often use the behaviorist and social learning terms of models, reinforcement, and punishment. Gerontological social workers often blend theories associated with cognitive psychology, characterizing mental processes with theories associated with human biology, especially those explaining the physical correlates of aging and disease trajectories. Social work students who try to connect theory to practice can use a theoretical perspective and its language as a versatile tool. In the final chapter, I will discuss how practitioners might integrate different theoretical languages as needed for work in particular practice domains or fields.

The value of theory for practitioners should be determined by the pragmatic standard: Does the system of ideas facilitate the work of theorists, researchers, and practitioners in solving pressing public problems? Let's give an explicit nod to the needs of our clients in these formulations. The professional use of theoretical knowledge should result in observable and measurable improvements in clients' experiences as members of various groups and organizations. Theoretical frameworks may differentially contribute to the realization of particular membership goals: promoting democratic practices and freedoms, ensuring the material and social prerequisites for community survival, deepening self-understanding, or extending human dignity and respect. Whatever the goal, a useful theory is one that will help the theory's users achieve political, social, or ethical ends consonant with the social work mission, in a way that is responsive to client groups and backed by scientific evidence. Theories may increase practitioner effectiveness in several specific ways (Gitterman, 1988; Skidmore, 1979).

REFERENCING

A theoretical tradition, like a language, serves as a frame of reference or perspective shared by a particular group of practitioners. Ministers and priests working with the elderly can organize their observations of nursing home residents by **referencing** a theoretical system of spiritual beliefs and principles. The social worker familiar with this tradition can better understand the assessment and intervention recommendations of spiritually minded team members than the social worker with no grasp of such a viewpoint. The social worker familiar with multiple theories can go further, shifting perspectives and understanding the viewpoints and referencing systems of the priest, the doctor, the nurse, the office manager, and other allies involved in case deliberations.

CLASSIFYING

Language users classify and group experiences into manageable categories. Theoretical traditions provide schemes for systematizing and **classifying** large amounts of information about clients and client groups. Mental health workers, for instance, use diagnostic categories influenced strongly by the psychodynamic tradition. Configurations of a client's physical actions, verbal statements, and nonverbal communication are matched with categories of "mental disorder." Then, workers use such categorizations as a guide to treatment in psychiatric clinics and hospitals. Social workers use many theory-based classification schemes.

Classification may use a temporal principle to organize data. For example, structural functionalists might classify societies according to their degree of social evolution, from very primitive like the societies of the first humans to highly complex like contemporary advanced industrial societies. Physical proximity to a central place is another classificatory principle. Ecological theorists sometimes categorize human settlements by their distance from an urban core. Theorists might also use a set of logical ideas to organize information. Family systems theorists have developed strengths-oriented categories related to family system functioning. One tool helps practitioners judge how well a particular family's systemic processes fit in a typology of 16 family types organized in relation to standards of ideal adaptation, ideal cohesiveness, and ideal communication.

EXPLAINING AND INTERPRETING

Theoretical traditions and their associated theories and concepts help us explain biopsychosocial patterns, and they help us interpret or make sense of social worlds different from our own. Theories help workers generate ideas to better understand challenging practice situations (Skidmore, 1979). This **explaining and interpreting** function will be reviewed in detail in Chapter 3. The use of theory in its deductive form is associated with positivism. Explanations are stated in terms of cause and effect. Explanations that can be generalized widely are most highly regarded, and explanations are considered valuable when supported by scientific research conducted according to carefully controlled procedures for sampling, measurement, data collection, and data analysis. Cognitive-behavioral explanations of client problems such as phobia, wife abuse, or learned helplessness are often presented in deductive form.

In the inductive form of theory construction, theory helps practitioners understand the particular meanings, definitions, or social processes of a particular group embedded in a specific social context. Specifics are accumulated and organized as general statements. Professional interpretations only follow lengthy, up-close immersion in the natural settings inhabited by these group members. Such "grounded theories" also make use of the concepts close to the meaning system of the group.

A skilled theory user can use either the deductive or inductive mode of explanation. A skillful theory user can explain and interpret in parsimonious ways and in ways that can be communicated to others.

PREDICTING

Theories allow for the prediction of action or interaction following the observation of some aspect of a client's life. Theoretical traditions, for example, are a source of **hypotheses,** testable statements about predicted relationships between two or more variables (Skidmore, 1979). When a theoretical language is applied to a particular theoretical problem or practical challenge, predictions are generated. For example, a correctional social worker might select an interactionist framework to make judgments about which first-time offenders are most likely to become career criminals. Propositions about the negative impact of court-imposed labels on self-concepts and the relevance of a history of brutalization by parents can be converted into specific testable hypotheses. The worker can also refer to studies testing such hypotheses or conduct her own studies and begin to accumulate information about the predictors of recidivism.

Psychic hotlines claim to make accurate predictions but would fail any scientific test. Theoretical predictions offer social workers the possibility of changing client system futures. Bloom (1975) remarks that prediction gives us "the ability to intervene in the course of events purposely so as to influence a new consequent event which is closer to a desired event than a natural event would have been" (p. 56).

THEORIZING COMPETENCIES

Communication competence is a linguistic term used to refer to a speaker's knowledge of a language, including its pronunciation, grammar, and vocabulary, and the rules for using the language in socially appropriate ways (Romaine, 2000). This competence is necessary for successful participation in the speech community. Theorizing competence is similar, and novices must demonstrate competence to earn acceptance as a full member of most professional communities. I have adapted B. S. Bloom's 1956 taxonomy of educational objectives to help us think about theorizing competencies. I have added theorizing communication to his list.

THEORY KNOWLEDGE

This competency is similar to learning the basic words of a new language. Knowledgeable theory users know the key terms or concepts of many theoretical perspectives. They know about the exemplars and pioneers within various theoretical traditions, and they know something about the historical, cultural, economic, and political context associated with the formulation of the framework and its path into social work. Knowledgeable theory users are familiar with the resources for increasing their understanding of various theoretical frameworks: case studies, theory-based evaluation studies, journals, articles, websites, books, and conferences.

THEORY COMPREHENSION

This competency is similar to grasping the basic rules and structures of a spoken language. Theoretical comprehension involves understanding the foundation assumptions and the root metaphors from which various theoretical frameworks have grown. Those with high comprehension can translate into plain English the terminology and middle-range theories of many different theoretical languages. They can begin to identify the components of various theoretical languages and how these are organized or structured, and they can understand the small differences distinguishing variations or dialects within theoretical frameworks. Good theoretical comprehension competency enables us to identify the everyday and informal theories used by clients (Payne, 1997).

THEORY APPLICATION

This competency is similar to the use of language to solve real-life problems. Theory application relates to every phase of the planned change process (Mithaug, 2000). Theory appliers can identify a practice challenge, see the discrepancy between what is known and what needs to be known, and search for the relevant theories. Theory appliers can construct a theory to explain client troubles and use a theory (or theories) for assessment and for intervention planning. Theory appliers can evaluate a theory for its significance (reduction of knowledge discrepancy), its scope (coverage of all aspects of practice challenge), and its utility (guide to the helping work). Theory appliers can adjust a theory by using data collected after its application, and revise the theory to better fit the facts.

Theory appliers develop some other theorizing skills too. They know how to create theory-based models (qualitative and quantitative) to organize information about client problems or change processes (Britt, 1997). They can engage in theory-based practice evaluation and program evaluation. They can map the "client system in the environment configuration" in multiple theory-specific ways. Theory appliers can use multiple theoretical languages to develop alternative assessment formulations about the nature, conditions or causes, likely trajectories, and dynamics of client challenges or problems, and to propose alternative intervention strategies.

THEORY ANALYSIS

This competency builds on theoretical comprehension and is like language parsing, the analysis of the grammatical structure of sentences and paragraphs. This capacity includes the ability to formally identify the building blocks or components of a theoretical framework or theory. These components include the central assumptions and images, root metaphors, concepts, propositions, and models used by the theory's architects. Theory analysts can also create diagrams and other visual representations of the organization of a theory.

THEORY SYNTHESIS

This competency is like the ability to combine ideas and words from different languages in ways that enhance communication. The theory synthesizer can compare and contrast different theoretical languages and their theory-derived concepts and propositions, and recognize similarities and differences. In addition to comparison, theory synthesizers can create middle-range theories to explain client troubles by blending elements from different languages. Advanced synthesizers can mix and match ingredients from different theoretical languages to build innovative and effective practice models.

THEORY EVALUATION

Remember the controversy about the language spoken by some African Americans in Oakland, an inner-city variation on English. Commentators argued about whether such language use was an acceptable cultural variant of standard English, a distinct Black English, or an inferior language, Ebonics.

Theory evaluation is like the ability to appraise the quality of a language and of its use. Theory evaluators can judge the best uses and limitations of various theoretical languages relative to particular practice challenges (matching to client preferences, problem, or setting, for example). Theory evaluation includes the ability to appraise the suitability of different theoretical languages for social work use according to our profession's standards (ethics and values, holistic, strengths, justice, diversity, and empirical support). Theory evaluation includes the ability to use research methods to test and correct the critical elements of theoretical frameworks and theories (Reid, 1998). Good theory evaluators can also judge how well a theoretical orientation fits with a worker's personal and professional style, character, and life experiences.

THEORY COMMUNICATION

For practitioners, this competency is a critical component of theorizing. Language fluency can be demonstrated only by speaking. Theorizing competency becomes apparent during moments of theoretical discourse. Theory communication includes the ability to recognize the theoretical preferences and orientations of colleagues, collaborating professionals, and agency administrators by careful listening; the ability to speak, understand, and be understood by experts in various theoretical languages (Marshall, 1989); the ability to explain theoretical frameworks, practice theories, and theory-derived concepts, principles, and models to clients and other laypersons; and the ability to modify theory use based on conversations with supervisors, clients, and colleagues.

Effective theory communicators can discuss theoretical issues at case conferences with team participants who have different theoretical orientations. They can also read and understand case notes and logs created by colleagues and agency professionals with a variety of theoretical orientations. They can read professional articles and books and determine the theoretical underpinnings of the research study, policy statement, practice illustration, or agency report. They can deepen their theoretical comprehension by communicating about assessment formulation, working agreements and plans, and interventions with theory users who speak different languages (Turner, 1999). They can write a resume that summarizes theorizing competencies in a way that is tailored to a particular potential employer. They can inform the general public on radio talk shows or at community meetings about the theoretical perspectives and practice theories used by social workers and, thus, demystify theory (Deflem, 1999).

THE PROFESSIONAL CAREER AND THEORIZING MASTERY

This book will not result in your attainment of theorizing competencies in all seven areas. Mastering theorizing is a career-long project (Fook, 2002). However, we can identify some of the steps on the path to mastery (Forte, 2001).

Mastery of multiple theoretical languages is comparable to the process of gaining language proficiency (Gergen, 1982). We progress from the limited vocabulary and simple grammatical structure of the child to the adult's richly differentiated vocabulary, ability to execute complex grammatical forms, comfort in employing various communication forms such as sarcasm, and capacity for using language as a means to varied social achievements. Language lovers even learn how to add second or third languages to their language repertoire.

Immersion in a new culture is necessary for progress toward language proficiency (Britt, 1997). The same applies to progress in learning theoretical languages. Theory learners must immerse themselves in the literature of a theoretical language, in discussion groups (online and face-to-face) with theory users, in theory-oriented workshops, and in deliberations about the practice cases illustrating and articulating theory application. With patience and hard word, significant achievements are possible.

Social work educational programs can prepare practitioners for communication with scholars of diverse theoretical allegiances if they introduce students to multiple theories at the bachelor's, master's, and doctoral levels (Forte, 2001). The steps toward multitheory mastery can be conceptualized in terms similar to those necessary for mastering a new language: reading and understanding the theoretical language, communicating in the theoretical language, and teaching others the theoretical language (Marshall,

1989). Expectations might be progressively toughened at each educational level.

NOVICE THEORY USERS

As an undergraduate or first-year graduate student, you have made the decision to become a student of theories. Your first step is to master the profession's natural language, the ecosystems paradigm. You must learn to apply that theoretical language to different practice situations, and to differentiate in a basic way between ecosystems language and other theories that are taught in school or used at your field agency. In keeping with the generalist approach and its emphasis on breadth of knowledge, skill, and technique, novice theory users should take advantage of opportunities to increase their theoretical knowledge, comprehension, and communication capacities.

Here are some possible indicators of progress at the novice level: The novice theory user can indicate that he or she is a theory language learner and seek help and support from fluent speakers of various theoretical languages. The novice has learned and can use the concepts of the ecosystems theoretical language. The novice can identify and use the ecosystems theory concepts in relation to problem understanding, assessment, and intervention. The novice is building a small dictionary of concepts and their meanings from a few other theoretical languages. The novice can ask questions and make simple statements in the classroom and in the field using theoretical concepts and propositions.

INTERMEDIATE-LEVEL THEORY USERS

Second-year or concentration-level graduate students might be expected to become fully conversant in the professional language of ecosystems and two additional theoretical languages, and to begin learning to apply an integrated approach using multiple languages to practice situations. Intermediates are deepening their knowledge of these particular theories and improving the theorizing skills related to analysis, application, synthesis, and evaluation (Turner, 1999). In addition, intermediate-level theory users are progressing rapidly in their theory communication capacities.

Here are some indicators of progress at this level: Intermediate-level theory users can initiate and participate in theoretical conversations with colleagues and supervisors. They can pronounce and use a variety of theoretical concepts correctly almost all the time. They can make theoretical statements (propositions and hypotheses, for example) following the conventions of the relevant theoretical language. They can answer basic questions about several theoretical languages, including questions about their histories, assumptions, middle-range theories, applications, and performances in evaluation tests. They can translate the ecosystems theoretical language and one or two other languages for the sake of clients and collaterals. They can join in theoretical deliberations at the conference or in a web discussion with fluent theory users.

Doctoral candidates might be expected to become conversant in a significant number of major theoretical languages and to identify emerging theoretical languages such as Afrocentric theory, queer theory, or postmodernism. Doctoral-level theory users know how to apply theories differentially to particular fields of practice or public problems and how to develop tools and strategies for translating across theories.

Indicators of progress at the advanced level include the following: Advanced theory users can offer alternative theory-based options at each phase of the planned change process. They have developed an extensive vocabulary in multiple languages and can use concepts precisely. They can adeptly participate in or lead multidisciplinary team meetings and case conferences. They are expert in theorizing skills, including analysis (the ability to identify the deeper assumptions and metaphors on which multiple theoretical languages are built and to diagram theoretical linkages), synthesis (creative formulation of new approaches to understanding or helping that combine multiple theories), and evaluation (the use of logic and scientific research to test theoretical languages and their components). Advanced users demonstrate their expert understanding in the theoretical discourse.

Advanced-level theory users are also expert theory communicators. They have progressed in several theoretical languages toward "native competence," the ability to communicate as well as an educated specialist in the languages. They can also do sophisticated theory translation work for laypersons, colleagues, and the profession.

STANCES TOWARD THEORETICAL DISCOURSE

Your choice of an orientation toward theory depends on many factors. Social work programs differ in their approach to theory. In my graduate program, almost every course included content on the psychodynamic object relations theory. Students were discouraged from exploring alternative theoretical frameworks. This approach hindered my development of a multitheory outlook.

Social work educators and field instructors assume different stances toward theory. Chance and luck may play a part in who become our role models. A faculty member on my dissertation committee, for instance, turned out to be a devoted member of the Society for the Study of Symbolic Inter-action. Over the past 15 years, he has shared his extensive knowledge of this tradition with me.

Social work administrators make choices about the agency's theoretical orientations that affect student interns. Some agencies prefer theoretical orientations that do not question current political arrangements (correctional settings tend to endorse behaviorism); others prefer those that radically challenge the dominant ideology (shelters for battered women often adopt a feminist-emancipatory perspective). Agency economies influence the selection of a theoretical orientation. Practitioners in private practice groups and in for-profit mental health settings must grapple with the medicalization of most psychosocial conditions to earn reimbursement from health management organizations. They often choose theories that lend themselves to short-term problem-solving work.

A social work practitioner can attempt to choose a theoretical orientation that complements his or her personality, value system, and worldview. Two such social workers assisted an undergraduate program where I worked. One African American practitioner with great pride in his heritage and a commitment to serving at-risk youth advanced the Afrocentric theoretical perspective. Another had strong religious convictions and confidence that prayer, Bible studies, and worship are practices that can supplement traditional social work methods. She developed a spirituality-based framework and works in a Christian counseling center.

Your decision about the best stance toward the use of theory for practice, then, will be affected by your relationships with the teachers, field instructors, employers, peers, researchers, and textbook writers who become significant during your professional career. After accounting for agency and social constraints, social work practitioners can select from dozens of theoretical frameworks. You can deal with this multiplicity in several different ways.

PHILOSOPHICAL POSITIONS

Practitioners may endorse three different philosophical postures toward the pluralistic practice universe (Cronen, Chen, & Pearce, 1988). First, they may assume theoretical incompatibility. Team members, for example, may be familiar with the same papers and books, use a similar theoretical logic, and communicate with each other in a common vocabulary. However, within the common framework (psychodynamic theory, perhaps), members still argue over the correct interpretation of classic texts, often to the point of splitting into separate and irreconcilable camps (the ego psychologists versus the object relations psychologists, for instance). Congenial collaboration is unlikely.

Second, practitioners may assume that theoretical orientations are incomparable. Theory users claim that their traditions are so different that comparisons and cross-theory translations, even for practical purposes, will be fruitless. Social work behaviorists and social constructionists often engage in bitter debates about theory, asserting that any reconciliation of the two languages is impossible.

Finally, practitioners may assert that their different viewpoints are incommensurable. Theory users may lack a neutral language that bridges the two theoretical perspectives and allows translations that do not distort any theoretical perspective. Although the theoretical languages are different, comparison is considered possible. The means of translation must be invented, and useful translations will require comparison by means of multiple tools. George Herbert Mead and Jane Addams assumed this stance toward the membership differences common in Chicago. Their innovative work at cross-boundary translation will be adapted in this book to the current problem of knowledge fragmentation.

PROFESSIONAL THEORETICAL COMMITMENTS

Ask your field instructors about their orientation to theory. If you talk about the answers with your fellow students, you will discover that social workers approach theory in many different ways. In the following subsections, I present my typology of the major approaches. Here I will break a writing rule and mix metaphors. Each type of theoretical commitment can be compared both to the stance a person takes toward religious belief and to a person's language proficiency.

ATHEORETICAL PRACTITIONERS   Some practitioners, educators, and administrators are **atheoretical.** They are like atheists, those who do not believe in God or a higher being. Atheoretical practitioners may also be compared to speech-impaired adults who have difficulty in fully using the culture's language.

Atheoretical practitioners discourage any intellectual conversation about theory. These practitioners walk out when others start speaking theory. Atheoretical practitioners claim that good social work can be practiced without reference to theory. Theories have little relevance to the necessities of day-to-day practice. Practice wisdom and intuition can guide work. Why talk when there is so much to do? End of discussion. Atheoretical practitioners are theoretically inarticulate (Specht, 1977). They received minimal training in theories and theorizing, or they rejected or forgot the training. Atheoretical practitioners cannot identify and talk about concepts, propositions, models, or other theoretical elements of theoretical language that guide practice.

ONE-THEORY MONISTS   Theoretical **monists** talk, but they prefer monologues, and they will speak only one language. They are dogmatic about their faith, believing in one God but assuming that all other gods and religious beliefs are false. Theoretical monists are monolingual (Romaine, 2000), and they are content with their language. They speak the language of the one true religion.

Monists are sure that they have found the best theory. Open and reciprocal exchanges with those who speak other languages are discouraged as pointless, or as hazardous and contaminating (Turner, 1996a). Complete loyalty to the theory is expected, and the disciple is challenged to master the one true theory and its distinctive jargon (Payne, 1997). Monists are very selective about their choice of ideas (Payne, 2002b). They are convinced that the ideas of their belief tradition can explain every kind of practice situation or challenge. Monists are prone to dualistic or either/or thinking (Prochaska & Norcross, 1999). Their approach is good, and all other approaches are bad. Either you are a true believer like them, or you are deluded and condemned to a life without the possibility of salvation.

THEORETICAL PROSELYTIZERS   Some practitioners are theoretical proselytizers. Like monists, they speak only one theoretical language, but they are fanatics. Not only are they sure they have found the best theory, but they are determined to convert everyone else to this theory. Theoretical proselytizers always define their own theory as superior when contrasted to others (Safran & Messer, 1997). Theoretical proselytizers want to monopolize and control the search for understanding (Merton, 1975). In struggling for the supremacy of their theoretical perspective, they embrace the "wheeling and dealing, personal manipulation, threats, and cajolery involved in promoting that worldview" (Rule, 1997, p. 195). A social work educator recently told me, for example, that political leaders in the state of Michigan were demanding that all social workers embrace a solution-oriented practice model.

Theoretical proselytizers endorse one theory and prefer a competitive, aggressive, forced conversion to gentle persuasion. As champions of a theoretical perspective, they eagerly seek opportunities for debate. However, instead of offering carefully developed arguments about how their theoretical perspective best solves social work's theoretical puzzles and practical problems, they exhort or entice potential converts. Thus, the superiority of their affiliation (and inferiority of that of their rivals) is arrogantly and continually demonstrated in official edicts (Payne, 1997). Missionary work to convert others to the correct doctrine and the political campaign for theoretical dominance are never ending. Influence seeking, name calling, grand promising, and disciplining those who stray from the line of the faithful are additional tools in jockeying for glory.

THEORETICAL CULTISTS   An **eclectic** approach means either that the social worker selects parts of different theoretical languages and tries to use the parts together in one helping situation, or that the worker uses different theories for different practice situations depending on the fit between the theory and the case (Payne, 2002b). Many eclectic theory users are semiliterate in a variety of languages (Romaine, 2000) but do not possess the complete set of skills and vocabulary necessary for effective communication in any one language. They are like religious cultists following the latest system of religious beliefs and rituals for a while, then losing interest and moving on to the next fad.

Theoretical dilettantes take eclecticism to the extreme. Allegiances to a theoretical tradition are short-lived. Dilettantes prefer talking in terms of the latest theoretical trend one season but soon forget it and move on to the next glamorous fad. Or dilettantes may mix and match theoretical languages with little awareness of or attention to their compatibility. Dilettantes prefer speaking the transactional analysis talk one season and the vocabulary of the new favorite, neurolinguistic programming, the next season.

THEORETICAL INTERNATIONALISTS   Theoretical internationalists are practitioners, teachers, supervisors, and colleagues who stand apart from the atheoretical, the fanatics, the proselytizers, and the dilettantes. They can be compared to people who speak multiple languages and enjoy world travel. They are like ecumenical religious believers who accept those with other faiths as having a legitimate conception of ultimate reality and who are eager to worship respectfully with devotees of other traditions.

Theoretical internationalists believe in a "United Nations of scientific theory." Contact with different theoretical societies presents an exciting challenge, not dread or disdain. Boundaries to communication between rival theoretical traditions should be removed, and bridges for respectful encounters built (Ritzer, 1991). As skilled diplomats, the theoretical internationalist aims to understand the "culture" of other theoreticians on their own terms. Each theoretical language can contribute to a dialogue that helps social workers better solve membership problems. Rigid segregation of theories by discipline, tradition, and conventional occupational categories stifles the social work imagination. Theoretical internationalists believe that practitioners who seriously and carefully listen to those from diverse conceptual traditions avoid wasteful work duplication, stay informed about social science developments, increase their theoretical understanding through contrast and comparison, cultivate a reflective and critical stance toward their preferred theoretical orientation, and most important, broaden the repertoire of theoretical tools that they can bring to practice (Payne, 1997; Turner, 1983, 1996a).

For internationalists, reality is multiperspectival. There are many gods. William James asserted about social life, "the universe is many" (1907/1958, p. 92). Different spheres of reality are associated with different human enterprises: art, science, religion, dream states, sexuality, ritual, play, commerce, and so on. Each sphere makes use of a distinctive language, a set of symbols and rules for ordering these symbols. Distinctive experiences are generated for members of each symbolic world. George Herbert Mead agreed with this view and added that social understanding is enhanced by appreciation of plural perspectives (Weigert, 1995). Theoretical internationalists believe that we develop larger selves through cross-theory dialogue. The internationalist applauds and supports efforts to gain familiarity with the symbolic worlds of minority groups, of powerless peoples, and of those who present theoretical alternatives to the dominant versions of reality (Schriver, 1998). They appreciate diversity and uncertainty (Prochaska & Norcross, 1999).

This stance of "theoretical internationalism" or "enlightened cosmopolitanism" can be emulated by social work practitioners. As a new theory user, you can begin a trip toward the destination of theoretical internationalism. Your natural slant on theorizing during field internship and other professional projects will be a valuable starting point. This slant reflects the particulars of your socialization experiences (Seigfried, 1996). However, any student's "angle of vision" is partial and incomplete. Professional socialization, including your use of this book, can advance your theoretical intelligence and fluency. Generalist social work practice fits well with the internationalist's commitment to becoming bilingual or multilingual (Romaine, 2000) and able to converse about the challenges or opportunities facing a client system in a number of theoretical languages. In the remainder of this book, I intend to promote the values of an internationalist approach to learning theories for practice and invite you to learn the basics of 10 different languages.

PREVIEW OF THEORETICAL TRANSLATION TOOLS

Theories about the person, the social and environmental context, and common membership problems are excellent and essential tools. However, no one theoretical framework can explain all practice challenges, and social work practitioners can no longer afford to follow outdated directives regarding the teaching of theory: Don't learn any theoretical language; learn only my preferred theoretical language; learn the trendy language this week, and then learn the next theoretical language in vogue; learn systems theory and life course approaches, and somehow you'll incorporate knowledge about multiple theories.

As with nations striving to succeed in the global economy, social workers will never prosper by embracing belligerence or isolationism. Novice social workers can aspire to become theoretical internationalists and work to attain familiarity with multiple theoretical languages while developing a commitment to lifelong expansion of across-tradition language skills.

In the next two chapters, I will make use of my dialogical approach to scientific theories (Duncker, 2001; Norcross & Thomas, 1988; Sarukkai, 2002) and introduce you to a variety of translation tools models (theoretical exemplars or role models, root metaphors, theoretical maps, theory-based eco-maps, and theoretical models) that will help you learn various theoretical languages and will help you relate these languages to the professional language of social work. In Chapters 4 through 13, I present translation mechanisms for facilitating your understanding of 10 theoretical languages. Chapter 14 will summarize some of the latest routes and strategies for integrating knowledge in a multitheory world.

LEARNING ACTIVITIES

1. Many social workers assist older clients who live in nursing homes. These social workers often work on interdisciplinary teams. What occupational groups might be represented on such a team? What different ideas and words (theoretical perspectives and languages) about helping residents might team members bring to a group meeting?

2. Identify two empirical generalizations about membership in your society. Discuss the relevance of each to social work practice.

3. Interview your field supervisor or some other professional social worker. Find out how he or she defines the concept *theory*. With what theoretical tradition and/or practice theory does the social worker identify?

4. Let's begin thinking metaphorically. Have you noticed that some agencies refer to clients as *customers* and others use the term *patient*? Mental health clubhouses prefer the word *member*. Review what you know about your field placement agency or some other human service organization. Make some comparisons referring to this agency that complete the following phrases: A social worker is like _____. A client is like _____. The agency is like _____. Discuss your comparisons with students reporting on different agencies, and summarize your work here.

5. The social role theory uses the metaphor of drama. A client is like a performer in a play,

and the social environment is like the stage of a theater. Think metaphorically. Use the social role theory and discuss what a social worker might be like.

6. The concept *reference group* is familiar to many social workers. Develop a nominal and operational definition of this concept. What might a reference group theory look like? What social system level or levels (micro, mezzo, or macro) might reference group theory address?

7. Social workers pay special attention to clients who are members of "populations at risk," such as lesbian, gay, and bisexual people. Develop a middle-range deductive theory that explains hate crimes against people with an alternative sexual orientation. Identify several concepts, and relate these concepts to each other in propositional form. Finally, propose a testable hypothesis about specific social groups or actions that might be deduced from a general premise in your theory. Summarize your theory here.

8. Look at Tables 1.2 and 1.3. What observations about the stated theoretical preferences of theory users can you make? How do the preferences of social workers compare to the preferences of those who are not social workers? What lessons do you draw from your examination of these summaries of theoretical preferences?

9. Search for examples of the different ways that social workers use theory. Check with workers in your field agency. Look through your textbooks or talk to your teachers. Make use of social work search engines. Attempt to find an example of how social workers use theory to classify. Identify an illustration of the use of theory for explanatory purposes. Finally, record social workers' use of theory, and perhaps of the research literature, to help in predicting client actions.

10. Think about your experience as a social work student so far. Identify some teachers, agency-based social workers, and fellow students who have talked to you about theoretical orientations. Characterize their overall stance toward theory. What did you learn from these interactions? How have they influenced your own ideas about approaching theory for practice?

11. Develop a vision of your progress toward multitheoretical fluency. Review the theorizing competencies and the levels of theorizing achievement presented in this book. Identify your short-term and long-term goals for learning theories and theorizing. Create a timetable for goal achievement, and select three or four strategies for staying on course toward your goals.

ADDITIONAL RESOURCES

Additional resources are available on the Book Companion Website at **www.thomsonedu.com/social_work/forte**. Resources include key terms, tutorial quizzes, links to related websites, and lists of additional resources for furthering your research.

2

CHAPTER

Tools for Translating and Practical Theorizing

Models and Metaphors

Members of the social work profession belong to a mutual aid community. Social workers help each other. Many dedicated social workers are eager to help you find the tools and resources necessary to apply theory to practice. Your college or university has social work professors, and even teachers from allied disciplines like psychology and sociology, who will help you. Your field placement agency has experienced direct service practitioners and administrators who have much to offer. Of course, your field instructor or supervisor has agreed to guide you, too. Other social workers, human service professionals, and social scientists you may never meet in person can also help you. These experts have contributed their theoretical ideas, their research studies, and their lessons from practice experiences to our professional knowledge base. Their advice and help are available in books, articles, and other published works. The process of connecting theory to practice, for novice social workers, requires you to seek and use the expertise and advice of these mentors.

In this chapter, I will begin to teach you how to use role models to facilitate the theory application process. I will also introduce you to the "root metaphor" tool. Additionally, I will present an approach for organizing your career-long efforts to connect theory and practice.

TOOLS FOR TRANSLATING AND PRACTICAL THEORIZING

I would like to review some of the tools and strategies that you can use during your own theory application. These can help you understand many different theoretical perspectives. Theoretical traditions and theories are like languages. When you travel in Europe or Africa, you use translators to help you negotiate new terrain and cultures. Theoreticians have also developed tools that can be used as "universal translators."

The effective scientific practitioner talks to himself or herself continually (Forte, 2001). Inner dialogue is an important part of the theorizing process. I hope that this book stimulates such private conversations and makes the self-talk of many practitioners richer and more multivocal. Reading the seminal works of human behavior theorists, for instance, brings us into subvocal contact with the voices of those who have long pondered issues of interest to practitioners. The reader might even pause and speak an important passage aloud.

When faced with a practice challenge, the practitioner can engage in inner deliberations that incorporate the internalized voices from a choir of theoretical and practice ancestors. How might Sigmund Freud proceed in this case? What contribution might Karl Marx make to understanding the current political and economic scene? Could George Herbert Mead provide a useful hypothesis here? While talking to himself or herself about how to best understand the client system and the environmental context, the practitioner can also call up the voices of the exchange theorists, the feminists, the evolutionary biologists, and the other spokespersons for various theoretical frameworks. The practitioner can then ask himself or herself: What might each of these contribute to a full understanding of the practice situation? Which theoretical perspective or perspectives might be most useful? Which combinations of perspectives could help? In what ways do competing theorists and theoretical perspectives offer contradictory or irreconcilable advice about how to assess and to intervene?

When practitioners are stuck with a theoretical puzzle, research question, or practical problems, they might ask themselves, "Who am I going to call for help?" The list of potential allies should be long (Forte, 2001). It might include sociologists, psychologists, biologists, geneticists, ethologists, ecologists, geographers, demographers, economists, architects, political scientists, philosophers, dramatists, actors, computer scientists, anthropologists, marketing and advertising professionals, revolutionaries, and many others. Talking to specialists associated with these allied disciplines and diverse theoretical frameworks need not weaken our sense of professional identity. Social workers stand on a "common base." This distinctive orientation to helping work includes a widely agreed upon sense of professional mission, a set of core values, an inventory of relationship-building skills, and a commitment to the planned change process.

These specialists can benefit also from public conversations with social work and sociological practitioners. If they listen more to practitioners, for example, they might learn valuable lessons from those who take seriously the pragmatist maxim of putting knowledge to the test of use. Such lessons can strengthen both theory and research. This chapter will introduce three theory translation tools. First, I will describe how you can purposefully supplement public dialogues with theory experts and engage in imaginary conversation with **role models,** the theorists and practitioners who exemplify the development and application of theory for public problem solving. They can become internalized guests during your professional deliberations. Let me digress briefly and discuss my understanding of social work.

SOCIAL WORKERS AS COOPERATIVE KNOWLEDGE USERS

Cooperation is an essential ingredient of professional social work (Aronoff & Bailey, 2003; Graham & Barter, 1999). We cooperate with our clients to learn about their needs and to develop helping plans. We talk and work with the significant others of our clients: friends, family members, and co-workers. We cooperate across professional allegiances and occupational memberships and work together at times with clinical psychologists, nurses, doctors, accountants, applied sociologists, priests or ministers, and others. We cooperate as members of professional associations with our fellow association members (the National Association of Social Workers, Association for the Advancement of Social Work with Groups, the Environment for Social Work and Research, and others), and we cooperate with members of other associations.

Social work borrows knowledge from other disciplines. For example, the Council on Social Work Education's Educational Policy and Accreditation Standards includes the following mandate:

> Social work education programs provide content on the reciprocal relationships between human behavior and social environments. Content includes empirically based theories and knowledge that focus on the interactions between and among individuals, groups, societies, and economic systems. It includes theories and knowledge of biological, sociological, cultural, psychological, and spiritual development across the life span; the range of social systems in which people live (individual, family, group, organizational, and community); and the ways social systems promote or deter people in maintaining or achieving health and well-being. (Council on Social Work Education, 2001, p. 7)

When borrowing and using this knowledge, we are cooperating and learning from the knowledge developers of different academic enterprises, including education, nursing and medicine, business, psychology, and sociology. This is how social work expands its knowledge base.

Complete agreement on a list of the major disciplines does not exist (Smelser, 2004). However, social workers may find themselves borrowing and using ideas from the biological sciences, including genetics, evolutionary biology, and biochemistry; psychology and the related sciences, such as behavioral psychology, humanistic psychology, ego psychology, cognitive science; the sciences of the environment and of social structure, including sociology (social role theory, social systems theory, conflict theories, social exchange theory), economics, and political science; the sciences of culture, such as anthropology and symbolic interactionism; the fine arts and humanities, including philosophy (pragmatism, existentialism, postmodernism) and religion; the sciences of ecology, including demography and geography; and hybrid disciplines such as child development, sociobiology, race and ethnic studies, gender studies, and environmental sociology.

Effective cooperation and collaboration with clients, with client collaterals, with representatives of different disciplines, with colleagues from other professional groups, and with social workers who speak different theoretical languages require exceptional communication skill. In this chapter, I will introduce you to three theory translation tools that will facilitate cooperative communication. First, I will suggest how you might make purposeful use of role models to enhance your private and public deliberations about practice challenges. Second, I will show how you can exercise your metaphorical imagination, the use of metaphor, to make comparisons between the complex and abstract parts of a theoretical perspective and everyday events, things, and processes. Third, I will introduce you to theoretical modeling, the construction of organized structures of concepts and propositions to help you assess and serve clients with particular problems.

Chapter 3 will present theoretical mapping, a translation tool for visually displaying the concepts and the relationships between concepts that constitute a particular theoretical perspective, and ecosystems mapping, a translation tool for transforming a theoretical language into the familiar terminology of ecosystems theory. These tools will prepare you for cooperating with professionals who speak different theoretical languages and laypersons speaking nontheoretical languages. In Chapters 4 through 13, I will demonstrate the use of these metatheoretical tools by translating 10 different theoretical frameworks into comprehensible terms and into the language of social work.

ROLE MODELS: USEFUL THEORISTS AND SCHOLARLY PRACTITIONERS

Imagine that you could confer with some of the most educated, creative, hardworking, moral, and compassionate theorists and theory users of the last century. These theorists are like the language innovators who enrich a culture's working vocabulary (Romaine, 2000). They have been instrumental in creating the theoretical and professional terminologies that have been transmitted across history and throughout the global social work community. Imagine that you could ask them for their advice and then use this advice to increase your professional sensitivity and effectiveness. Imagine, for example, that Jane Addams, the great social theorist and social worker, could respond to your summons and join you in deliberations about practice. To your inaudible question, "What would Jane do (WWJD) in this situation?" you would hear an answer echoing from her practice experiences, her theorizing at Hull House and the University of Chicago, her professional writings, and her personal setbacks and triumphs.

I shall introduce you to a new way of thinking about your professional "self," one that gives central importance to communication with real others and with our imaginary reconstruction of others. Symbolic interactionists view the self in conversational terms. The major participants in intrapsychic discussions are the "**I**," the impulsive or spontaneous aspect of the self, the "**me**," the internalized perspectives of particular others and generalized groups and institutions, and "**guests**," the representations of real or imagined others who participate in a temporary way in our inner deliberations.

The **professional self** is like a noisy and active forum where the practitioner debates, deliberates, and decides about various practice matters with many imaginary people. I will acquaint you in this section with a mental procedure for inviting others to become part of your "inner forum." This procedure will equip you to personify **useful theorists** and **scholarly practitioners** and to cultivate working relationships with them; to use them as supports, models, and fellow fighters for social justice; and to learn from your imaginary interactions with these guests to become a better social worker. In each of the chapters following the next one, I will profile exemplary useful theorists and scholarly practitioners in ways designed to stir your imagination and to entice you to employ these role models as professional consultants.

THE PROFESSIONAL SELF AND THE CONSTANCY OF SELF-TALK

What do we mean by **inner conversations?** All humans interact with themselves (Athens, 1994). Verify this assertion by asking yourself, "Do I ever talk to myself?" Verify it by listening to yourself answer the question "What am I thinking?" (Honeycutt, Zagacki, & Edwards, 1989). Social work practitioners can engage in numerous types of private conversation. We can pose questions to ourselves and answer them. We can play with words and sounds. We can make remarks to absent or nonhuman others. We can label and describe our own activity or that of others. We can talk about what we are thinking. We can curse silently. We can respond to environmental or bodily stimuli with self-talk. We can speak to ourselves instead of muttering damaging remarks to others. We can talk to ourselves as a way to savor and collect delightful life experiences. We can ask ourselves questions about how to handle a social work practice situation.

Contemporary practitioners are members of complex and pluralistic societies. Our social worlds include numerous and specific others with whom we have formed personal or social relationships. We are members of many different social groups and of many large social organizations and societal institutions. Our memberships involve real relationships, real groups, and real institutions, but we also share memberships with imagined others and imaginary social systems. Those memberships that have importance to our daily psychosocial functioning, and our social work practice, are the internalized ones endowed with special symbolic significance. **Significant others** is the technical term for those people designated internally as mental representations who participate as the most influential voices in our inner deliberations (Anderson & Glassman, 1996). They live in us as the "me" part of our personality. These significant others are present to us no matter where we move in our social ecology, or when we met them on our personal time line, whether they are living or dead, real or artificial.

For present purposes, I would like also to stress the importance of one set of unseen members of the self's inner forum: role models. Role models are actual associates or fantasized others who signify or symbolize for us the values and behaviors of the culture that we affirm (Rochberg-Halton, 1984). They can be, for social workers, the great theorists and practitioners from the past. They are the heroes and heroines of our time. They are the exemplary performers of important social roles. They are the social workers, political leaders, and educators who represent in unique and distinctive ways what we would like to become. We admire these role models as exemplars, imitate them, and invite them to become critical participants in our inner deliberations. We listen carefully to their subvocal recommendations for action (Caughey, 1984).

Some exemplars and role models become so significant that we internalize them as part of the "me." However, some members of the set of role models and exemplars profiled in this book may be only visitors or guests in the practitioner's inner forum (Wiley, 1994). These are temporary participants invited for particular purposes and special conversations. We might eventually ask them to take up permanent residence in our minds so that they are continuously present and ready for any internal conversation (Wiley, p. 55). These imagined others speak from the perspective of their real-life counterparts until they may become absorbed into the "me" and lose their distinctive identity and voice. The imaginary guests are the perfect professional consultants. They work free. They are available 24 hours a day. They have excelled in scholarship and service. They are committed to democratic ideals, social justice, and the alleviation of human suffering. They speak from a lifetime of distinguished service, and they offer us their words and deeds as tools for sharpening our assessment abilities and increasing our intervention effectiveness.

THE USE OF THEORISTS DURING IMAGINED DIALOGUE

Imaginary guests can support us in our work. During the moments of confusion, indecision, and blocked action that emerge in assessment and intervention processes, we can invite them to join our inner dialogue and offer novel perspectives and valuable solutions. Figure 2.1 suggests that we often begin to talk to ourselves when we face practice situations that challenge us, especially when our work habits and past training provide no remedy. During such impasses, the spontaneous and flowing action of the professional stops. At these moments, we begin talking to ourselves (theorizing tentatively), and we start to search our past relationship experiences, the "me," for helpful definitions of the situation. We might consciously invite real and imaginary mentors, theorists, and practitioners, the "guests," to assist us during these deliberations. It is quite likely that consideration of their perspectives will provide us new definitions and solutions, and thus increase our creativity, accountability, and effectiveness. They can help us progress despite the obstacle. Jane Addams and George Herbert Mead advise me often during my unspoken and imaginary dialogues.

Next time you face a life challenge, pause. Check your impulses. Think about significant others in your life and how they could offer guidance. Think about exemplars across historical periods and societies who could comment helpfully. Imagine yourself conversing with these consultants. Reflect on what they suggest you think, feel, and do. What creative options do they propose?

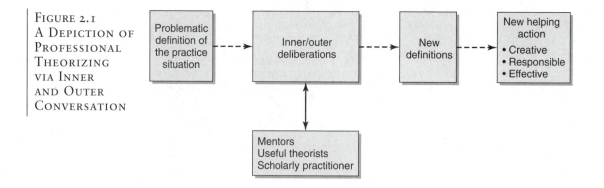

FIGURE 2.1
A DEPICTION OF
PROFESSIONAL
THEORIZING
VIA INNER
AND OUTER
CONVERSATION

Summarize the possibilities for productive action that emerge during this inner conversation. Pick the best course of action. End the pause for inner reflection and meet your challenge.

THE USE OF MENTORS DURING PUBLIC DIALOGUE

Mentors are people who guide us and help us develop our potentials as students, workers, and people. Many seasoned social workers are experts in a particular theoretical language, even if they take their fluency for granted. Novice theory users can turn to mentors in the same way that those learning a new language turn to language informants: the community elders, the tour guides, the local officials and other people who are willing to help us learn their way of communicating (Marshall, 1989). You can ask a mentor to quiz you on your understanding and pronunciation of theoretical terms. You can ask your mentor to explain terms used in the practice setting that you do not understand. You can work with the mentor to create a list of the most frequently used theoretical terms. You can ask your mentor to observe you and provide feedback when you use a theoretical language to discuss a case at a meeting. You can ask your mentor to recommend workshops and classes designed to increase your theoretical fluency. You can report back to your mentor on your understanding of a published theory-based practice case or research study. You can practice mapping or diagramming a theory of a client problem with your mentor. You can ask your mentor to create an opportunity to explain some part of a theory to a receptive public audience.

The mentor may be a theoretical expert and a fluent speaker of the theoretical language. Medical social workers, for instance, are often quite adept at teaching the biological language of diseases and medications to their apprentices. Agency administrators are often conversant with and can teach the economic vernacular. The mentor is often a field instructor. He or she will probably agree to socialize you to the use of the local theoretical orientations; to drill you on specific theoretical concepts and definitions; to show you the ways that the theory has been translated for assessment and intervention purposes; and to help you converse with professionals from various disciplines who work in your agency. Even when you are not in the physical presence of your mentor, you can think about what advice and supportive words he or she would offer. One field instructor in the psychiatric unit of a Veteran Center, for example, challenged his intern to prepare for each team case meeting by formulating diagnostic assessments based in the psychodynamic theoretical framework. After every meeting, the instructor and student compared the student's use of diagnostic terminology with that of the experienced diagnosticians and of the diagnostic manual.

You might also look for a field instructor or other social workers at your field agency to tutor you in the use of a theoretical language. Apprenticeships with agency instructors who speak several theoretical languages might be arranged for advanced students. Make a plan to identify mentors and seek their help.

Students can also observe and listen to social work practitioners who are adept at different theoretical languages. These are practitioners with a special interest in and aptitude for the daily application of one theoretical approach. They can act like translators during your travels abroad and teach you the theoretical terms necessary for successful cooperation with others. Make a plan to find one or two helpful translators.

For an HBSE course that I taught several years ago, a group of experienced social workers were invited to discuss with the students their theoretical allegiance, the process by which they learned their preferred theoretical language, the ways that their language guides an assessment and intervention, and the communication challenges in their agency. Presentations by the guests were followed by discussion. Guests presented the Afrocentric perspective, the language of spirituality based social work, and feminism. Students were enthusiastic about the exposure to these practitioners and their approaches, and comforted to hear how complex theoretical languages could be learned and used competently to carry out various normal work duties. Over time, you too may internalize both the new concepts and the translation skills taught to you by your translators.

You can also look for allies in your efforts to master theories at your college or university. Your classroom instructors and teachers from other disciplines and departments have special theoretical expertise that they can share with you. The social work faculty may include members with various areas of expertise. During my graduate studies, I learned from experts in ego psychology and object relations theory, experts in the existential-humanistic approaches, and experts in symbolic interactionism. The faculty at your school associated with allied departments such as biology, sociology, psychology, economics, nursing, and political science may be willing to answer your questions about theory and tell you about particular theoretical terms, resources, and applications. Consider who might teach you more about your favorite theory.

To learn more about theoretical languages at my university, for example, a student could pick from a wide array of courses. Here are a few: physical anthropology; human psychophysiology; biology and environment; ecology; genetic analysis; biology and environment; evolutionary biology; energy and the environment; humans and the environment; communication theory; theories of conflict and conflict resolution; macro theory (economics) and micro theory (economics); the history of economic thought; development, learning, and assessment; introduction to environmental science; survey of finance (theories); introduction to human geography; environmental hazards; information systems concepts for management; interdisciplinary general education; social science; organizational theory; nursing theories; theory of knowledge (philosophy); political theory; developmental psychology; history and systems in psychology (theories); sociology of the environment; foundations of sociological theory; and contemporary sociological theory.

You can also seek mentors in the past. Many ideas and theories only became part of the professional knowledge base because of the creative thinking and actions of exemplars, great or "key" figures in history. Jay Haley (1969), a family therapist, used Jesus Christ as his role model and showed how Christ's life exemplified the use of ideas and tactics to bring about revolutionary social change. When facing professional challenges, Haley could converse imaginatively with Christ and reflect on the lessons taught by the Bible. Jesus is one of my heroes, too, and his teachings remind me of the importance of accepting people who are different, fighting for the downtrodden, and showing compassion to all.

Each theoretical "school of thought" or tradition traces its development back to original founders. The associations and journals of different schools of thought also recognize and applaud the work of outstanding contemporary theorists. You can learn about the lives, theories, and contributions of these exemplars, and about how their personal histories shaped their theoretical viewpoints (Lengermann & Wallace, 1981). You might pattern your own professional thinking after that of an exemplar. Many possibilities will be discussed in this book; in addition, the References section lists numerous books that offer profiles of exemplary theorists and practitioners.

TWO KINDS OF EXEMPLARY MODELS

Useful theorists is my term for exemplary theorists who developed knowledge with utility for social workers. George Herbert Mead was a most useful symbolic interactionist. *Scholarly practitioners* is my term for practitioners who wrote about practice experiences, and formulated these ideas as practice theories, models, and guidelines. Jane Addams was a great scholar and practitioner.

Each chapter in this book on a theoretical framework will summarize the work of the tradition's great theorists and practitioners. Theoretical languages are created and developed by individuals, and my biographies of useful theorists will help you learn about the theories by introducing you to the historical context, major scientific works, service activities, and styles of theorizing of these exemplars. Reading these biographies can show you also that useful theorists and scholarly practitioners shared a common human condition despite their intellectual differences, and the biographical information may assist you as you try to translate the theoretical frameworks into your own language (Ritzer, 1991a).

I hope that some of these useful theorists and scholarly practitioners, whether living or dead, will become imaginary guests at your inner conversations, and especially during your reflections on practice. You might ask them theorizing questions as if you were really talking to them. What concepts and theories can you contribute to my professional theoretical toolbox? What can I learn from the way you responded to the intellectual challenges and public problems of your day? Were there particular theoretical puzzles or practice dilemmas that attracted your attention, and how might your solutions have relevance to me? How did you deal with tough moral or ethical quandaries? What side would you take in contemporary social work debates about the best approach to research or the tension between clinical practice and political advocacy? In what ways did you effectively make changes in your physical and social environment? What specific suggestions might you offer to help me better assess, intervene, and evaluate?

I am recommending in this book that you select a number of exemplary, and effective, useful theorists and scholarly practitioners from the scientific and social worker traditions. Imagine that each is joining a network of significant others that will support and help you, your personal team of theory consultants. I encourage you to open yourselves to their positive influence and nurture these relationships across your career.

THE METAPHORICAL IMAGINATION: A TOOL FOR LEARNING THEORETICAL LANGUAGES

Metaphors are imaginative comparisons between one object and another object based on a perceived similarity (Pugh, Hicks, Davis, & Venstra, 1992). A metaphor links two objects, ideas, or processes that are similar in some ways (Rosenblatt, 1994). The compared entities have similar elements, patterns, associations, or implications. Useful metaphors have extended applicability and relevance.

The **metaphorical imagination** is the use of a mode of theorizing wherein we interpret one domain of experience through the language of another, creating a fusion of images and associations between the two (Rigney, 2001). Lakoff and Johnson (1980) explain that we theorize about ourselves and we experience (perceive, think, and act in) the world by use of metaphors. Consider the powerful influence of self-conceptions based on two different metaphors: "I am the captain of my fate" versus "I am a small boat tossed about in a large sea." Daily life will be very different for the client who uses the first metaphor compared to the one who uses the second one. In this book, we will use the metaphorical imagination to enhance our theorizing competencies.

Metaphorical thinkers can use different types of metaphors: **similes**—A is *like* B in certain ways; **analogies**—the detailed identification of the points of similarity between A and B; **personifications**—the assignment of human qualities to an animal, inanimate object, or idea; and **symbols**—stylized but arbitrary representations that have become an agreed-upon part of a community's communication system (Pugh, Hicks, Davis, & Venstra, 1992; Rigney, 2001). Since we are not English majors or experts, the use of metaphor in this book will follow the recommendation of Pugh and her associates. They suggest that the differentiated use of the four language tools is unnecessary. Instead, the common element of each tool, **comparison,** will suffice for novice theory learners. Our emphasis, then, will be on the imaginative use of comparison as a way to gain basic familiarity with ten theoretical languages. Fine distinctions between the different types of metaphor will not be required for professional social work purposes.

Root Metaphor: The Sustainer of a Theoretical Language

Social work students often view theories as complicated codes almost impossible to decipher. Theoretical languages, like everyday languages, make much use of metaphor. Metaphors are omnipresent in scientific discourse (Rosenblatt, 1994). Theoreticians often use ideas with vivid associations to everyday life (ego defenses and military defenses, for example). Variable names often have metaphoric connections (societal stratification involves a comparison to strata, levels of a rock formation). Research methods are rich with metaphoric imagery. Think of the associations to *focus group* or *interview*. Applied scientists such as social workers use comparisons frequently. Some take issue, for example, with the use of *diagnosis* as a term for social work assessment because of its medical meanings. I have always had unpleasant associations to the practice concept of *client termination* because it reminds me of the *Terminator* films.

In this book, we focus on a particular use of metaphors in theorizing. Pepper (1942), a philosopher, helps simplify the task of decoding complicated theories. He argued that each framework of thought or paradigm about the world is built on a **root metaphor.** The theory and all its branches depend, like a tree, on the root system for support and nourishment. The tradition's assumptions, concepts, and propositions grow from its metaphorical roots or foundations. Members of each theoretical tradition explicitly or implicitly compare the person, the environment, and the change agent to different objects, events, or processes. It will be easier to learn theory, I propose, if we start by thinking about how each theoretical language expands in these three ways on its root or central metaphor. Each of my theory chapters will identify the theory's metaphor of the person, the environment, and the change agent. Once you learn the root metaphor, you can practice theorizing by shifting in your thinking back and forth between what is well known to you and the abstract, theoretical ideas that are strange or hard to understand.

The Use of Theoretical Metaphors

Metaphors are central to our mastery of scientific theories. Developing the metaphorical imagination means looking for and noticing the similarities or relationships between theoretical knowledge and knowledge from the social world. Metaphors have a variety of specific uses.

The metaphorical imagination can foster theoretical synthesis. Shoemaker, Tankard, and Lasorsa (2004) tell us that metaphors are very helpful in the early stages of theorizing and theory building. If we have not yet found a way to express our ideas about a client problem or practice challenge in words, then generating metaphors and their associated images may facilitate the creative thinking process. We can assemble all the information we have obtained about the client–environment configuration and summarize it in metaphorical terms. Our theory might build to the metaphor of "boundary issues" or "poor adaptation."

Rosenblatt (1994) adds that applying your metaphorical imagination can lead to new discoveries and insights. Some great theoretical scientists, for example, have used imagery and ideas from everyday activities that were generated while dreaming to solve theoretical and research puzzles. Metaphors "stretch" our minds into new places. The boundary metaphor can alert you to the symbolic and physical barriers created by a family to resist the influences of others, for instance.

The metaphorical imagination can foster the retention of theoretical knowledge. Metaphors are valuable memory devices (Shoemaker et al., 2004). They are often catchy and vivid. The translation of theoretical knowledge by metaphor will help novice and expert practitioners remember a large set of theoretical perspectives by creating associations between root metaphors and evocative memories (Wickman, Daniels, White, & Fesmire, 1999). Social work students, I believe, will find it possible to remember the general themes and the specific details of the ten theoretical languages reviewed in this book if they start with each theory's root metaphor.

The metaphorical imagination can foster theoretical evaluation. Identifying and exploring the metaphors implicit in a theoretical language can help us appraise the strengths and limitations of the theory. Think about the social role theory metaphor of life as a drama. Much of the theory is based on the imagery of the stage and of actors learning scripts. This imagery helps us understand much about the scripted nature of client behavior and development across role careers. However, critics argue that the metaphor is limited and that many of our role performances are improvised. In some ways, life is more like participation in an improvisatory comedy troupe than in a Shakespearean acting company.

Rosenblatt (1994) proposes some questions that can be used for appraising the quality of a theory's underpinnings. Do the comparisons and distinctions made by a new theoretical metaphor differ from those of existing root metaphors? For example, do new models of social work organized around the imagery of storytelling differ from older models? Are the parts of the metaphor organized in a coherent fashion, or are they disconnected? For example, does the new "narrative social work model" meld images of stories, storytelling, story revision, listeners, and storytelling sites coherently? Is there a good match between the theoretical abstractions and the life experiences linked metaphorically? In what ways is social work practice, for instance, like listening to a story and suggesting areas for story improvement? Does the root metaphor provide new and useful ways of conceptualizing the social work planned change process? If social work is like listening to the client story, what does that metaphor add to conventional notions of data gathering, assessment formulation, contracting, and so on? Does the root metaphor connect with and evoke a theory user's feelings as well as cognitions? How well does the narrative metaphor work for you? What feelings and thoughts have you experienced while reading this paragraph?

The metaphorical imagination can improve theory application. Practitioners who are stuck and looking for insights into public problems, client system difficulties, research barriers, or the helping process might consider the metaphors from alternative theoretical languages. Shuffling from one to another can lead to new insights, solutions, and discoveries (Rosenblatt, 1994). This process requires the sequential consideration of each theoretical concept's entailments. Entailments, according to Rosenblatt, are the automatic associations to a concept; "using a metaphor makes entailed associations, connections, and creative leaps likely, if not certain" (p. 23). Using multiple metaphors will help us develop more comprehensive assessments and enable us to select from a wider range of possible interventions than if we rely on one theoretical language and its root metaphor. Shuffling between images of a particular family member as a part of a machine, as an organ in a body, as an actor in a play, and as a fighter in a war, for example, will enrich our understanding of the client and her family.

Let me summarize by quoting Rosenblatt (1994) on the value of the metaphorical imagination for the attainment of theorizing competency: "it is a step toward more powerful, creative, and flexible theorizing to be able to recognize the metaphors we use for what they are, to explore what they highlight and obscure, and to acquire fluency in developing and applying alternative theoretical metaphors" (p. 11).

A PREVIEW OF THEORETICAL ROOT METAPHORS

Here is my recommended starting point for developing our metaphorical imaginations. Try to learn first the specific way each theoretical language is built on a central metaphor. Remember that a metaphor makes a comparison between two unlike things. Then attempt to discover how each different theorist fills in the following sentences: The person or client is like _____. The environment is like _____. The social worker is like _____. The key assumptions, concepts, and propositional statements for each theoretical language can often be sensibly linked to these metaphors.

Contemporary social life is very complex, and no root metaphor captures all aspects of this reality (Rosenblatt, 1994). You are invited to learn multiple metaphors. The following summary of the root metaphors used by theorists and practitioners who have developed the ten different theoretical languages explored in this book will serve as a preview for our metaphorical imagining in Chapters 4 through 13.

Behaviorists emphasize the commonality between humans and other animals. Much of their early research, for example, examined the learning process in rats, pigeons, and dogs. Lessons from this research were later extended to human learning. Behaviorists conceive of the environment as a laboratory where the major variables associated with learning can be controlled. Social workers are like the laboratory scientists or behavioral engineers who manipulate various contingencies to obtain desired results. Clients are like the animals conditioned by Pavlov and the other behaviorists. Concepts such as *learning, behavior, behavior training, behavior modification, rewards for behavior,* and *punishment* grew from the theory's root metaphors.

Cognitive psychologists often compare humans to computers. Our brains are the hardware, and our patterns of thinking are the software. The environment is conceptualized as a network of computers. The social worker is the computer programmer who helps community members install new software programs in the young (initial socialization) and fixes problems in the software programs of older clients (resocialization). The addition of more and better software equips the client for executing complex programs of action. Concepts such as *schemas, accessibility of cognitions, cognitive capacity, memory storage,* and *mental plans* are related to this metaphor.

Critical theorists, such as Marxists and feminists, see all social processes as marked by contention. The environment is like a battleground where warring groups fight for territory, wealth, prestige, and control of the media. The client is like a combatant in one of two armies: the army of the privileged or the army of underdogs. Most social work clients are underdogs. The privileged control most of the machinery for combat and so prevail in almost all struggles. Practitioners are strategists and advocates who try to help the underdogs defy the odds and win some battles. Words such as *conflict* and *struggle* characterize the social environment. Words such as *hegemony, dominance,* and *exploitation* point to the power of the privileged; *oppression, alienation,* and *revolution* refer to possible outcomes of the battle for those without privilege.

Ecologists compare the person to other living organisms. Every organism or client depends on reciprocal interchanges with the natural environment, and for humans the social environment, to grow. Organisms that fail to thrive are those subject to noxious or deficient interchanges. Social workers are gardeners or park rangers who tend to the whole environment so that it can best support all life. Concepts such as *nature, ecology, life space, place,* and *territory* characterize this theoretical community.

Economic and social exchange theorists conceive of human beings as calculators and traders who continuously attempt to maximize profit and minimize loss. The environment is like a marketplace where wheelers and dealers meet to exchange material and symbolic goods. Each client is looking for a good bargain. The social worker might be like a financial adviser assisting those vulnerable to unfair market policies and those with little capital. Concepts such as *cost, benefit, comparison ratios, investment, negotiation,* and *exchange networks* flow from this metaphorical starting point.

Evolutionary and biological theorists categorize all living beings according to their species membership and, thus, think in terms of evolutionary eons rather than days, months, or years. In the harsh version of evolutionary theory, the environment is compared to a jungle where species members are competing for survival. The survivors are those who have best adapted to jungle conditions. The weak—often those who seek social work services—perish, and their genes are removed from the gene pool. The social worker might be like the geneticist who considers the likely hereditary impact of a match between potential mates or the genetic contribution to patterns of cultural adaptation. Concepts such as *survival of the fittest, evolution, heredity, mutation,* and *adaptive mechanisms* are common in the discourse of evolutionary biologists, psychologists, and sociologists.

Psychodynamic theorists have likened the person to a wild man or beast. Freud, for example, compared the person to a runaway horse with a small and relatively ineffective rider (ego) trying to slow it down. The environment is like the circus or horse stable where the energies of wild beasts are channeled into acceptable, civilized patterns of action. The social worker is like the tamer of these animals, helping each client control primitive urges and passions. Concepts such as *instincts, aggression, sex drives, unconscious desires, repression*, and *suppression* reflect this metaphorical view.

Social role theorists think of the person as a social actor. Each client plays various parts in and acts in many different social dramas. The environment is like the stage for our various performances, and members of our social networks are the audiences. Some performances are reviewed positively by the audience, but some are judged failures. The social worker is like a theatrical director or acting coach who helps prepare the client to play a difficult part. Concepts such as *role, script, rehearsal, impression management, sincere performances*, and *cynical performances* are common in this dramaturgical tradition.

Social systems theorists make frequent use of the root metaphor of a machine with parts. The person or family is one part in a larger machine. The environment or social organization is the whole machine. If the parts of the environment work well together, the societal machine will do its jobs well. However, if any part breaks down, then the environment or organization (the assemblage of all working parts) will do its job poorly or cease to run. The social worker is like a mechanic trying to find the broken parts and fix them so that the machine returns to a state of efficient operation. Concepts such as *systems, subsystems, function, dysfunction, energy, steady state*, and *integration* are used by systems thinkers.

Symbolic interactionists emphasize the human capacity for symbol use. The human species has evolved so that its members can interact with each other using words, gestures, and sensible actions. Humans are the best conversationalists on the globe. An environment is like a conversation, one that started centuries ago, now involves thousands or millions of people, and focuses on many different topics. The social worker is the interpreter and discussion leader who helps people converse with one another. For instance, the social worker helps members of language communities that are outside the mainstream (working-class Hispanic American or African American groups in the United States) join in and influence the national conversation. Concepts such as *communication, definition of the situation, vocabularies of motive, working consensus, misunderstanding*, and *perspective taking* are part of the language of this tradition.

These metaphors can provide clues that help you match concepts to theories. Be aware that theories are expressed in a continually changing language. Members of a different theoretical community may disagree about the right words and best metaphors to use. Some concepts have been retired, and new concepts are continually recommended. We will return to our translations by use of the metatheoretical tool, root metaphors, later in the book.

STRATEGIES FOR DEVELOPING THE METAPHORICAL IMAGINATION

Skills at identifying the explicit and implicit root metaphors, images, and symbols that organize varied theoretical perspectives can be increased. Each theoretical language typically uses a small number of metaphors to explain biopsychosocial phenomena (Lakoff & Johnson, 1980). Translation by metaphor can be used to link complex and abstract theoretical ideas to concrete, everyday experiences (Wickman et al., 1999). Readers of this book will learn to make cross-domain comparisons. These translations connect the properties of something in a "source domain" to properties in the abstract "target domain." The **source domain** includes conceptual knowledge derived through bodily experiences, familiar events, objects, and what the student or practitioner has learned from others. These are your sense and abstract memories. The **target domain** includes theoretical constructs and propositions. These are the ingredients of the lectures, articles, and books about theory that you have a hard time understanding.

Rosenblatt (1994) provides some tips for recognizing metaphors. First, when you are reading or listening to a theoretical discussion, ask yourself where else the theoretical terms are used. When systems theorists communicate, they refer to *feedback*. Where have you heard this term? How are the everyday meanings similar or dissimilar to those associated with the systems theorists' linkage of feedback to their root metaphor of a self-regulating machine?

Second, consider whether the concept makes sense when used literally. If we take the psychodynamic imagery of the person's id or set of core impulses as an "unruly beast," does this make literal sense? Your body has many different internal parts, but no surgeon will find an inner beast if she or he operates. The term is metaphorical.

Third, try extending the implications of a theoretical concept. For example, interactionists often use images and symbols characterizing the person as a *member*. Can you identify recruitment and screening processes operative in a group's life? Can you think of groups to which you belong, and groups that refused you membership? Is it possible to lose your membership privileges? If you are able to answer such questions, then the theoretical concept is metaphorical, and comparisons between the abstraction and everyday life are valuable.

Fourth, seek information about the source domain (an occupation, a realm of activity, an artistic pursuit, for example) from which theoretical comparisons are made. If you learn more about this domain, you will more easily recognize the theory's associated metaphors and the implications of these metaphors. For example, when I try to make sense of the system concept of feedback, I reflect on my experience with my home's furnace, its operation, its breakdowns, its parts, and its need for servicing. This helps me grasp more fully what systems theorists mean by feedback mechanisms.

Finally, Rosenblatt recommends that you learn how to identify theoretical metaphors by creating some metaphors yourself. Let's try this out with a psychodynamic root metaphor. Refer to your own personal experience and imagine a "beast." Be specific and detailed. You might think about an unwanted bear at a campsite or the wild horses of Chincoteague walking up to your beach blanket. Then, imagine this beast living inside you and behaving badly. Now, connect these images and ideas to the theoretical domain: the psychoanalytic concept of the *unconscious,* a beast within. Draw out the associations and implications of this comparison. In what ways does your unconscious behave like a beast? In what ways is your unconscious unlike a beast? You have used your metaphorical imagination to start to grasp several of the complex ideas of the psychodynamic tradition.

METAPHORS OF MULTITHEORY PRACTICE

Let's try once more to begin using our metaphorical imagination, and to understand better the idea of multitheory social work practice. I am going to develop some comparisons between multitheory social work and everyday jobs and activities.

You have already been introduced to two basic metaphors that help me make sense of theorizing in a pluralistic practice world: translation and toolbox. First, the multitheory social worker is like a linguist or translator who is fluent in several languages, can converse effectively with persons from various speech communities, and can translate the communication of non-English-speaking persons to English listeners. Let's expand on this metaphor with some concrete images. The social work linguist can participate in a family assessment planning team with representatives from five different departments and from multiple professional groups in a large hospital. The social work linguist can understand the language of the priest from the pastoral counseling center speaking of a patient's faith-based beliefs and convictions related to an afterlife. This social worker can understand the physician speaking in terms of disease, medication, medical treatments, and prognosis. Finally, the multi-lingual social worker can even understand the program administrator who articulates an agency policy position using the language of tight budgets, fiscal accountability, sliding scale fees, and reimbursement plans.

Second, the multitheory social worker is like a carpenter with a large toolbox. In everyday life, a tool is a physical device designed to serve a particular purpose (White, 2005). Theories are the social worker's tools. They serve specific purposes such as the production of knowledge for use. The carpenter selects the right tools (hammer and nails, power saw and ruler, or screwdriver and screws) for each job; so does the multitheory social worker. The carpenter knows that tools (like theories) may need replacing at some time, and the carpenter knows that new and replacement tools are available at a hardware store. Theories are available in the professional literature. Here are a few concrete images of the multitheory social worker as tool user: The social work theory user can use an ego psychological life review to help nursing home residents give new meaning to their lives. She can use a behavioral observation checklist to help public school teachers track progress toward appropriate classroom behavior by their special education students. She can use a family-oriented eco-map to identify the environmental stressors and supports, the internal family subsystems, and the boundary regulation issues faced by a family joined by a former member returning from a state mental hospital. She can use economics and create a marketing plan as a tool to publicize and promote a program teaching safe sex practices.

Many other metaphors help me understand multitheory social work. The multitheory social worker is like an actor who continually expands his repertoire of parts so he is invited to participate in many different theoretical performances. He can use the economic framework as administrator to guide the board of directors as it conducts a cost-benefit analysis of a new program to divert nonviolent offenders from the criminal justice system. He can learn the critical theory scripts and perform as an advocate to document laws regarding drug use that treat members of minority cultural groups (crack users) differently than members of mainstream groups in suburbia (cocaine users). He can refer to social learning and role theory as a coach who prepares those recently released from prison for community roles of worker, tenant, roommate, and friend.

The multitheory social worker is like a camera operator who can shift lenses during a photo shoot depending on the changing conditions and goals of the model and the light. The social worker can use a certain lens for close-ups, the applied biological approach, to capture micro-level images of body chemistry associated with a client's anger management problems. The social worker as photographer can use another lens for standard-range photos—applied symbolic interactionism, for example—to study the patterns of interaction between the angry client and his family. Finally, the social worker can use a special long-distance lens, applied critical theory, to snap shots capturing the ways that social structural variables such as social class and minority group membership relate to individual member problems with rage, resentment, and repressed feelings of humiliation.

The multitheory social worker is like a diplomat with the knowledge and experience to participate in celebrations and ceremonies in various countries with grace and sophistication. The diplomatic social worker can work adeptly in many fields of practice and earn the regard of agency directors in each. He or she can use the behavioral framework as part of a behavior modification program in a school for children with behavioral problems. The same diplomat can work in a neighborhood center providing a nutrition and activity program for elderly persons and use the biological approach to understand the health needs of these clients.

The multitheory social worker is like an experienced map user who can select the map that best describes the terrain where he or she is traveling: a street map, a map of navigable waters, or a map of trails through the woods. So, too, the multitheory social worker can use different maps: a physical ecology map that traces the homeless client's daily routines in a neighborhood, locates resources in the community space, identifies dangerous spots, and describes paths for travel, physical features, and major buildings; a systems map that identifies all the large systems that indirectly influence family functioning of a recently evicted client family, and characterizes the nature of family system connections to the larger systems; or a map of the client's brain functioning presented in simplified form by the medical consultant to the homeless shelter to help workers understand the impact of Alzheimer's disease on an elderly alcoholic who has wandered repeatedly from the agency's house.

The multitheory social worker is like a perspective taker. Think of the proverbial elephant handlers who all took a look at the elephant from a different perspective (snout like a hose, leg like a tree trunk, tail like a fly swatter) and defined the animal in ways that fit their perspectives. The multitheory social worker can use different theoretical frameworks to shift perspectives on the client–environment configuration. She can use the applied ego psychological framework to aid in taking the perspective of the client's intimate others, mother, father, and siblings, and in taking client perspectives of which the client may not be fully aware. She can use the applied symbolic interactionist framework to aid in taking the perspective of significant others (teachers, best friends, lovers, spouses) who have influenced the client's identity formation process; reference group others whom the client uses to develop standards for success and life aspirations; and generalized others (such as religious organizations or the legal system) that the client uses to appraise the appropriateness of varied lines of conduct. She can use a critical or feminist framework to help take the perspective of marginal, exploited, oppressed, or powerless group members.

Finally, the multitheory social worker is like a bridge builder constructing connectors across rivers. The rivers are the divides separating those who speak different theoretical languages. You might expand on these metaphors or add your own. I can even imagine graduating social work students tailoring their presentation of self to a potential employer and the potential employing agency by using some of these metaphors.

FINAL THOUGHTS AND CAUTIONS FOR METAPHORICAL COMPARISONS

In this book, our metaphorical analysis of theoretical languages will look for **positive comparisons**. These comparisons identify attributes that A, a theoretical framework, shares with B, an everyday object or event. However, we will also consider the limits of each root metaphor (Rigney, 2001). These are neutral or negative comparisons. **Neutral comparisons** refer to metaphors for the framework's abstract conceptions of environment, social worker, or client that are yet unknown. For instance, you might not have yet discovered how exchange theory conceives of the worker role. **Negative comparisons** refer to differences between A and B, attributes that are not shared by the abstract theoretical idea and the object in the empirical world. Social scientists and social workers should be aware of a theoretical language's neutral and negative comparisons. These are the limits or deficiencies of the theoretical framework.

Cultivating your metaphorical imagination will help you theorize. How-ever, the use of metaphors can cause problems too. Shoemaker and associates (2004) offer a few cautions. Metaphors may be misleading, directing the theory user to see false similarities. Behaviorists, for example, have been tempted to take the comparison of human learners to animal learners (dogs, rats, and pigeons) too far. Humans' use of higher mental capacities during learning differentiates them from other animals in many important ways.

Metaphors may also tempt theorizers to engage in lazy or simplistic thinking. For example, a theorizer may make use only of positive comparisons and fail to do the hard work of studying the neutral and negative comparisons between everyday life and the theoretical abstractions. Theorizers may also fail to identify the aspects of a theory or theoretical framework not clarified at all by the metaphor.

MODELING: TRANSLATING THEORETICAL LANGUAGES INTO GUIDING CONCEPTIONS

I discussed earlier how you might use exemplars, people known for the skillful and intelligent application of theories to practice, as role models. In this section, I will discuss another use of the term *model*.

One of my friends is both a sociology professor and a model airplane enthusiast. He often spends one or two months designing and building a miniature version of a famous warplane. Each new construction is added to his large fleet of toy aircraft. He then joins with similar hobbyists and flies his planes. His planes are less than two feet long and have a rubber band propeller. However, each can fly several miles with a good wind. Of course, his planes cannot carry passengers, but they resemble actual planes in many ways.

A **model** is a small-scale or partial representation of something concrete in the world. There are models of airplanes, railroad trains, cars, and buildings. A model can also be a representation of something more abstract, such as the process of reconstructing a social network after a husband dies or the way that social workers find knowledge and translate it for use in practice. Shoemaker and associates (2004) define a **theoretical model** in this way: "a model simply represents a portion of reality, either an object or a process in such a way as to highlight what are considered to be key elements or parts of the object or process and the connections among them" (p. 110). Theoretical models provide a picture or partial representation of a scientific theory (White, 2005).

Theoretical models are good translation devices. Models, Britt (1997) shows in his book on conceptual modeling, "facilitate continuing dialogue about which concepts are important and unimportant, what their nature is and is not, and how they may and may not be related to one another" (p. vii). Theoretical models facilitate conversations across theoretical languages by providing a common and simple mode of communication, and theoretical models facilitate translation within a language by transforming complex ideas and patterns of ideas into verbal and visual summaries.

TYPES OF THEORETICAL MODELS

Max Black (1962) and other experts on theoretical modeling describe various kinds of models. **Scale models** are models like the fighter planes and bombers designed by my friend. They preserve the relative proportions between the model (the 18-inch, balsa wood dive bomber) and the material object or biopsychosocial system (the full-size plane preserved at an Air Force base). **Mathematical models** are very popular in the sciences. These use mathematical logic, symbols, formulations, and equations to illustrate and explain the relationship of variables in some biological, psychological, or social system. These are also sometimes called *formal models* (Humphreys, 1998; Land, 2001). **Conceptual models** use ideas and images expressed as concepts to make intelligible important aspects of some practical problem (Skvorertz, 1998). These models can be talked about by both scientists and practitioners. They are also called *semantic* (Shoemaker et al., 2004) or *expository models* (Lathrope, 1969) because the representation is restricted to words, and the model is presented in conventional sentence and paragraph form. Expository models, Lathrope advises, can be transformed into **research models** when propositions and their suspected relationship to empirical data are specified in a form identifying testable hypotheses.

Theoretical modeling has also been adapted for use by practitioners (Breakwell, 1982; Mullen, 1983; Reid, 1979). Mullen (1983) proposed that each social worker develop a set of **personal practice models,** "explicit conceptual schemes that express an individual social worker's view of practice and give orderly directions to work with specific clients" (p. 623). These models would summarize what a worker had learned from personal experience, theory, research, and practice wisdom about how best to work with particular clients with particular problems in particular agency settings. Each model in the set of personal practice models would organize its ingredients—theoretical concepts, research and practice generalizations, and practice guidelines—into a concise and usable verbal and visual form. Each model would be continually revised during practice.

Here is an example of a personal practice model: Reid (1979) guided his student, Ronald Rooney, in the development of a task-centered practice model. This model organized concepts and directives for helping natural parents secure the return of their children from foster care. The model gave central place to the worker–client tasks essential to family reunification.

The theoretical model has several other variations (Shoemaker et al., 2004). The **path model** represents the temporal order of causal processes for a set of two or more variables. For example, a loved one's death precedes the initiation of a grieving process, which precedes the initiation of an identity and a social network reconstruction project. This sequence can be displayed easily. A **structural model** describes the structure of some object or organization. For example, a sketch of the layout of a social work agency and an organizational chart depict, respectively, physical and social arrangements. A **functional model** describes the relationships among the parts of a larger system and suggests how each part functions for the benefit of the whole system.

In everyday life, we use category systems to understand ourselves and our social relations. We might have a simple way, for example, of classifying associates as friends or enemies. A scientific **taxonomy** is another way that theorists model the real world. Chafetz (1978) defines a taxonomy as "a classification scheme which is developed systematically by specifying a series of attributes and creating categories that exhaust the logical combinations of those attributes" (p. 67). In the chapter on applied systems theory, I will introduce you to a scheme for classifying families in terms of two attributes: cohesion and adaptiveness. In this book, I will use the term *theoretical model* to include mathematical, conceptual, research, personal practice, path, structural, and functional models, as well as taxonomies.

Theoretical models can be categorized in one other way, according to the model maker's approach to science. In the conventional or quantitative approach to scientific theorizing, theoretical models are described in terms of a number of related variables (Aneshensel, 2002; Shoemaker et al., 2004). A model may show the relationship between two variables—for example, the death of a loved one and the intensity of grief. The model may create linkages among three different variables: death, the suddenness of the death, and grief. Here, the sudden and unexpected death of a loved one is expected to have a greater negative impact on the grieving process than a long expected death. The model may portray the relationship of four or more variables. For example, theoretical linkages among a loved one's death, the suddenness of the death, the number of supportive others in the bereaved person's social network, and grief might be conceptualized, displayed, and eventually used to generate and test hypotheses.

Qualitative theoretical models summarize patterns identified in inductively generated theories, theories grounded in multiple observations of the social world (Soullier, Britt, & Maines, 2001; Strauss, 1987). Qualitative models may explicate and illustrate a relationship between concepts (stance toward an emergency shelter and thematic characterizations of the homeless); a trajectory in a client system's life or condition (a common path from home ownership to homelessness, for example); a sequence of actions (the routine interactions of a group of homeless persons in Austin, Texas); or the way ideal types are clustered (grouping homeless persons by the way each deals with shame). Qualitative models tell the model user what concepts are important to the grounded theory and what concepts are not important. Soullier and her colleagues used qualitative modeling to make sense of a large set of research observations. They diagrammed a model indicating the nature of the relationships between the status of customers (regular or not regular) at a business place, the amount and depth of personal talk with the customer, and the degree of comfort clients felt about the service provided.

The Uses of Modeling for Theoretical Translation

Each theoretical language or school of thought can be viewed as a family of related theoretical models (Land, 2001). If concepts are the bolts, bricks, and mortar of theories, then models are the interconnected beams and walls that hold these theoretical frameworks together. Practitioners may have difficulty fully understanding everything about a theory, and they will never apply an entire theoretical perspective to a particular practice challenge. However, theoretical models associated with a perspective are practical tools, and these tools can be used by social workers. Lathrope (1969) summarized their utility: "Models and model construction represent a highly general and versatile approach to the extraction, verification, accumulation, codification, presentation, transmission, and use of knowledge" (p. 46). Theoretical modeling helps us theorize and communicate about our theorizing in several specific ways.

First, models help social workers order and organize the profession's experiences and observations in a particular arena (Land, 2001; Shoemaker et al., 2004). For example, the task-centered model is a sophisticated organization of the profession's practical and research experience as problem solvers. It can be quickly taught and explained to students, workers, and clients.

Second, models help us see and talk about connections among biological, psychological, social, and spiritual processes as these relate to a problematic situation (Black, 1962). A model of alcohol relapse, for instance, may highlight the linkages among brain changes, stimuli, information processing, behavior chains, social pressures, and existential anxieties. Such a model communicates concisely how these related processes complicate attempts by alcoholics to abstain.

Third, theoretical models may suggest new "working hypotheses" that can guide us in our efforts to better understand the person-with-problem-in-a-place dynamics (Black, 1962). They are tools to stimulate theorizing and the theoretical imagination (Shoemaker et al., 2004). Lofland's (1985) model of grief work, for example, suggested the following proposition to my team of social workers: The greater the disruption to the social network of significant others caused by loss, the more difficult is the resolution of grief and its symptoms (Forte, Barrett, & Campbell, 1996). We transformed this proposition into a hypothesis and tested it with members of a bereavement group. This model will be discussed in detail in the chapter on psychodynamic ego psychology.

Modeling can be valuable to social workers in additional ways (Land, 2001; Shoemaker et al., 2004). Models can help us decide what needs to be assessed or measured. They can help us collect, assemble, and make sense of our assessment data. They can help us make comparisons between practice in one situation and practice in different situations, places, and time periods. Models can help us make predictions about the likely course of helping processes or the probable outcomes of a planned change process.

STRATEGIES FOR THEORETICAL MODELING

Theoretical model building involves a series of tasks (Black, 1962; Shoemaker et al., 2004). First, the model builder must identify and define a set of concepts that will help you understand a practice challenge. Books and articles about the theory, the research literature on the practice challenge, discussion with colleagues, or the builder's experience and logic can guide this process of identification. Second, the model builder must decide how the concepts are related to one another, and express these relationships as theoretical statements. Third, the model builder must create a visual equivalent for his or her understanding of the network of theoretical statements and propositions. Fourth, the model builder must devise ways to appraise the model's fit with the larger theoretical framework and with that part of the practice world represented by the model. Finally, the model must be revised and improved when new knowledge is acquired.

These steps for modeling can be cast in social work terms. First, social work theorizers identify theoretical concepts that help them organize the facts and patterns associated with a client's particular personal or public problem. Second, the worker begins to organize these concepts in a way that scientifically explains the problem. Third, the worker begins to transform the theoretical statements into images of the entities associated with the problem and images of the interrelationship of these entities. Fourth, the social worker proposes some rules for correlating the descriptions of the problem with evidence obtained in the actual helping situation. Last, the descriptions and predictions expected from the model are tested in the practice arena.

In each theory chapter of this book, I will share a theoretical model that has helped me during my social work research, practice, and teaching. These personal practice models will include a systems model for appraising military families, a biological model of alcohol addiction, a psychodynamic model of grief management and identity reconstruction, a cognitive model for work with neglectful mothers, an interactionist model for group work with the chronically depressed, a role theory model for promoting altruism, an economic model for web-based advocacy, a behavioral model for substance abuse treatment, an ecological model of homelessness, and a critical theory model of political justice. Although theoretical models differ in their conceptual language and their selection of relevant statements and linkages from that language, they share certain similarities. I show how each of my personal practice models provided guidance to the planned change process, including explanation of the focal problem or challenge, directives and methods for assessment, and intervention rationales and strategies.

Hobby model builders follow the conventions common to their leisure time pursuit. If my model plane builder friend violated a convention (engines are constructed of rubber bands), his plane would be disqualified from a show or competition. Social work model builders are bound by construction rules, too. These are like the rules of grammar that help us speak our native language correctly. Following are some of the common conventions for theoretical model building (Britt, 1997; Burr & the Editors, 1979; Shoemaker et al., 2004).

Models contain concepts for actors, social systems, activities, and goals. Brief name labels should be added to the model to identify these concepts.

Causal patterns should be displayed. For causal relationships, the independent variable is labeled *X*, and a dependent variable is identified as *Y*.

Modelers may use lines to show connections between different entities or processes. Arrows may be attached to the end of lines to show the direction of influence. Sets of arrows map the set of relationships. Line length or line width may be varied to communicate information about magnitude: the thicker the line, the stronger the influence of the independent variable on the dependent variable. Lines may be placed at different angles (for example, a vertical line pointing to a horizontal line) to indicate a conditioning relationship, and lines may be drawn as circling back to a starting point to indicate a feedback loop.

Plus and minus signs may be added over lines to indicate a positive or negative relationship. Propositions are usually ordered in levels when displaying a deductive theory. The more general propositions are higher than the more specific theoretical statements. A vertical dotted line can be used do connect the propositions from top to bottom.

A box or block in which several variables are clustered indicates that these variables are part of a larger construct. Influence and time are shown by convention as flowing from left to right.

FINAL THOUGHTS AND CAUTIONS FOR THEORETICAL MODELING

Models should not be confused with the entire theoretical language, with an aspect of client reality, or with a portion of the social worker's practice world. They are not mirror images but partial representations that focus on certain aspects and ignore other aspects of a whole. Rubber band propelled airplane models will not take you to Philadelphia. Good practitioners make use of theoretical models, but also of additional tools: research, practice wisdom, and the client group's conception of their troubles. Good practitioners remember humbly that a model will never help them totally grasp the client's situation.

Several other cautions relate to modeling and model use (Shoemaker et al., 2004). Remember always that models are simplifications and do not capture the complexity of a client system's interaction with the physical and social environment. Remember that models are like fashion in some way; the tastes and preferences of theorists for different types of models and for modeling conventions change over time. Remember, therefore, that a conceptual model located in the theoretical or empirical literature must be understood and evaluated within its historical context. Remember that model borrowers can become lazy and sometimes stick to tried and true models instead of breaking with tradition and creating innovative models that challenge contemporary convention and theorizing. In this book, you will learn about a variety of theoretical models and how they can guide your inquiry into the difficulties, goals, and social context of people who need your help. In the next chapter, I will introduce you to theoretical mapping and ecosystems mapping, two more translation tools for connecting theory to practice.

A MODEL FOR CONNECTING THEORY AND PRACTICE

The process of connecting theory to practice is a creative and complex one. Earlier I talked about models as guiding conceptions. The following model provides one way of conceptualizing the tasks central to the theory application process. This approach was created initially by a social worker, Martin Bloom (1975), and now includes some of my embellishments and those of Gordon Hearn (1979), Daniel Fishman (1999), and Dennis Mithaug (2000). I encourage you to use this model or develop your own model to guide your efforts to apply theory to challenging practice situations.

IDENTIFICATION OF THE CHALLENGING PRACTICE SITUATION

Practical theorizing requires an orientation phase (Hearn, 1979). A good theory will help you orient yourself toward and solve everyday practice problems. A difficulty in serving a client should provoke your urge to theorize. The difficulty may be experienced as a discrepancy between what you know and what you need to know to help the client confidently and competently (Mithaug, 2000). Your practical theorizing always occurs in a particular place at a particular time. You can begin connecting theory to practice by learning about and describing the relevant ecological and temporal features of the case.

Fishman (1999), borrowing a term from the qualitative researchers, calls this a **thick description.** It includes your description of the agency context and agency factors (mission, focus on macro- or micro-level problems, political stance, finances). The agency context and factors influence your choice of a theoretical language and your creation and application of a theoretical model. The thick description includes also your summary of information about the client system. Particular client system characteristics such as size (individual, family, or community), life stage (adolescence or middle age, for example), and salient social memberships (race, ethnicity, social class, sexual orientation, religion, and so on) often influence your search for useful knowledge. Information about the relation of the client system to larger social systems and to subsystems is also important. Your decision—with input from the client—to focus on changing either one social system or multiple social systems will be relevant to the theory selection process. Your description should also summarize the client's request for help and any information about the initial definition of challenges or problems that provoked contact with the social agency. One client system may complain about poor family communication while another client wants help in managing an intense grief reaction following the loss of a beloved husband. Your thick description might report on worker characteristics—your relevant social memberships, for example—and how these may influence the helping relationship and process and your theoretical choices. Include also your preliminary understanding or hunches about what specific theoretical knowledge you need and the likely uses of that knowledge.

Social workers and social scientists have developed languages for communicating within specialties that are unlike everyday English or French.

Many social workers, for example, use the terminology of the ecosystems theoretical perspective and a strengths or empowerment value stance. Write your preliminary thick description of the case by using the ecosystems or strengths perspective concepts and variables familiar to you and other social workers. This will help you in the next phase when you begin the search for relevant knowledge, and later you can incorporate more concepts and propositions from a selected theoretical language and its models.

IDENTIFICATION OF POTENTIALLY USEFUL KNOWLEDGE

Social workers make use of various forms of knowledge. We use the research findings of social work and social science researchers. We use ideas and techniques that have been developed by reflection on practice experiences (practice wisdom) even if they have not yet been transformed into theory or confirmed empirically. We listen to, respect, and use our clients' everyday theories about their predicaments, and we use scientific theories about the social world, about public and personal problems, and about intentional change. The research sequence in your school will help you increase your ability to identify and retrieve scientifically based knowledge. The practice sequence and field internship will expose you to the profession's accumulated practice wisdom. The policy sequence will alert you to theorizing and knowledge use necessary to advocate for policy changes. This book presents knowledge appropriate to the Human Behavior and the Social Environment sequence; therefore, we will concentrate on the search for relevant theoretical knowledge.

Let's use the notion of levels of theorizing from the first chapter. Connecting theory to practice requires that you identify a theoretical tradition or language that is relevant to your case. Bloom (1975) recommends that you seek a theoretical orientation that includes knowledge offering a parsimonious (or simple), clear, consistent, and testable explanation of the challenging situation. Ideally, the theoretical knowledge has also been supported empirically by research. The social work and scientific literature on matching theoretical traditions to practice challenges is still somewhat sparse and disorganized. So, your thick description, especially your appraisal of the client system problems, will be an important aid in directing your search.

After selecting the framework, you can search for a theoretical model derived from the larger tradition and developed specifically to guide your inquiry and helping action with this kind of client and this kind of problem. Study the conceptual model to become familiar with its set of concepts as well as its propositions (or processes, for inductive theories) showing how the concepts relate to each other. If the literature from the social work profession and allied disciplines does not offer a relevant model, then you may need to develop your own (Hearn, 1979). Select concepts and propositions from within a theoretical language, and begin to think about hypotheses generated from this model that are useful for your practice case.

It will probably help if you create a diagram or map of the theoretical model. This can take several forms (Fawcett & Downs, 1986). You might create a diagram of the propositions linking central concepts. You might draw a diagram of the path of influence, including independent, intervening, and dependent variables. You might create an inventory of the causes of the client's condition; or an inventory of the effects of the condition; or a row-and-column matrix in which the intersections of concepts linked to each other are checked and those with no relationship are unmarked. Theoretical mapping of this kind will be discussed in detail in the next chapter.

Practitioners next take a step unfamiliar to academic theorists. You need to look for ways in which the theoretical language has been translated from abstractions into actual tools or strategies for practical use or into a practice model (Bloom, 1975; Fawcett & Downs, 1986). Specifically, is there any knowledge associated with this theory that can direct every phase of the planned change process, including your assessment, intervention, and evaluative activities? Or must you undertake the translation process yourself? If you are fortunate, some useful theorists or scholarly practitioners have operationalized the concepts in the theoretical model. Perhaps theory-specific measurement or assessment tools have been developed, too. Sometimes theory users have explicitly linked theoretical traditions, theoretical models, and practice directives and formulated these as coherent approaches to addressing particular client problems and goals. You can borrow (after giving credit) from these innovative theory users.

The task for this phase of the connecting-theory-to-practice process, then, is developing a preliminary theoretical conception for understanding and solving the practice challenge in a way that is responsive to the specifics of the case (setting factors, client system factors, and practitioner factors). You should also be able to justify your choices of a theoretical language (or languages), a theoretical model, theory-based concepts, and translations of the theory into planned change procedures. This rationale might include your preliminary ideas about how to adapt the theory for social work use and your ideas about any limitations of the available knowledge. A written proposal of the approach to understanding and improving the problematic situation that flows from the theoretical conception could be reviewed with colleagues and instructors.

For instance, several years ago I agreed to assist several of my students with their work in a hospital-based bereavement support group (Forte et al., 1996). They were serving family members who had experienced the death of a loved one as a result of illness or accident. My literature search indicated that symbolic interactionism presented a usefully and carefully developed perspective for understanding grief and one compatible with the object relations and attachment frameworks familiar to social workers. Lynn Lofland (1985) had created a mid-range interactionist theoretical model that specifically explained difficulties in managing grief reactions. Her model included concepts such as *sense of self, significance of the deceased, interactional connections, pattern of interactional connections, definition of death, feeling rules,* and the *grief experience.* She conceptualized the grief experience as multidimensional and highlighted variables such as intensity of grieving and duration of grieving. The theory offered a way to predict which group members would need the most help.

Lofland also offered several useful propositions. The more connections a person has to a network of significant others (an "eggs scattered among many baskets" pattern), the less the intensity and duration of the group experience will be. Conversely, the fewer connections to others (an "all eggs in one basket" pattern), the greater will be the difficulty of managing grief following the loss of a highly significant partner.

Interactionist tools existed that made possible the translation of Lofland's major concepts into assessment devices. Our team was able to use these to construct a multi-instrument survey for use in appraising each bereaved person. Several practitioners had developed bereavement support groups that incorporated interactionist ideas about grieving. These enriched the hospital social workers' intervention plan. Lofland's modified model of grief and social connections guided both the helping work and the team's evaluation of their effectiveness.

TRANSLATION OF KNOWLEDGE INTO CHANGE STRATEGIES

Connecting theory and practice means that you try to translate the concepts, propositions, and theoretical models associated with a theoretical language into a form that you can use. For certain theoretical languages and for certain client problems, good translation work has already been done. Cognitive-behaviorists, for instance, are excellent at transforming basic scientific knowledge into knowledge for use. In some cases, however, you may have to do the translation work yourself.

You can proceed in one of several ways. I have already referred briefly to some of these ideas. Take a theoretical model that you have discovered in the professional literature. Pick one that explains a personal or social problem affecting your client. Read and reread articles, chapters, and books on this theory, and then attempt to identify the root metaphors and major assumptions, concepts, and propositions. Show how they are interrelated in a way that explains the challenge facing the client system: depression or domestic violence or an unfair housing policy.

Next, I'll expand on some ideas about how theoretical knowledge can inform all phases of the helping process. The professional literature often includes knowledge associated with various theoretical languages that identify the major causes of client troubles or the meanings that clients attach to problematic life circumstances. This knowledge can assist you and the client in the problem identification and formulation phase of the planned change process. For example, you might develop a visual display or table that identifies the independent variables (causal factors), the dependent variables (effects on client membership experiences), and the intervening variables (factors that qualify or change the causal relationship). You can use arrows to depict the direction of influence, and mathematical signs for plus or minus to indicate whether the cause results in an increase or decrease in the dependent variable. Here is a very simple display of a factor that contributes to the development of a commitment to volunteer service.

	Rank	Theme
TABLE 2.1 SALIENT MEANINGS OF CONTESTANTS IN HOMELESSNESS SYMPATHY BATTLE	1	We are capitalists or anti-capitalists.
	2	We are soldiers at war.
	3	We are law followers; they are law breakers.
	4	We are made of flesh and blood.
	5	We are strangers or brothers and sisters in Christ.
	6	We are creatures of the natural and built world.
	7	We are lifters and carriers.
	8	We are competitors.

Rewards for volunteering $\longrightarrow$ acts of volunteer service

Some theories are "grounded" in an intensive and lengthy study of the client system's participation in its natural setting. These theories present an interpretation of the problematic membership experiences of a particular group or subculture. Such a theory might be summarized as a sequence of social processes (those actions and interactions that lead to homelessness) or as a set of symbols or meanings. Table 2.1, dealing with homelessness, summarizes the themes that I identified by examining numerous newspaper stories about the siting of a shelter for the homeless. My grounded theory indicated that community members communicated by eight different symbolic representations of themselves, their opponents, and the homeless clients.

Besides conceptualizing a challenge or problem from a particular perspective, a theory can often help you organize the assessment process. First, a theory identifies the factors or variables most relevant to the membership troubles or opportunities. Therefore, the worker can gather information in a selective and purposeful way and avoid being overwhelmed by the complexity of the client's predicament. The theory of grief management that I discussed earlier, for example, directs worker attention to social connections, patterns of social connections, the ways that these social connections confirm and sustain one's sense of self, and the damage to the self-system that occurs when a highly significant connection is severed by the death of a loved one. Therefore, the grief counselor is directed to give priority to collecting assessment information on these factors.

Second, the professional literature includes the work of many social workers and social scientists who have operationalized the concepts associated with particular theories and theoretical frameworks. Operationalization connects the abstract theoretical idea to empirical (observable by the senses) indicators and shows how to measure the quantity or quality of the phenomenon (Hearn, 1979). Theory-based concepts have been translated into self-report paper-and-pencil surveys, observational checklists, interview guides, and other measurement procedures. Let me return to an example from my own experience linking theory and practice. Lofland did not specify how her theory could guide the assessment process. However, other interactionist researchers have operationalized each of the seven types of symbolic connections that she identified. Moreover, social workers have developed an assessment tool called the Social Network Grid that gathers information on a client's perception of his or her social network. We modified this grid by replacing the original variables with interactionist variables but then used the modified grid according to the original instructions.

Here is a suggestion for translating theory for use during the intervention process. Search the literature on your theoretical model for propositions supported by some research evidence and rewrite them as if–then generalizations. The "if" part refers to social system processes and structures that might be the focus of intervention. The "then" part refers to the probable outcomes of an intervention for improving the quality of social system membership. For instance, we might translate an interactionist theory of small group solidarity as an if–then generalization. If the practitioner can increase the role-taking abilities and inclinations of diverse members of a small group, then the quality of communication among these members will increase. An interactionist theory that relates power and role-taking to the troubles of battered women includes the following if–then generalization: If the worker can help the batterer take the perspective of the woman frequently and accurately and empathize with his abused partner, then the batterer will internalize the partner's perspective and use this to control his violent impulses. This translation process can be adapted to your practice needs.

Each theoretical tradition includes some conception of personal and social change. Many specify how a social worker or other change agent might facilitate the transformation process. The recommendations of these traditions and their associated theories can be treated as strategies for action. During the intervention process, the worker and members of the client system can include them as alternative ways to rectify the problematic membership conditions. Ideally, these strategies have been tested empirically and shown to be effective with many client types in many social contexts. Ideally, the strategies include specific directions for what to do, how to do it, and when to do it. Advocates of the behavioral tradition, for example, have been especially diligent in developing theory-based and research-tested intervention strategies, such as systematic desensitization and the timeout procedure, that meet these standards.

Your job is to select a theory-based intervention, present a rationale for your choice (what evidence shows that this strategy will help the client achieve her goals, for example?), and judge whether you have the knowledge and skills necessary for effective and responsible use of the intervention strategy. In my work with the bereaved, for example, my colleagues and I used the strategies for "shared grief work" recommended in the literature by expert grief counselors and compatible with my interactionist case conception. Group leaders used these strategies to help group members reconstruct both their sense of self and their network of significant connections through facilitated mutual aid discussions.

APPLICATION OF THE THEORETICAL KNOWLEDGE

Your work during every phase of the planned change process can be enhanced by the use of theoretical knowledge. Your theoretical framework provides resources for the goal-setting phase. Each framework provides its own conceptions of the ideal client and community. The psychodynamic framework, for instance, directs workers to recommend client goals related to insight; the ability to verbalize beliefs, feelings, and desires; the ability to handle ambivalence; ego strength; romantic intimacy and maturity; and the sense of identity (Messer, 2000). You will make use of theoretical knowledge to direct and structure the data-gathering and assessment process (Bloom, 1975). At times, you will think deductively and start with theory-based general statements, such as "The powerless often develop role-taking abilities and inclinations to meet the demands of the powerful," but then you must seek information about the specific ways that your clients, battered women, use role taking to anticipate harm from their partners. At other times, you will think inductively and gather information about numerous events—for example, opinions about the relocation of a shelter for the homeless—and then judge whether the patterns you detected correspond with those of a grounded or inductive model that you are using.

Problem formulation and classification vary by theoretical framework. Behaviorists recommend categorizing problems as behavioral deficits or behavioral excesses. Psychodynamic theorists and practitioners recommend the use of classes or diagnoses of mental and emotional disorder. Interactionists suggest starting with the symbolic meanings that the client attaches to his or her problems.

Each theoretical model provides different directives for your selection of an intervention strategy and for implementing the intervention. Role theorists, for instance, have inspired the development of psychodrama and sociodrama. These approaches emphasize the active and creative involvement of clients in the reenactment of challenging life scripts. Psychodrama offers dozens of interventions for enriching the client's ability to perform social roles successfully.

Finally, each theoretical framework and its associated model direct how you conduct your evaluation of practitioner effectiveness and client satisfaction. Theoretical advocates have different preferences for conducting scientific inquiry. Behaviorists prefer experimental or quasi-experimental design and the use of valid and reliable measures for changes in observable behaviors. Interactionists prefer participant-observation methodologies, such as focus group interviews with clients soliciting qualitative data on the meaning and significance of the helping experience. Systems theorists prefer functional analysis and the search for feedback loops.

To summarize, you can use a theoretical perspective and its specific theoretical model to direct your goal setting, data gathering, problem formulation, review of intervention possibilities, intervention, and effectiveness evaluation (Hearn, 1979). Social work involves both science and art. Theory application is an important part of the helping process, one that complements the use of your experience, emotion, and intuition. Each theory chapter in this book will offer a concise presentation of the theory's approach to the phases of the planned change process.

EVALUATION OF THE USEFULNESS OF KNOWLEDGE

You have probably become familiar with the social work approach to program and practice evaluation. You are joining a profession with members who try hard to be accountable to their clients and the larger environment. Most social workers now recognize that it is important to evaluate the impact or outcomes of their helping work. Can we show that the program or helping action achieved the desired results? Social workers also aim to show that the process of helping meets the highest professional and community standards. Can we demonstrate that the service was provided in a fiscally responsible way, in accord with agency standards, and in response to changing client needs and concerns?

If we are concerned about connecting theory to practice, then we should also try to demonstrate that the particular theoretical language and theoretical model that we used were helpful. Here, we put it to the utility test (Mithaug, 2000). Was the theoretical conception that guided problem formulation, assessment, intervention, and evaluation critical to the success (or the failure) of the planned change process? There should be logical and reasonable evidence that the application of theory helped bring about the desired outcomes (Fishman, 1999). Additionally, the social worker might appraise the usefulness of the theory as compared to other theories. Might another theoretical approach have produced significant benefits for the client system too, but in a way that allowed easier translation into practice strategies, or clearer and more precise guidelines for effectiveness testing? Social workers often consider the use of a theory in terms of a suitability test. Did the theoretical conception and its use affirm the core social work values like appreciation for diversity and commitment to social justice? These tests will be discussed further in the next chapter.

Although my colleagues and I did not formally and extensively evaluate the utility of Lofland's interactionist theory of grief management in achieving client goals, we did obtain some useful evidence. Her theory accurately predicted that those clients who were connected in many ways to only one person and then lost this loved one would report the greatest difficulty with grief management. From this starting point, workers were able to identify effectively group members who needed extra support in reconstructing their interaction network and their sense of self-coherence following the severance of ties to the significant other.

CONTRIBUTION OF THE LESSONS ABOUT THEORY APPLICATION

The process of connecting theory to practice involves another step. You have learned important lessons about the choice of a theory, about judging the limitations of the approach, and about how to modify a theory for social work use in your agency with your client system. These lessons can benefit other members of the social work community. Therefore, please share your work with others. You might write a paper and submit it to a journal (*Social Work Perspectives,* http://userwww.sfsu.edu/~swpersp, for instance, publishes only articles by students). Or you might organize a workshop for presentation at a regional conference. At least report on your theory application to your field instructor and other social workers in your agency. Include some discussion of how your theoretical conception of the practice situation might be generalized to other cases, other social agencies, and other workers.

CONNECTING THEORY TO PRACTICE: THE DIALOGICAL TEAM APPROACH

My model has shown you how to use theory as an individual practitioner. Much theory application, however, occurs in teams. I will provide a few guidelines for connecting theory and theories to practice in collaboration with interdisciplinary and interprofessional teams. This team approach will be reviewed also in Chapter 14.

First, interdisciplinary teams need to create a common language or "universe of discourse." According to Mead (1929/1964), these are "intelligible common objects" (concrete and conceptual objects) that can be understood in similar ways by diverse members. The translation strategies (communication by event, art, and gathering) developed by Mead and settlement house workers produced shared understandings between different immigrant and native communities. For interdisciplinary teams, "bridging narratives" or "synthesizing discourses" are concepts and language devices that "facilitate mutual translation and interpretation of each other's scientific narratives and practices" (Weigert & Gecas, 1995, p. 144). These concepts become a metalanguage, a language about theoretical languages transcending the vocabulary of specific theoretical traditions. The common language allows each member to take a perspective outside his or her own standpoint and view things from the perspective of a larger commonwealth, a team. In the next chapter, I will propose that ecosystems terminology might serve such a bridging function.

Team members should then seek agreement about intervention goals. Critical and self-reflective practitioners can discuss, deliberate, and negotiate alternative theoretical perspectives on the problem and theory-based problem-solving strategies (Bohman, 1999b). Dialogue rather than monologue is the norm. Dialogical communication is modeled after the dialogues of the great Greek philosopher Plato (Turner, 2004). It requires team members to assemble a variety of opinions, engage in careful analysis of and reflection on the opinions of different members, make a selection of the best contributions as errors are illuminated, progress toward deeper and more accurate understanding of client system challenges, and select the best interventions. Consideration of a plurality of theoretical orientations helps rather than hinders democratically and dialogically structured group processes. Disagreements, for example, become assets in the search for practical solutions to personal and public problems. From dialogue about such disagreement, team members can generate multiple explanations of the problem at hand, varied directives for assessing the person and social situation, and a wide range of solutions and policies. The group's "working hypotheses" (Mead 1899/1968) represent team members' tentative agreements in each of these areas. These hypotheses can be publicly verified by the practical test of their useful and liberating contribution to improving membership processes and conditions.

The negotiation of differences during practical inquiry will be most successful when organized according to the same democratic and dialogical principles and norms that guide scientific inquiry. Bohman (1999b) proposes specifically that ideals such as unimpeded communication, mutual understanding, the decentralization of power, and deliberations free from unconscious constraints or force maximize team effectiveness. Team members should also reflect continuously on the ideals, the norms, and the communication patterns that characterize their cooperative inquiry and problem solving and use these reflections to improve team theory application.

PRACTICAL SUGGESTIONS FOR LEARNING THEORETICAL LANGUAGES

Next, I will briefly review some additional tools and suggestions that may aid you in learning to connect theory and practice.

THEORY-SPECIFIC WEBSITES

You can learn more about theoretical traditions, theories, and the concepts common to each approach by joining in theory-specific web conversations. The World Wide Web includes numerous sites devoted to particular theoretical languages. These may include biographies of key theoreticians, archives of articles on the theory, links to related sites, and chat rooms where participants can discuss issues related to the theoretical framework. The World Wide Web also includes some metasites that allow you to search from one virtual place for information about many different theories.

An example of a website with resources on multiple theoretical perspectives is Sociosite (http://www.pscw.uva.nl/sociosite/ TOPICS/ Theory.html). This site focuses on various theoretical perspectives used by sociologists. It presents information about Marxism, rational choice theory, sociobiology, ethnomethodology, and game theory. Links enable the student to access additional information about the theories, including bibliographies, online articles and papers, biographies of major theorists, associations devoted to the advancement of each theory, and links to related sites.

Other websites are devoted to a particular theoretical perspective. The Society for the Study of Symbolic Interaction, for example, sponsors a website (http://sun.soci.niu.edu/~sssi) devoted to the interactionist theoretical perspective. The website includes information about conferences sponsored by the society, archives with debates on issues of concern to interactionists, a small collection of online articles, links to related sites, and resources for teaching about symbolic interactionism.

The Red Feather Institute sponsors a website (http://tryoung.com) devoted to critical theories, including Marxism, neo-Marxism, feminism, and post-modern theories. This website includes a dictionary of critical concepts, lectures on the use of critical theories to understand religious practices, discussions of crime and punishment and social justice issues, biographies of progressive women, worksheets for analyzing contemporary films from a critical perspective, an online journal for and by graduate students, a set of teaching materials, and "left links" that connect site visitors to other sites committed to a radical perspective on politics.

THEORY-SPECIFIC BOOKS AND ARTICLES

Social workers and social scientists share what they have learned about theory application by writing and publishing their discoveries. You can make use of these resources.

Some social work writers have organized surveys of the major theoretical traditions. A few of these social work texts provide lexicons of theoretical languages. Francis Turner's (1996) *Social Work Treatment: Interlocking Theoretical Approaches* is probably the leading book, but its breadth and sophistication of coverage may be overwhelming to undergraduate social work students. The more recently published *Contemporary Human Behavior Theory* by Robbins, Chatterjee, and Canda (1998) is excellent. These authors recommend the use of multiple theories and offer a critical appraisal of different theoretical approaches. Greene is the author/coauthor of two useful books on *Human Behavior Theory* (Greene, 1994; Greene & Ephross, 1991). These books are relatively inexpensive, offer glossaries defining the terms of each theoretical language, and provide tables with theory-specific assumptions, assessment guidelines, and intervention guidelines. You might take a survey book, find a theory that you are considering for use in your agency, and read the appropriate chapter. Such reading will introduce you to the basic features of the theory, including some of the founding figures and role models. Survey chapters often identify some of the major social workers associated with each theoretical tradition, the theory's root metaphors, and theory-specific practice models for understanding clients and their problems. Surveys also provide an extensive reference list for each theory. These lists may include citations useful for your theory application project.

Thousands of published articles report on the application of theory to practice. Effectiveness studies report on empirical tests of the usefulness of a theory for practice purposes. *Research on Social Work Practice*, for instance, is a journal that publishes many such studies. These studies might compare the effectiveness of practice based on different theories in solving specific problems. Other research studies might compare the effectiveness of practice based on one theory to practice based on multiple theories. Meta-analyses or summaries of a collection of effectiveness research studies match particular client system problems to the best theory-based practice approach for solving the problem. Case studies are detailed reports on the use of a particular theoretical approach with a particular client in a particular setting. They may or may not include research evidence. These case studies can be very helpful because they illustrate the actual decisions and actions of a practitioner. Theory-informed case studies related to homelessness, grief management, worker alienation, volunteer recruitment, and other subjects are reviewed in my earlier book (Forte, 2001). Among other topics, the writer of the case study may summarize the theoretical framework and its key concepts, the rationale for using this theoretical language in the particular practice circumstances, and the particulars of how the theoretical approach infused all phases of the planned change process. The following references provide illustrations of some published social work articles that report on the use of theory for practice.

APPLICATION OF A SINGLE THEORY

Compher, J. V. (1982). Parent-school-child systems: Triadic assessment and intervention. *Social Casework, 63*(7), 415–423.

Munson, C. E. (1977). Consultation in an adolescent group home using a role theory perspective. *Offender Rehabilitation, 2*(1), 65–75.

Seinfeld, J. (1989). Therapy with a severely abused child: An object relations perspective. *Clinical Social Work Journal, 17*(1), 40–49.

Tolman, R. M., & Edleson, J. L. (1989). Cognitive-behavioral intervention with men who batter. In B. A. Thyer (Ed.), *Behavioral family therapy* (pp. 169–190). Springfield, IL: Charles C. Thomas.

USE OF TWO OR MORE THEORIES FOR A SOCIAL WORK PURPOSE

Delon, M. (1989). An integrated theoretical guide to intervention with depressed elderly clients. *Journal of Gerontological Social Work, 14*(3/4), 131–146. (Integrates social role theory and Erikson's psychosocial theory)

Pinkston, E. M., Green, G. R., Linsk, N. L., & Young, R. N. (2001). A family eco-behavioral approach for elders with mental illness. In H. E. Briggs & K. Corcoran (Eds.), *Social work practice: Treating common client problems* (pp. 339–370). Chicago: Lyceum.

Rank, M. R., & LeCroy, C. W. (1983). Toward a multiple perspective in family theory and practice: The case of social exchange theory, symbolic interactionism, and conflict theory. *Family Relations, 32,* 441–448.

EVALUATION OF THE EFFECTIVENESS OF A THEORY APPLICATION

Gerdtz, J. (2000). Evaluating behavioral treatment of disruptive classroom behaviors of an adolescent with autism. *Research on Social Work Practice, 10*(1), 98–100.

THEORY-SPECIFIC WORKSHOPS AND CONFERENCE PRESENTATIONS

Social worker experts frequently offer professional education events. These specialists explain the use of a theoretical approach in practice situations. Sometimes, reports on these presentations are available from the presenter as an unpublished manuscript or from the conference host as written proceedings or as audiotapes. The New England Educational Institute, for instance, offers summer workshops on Cape Cod, Massachusetts. These four-day intensive educational sessions are geared to the needs of mental health professionals who want to incorporate the latest theory and research into their knowledge base. The summer 2000 series included workshops such as "A Spiritual Approach to Couples Therapy," "Challenging Cases: Schema-Focused Innovations in Brief Cognitive Behavior Therapy," and "Attachment and Developmental Research: Applications to Psychotherapy." Students might also consider attending national conferences sponsored by the social work profession or local agency–sponsored workshops. These forums enable participants to interact with social workers advancing the use of theory for practical purposes. The Association of Baccalaureate Social Work Program Directors, Inc. (BPD) hosts a yearly conference attended by more than 500 undergraduate educators and some students. The 2001 conference in Denver, Colorado, included workshops such as "An Ecological Perspective on Women's Depression: Engendered Risks, Empowered Solutions," "Case Study Illustrations of System Dynamics Modeling," and "Settlement Houses and the Women's Movement: A Network Analysis."

Conferences are like the local places where language learners go to immerse themselves in another culture. At conferences, you can hear many fluent speakers use the language that you are learning. You can make beginning attempts to ask questions or even offer comments or suggestions in the theoretical languages of the conference participants.

THEORY-SPECIFIC MERCHANDISE

Those trying to learn a foreign language often start by identifying the cultural objects common to a given environment and learning the terms for these items. We can adapt this approach to the task of learning theoretical languages. The practice community in our market-driven environment is flooded with informational materials about theoretical languages. These include advertisements for theory-specific workshops, books, and journals about theory application (cognitive approaches to depression management, for instance); news stories about theory-based social experiments (ecological-behavioral wilderness training); and television programs about theoretical innovations (spirituality and healing, biochemical and genetic alterations of basic human dispositions). Watch for advertisements for specials and books that explain theory-specific approaches to theorizing about client system challenges and problems. These might help you begin to think about matching theoretical language to client particulars. They might also help you to see the diversity of theoretical languages used in the larger social work community. I recently received, for example, a brochure listing PBS videos available for sale (www.shopPBS.com/teachers). Two videos, *W. E. B. DuBois of Great Barrington* (DuBois contributed much to the Afrocentric perspective) and *Evolution* (a nine-hour special on the latest theories of evolutionary scientists), caught my attention.

SEARCH ENGINES FOR CONNECTING THEORY TO PRACTICE

How do you find the best and most relevant written theoretical knowledge? Many new tools can help you search through millions of books, articles, dissertations, and unpublished presentations to identify information about theories and their application.

Your college or university probably has a set of academic search engines that you can use. *Social Work Abstracts,* for instance, facilitates searches for books and articles from dozens of different social work journals and journals in related fields. A CD-ROM version is available that your library may have purchased. Or you can search by looking through the journal itself on your library shelves. The software program allows you to search by keywords. My search using the keyword *theory,* for instance, resulted in a report listing 2638 books and articles for the period from 1977 to 1999. Narrowing your search by adding other keywords will help you identify sources about specific theories and particular client problems. Many libraries now offer access to other search engines; sometimes you can use them from home by connecting to your library's website. OVID, for example, includes databases for sociological abstracts, educational abstracts, nursing abstracts, and psychological abstracts. These databases include articles from many social work journals and facilitate access to archives of citations from related disciplines.

Commercial search engines are available to you for free. Many web-based booksellers include search engines at their home page. They can search very large archives, identify books on a particular topic, and indicate whether the books can be purchased. Two of the largest companies selling new books are Amazon.com (www.amazon.com) and Barnes and Noble (www.barnesandnoble .com). A search at either of these sites usually results in a list of numerous relevant books. The site provides publication information for each book, a summary of the book, and a table of contents. Students can use these engines to identify the latest theory-based publications and to examine topics and keywords. The Advanced Book Exchange (www.abebooks.com) is a network of independent booksellers with a very large catalog. This archive includes many older and used social work and social science books. Searching ABE will help you trace the historical coverage of a theory. These books can be purchased at prices much lower than the newer versions.

LEARNING ACTIVITIES

1. Who are two or three role models who have influenced you? Choose from your family, your friendship network, your school, or any other membership groups. What lessons did these models teach you? Describe how each contributed to your inner conversations, including your deliberations about your values, your life goals, and your lifestyle?

2. Practice thinking metaphorically. A recent movie, *American History X,* documents the organization of "skinhead" groups in Southern California in the early 1990s. The skinheads viciously attacked anyone in a different group, Mexican Americans, and the illegal Mexican workers in a local grocery store. Offer different explanations

of this crime using two of the following: the behavioral, conflict, social systems, and symbolic interactionist frameworks. First, fill in the following applications of the metaphors associated with each framework. The community where the violence occurred is like _____. The groups causing and affected by the act of violence are like _____. The acts of violence are like _____. Social work intervention would be like _____. Your explanation should integrate ideas from your four answers. Compare and contrast your two ways of explaining attacks on members of minority groups.

3. Now apply the metaphorical imagination closer to your professional identity. Reflect on different ways of thinking about the client: as customer, as patient, as member, as detainee. What are the implications of the comparison between service user and each of these roles? What would the expected role for the social worker be for each metaphorical comparison? If a client is like a customer, for instance, should a social worker act like a salesclerk?

4. Check out two different websites devoted to theories about human behavior and the social environment. Describe each website. Who sponsors it? What kind of information is provided? What are some positive and negative features of the website?

5. Reflect on what information might help you apply theory to a practice situation. Go to a website for a bookseller and search for books that might be useful. Report on your search to your classmates.

6. Look through classroom textbooks (if they include a survey of different theoretical traditions), or borrow a survey book from the library. Pick a chapter on a theoretical approach that interests you. Carefully examine the chapter title. Look at the headings and subheadings. Skim the references listed at the end. Identify three or four concepts associated with the theory that you discovered during your examination.

7. Develop a plan for searching the professional literature. Be as specific as possible in identifying what you want to find and what sources might have the relevant information. Use one of the search engines at your school to conduct the search. Summarize your experience.

8. Develop a report on one founding figure of a theoretical tradition (George Herbert Mead, Sigmund Freud, B. F. Skinner, or Talcott Parsons, for example). Use any of the tools and resources recommended in this chapter to help you. Report on three or four terms that this theorist contributed to the theory's vocabulary. Summarize how you might approach a social work topic using this theorist's perspective. What else did you learn that was helpful? Did you notice, for instance, that most of the founding theorists are men? What might feminists say about this pattern?

9. Write a letter to one of your favorite useful theorists or scholarly practitioners. Ask this person for advice on a practice challenge that you are facing or anticipate facing. Pose specific and detailed questions in your letter. Imagine the person's response.

10. You can be a role model or exemplar for a future generation of social workers. Imagine that you are giving a retirement speech that reports on your accomplishments in the theory/research/practice realms or in contributing to the social work knowledge base. Summarize in several paragraphs your achievements as a member of the social work profession.

ADDITIONAL RESOURCES

Additional resources are available on the book companion website at **www.thomsonedu.com/ social_work/forte**. Resources include key terms, tutorial quizzes, links to related websites, and lists of additional resources for furthering your research.

TOOLS FOR TRANSLATING AND PRACTICAL THEORIZING

CHAPTER 3

Theoretical Maps and Ecosystem Maps

Photos.com Select/IndexStock

INTRODUCTION

Have you noticed what happens in so many scenes from the television series *Star Trek* and in scenes from most science fiction movies? Not once but a zillion times, intrepid space explorers from Earth meet alien beings from faraway galaxies and from alternate time lines. The alien may look like a mobile robot, a two-footed reptile, a little doll, a prehistoric giant, a blue amphibian, a medieval angel, or a sparkling cloud. The alien may differ from humans in every conceivable way— size, shape, color, sound, and smell. However, each representative of the new alien species shares, somehow, the same capacity: the ability to speak in English. This miracle is generally taken for granted, but if explained, the marvelous transformation of all beings in the universe into 20th-century Americans is attributed to an invisible "universal translator." Thanks to instantaneous and perfect translations, mutual understanding between earthlings and aliens is possible. Dramatic consequences usually follow these auspicious encounters and cross-species translations.

Social work students, in one way, are like these future adventurers. You will meet and work with men and women trained in disciplines and professions other than social work, and you will collaborate with social workers speaking varied theoretical languages. Your partners might have been trained in other disciplines, and they may draw on biology, economics, political science, anthropology, ecology, philosophy, theology, or some unfamiliar disciplinary tradition to do their work with you. Collaborative projects may bring you into contact with nurses, psychologists, rabbis, attorneys, community planners, and doctors. Your social work professors may talk specialized and hard-to-understand languages, such as psychoanalytic ego psychology or existential humanism. You may attend national conferences crowded with family social workers versed in the jargon of the family process theory, or you may participate in meetings of a local social group work association where the dialect of "mainstream group work" is the only language spoken. Your clients will speak about their own theories of everyday life, and they may do so in English or in a native language that you do not speak.

If each theoretical perspective is like a language with its own words, rules of grammar, and pronunciations, then how can you possibly hope to understand and work with clients and colleagues from dozens of different speech communities, professions, academic backgrounds, and theoretical traditions? It will not be easy. However, there is hope. Chapter 1 discussed how scientists use various symbol systems to cooperate with one another and to accumulate valid knowledge. In Chapter 2, I introduced several translation tools— exemplary models, root metaphors, and theoretical models—for learning different theories.

Theory experts have also developed something that can work like Captain James Kirk's universal translator. It is called a **map.** Theoretical maps identify and display all the major components of a scientific theory and the paths connecting these components. Social work educators and practitioners have created and refined a similar mapping procedure, the **eco-map.** The eco-map is a graphing tool that depicts the relationship of a person or family to the environment. This tool has been developed to help social workers use the ecosystems theoretical language to organize their thinking and their practice.

In this chapter, I will explain and illustrate the translation tool of theoretical mapping. In the remainder of the book, I will use theoretical mapping for "within-theory translation" to translate 10 theoretical languages into English words and patterns of words that will make sense to you. In this chapter, I will also remind you of the basic components of the eco-map visual display and the guidelines for its use. I will then demonstrate how the eco-map can be adapted to serve as a universal translator for "cross-theory translation." Each theoretical language presented in this book will be translated into the ecosystems terms and images used by this eco-map translation device. The chapter will end with a review of the values language that social workers use to evaluate theories and a brief introduction to the process of theory evaluation.

MAPPING

Scientists and social workers often use visual aids to depict theories and causal models (Mattaini, 1993; Sarukkai, 2002). These displays can be drawings, pictures, or diagrams, and they are designed to represent in a simple fashion a complex set of ideas. The visual aid offers a shorthand version of the numerous sentences and paragraphs that describe the theoretical model in words. Earlier, for example, we talked about a display depicting the relationships among variables. The independent variable (association with delinquent peers, for instance) is placed on the left of the display. An arrow points from the independent variable to the dependent variable (delinquent behavior). The display might use a plus or minus sign to indicate whether the correlation between the two variables is positive or negative. Often, other variables (social class, age, receptivity to peer suggestion) that intervene between the causal force and the consequence of this cause are added to the visual tool. We discussed these kinds of modeling conventions in Chapter 2. Maps supplement or enhance the theoretical modeling process.

A map can be a very useful visual tool. Let me provide an example of the power of maps from recent history. The Allied forces created huge map rooms during World War II with three-dimensional replications of battle areas. Generals used the maps in these rooms to display the contested terrain, to show the movement of their troops and enemy troops, and to consider alternative strategies for advancing soldiers toward desired objectives. These maps were important contributors to victory over Nazi Germany.

Social workers use maps in practice. Hodge (2005) describes a mapping procedure for identifying a client's spiritual journeys. Life paths and meaningful events are depicted pictorially, and the worker uses a spiritual lifemap to assess the client's spiritual choices and beliefs and to mobilize spiritual strengths for fostering personal growth. Such maps help clients identify where they are on their spiritual path in relation to their desired spiritual destination. The extensive use of eco-maps by social workers will be reviewed later.

Theoretical maps can be equally useful. Dewey (1902/1990), an educational expert, valued cartography and wrote that a map, as "a summary, an arranged and orderly view of previous experiences, serves as a guide to future experience; it gives direction; it facilitates control; it economizes effort, preventing useless wandering, and pointing out the paths which lead most quickly and most certainly to a desired result" (p. 198). These values apply equally to directional maps and theoretical maps.

Theorists are mapmakers (Goldfarb & Griffith, 1991; Toulmin, 1953). Each theory provides a representation of some aspect of physical, psychological, or social reality, although sometimes the mapping is not explicit. Charles Hampden Turner (1981), for instance, developed a set of maps representing 60 different scientific, religious, and philosophical ways of understanding the human mind. Each creatively and visually summarized a way of conceptualizing and understanding mental functioning. A theorist might imitate Lewis and Clark. These great explorers sought to fill in the details of early American maps and describe previously vast and unknown spaces. Theorizing as conceptual or **theoretical mapping** accepts a similar mission and tries to fill in the blank spaces in the social work knowledge base, those areas of human biopsychosocial functioning in the environment that have not been previously explained (Rule, 1997). Social work cartographers aim to discover and document the landscapes of client reality, the territory of social agencies and the helping process, and the terrain of the large social contexts that constrain social worker and client activity.

Theoretical maps, like directional maps, vary in their scope and detail. A theoretical language or tradition maps a vast conceptual terrain, an entire world of ideas. Each major framework might be likened to a geographer's depiction of one continent on the globe. Role theorists, for example, attempt to map all that has been discovered about roles, role processes, role structures, role careers, and role change. **Theoretical models** provide, in contrast, much detail but only about a limited area or set of ideas. Each theoretical model could be compared to a map of a city and its major connecting highways and streets. The psychodynamic model of emotional catharsis and grief work discussed in Chapter 8 attempts to map fully the human grief process, including its components and its healthy and unhealthy variants. Theoretical propositions are like the small-scale maps that you download from the web to get from point A to point B. A social worker, for example, might teach the behavioral proposition "Positive reinforcement increases desired behaviors" to help a parent progress in the direction of effective control of an unruly child's conduct.

Directional maps vary according to the mapping preferences of the cartographers who design them and the needs of those traveling by means of the map. Theoretical mappers also have different mapping preferences and anticipate different needs of the theory users (Toulmin, 1953). You might print a direction map from a website providing such a limited service. Here, the cartographer focused on the starting point, the end point, and the best route to traverse the distance between the two points. Theoretical maps of causal patterns often use such simple mapping conventions. You might buy a state map. The cartographer created a detailed and comprehensive display of all the state's highways and major streets. Imagine here a book-length analysis of a theoretical framework with a series of visual displays representing each of the framework's theoretical models. You might purchase a topographical map to learn about a region's mountains, lakes, and plains, the ecological features supporting human and nonhuman life. Think here about a grand theory such as Parsons' structural functionalist approach discussed in Chapter 5 and its mapping of the cultural, social, and personality systems that make social order possible. When you decide to use either a geographic map or a theoretical map, you must select the map appropriate to your purpose, and you must acquaint yourself with the mapping conventions used. Then the map will serve as a tool guiding you on your journey.

This overview of theoretical mapping ends with a few cautions. Directional and theoretical maps may have some details wrong without seriously damaging their usefulness. No map includes every detail that characterizes the total road system or topography of the United States, for instance. Likewise, a map is not a complete summary of a theory but a display of selected aspects. Often maps are not revised as frequently as developers add communities or legislators initiate new road construction projects. Theory mapmakers may also fail to change maps to correspond with revisions and improvements in the theoretical framework. The accuracy of maps must be continually tested. Social workers, too, should regularly examine the correspondence between theoretical maps and the facts of social life and of particular cases. Finally, a map is not a substitute for experience (Dewey, 1902/1990). Your family would be quite disappointed if your trip to the beach consisted of a half-hour examination of a map showing the beach route. A theoretical map is no substitute for careful and thorough study of a theory's original texts and the best commentaries on the theory.

THEORETICAL MAPPING: ARCHITECTONIC ANALYSIS OF A THEORY'S STRUCTURE

Theoreticians are "structure producers" (Harre, 1978). They have created a structure, or **architectonic** (Ritzer, 1991a; Rock, 1979; Watson, 1985), around which each theoretical approach to understanding human conduct is built. The word *architectonic* refers to matters dealing with building construction or architecture. A theoretical structure is like the architect's design for a complex building. A theoretical domain is built by following a blueprint with its interconnected set of "categories, structures, and dynamics" (Weigert & Gecas, 1995, p. 142). The overall structure facilitates "generalized discourse" among those interested in the framework. For instance, symbolic interactionists from around the world can communicate easily with one another, even

about new areas of inquiry, because they are familiar with the basic architectonic, or configuration, of the interactionist approach.

However, the structure or architectonic of a theoretical school of thought,
unlike an architect's plan, is continually refashioned. Clinical social workers,
for instance, have replaced the original psychodynamic foundations (built on
the construct *instinct*) with new beams and joists (built on the construct *ego
coping with reality*). The architectonic is not fixed in ink on drafting paper.
Instead, it is like a conversation. It will sound different to different participants
in the conversation, and it will serve those who speak the theoretical language
in different ways at different periods of time. Theorists act at times like
architects working on a big project and arguing about the best building design.
Theorists argue about the ideal structure for the tradition and about the
conformity of theory users to the dictates of this ideal structure. A theory's
structure changes in response to the questions, criticisms, and recommendations of insiders who specialize in the framework and of outsiders who
challenge the framework (Colomy, 1991).

Generally, the structure of a scientific tradition brings some order to a
relatively abstract set of theory-building elements. Social science architects
construct their theories using the "presuppositions, the methodological underpinnings of social scientific practice, general models purporting to describe and
explain social processes and systems, and ideological commitments, explicit or
otherwise" (Colomy & Brown, 1995, p. 18). The final structure of a theoretical
language is a distinctive assemblage of root metaphors, assumptions, concepts,
explanations, middle-range theories, and rules for representing the structure in
words or images (Burr, 1995; Fararo, 1989).

THEORETICAL MAPPING: THE BUILDING BLOCKS OF THEORETICAL CONSTRUCTIONS

A team of architects will meet to discuss the best elements and the best arrangement of elements for a planned school or health center. The architects will use
drafts (sketches of parts of a building project) and blueprints (a portfolio of
plans or technical drawings for a construction project) to understand and
communicate with one another and with their customers during this design
phase. The general contractor will use the blueprints to guide the work of the
carpenters, electricians, plumbers, masons, and drywall installers. After the
project is complete, the building's users might go back to the displays and reflect
on or critique the choices made by the architects.

Theory users can engage in a similar process. In most cases, generalist
social workers will use existing theories rather than build new ones. I will focus,
therefore, on theoretical mapping, strategies for analyzing and describing a
theory in terms of its architectonics. We will learn to identify a theory's basic
building blocks or components and their patterned arrangement. Fawcett and
Downs (1986) call this process **theory formalization,** a tool to "determine
exactly what a theory says. It is a way of extracting an explicit statement and a
diagram of a theory from its verbal explanation" (p. 15). Turner (1986) calls

this process **analytic theorizing,** by which he means identifying how concepts, propositions, and sometimes theoretical models are connected in overarching schemes to explain some aspect of reality.

The final product of the theory formalization process is the creation of a theoretical map. Theoretical mappers might map out the entire knowledge base of the social work profession and the overall interrelationship of theories. Howe (1997), for instance, believes that "mapping out social work's theoretical terrain helps practitioners locate themselves intellectually and invites them to explore new areas of thought and practice" (p. 173). In practice, you will more often need to map only a theoretical language or a theoretical model for use as a guide to the helping work. That will be our focus in this section.

Effective language learning necessitates mastery of the words, phrases, and sentence structures of the language studied (Marshall, 1989). One important theorizing competency is theoretical analysis. Effective theory learning and theory use involve learning the elements and structured linkages between the elements of a studied theory. A theory can be analyzed in terms of these elements and the distinctive way that these parts are organized into a whole (Shoemaker, Tankard, & Lasorsa, 2004). These elements or parts of a theory are commonly called root metaphors, assumptions, concepts, and explanations. If a theory is an intellectual structure for understanding human membership, then these parts are the building blocks necessary to create a stable, pleasing, durable, and useful theoretical construction. I will briefly discuss each of the parts.

ROOT METAPHORS   A careful study of the major theoretical traditions indicates that they often can be differentiated by their **root metaphors.** These are the analogies or images that express the similarity of some aspect of the theory's philosophical ideas or methodological preferences to some concrete aspect of everyday life. Interactionists, for example, compare society to a conversation among hundreds of groups and individuals. The person is compared to a competent conversational participant who alternates between speaking and listening. Marxists compare society to a war between groups competing for scarce or cherished resources. A person is a winner or loser, a super dog or underdog. Chapter 2 discussed fully the use of root metaphors to deepen our understanding of theory.

ASSUMPTIONS   Assumptions are like the deeply held cultural beliefs that shape the way cultural members use language. For example, Americans assume that community members generally endorse an individualist social philosophy. Our communication is dominated by the use of words indicating our belief in the separateness of community members: *I, me, mine, individuals,* and *individual responsibility.* If a client has work or relationship troubles, we tend to assume that the troubles are caused by personal failings, not by deficits in the society.

Theoretical traditions, like cultural groups, can be understood by reference to basic assumptions. Chafetz (1978) defines theoretical **assumptions** as "statements taken as given and not subject to direct empirical verification"

(p. 33). In everyday life, we are careful when we make assumptions. Remember the slogan "*Assume:* assumptions make an ass out of you and me." Theorists must accept some assumptions, but they try to remain aware of their working assumptions. Theorists assume that the universe is orderly, for example, and many theorists assume that laws of cause and effect govern all phenomena in the universe. However, theorists are careful too. Theorists know, for instance, that scientists will never collect the evidence necessary to prove foundational assertions conclusively.

Theorists also know that theories differ in their stated and unstated assumptions about the person, the environment, the interaction between the person and the environment, and the change process. Symbolic interactionist social workers, for instance, assumed (until recently) that many social interactions were harmonious and that people use words and gestures to talk together and cooperate in the pursuit of shared goals. Marxist and critical theory social workers, in contrast, assume that most social interaction is characterized by conflict, and that the privileged members of a society maintain their wealth, power, and prestige by the strategic use of force, threat, deception, and other tactics of dominance. Communication across theoretical languages will be very difficult unless interlocutors understand and respect each other's basic assumptions. The core assumptions of 10 major theoretical frameworks will be reviewed later in this book.

One type of theoretical assumption is called an **axiom.** This is "the assumption that a given trait is common to all cases of a particular analytic type (e.g., all people, all organizations, or all societies)" (Powers, 2004, p. 14). Social exchange theorists discussed in the chapter on applied economics, for example, accept the axiom "All people try to maximize profit."

Social work theory users can learn to ask questions about each theoretical perspective's assumptions (Howe, 1997). What does the perspective assume about human nature? (Are our basic inclinations toward responsible social membership or toward deviance? Are they malleable or fixed?) What does it assume about the relative influence of biological factors and environmental factors on human behavior? What assumptions does it make about psychosocial development? What does it assume about the basic ingredients or processes necessary to change? What does the perspective assume about the ideal or desired relationship between the person and the larger social and political order? Theoretical mapping is a way to identify the answers to these questions.

CONCEPTS   Theories are built from **concepts.** These are "ideas about cases of ideas derived from experience and expressed through symbols (Bloom, 1975, p. 38). Concepts point to or represent something in empirical reality. Concepts might be stated in **nominal form,** as in a dictionary definition that uses words to define other words. Some experts on theory use the term **construct** to refer to a very abstract or general concept (Shoemaker et al., 2004). For example, family systems theorists might consider *health family functioning* as a construct that includes more specific concepts such as optimal adaptability, cohesion, and communication.

Concepts, unlike everyday words, are technical terms, and theorists try to develop precise and agreed-upon definitions and rules for a concept's use. Concepts might be stated in **operational form** as variables. These operational definitions include empirical indicators of the concept observable by a practitioner, and measurement procedures that allow one to detect variation in the phenomenon pointed to by the concept. Key concepts in the interactionist tradition include *mind, gesture, symbol, interaction, act, society, culture, role, self, reflexivity,* and *definition of the situation. Self-esteem* is a concept characterizing one dimension of the self. It might be defined, dictionary style, as a person's evaluation of his or her worth. It might be measured by a multi-item self-report questionnaire such as the Rosenberg Self-Esteem Scale. Scores on this device would indicate whether a client has low, moderate, or high self-esteem. Each theory chapter in this book will list the major concepts or terms that constitute the language of the theory.

When studying a culture, linguists attempt to identify its **key words.** These are the "words which are particularly important and revealing in a given culture" (Wierzbicka, 1997, pp. 15–16). Key words are used frequently and often serve as the center of many clusters of phrases. For example, *freedom* is a very important concept in the United States. It is commonly used by politicians, by advertisers, and by citizens, and it is associated with many common phrases, such as *freedom of speech, freedom from hunger,* and *freedom to act.* Wierzbicka, a linguist, recommends studying key words as focal points to understand particular domains of a culture.

Theoretical concepts are expressed as words. Theoretical languages include key concepts or words, and those who speak the theoretical language must understand and be able to use these key concepts. In each theory chapter in this book, I have attempted to identify and define the theory's key words. As you master these key terms, you will become better able to converse with professionals who speak diverse theoretical languages.

EXPLANATIONS   Theories offer **explanations,** sense-making statements and sets of statements. No explanation is perfect or total. Theoretical explanations are always limited, and questions about the rigor of the methods used to arrive at an explanation are common (Skidmore, 1979). Theoretical explanations are like paragraphs. Paragraphs are constructed from words. The words are organized into sentences, with punctuation breaking up the flow of the words into manageable bits. Explanations are constructed from concepts. Concepts are organized into propositions and other general statements, with symbols indicating the relationship of concepts and the linkage of propositions.

Explanations can take a propositional or **deductive** form. Burr (1973) defines deduction as

> an attempt to increase human understanding by providing explanations for why certain things occur. It provides this explanation by having a set a propositions and then deducing, that if these propositions are true, and if certain other conditions are

met, certain specific and observable events occur. The more specific events are then "explained" by the more general propositions that have been used as premises in deducing that specific events occur. (p. 3)

How, for example, do we explain an observation that social workers vary in their ability to empathize with clients from different membership groups? Four concepts are necessary for a provisional answer: perspective taking (empathic tuning-in), cultural difference, encounter, and interpersonal competence. Next, these concepts must be related to one another in a general statement: The more frequently a person tunes in to the perspective of clients who are culturally different, the more competent the person becomes in managing encounters with culturally different clients. We can deduce (and test by research study) that this general pattern would hold for any specific set of social workers. Let me reverse the proposition's wording and deduce the following specific and testable statement: The most empathic social workers are those who have participated in much cross-cultural interaction and have worked hard and often to understand the thoughts, feelings, and inclinations of people who are different. Theorizing as deduction might be mapped in this way: This general pattern _____ suggests this specific manifestation _____.

Explanations can also take an **inductive** form. Inductive reasoning is reasoning from specific premises or observations to general conclusions. Burr (1973) explains inductive logic this way: "it is used by having one or more specific propositions, or even somewhat general propositions, and then inducing that there is a more general proposition (or propositions) that explains why the relationship in the more specific propositions occur" (p. 20). We might add the phrase "or observations" to Burr's notion of specific propositions to cover inductive research and grounded theory. For example, Carl Couch (1989) and his associates used videotaping technology to make repeated and intensive observations of numerous episodes of social interaction in their social laboratory. Their inductive theory identified six essential ingredients of cooperative action: co-presence, reciprocal attentiveness, social responsiveness, shared focus, social objective, and congruent functional identities. Their general conclusion was that any cooperative effort—the coordination of efforts by two different social workers blocked by a fallen table in a meeting room, for example—involves the carefully sequenced use of these elements. Theorizing as induction might be mapped in the following way: This set of specific manifestations _____ suggests this overall and general pattern _____.

Theorizing also has a creative aspect. Some theorists and researchers search for new statements of the relationships between variables to help us understand some mysterious aspect of social life. They can develop such explanations by alternating creatively between induction and deduction.

A few explanations have passed various tests and earned the prestigious title of **empirical law**. This is a general propositional statement that has been shown to describe uniform patterns across ecological settings and historical periods (White, 2005). Scientists have great confidence in the truth of such statements (Tomey, 1998). The laws of gravity and of evolution are explanations that have achieved this status. Empirical laws, however, are rare in scientific theories used for social work purposes.

THEORETICAL MODELS   The definition of theoretical models and the use of models to understand theory were described in Chapter 2. Here, I will add information about one other kind of theoretical model called a "working model" (Lathrope, 1969), a "guiding conception" (Fishman, 1999), or a "case conceptualization" (Meier, 1999). This type of theoretical model is designed to provide a composite picture of a social worker's observations, information, ideas, insights, and reflections about a helping system and its needs in a particular case. I prefer the term **guiding conception,** because it suggests that this tool helps the worker map the theory necessary to achieve his or her helping goals (Egan, 1979).

THEORETICAL BOUNDARY STATEMENTS   The basic architectonic of a theory ideally includes **boundary statements,** or scope conditions. Linguists use the term *language domains* to refer to social settings in which different sublanguages are used (Romaine, 2000). In your daily routines, for instance, you may enter and exit places characterized by the use of formal English, professional jargon, and casual in-group slang. In boundary statements, the theory's experts indicate the helping contexts or fields of practice to which the theory is most relevant, as well as those contexts and practice challenges to which the theory has not yet been extended successfully (White, 2005). Few boundary statements have so far been developed for the social work use of theoretical languages, with the exception of cognitive-behavioral approaches.

THEORETICAL MAPPING: PARSING AND DIAGRAMMING A THEORY'S STRUCTURE

Fawcett and Downs (1986) use a linguistic metaphor for theory analysis similar to the dialogical approach that I introduced in the first chapter:

> Theory formalization is similar to grammatical parsing of a sentence. Just as parsing identifies nouns, verbs, adjectives, adverbs, and other parts of a sentence, theory formalization identifies the concepts, definitions, and propositions that make up a theory. . . . Theory formalization may even involve the translation of a verbal theory into a mathematical or computer language. (p. 15)

Parsing is the act of analyzing the grammatical arrangement of words in a sentence.

In this section, I will review the steps and strategies for parsing theories. Theoretical languages are very complex and hard to parse and diagram. My theory-based chapters will attempt a basic parsing of 10 languages. Middle-range theories and theoretical models, including personal practice models and guiding conceptions, can also be mapped and represented pictorially (Fawcett & Downs, 1986). Examples in this section will be of modest and small theories.

Chafetz (1978) outlines the commonly followed components of a map of theoretical structure as follows:

A. Theoretical assumptions
B. Theoretical concepts and their nominal definitions
C. Theoretical propositions and their linkages
   1. Proposition 1
   2. Proposition 2
   3. Proposition 3
   4. Additional propositions

I will discuss strategies for identifying each of these components. Social workers also test their theories. To prepare you for theory evaluation, I will add an additional component, D, for mapping during theoretical parsing and diagramming activities:

D. Empirically verifiable statements
   1. Theoretical concepts converted to variables with operational definitions
   2. Propositions converted to hypotheses

Parsing is the effort to identify each component, and diagramming involves representing the structure in a hierarchical manner from A to D. Modeling conventions discussed in Chapter 2 may also be incorporated into your theoretical diagrams.

IDENTIFYING ASSUMPTIONS   Chapter 2 includes an extensive discussion of strategies for identifying a theory's root metaphors. I will begin this discussion of how to map theories with assumptions. Assumptions are like the foundation of a building. Different foundations are necessary for but limit the possibilities of different kinds of structures. A beach house may have a foundation of wooden piers sunk deep into the sand, allowing some flexible house movement during storms and raising the house above storm water. An apartment building may use massive steel-reinforced concrete footings to provide support for the heavy weight load. Similarly, theorists make assumptions that constrain the theory's explanatory possibilities. For example, early behaviorists assumed that cognitive processes were not relevant to the processes of understanding and changing human behavior. This assumption helped behaviorists develop procedures to change observable behavior. However, it limited the behaviorist's explanations of human choice.

Honest social work theorists take care to identify the core assumptions of the theoretical languages they use. By accepting that different theory users make different assumptions, and by identifying our assumptions and how they differ from those of collaborators who speak different theoretical languages, we increase the likelihood of maintaining cooperative communication when theorizing, researching, or practicing.

The habit of identifying one's assumptions can also contribute to reflective practice (Britt, 1997). Social work theory users should try to be as alert and sensitive as possible to their own theoretical assumptions and biases. For example, I tend toward a systems theory bias and often suspect that client problems are the result of system problems not bad decisions. Theory users should try to minimize any negative impact of these assumptions on theoretical discourse, practice, or research. They should continuously examine and revise their assumptions through dialogue with theorists and practitioners who make other assumptions and through feedback from empirical data.

Theory mapping is richer when theory users search for the social, political, and cultural orientations embedded in theoretical assumptions (Chafetz, 1978). For example, does a theoretical assumption suggest a conservative, liberal, or radical political stance? The critical theory assumption that privileged community members rule for their own benefit is associated with radical politics. We might also increase our tolerance for those who make different theoretical assumptions if we appreciate the relevance of cultural background to theorizing. Africans and African Americans allied with an Afrocentric theory of cross-cultural adoption, for example, bring their distinctive experiences of oppression and their distinctive tribal heritages to theorizing about family social work (Hollingsworth, 1999). While avoiding stereotypes, we can attempt to understand the historical and social context of a given theorist and speculate about connections between the theorist's lived experience and his or her theoretical assumptions. George Herbert Mead's youthful interest in ministry, his interaction with Hull House social workers in a rapidly changing Chicago, and his friendship with John Dewey, the great philosopher of pragmatism certainly influenced his theorizing about social change and his optimistic assumption that theory can and should be used to ameliorate human suffering and political injustice.

Identifying assumptions is one of the most difficult parsing tasks. Theory speakers and writers only rarely help us by explicitly stating their basic assumptions. We must look and listen for general statements that the theorist assumes to be true (Burr, 1973). Theorists often present these statements without supporting research evidence and without reference to relevant theoretical literature. More often, we must turn to the commentators on a given theory for help. They have studied a theory deeply and thoroughly and often include a section enumerating theoretical assumptions in their commentaries. We might also look for books and articles by speakers of different theoretical languages arguing about the relative merits of their approaches, and the lack of merit of their rivals'. These discussions often make explicit the theories' assumptions as well as their weaknesses and strengths.

IDENTIFYING CONCEPTS AND DEFINITIONS   Like the materials or basic elements (pieces of lumber, crates of nails, truckloads of concrete) necessary to build a house, concepts are the basic elements of a theoretical construction. Fawcett and Downs (1986) suggest that it is not easy to distinguish theoretical concepts from the words in the narrative that surrounds the concepts, but a few practical strategies may facilitate your parsing and diagramming work. Chapters reviewing theoretical languages like those in this book and the theory textbooks referenced in Chapter 1 often include a list of key terms. Such a list is similar to a builder's list of materials and supplies. Concepts may be typed in bold in commentaries or overviews of theoretical frameworks. Those writing or talking about a concept often bracket or identify the theoretical word by explicitly indicating that they are using an accompanying definition. Read and listen for these key terms.

Written theoretical statements are good places to track down a theorist's concepts and their meanings (Bloom, 1975). Theory-based practice articles and research reports generally include an abstract with a short list of key words. This list may include the theoretical concepts referred to in the paper. The title of this kind of scholarly paper may also include the theoretical concepts used by the writer. Research studies often include theoretical concepts in the hypotheses or the research questions that guide the scientific inquiry.

Theoretical concepts are often expressed as **jargon,** a specialized terminology used by members of the theoretical speech community (Chafetz, 1978). Common words have emotional associations and multiple meanings, and thus do not lend themselves to precise and consensual use by scientists and applied scientists. So theorists sometimes like to coin new terms (bizarre and difficult concepts, at times) for the sake of science (or to appear profound). Later, you will learn some of the unusual terms created by Sigmund Freud and Talcott Parsons, for example. Look for the words that are not often used in everyday, normal language use. Underline these terms as likely theoretical concepts.

The definitions of theoretical concepts may also be difficult to identify (Fawcett & Downs, 1986). They are not always clearly and explicitly labeled as nominal or operational definitions. In theory-based articles and books, search the narrative surrounding the concept for the nominal definition. In theory-based research reports, definitions are often provided in the methods section. Here the researcher reports, for example, on how theoretical concepts were operationalized and on the quality of the measurement procedures. You need to check on whether the concept's definition accords with common scientific usage. The dictionaries and encyclopedias of the scientific disciplines and of social work are good places to check on the standard definition of theoretical concepts. See, for example, *The Social Work Dictionary* (Barker, 2003), *The Penguin Dictionary of Sociology* (Abercombie, Hill, & Turner, 1994), or *The Dictionary of Personality and Social Psychology* (Harre & Lamb, 1986).

As you learn more about theories, you can create your own mini-dictionaries of key terms. These are like the language guides that travelers use to assist them when visiting Italy or China. Record definitions that you have discovered, with citation information. When possible, check on the proper pronunciation of theoretical concepts and note this in your mini-dictionaries. Practice saying the words that make up a relevant theory. This will prepare you for conversations about theoretical mapping with others.

IDENTIFYING PROPOSITIONS **Propositions** are sentences. They might be likened to an architect's or general contractor's statements about how different construction elements should be joined together: Two-by-four pieces of lumber will be connected by nails to construct a wood-framed wall. Propositions are statements about the joining of concepts within a theoretical language. They are declarative sentences that state something about the nature of theorized connections.

When you participate in theoretical discourse or the study of theory, you can listen and look for theoretical propositions. Several major kinds of **relationships** are stated in propositional form (Burr, 1973). A proposition might state the **existence** of a relationship between two or more concepts. Burr reports, for example, on the exchange theory proposition: "the amount of interaction between intimates is related to the degree of positive sentiment or liking." A proposition might state the **direction** of a relationship. In the positive case, for example, exchange theorists submit the proposition "the greater the interaction between intimates, the higher the degree of positive sentiment or liking." In the negative or inverse direction, exchange theorists propose that "the more costly an intimate relationship in the currency of physical or mental effort, the lower the degree of positive sentiment or liking." Look for directional propositions when studying theory. Theorists might even develop propositions in a form indicating the **strength** of a relationship. This might be stated in words or in the language of applied statistics: correlations. Symbolic interactionists, for example, posit a very strong relationship between a husband's disposition toward empathy and his abusive behavior. They suggest a direction, too: the greater the empathy, the lower the verbal and physical abuse of a partner. A proposition might also indicate the **shape** of a relationship. Here are two contrasting propositions: "Marital satisfaction increases over the couple's life together" communicates a linear relationship. "Marital satisfaction shows a U-shaped pattern over a couple's lifetime: high early in the marriage, lower in the middle phase of the marriage, and high again in the later stage of life" suggests a curvilinear pattern.

Practice models are often built from propositions specifying the likely effects of an intervention (Specht, 1977). Burr, Klein, and their associates (1994) discussed one more kind of proposition that can inform practice: **if–then statements** relating some theoretical concept to likely results following a planned intervention. The "if" part of the statement might refer, for example, to social membership processes and the structures where intervention is possible; the "then" part would refer to the probable outcomes of such intervention for the quality of social membership. For instance, an interactionist theory of small group interaction provides a useful practice directive: "If the practitioner can increase the perspective-taking abilities and propensities of diverse members of a collective, then the quality of communication among these members will increase." Theory developers often fail to think about theory application. Therefore, these kinds of propositions are rare. However, they are especially valuable. If you do not find such explicit if–then propositions, you might try using a theory's major concepts to generate them yourself.

You can practice searching for theoretical statements that combine concepts. Look in theory-based research studies, in practice theory articles, and in case studies. You can create your own theoretical statements to help explain a client problem or some phase of the helping process. Try these out with a fellow student and ask for feedback on how well you combined ideas.

IDENTIFYING THEORETICAL LINKAGES   Theoretical linkage refers to the interlacing of all concepts and propositions to create the overall edifice or theoretical structure (Fawcett & Downs, 1986; Shoemaker et al., 2004). It is the arrangement of a set or network of theoretical statements (Bloom, 1975). Parsing a theory's linkages is like analyzing the way a good storyteller arranged words, sentences, and paragraphs into a compelling narrative.

Several types of theoretical linkage are common. A theory may be arranged by its explanatory logic. Parsing requires you to look for the logic of theoretical linkage—deductive, inductive, or a combination of both—in the set of propositions. These forms of logical reasoning were discussed earlier. A theorist using inductive logic proceeds from specific observations or propositions to more general ones. A theorist using deductive reasoning proceeds from general propositions (premises, postulates, or statements) to more specific propositions or conclusions. You can parse or summarize these linkages as an "informal system of sentences related by simple deduction using proposition logic" (Skvoretz, 1998, p. 251). A theorist may creatively alternate between induction and deduction (Tomey, 1998).

Theorists who use a mathematical language might characterize the linkages as a set of equations. The job of parsing and diagramming theories composed of mathematical formulas and arranged as mathematical theorems can be reserved for advanced theory users.

Several other linkage patterns are common. Theorists may organize linkages to communicate the path of a series of actions. A theory of the career of heroin abuser from non–drug user to drug addict details a typical pathway. Theorists may organize concepts and propositions to communicate an interrelated network of cause and effect. Or a theorist may organize theoretical statements to communicate all the factors or independent variables that influence one dependent variable or outcome. A theory of the predictors of criminal recidivism by child molesters uses this pattern. A theorist may arrange theoretical elements to communicate an information transmission system with feedback loops. For instance, family systems theorists might trace the complex patterns of communication within families with schizophrenic members. A theorist may order theoretical concepts and propositions to communicate a temporal sequence of events. For instance, an agency theory user might map the expected 16-week progression through an alcohol rehabilitation program. Finally, a theorist may arrange theoretical building blocks in the form of typology or classification system. Psychiatric social workers use many diagnostic categories to map the various types of mental disorder.

Unfortunately, scientists and applied scientists do not often present their theoretical papers, theory-based practice reports, or theory-based research studies with a formal delineation of theoretical linkages (Fawcett & Downs, 1986). Here are a few strategies for theory parsing that you may find helpful. Look for references in the narrative and the citations that indicate where the theory user found guidance for the theory design process. Was the design supported by literature from an existing theoretical framework, supported by previous empirical research, or supported by the theorist's logical thinking? You can turn to these original sources for a better understanding of the theory's architectonic.

Look for the theory user's approach to science. Theorists using a logical positivist paradigm (the language of determinism, variables, hypotheses, measurement, and findings) tend toward deductive theoretical structures. Theorists embracing the postpositivist or qualitative paradigm (the language of choice, research questions, observations, interpretation, and patterns or themes) are more likely to use inductive logic (Britt, 1997; Gubrium & Holstein, 1997).

Study the theoretical text. Identify all the propositions relating two or more concepts associated with the theory. Separate these propositions according to their level of generality, from the most general to the most specific statements. Then, arrange them in words or in a diagram into the appropriate hierarchical order (specific to general, or general to specific).

Boisen and Syers (2004) have developed an integrative case analysis method that incorporates theory-mapping strategies. This tool is used in the classroom, in field seminars, and in practice settings. It challenges students to learn how to consciously apply theory to their helping work in a field internship. The structured format requires that the student pick a field case, identify a client system's presenting problem and the relevant data, and then describe the "human behavior and the social environment" guiding theoretical conception that guided the data collection phase. Students also identify the practice theories and models that served as the conceptual foundation for goal setting and for the selection of intervention strategies. You might use this procedure with your own casework, or you might examine an experienced practitioner's case report and disassemble the guiding conception into its concepts, propositions (often stated as practice directives), and theoretical linkages.

Practice describing the linkages or structure of a theoretical model to a friendly audience. At first, it may seem as though you are trying to tell a story in a foreign language, but with repeated attempts you will increase your confidence in talking about a complicated theory's patterns and designs.

JUDGING THE VIABILITY OF A THEORY'S DESIGN

Architects and builders wonder how well their design will perform when built in a specific location and required to meet specific environmental challenges and use demands. Will the bridge hold the weight of thousands of automobiles? They run tests under varying conditions on simulations and models of their structures before finalizing the blueprints.

Theorists also seek tests of the usefulness and likely performance of theories in real circumstances by using research methods. They seek empirical support for the proposed relationships and for the set of linked propositions (Bloom, 1975). They are trying to forge connections between theorizing and researching that improve the theory (White, 2005).

IDENTIFYING VARIABLES   When mapping a theory, you can decide if the theorists have taken this step. Have concepts been formulated as **variables,** social phenomena that vary in quantity, quality, or condition? Has a symbolic interactionist concept of marital satisfaction, for example, been operationalized as a variable using the client ratings low satisfaction, moderate satisfaction, and high satisfaction? Also try to identify whether the theory user has specified an **independent variable,** one that influences or causes changes to happen, and a **dependent variable,** one that is influenced or changed by the action of the independent variable. For example, Burr's (1973) review of marital satisfaction theories indicates that empathic communication between spouses, the independent variable, influences the degree of marital satisfaction, the dependent variable. Also look for evidence that the measurement strategies for each variable in a theory are valid, reliable, and sensitive to social work client groups.

IDENTIFYING HYPOTHESES   To test a theory, theorists and theory researchers can transform propositions into **hypotheses,** testable statements that predict a relationship. Burr, for example, might have tested the hypothesis that good marital communication as measured by a high-quality measurement tool is associated with high marital satisfaction as measured by the Kansas Marital Satisfaction Scale. Qualitative theory testers use carefully developed research questions instead of hypotheses.

I have added the notion of judging the viability of a theory's construction to this section on theoretical mapping, However, we are shifting into the territory of social work research methodology. Let's turn our attention back to theorizing for practice.

ECOSYSTEMS MAPPING: TRANSLATING THEORIES INTO A COMMON LANGUAGE

Social workers can become cartographers and translate theories into social work language and social work maps. These maps can improve our practice. Ann Hartman (1978; Hartman & Laird, 1983) and her associates, for example, have created a two-dimensional mapping tool for representing the relationship of families to the social environment. This **eco-map** can serve as a shorthand communication device for characterizing the person's behavior in the ecosystem and as a substitute for hundreds of words.

The eco-map has been used in many fields of practice and with clients of all different ages. Beckett and Coley (1987) demonstrated its utility, for example, in mental health work with elderly members of African American families. The reference section on the book's companion website includes a list of articles describing other uses of eco-maps by social workers and human service professionals. Most textbooks on social work practice present the eco-map. You might have even completed one yourself (perhaps a genogram too) to learn about your likely strengths and vulnerabilities as a worker.

The eco-map is associated with the ecosystems paradigm. This abstract conceptualization of "human behavior and the environment" has become a primary and common language for most social workers. The research discussed in Chapter 1 found that many social workers identified the ecosystems paradigm as the most important theoretical influence on their current practice (Ephross Saltman & Greene, 1993). Citizens of the United States can travel almost anywhere in North America, Central America, or Europe and find people who speak English. Social workers, too, from distant parts of the globe (and galaxy?) should be able to use the ecosystems language to communicate. The novice social worker's ability to interpret speakers using different theoretical languages will be enhanced if she turns on this universal translator. The ecosystems paradigm can facilitate communication across traditions, professions, and disciplines, and among team members from diverse educational backgrounds. The language of ecosystems can be used to reference the social work self-identity, to articulate social work's common language, and to guide mapping of clients' relationships to their life spaces. I will next review the basic features of the eco-map and then describe its potential for translation.

THE ECO-MAP

The eco-map is a visual representation of ideas from the ecosystems paradigm. The ecosystems paradigm combines ideas from two different theoretical traditions: the ecological perspective and the systems approach (also known as structural functionalism). These traditions will be reviewed fully in Chapters 4 and 5. The ecological perspective builds on a metaphor that characterizes humans as like all living organisms. Human organisms depend on continuous interchange with the surrounding environment for survival and growth. The systems approach compares humans to machines or bodies. The whole is made up of many interrelated parts; problems with one part affect every other part and the whole system. The eco-map relies on one other metaphor: The social worker is like a geographer. The social work job involves helping clients map the important locations in their ecology and the pathways from one location to another location. Good social workers help clients develop a map of the ideal ecosystem, too.

CENTRAL THEORETICAL TERMS USED IN THE ECO-MAP

The social worker using the eco-map makes use of various concepts derived from the ecosystems paradigm. These concepts include *system, subsystem, suprasystem, connection, quality of connections, focal system, boundary, resource, resource flow and direction of resource transfer,* and *environment.* I will use these concepts in the same way that communication experts use **conceptual universals.** Conceptual universals are meanings that are common across cultures (Wierzbicka, 1997). They can be used as a common measure or a translation device for comparing language systems. For example, Wierzbicka suggests that the term *friend* refers to a concept that transcends cultures even if different language communities use different words to signify *friend*. I will assume that terms used to characterize an eco-map are conceptual universals among the social work community, and I will assume that we can use these terms to compare and contrast many different theoretical languages.

The set of ecosystem terms is offered as a theoretical Esperanto. Esperanto is an artificial language based on words common to all European languages (Albeniz & Holmes, 1996). It was designed to be easier to learn than any one of the European languages or English and to allow for conversations between people across the globe. The theoretical Esperanto built from ecosystems terminology can be used to facilitate communication among practitioners from different theoretical language communities. Social workers have a speaking dictionary that uses ecosystems terms. Speakers of different theoretical languages have their own dictionaries, and theorists aligned with each theoretical language use the theory's dictionary.

The task for practice in a multitheory work is to create a new dictionary (Duncker, 2001). I propose that this new dictionary can be composed of the ecosystems conceptual universals from the social work dictionary and the theoretical translation of the key terms of 10 major theoretical languages into these conceptual universals. Chapter 13, for example, will include a section that starts with a social work term, *connections,* and then defines this term from the perspective of applied critical theorists. As much as possible, I will also take terms that are strange to us from a theoretical dictionary and transform them into common English words and words that are familiar to social workers. Combine the translated concepts from each of the 10 theory chapters into an overall dictionary, and you have a metatheoretical dictionary, one that can make many cross-theory conversations possible.

MAPPING CONVENTIONS FOR THE ECO-MAP

Figure 3.1 presents the conventional empty eco-map. A cartographer must choose a system of conventions—a baseline or point of reference, an orientation scale, a system of signs, and a method of projecting geographical information—before mapping an area (Toulmin, 1953). Hartman (1978) has provided a set of mapping conventions that social workers can use when mapping client systems and their relationships to the environment. The following discussion summarizes the parts of the eco-map and the basic mapping conventions.

The large circle in the center of the map represents the **unit of attention:** the individual, the couple, or the family that is using the services of a social worker. The eco-map was developed specifically to help workers in public child welfare agencies. Many social workers follow this tradition and place the family or the household in the center circle. Members of this focal system can also be

FIGURE 3.1
SAMPLE BLANK
ECO-MAP

Source: *Family-Centered
Social Work Practice*
(p. 160) by A. Hartman
and J. Laird, 1983.
New York: The Free
Press. Copyright 1983 by
The Free Press. Reprinted
by permission.

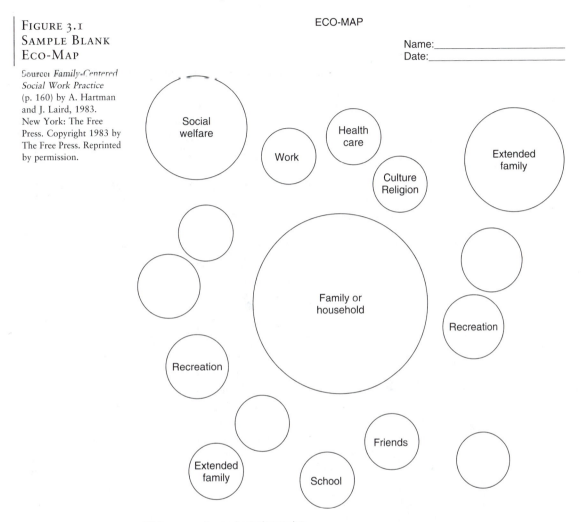

ECO-MAP

Name:_____
Date:_____

Fill in connections where they exist:
Indicate nature of connections with a descriptive word or by drawing different kinds of lines:
———————— for strong ----------- for tenuous +++++++ for stressful.
Draw arrows along lines to signify flow of energy, resources, etc. ➝ ➝ ➝
Identify significant people and fill in empty circles as needed.

symbolized by genogram conventions—a small box for a male, a small circle
for a female, and lines connecting marital partners and parents to children. The
focal system might even refer to a larger social system that the worker intends
to help: a social organization, a community, or perhaps even a society.

The entire eco-map figure represents the **environment,** or life space, of
the client or client group. The circles surrounding the unit of attention are the
major social systems—the groups, organizations, and institutions that influence
and are influenced by the client(s). Hartman (1978) identifies common social
systems such as school, friends, work, health care, recreation, and cultural or

religious organizations by small circles. Circles without names are available so that the practitioner can identify and label distinctive or unusual social systems. Two circles of moderate size indicate the importance of the social welfare system and the extended family network to most social work clients. A contemporary eco-map creator might include even larger circles to represent the macro-level social systems such as corporations or labor markets that affect many clients' life chances. The circles are drawn with solid lines to indicate the boundaries between one system and external systems. Dashed lines could be used to convey the ecosystems notion that all groups of living organisms have permeable **boundaries.**

The worker must add to the eco-map form by drawing in lines suggesting the connections between the focal system and external systems. These **connections** have been referred to in various terms as the exchanges, interfaces, relationships, linkages, and transactions between the client system and its environment. The nature or quality of the connection is represented visually in three different ways. A solid or thick line indicates a strong or **positive connection.** A dashed line indicates a weak or **tenuous connection,** and a line made up of crosses indicates a conflict-ridden or **stressful connection** or relationship. Transactions between the systems are described as transfers of **resources,** including energy, opportunities, and interests. The direction of the flow of resources is mapped as an arrow placed alongside the connecting line.

The worker can increase the utility of the eco-map in several ways. The date on the eco-map records the time when the ecosystems assessment was completed. However, the worker and client or clients can select the most useful **temporal focus** for their purposes. The eco-map might depict life space systems and processes in the present, or it might be retrospective, attempting to capture client–environment exchanges at an earlier historical period. Finally, the eco-map might be prospective and attempt to depict visually a future or ideal ecosystem.

The fact that different members of the focal system construct social reality differently can also be depicted. When all members of the family have connections to the same external system, then a line can connect the family boundary and the system boundary. However, if the focal system includes multiple members rather than one client, the practitioner might use a color code during mapping and draw lines of different shades from each member to show the salient systems for that person.

THEORETICAL PROPOSITIONS AND ECOSYSTEMS PRACTICE

We reviewed the notion of theoretical propositions in an earlier chapter. Several propositions derived from Hartman and Laird's (1983) discussion of the eco-map can guide ecosystems assessment and intervention. Let's do some theoretical mapping here. I'll parse the ecosystems theory used in the eco-map and identify a few simple propositions. The first refers to the concept of connections. The greater the quantity of positive exchanges between the client and the environment, the more likely it is that the client will adapt to the environment and grow. Conversely, a large number of stressful and harmful connections will be associated with problems in adaptation. The second refers to the concept of boundary and the idea of an optimal degree of boundary permeability for client systems. Families with relatively closed boundaries, for instance, will lack the resources and supports necessary for meeting family member needs. The last refers to the multidirectional nature of ecosystems change. Change in the system contributing to the most salient client problem (the family, for example) will reverberate and stimulate changes in other systems (the workplace and the peer group) and in the total life space.

Verbal summaries can add important detail to the eco-map's depiction of client system–environment exchanges. This detail can help with the ecosystem assessment and intervention planning. The worker can add case notes to the eco-map that summarize her conceptual thinking about the overall quality of family–environment exchanges, about a client system's problem areas and potential strengths, about the factors for change, and about resources for change in the ecosystem that might contribute to achieving desired changes. The worker can also add notes that use the theoretical mapping of the paradigm's propositions to direct helping action. For instance, if I can help the family better manage their boundaries, then the family members will make better use of various resources and opportunities provided by external systems, including the social service agency.

Social workers might develop two different eco-maps for their clients: an **actual eco-map** depicting current conditions and another depicting ideal conditions. The **ideal eco-map** can be used to set goals for positive changes in the client, the social systems, the connections, and the resource exchange patterns.

THE ECO-MAP AS UNIVERSAL TRANSLATOR

Many social workers have learned that the eco-map can help them communicate with other social workers quickly and efficiently about the total situation of a client system. I propose that the eco-map can also work as a communication tool that helps social workers understand team collaborators from other disciplines and theoretical traditions and that helps them understand us. Why might the eco-map and the ecosystems ideas that it uses serve as a good cross-theory translator?

The first reason is a practical one. The language of person-in-the-environment is the most widely spoken language in the profession of social worker. Europeans and Chinese may regret that English has become the dominant language on the globe, yet they are realists. Mastering English enables them to benefit from the economic ventures, cultural entertainment, and scientific inquiries offered by citizens of the United States and by our English-speaking friends. Therefore, they are working hard to learn English. Some of us might prefer that social workers develop a primary language different from the ecosystems paradigm. I prefer symbolic interactionism, for instance. However, many complicated decisions by leaders of the profession related to our history, our place as a vocation, and the composition of our associations' membership have resulted in the pervasive spread of the ecosystems language. Today, social workers can converse most effectively with their diverse colleagues, I contend, using terms generated by this combined ecological and systems perspective.

Second, the ecosystems perspective and eco-map are designed to emphasize the transactional nature of human action and social life. This philosophical stance fits well with the social work mission of improving both the quality of membership experiences for our clients and the quality of the membership organizations in which clients work, live, and play. **Transactionalism** is the assumption that all human action must be seen as the interplay of personal processes and ecological processes. The concepts *person* and *environment* cannot be separated. The eco-map forces the worker to translate other theoretical languages in ways that avoid either downward or upward reductionism. **Downward reductionism** occurs when theorists focus only on individual factors and processes. All human behavior might be explained, for instance, as the operation of inner inclinations to seek fulfillment of sexual and aggressive drives. Or a homosexual orientation is fully explained, according to downward reducers, by a genetically structured part of the brain; the environment is left out of the equation. **Upward reductionism** reduces complex explanations of the person-in-environment interface to the pervasive influence of large-scale social systems. The person is left out of these equations. For instance, all human behavior is determined, Marxists sometimes assert, by one's place in the larger political and economic structure; personal choice is irrelevant. Material arrangements—access assigned at birth to wealth, housing, good jobs, and other life necessities—preordain us for prosperity and health or poverty and early death. Human choice has little relevance.

Third, look at the eco-map closely. The center circle is large enough to contain multiple family members or various subgroups. Note the 13 small-size external systems and two moderate-size systems. One can draw dozens of lines indicating various connections among these systems. The social worker can choose how to describe the resources transferred between the major social systems and the client system. These resources may relate to basic biological needs for food, shelter, and physical security. They may refer to psychological needs for meaningful experiences or for intellectual challenge. Resources may relate to social needs for gratifying work and supportive friends, or they may be spiritual and relate to how people meet their needs for congress with God or other transcendental divinities. The eco-map thus represents the client's ecology as one of great complexity and variability. The eco-map, then, makes it possible to think of each different theoretical language as contributing to social work knowledge about certain social systems, certain kinds of connections, and certain types of resource transfers. Each can help social workers understand a different aspect of the whole person and environment configuration. Symbolic interactionism, for instance, contributes many middle-range theories and research-supported concepts about the influence of the family and the small group on the client's self-conceptions. It directs attention to the connections forged by verbal and nonverbal communication that result in shared understanding, and it characterizes the ecology as a symbolic environment rich with resources for communication—symbols and systems of symbols.

Finally, the eco-map uses ecosystems concepts that are at a high level of abstraction. The notion of connections, for instance, is quite general and vague. Resources is another concept without precise, specific, and easily agreed upon empirical referents. However, the generality of eco-map concepts can be an asset, enabling these concepts to be used to translate the more clear cut and definitive concepts of other theoretical traditions.

The remainder of this book will build on these observations about the versatility of the eco-map. Each theoretical tradition will be displayed on a modified eco-map. Each tradition will also be translated by the use of eco-map terms. Theoretical equivalents for ecosystems conceptions of the environment, the external system, the focal system, the helping system, the connection, and the characteristics of the connection will be identified. Our major question will be: How would adherents to each different theoretical tradition label the elements of the conventional eco-map, fill in connecting lines, and add descriptive words? Theory-specific eco-maps will explicate the notion of the connectedness of clients to various groups (and how theorists talk differently about connectedness and isolation); the various theoretical conceptions of the linkage; issues and resource-need discrepancies central to client problems; and the theories' various recommendations for helping clients meet challenges and change transactional patterns. The examination of these theory-specific eco-maps will result in an appraisal of the contribution of each theoretical language to a complete depiction of client system-in-environment dynamics. Table 3.1

TABLE 3.1 KEY ECO-MAP QUESTIONS FOR TRANSLATING THEORETICAL LANGUAGES	1. In what ways do adherents of the theoretical framework conceptualize *connections* between the focal group and other groups, organizations, or systems?
	2. Do they differentiate the *quality of connections* as positive or negative? If so, how?
	3. Who and what do they typically include in the *unit of attention* (the focal system)?
	4. How do they conceptualize the *environment*? What groups, organizations, or systems would they include?
	5. Do they give greater *emphasis* to particular groups, organizations, or systems in the environment? Which ones?
	6. How do they conceptualize *resources* and indicate the flow of energy, resources, and opportunities between the focal system and other systems in the client's life space?
	7. What *descriptive words* would they add to characterize systems within the environment and connections between systems?
	8. How do they conceptualize (and visualize) *changes* in the interface of the focal system and major systems in the environment? How do they conceptualize the social work role in the change process?
	9. How would they contrast eco-maps that characterize *actual and ideal conditions*?
	10. How do they address *issues of diversity, color, and shading*?
	11. Would they *add or delete* any elements of the conventional eco-map?

summarizes the translation questions that we will use to compare and contrast different theories of human behavior in the environment.

SOCIAL WORK LANGUAGE AND UNIVERSAL STANDARDS FOR THEORY EVALUATION

We need to consider one more topic before we conclude this chapter. Social workers will work with professionals and semiprofessionals from numerous different theoretical traditions, and it is important that we know how to communicate with them no matter what theoretical language they speak. For instance, after I graduated from college I worked in a school for preteens from a poor neighborhood in central New Jersey. The school was committed to the behavior modification approach, and these children were understood in terms of their behavior disorders. I was required to use the language of "Good sitting, Nigel"; "You have earned one token, John, for raising your hand before speaking"; and "If you throw that desk, Ricky, you will be put in timeout." However, some theoretical languages are better for social work purposes than others, and we need to be thoughtful about which knowledge we borrow (Garvin, 1997). I wondered, for instance, during my work at the training center whether the exclusive focus on observable classroom behavior prevented us from exploring the contributions of poor neighborhoods, disorganized families, and psychological confusion to the troubles displayed by these boys. Borrowing knowledge from critical theorists, family systems theories, and ego psychology would have enhanced our assessments and interventions.

GENERAL STANDARDS FOR THEORY EVALUATION

Experts in theoretical languages offer general **standards,** criteria for evaluating theories. Shoemaker, Tankard, and Lasorsa (2004), for example, propose that you ask the following questions about a theory: Is the theory testable? Is it parsimonious, stated as simply as possible? Does it have explanatory power, explaining a great deal of the topic or challenge of interest to the social work theory user? Does it help us make accurate predictions? Is it broad in scope, helping us understand many important public problems and social work topics? Have its proponents taken a cumulative approach and revised the theory whenever new evidence is discovered? Has the theory been developed formally and precisely—that is, have assumptions, concepts, nominal definitions, operational definitions, propositions, and the linkages between propositions been explicitly articulated? Does the theory have heuristic value, generating ideas for social work practice and research?

Chafetz (1978) adds criteria focused on the communicability of the theory. Clarity is critical to effective theory development. Are the assumptions explicitly stated? Are the concepts carefully defined and used in a consistent manner? Is the nature of the explanation(s), the theoretical linkages, spelled out clearly and without ambiguity?

Fawcett and Downs (1986) recommend a set of standards related to the theory's suitability for and support by scientific testing. Was the theory developed with reference to a sample representative of the theory user's population of interest? Are the theory's concepts defined using empirically observable indicators? Are valid and reliable measurements of the indicators available? Are the hypotheses falsifiable? Are the theoretical statements backed by empirical evidence?

These criteria are important for theory evaluation. Be alert for commentaries on the degree to which your favorite theories earn favorable answers to these evaluative questions. Using these standards to evaluate theoretical languages and specific theories requires advanced theory knowledge and theorizing skill. As theory users proceed to the intermediate and advanced levels of theorizing competency, such theory evaluation becomes manageable.

SOCIAL WORK STANDARDS FOR THEORY EVALUATION

In this book, I will focus on the distinctive social work contribution to theory evaluation. Social workers share a set of preferences regarding theory, expressed through our language of values and ethical guidelines (Bloom, Wood, & Chambon, 1991). All social workers must confront value issues during the research, practice, and policy analysis processes. Professional values are also relevant to theorizing and theory use. Social work theory users can learn to take a critical approach to theory, inquiring "how consistent is the theory with social work values and ethics?" (Robbins, Chatterjee, & Canda, 1998) Students need to learn to evaluate each theoretical language in terms of its fit with social work by using our value language and its universal standards.

Although we are a profession that borrows much knowledge from other professions and disciplines, we are also discriminating in what we borrow. When our theory builders enter trading zones to acquire theory for social work use, they make deals only after checking the theoretical merchandise against the values and principles at the core of our professional identity. In this way, we avoid careless borrowing. We select theoretical languages, models, and concepts that will contribute to successful and responsible practice (Berger, 1986).

The evaluation standards shared by almost all social workers (strengths orientation, appreciation of social justice, sensitivity to diversity, biopsychosocial explanations, ethical integrity, attention to various-size systems and life stages, and empirical support) transcend particular theoretical languages. These standards can be used as translation tools to guide us as we consider using these theories in practice. Most of these criteria are codified in the policies of the Council on Social Work Education, a body that accredits social work education programs (Council on Social Work Education, 2001). We might use the following specific standards to judge the suitability of a theoretical language or one of its theories.

STRENGTHS PERSPECTIVE   Is the language of the theoretical tradition compatible with central social work value commitments? Does the theory share the social work emphasis on health, human possibility, and personal **strengths**? We should be wary of theories that dwell on illness, deficit, or psychopathology. We should only use with caution theories that place very narrow limits on human capacities for creativity and freedom.

COMMITMENT TO JUSTICE AND APPRECIATION FOR DIVERSITY   Social workers are committed to the fight for **justice** and the fight against all forms of injustice—social, economic, and political. The profession prefers theories that prepare social workers to understand and change oppressive community practices and policies. We pledge to work with diverse clients and serve them respectfully and without discrimination, whatever their age, social class, skin color, cultural and ethnic background, national origin, gender, sexual orientation, or level of physical ability or disability. Therefore, we also prefer theoretical languages that prepare us to appreciate **diversity** and to work in a pluralistic community.

ETHICAL INTEGRITY   The social work profession is committed to practice in accordance with **ethical standards** related to the client's rights to dignity, respect, privacy, and self-determination. Theoretical traditions that suggest any assessment or intervention practices that humiliate or coerce clients are suspect. Theory-based practice models that conceive of the worker as controlling rather than cooperating with those who need our help deserve a negative evaluation.

HOLISM   Social workers take a **holistic stance** in our work with clients. We appreciate that humans are complex, multidimensional creatures, and we prefer theories and knowledge that contribute to our understanding of all the dimensions of the human experience (biological, psychological, socio-logical, and spiritual) and the interrelatedness of these dimensions. Theoretical perspectives that restrict attention to only one dimension are less useful than holistic theories.

ATTUNED TO VARIOUS SYSTEM SIZES AND LIFE STAGES   Social workers endorse generalist practice, acknowledging that some will build special knowledge and skill on the generalist foundation. The profession expects that all social workers can help **social systems of various sizes** and people at **various stages of life.** Therefore, we need theoretical languages that speak about the multiple levels of social organization: individual, dyadic encounter, dyadic relationship, peer and family group, community, formal organization, social movements and collectives, society, and the global aggregate of societies. We also prefer theories that can help us understand human development across the life span. This is a large order, and no one theoretical tradition can fill it. However, social workers can listen carefully to the language used by adherents of different theoretical traditions and judge whether the approach contributes to a multisystem, multistage knowledge base for the profession.

EMPIRICAL SUPPORT   Lastly, social workers are responsible and accountable professionals. We realize that the viability of our profession and of our agencies is related to our ability to prove that we solve public problems and meet human needs effectively and efficiently. Science is the best tool devised for ensuring that our theories work and for improving them. Therefore, social workers strongly prefer theoretical traditions, mid-range theories, and theoretical models including practice models that are scientifically or **empirically sound.** These theories and models are supported by empirical evidence and can be applied in testable ways to practice. They are also structured in a way that allows us to evaluate program outcomes and our practice effectiveness.

APPLYING STANDARDS DURING THEORY EVALUATION

Social work students who use this universal set of standards and internalize this distinctive social work approach to appraising, selecting, and modifying theoretical languages will best advance the profession's interests and values. In social work schools and agencies, we can try to choose the most suitable theoretical traditions developed by the profession or adapt alien approaches for social work use. In private practice, we can deliberate carefully and select a theoretical orientation that suits our personal preferences while meeting the profession's standards. We may have little influence, however, over what languages other professionals speak. Yet, as a member of an interdisciplinary team or a practitioner in a multiprofessional setting, the social worker should model the critical and principled use of theory and offer constructive and, if necessary, forceful feedback to those who use theories at odds with social work convictions.

Besides translating theories into theoretical maps and into eco-map terms and symbols, the remainder of the book will include some consideration of the suitability of each theoretical language for social work. Here are some sample questions to suggest how this appraisal process will work: How do the metaphors and terms of behaviorism, ego psychology, and economic theory shape each theory's conception of client potentials and strengths? In what ways do advocates for critical theory, structural functionalism, and evolutionary biology talk about social justice and the ideal society? How do interactionists, role theorists, and cognitive scientists consider the notion of scientific proof, and how does each of these three approaches demonstrate its utility and effectiveness for social work practice?

LEARNING ACTIVITIES

1. Think of how you have used a road map to travel to a new place. How did the map help during the trip? Did your use of the map make the trip difficult in any way? What lessons can you take from your experience that will improve your use of theories?

2. Take one of the middle-range theories that you have already learned in a practice, policy, research, or ethics class (a theory of homophobia, an explanation of welfare dependency, a model of the influence of spiritual beliefs on coping with illness). Attempt to parse or identify the major building blocks of

this theory: assumptions, concepts, and propositions. Discuss how the concepts and propositions are linked. Speculate about ways to test the theory.

3. Identify a personal change goal and a practice theory that you might use to attain this goal. List and define the major concepts selected from this practice theory that you can use for specifying your goal, assessing your progress, and implementing a self-change intervention. Create a diagram or map depicting your personal theory's building blocks, their connections to each other, and their connection to your target goal or problem.

4. Make a copy of the eco-map in Figure 3.1 Use it to characterize your current social situation. Follow the instructions presented earlier. After you are done, summarize what you have learned about your personal life space: What are the major social systems? How would you describe your connections to each of these systems? What resources are exchanged between you and members of the outside systems? How is your pattern of connections similar to or different from those of other members of your family or household?

5. Consider your eco-map again. This time, create an ideal eco-map that includes improvements in your relation to the environment associated with the perfect life space. What social systems might you like to add to your life space? Which social systems would you delete if possible? How would you change your connections to different social systems?

6. Compare the eco-map of your actual situation to the eco-map of your ideal relationship to the ecosystem. Develop two or three goals, and then develop several action strategies that would help you reduce the discrepancy between your real situation and your possible social situation.

7. What aspects of your overall relationship to the environment, your connections to systems in this environment, and your personal functioning are not well represented in the actual or ideal eco-map? Summarize in words the themes, issues, problems, or qualities that are not represented on the visual display. Identify some ways that these might be depicted in graphic form.

8. How well might the eco-map record the relevant information for clients of different ages, racial/ethnic backgrounds, social classes, or sexual orientations? What modifications might help you map information related to diversity and social justice?

9. Reflect on some piece of theoretical knowledge that you have acquired in one of your classes. You might reflect, for example, on an explanation for social problems such as poverty, violence, crime, or discrimination. How well did this knowledge meet the evaluation criterion shared by most social workers for good theory (strengths orientation, appreciation of social justice, sensitivity to diversity, biopsychosocial explanations, ethical integrity, attention to various-size systems and life stages, and empirical support)?

ADDITIONAL RESOURCES

Additional resources are available on the book companion website at **www.thomsonedu.com/ social_work/forte**. Resources include key terms, tutorial quizzes, links to related websites, and lists of additional resources for furthering your research.

Applied Ecological Theory

CHAPTER 4

John Riley/IndexStock

INTRODUCTION

Ecology is the interdisciplinary science that studies the relations between organisms and their environments (Germain, 1990; Ungar, 2002). Ecological theorists incorporate ideas from biology, sociology, psychology, social psychology, geography, and other academic disciplines. Applied ecological theory, often called the ecological perspective, helps social workers examine the nature and consequences of transactions between organisms, including humans, and their physical and social environments (Germain, 1979). Ecological social workers direct their practice efforts toward improving the transactions between people and environments, nurturing human development within particular environments, and improving environments so that they support the expression of client systems' positive dispositions and potentials.

The ecosystems approach blends assumptions, concepts, and propositions from both the ecological theoretical framework and the systems theoretical framework (Grief, 1986). The ecosystems approach serves many social workers as a **paradigm,** an overarching system of beliefs about the nature of reality and about helping work suited to this reality. You have been briefly introduced to the ecosystems approach in my earlier discussion of the eco-map.

In this book, we are reviewing the major theoretical frameworks for use by social workers. Therefore, the ecosystems paradigm will be separated into its two theoretical components. This chapter will introduce you to applied ecological theory, with primary attention to human ecology. Chapter 5 will report on social systems theory and how you might best understand it using the theory-mastery tools of exemplars, metaphors, maps, and models.

RELATED DIALECTS, ASSOCIATED SCHOOLS OF THOUGHT

The ecological theoretical framework is an important school of thought. It provides a coherent way of organizing our understanding of human behavior and the social environment, of social work practice, and of scientific inquiry. The school incorporates the theoretical contributions of diverse departments, but these departments use different names. Social workers use terms such as the **ecological perspective** and the **life model** (Germain & Gitterman, 1996). Psychologists prefer the term **ecological psychology,** defined as the study of how "the behavior of people is influenced by the symbolic, sociocultural meanings people attach to physical environments" (Freese, 1997, p. 24). Ecological psychologists also study the effects of the environment, especially as a behavioral setting, on human thinking, feeling, wishing, and acting (Ungar, 2002). Sociologists have developed a version of the ecological framework, **environmental sociology,** through which they study interaction between the environment and society. Sociologists show special interest in the relationships between social variables such as race, social power, or status and environmental variables such as pollution or land use (Dunlap, 1997).

Some theorists have merged ecological theories and critical theories. **Social ecologists,** for example, like other ecologists, study the interrelationship between human organisms and the environment. However, they add the critique that environmental problems such as ecosystem degradation and resource depletion are the consequence of the human arrangements associated with social hierarchy and capitalistic markets (Freese, 1997; Ungar, 2002). Social ecologists propose that the creation, spread, and empowerment of direct democratic assemblies are necessary if we are to solve ecological problems (Treesong, 2004).

This chapter will translate knowledge from **human ecology,** the "study of the spatial and temporal relations of human beings as affected by the selective, distributive, and accommodative forces of the environment" (McKenzie, 1924, p. 288). Plant ecology and animal ecology are important, too, but social workers can benefit most from knowledge about the relations of humans to their environments. I will concentrate next on introducing you to some exemplars in this tradition, and then review the assumptions, concepts, propositions, and models that characterize humans as developing organisms and that explain the human relation to physical environments.

APPLIED ECOLOGICAL THEORY: EXEMPLARY MODELS

Let me introduce you now to some of the major contributors to the ecological school of thought. I will tell you about their ideas, their lives, and their application of ecological theory.

ROBERT PARK

Robert E. Park (1864–1944) was a very influential sociologist. In the 1920s, Park had the distinction of contributing to both the consolidation of the Chicago School of Sociology and the development of the field of human ecology (Freese, 1997; Lyman, 1995). In a 1921 textbook, *An Introduction to the Science of Sociology,* coauthored with Ernest Burgess, Park made the first use of the term *human ecology* (Catton, 1992; Gaziano, 1996).

Robert Park was an important theoretical innovator. He extended the work of plant and animal ecologists to the study of social patterns (Gaziano, 1996). Using metaphors generated by ecologists, Park (1926/1967, 1936/1979, 1938/1972a, 1939/1972b) proposed a set of new concepts for understanding the relationship of the person to society. He referred to human ecology as a "web of life." Expanding on this Darwinian image, Park (1926/1967) wrote that "all living organisms, plants and animals alike, are bound together in a vast system of interlinked and interdependent lives" (p. 79). When constructing a society, humans, like other creatures, create shared habitats and develop a natural economy. Societal labor, Park suggested, is divided in two ways: ecological and cultural. Through **ecological processes** such as competition and cooperation, members accommodate themselves to the requirements of their environment. They develop adaptive patterns of group specializations, resource uses and exchanges, land-use decisions, and population constellations. The differentiation of social activity into such patterns contributes to a balanced and stable community (Maines, Bridger, & Ulmer, 1996).

However, Park (1938/1972a) also recognized that humans are unlike other organisms in that human transactions with the environment are not driven by instincts. Humans have distinctive symbolic and cultural capacities. Park noted, for instance, how members of human ecosystems use various social tools to facilitate their adaptation—newspapers, films, conversation, electronic media, telephone, radio, and travel. Thus, **cultural processes** facilitate the socialization and integration of new members into the larger ecosystem. Novices learn to understand one another and to be useful to one another, and this makes possible the subsequent subordination of individual interests to the collective purpose and the coordination of action in common environments.

Human territorial changes, Park explained (1926/1967), can be likened to the population movements of other species. Using the concept of **succession,** Park described how one ethnic or racial group competes with another for control of a **natural area** of a city. A city is best characterized, he theorized, as a set of territories inhabited by conflicting groups. One group prevails temporarily in an area. Then, new groups invade the territory. A struggle for domination ensues. If the new group is better able to survive and flourish in the ecological niche, it displaces the original group and gains territorial control. The original group is vanquished; it dies out or is banished to a territory lower in the hierarchy of desired places. Park and Burgess also believed that a spatial pattern characterized the growth of cities. This pattern could be represented as a series of concentric circles. The business district was at the center (Guest, 1984). Housing types, land-use preferences, and problems of personal and social organization varied with the distance of a residential community from the city center.

Park's innovative ecological work stimulated the examination of many important topics in the field of human diversity (Lal, 1995), including geographic patterns of racial segregation, the interaction of territorial boundary violations and racial prejudice, the effects of physical and social isolation on minority group life, and the origins of racial disturbances in inequitable inclusion and exclusion practices. Park contributed to theorizing about the person, urban environments, social distance, ecological processes, natural histories, the ecological order, and marginality—the experience of the immigrant on the border of two different cultures.

Park (1939/1972b) presented an influential depiction of the components of the dialectical relationship between humans and their natural and social community. He suggested a pyramid or cone image. The base of the pyramid is the **biotic community,** "the ecological organization of human beings living together in a territorial unit, region or natural area" (p. 140). From this base, as directed by the ecological and cultural processes of competition, cooperation, and communication, the social community emerges. Specifically, human associations develop in the economic, political, and moral realms. These associations solidify and serve as catalysts to the formation of stable social organizations. The continuous interaction of four factors—"1) population, 2) artifact (technological culture), 3) custom and beliefs (nonmaterial culture), and 4) the natural resources" (Park, 1936/1979, p. 84)—maintains both the biotic balance and the social equilibrium of the community.

Park (1926/1967) demonstrated that community life is both a moral order and a spatial pattern. He melded the sociological conception of social arrangements existing in and through communication with the ecological notions of spatial patterning and organism–environment interdependency. He demonstrated that geographical barriers, physical distance, sustenance needs, and distribution of populations and other ecological factors "define the conditions under which communication and social life are maintained" (Karp, Stone, & Yoels, 1991, p. 33).

Robert Park had other notable interests. Park and Burgess taught their students how to map the settlement patterns and distinctive niches of ethnic groups in Chicago, and thus to create physical and social topographies of the city environment. As a former newspaper reporter, Park actively promoted direct, firsthand observation of social life in natural settings, and he guided social inquiry that required students to get their hands dirty with real and messy research (Bulmer, 1984).

Unfortunately, Park was opposed to "do-gooders" and theory application (Faris, 1967), preferring pure scientists. He complained that helping professionals did not understand ecological processes and problems as fully as scientific sociologists. Social workers, in his view, generally failed to appreciate the limits of the possibilities for social and environmental change and worsened problematic situations by their interventions. However, Park's civic involvement indicated a commitment to social involvement and activism that contradicted his public statements. He traveled widely and paid special attention to the problems of race and poverty as they were illustrated in numerous countries. Many of his theoretical efforts emerged following firsthand attention to pressing public problems, including those related to hoboes and housing shortages, the consequences of war, and isolationist immigration laws (Reitzes & Reitzes, 1993).

Park demonstrated a lifelong commitment to the improvement of social conditions. From 1922 to 1924, he was president of the National Community Center Association, and in 1924 he helped create the Park House, a youth center that emulated settlement houses (Deegan, 1988). Park had a career-long interest in oppressed groups and in the dynamics of race prejudice. He was an active member of the Congo Reform Association and wrote many articles exposing exploitation of the Congolese. He led the research efforts of the Chicago Commission on Race Relations, a group started after the 1919 race riots. Park convinced commission members of the importance of African American betterment, and that the best means was involvement in social agencies (Carey, 1975). He supported some of the first African American sociologists. Park worked, for example, for seven years as a publicity agent to and close collaborator with Booker T. Washington and contributed substantially to the writing of Washington's *The Man Farthest Down,* a research-based account of Europe's underclass (Hughes, 1984).

RACHEL CARSON

Rachel Carson (1907–1964) has earned a place in the Ecology Hall of Fame (www.ecotopia.org.ehof/carson/bio.html). *Time* magazine identified her as one of the 100 most important people in the last century. Born and raised on a farm in a river town in Pennsylvania, Rachel Carson studied marine biology, earned a master's degree in zoology from Johns Hopkins University, and taught zoology at the University of Maryland for several years. She then worked for 15 years for the United States Bureau of Fisheries, later renamed the U.S. Fish and Wildlife Service, as a scientist and editor of federal publications (Lear, 1997).

Rachel Carson's books have influenced ecological theorizing and pro-environment political organizers. In *The Sea Around Us* (1951/1961), she explored the origins and the geology of the sea. In *Silent Spring* (1962), she described the dangers and long-term effects of pesticides such as DDT and condemned the chemical companies that ignored the problem. This book began with a chilling fable of a town where all the voices of nature had been silenced by ecological blight. Before her exposé, scientists, political leaders, and the public spoke not at all about the impact of pesticides and chemicals on the environment (Gore, 2002). After its publication, Carson and her work were attacked viciously by the chemical industry. However, she continued to speak out courageously, testifying before Congress in 1963 (Lear, 1997) and recommending environment-friendly policies. *Silent Spring* invited the general public to change its way of viewing the natural world and environmental dangers. In today's terms, she challenged the prevailing theoretical assumption that humans dominate all things (Gore, 2002), and she facilitated the shift to an ecological paradigm that recognizes that the balance of nature determines human survival. Her book was a critical stimulant to environmental theorizing.

Carson's work also had a practical impact. Vice President Al Gore (2002) credited Rachel Carson with identifying ecological concerns and raising public consciousness in ways that prompted the government to create the Environmental Protection Agency. Gore also reported that a 1992 panel of distinguished Americans had identified Carson's *Silent Spring* as the most influential book in 50 years.

Rachel Carson was a natural scientist, teacher, writer, aquatic biologist, and vocal advocate for planet Earth (Lear, 1998). Lear reports that Carson encouraged students to seek ecological lessons in nature, in the writings of the great naturalists, and in the scientific laboratory. Her commitment to the ecological paradigm, her anxiety about nuclear technology, her support for wilderness preservation, her interest in animal rights, her concern with global climate change, and her exposure of the role of corporations in creating environmental hazards have earned her the title of the mother of the modern environmental movement.

Rachel Carson may have been a theory popularizer and a paradigm promoter more than an ecological theorist. Nevertheless, she provided the foundation for applied ecological theory. Carson rejected the conventional view of human dominance of nature, writing that "the 'control of nature' is a phrase conceived in arrogance, born of the Neanderthal age of biology and philosophy when it was supposed that nature exists for the convenience of man" (Carson, 1962, p. 261). She eloquently made the case for a holistic and interdisciplinary conception of the person–environment relationship. She wrote, for instance,

> I have been thinking about the relations of one animal to other animals, of animals to plants, and of the animal or plant to the physical world about it. Always in such reflection is one made aware of the complex pattern of life. No thread is found to be complete in itself, nor does it have meaning alone. Each is but a small part of the intricately woven design of the whole, for the living organism is bound to the world by many ties, some of them relating to biology, others to chemistry, geology, or physics. (Carson, 1953/1998, p. 134)

CAREL GERMAIN

Social work has an exemplar from the ecological tradition. Carel Bailey Germain (1916–1995) was born in San Francisco and taught at social work departments in several universities (*Carel Bailey Germain Papers,* 2004). She was an educator at the University of Maryland and in the later part of her career earned the rank of Professor of Social Work Emerita at the University of Connecticut. Germain first developed her conception of applied ecological theory at Columbia University in the mid-1970s. She pioneered and taught many graduate courses focusing on this ecological perspective on social work practice and theory.

Reviewing her life, Germain reported that her childhood involvement with the Campfire Girls in California was an inspirational experience. Outdoor activities at Camp Deep Woods instilled a love of nature that later contributed to her development of the ecological model of social work (*Carel Bailey Germain Papers,* 2004).

Before Germain's ecological theorizing, most direct practice workers gave primary attention to a client's internal psychological processes or to a family's interactional processes (Marson, 2004). Germain (1973) suggested that the ecological metaphor could help social workers expand their conceptualization of the person-in-environment construct. She wrote numerous articles and seven books building on this root metaphor. In *The Life Model of Social Work Practice: Advances in Theory and Practice* (1996), coauthored with Alex Gitterman, Germain showed the relevance of ecological ideas to practice. Her *Human Behavior in the Social Environment: An Ecological View,* published in 1991, presented the ecological perspective as a comprehensive intellectual framework for understanding the person, the environment, and transactions between person and environment.

Germain repeatedly urged social workers to give greater consideration to client systems' physical and social environments and to the reciprocal influences of life processes and human action. She asserted that all human behavior is situated in a particular space and a specific time. She urged the use of the construct *person:environment* instead of *person-in-environment,* arguing that the colon better indicates the unified nature of person and environment than the hyphen. The hyphen suggests visually the distinct nature of each aspect, person and environment, and conceptually fractures Germain's ecological emphasis on indivisibility (Germain & Gitterman, 1996). Her colleague Alex Gitterman praised Carel Germain for her unparalleled commitment to integrating ideas from various academic disciplines into a comprehensive and innovative ecological framework (Germain & Gitterman, 1996).

APPLIED ECOLOGICAL THEORY: ROOT METAPHORS

In this section, I will introduce you to some of the metaphors that root the concepts, propositions, and theories of the ecological framework. I will review comparisons between real life and the theoretical framework's conception of the person, the environment, and the social worker.

THE PERSON AS A LIVING ORGANISM

Ecologists compare human beings to plants, animals, and other living organisms (Quinn, 1934). All organisms live and "every living creature must secure from its environment sufficient resources to meet its needs if it is to survive and reproduce" (Quinn, p. 569). All organisms consist of interdependent parts that allow for the functioning of the whole. An organism develops and actualizes its biological nature in an environment.

Ecologists use the metaphor of the living organism in other ways. A tree has a predictable cycle of birth, growth to maturity, decay, and death. Humans also have predictable physical life cycles. Flowers, fruits, and vegetables need nutrients from the soil and air to grow. Humans need psychological stimulation and social support from their physical environment and their communities to grow. Many organisms, like the tree that flourishes in a shady park, thrive in a particular kind of environment and in a place in that environment with special characteristics. Successful organisms and successful environments arrive at a mutual accommodation. Humans, too, grow best and prosper in certain niches. We seek the ideal "occupation" in the ecology's economy. Many organisms are strongly linked to particular places. A plant sends down roots that anchor it in rich soil; an animal follows a set of daily rounds that increase its access to food and its safety. Displacement of the plant or animal can have dire consequences. Humans form place attachment and are often traumatized by severance of their roots to cherished places. Older persons compelled to move from a home to an institution are more prone to death than if left alone. Organisms often exist in a web of interdependence. The flower depends on the bees, and the bees depend on the flower. As with a spider's web, a blow to one set of strands of the web affects all the other strands. Humans are social organisms, caught in a web of culture and social structure. Humans depend on their culture to provide a sense of meaning. An attack on the whole web, an unexpected clash with an invading culture or a sudden redistribution of vital resources, reverberates and changes all the human web dwellers

This root metaphor is limited. Most applied ecological theorists recognize that humans are distinctive and unlike all other living organisms. In comparison, plants and animals and insects leave vary small traces of their passage through the environment. Humans leave large footprints in both cultivated and uncultivated areas, and as societies increase their technological abilities to exploit the physical environment, the footprint is becoming bigger and bigger (Ungar, 2002).

The Social Environment as a Natural Area

The early human ecology theorists consciously borrowed ideas from plant and animal ecologists to understand the relationship of humans to their environments (Gaziano, 1996). Societies and social settings were compared to the fields, gardens, woods, and other natural areas where plants and animals lived.

The ecological processes of succession common to natural areas were used to explain human activity. A field, for example, may be invaded by new species, and repeated invasions contribute to the variations in vegetation in the space and to changes over time in the predominant vegetation. This ecological concept of succession refers to the "temporal sequence of displacements of various species" (Freese, 1997, p. 8) and the colonization of a site by certain species accompanied by the extinction of other species (Townsend, Harper, & Begon, 2000). This concept helps us understand diverse human activities. Human ecologists have used it, for example, to increase our theoretical understanding of many features of urban life, including immigration patterns, racial contact, community conflict, and land-use decisions. Here, the invader is a new ethnic or racial group rather than a plant or animal species.

The ecological processes of competition for existence between plants and animals in the natural sphere have human parallels. In cities, members of different social groups compete for good work, for desirable housing, and for other resources in their urban environments. Some human groups, like some animal groups, may prevail and crowd out the less fit competitors.

The ecological processes of symbiosis refer to the ways that plants and animals of different species develop close and mutually beneficial associations. These processes operate too in human societies. Symbiosis helps us understand, for example, how humans use division of labor to coordinate the actions of diverse community groups and members for the sustenance of the whole community.

The ecological processes of cooperation are important too. Think about how a flock of birds protect themselves against threats by using the eyes and claws of each bird as a defensive grid. The flock increases its strength by fighting together. In human settlements, people also engage in mutual aid and use their combined talents, strengths, and intelligence for defensive purposes.

These ecological processes affect the distribution of plants and animals in a given natural area and the physical order created by these living organisms. Ecological theorists assert that ecological processes also determine the orderliness of human communities and societies, the distribution of different human populations in the settled environment, and the opportunities and constraints influencing how well different human groups adapt to these environments.

Besides the imagery of diverse species (frogs, rabbits, ducks, sunflowers, roses, and humans) competing and cooperating in a natural area, other symbols and images associated with this root metaphor are available for our creative use. A fence often protects a farm field or a garden. Such a boundary protects what is inside the fence from the outside or wilderness areas (Hawley, 1986). Human societies use both physical and symbolic boundaries to differentiate insiders and outsiders.

The natural areas of plants and animals show highly visible spatial patterns (Hawley, 1986). At the beach, the observer can clearly differentiate between the life forms at a distance from the ocean, in the dunes, on the sandy expanse, and at the water's edge. Societies are divided into recognizable areas, too. Social workers, for example, might map a region into urban, suburban, small town, and rural districts.

Gardens and fields vary in their degree of organization from the simple to complex. Human societies and communities can be compared to different types of gardens. The city, for example, is a very active, dynamic, and crowded garden filled with species of all kinds competing vigorously for available nutrients (Rigney, 2001).

Natural areas vary in their degree of cultivation, from the most planned and cared for garden of a gardening expert to an isolated wilderness. Similarly, societies and subsocieties might be appraised in terms of their degree of cultivation or enculturation. Some cultural groups are composed of people with refined sensibilities, comparable to highly prized plants. Others include coarse and violent people, similar to weeds.

Ecologists, gardeners, and farmers can make judgments about the quality of a natural area. Are the air, water, and soil characterized mostly by toxic or nourishing ingredients? Connections can be made between the area's qualities and the degree of support for living organisms. A society may also be judged as toxic or nourishing. In some, human life is difficult. The average life span is short. Societal members are damaged mentally, socially, or spiritually by the poor quality of their social environment. In a few, almost all members are abundantly nourished and prosper.

The natural area, whether field, forest, or lakefront, provides a useful root metaphor for applied ecological theorists. Other metaphors have also been identified (Dunlap, 1997). For some theorists, society is like a resource depot. Cynical observers compare society to a waste repository. Kurt Lewin, an ecologically minded social psychologist, compared society to an interacting field of forces and recommended that practitioners study the forces that pattern human activity in a societal field at a given time (Brower, 1988).

THE SOCIAL WORKER AS GARDENER

I have invited you to use your metaphorical imagination to try to see, smell, and feel how society might be like a field, garden, or other area in nature and how a person might be like a plant, animal, or other living organism. Let's take the ecological root metaphor one step further and compare the social worker to a gardener or family farmer.

Good gardeners appreciate the intricate relationship between the growth of each plant and the conditions that form and maintain the entire garden. Good social workers remember Carel Germain's advice and affirm the indivisibility of individual community members and the community as a whole.

Good gardeners recognize the limits to growth that characterize their gardens. They avoid planting so many flowers, bushes, and trees that the garden's supply of nutrients becomes quickly depleted and the garden loses its ability to sustain the health of all the living things it contains. Good social workers are also concerned with issues of sustainability and promote practices, programs, and policies of stewardship.

Good gardeners become adept at reading signs that flowers or plants are in danger, such as patterns of spotting on a leaf or evidence of infestation by a particular insect, and use these signs to prevent problems. Good social workers learn to decipher the signs available in client households, local neighborhoods, social agencies, or other human environments indicating a threat to the quality of human–environment transactions. Like the alert gardener or farmer, they can initiate corrective action before the environment is irreparably damaged.

Expert gardeners can transplant fragile plants and help them grow in new spots in the garden. Expert social workers can help clients manage the grief associated with "pulling up roots" and moving to a nursing home or relocating after a destructive hurricane and then trying to start life again in a new place.

Dedicated gardeners protect their gardens from deer or other predators and from careless neighbors who throw their garbage on the wrong side of the fence. Social workers are similarly dedicated to protecting the territory of poor and oppressed client groups from regional politicians offering sites cheaply for medical waste, radioactive materials, or large-scale trash disposal operations. Ecological social workers can also become like the watchdogs that scare away corporate predators interested only in exploiting human and environmental resources.

CORE ASSUMPTIONS OF APPLIED ECOLOGICAL THEORY

Applied ecological theorists are attempting to develop a new paradigm, one that differs from the dominant paradigm informing many theoretical frameworks. Remember that a paradigm is a fundamental way of seeing reality. The assumptions of various theoretical champions are linked closely to their basic paradigms. Dunlap (2002) refers to the dominant paradigm or worldview as the "human exemptionalism paradigm." Adherents to this dominant paradigm are anthropocentric. They conceptualize human beings as the central focus of theorizing, as separate and distinct from all other creatures, and as exempt from the laws of nature that determine and limit lesser species. Proponents of this paradigm maintain that humans' cultural heritage, language facility, and ingenuity earn the species a privileged place in the ecological order. Therefore, humans legitimately dominate all other animals and the rest of nature. The environment exists for human control and use. The human exemptionalism paradigm attacks environmental pessimists because the paradigm assumes that humans can solve any problems in the social or physical environment by the clever application of science and technology. Exemptionalists focus theoretical inquiry on the individual's relation to self if they are psychologists and on the individual's relation to social groups if they are sociologists. The relationship of humans to the earth, the central topic of ecological theorists, does not interest the exemptionalists.

Dunlap argues that theorists began to articulate a "new ecological paradigm" in the 1970s as environmental threats and problems became too serious to ignore. Rachel Carson and Carel Germain helped begin this new conversation about the underlying assumptions of social theory. The following assumptions are shared by adherents to the new ecological paradigm and applied ecological theorists.

The Human Organism and the Environment Are Interrelated

Humans evolved as beings connected to the physical environment (Freese, 1997), and ecological processes continue to connect humans and other systems of living things to the systems of nonliving things with which they interact. People are grounded in a biophysical reality. Our lives are fused with the resources that sustain our basic functions. Just as we cannot imagine a human living without air, ecological theorists cannot imagine a human adrift from an environment.

Human beings depend on the environment for air and also for water, food, and shelter. Every human society depends on resources provided by its ecosystem. Although humans may have exceptional characteristics related to our capacities for symbolic communication and tool use, we are like every other species in our interdependent relationship with the global ecosystem (Dunlap, 2002).

This assumption of interrelatedness is also called **holism.** Holistic theories assume connections, linkages, and relationships between people and their environments. This philosophy acknowledges the existence of individual entities but has a theoretical preference for individuals-in-relations (Young, 1998). The person, for example, is understood as a living organism in constant interaction with the world around her. The person and her environment constitute an indivisible unit, and neither can be understood independently of their relationship to each other (Germain, 1991). Germain and Gitterman (1996) summarize this holistic philosophy:

> From a holistic view, people (and their biological, emotional, and social processes) and physical and social environments (and the characteristics of these environments)

can be fully understood only in the context of the relationship between and among them, in which individuals, families, and groups and physical/social environments continually influence the operations of the other. (p. 6)

Dunlap (2002) makes the point that the biophysical environment is finite. Because of our ecological dependence, we are constrained by the **carrying capacity** of planet Earth. Recent and troubling changes in the global environment, such as atmospheric warming, support this holistic assumption of interrelatedness. Carrying capacity is the ecological concept for "the largest number of any given species that a habitat can support indefinitely" (Postel, 1994, p. 4). Human inventiveness has allowed social groups to test and often extend environmental limits, but humans have not repealed ecological laws. As the population size that can be carried in a physical environment is surpassed, the resource base (available supplies of water, oil, or food, for example) in some societies has started to decline, with negative consequences for the population and for the environment. Failure to respect the natural limits on the number of specific organisms an ecosystem can support causes a "significant and perhaps irreversible lowering of its capacity to sustain its populations" (Weigert, 1997, p. 137).

Causation Is Best Characterized as a Reciprocal Process

Nonecological theoretical orientations often assume that x, the independent variable, causes y, the dependent variable. This assumption is portrayed as a simple linear relationship: $x \rightarrow y$. Ecological theorists assume that causal processes are much more complex. People and environments reciprocally influence and change each other (Germain, 1991). The ecological setting for social activity, for example, has a determining influence on a person's behavior; thus, we often find consistent and enduring setting-specific patterns. Males consistently use the men's bathrooms and females use the women's bathrooms at rock concerts. The person has the capacity, however, to act on the perceived environment, influence the setting, and lessen its constraining power (Gutheil, 1992). Women tired of waiting in line can begin to break cultural conventions about space use and crash the men's bathroom. The pattern is not linear but circular: x influences y, then y influences x, and so on.

Dunlap (2002) explains the ecological approach to causality by arguing that human actions and social arrangements are influenced by cultural and technological variables but also by "intricate linkages of cause, effect, and feedback in the web of nature" (p. 333). Freese (1997) adds that humans have two masters, physical nature and the human group, but humans can tap their ingenuity to escape their enslavement to each.

The Environment Has Nonsymbolic and Symbolic Features

The environment includes both conditions and resources that are independent of human interpretation (Townsend et al., 2000). **Conditions** are physico-chemical features of the environment such as temperature and humidity.

Environments can be objectively characterized as presenting benign, harsh, or extreme conditions to their human inhabitants. **Resources** are the energies and materials that are consumed by living organisms in the course of growth and reproduction. These and other nonsymbolic qualities of the environment have an impact even if humans are not aware of them. Carbon monoxide released in a closed garage will act lethally whether or not the trapped person detects the gas.

However, the environment also has symbolic or information-giving functions. The exterior and interior features of a social agency, for example, communicate much about the activities, operations, and cultural preferences associated with the physical structure (Resnick & Jaffee, 1982). The purpose of a social organization is often symbolized by the arrangement of its physical elements. The thick walls and bars of a prison communicate messages about security, control, and detention. The characteristics and relationships of the members of the social organization are also communicated by physical arrangements. The high status attached to the agency administrator is demonstrated by her position at the head of the conference room table. Organizational patterns and processes are communicated through environmental design. The power distribution (the size of offices and chairs of administrators contrasted to those of direct service workers) and the social norms (expectations to sit and wait in agency reception areas conveyed by signs, seating arrangements, and the placement of imposing security guards) are two illustrations.

The human capacity to use symbols will be discussed more fully in the chapter on symbolic interactionism. Here I will illustrate only briefly this assumption of a symbolic dimension to the environment. Fine (1998) studied how mushroom collectors and other users of the environment interpret nature. Members of different social groups attached images and meanings to diverse objects (trees, plants, lakes, animals) and places (home, abroad, work) in the environment in line with their social values, cultural beliefs, and experiences with the "natural world." These symbolizations took on power and governed how members relate to nature. Some groups defined nature as a preserve and thus something to be protected. Other groups defined nature as a source of riches and dangers, and thus something to be used and controlled.

Two particular forms of assigning meaning to environments—territoriality and place attachment—further illustrate the assumption. Lyman (1997, 2002; Lyman & Scott, 1967) argued that humans have a tendency toward **territoriality,** controlling space by assigning it cultural meanings. Humans invest the environment with emblems and other sociocultural symbols communicating information about inhabitants' identities. Lyman differentiated four possible meanings attached to areas in the environment. **Public territories,** such as community playgrounds, are defined areas where all citizens have free access and can engage in legal activity. Symbolizations of public areas are created by official designation and authoritative legislation. **Home territories,** such as teenagers' clubhouses or homosexual bars, are defined as arenas where participants can behave freely in an intimate setting over which they have some control. Gathering, communicating, and celebrating on behalf of the groups' interests and beliefs occur freely here. **Interactional territories** are those temporarily defined and designated as appropriate for social gatherings. Public streets are closed for a riverfront party, or a city boulevard becomes the promenade for the Easter Parade. **Body territory** is that space encompassed by the body and defined as private, yet subject to creative adornment by its owner through fashion, tattoo, and other forms of imagery.

Much social behavior has a territorial dimension. Lyman and Scott (1967) insisted that conflict over territory and its meanings is common. Aggressors engage in various **territorial encroachments.** These include violation and uninvited trespass, invasion with the intention to change territorial meanings, and physical or symbolic contamination. Protectors respond with **territorial reactions.** These include a turf defense against intolerable intruders, insulation from potential intruders, and linguistic collusion by which defenders unite in labeling all invaders as outsiders. Lyman (1995) later expanded on this notion that meanings are attached to land surfaces in his exploration of the global aspects of territory. New global patterns of migration, the dispersal of indigenous groups, and imperialistic efforts to expand settlements indicate the symbolic, social, and geopolitical importance of territory.

Lyman delineated various modes of **territorialization,** ways "by which one or more peoplehoods become attached to a land surface" (p. 128). First is "domestication," the conversion of an undefended or uninhabited piece of the earth into a home territory. Promulgating a new name for the territory and enforcing the name's use are keys to successful domestication. Naming issues, for example, are prominent for peoples in lands formerly included in the Union of Soviet Socialist Republics. Second, Lyman discussed "boundaried communication," the creation of borders, border patrols, and border defense practices that enclose and insulate insiders, restrict exit, and discourage entrance by undesirable outsiders. The former Berlin Wall stood as such a boundary. Third, Lyman discussed the territorialization of the bodies of a collective group. Identifiable markers are used to symbolize the rights and duties, the legitimacy, and the merit of inhabitants of a given territory. The Nazis used badges, tattoos, and catalogs of ethnic facial features to mark European Jews as vermin and to justify relocating them to segregated extermination camps.

Place attachment, the identification with and emotional bonding to certain places, also illustrates the assumption the humans invest environments and parts of the environment with personal meaning. Milligan (2003) formally defines *place attachment* as an "emotional bond formed by an individual to a physical site" (p. 118). The attachment includes positive memories of experiences in the place and expectations for future positive experiences in the place. Social work clients may form attachments to a residential dwelling, to a social agency or church building, to a street corner, to a neighborhood, or to a region. Place attachment contributes to the sense of personal and social identity ("I am a New Yorker" or "I am a Southerner") and fosters a sense of identity continuity, the recurrent feeling of being at home in an environment. Moves that sever place attachments are often experienced as psychosocial losses. Relocation, for instance, signifies a destruction of place meanings that were central to identity and identity continuity. When I served as executive director of a clubhouse for the mentally ill, many of our clients and workers were deeply disturbed by our eviction from our facility of 10 years. It took much time and many healing activities to let go of the old place and settle into the new agency location. Social workers act on this ecological assumption when they help individuals, families, and groups deal with the identity disturbances and difficult emotions that follow the loss of an important place attachment.

PRACTITIONERS SHOULD MAKE USE OF NATURAL LIFE PROCESSES

Applied ecological theorists assume that the principles and methods that guide social work practice should be congruent with the basic tenets of the ecological theory (Germain & Gitterman, 1996). Assessment will be most accurate and useful when it includes naturalistic observation of behavior in the undisturbed client–environment setting. This type of assessment is necessary to understand fully the client and relevant others in their interactive context and in terms of all their connections to the environment.

Ecological social workers make use of various naturalistic assessment procedures. **Experiential sampling** is a method of collecting information about a person's thoughts and actions in a particular environmental setting (Hektner & Csikszentmihalyi, 2002). The worker gives the client an electronic signaling device such as a pager. The worker then sends signals at random intervals to the person as he or she participates in daily routines, and the client records information about location, thoughts, activities, and other variables in a booklet. This recording helps the worker and the client learn about the connections between the person's external landscapes and internal landscapes (inner experiences). The worker might track and assess, for example, a person's positive emotional states across home, workplace, school, and leisure settings to relate patterns of social interaction, psychosocial development, and environmental contexts. Naturalistic assessment might also include **specimen records.** The worker closely observes a client's activity for a significant period of time, such as a full day, to learn about and record the typical or characteristic way the client relates to his or her environment (Wicker, 2002).

The ecological social worker assumes that every client has an innate inclination toward development and health. The practitioner should focus helping efforts simultaneously on releasing the growth potential of the client and on the capacity of environment to sustain and nourish the client. The worker uses and changes the person–environment interrelationship to promote improved persons, transactions, and environments.

When possible, the ecological social worker provides services in the client system's **life spaces**—home, playground, or workplace. The social worker also invites natural helpers, such as concerned family members and indigenous community leaders, to participate in helping processes. Principles and procedures for social work practice based on ecological theory will be discussed further in the next section.

THE ECOLOGICAL MODEL OF HUMAN DEVELOPMENT

In this section, I will discuss the ecological approach to human change across the life span. The section will include a profile of the exemplary scholar in this tradition; a review of the assumptions, metaphors, concepts, and propositions of the ecological model; and a brief overview of its applications.

URIE BRONFENBRENNER: EXEMPLARY ROLE MODEL

Carel Germain (1987), the premier social work ecological theorist, recommended Bronfenbrenner's ecological theory of human development. His model, she believed, offered one of the few "non-stage approaches to the total life course" (p. 576). Bronfenbrenner, she said, "recognizes the influence of biological and cultural factors on development and the significance of psychological processes such as perception, motivation, emotion, thinking, and learning" (p. 576).

Urie Bronfenbrenner (1917–2005) was born in Moscow and came to the United States at the age of 6. During World War II, he served as a psychologist and carried out a variety of assignments. Bronfenbrenner traveled widely; his ideas about human development were influenced by studies in China, the Soviet Union, Nova Scotia, Israel, and both Eastern and Western Europe. At the time of his death in 2005, he was the Jacob Gould Sherman Professor of Human Development and Family Studies at Cornell University. In his scholarly work, Bronfenbrenner developed a very influential ecological theory of human development.

Bronfenbrenner also worked industriously to demonstrate the utility of his theory for practitioners and policy makers. For example, he contributed actively to the design of developmental programs in the United States, including Head Start. He earned numerous honors and distinguished awards, including an award for his lifetime contribution to developmental psychology from the American Psychological Association.

ASSUMPTIONS OF THE ECOLOGICAL MODEL

Later in this book, I will introduce you to Piaget's stage model of cognitive development and Erikson's stage model of psychosocial development. Carel Germain (1997; Germain & Gitterman, 1996) preferred models like Bronfenbrenner's because it rejects the assumptions of the stage and life cycle models of biopsychosocial development. Ecological theorists like Bronfenbrenner assume that individuals transact with many environmental contexts over the life span; stage models cannot account for such complexity. Germain preferred the image of a **life course,** which she defined as "the unique paths of development people take and their diverse life experiences in various environments" (cited in Bloom, 1992, p. 408). Imagine the varied main trails and branching trails traversing a large national park. A group of hikers starting from the same point may travel many different pathways. The ecological understanding of great diversity in physical and social environments requires social workers to think also of the great diversity in courses or paths across the life span.

Ecological theorists assume unpredictability in the life course. They reject the assumption of developmental theorists such as Freud, Erikson, and Piaget that all people experience familiar, fixed, and predetermined stages of development (Bloom 1992). The complexity of transactions between persons and environment and the rapid change in the environmental contexts for development add a capricious quality to the progression of life not captured in stage models.

Ecological theorists doubt the assumption of universal stages. Germain (1987) believed that factors such as culture, race, ethnicity, and sexual orientation influence transactions with the environment and result in "nonuniform pathways of individual development and collective life" (p. 577). Human development theories should account for this remarkable variety in complex contemporary environments.

Urie Bronfenbrenner made compatible assumptions. All human development, Bronfenbrenner (1979) proposed, must be understood ecologically as "development-in-context," defined as a "progressive accommodation between a growing organism and its immediate environment and the way in which this relation is mediated between forces emanating from more remote regions in the larger physical and social milieu" (p. 13). Because there are many different environmental contexts, there must be many ways to develop as a person.

Bronfenbrenner (1979) also assumed that the particulars of human development must be gleaned from ecologically styled research. Psychologists, sociologists, and social workers who study developmental processes are more likely to achieve scientific validity if their study is carried out in natural settings and if the inquirer attends to the objects and activities common to the client's life space.

In accord with the ecological theory's assumption of reciprocal causality, Bronfenbrenner (1979) used the notion of bidirectionality to describe the influential interactions that take place between mother and child, child and father, child and teacher. Emotional management preferences are transmitted, for example, from parent to child but also from child to parent because of the child's distinctive personality style and way of responding to the parent. Bronfenbrenner assumed, then, that developmental influences go in two directions. Bidirectional influences take place when individuals and groups of individuals interact and directly affect others who exist within the same environment, as well as when those who are in larger environments influence and are influenced by members of the immediate or focal setting.

ROOT METAPHORS OF THE ECOLOGICAL MODEL

The ecological model of human development makes implicit use of the metaphor of species adaptation applied at the level of the individual developing person. Development for humans is like the development of plants and animals because it occurs within an environmental context. Elaborating on Kurt Lewin's axiom that behavior is a function of the person and the environment, Bronfenbrenner (1979) argued that human behavior evolves as a function of the interplay between the person and the environment; he defined human development as "a lasting change in the way in which a person perceives and deals with his environment" (p. 3). Ecologists believe that different environments evoke different adaptive potentials (Thomas, 2001). Environments may vary in weather, modes of transportation, distance between locations, complexity of the environment, the human activities for which the environment is suited, and so on. Species adapt to the particular conditions of their environments. Differences in environments explain the great diversity of ways in which cultural members raise the next generation and the great diversity in the development of talents, temperaments, and relationship skills across societies (Bronfenbrenner, 1979).

Bronfenbrenner (1999) also compared the environment to a set of nested structures. The developing child grows up in this nested environment. The child, who also contains various substructures within him- or herself, is like the egg at the center of a nest. The family nest is surrounded by larger layers including the neighborhood and school, and this nest of local settings is nested in the even larger society and culture.

The interrelated systems can also be imagined as a force field (Thomas, 1999). Bronfenbrenner (1979) encouraged ecological developmentalists to learn about all the forces, the total life space, influencing a developing person's behavior at a given time. He also advised awareness of the interacting effect of disturbances to any one part of the field of forces as these affect all other parts (Bronfenbrenner, 1979). To couple the imagery of a bird in the nest and interacting forces, imagine a storm building off the coast. It generates winds and rain clouds, which move inland. Soon the birds, once secure in a nest high in a riverside television antenna, are buffeted by the new weather conditions.

BRONFENBRENNER'S MODEL OF HUMAN DEVELOPMENT

Developmental science is "the systematic scientific study of the conditions and processes producing continuity and change over time in the biopsychological characteristics of human beings" (Bronfenbrenner & Evans, 2000, p. 117). Remember that a theoretical model provides a selective portrait of some aspect of reality by showing how a set of variables and propositions are interrelated. Bronfenbrenner (1992) expanded on Lewin's axiom, behavior is a function of the person and the environment, by providing his own formula: $D_t = f_{t-p} PE_{t-p}$. Thus, he proposed that human development is a function of interrelationships of person, physical environment, process, and time. Development (D) is defined in this model as "the set of processes through which properties of the person [P] and the environment [E] interact to produce constancy and change in the characteristics of the person over the life course" (p. 191). Let's elaborate on the basic concepts of this model.

DEVELOPMENT Ecologists define development as "the person's evolving conception of the ecological environment, and his relation to it, as well as the person's growing capacity to discover, sustain, or alter its properties" (Bronfenbrenner, 1979, p. 9).

PERSON Bronfenbrenner (1992) described the developing person as composed of attributes that influence subsequent development. Some attributes are more consequential than others; those personal qualities that have the power to affect subsequent psychological and social growth are called developmentally instigative characteristics. Three types are important. **Personal stimulus qualities** are personality features that invite or discourage particular kinds of reactions from persons in the environment. These reactions can either disrupt or foster the child's development. Such qualities include temperament, such as fussy versus content, and personality traits, such as socially alert versus withdrawn. The person also has **developmentally structuring attributes,** characterized as one's orientation toward interaction with the environment. Sontag (1996) provides several examples of these attributes in infants, including the tendency to initiate and maintain patterns of reciprocal interaction with the caregiver, intellectual curiosity, exploration of the environment, and self-concept as an active agent in the world. Physical features of the person, including body characteristics (such as size and weight), previous organic injuries (congenital anomalies or physical disabilities), and body-based statuses related to age, sex, or race are also relevant to development.

PHYSICAL ENVIRONMENT OR CONTEXT Bronfenbrenner (1979, 1986) describes the environment as including various level systems. His conception varies somewhat from the social work depiction of micro, mezzo, and macro systems that will be discussed in the next chapter.

The **immediate setting** includes systems such as the home, the classroom, and the neighborhood in which the person develops. This setting is a specific place or "life space" with identifiable physical features where developing persons participate in specific activities for a particular time. The person participates directly as a son, daughter, student, or peer in activities that are critical to human development.

The **mesosystem** is a system of relationships between two or more immediate settings. Bronfenbrenner (1979) was interested here in the linkages and processes between settings and how these linkages may conflict with or complement each other. Starting with Bronfenbrenner's example of the student, for example, an ecological investigator might consider the connections between the home, the school, the local hangouts, and all the participants in these settings. Bronfenbrenner (1986) later urged ecological developmental scientists to study linkages between the family and the hospital, the family and the child's peer group, the family and the school, the family and support systems such as day care, and the family and the neighborhood.

The **exosystem** is the collection of those systems that do not involve the developing person as an active participant but that nevertheless influence what occurs in the immediate setting. Government policies regarding testing and promotion by school administrators influence a student's progress. Bronfenbrenner (1986) identified other important elements of a developing child's exosystem: the parents' world of work, the parents' network of friends, the residential community, the mass media, and the economy. All indirectly influence the child's development.

The **macrosystem** refers to the consistencies or "generalized patterns" that exist at the level of culture and ideology, including values, laws, and customs (Bronfenbrenner, 1979). For example, the characteristics and functioning of school systems and their interrelated settings in France might be compared to the macrosystem in the United States. In relation to adolescent child rearing by African Americans, Merrick (1995) reviewed research about the relevant macrosystem features. These include cultural patterns related to motherhood and child rearing traced to West African heritage and philosophy and to sharecroppers in rural areas of the United States who moved to urban areas; social norms regarding the acceptable age for childbearing; cultural beliefs about the values of children and parenting common in lower socioeconomic African American communities; and the sexual permissiveness of the United States.

PROCESS   In Bronfenbrenner's formula, development is also a function of developmental processes. He was most interested in **proximal process**, "the transfer of energy between the developing human being and the persons, objects, and symbols in the immediate environment" (Bronfenbrenner & Evans, 2000, p. 118). Proximal processes include the activities that others engage in with the developing person or in the presence of the developing person that stimulate development, such as family members' speaking directly to the child and listening to his responses (Bronfenbrenner, 1979).

TIME   Temporal factors influence human development. Many development changes, Bronfenbrenner (1979) postulated, are triggered by ecological or **life transitions,** shifts in one's position in environmental contexts (the settings and the roles played in these settings) that occur at particular times in the life course. A person's entry into high school or graduation from college necessitates adaptive change. Bronfenbrenner (1986) coined the term **chronosystem** to refer to the changes in the developing person and the developing person's environment that occur over time. These changes can be imposed externally, or they can arise from within the organism, because children select, modify, and create many of their own settings and experiences. Examples include life transitions, such as the parents' divorce or the person's first job, and historical influences, such as being born during the Great Depression. Bronfenbrenner also recommends attention to the timing of biological and social transitions (age-based expectations and opportunities) and to personal history, the long-term impact of interactions between environmental characteristics and the developing person.

Other applied ecological theorists believe that **time** is a factor that conditions human development (Germain, 1990). The human organism is time-bound and characterized by a finite life span, a rhythm of life activities related to the needs for food and rest, a set of identifiable biological changes related to immaturity, maturity, and senescence, and an imperative to economize the time allocated to various activities (Hawley, 1986). Germain introduced three notions of time that are similar to Bronfenbrenner's approach to the temporal aspects of human development. **Historical time** refers to the effects of major societal and global changes on group and individual life experiences. For example, many migrations in Africa over the past two decades have been caused by an increase in vicious tribal warfare. A **cohort,** the collection of people born at a particular time in history, experiences very different life chances, life challenges, and life courses than another cohort. **Social time** refers to the norms governing the timing of ecological transitions in a particular community (the appropriate ages for marriage or retirement, for example), and variability in how fixed these norms are. Note how the American expectation that children move from their homes when they become adults was relaxed as housing prices rose in the late 1990s. Life courses will differ depending on the relevant social timetables. **Individual time** refers to the choices related to educational, work, family, and leisure pathways that each person makes and that influence the flow of one's life. Thus, each person has the power to pick uniquely significant paths for his or her life course.

PROPOSITIONS

This ecological model of human development generates numerous propositions. Here are a few samples. First, the basic formula can be restated as a proposition: There is a relationship between a development outcome (competence or dysfunction) and the proximal process, the characteristics of the person, the nature of the immediate setting, and the length and frequency of the time interval during which the person is exposed to the proximal process. Second, interactions between the human organism and the persons, objects, and symbols in its immediate external environment will have a greater effect on human development if the interactions occur on a fairly regular basis over an extended period of time (Bronfenbrenner & Evans, 2000)—for example, every day for the child's first three years of life the other family members speak to and listen to the baby.

Third, Bronfenbrenner (1990) extended his model to the public realm. The effective functioning of child-rearing processes in the family and other child settings, he stated, requires public policies and practices that provide place, time, stability, status, recognition, belief systems, customs, and actions in support of child-rearing activities not only on the part of parents, caregivers, teachers, and other professional personnel, but also by relatives, friends, neighbors, coworkers, communities, and the major economic, social, and political institutions of the entire society. These are complex and multifaceted propositions. Researchers and practitioners using the ecological model have much work to do before the propositions will serve as working hypotheses or practice directives.

CRITICAL COMMENTS

Bronfenbrenner's ecological model transformed the scientific study of human development (Lerner, 2005). It pioneered theoretical conceptualizations related to the environmental embeddedness of personal change, the multilevel and integrated quality of the ecology of development, and the active reciprocal influence of individuals and social systems on the developmental process. During a 60-year career, Bronfenbrenner continuously refined and validated his model. He also demonstrated repeatedly how social policies and programs might be designed to promote healthy individual and family development. Lerner characterized Bronfenbrenner as "both the standard of excellence and the professional conscience of the field of human development" (p. x).

Most social workers share Bronfenbrenner's theoretical and policy commitments. However, the profession has done little to advance the ecological model of human development. Cairns and Cairns (1995) provide direction. The remaining tasks include studying the links between dyad, family, peer group, community, organization, and individual development for specific client groups; creating measurement tools and assessment methods to track multi-dimensional and context-based development; and determining how to use Bronfenbrenner's ideas to promote individual and social health.

APPLICATIONS OF THE ECOLOGICAL MODEL OF HUMAN DEVELOPMENT

Head Start was based on an ecological philosophy, and embraced a number of goals. Each Head Start preschool center aimed to improve children's mental and physical health, enhance their cognitive skills, encourage their social and emotional development, build healthy relationships and social responsibility, and foster a sense of self-worth for both the child and the family. Parents were involved as teacher aides; they were offered parent education classes and access to family support services. The distinctive idea in the design of Head Start was the central role accorded to parents as planners, administrators, and activity leaders in their children's centers. Community members were also expected to become involved. This strategy was attributed to the influence of Urie Bronfenbrenner, who advocated an intervention focusing on the total ecology of the developing child (Tomison & Wise, 1999). He inspired the Head Start commitment to partnerships among service providers, children, parents, and the local community.

More recently, Bronfenbrenner used his ecological model to identify harmful changes in the environments for child development in the United States. These changes include family members' physical distance from one another, chaotic homes, unsafe neighborhoods, violent schools, and the "progressive decline over time in concern for the well-being of others" (Bronfenbrenner & Evans, 2000, p. 121). The bridges between home, school, and neighborhood necessary to optimal human development are crumbling, he warned.

MAPPING APPLIED ECOLOGICAL THEORY

Figure 4.1 presents the eco-map adapted for applied ecological theory. This section offers answers to our translation questions from the perspective of applied ecological theory.

How Are Connections Conceptualized?

Connections are conceptualized as **transactions,** reciprocal exchanges between entities in the environment (Germain, 1991). The philosophers Dewey and Bentley (1949) provided the basic transactional framework for conceptualizing

FIGURE 4.1
THE
ECOLOGICAL
THEORY
VERSION OF
THE ECO-MAP

Source: Adapted with permission from *Family-Centered Social Work Practice* (p. 160) by A. Hartman and J. Laird, 1983. New York: The Free Press.

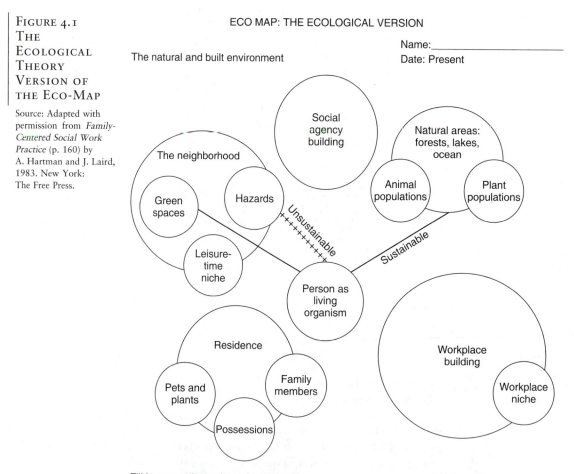

ECO MAP: THE ECOLOGICAL VERSION

Name:_____

Date: Present

The natural and built environment

Fill in connections where they exist.
Indicate nature of connections with a descriptive word or by drawing different kinds of lines:
————— for sustainable transactions
+++++++ for unsustainable transactions
Draw arrows along lines to signify flow of natural resources → → →

the relationship between person and environment (Emirbayer, 1997; Tibbetts, 1981). They analyzed three major types of human action.

Self-action refers to humans (and other living organisms) acting by means of their own powers. Rational choice theorists, discussed in the chapter on the economic framework, emphasize self-action. Subjects act in relative isolation from one another. They choose the most rewarding or profitable course of action, and this calculated choice propels their movement in the environment. Persons are capable of generating their own locomotive steam. Scientists analyze self-action by identifying the essential substances or qualities of the acting agent and the properties of these substances. The individual is the focal system. Choice is independent of context, and the person movements are not related theoretically to the surrounding environment.

*Inter*action assumes that human beings are independent and distinct organisms but that a related set of humans influence one another as causal agents. Emirbayer (1997) compared such relatedness to that of billiard balls colliding and causing change in the trajectory of each. Dewey and Bentley (1949) referred to marbles. Modern proponents of the interactional view, an approach different from the symbolic interactionist theoretical framework presented in a later chapter, use "variable analysis" to identify the correlated variables that generate movement. Scientists analyze interaction by focusing on the causal interconnections of fixed entities with identifiable attributes. The interrelated variables make up the focal system. Choice is influenced by external causes, and a "thing is balanced against a thing in causal interconnection" (Dewey & Bentley, 1949, p. 108). However, the interacting elements or relations are still conceptualized as independent of the environmental context for the interaction.

The *trans*action concept assumes that persons are inseparable from their context. The persons or units involved in a transaction "derive their meaning, significance, and identity from the (changing) functional roles they play within the transaction" (Emirbayer, 1997, p. 287). Scientists analyze transactions by focusing on the dynamic and unfolding person–environment process, not by focusing on the individual elements. Scientists can learn to use names and conventions for description to deal with the various aspects and phases of this complex joint process, but choice is viewed as inseparable from the context for decision making. Actors meet and change challenging environmental conditions, and environments, in turn, respond dynamically to the actor's choices. The transactional credo asserts, "Our position is simply that since man as an organism has evolved among all other organisms in an evolution called 'natural,' we are willing under hypothesis to treat all of his behavings, including his most advanced knowings, as activities not of himself alone, nor even as primarily his, but as processes of the full situation of organism–environment" (Dewey and Bentley, 1949, p. 104). The living organism and the environment are like a circuit (Tibbetts, 1981), phases of a single natural transactive process. Neither aspect of the organism–environment circuit can be specified and described fully apart from the other aspects or constituents.

Dewey and Bentley (1949) give several vivid illustrations. Taking an example from the sport of hunting, they suggest that the transactional view requires attention to the hunter and the hunted united in the act of hunting, an act occurring in a particular hunt club and season. They also use the illustration of trade: "no one exists as a buyer or seller save *in and because of* a transaction in which one is engaged," and "things *become* goods or commodities because they are engaged in the transaction" (p. 270). Finally, they discuss the organism–environment transaction using the following imagery: "living body and environing conditions cooperate as fiddle and player work together" (p. 286).

Emirbayer (1997) uses Dewey and Bentley's scheme to contrast three views of personality. The self-action approach conceives of personality as a set of fixed traits enduring across time and space. The interaction approach defines personality as a collection of dispositions activated by causal factors external to the person. The transaction perspective views personality as a stable configuration of characteristic patterns of behavior within distinct environmental situations. A personality is the person's signature set of "if this ecological situation, then this behavior." The personality may appear to exist independently of its transactions, but such a conclusion represents a superficial observation and ignores the varied and complex transactions engaged in by the person across space and time. A client may be identified as a "businesswoman" detached from transactions, but naturalistic observation grounds this identified specialization in the various business transactions that constitute the client's patterned way of engaging the environment.

Dewey and Bentley (1949, p. 271) extend their transactional philosophy to the life course and argue, "From birth to death, every human being is a *Part*, so that neither he nor anything done or suffered can possibly be understood when it is separated from the fact of participation in an extensive body of transactions."

HOW IS THE QUALITY OF CONNECTIONS DIFFERENTIATED?

Like the evolutionary biologists presented later in the book, ecological theorists differentiate positive from negative transaction in terms of person–environment fit and adaptation. However, they also contribute the concept of sustainability to differentiate connections.

Positive transactions indicate a **favorable fit** between the client system and the environment. The needs, goals, and capacities of the client system and the qualities and operations of the environment are matched in such a way that the individual or collective develops continuously and functions effectively while the environment is sustained or enhanced (Germain & Gitterman, 1996).

Positive transactions are also sustainable transactions. **Sustainability** involves balance. Interests in human prosperity are balanced against concerns with the prosperity of ecosystems. Sustainable transactions are built from scientific practices, economic patterns, social policies, and human lifestyles that use the resources necessary to provide for human needs while maintaining or improving the environment (Hoff & Polack, 1993). Sustainable community development, for example, promotes environment-friendly housing, transportation, farming, heating, cooling, and manufacturing. Sustainable societies recognize their dependence on life-supporting biogeochemical exchanges with the ecosystems (Freese, 1997).

Sustainability also involves a temporal judgment. Can the transactions be continued into the future, and does the environment have the capability to continually provide the resources necessary for human subsistence and to absorb human waste products (Freese, 1997)? Sustainable person-to-person transactions and person-to-system transactions improve the environmental conditions relevant to contemporary social and economic processes while safeguarding the quality of conditions for future generations (National Association of Social Workers, 2003). Sustainable transactions meet the needs of members of the present generation without jeopardizing or compromising the ability of future generations to meet their needs.

Negative transactions indicate a poor or **unfavorable fit** between the client system and environment. Such negative exchanges impair the health, functioning, and development of the client system while also damaging the environment (Germain & Gitterman, 1996). Negative transactions are unsustainable transactions. They jeopardize the future functioning of the local, regional, or global ecosystem. They have a disorganizing influence on the environment's equilibrium and result in environmental degradation. Unsustainable transactions cannot be continued indefinitely. The well runs dry. The soil won't nourish any more plants. The air cannot be safely breathed.

Applied ecological theorists do not generally talk about neutral transactions. Transactions are differentiated into the dichotomies of good fit or poor fit, sustainable or unsustainable.

What Is the Typical Focal System?

Some theoretical perspectives direct the worker to focus on the client. Some theoretical perspectives direct the worker to focus on the environment. Ecological theorists challenge social workers to cultivate a dual focus. The focal system is both the identified client and the relevant aspects of the environment. The worker concentrates his attention on the client's coping capacities and limitations. The worker also adjusts his vision to determine environmental constraints and opportunities. Anderson and Carter (1990) used the term **holon** to characterize the dual nature of the focal system: the client system has a distinctive identity and integrity, and the client system is part of a larger environment. Using Dewey and Bentley's (1949) ecological conception, the worker assesses and helps a living organism transacting dynamically with an environmental situation.

How Is the Environment Conceptualized?

Ecological theorists give theoretical emphasis to the physical environment, comprising both the natural and built worlds. The **natural world** includes plants, animals, geographic aspects, soil, minerals and other materials, and climactic features (Germain, 1991; Hawley, 1986). It is "the sum of all the elements, processes, and resources that support human life and social development" (National Association of Social Workers, 2003, p. 116). The natural world can also be conceptualized as various spheres (Hoff & McNutt, 1994). The geosphere is the solid matter of the earth, including the soil. The hydrosphere is the liquid portion of the earth, including its lakes, rivers, oceans, and atmospheric water. The atmosphere is the mixture of gases that surround the earth. The term **biosphere** refers to all the living creatures, including humans, that inhabit the earth's surface, plus the atmosphere, waters, and other systems in contact with and supportive of living organisms (Weigert, 1997). The biosphere extends "from the ocean depths, where the primitive forms of life exist, to the upper stratosphere" (Rifkin, 1991, p. 259).

Ecologists recognize that cultural groups vary in their conceptions of the natural world. Weigert (1997) provides the following typology: The cosmic environment is the brute and obdurate world that exists and continues even if humans die out. The species environment is the physical environment shared by all humans as members of the same species. The institutionalized environment includes the selected and constructed aspects of the world in which institutions such as government or church operate, and the personalized environment refers to aspects of the naturally occurring world within which the individual lives, the personally seen and felt world.

Ecological theorists also study the **built world,** including "urban and rural layouts, city squares and village greens, dwellings and other structures, aesthetic and utilitarian objects of all kinds" (Germain, 1991, p. 29), and the buildings designed by people and the spaces that contain such structures (Germain & Gitterman, 1996). The built world emerges because of the application of craft or technique that transforms the physical world in accordance with intentional human design (Weigert, 1997). Social workers might use ecological theory to understand the qualities of rooms, houses, office buildings, hospitals, or cities and the relation of these constructions to human activity.

Some ecological theorists theorize about the **social environment.** This is the "network of human relations at various levels of organization" (Germain, 1979, p. 13) and the cultures developed by people in these networks (Hawley, 1986).

Applied ecological theorists focus on the person and environment as the primary unit of attention. Special emphasis is given to the **interface,** or point of contact. This is the field of action where the client transacts with some delimited aspect of the physical and social environment. Social workers might study the client and his or her personal space—the area around the person's body into which others should not enter without invitation, and where intrusion evokes feelings of discomfort (Gutheil, 1992). Visualize the large and noisy support group member who steps up close to the faces of his visibly ill-at-ease peers. Social workers might study the interface of client and home—the client's use of his or her house to control the climate, regulate the movement of family members, regulate light and dark, showcase treasured objects, and indicate social status. Germain (1978), for example, studied homes in public low-income, high-rise apartments and noted that these do not communicate that residents are people of worth and dignity. They do not provide public places for social interaction, and they do not protect residents from dangers and vandalism.

Social workers might study the interface of clients and buildings such as social agencies. We might assess, for example, the physical aspects of our employing organization, including the people, equipment, furniture, floor plans and spatial arrangements, paint and wallpaper, interior design, and flow of work activities, and then assess the systems of meanings associated with these physical elements. Gutheil (1992), a social work expert in ecological theory, differentiated **fixed-feature spaces** in organizations—permanent walls separating resident space from staff space in an institutional dining room for chronically mentally ill patients, for instance—from **semi-fixed-feature spaces**, arrangements in an institutional setting that are movable like the furniture in a nursing home's dayroom. She reported that other spacing choices also have an ecological impact on the quality of interaction. An agency can be designed to welcome and encourage interaction, as by creating large, airy, and well-furnished offices for social workers. An agency can be designed in ways that discourage interaction, as in the long corridors and large, partitionless, privacy-free spaces common to areas for congregation in mental hospitals or jails.

Social workers might study the interface of person and community. What is the settlement type: rural, suburban, town, or urban? How do variables such as distance from the central urban core, size of settlement, density of population, sprawl, and the flow of resources within the settlement and across settlements influence human transactions?

Social workers who use ecological theory might also study the interface between the client and regional or larger land areas. **Human geography,** the study of spatial organization, can be used to assess spatial variations in social welfare, "who gets what where, and, how" (Smith, 1977, p. 7). The "who" question deals with human populations, especially vulnerable populations, and considers social class, race, ethnicity, and other population characteristics influencing the distribution of social welfare. The "what" question directs inquiry to resources, income, and other contributors to human well-being and social welfare, including good health, gainful and satisfying employment, leisure time, pleasant and safe housing, access and command over goods and services, personal safety and fair justice administration, educational and self-development opportunities, and chances to participate in community life, and how these resources are distributed spatially. The "where" question suggests an investigation of the relationship between subdivisions of territory, aggregations of social groups, and access to resources in particular areas. The "how" question asks about the processes and causal mechanisms that result in particular human geographic patterns of social welfare.

Smith (1977), for example, used human geography to develop an index of economic and social well-being, and to map the city of Tampa. He documented dramatic variations in social well-being and found that Tampa's inner city was a "pit of deprivation" (p. 282). Robert Park and Chicago School ecologists in the 1920s and 1930s initiated the ecological study of social problems and how they were distributed in cities (Jackson & Smith, 1984). They discovered a clear relationship between patterns of physical distance between different ethnic and racial groups and patterns of social distance. They also conducted or inspired geographic studies of crime, poverty, mental illness, conflict between social groups, homelessness, social well-being, and other psychosocial variables. They taught us that a physical map of a human settlement such as a city might be used as a starting point for mapping the opportunities and constraints faced by various community members. Social workers might also advance human behavior and practice theory by beginning to study the interface between client systems and planet Earth.

Is Particular Emphasis Given to Any Systems?

Applied ecological theorists conceptualize and emphasize places and systems not included in other theoretical frameworks. Applied ecological theorists are interested in **habitats,** those places in the ecosystem where particular organisms live and act. Habitats include nesting places, home ranges, and territories (Germain & Gitterman, 1996). Human habitats include dwelling places, workplaces, schools, and parks. The habitat can be compared to a species' address. For example, certain microorganisms have converted your gut into their habitat (Townsend et al., 2000).

Each habitat provides many **niches.** A niche is the "unique place in which one 'fits' into the environment, the workplace, or the community. It is the special place within which one feels comfortable; one has made it 'one's own' " (Brower, 1988, p. 412). The concept of niche refers to an ideal relationship to a place. The niche in a habitat has characteristics, conditions, and resources that best meet an organism's tolerances and requirements (Townsend et al., 2000). The niche allows existence and growth. A lion roams freely and proudly in a particular realm in the jungle but loses all vitality when captured and imprisoned in a small zoo. If the habitat is like a person's address, the niche is like finding an occupation or profession perfectly suited to the person at that address (Germain & Gitterman, 1996).

A **population** is a collection of individuals of the same species. Demographers study systematically the characteristics of human populations, including their size, their growth, their density in a given environment, the patterns of birth, death, marriage, divorce, and illness, and the memberships in various categories (race, ethnicity, sexual orientation, and gender, for instance). Social workers often use the term *population* in a slightly different way to describe vulnerable, disenfranchised, and excluded groups that are most afflicted by major social and environmental stressors (Germain, 1991). The poor children in the valleys of Los Angeles or Mexico City who experience asthma and other breathing difficulties because of air pollution might be grouped together as a population.

A **community** is the ecological term for a place where multiple populations live in organized and functional relationships (Freese, 1997; Townsend et al., 2000). You might consider your local neighborhood a small community. Members of the same population, humans, live and cooperate together to keep the neighborhood safe and friendly while members of different populations (cats, dogs, birds, squirrels, rabbits, and geese) coexist peacefully, providing a tranquil and rural flavor to the neighborhood.

The ecological system, or **ecosystem,** is the larger conglomeration of the various ecological settings in which a living organism functions. An ecosystem is an organized system of members of a living community plus the geochemical and geophysical influences on it (Freese, 1997). Defining the boundaries of the ecosystem depends on the purposes of the social worker. Boundaries may be set for constructed human environments—neighborhood, human settlement, or society (Hawley, 1986)—or for natural terrestrial, freshwater, marine, or global environments (Moran, 1990). Technically, the ecosystem is defined by the character of the relationships among its constituent organisms and species. An ecosystem is a network of interdependences, a place where members function together as an adaptive unit in a given environment. The joint operations of the members enable the unit as a whole to maintain a viable relationship to the environment (Hawley, 1986). Continuous cooperation among the members results in a structured or patterned way of engaging with environmental challenges. Applied animal and plant ecologists use the ecosystems concept to help them manage forests and fisheries. Human ecologists understand also that ecosystem boundaries may transcend conventional organizational units or geographical sites. A coastal ecosystem, for example, might stretch across numerous towns, cities, and counties. The biosphere can be considered the mosaic of all ecosystems on the earth, and the boundary between us and space.

How Are Resources and Their Flow Conceptualized?

Resources are the "goods or bounty or some other quantity of material that may be in the actual or potential possession of some agent, that is provided by the environment of that agent, and is exploitable for that agent's purposes" (Freese, 1997, p. 232). Applied ecological theorists are interested in resources such as air, food, soil, water, and natural areas (forests, pastures, rangeland, and woodlands); energy for heating, cooking, and transporting; and materials for tool construction. Ecologists are mindful also of the services that these resources provide. Wetlands filter pollutants, for example (Postel, 1994).

Human subsistence depends on the ecological processes of converting ecosystem energy stocks (solar energy, for example) into resources (food). Natural resources are the base that provides the life support used by humans for meals, breathing, travel, and other essential activities. Natural resources make human organizations, institutions, and traditions possible (Freese, 1997).

Applied ecological theorists make a distinction between **renewable resources** and **nonrenewable resources.** Resources are renewable if steady-state ecological processes ensure a continual supply, although this supply is not necessarily infinite or permanent (Freese, 1997). Nonrenewable resources are resources such as fossil fuels, including petroleum and natural gas. Supplies of these resources are finite, and their quantity will not be increased by ecological processes.

Humans are resource dependent. Ecologists worry that some economic philosophies and human technologies rapidly use up nonrenewable resources (biological entities, species populations, and geochemical entities) and thus jeopardize the functioning of our ecosystems. Organic resources extracted from forests, grasslands, and fisheries can be depleted and become nonrenewable if human exploitation disrespects their natural systemic rates of renewal (Freese, 1997). Few can make a living, for example, fishing in the Chesapeake Bay of the United States because of the depletion of fish stocks.

WHAT DESCRIPTIVE WORDS ARE USED?

Ecological theory is interdisciplinary, incorporating terms from various professions and disciplines (Choldin, 1978). The framework uses some concepts familiar to ecologists and environmentalists: *ecology, natural, adaptation, cooperation, succession, carrying capacity,* and *sustainability.* Designers including architects, landscapers, and city planners have contributed to its vocabulary, offering terms such as *zoning, sprawl, land use, green spaces, defensible spaces, designed environments,* and *housing styles.* Psychologists have popularized many concepts, including *density, crowding* (neighborhood and household), *privacy,* and *isolation.* They have also related these variables to social and individual pathologies, including crime, stress-related diseases, and psychosocial development. Sociologists have contributed concepts such as *natural areas, concentric zones, front regions, back regions and props* (the dramaturgy of space), and *territorial meanings.*

HOW IS CHANGE CONCEPTUALIZED?

Let's break this answer into two parts: ecological assessment and ecological intervention. Applied ecological theorists prefer naturalistic assessment. Besides the methods discussed in the section on theoretical assumptions, ecological social workers might use **home visits.** A systematic inspection of the client's residential environmental allows the worker to learn about the client's physical environment, the meaning of this environment to the client, the ways that the environment promotes or hinders client growth, and areas for social and environmental change. Ecological social workers might also use aspects of the home setting to facilitate the change process (Norris-Shortle & Cohen, 1987).

Ecological social workers might assess targets for person–environment change by **mapping.** For example, in my study of members of a bereavement support group, I used the Social Network Map to identify changes in each member's connections to his or her environment after the death of a loved one (Forte, Barrett, & Campbell, 1996). During our interviews, we discovered that the loss of a significant other damaged group members' perceived social networks in many ways. Shared grief work was interpreted ecologically as the communal construction of a new network or map of symbolic, identity-sustaining social bonds. As a prelude to intervention, social workers might also map the changing availability of jobs in a community, the distribution of preferred languages, the clustering of different religious institutions, or the spread of HIV infection. Social workers might map the neighborhoods adjacent to a social agency and try to learn about spatial differences in the quality of streets, upkeep of homes, and public behavior.

Ecological social workers might initiate **environmental impact assessments** and investigate the effects that a corporate project or policy has on the physical environment, on social welfare, and on cultural heritage. When necessary, the assessment can be followed by recommendations for corrective or preventive measures to minimize negative impacts (Pol, 2002). Such assessments might also be directed at the detection of difficult-to-detect household, workplace, neighborhood, and regional hazards that endanger the physical and mental health of clients.

Ecological intervention might use the environment as either the context for or the target of planned change efforts (Neugeboren, 1996). The environment is a context that either constrains or facilitates helping activities. Social workers can build on the healing qualities of environmental contexts. In various forms of **nature therapy,** aspects of the natural environment are made part of the helping context (Lovell & Johnson, 1994). Horticulture therapy makes use of plants. Community groups might enrich their lives through neighborhood farming or gardening activity. Pet therapy makes use of the human inclination to bond with animals to help patients in hospitals, to help children develop, to help the elderly in nursing homes, or to help prisoners become caring citizens. My wife brought our puppy to work at the Ronald McDonald House, and he had a positive influence on many children diagnosed with cancer. Some prison farms allow inmates to train and tend horses. Animals can provide companionship, assistance, and nonthreatening relationships. **Wilderness therapy** provides therapeutic experiences in natural environments where delinquent or disturbed adolescents, for example, can camp, hike, and canoe in secluded parts of nature without the diversions or dangers of city life. Often exposure to such physical environments uses the fresh air, fresh views, and fresh new experiences to challenge clients to learn new ways of relating to their home environment. **Milieu therapy** is a helping approach that involves the environmental treatment of persons in mental hospitals. The physical and social features of the hospital milieu are intentionally designed to maximize their healing powers (Germain, 1979).

The environment may also be the target of a social work intervention. Social workers can engage in planned change efforts toward some aspect of the natural or built environment to produce a positive impact on the ecosystem, the social structure, or the social interaction of a population or of some of its members (Pol, 2002). Social workers might teach **lifestyle changes** and work to improve the client system's use of the environment by influencing purchasing decisions, recycling practices, and home energy consumption patterns. The National Association of Social Workers (2003), for example, encourages practitioners to reject lifestyles organized around material consumption and based on the assumption of the plentiful and eternal supply of natural resources.

Social workers might initiate an **environmental modification,** helping clients improve the quality of their lives by altering spatial arrangements and their use (Germain, 1979). The worker can change the organizational environment so that it better accommodates clients' spatial and psychosocial needs (Germain & Gitterman, 1996). Agency meeting places can be redesigned so that clients can talk with workers in private, rather than in cubicles with thin and short dividers crowded into one room. Workers can teach clients to make better use of the natural and built environment. For example, I once helped adult offenders who feared no one but who came from the rural counties meet the great and dreaded challenge of negotiating the confusing and elaborate city system of bus routes. We rehearsed ways to travel through potentially difficult new physical environments by mapping routes to various work sites, and we joined the clients on their first trips through these routes. Gutheil (1992) urged social workers to identify and remove obstacles in the environment that impede clients' ability to function. Blind clients often must traverse community areas with confusing and multidirectional pathways. Older residents in five-floor apartment buildings without elevators find that steps become barriers to their mobility. Social workers can advocate for environmental changes to accommodate physically challenged clients.

Social workers might use crisis intervention and other direct practice knowledge and skills to assist in community responses to environmental disasters. Hurricanes, floods, and technological disasters such as nuclear power plant leaks or meltdowns have devastating effects on the environment and on the people who live in the affected areas (Hoff & Rogge, 1996). Social workers can ameliorate the damage.

Practitioners can engage in **environmental justice work.** We can capitalize on our environmental knowledge, our commitment to sustainable development, and our awareness of the likely impact of ecological changes on vulnerable populations to contribute to the planning of improvements in the built environment. We can fight to ensure that city planners and zoning officials, transportation planning boards, park developers, and political leaders consider the needs of all stakeholders and of future generations (Hoff & Rogge, 1996).

How Are Actual and Ideal Eco-Maps Contrasted?

Applied ecological theorists express great concern about the actual eco-maps that depict the relationships of clients to their ecosystems. Ecologically oriented eco-maps, for example, would frequently show the presence of environmental hazards such as **toxic waste,** including pesticides and heavy metals that are the by-products of industrial processing. Acute or continuous "exposure to these substances threatens human health by increasing the risk of irreversible and incapacitating illness or death" (Rogge, 1993, pp. 111–112). Rogge (1993, 1994) identified several extremely hazardous areas in the United States, including an immigrant community in McFarland, California, surrounded by agricultural fields and exposed to dangerous pesticides; a New York community called Love Canal, where residents were exposed to various toxic substances and the community saw increases in fetal deaths, miscarriages, and birth defects; and the community of Grassy Narrows on the Canadian Ojibwas Indian Reservation, where mercury contamination in the river destroyed the fishing and hunting economy. Low-income groups and people of color are exposed more often than other groups to hazards related to air, water, and ground contamination. American Indian lands, for example, are frequently targeted as sites for dumping toxic materials, for mining, and for nuclear testing (Hoff & Rogge, 1996). Rogge (1994) also reported that in eight states in the southeastern United States, three of four communities housing toxic waste dumps were in African American communities. Rogge (1993) argued that social workers must learn to fight environmental racism and class bias through advocacy for these hazard-endangered communities and groups.

Contemporary eco-maps would display other worrisome signs of threatened environments. Wars cause significant environmental destruction of people and environments. The chemical weapons used by Saddam Hussein against Kurds and Agent Orange used in Vietnam by the United States had immediate and lasting harmful effects. The minute dust particles created by the attack on New York's World Trade Center damaged the respiratory systems of many rescue workers, firefighters, and construction workers. Military activities around the world are responsible for stockpiles of dangerous weapons, nuclear contamination, and the distribution of land mines. Other hazards such as ozone depletion, the extinction of animal and plant species and resulting loss of biodiversity, the elevation of sea level, and problems with disposal of solid wastes and nuclear materials would become apparent through careful eco-mapping of regional environments.

Actual eco-maps of client systems in human settlements would display the ineffective collective effort to control the spatial conditions of built environments. Many urban clients live in habitats of very high **density.** Density is a measure of the ratio of people to space. **Crowding,** "an unpleasant psychosocial state" experienced when "a person's demand for space exceeds the available supply" (Germain, 1991, p. 34), occurs in their households, their neighborhoods, and their cities. Other individuals and families experience **isolation,** "an unpleasant state" that "occurs when space is in excess so that one is more distant from others than one wishes to be" (Germain, 1991, p. 34). Old and poor clients in rural communities with poor public transportation systems, for example, are often troubled by their distance from social, recreational, and service centers.

Applied ecological theorists should describe the actual physical environment in client system eco-maps. Such descriptions would reveal a widespread pattern of **environmental degradation.** Berger and Kelly (1993) asked that social workers develop maps that account for the continuing population growth in developing countries, the accumulation of synthetic organics such as plastic that do not biodegrade rapidly, and changes in the planetary surface because of improper farming, urbanization, and deforestation. Although such environmental changes may be subtle and require a new form of observation by social workers, they have important negative effects on client systems in the form of forced geographic migration, health problems, and economic displacement. Hoff and Polack (1993) directed our attention to the depletion of natural resources, environmental discrimination (the location of garbage disposal facilities, for instance), and shortages of food and water. Freese (1997) contended that the rapid loss of many species harms our ecosystems, and he predicted that between 1980 and 2020 more than 1 million species will have been lost to extinction. Lovell and Johnson (1994) suggested that careful eco-mapping would show the ways that dangerous pesticides and toxic chemicals reduce the quality of life of some social groups. Shove and Warde (2002) advised ecosystem cartographers to show how the excessive consumption of energy and water, and the frequent purchase and excessive use of goods (refrigerators, automobiles, stoves, televisions, dishwashers, air conditioners, vacuum cleaners, lightbulbs) and services (lawn care, car washing) that deplete our natural resources, are damaging client environments.

Applied ecological theorists offer a clear vision of ideal ecosystems and of what ideal eco-maps would look like. A new philosophy would guide human action in the environment. This new ecological paradigm values harmony and harmonious relationships between people and nature and respect for the diversity of life forms. The new philosophy calls for a commitment to the principle of sustainability (Weigert, 1997) and the development of our sense of **stewardship,** "a notion of moral responsibility to live harmoniously with the biosphere, with full responsibility to care for the planet as we would care for a beloved parent" (Berger & Kelly, 1993, p. 524). This philosophy is promulgated by ecological theory users involved in **environmentalism,** "the ideologies and the organizations that serve a worldwide social movement whose broad intent is to promote environmental protection" (Freese, 1997, p. 240).

Applied ecological theorists offer more specific guidelines for operationalizing this philosophy in various size environments (Germain & Gitterman, 1996; Gutheil, 1992; Hoff, 1998; Lawrence, 2002; National Association of Social Workers, 2003; Neugeboren, 1996). If you are a middle- or upper-class social worker, some of these guidelines may seem obvious. Extend your vision, however, to the environments of poor people in the United States and in countries around the world.

Human residences would be designed with adequate space allowances, avoiding the extremes of isolation or crowding. Acceptable levels of household occupancy would remove conditions, for example, that contribute to the transmission of infectious diseases. Residences would include the features necessary for safely inhabiting the environment. Homes and nursing homes for the elderly, for example, would have nonskid surfaces on stairs and in bathtubs, call buttons or beepers to request help, one-level room layouts, and smoke detectors. Residences would be stocked with stimulating physical objects—toys, books, games, art, and so on. Ideal housing would provide protection from intruders, rodents, and dust and shelter from extremes of temperature. Household members would ideally learn consumption habits and practices geared primarily to resource frugality, efficiencies in resource use, and the durability of commodities and secondarily to comfort and convenience.

The buildings housing social agencies or other organizations would satisfy ecological principles in their design. They would include physical amenities, features of the environment that add convenience and comfort and foster interaction and recreation. The USO center in Dallas for military veterans returning from the Iraq war, for example, provides phones, computers, cots, televisions, and CD and DVD players. The physical aids necessary to mobility and physical independence (prosthetic aids, for example) are also provided. People often need help in traveling through large public facilities. Directional signs, facility maps, and nightlights at exits would aid in orienting clients. The indoor air quality should be high. Workers in hazardous workplaces would be educated and protected to minimize risks. Hazards related to the choice of building structures and materials would be avoided. Accommodations in work, school, and other public buildings would protect persons who suffer from multiple chemical sensitivities.

Neighborhoods can be designed following ecological lessons. All community groups should have access to environmental and social resources, to community facilities, and to basic services. The community's members should be able to depend on an affordable food system free of toxic chemicals and pesticides. Communities can be sited and designed to maximize safety from natural disasters such as flooding and landslides. Ideal neighborhoods provide a safe and continuous supply of water and ensure the maintenance of sewage and waste disposal systems. Ideally, neighborhood planners eliminate environmental practices that differentially spread the negative effects of degradation, forcing communities of the poor and people of color to assume a disproportionate share of risk and danger compared to communities of wealthy persons. Human settlements should be designed or redesigned for sustainability, reduced and reused waste, plentiful green spaces, and human-scale buildings.

Societies can be reconstructed to meet ecological standards. Societal leaders can reduce reliance on fossil fuels and replace this reliance with clean energy derived from the sun, wind, and water. Governments can rigorously and effectively regulate chemicals and the products that contain them. Public policy can minimize the production of waste and encourage full recycling. National political leaders can work to protect the supply of clear air and water, arable land, and food crops and to reverse the trend toward rapid extinction of species. The preservation of biodiversity can be promoted as a public good. Politicians might also support the development of transportation systems that move masses and rely on renewable resources.

Ecological social workers can help to create ideal residential, organizational, community, and society environments. These environments are compatible with the population's basic needs and with their full and healthy functioning, including biological reproduction, over a long period of time.

Social workers might ask: Is the layout, design, and maintenance of human environments responsive to the requirements of all groups who use them, including those with special needs and vulnerabilities?

How Are Issues of Diversity, Color, and Shading Addressed?

Applied ecological theorists take a very positive stance toward diversity. They imagine a world of many hues and shades, a world rich in natural colors like the green of leaves and grass, the blue of clear skies, and the reds, yellows, or purples of flowers. Applied ecological theorists fight against the creation of an environment with colors bleached out by smog, artificial additives, and waste materials.

Ecological theorists consider the variety of colors, species, and human groups an asset. **Biodiversity** is the number and variety of distinct species and populations that exist (Freese, 1997). Biodiversity is an indicator of species richness (Townsend et al., 2000).

Diversity protects plant, animal, and human ecosystems from destruction (Ungar, 2002). The diversity of social organizations and human groups in an ecosystem increases the likelihood that effective and creative solutions to environmental challenges will emerge. Natural diversity increases the pool of resources (sources of medicines, industrial chemicals, biological control agents, and other valuable stocks) available for human use (Freese, 1997). The diversity of ecological niches and life forms increases the resilience of life and the stability of the ecosystem (Berger & Kelly, 1993), and the complexity and diversity of ecosystem populations and systems contribute to ecological functions related to gaseous composition of the atmosphere, water recycling, the generation and maintenance of soils, the self-regulation of global ecological processes, and other life support services (Freeze, 1997; Hoff & Polack, 1993). Diversity creates the conditions for the long-term adaptability and survival of our species.

Applied ecological theorists appreciate the diverse ways that human groups symbolize the environment. Cultural groups live in different **landscapes,** "the symbolic environments created by human acts of conferring meaning to nature and the environment, of giving the environment definition and form from a particular angle of vision and through a special filter of values and beliefs" (Grieder & Garkovich, 1994, p. 1). When multiple groups share a geographical space, one physical place in that environment may have multiple landscapes. Yucca Mountain, Nevada, is viewed by engineers as a potential high-level radioactive waste repository but by Southern Paiute elders as a sacred site and a place of healing. Applied ecological theorists encourage social workers to learn about how various groups define, value, and use the environment.

Proxemics teaches us about cultural and group-based differences in preferred interactional distance (Albas & Albas, 1989). Research evidence indicates a range of symbolic orientations toward physical closeness during social interaction. Members of contact cultures, such as Arabs, Latin Americans, and the French, often prefer closer physical distance, more frequent eye contact and touch, and more direct angle of orientation. Members of noncontact cultures, such as the British, Pakistanis, and Northern Europeans, interpret such physical closeness as threatening or uncomfortable. These differences have clear implications for social work counseling.

Applied ecological theorists recognize that various social and personal problems emerge from human difference. Physically and mentally challenged persons relate to the environment in ways different than the physically able. Walker (1995), for example, used the tools of geography to learn about the places where persons with developmental disabilities spent time in the community. She learned about the stores, restaurants, workplaces, homes of friends and relatives, churches, and social service agencies visited by these people and about the characteristics of these places. Places in the environment varied in their support for the efforts of the studied individuals to interact with others, to achieve a degree of independence, to develop interests, and to expand their social networks. Her maps of "the personal geography of lives" can provide guidance to social workers trying to help physically and mentally different clients increase their social connections and improve their quality of community membership.

Social groups vary in their access to places of privilege and status. Feminists use the image of a glass ceiling to indicate that women cannot easily obtain positions at the highest levels of corporate hierarchies. In some organizations, the boundaries are both symbolic and physical. In one of my former university positions, I noticed that no women held an office or position of administrative leadership on the fourth floor of our administration building. In one city, the leaders of the nearby wealthy county refused to allow public bus transportation across their boundaries. City residents (often poor African Americans) seeking employment in the prosperous and mostly European American suburbs hit an invisible wall. Segregation in housing and the geographical partitioning of land to favor certain social classes and ethnic groups provide further examples of the ecological dimension of public problems. The exclusionary practices of apartheid, the restrictions on the rights of certain groups to move into and out of or across public territories, and the fencing in of a group by means of a ghetto or a reservation also typify methods of using the environment to discriminate against certain groups (Lyman, 2002).

The difficulties of minority ethnic and racial groups in those societies dominated by a majority have a territorial dimension. Lyman (1997) proposed that the argument over accommodation versus assimilation illustrates basic symbolic ecological issues. For pluralists, the advocates of accommodation, minority ethnoracial groups merit a home territory where they can freely live out their cultural customs and practices without any surveillance by the majority. The tolerant city with various ethnic neighborhoods—Little Italy, Chinatown, Harlem—typifies this ideal in its spatial patterns. In this city's neighborhoods, each ethnic group can affirm its identity by decorating the stores, homes, and parks "with emblems of their particular peoplehood" (Lyman, p. 34). The assimilationists prefer the root image of the Greek agora or central, public meeting place. All people dwelling on society's periphery or margins—in spatial terms or in terms of custom—must be civilized so that their cultural, social, economic, and political distance from the center is minimized. Hence, those gathering at the agora can relate, interact, and communicate easily and freely with all their fellow city dwellers. The shopping mall, in the modern version of this kind of city, becomes the integrative place where rough-edged ethnic identities are smoothed into a common "shopper" identity. In France, lawmakers demanded that Muslim children move to the culture's center, forsaking scarves and other traditional clothing when entering the public school system.

WHAT WOULD BE ADDED OR DELETED?

When drawing the eco-map, applied ecological theorists would want to consider not only local environments but also the largest environment, the earth. The world is a biosphere, and this largest living system influences all smaller and local systems (Rigney, 2001). Animals and plants might also be added to the conventional eco-map.

Applied ecological theorists assert that **objects** and nonhuman things are critical to human functioning. In contemporary physical and social environments like those in the United States, cherished possessions play an important role in people's self- and social definitions. Csikszentmihalyi and Rochberg-Halton (1981), for example, researched how families in Chicago invested manmade things and natural objects with special meanings. In the ecology of these households, family members used furniture, art pieces, photographs, books, stereos, musical instruments, televisions, plants, plates, and other objects to represent their identities, memories, and aspirations. The set of cherished objects provided physical form for what the human inhabitants considered most meaningful in their habitats. During home visits, social workers might appraise the objects collected and cherished by clients. Csikszentmihalyi and Rochberg-Halton (1981) suggested that the household's symbolic ecology provides clues to a family's emotional integration (warm or cool), their degree of membership in social organizations, their role models, their status aspirations, and their goals. We have already discussed the importance applied ecologists give to identifying dreaded, dangerous, and hazardous objects in the client's environment (Lovell & Johnson, 1994).

Applied ecological theorists would encourage us to make the invisible "generations of the future" visible on contemporary eco-maps. Children and grandchildren and the future earth we will pass on as an inheritance can be ignored only at their peril (Hoff & Rogge, 1996). Adding such elements to conventional eco-maps would demonstrate the practitioner's commitment to "intergenerational environmental justice" and support for consideration of the resource needs of persons not yet born and the impact of our current environmental practices on these generations.

Weather, the momentary or temporal variations in meteorological conditions, and **climate,** the spatial or geographical variations in meteorological conditions, are also important ecological variables. The creative social worker might add these to a conventional eco-map and make judgments with the client about the effects of weather and climate on his or her relations to the physical and social environment.

THE LIMITS OF APPLIED ECOLOGICAL THEORY: A SOCIAL WORK APPRAISAL

In this section, I will briefly offer some critical reflections on the applied ecological theoretical framework.

Some social workers have put forward the ecological perspective or life model as a generic practice paradigm, a way of thinking about helping work that can serve social workers in a variety of settings and that can incorporate other, less abstract theoretical perspectives. The ecological perspective usefully accentuates the indivisibility of person and environment. However, the ecological framework is built from very high-level abstractions about ecosystems, transactions, human adaptation, and human development. Social workers need more domain-specific knowledge for assessment and intervention purposes, specific and concrete practice guidelines to direct efforts to help battered women, chronically depressed adults, or minority group delinquents (Wakefield, 1996). The ecological perspective may be too abstract (Brower, 1988). Faithful adherence to the ecological perspective also requires social workers to collect and consider an overwhelmingly large amount of information. For example, Bronfenbrenner's approach to human development necessitates assessment of client–environment exchanges at the levels of immediate system, mesosystem, exosystem, and macrosystem. Many social workers may not have the time or ability to engage in such a comprehensive data collection project for each client.

Adherents to conventional causal models complain that the ecological perspective provides too little explanatory power in relation to a variety of specific personal and social problems (Wakefield, 1996). What, for example, are the nature, strength, and malleability of the specific causal processes activated in a case of domestic violence? Applied ecological theorists prefer reciprocal, emergent, and complex models of causation. This approach may accurately reflect reality, but lack practicality. A cognitive-behavioral model pinpointing the batterer's power advantages, deficiencies in empathic skills and dispositions, tendency to blame the environment or partner, and learned use of violent behavior to control intimate others more simply identifies relevant determinants.

The ecological perspective's emphasis on both the person and the situation may divert practitioners from two alternative interpretations of client difficulties. In some practice circumstances, the major causes of social functioning failures reside in the person. Clients have free will and the capacity for choice, and they may make decisions that lead to social and environmental predicaments (Gaziano, 1996). In other circumstances, the environmental constraints may be so great that clients have almost no room for adaptive decision making (Wakefield, 1996).

Unfortunately, there is little empirical support for the ecological perspective. I did not find one study that demonstrated the efficacy of a social worker's use of concepts, propositions, and middle-range theories related to the physical environment or the basic tenets of this framework. Ecological social workers offer many case studies demonstrating theory application, but the profession's turn toward evidence-based practice approaches requires more scientific tests of the ecological framework.

Let's end by summarizing some of the strengths of applied ecological theory. The perspective has a strong emphasis on contextual understanding, a hallmark of the social work tradition. It theorizes extensively on how the person, like all living organisms, is embedded in the physical and social environments. The ecological perspective's commitment to uncovering the reciprocal influences between person and environment avoids the extremes of individualistic theoretical frameworks that endow the individual with excessive agency and collectivistic theoretical frameworks that consider social structures and environments as inescapable shapers of our life chances. Finally, the commitment of applied ecological theorists to expanding the profession's knowledge base by collaborating with theorists, researchers, and practitioners aligned with many disciplines coincides with the core conviction of this author. Contemporary social work practice requires social workers to learn multiple theoretical languages and to jump disciplinary and professional fences.

A MODEL OF HOMELESSNESS, CONTESTED TERRITORY, AND SHELTER SITING PREFERENCES

Ecological theorists have given increased attention to the **NIMBY** (Not In My Back Yard) phenomenon, organized resistance of community members to the siting of controversial land uses and social agencies in their neighborhoods or "home places" (Takahashi, 1997). Powerful groups increasingly work to place social and environmental hazards such as toxic waste, land mines, the homeless, and HIV-infected persons far away from their homes but often in the backyards of less powerful community members (Weigert, 1997). This section presents a conceptual model that makes practical use of applied ecological theory.

THE ECOLOGICAL PERSPECTIVE ON THE PROBLEM OF CONTESTED TERRITORY

As indicated earlier, ecological theorists inform us that place meanings are collective creations, and meaning assignment varies by culture, historical period, and location in the social structure. Certain places can become stigmatized and defined as undesirable, unworthy, unproductive, or dangerous (Takahashi, 1997). Shelters for the homeless, for example, often attract this stigma. Residents of some neighborhoods worry that worthy and nonstigmatized places will become polluted by the arrival of outsiders and nonconforming people (Takahashi, 1997). The negative characteristics attributed to a stigmatized population such as the homeless may rub off and become attached to the place. Undesirable people, according to mainstream community members, lower the value of places to which they migrate. Therefore, community members are more frequently joining NIMBY efforts to keep stigmatized social work clients at a distance from their homes. Social workers are advocating in return for the rights of client groups as community members to live and receive service in our communities. Sites for the location of homeless shelters or group homes become **contested territories,** and a planned relocation often activates the negative attitudes and oppositional collective action of neighbors.

The losers of the territorial definitional contest—the homeless, for instance—are likely to experience more than a setback in the fight to define a public problem and solution. In a case that I studied (Forte, 2002b), surrender to the NIMBY forces had the possible consequences for homeless persons of a three-mile walk to a shelter, increased episodes of hunger, frequent arrests for loitering, scorn from the public, and possible death.

ECOLOGICAL ASSESSMENT: MAPPING TERRITORIES AND TERRITORIAL MEANINGS

Social workers engaged in territorial contests might start with a spatial map of relevant places and their valuation, including the particular meanings attached to each place by various community groups (Takahashi, 1997). Here's a brief summary of my mapping effort. After building a headquarters on a former downtown prison site in Richmond, Virginia, in 1992, a large corporation requested that the nearby multipurpose service center vacate its shelter/drop-in building. Community groups differed in their reactions. For almost five years, advocates for the homeless, leaders of neighborhood associations, downtown businesspeople, local politicians, and representatives of area churches argued about the problem. The best location for the agency was the central issue. The NIMBY chorus yelled loudly, but calls for Christian compassion and for community responsibility were also heard.

Ecological and cultural features of the city were central to the agency siting contests. As the city developed, the agency's location was invested with contradictory meanings and values. In brief, the multipurpose center, called the Daily Planet, leased an empty city building at the city's downtown edge in 1985. Here, it offered meals, clothing, food, job training, employment counseling, physical and mental health care, drug treatment, and limited temporary housing in the winter. Roughly 300 clients used this agency each day—an unruly crowd in the eyes of agency detractors. Two blocks to the east was a public university of 17,000 students in an expansionistic phase. A bit farther to the east was an upper-middle-class neighborhood of restored, highly valued homes. To the north of the Planet was the downtown business district. This area included the headquarters of the major city newspaper and several business owners determined to facilitate a downtown revival. Most service agencies and many churches offering feeding programs were also downtown.

Slightly to the north were several small working-class, mostly African American, neighborhoods. Directly across the highway to the south of the Daily Planet was a large corporate facility. Farther south was the James River, and on the other side of the river was a very poor business and residential section of the city. To the east of the city center was an industrial area with many railroad crossings and the city jail. This area lay at the bottom of a large hill.

Advocates of the homeless wanted the Daily Planet to stay where it was in the central city district. This location provided the homeless with access to the agency's varied services and to nearby health and social services. Opponents, including those associated with the large corporation, challenged the legality of the siting. They wanted the agency moved to the poor south side neighborhood, moved to a desolate spot near the city jail, moved to the African American north side, or closed. Powerful advocates from the associations of white neighbors were most determined to prevent the agency from being moved near their backyards.

Besides geographical mapping, I assessed some of the cultural meanings community members attached to the shelter site and related territories. My assessment was based on a content analysis of a multiyear media battle over shelter siting preferences—138 position statements identified in 79 articles obtained from four newspapers. Many letters, editorials, and feature stories used negative symbols to characterize the homeless and their use of space. To critics, the agency was like a "pigsty," and the surrounding natural area spoiled by "a dozen empty bottles of Colt 45 and Magnum 12 lying among the piles of crisp autumn leaves." Opponents asserted that the agency location for the homeless was an "enabling magnet" and argued that they didn't want their neighborhoods "to become a magnet." Construction of downtown parks and other green spaces should be stopped because these spaces attract the homeless.

Members attached meanings to the larger region, too, and complained of the geographical distribution of the community burden. A critic complained that social workers failed to see the extent to which they burdened others: "liberal do-gooders" don't understand or "appreciate" people's neighborhoods. Those against agency relocation to sites close to their homes worried about "fragile neighborhoods" with "more than a fair share of problems" and believed that the agency would "drag down a neighborhood." Many recommended a more equitable distribution of burden by recognizing "the regional nature of homelessness and the need to develop a regional solution." They would have been pleased if the shelter and the services were located in a distant county or across the river.

Contestants in the fight over territory made various claims about the homeless. Components of the total claims package were coded as follows: overall stance toward the homeless (sympathetic or not sympathetic); characterization of the moral features of the actors in the controversy (homeless to blame or not to blame); attribution of blame for the problem (bad luck, deficits of the homeless, societal conditions); and recommended policy toward the agency serving the homeless (leave the Planet in the city center, move the Planet outside the city center, close the Planet). Proximity to the current shelter and to the downtown relocation site seemed very influential in the stakeholders' positions. Downtown business representatives were vocal. Those with probusiness affiliations were divided, however, in their siting preferences: 50 percent (N = 13) recommended leaving the Planet at the current location (this site on the edge of downtown probably seemed less threatening than relocation closer to the business center), and 50 percent (N = 13) suggested that it be moved out of the city center or permanently closed. Membership in a nearby neighborhood association and home ownership were linked to writers' stances in 74 published positions. Almost 90 percent (N = 17) of the residential stakeholders preferred to leave the Daily Planet at its current location. The current location was not residential and, therefore, clearly preferable to relocation in the far northside, west end, or north-of-downtown neighborhoods.

ECOLOGICAL INTERVENTION: MULTI-ROLE COLLECTIVE PROBLEM SOLVING

Advocates for the homeless had clear preferences about the agency siting solution. They were seeking a location that accommodated the "daily rounds" of the homeless. This ecological concept has been borrowed from animal ecology to understand the range of activities by a homeless person and the spots and routes significant within this range (Stein & McCall, 1994). Social workers and allied advocates preferred a downtown location because resources such as phones, mailboxes, lockers, and laundry facilities could be centralized, reducing travel by the homeless. Also, a downtown location provided easy assess to social services and meal programs. The downtown location was close to several other shelter programs, offering the homeless some options when they needed protection from harsh or dangerous weather conditions. Finally, many downtown places had been legitimized by the police and other community leaders for the physical and social use of the homeless. The site in the distant industrial area satisfied none of these criteria.

The general thrust of ecological intervention involves helping community members engage in processes of negotiation and mediation with a focus on exploring and resolving differences in sociospatial meanings (Takahashi, 1997). From my analysis of the media contest over the siting of the Daily Planet, it became clear that social workers must enact multiple change-agent roles. As good listeners, ecological social workers cultivated their ability to take the role of all community groups, with a special ear for the place identifications, attachments, and other meanings that are central to personal and social identities. As symbolic geographers, the workers needed to map both community locations and their meanings as these related to the general problem-solving process and to specific service-siting recommendations. As media analysts, the workers needed to identify the media vehicles covering the homelessness controversy, interpret and classify the major claims about homelessness, relate these perspectives to the location of various groups in the larger ecosystem, and trace the influence of the media on problem-defining and -resolving processes. As political brokers, the workers had to mobilize symbolic resources on behalf of the locations desired by homeless clients and service providers. For instance, the workers might weigh the relative cultural power of favorable depictions of a downtown location in terms of rhetorical effectiveness, resonance with existing community opinions, and likelihood of being retained in social institutions. In the Richmond community, for example, social workers recognized that faith-based arguments about members' bonds with and obligations to the homeless seemed to have special symbolic power. So, social workers were wise to ally with leaders of spiritual organizations and to include religious imagery and language in some of the activities designed to increase sympathy for the location of a shelter for the homeless in a downtown location not far from many backyards.

The leaders of the homeless shelter and other advocates for the homeless enacted these roles. They arrived at a compromise solution that responded to the NIMBY concerns of homeowners and businesspeople without moving the agency to a site that would disrupt the daily rounds of the homeless. A building on a different edge of the downtown area, one where several other agencies and a large police department are located, was picked. The shelter had again become accepted because it was a "close but not in anyone's backyard" neighbor.

LEARNING ACTIVITIES

1. Use your metaphor imagination to better understand one of your clients and his or her environment. How is this client's neighborhood environment like a well cared for and nutrient-rich garden? How is it not like the ideal garden (harsh conditions, nutrient deficiencies, or vulnerabilities to dangerous and damaging intruders)? What are some of the environment's positive influences on the growth and the flowering of your client? How might you tend to the environment like a gardener enriching the soil, watering the plants, and pulling the weeds?

2. Use Kurt Lewin's metaphor of a force field to understand the prospects for a successful personal change in your life space. Consider the desired change. Now identify all the forces in your total situation that will make change difficult. These can be internal and part of your personality or external and part of your environment. Next, identify all the forces in the total situation that will facil-

itate your change efforts. What is your verdict? Will constraining or facilitating forces prevail?

3. Think about the influence of the environment's climate on human development. How might your personal and social development have differed if you had grown up in Alaska and had to cope with dangerous terrain and extremely cold weather? What if you had grown up on the edge of the Sahara desert in North Africa?

4. How might your development have differed if you had been raised in a very different environmental milieu? Picture a very different ecological setting—for example, a house where cocaine was manufactured and sold; a neighborhood where the major occupations were gambling, drug dealing, and bookmaking; or a community where the curfew law required minors to be off the street by 10:00 P.M. yet gangs were continuously pressuring teens to join.

5. Take a tour of your apartment or home as if you were a social worker conducting a home visit. What are the furnishings, and how are they arranged? What private spaces are available? How do you and your family or roommates or pets mark different territories? Are boundaries respected? Are there any barriers to mobility or hazards? What is the quality of the home environment? Summarize what you learned about the ecological features of your home and what your assessment tells you about yourself, about safety and security, about privacy and crowding, and about preferred patterns of interaction.

6. Take a tour of your field agency or a nearby social agency. Assess the aesthetic and functional qualities of office spaces, waiting rooms, and hallways. How well does the air flow and lights illuminate? What do the building design, landscaping, and arrangement of the parking spaces communicate to community members, clients, and workers? How do workers personalize their office territories? Mizrahi (2001) advises that you use all your senses to enrich your assessment of the likely impact of the agency environment on its users: sight (colors, cleanliness, appearance of staff and clients), hearing (level of noise, voices, machinery sounds), smell (odors of people and of things,

cigarette smoke), taste (agency food), touch (closeness of bodies, temperature, textures of walls). How well do the signs help clients find their way? Find out if the agency has any written policies regarding the physical environment.

7. Identify your "niche." Where do you fit best? How have you transformed this part of the total environment into a harmonious and comfortable place? How can you use what you learned about your niche to better understand your clients and their problems related to niche?

8. Observe the patterns of association and interaction on your campus. Are there some places (dining hall, library study areas, lawn benches) where members of different ethnic groups associate separately from other groups? Are there places where participants from diverse backgrounds mingle and interact with one another?

9. Develop a simple map of the neighborhood or community surrounding your field internship or an agency that you have visited. Locate community resources and potential environmental problems. Can residents easily access resources and services? Where are the community meeting places and recreation centers? Characterize the density of the local population. Does the neighborhood include green spaces such as parks?

ADDITIONAL RESOURCES

Additional resources are available on the book companion website at **www.thomsonedu.com/ social_work/forte**. Resources include key terms, tutorial quizzes, links to related websites, and lists of additional resources for furthering your research.

5

APPLIED SYSTEMS THEORY

Bob Scott/IndexStock

INTRODUCTION

Some social workers consider the systems approach a paradigm or metatheory (Anderson & Carter, 1990), one often joined with the ecological theory to form an ecosystems philosophy for all social work practice. In this chapter, I shall treat applied systems theory as a theoretical perspective organized as a coherent set of assumptions, concepts, propositions, and middle-range theories. This chapter will introduce you to these building blocks and help you understand the essentials of applied systems theory by using the theory-mastery tools of exemplars, metaphors, maps, and models to translate it into comprehensible images and terms.

RELATED DIALECTS, ASSOCIATED SCHOOLS OF THOUGHT

Contemporary systems theorists have integrated conceptual influences from several related streams or schools of intellectual thought. **Cybernetics** is a science of information processing and system self-regulation developed in the 1940s by Norbert Weiner (Chetkow-Yanoov, 1992; Hanson, 1995). It has contributed to our understanding of "the nature of control systems in machines, organisms, and (more recently) social systems" (Gergen, 1990, p. 292). Cybernetic theorists study, for example, how thermostats, automatic pilots, missile guidance systems, cruise control devices, and the human brain use information from the environment as feedback to guide actions toward desired targets or goals.

General systems theory has been defined by its founder, Ludwig von Bertalanffy, as "a logico-mathematical field, the subject matter of which is the formulation and derivation of those principles which hold for systems in general" (Bertalanffy, 1952, p. 199). Advocates of this complex perspective claim that general systems theory offers a philosophy of science, a scientific method, a framework for integrating knowledge from different disciplines, a theory explaining the way systems function, a collection of guiding principles, and an approach to life (Bertalanffy, 1969; Buckley, 1998; Meyer, 1976). Many concepts from general systems theory will be presented later.

Talcott Parsons, one of America's greatest social theorists, developed a sociological version of systems theory called **structural functionalism.** This theoretical framework examines how a social system is characterized by structure and function. Structure refers to formal and informal patterns of action. The structure provides an order and predictability to system processes and functioning. Client and worker behaviors in a social agency, for instance, are patterned and constrained by the set of norms, the role arrangements, and the distribution of power that constitute the agency structure. Structural functionalists also believe that every system—a society, for example—consists of parts (police departments, hospitals, schools, mutual aid associations, families, farms). Each part carries out an important function or set of functions that contribute to the survival and stability of the social system. The family socializes children for participation in the larger society.

New developments related to applied systems theory include **chaos theory** and **complexity theory** (Franklin & Warren, 1999). These theories seek to explain how apparently chaotic or disordered systems may eventually exhibit a degree of order, but with ordered patterns that are hard to predict. My presentation of applied systems theory in this chapter will offer an amalgam of general systems theory, structural functionalism, and cybernetics, but with a focus on social systems rather than biological or mechanical systems.

APPLIED SYSTEMS THEORY: EXEMPLARY MODELS

My major exemplars of applied systems theory are two scientists and a social worker. Next, I will report on the lives, the theories, the approaches to theorizing, and the applications of these practical theorists.

LUDWIG VON BERTALANFFY

Karl Ludwig von Bertalanffy (1901–1972) was born in a village near Vienna (Brauckmann, 2004). He was educated at home by private tutors before entering school at the age of 10. He wrote his first book, *Modern Theories of Development* (1928/1962), when he was 27. During his career, Bertalanffy taught at many different institutions, including the University of Vienna, the Menninger Foundation, and Mount Sinai Hospital. Bertalanffy was a versatile scholar and researcher. He contributed to theoretical biology, theoretical psychology, cancer research (especially by pioneering techniques for detecting cell malignancies), the philosophy of science, and scientific methodology.

Ludwig von Bertalanffy created and named general systems theory (Hearn, 1979). He imagined the possibility of a framework of concepts and principles applied universally to all systems: mechanical systems, biological systems, and social systems (Martin & O'Connor, 1989). Bertalanffy's life work was a reaction against the splitting of the scientific enterprise into numerous disciplines and fields. He hoped that his general systems theory would serve as a new paradigm for theory development and stimulate the reunification of physicists, biologists, chemists, psychologists, and social scientists. Bertalanffy (1952, p. 176) argued specifically that "the principles of wholeness, of organization, and of the dynamic conception of reality become apparent in all fields of science." He searched for similarities across systems of all sizes and believed that "a unitary conception of the world may be based, not upon the futile and certainly farfetched hope finally to reduce all levels of reality to the reality of physics, but rather on the isomorphy of laws in different fields" (1969, p. 48). Bertalanffy (1952) also rejected conceptions of living systems rooted in metaphors comparing human beings to machines or robots. He preferred dynamic and holistic conceptions focused on human activity rather than reactivity, human becoming rather than being, and human goal directedness rather than purposelessness.

Advancing his organismic approach to theoretical biology, Bertalanffy formulated a theory of **open systems** (Davidson, 1983). These are systems that continually exchange matter and energy with their environment. He documented the dynamic processes that characterize the internal operations of such systems, the tendency of such systems to seek a steady state, and the hierarchical organization of their structures. Bertalanffy championed thinking about wholes not parts. General systems theory was a science of wholeness, and he asserted that the systems expression "The whole is more than the sum of its parts" means that "constitutive characteristics are not explainable from the behavior of the isolated parts. The characteristics of the complex, therefore, appear as 'new' or 'emergent'" (Bertalanffy, 1969, p. 55). Scientific inquiry about a living thing requires the analysis of parts, but more important, the study of the whole, and the emergent "properties that are absent from its isolated properties" (Bertalanffy, 1952, p. 12). You might understand four musicians as individuals—John, Paul, Ringo, and George of the Beatles, for example—but you can only understand and appreciate a Beatles song in terms of the dynamic and innovative operations of the whole band.

Bertalanffy devoted himself fully to his theorizing activities. He rarely watched television and was not interested in movies. He spent his free time reading, taking notes, and writing. A complete bibliography of his life's work on theoretical biology and general systems theory demonstrates his industrious commitment to theorizing. It includes more than 275 items.

Bertalanffy was a useful theorist. He was a member of many prestigious intellectual societies, including study groups of the World Health Organization. The United Nations and British fisheries used Bertalanffy's equations specifying the likely growth rates of varied species as a method of forecasting yields. In 1954, Bertalanffy and three other sympathetic systems theorists founded the Society for the Advancement of General Systems Theory, later renamed the Society for General Systems Research (Boulding, 1983). In 1956, he founded and helped edit the society's yearbook, *General Systems*. In 1962, Bertalanffy established the International Center for Integrative Studies, an organization dedicated to integrating all knowledge and to resisting science's tendency toward overspecialization and fragmentation (Davidson, 1983). True to his interdisciplinary convictions, he became one of the first scientists to apply systems theory and methodology to psychological and sociological topics.

Bertalanffy took risks and acted on his principles. Before World War II, he wrote an essay denouncing the biological theories used by the Nazis to justify their racist policies. During this time, he argued frequently with Nazi sympathizers (Davidson, 1983). Bertalanffy was a critic of the technological approach to the Vietnam War and suggested that if military and political leaders had assumed a systems mindset they would have considered nonmilitary dynamics related to history, culture, and nationalism. Naive assumptions about quick and decisive victory would have been tempered, and a commitment of the country to war avoided (Davidson, 1983). Bertalanffy advocated a new global morality and systems consciousness, one appreciative of the systemically interdependent relationship of members of the world community. His systems theory and advocacy inspired ecologists, scientists, organizational managers, inventors, historians, and school administrators. Buckminster Fuller (1983) nominated him for a Nobel Prize, but Bertalanffy's unexpected death derailed the nomination process.

Before his life's end, Bertalanffy voiced eloquently to a group of students his commitment to useful theory: "The only thing we can hope for is perhaps getting a little bit wiser about our problems and what can be done. So let us discuss these things as far as you and I are able to do so—because you see, I want to be of some use to you. If I succeed in making a very tiny contribution in that way, then I would be very satisfied" (Davidson, 1983, p. 221). The full value of Bertalanffy's inspired scientific work was not appreciated by the scientific community, unfortunately, until after his death (Davidson, 1983).

Talcott Parsons

Talcott Parsons (1902–1979) was born in Colorado Springs to middle-class parents (Martindale, 1975). His father, a Congregational minister, later progressed from a position as dean at Colorado College to the presidency of Marietta College in Ohio (Lidz, 2000). Because of an interest in social reform and justice, Talcott Parsons switched from studies in biology at Amherst College to course work in economics. As a young scholar, Parsons studied abroad at the prestigious London School of Economics and the University of Heidelberg. His doctoral dissertation was completed for the Heidelberg program. Parsons served as a professor at Harvard University from 1927 until 1979. Like Bertalanffy, he preferred an interdisciplinary slant to theorizing. He founded the Department of Social Relations at Harvard University as a way to integrate diverse fields, including psychology, anthropology, and sociology (Ritzer, 1996).

Parsons' theorizing efforts were directed toward a "grand theory," a comprehensive framework for integrating all knowledge about human behavior and the social environment. He believed that explicating the basic premises of applied systems theory and the theoretical categories that cross system levels should precede the empirical investigation of social life at any particular level of social organization (Lidz, 2000). Parsons' writing style challenged many readers and has been characterized as abstract, complex, hard to follow, and full of unnecessary new terms (Holton, 1998; Martindale, 1975). In the 1950s, Talcott Parsons was ranked, nevertheless, as the most prominent sociologist in the United States (Martindale, 1975) and is considered by some to be the greatest American sociologist (Ritzer, 1996).

Parsons' overarching theoretical framework, structural functionalism, defined the properties of social systems, identified the functional imperatives of every system (adaptation, goal attainment, integration, and latency or pattern maintenance), outlined an explanation of the structuring of systems, examined the interrelationship of the major systems (personality, social, and cultural), and presented a model for understanding system change and stability. He wrote numerous influential essays and books developing and amplifying these systems ideas, including *The Social System* (1952), *Sociological Theory and Modern Society* (1967), and *Politics and Social Structure* (1969).

Parsons was interested in theorizing and in service. During the Great Depression, he supported President Roosevelt's New Deal policies because of their emphasis on reducing the deprivations associated with poverty and discrimination (Lidz, 2000). He again demonstrated a commitment to civic engagement by taking public stands for liberal democratic values against Nazism in Germany and the totalitarianism of the Soviet political system (Holton, 1998; Lidz, 2000). For the last few years of World War II, Talcott Parsons helped prepare U.S. military, intelligence, and diplomatic officers for roles in governing occupied Germany and Japan. In 1949, he was president of the prestigious American Sociological Association. In the 1960s, Parsons participated in conferences with U.S. and Soviet scientists discussing methods for the control of nuclear weapons. Attentive to issues raised by civil rights leaders in the late 1960s, Parsons wrote on citizenship and the experiences of excluded groups such as African Americans. He linked citizenship rights to the full inclusion of social groups in community life and political processes. Parsons has been criticized for right-wing political tendencies and an inclination in his theorizing and practice to defend the status quo (Martindale, 1975). However, Lidz (2000) rejects this stereotype and argues that Parsons was a liberal democrat who believed that expanding the prosperity of middle-class citizens would reduce social inequality.

Although a grand theorist, Talcott Parsons applied his concepts to practical issues, including the illness experience, the interaction between doctors and patients, the development and regulation of the professions, and the division of labor and responsibility within families (Holton, 1998). Parsons also contributed indirectly to the development of social science theory by mentoring numerous graduate students who became important theorists (Ritzer, 1996). His students included Clifford Geertz, Robert Merton, Kingsley Davis, and Neil Smelser.

GORDON HEARN

Gordon Hearn (1914–1979) introduced social work theorists and practitioners to systems theory (Longres, 1995). Born in Canada, he gained practice experience working with boys at the Young Men's Christian Association. Hearn completed his doctorate work under the direction of the great social psychologist Kurt Lewin at the Massachusetts Institute of Technology (Chetkow-Yanoov, 1992). Before becoming an educator, Hearn was a social group worker, and he maintained his involvement in service as an associate to the staff at the National Training Laboratory, an organization advancing the use of small groups for human relations training.

Hearn was a social work professor and theorist at Portland State College (Hearn, 1958), and the first person to advocate for the centrality of the construct *system* to social work knowledge building and practice (Payne, 2002a). Professor Hearn had been inspired by the theoretical work of Ludwig von Bertalanffy and of James Miller, a systems-oriented behavioral scientist (Hearn, 1974). When given a yearlong sabbatical to think and theorize, Hearn began his project of identifying the central properties of living systems, outlining how general systems theory might direct social work theory building, and helping his students conduct research studies of systems interventions and their usefulness with individuals, groups, organizations, and communities. At the time, social work knowledge and practice were organized by distinct methods: casework, group work, and community organizing. Hearn (1974) broke from this tradition and created a conceptual model based on systems theory, a model designed to unify all social work by showing "there are living systems at the level of human individuals, groups, organizations and communities, those entities with which social workers do their work, and as systems they have certain characteristics in common" (p. 345).

The social work profession responded slowly to Hearn's theoretical innovations, but five years after the publication of *Theory Building in Social Work* (1958), interest began to grow. In 1968, social work educators eager to learn participated in a one-day seminar at the Annual Program Meeting of the Council on Social Work Education on applied systems theory. Hearn (1969a) edited an influential collection of papers that had been presented at the seminar, *The General Systems Approach: Contributions Toward an Holistic Conception of Social Work*. He also contributed a summary paper and an introductory bibliography to this publication. Gordon Hearn spread his ideas about systems theory by presenting workshops in Denver, Portland, Miami, and other cities. In these workshops, systems principles, concepts, and techniques were applied to client systems of various sizes. Social worker practitioners learned how to deal more effectively with difficult practice situations from Gordon Hearn, the expert.

APPLIED SYSTEMS THEORY: ROOT METAPHORS

In this section, I will introduce you to some of the metaphors that root the concepts, propositions, and theories of the applied systems theoretical framework. I will review comparisons between real life and the theoretical framework's conception of the environment, the person, and the social worker.

The Environment as a Whole (Machine, Body, or Species)

Systems have been compared to machines, bodies, and species. The mechanistic tradition assumes that a system is like a machine (Buckley, 1967; Gergen, 1990). Call to mind images of your car, washing machine, or furnace. Characteristic of a smoothly running machine are coordination and an integration of parts; you, the owner, can assume a reliable cause-and-effect relationship among these parts of the machine. Turn the key, and the ignition system causes the car to start. Societies and other social systems are made up of parts that can work well together. Applied systems theorists make frequent use of images of machines with control or feedback mechanisms. Departures from the machine's state of equilibrium or optimal operational parameters result in corrective actions. The automobile detects unacceptable increases in engine heat after fast driving and activates a fan to cool down the motor (Martin & O'Connor, 1989). Machine operators can program the control devices to achieve desired outputs. You can set your washing machine to direct electricity, water, and other resources so that the parts operate toward the desired goal of clean permanent-press clothes (Rigney, 2001). You can set your home's thermostat at 70 degrees to regulate the internal temperature during winter. Societies also use feedback mechanisms to adjust system operations: economic indicators to regulate business activity or voting records to improve election procedures. Machines depend on an energy source; as energy supplies diminish (batteries in the camera are used), the machine becomes inert. Social systems need supplies of physical and psychological energy to maintain a level of dynamic activity. Finally, applied systems theorists use machine imagery to judge the quality of system processes. Some social organizations, such as a decorated army division, function very effectively and might be compared to a well-oiled, technologically refined, high-performance machine (Rigney, 2001). Images of machine breakdown, damage to its parts, poor engineering or design, and insufficient power to ensure effective operation are used also to characterize dysfunctional societies or smaller social systems (White & Epston, 1990).

The organic tradition of systems theorizing compares society and other systems to an organism's body (Buckley, 1967). The parts/whole relationship is central to bodies and to social systems. Each can be characterized as interdependent parts that work together to produce a functioning whole (Rigney, 2001). Each includes smaller systems. The body has organs, such as the heart, and organ systems, such as the nervous and digestive system. A society includes individual members or citizens, families, friendship groups, and larger forms of association and organization. Bodily systems and societal systems have identifiable functions. The heart, for example, is an organ whose job is to pump blood throughout the body. The digestive system consists of various organs that enable the body to use food. The nervous system is made up of organs that carry messages from one part of the body to another. Just as the organs of the body are differentiated to perform the specialized functions necessary to the growth of the living organism, society has differentiated institutions (family households, business firms, governments) that are necessary to its effective functioning and to the well-being of its members (Holton, 1998; Martin & O'Connor, 1989).

Bodies and social systems have identifiable structures. The bodies of many species, for example, have skeletons. The skeleton is a bony and cartilaginous structure that orders the way that the body's internal systems are interrelated. A society's internal structure includes its gender structure, power and status hierarchy, and channels of communication. Many bodies have an exoskeleton, an exterior protective or supporting structure or shell. This structure influences how the organism connects to other systems in the environment. Societies have external structures, such as great walls, military fortifications, and checkpoints, that protect and that regulate the flow of people and goods into and out of the society.

Human bodies depend on feedback mechanisms. The brain, for example, automatically monitors significant departures from a state of homeostasis and activates corrective action to return the body to a balanced state. A body with an infection as indicated by a fever begins a healing process. Like the body, social systems have regulating mechanisms that can enable the system to return to a state of equilibrium after a disturbance. In the body, breathing regulates after a quick run, and body temperature returns to normal soon after stepping outside in very cold weather to pick up the newspaper. Social systems have similar social control and regulatory processes. When deviations from the "ideal" state of the country were caused by the political rebellion of counterculture advocates during the 1960s, the leaders of U.S. society mobilized responses using politics, media propaganda, and force to neutralize the elements that were disturbing the body politic and return the social system to a state of social order (Rigney, 2001). Applied systems theorists assume that alteration or removal of any element of a body or social system can change every other part, or even destroy the whole body or social organization (Pepper, 1942).

Finally, images of the quality of system processes are drawn from common understandings about the body. In a healthy body, all the organs operate together and effectively for the body's vitality and survival. In a healthy society, all parts of the society (the government, the educational institutions, the social welfare system) function smoothly with one another for the efficiency and survival of the whole society (Rigney, 2001). In a diseased or injured body, pain associated with one part is felt throughout the whole body; if the problem with the part is not remedied, then deterioration or death of the body may result. Societies and social systems are similar. Systems-oriented social workers watch for symptoms of social malaise and societal dysfunction (White & Epston, 1990).

Buckley (1967, 1998) believes that social systems are so complex that comparisons to machines and bodies are misleading. He proposes that we imagine a society as being like a species evolving in a particular environment. Societies and other forms of social organization are complex adaptive systems. The constant change, mutation, and inventiveness associated with species evolution provide apt images for understanding families, groups, organizations, and societies. Unlike mechanical systems, social systems and their members can create new and more complicated relations between parts. Social systems can regenerate when structures are damaged. They can devise and elaborate new and flexible structures in rapid response to changing environmental conditions. They can intentionally take actions to achieve new and more adaptive levels of organizational complexity. Unlike living organisms, a social system can change its structure extensively, not just within limited parameters. Like an evolving species, a social system, Buckley (1998) argues, "accumulates structures or internal changes, at the same time that new and competing or conflicting variations arise that may promote better, or worse, adaptation" (p. 32). Social work organizations can be compared to complex adaptive systems (Davidson, 1983). They display wholeness. They interact continuously with the external environment. They initiate strategies for adaptation and self-maintenance. They modify structures of labor, communication, affiliation, and power to fit into their environmental niches and to meet new internal and external challenges. They pass through phases of birth, growth, maturity, and decline. The best organized and most flexible agencies compete successfully and survive the longest.

THE PERSON AS A PART (MACHINE, BODY, OR SPECIES PART)

The person is a system, and applied system theorists compare people to machines, bodies, and species in the ways reviewed in the previous subsection. The person is also a part of a larger entity. The mechanical tradition compares the person to a robot programmed by a mechanical engineer to conform to a set of powerful societal directives (Holton, 1998). For human beings, however, the engineers are society's agents of socialization. The person's place in the community can be compared to a part of a machine. Parts are meshed and interlocked, and linkages cannot be easily broken (Rosenblatt, 1994). Completely severing ties from our neighborhood or family would be as difficult and problematic as removing a hard drive from a computer and expecting the computer to operate.

The person has also been compared to a body or an organ of the body. The person is not a freestanding and unchanging entity but is defined, like the heart or the eyeballs, by his or her interaction with other parts of a larger system (Rosenblatt, 1994). Finally, the person might be conceptualized as being like a species: a complex adaptive system continually restructuring him- or herself in response to changing environmental contingencies.

THE SOCIAL WORKER AS PARTS/WHOLE SPECIALIST (MECHANIC, DOCTOR, OR SYSTEMS ANALYST)

If a system is a machine, then the social worker is the mechanic. Social workers isolate the broken part causing problems with a family or group's functioning and repair the part (White & Epston, 1990). Social workers in leadership positions are like mechanical engineers who try to design smoothly functioning, efficient, and aesthetically pleasing machines. Social work activists and policy advocates attempt to make technical adjustments in the machinery of society so that the gap between our professional vision of an ideal social system and the performance of social machines is minimized (Price, 1997). Social workers might also be compared to a machine's feedback mechanisms. We help our clients steer toward desired goals, and we provide information to the system's decision-making centers by continual comparison of the current state of the client systems relative to social goals and policies (Rigney, 2001).

If a social system is like a body, then the social worker is a healer. We identify the pathology in a person, family, or larger social system. We develop a correct diagnosis of the specifics of the pathology and its contribution to system dysfunction. We operate or prescribe a medication that removes the pathological growth (White & Epston, 1990). Sometimes, a social worker becomes absorbed into a larger system (the client or organizational system) and, as a part of the larger system, loses some autonomy. As a part of a bigger whole, the worker's observations, helping skills, and reports become (like those of a doctor in a large hospital bureaucracy) subject to and influenced by the needs and constraints of that encompassing system (Gergen, 1990).

Finally, the social worker might be compared to a systems analyst or engineer. Systems engineering is the "scientific planning, design, evaluation, and construction of man-machine systems" (Bertalanffy, 1969, p. 91). Systems-oriented social workers specialize in the study of how the parts of a social system work together to ensure the system's adaptation. The mission of the social work systems analyst is to find the best way for a system to accomplish its task while maintaining optimal relations among the parts. For example, a social agency is a system that includes administrators, social workers, clients, and the physical building cooperating to actualize the agency mission. Systems analysts can help develop agency policies, procedures, and schedules that make the most efficient, effective, and harmonious use of the subsystems and the environment.

THE SYSTEMS THEORY AS A SKELETON

Systems theorists use their metaphoric imagination also to describe the contribution of this theoretical approach to the social work knowledge-building enterprise. Other theorists discussed in this textbook do not attempt this metaphorical project. Systems theory is like a skeleton (Anderson & Carter, 1990) to which social work theorists, researchers, and practitioners can add other theories and concepts. The additions are like flesh, and the combination of this flesh with the bones of the skeleton becomes a comprehensive theoretical perspective that explains all aspects of human behavior and the environment.

Systems theory is the skeletal framework for organizing other theories about the social world, from theories of the individual to theories of society and its policy-making organizations (Martin & O'Connor, 1989). Because systems theory is a general and content-free conceptual framework, benefits accrue from the addition to the basic skeleton of substantive theories appropriate to different levels of social organizations and different social processes. Applied systems theory is an abstract or conceptual framework that "can integrate the range of knowledge from various fields (biological, psychological, social, and cultural)" and thus "advance and unify social work theory" (Stein, 1974, p. 34). Social work theory synthesizers become like Doctor Frankenstein, adding some muscles from symbolic interactionism, some internal organs from behaviorism, and some brain tissues from cognitive psychology to turn the systems theory skeleton into a living creature.

CORE ASSUMPTIONS OF APPLIED SYSTEMS THEORY

Applied systems theorists such as Ludwig von Bertalanffy broke from the reductionistic models of human behavior and social life presented by Freud and Pavlov. They offered instead a "science of social systems" (Bertalanffy, 1969, p. 195) with its radically different set of core assumptions about the human organism, social organizations, and the knowledge-building process. This section summarizes the basic premises on which the logical edifice of applied systems theory is built.

THE REALM OF THE LIVING IS CHARACTERIZED BY ISOMORPHISM

Isomorphism refers to the theoretical expectation of basic similarities across systems of different types and sizes. Social work system theorists Martin and O'Connor (1989, p. 50) summarize this assumption by indicating that "all living systems share similarities of form or structure with all other living systems." Hearn (1969b, p. 2) offers a similar synopsis: "matter, in all its forms, living and non-living, can be regarded as systems, and systems as systems, have certain discrete properties that are capable of being studied. Individuals, small groups—including families and organizations—in short, the entities with which social work is usually involved—can all be regarded as systems, with certain common properties."

There is a general or common order in the world, and all living systems manifest this order (Norlin, Chess, Dale, & Smith, 2003). Whatever the kind of system, it participates in and is shaped by this greater order (Davidson, 1983). For example, all systems are purposive or goal-oriented. All systems are organized. Units or components of all systems are arranged in an identifiable way rather than in a random manner. All systems, whatever their size, process input, perform transformations, produce output, regulate energy flows, and manage boundaries.

The assumption of isomorphism creates the possibility of a common analytic approach and a common theoretical vocabulary—one that can be used to describe the human body, the person, the family, the social work agency, and the international partnerships of states (Chetkow-Yanoov, 1992). By adopting the systems approach, representatives of different scientific disciplines might communicate with each other using this shared language (Buckley, 1967). Social workers and applied scientists, who had been divided by their different languages (the lexicons of casework, group work, and community organization, for example), could use the general knowledge base provided by systems theory for cooperation despite specialization. My use in this book of the eco-map and ecosystems constructs as cross-theory translators assumes isomorphism.

EMERGENCE CHARACTERIZES SYSTEMS

New properties emerge from the dynamic interaction of the components of a system. These properties are not apparent when the components act independently of one another (Buckley, 1968). In the social sphere, cultural and interactional properties arise from the interaction of members of a newly formed social system (Martin & O'Connor, 1989). A sense of family emerges when two adults unite and create or adopt children (Rosenblatt, 1994). This family develops creatively shared purposes, role patterns, group rules, collective traditions, meaningful symbols, and ways of doing things that reflect the whole system. Friends could not have predicted the emergence of these properties using their prefamily understanding of each adult's personality.

The assumption of emergence can also be explained by use of the systems concept of **nonsummativity** (Hanson, 1995). The whole becomes greater than the sum of the parts. Just add up the parts, and something is missing. In the words of Bertalanffy's biographer, systems theorists assert that "in a system, one plus one equals two *plus*" (Davidson, 1983, p. 28). As discussed earlier, the musical group, the Beatles, for example, became significantly more than the sum of its four distinct musical personalities: John, Paul, George, and Ringo. Family social workers endorsing this assumption, then, would consider "How does the whole family operate?" and "What is best for the whole family?" when assessing and helping client families. Family social workers would also monitor the family group properties that emerge and change over time as family members interact and respond to environmental and developmental pressures and opportunities.

A DYNAMIC OR PROCESS ORIENTATION

Social systems are different from mechanical and nonhuman systems. In contrast to closed systems designed to maintain equilibrium, sociocultural adaptive systems are best understood in terms of continual change not stability (Buckley, 1968). Social systems are dynamic. They are characterized by the constant interaction of parts, the continual interplay of internal and external influences, and ceaseless accommodation of each part in the system to the other parts and of the system to the environment.

This dynamic orientation directs social work attention to "the actions and interactions of the components of an ongoing system, such that varying degrees of structuring arise, persist, dissolve, or change" (Buckley, 1967, p. 19). Even social structure should be conceptualized in process terms. Identifying a structure—for example, an agency's division of labor—is like taking a snapshot of arrangements frozen in time and place. It is an artificial observation. The organizational chart you create needs frequent revision because work arrangements are continually changing. Structure is a halted process. An ideal systems assessment would require videotaping and documenting the structural changes characterizing the organization, the "moving reality" (Buckley, 1967, p. 21). Then, you might capture the frequent adjustments in role definitions and expectations, the addition and departure of personnel, the changing work team alliances, and the emergence of new communication patterns and styles.

What appears to be structure in social systems is actually an ongoing set of social processes. For the observer, structure is a freeze-frame of the organization's changing life, an abstract construct providing only a "temporary, accommodative representation of it [ongoing interactive process] at any one time" (Buckley, 1967, p. 18). Structure depicts "a relative stability of underlying, ongoing micro-processes" (Buckley, 1968, p. 497). But change and instability characterize systems as much as freedom from variation. Society, for instance, is not a composite of stable structures but "a complex, multifaceted, fluid interplay of widely varying degrees and intensities of association and disassociation" (Buckley, 1967, p. 18).

Two primary and competing processes characterize social systems. The first set is **morphostasis,** the structure-preserving tendency. These processes maintain existing and characteristic structures of the system and tend to prevent significant change in its organization (Buckley, 1998). For example, a violent father has sufficient power and resources to overcome and counteract the mother's pleas and the social worker's efforts to change a family structure based on inequality and physical domination. The second is **morphogenesis,** the structure-elaborating and -changing tendency. Morphogenic processes are very important in social systems. Buckley (1968) summed up this basic principle: "the persistence and/or development of the complex sociocultural system depends upon structuring, destructuring, and restructuring—processes occurring at widely varying rates and degrees as a function of the external social and non-social environment" (p. 495). Effective systems change structure adaptively, resulting in improvements in system regulation and goal attainment. For example, the violent father chooses not to take defensive countermeasures to those of an allied team of children, mother, and social worker. He yields to their restructuring efforts designed to eliminate violence by distributing family power to all members and by accepting the role of the court as monitor. Whole family functioning improves.

The Social Universe Is Governed by a Cybernetic Hierarchy

This assumption has two parts. First, applied systems theorists assume that the social universe is like a ladder, with systems increasing in size and complexity as they are placed closer to the top (Martin & O'Connor, 1989). There is an order to the universe, with the smallest forms of life (chemical building blocks of cells, single-celled organisms) at the bottom of the ladder and the most complex forms (human societies, or the earth's biosphere) at the top (Davidson, 1983). The concept of **system level** refers to a particular system's place in this abstract hierarchy. Some systems theorists add to the metaphor of the ladder the imagery of nesting, with one system nested in the next bigger one like a set of Chinese boxes.

Second, the assumption of cybernetic hierarchy means that larger systems, those higher on the ladder, constrain or limit their included subsystems. Smaller systems, those lower on the ladder, are embedded in the larger systems, and the opportunities, choices, goals, and behaviors for the smaller system are influenced by pressures and preferences from the larger system. Talcott Parsons used the concept of **cybernetic hierarchy** to explain the ordered rule systems that integrate elements of a society (Turner, 2002). *Cybernetic* refers to the use of information for control or guidance purposes. At the high level, we find a society's culture, language, and generalized values. These forms of information provide very general statements of desirable action and direct the lower-level systems. At the medium level, systems such as social institutions and organizations generate more specific statements of preferred and prohibited action. Such norms may take the form of information about ideologies, ordinances, or professional codes of conduct. These norms direct lower-level systems. At the lower level, small groups define how to engage in specific role performances in socially acceptable or socially deviant ways. The lowest level of social interaction, two-person encounters in dyadic, group, or family systems, provides interpersonal information and guidelines for categorizing, communicating via talk and body language, and expressing emotions. These behaviors are responsive to higher-level information and standards transmitted from the culture and from institutions. However, the distance of encounters from the centers of decision making at the top allows some creative variation from orders. The hierarchy of information controls embedded systems. It changes from general to specific, from shared as a common culture to increasingly distinctive subcultures, from highly influential constraints on the entire society and subsystems at the top of the ladder to less powerful constraints on those lower in the hierarchy. The use of the prefix *sub* in *subsystem* refers to a system's place in the cybernetic hierarchy and indicates that it is beneath, less than, and part of something bigger (Rosenblatt, 1994). Whether a subdivision in a larger city or a subcommittee of a larger board of directors, the subsystem is constrained by its embeddedness in larger wholes.

A Parts/Whole Approach Is the Preferred Scientific Method

A **system** can be defined simply as "a whole made up of interdependent and interacting parts" (Stein, 1974, p. 3). We have discussed the assumption of emergence. Applied systems theorists also assume that parts and wholes cannot be meaningfully separated without destroying something essential. Systemic analysis or assessment, therefore, involves using our intellectual capacities to recognize the coherence of parts in relation to the whole. Systems analysis also involves a search for functional explanations, the identification of the contribution of parts to the adaptedness and survival of the whole (Hanson, 1995).

Holon is a concept indicating that a living entity can be both a part and a whole (Hearn, 1979). The family as a part contributes to the larger systems in which it is embedded, such as the neighborhood and the church. The family as a whole includes smaller subsystems such as the husband–wife dyad, the sibling unit, and the individual member. These subsystems are essential to the healthy functioning of the family. I have used the concept of **focal system** in a way equivalent to holon. The part/whole approach requires the social worker to shift perspective repeatedly from the holon to the larger whole and from the holon to its constituent parts. Assessment of the members as discrete or separate individuals is not sufficient. Relational units or subsystems are part of a "system of interweaving forces, all having reciprocity and feedback with each other" (Meyer, 1976, p. 135). To understand the behavior of members of a bereavement group, for example, the social worker will inquire about their relationships with each other in subsystems, their relationship to the whole group, and the dynamic characteristics of the counseling group.

For adherents to the parts/whole approach (Pepper, 1942), the part implies the whole and the whole implies the part. When we meet with an angry child, we appreciate that the child is a part of and influenced by the larger family. When we observe the family negotiating a conflict, we understand that successful negotiations depend on the commitment of each member and that agreements will affect each member. Applied systems theorists are reluctant to assign blame for interaction difficulties to only one member of a system (Buckley, 1998). Responsibility is both personal and shared. System patterns explain troubles, distress, or immorality, as does individual choice. Parts/whole thinking adds the notion of system self-determination to the social work value of individual self-determination.

CAUSATION IS REVERBERATIVE NOT LINEAR

Comparisons to echoes will help us understand this assumption. Imagine a noisy client on a field trip to an underground cave. We discourage his or her shouting. A loud and obnoxious shout not only may cause other cave explorers to react with irritation, but it may echo back and bother the original shouter. The noise may even bounce around the cave, gain in amplification, and cause some rocks to dislodge. The returning noise may cycle back and cause the initiator of the chain reaction to shout again, but this time in fear. Other actions of and communications by members of the field expedition may reverberate through the entire cave chamber, leading sometimes to unpredictable effects and sometimes to effects that are precisely the opposite of the desired or intended effect. The commotion may become so intense that park rangers outside the system of caves are alerted.

Small changes by a member of a social system are like shouts that can be amplified through systemic interactions and later make a big difference to the whole system (Franklin & Warren, 1999). Effects may be unpredictable. This approach to causation differs from the conventional linear assumption that an independent variable, x, causes changes in a dependent value, y. Events that happen to one part of a system affect all parts (y_1, y_2, y_3, and x), directly or indirectly (Martin & O'Conner, 1989). Causal paths are multiple and multidirectional: "A change in any part of the causal network affects other parts" (Anderson & Carter, 1990, p. 6). Identifying or predicting causal patterns is a very complex job. Such work requires sophisticated nonlinear mathematical tools such as logistic equations and fractal geometry (Franklin & Warren, 1999).

Systems theorists are interested in circular causal chains, in which "the effect of an event or variable returns indirectly to influence the original event itself by the way of one or more intermediate events or variables" (Buckley, 1967, p. 69). They also study more complex **feedback loops** in which goal states and standards are set. Test procedures are developed. Information as signals or symbols is checked continuously by the test procedures. Information is fed back to the decision centers. Behavior or output is continually adjusted because of the match or mismatch between the desired goal state and information regarding the actual state.

Components of a system are linked like points in a circle, with no indication of a beginning or end point and no obvious way of deciding that interaction patterns started with one person or another (Rosenblatt, 1994). A client's troubles are associated, for example, with an intricate network of direct and indirect influences rather than with a single causal agent. We can punctuate a sequence of interaction in a system. A child hits her brother—father yells—child cries—mother comforts—mother and father argue—child leaves—father follows child and resumes disciplining her—mother withdraws from interaction (Miller, 1997). The circle can be artificially broken by this punctuation for the sake of analysis. Causation can be traced conventionally in a line from a system member to a system member. But this vastly simplifies the actual reverberative causal processes operative in the family system.

Systems Principles Define the Social Worker Role and Relationship

Remember that the concept of **system dynamics** means that a social system, the relationships among its internal components, and its relationships with the external environment are in constant motion (Norlin et al., 2003). Systems theorists assume that the social worker becomes an "action intersystem" between the agency system, the client system, and environmental systems (Artinian, 1997; Gordon, 1969). As the worker system and client system form a helping system supported and constrained by the social agency, new system processes and dynamics emerge. The worker must monitor communication, value formation, norm creation and regulation, role allocation and other system dynamics and make judgments about whether these are functional or dysfunctional for the triad of related social systems.

Applied systems theorists assume, too, that the social worker influences and is influenced by the client system. The systems-oriented social worker negotiates a position in the helping system respecting the connections and obligations both to the agency and to the client. The social worker seeks a degree of interdependence with clients in the helping system but also a degree of autonomy so that client system imperatives do not determine worker action. In a sense, the worker straddles the client system fence and situates himself or herself both inside and outside the client system boundaries. I will discuss the applied systems perspective on social work and the helping process in greater detail in the mapping section.

THE SYSTEMS MODEL OF HUMAN AND FAMILY DEVELOPMENT

With the exception of Talcott Parsons, applied systems theorists provide little information regarding their theoretical approach to individual development and the human life cycle. However, many family scientists have been inspired by Parsons' work and used it to develop a model of family system development. I will review Parsons' model of socialization and its components, and I will provide a briefer overview of the family systems approach to change across the family life cycle.

EXEMPLAR: THE TRADITION OF DEVELOPMENTAL SYSTEMS THEORY

You have already met our exemplary human development theorist, Talcott Parsons. No single theorist or theory user is credited with the systemization of the model of family development. Reuben Hill and Paul Mattessich (1979) identify many contributors, however, including Evelyn Duvall, Joan Aldous, Roy Rodgers, and Reuben Hill.

ASSUMPTIONS OF THE SYSTEMS MODEL OF DEVELOPMENT

Talcott Parsons (1968) assumes that a human society is made possible because its members share normative beliefs and standards. The society's survival requires a high degree of integration of its members as parts into the whole society. Integrated actors share cultural values, expectations regarding appropriate behavior, and the motivation to meet societal demands. Thereby, they can contribute to the self-regulation and adaptation of the society and its smaller social systems.

This structural functionalist model assumes that societies aim to ensure that their central values and shared cultural beliefs are transmitted across generations (Lidz, 2000). Certain social institutions—family, kinship, religion, and education—take the central roles in carrying out this task. Parsons proposed that socialization is the major method by which individual members develop their commitments to systemic beliefs, values, norms, and behavior patterns. Socialization contributes to social continuity and order through an "interpenetration of social system, personality, and culture" (Parsons, 1968, p. 58). At the local level, for example, each social institution authorizes agents of socialization to engage members in socialization processes in specific socialization contexts. Parents function on society's behalf as socialization agents in the household and the family. Teachers function as socialization agents in school settings.

Structural functionalists assume that socialization is a lifelong process (Ritzer, 1996). **Primary socialization** during childhood induces children to adopt the society's general norms and values as transmitted through the family. In adolescence and adulthood, however, societal members will be required to participate competently in numerous other social systems. **Secondary socialization** meets this system need by providing the specific socializing experiences necessary for members to perform roles in peer groups, intimate relationships, the military, the workplace, a social work agency, and other social systems. Novices to the society, children or immigrants, participate in multistage, dynamic processes of learning the values and norms necessary for full membership (Lidz, 2000). The developmental progression in U.S. society typically goes from the mother–child system to the parent–child system, then the parents and siblings system, the extended family system, the peer system, the local community systems, and eventually to voluntary associations and business firms. The right to social membership as a participating citizen is earned through this long socialization process.

Parsons has been criticized for his characterization of the socialized member as a passive recipient in the process of psychosocial development (Ritzer, 1996). Ritzer notes that socialization as conceptualized by Parsons is a conservative process during which need dispositions are channeled to bind children to the social system. Allowance for the creativity of the societal member is minimal. Critics reject this assumption that system members are fully socialized and that powerful superegos compel them to obey all social dictates. Parsons depicts a harmonious interplay of the three major systems working to integrate all subsystems: The personality system assumes the task of internalizing core values; the social system assumes the task of coordinating the actions of diverse members thanks to shared values; and the cultural system assumes the task of facilitating the affirmation by social systems of the significant and central values of the superordinate society. This assumption of harmony downplays the conflicts, discontinuities, and failures common to the socialization process, especially in pluralistic societies.

Family theorists go beyond Parsons' foundational convictions. Family life cycle scholars and researchers assume that not only does the individual family member develop over time but family subsystems, such as the parent–child dyad or the husband–wife unit, and the entire family change in somewhat predictable ways (Klein & White, 1996). Family theorists also assume that the family is a semiclosed social group. The family system is affected in its development by external social systems such as the culture's norms for parental discipline. The family system and family dynamics are also influenced powerfully by within-group processes, activated often by the individual developmental transformations of each member.

ROOT METAPHORS OF THE SYSTEMS MODEL OF DEVELOPMENT

How does a society achieve a high degree of orderliness and integration? The core metaphor is socialization. **Socialization** is the process that facilitates member internalization of what is necessary for conformity to the social system. It involves teaching novices how to perform as competent and responsible system members (Parsons & Bales, 1955). The person is compared to either a socialized member or an agent of socialization. The environment is the context for socialization and includes numerous systems of socialization. Social workers and other human services professionals operate as consultants to agents of socialization such as parents, schoolteachers, and recreational leaders, or social workers may serve as agents of resocialization in correctional or psychiatric settings. When socialization is effective, the leaders of the social system need not use more severe methods of social control (imprisonment or banishment, for example) to bring the members' conduct in line with common standards.

Family systems theorists build on the imagery and ideas associated with the metaphor of "the family as a system moving through time" (Carter & McGoldrick, 1999, p. 1). In contrast to other social systems, members of the family group have a shared history and a shared future. Members are bound to the family—at least symbolically—for life, and members are connected across multiple generations. The family's movement through time requires continual system adjustments to the addition or deletion of members, to the maturation of members, to the age-based changes in the expectations associated with family roles, and to alterations in family members' linkages to external systems such as the school and workplace (Falicov, 1988). Family members may travel across time together, but the vehicle they use must be reconfigured regularly so that its structure and functions are suitable for the changing travel conditions. The two-seater Miata is replaced by a four-door Honda Accord, and then replaced again by a Ford sport utility vehicle, and the parents conclude their car purchasing with a silver Airstream motor home for recreational adventures.

Family theorists consider daily, weekly, and seasonal temporal changes as important in family studies (Duvall, 1962, 1977). However, this model prioritizes the assumption that "much as each individual who grows, develops, matures, and ages undergoes the same successive changes and readjustments from conception to senescence as every other individual, the life cycles of individual families follow a universal sequence of family development" (Duvall, 1977, p. 141). Recently, family theorists have tempered this assumption of universality by emphasizing the variations from the traditional family career and providing an "expanded family life cycle" (Carter & McGoldrick, 1999, p. 9).

THE SYSTEMS MODEL OF DEVELOPMENT

The applied systems model of human development uses concepts such as *socialization, social position, social norm, social role,* and *social system.* Parsons and Bales (1955) illustrate their model of socialization dynamics by reference to the family. The family structure includes positions such as husband, wife, father, mother, son, daughter, brother, and sister (Klein & White, 1996). The general procedure for socialization is straightforward, involving interaction between members in the complementary parent and child positions. Parents use social interaction to motivate their children to form attachments to the parents, to use the mother and father as role models of appropriate system behavior, and to learn to conform to the social norms related to smooth family system functioning.

Parsons and Bales (1955) outline the series of system and member changes necessary for successful socialization. The family begins in a stable state. Role allocation and the acceptance of role assignments, such as that of nurturing mother, precede the initiation of socialization activities. A disturbance occurs in the family's steady state. For example, the newborn infant begins to mature and the parents start to articulate new role expectations for the child's participation in the family system. The family then restructures itself by altering the roles in the primary socializing subsystem (the mother–child interaction system) to make possible the achievement of the parents' socialization goals. For example, the mother begins to use love and sanctions purposely to shape the child's membership performance. The child had also been in a state of personality equilibrium. New demands from the mother, however, shake the child out of her old personality equilibrium. The child changes in response to new system conditions by making preliminary adjustments in her behavior. Some changes result from trial and error. Some result from direct teaching. Some are functional, and some are dysfunctional. With the guidance of socialization agents, the mother first and eventually the father, according to Parsons and Bales, the child liquidates her old ways of integrating into the family system. She learns to channel needs into role performances that result in gratifications from the family system. The family achieves a new level of organization with this successful integration of the infant into the child role, and the child consolidates the personality structure necessary to maintain her contribution to family functioning. This socialization process is repeated across the family's development as new roles emerge.

Family life cycle theorists would add the concept of **family developmental task** to the Parsonian model. Every family must come to terms with tasks essential for the continuity of the family system (Duvall, 1962). These tasks include socialization and the physical care of members, the allocation of resources to meet member needs, the division of labor, the maintenance of orderly interaction patterns, the incorporation of new members and release of departing members, the linking of members to external social institutions and systems, and the maintenance of member morale and motivation to enact family roles. To return to our metaphor of a system moving through time, family system theorists add that family groups must continually find ways to mesh their developmental tasks as these change in importance and in difficulty for the individuals, dyads, and whole group (Aldous, 1978; Hill & Mattessich, 1979).

Family scholars have identified many propositions that link concepts in systems models of development. I will present here a few illustrations. First, social norms govern the sequence of family events across its life (Klein & White, 1996). If a member or family is "out of sequence," there is a greater likelihood of later problems with family functioning. For example, 20 years ago, Americans expected a couple to marry, then to cohabitate, and then to have children. Couples who violated this normative sequence were vulnerable to family dysfunction. Second, Hill and Mattessich (1979) posit that the interrelationship of number of persons, personalities, family rules, and position-based roles varies in complexity across the family's history. During family stages with a high degree of complexity, such as the "family with adolescents" period, the pressures of adapting to such complexity often results in individual and marital dysfunction. Finally, families face greater difficulty in reorganizing the family's structure and functions during the transitions from one family stage to the next than during the actual family stage (Falicov, 1988).

CRITICAL COMMENTS

In my presentation of the systems model of human and family development, I have identified several weaknesses. Parsons and his associates assume social harmony and underestimate the disagreements and conflicts that complicate the socialization process. They characterize the socialized member as passively subject to the wills of socialization agents. They conceptualize the family system using a conventional matching of males and females to group roles (mother as nurturing sustainer and father as breadwinner, for example) rather than allowing for the flexibility and variety of contemporary role assignments.

Yoels and Karp (1978) expand the critique of the Parsonian image of a passive and oversocialized person. The systems model assumes that a person is totally shaped by social forces and complies with communal rules. It offers no explanation of nonconformity. Yoels and Karp argue that a comprehensive model of socialization must account for human novelty and disobedience. Three social processes associated with the human capacity for symbolization contribute to instabilities in socialization. First, the person can replace the symbols taught by members of immediate social systems with symbols provided by remote or imagined reference groups. An artist, for example, can reject the values and norms of his family and friends while embracing those of innovative artistic predecessors. Second, the person belongs to many different membership groups, and contrary to Parsons' assumption of shared norms, each has a distinctive culture. The gay client rejected by his parents and the larger society can join a supportive circle of homosexuals and embrace their counterculture norms. Finally, each generation experiences a common set of historical events that differ from those experienced by previous and successor generations. Reality for parents socialized during an economic depression is unlike the reality of life for children maturing during an age of abundance. The human capacity for switching mental allegiances, the availability of divergent social worlds, and the conditioning effect of history on socialization agents add a degree of uncertainty to a society's socialization processes and outcomes neglected by Talcott Parsons.

APPLICATION OF THE SYSTEMS MODEL OF DEVELOPMENT

Contemporary social workers make infrequent use of Parsons' model of human development in practice. Models developed by Piaget or Erikson, discussed in later chapters, are much more popular. Social workers do make much use, however, of the family systems model of human development. At the end of this chapter, I present and discuss in detail David Olson's influential theory application, a blend of family systems assumptions and concepts with the assumptions and concepts of the family development model.

MAPPING APPLIED SYSTEMS THEORY

Figure 5.1 shows the eco-map adapted for applied systems theory. This section also offers answers from the perspective of applied systems theory to our translation questions.

FIGURE 5.1
THE APPLIED
SYSTEMS
THEORY
VERSION OF
THE ECO-MAP

Source: Adapted with
permission from *Family-
Centered Social Work
Practice* (p. 160) by
A. Hartman and J. Laird,
1983. New York:
The Free Press.

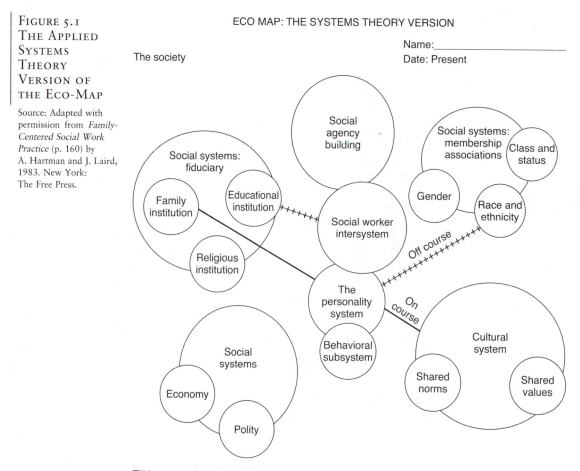

ECO MAP: THE SYSTEMS THEORY VERSION

Name:_____

Date: Present

Fill in connections where they exist.
Indicate nature of connections with a descriptive word or by drawing different kinds of lines:
——————— for on course and functional transactions
+++++++ for off course and dysfunctional transactions
---------- for unguided and nonfunctional transactions
Draw arrows along lines to signify flow of system resources → → →

HOW ARE CONNECTIONS CONCEPTUALIZED?

Living systems are connected to each other and the environment by energy
exchanges. For human systems and social systems composed of people,
information is the most important form of energy. **Information** refers to bits of
data conveyed in verbal language, written reports, nonverbal communication,
or other media formats (Hanson, 1995). Information exchanged between
systems serves as the binding or connecting force (Anderson & Carter, 1990).
The internal components of a social system are linked by information, and the
focal system's links to the environment are based on information (Buckley,
1967). Attending to all the information in the environment would cause a

system overload, so social systems continually sample and select subsets of the available information and then construct the signals and the symbols received into usable patterns (Buckley, 1998).

The following model describes the information processes that bind the social system to the environment. Applied social systems theorists assume that social systems are purposive (Walrond-Skinner, 1979). So, information selection and use vary depending on the system's **goal direction** (Artinian, 1997).

The system detects relevant information by scanning the internal and external environment. This information matches the system's goals, perspectives, and values. Selected information is called **input**. Informational input assumes various forms (grades, a recipe book, client satisfaction reports), and it is absorbed by the social system (Chetkow-Yanoov, 1992; Lathrope, 1969).

The social system activates conversion processes by which the system begins to make use of the input. Information transformation involves decoding, organizing, processing, integrating, and using the information according to the system's information transformation rules. The information is called **through-put** at this point in the cycle, and the **conversion operations** are defined as the means employed to transform inputs into outputs (Norlin et al., 2003). The social work student thinks about a teacher's comments regarding school performance. A couple uses the recipe and figures out how to prepare a meal. An agency team receives an accreditation report and appraises, deliberates, and decides what to do with the information.

Information **output** is the product exported from the system across its boundaries to the outside environment. Outputs might include homework, a meal for visitors, or a new intake policy. Information output is the outcome or results of the conversion process, the ways that a social system acts back on environment. Applied systems theorists differentiate output into desired or planned output and actual output.

Systems often feed back information output to the system decision centers. This helps the decision center judge and control system activity, and the information processing cycle begins again. **Linkages** are formed between internal subsystems and between the system and other systems in the environment when there are repeated information exchanges.

How Is the Quality of Connections Differentiated?

The quality of connections can be appraised in two ways: feedback and functionality. **Feedback** is the most critical form of information. Feedback is information from the internal and external environment used by the system to steer itself (Hanson, 1995; Rosenblatt, 1994). The example of a thermostat guiding the operation of a furnace to meet a temperature standard is often used to explain mechanical feedback. Biofeedback illustrates feedback in human systems. Biofeedback is the therapeutic use of information. A machine enhances monitoring of a client's heart rate and blood pressure. Using this information coupled with relaxation techniques, the client learns to intentionally change his or her body rates and thus reduce stress. Humans also engage in cybernetic self-guidance when they depend on feedback (real or imagined) from significant others, reference groups, and generalized others in response to their own actions during social interaction. Representative democracy institutionalizes procedures by which citizens provide feedback to elected officials about policies and programs.

Feedback processes allow a social system to be self-adjusting and regulate its behavior by using information to identify deviations or mismatches from desired internal states, desired overt behaviors, or desired environmental conditions (Buckley, 1967). Feedback serves system-correcting and steering purposes relative to the goal-directed activity. You can think of feedback also as a tool used by agency administrators to answer important questions. Is the organizational system on track in moving toward its goals? Is the organizational system maintaining itself in the ways desired by its members? (Norlin et al., 2003).

Feedback has been categorized as positive or negative, deviation amplifying or deviation reducing, match or mismatch, and error or correct appraisal, but these terms can be confusing. The judgment of positive or negative, for example, depends on the effects of the feedback on the system, not on its informational content. I will use the terms *on-course feedback* and *off-course feedback* to provide a simpler distinction.

On-course feedback indicates system movement toward its goals. The social system is moving in the right direction, producing a detectable reduction in the deviation between desired output and actual output (Rigney, 2001). An example would be a decrease in the distance between the family system and its ideal economic state (Rosenblatt, 1994). This information indicates that the system should maintain existing system arrangements and activities. If a client reports that the planned change activities are achieving desired result (a reduction in temper tantrums), there is no need to change the intervention or the helping relationship.

Off-course feedback indicates that a system is moving in a direction away from its goal. Achieving the goal is becoming more difficult; the distance between the actual state and the desired state is growing (Rosenblatt, 1994); the deviation between actual output and desired output is increasing (Norlin et al., 2003). Social systems can use such feedback to change directions. If a client reports that current interventions are not achieving the desired result (a reduction in temper tantrums), this feedback indicates a need to reassess and review interventions, and then to revise the planned change process.

Noise refers to information that cannot be used by the system. The data have no decipherable meaning. Internal or external events cannot be processed and converted into usable information (Buckley, 1998). The client reports confusing and mixed signals about his progress, or starts speaking in tongues, or lies so often that the worker cannot determine veracity. The worker has trouble deciding if the helping system is on course or off course. If this continues, the system becomes uncontrolled, like a runaway missile, and completely unable to use information from the environment to appraise goal-directed activity (Buckley, 1998).

On-course feedback is good from the point of view of the system, and off-course feedback is bad. However, systems-oriented social workers must consider the system goals, the system goal-achieving processes, and the surrounding context to know whether the course is a socially acceptable, cost-effective, and realistic path.

Applied systems theorists also judge connections by considering the functionality of ties between subsystems and between the system and other systems in the environment. **Function** refers to the contribution of a part to the operation or functioning of the whole, the contribution of system processes to the state of the whole system (Buckley, 1998). A system has functional prerequisites or imperatives, conditions that must be met for its persistence as a system (Buckley, 1967). Certain problems must be solved if a social system is to survive and maintain a viable organization. For example, a society has certain needs in that certain activities must be carried out for communal life to continue. Goods and services must be produced and distributed for an economy to remain viable. A society must have some administration of justice to ensure order, a political system to handle governance, and a family institution to reproduce the population. A society's parts—businesses, courts, governments, families—function for the society's benefit by performing tasks that meet critical needs.

Careful consideration of the function of an integrated mechanical-social system might help us here (Churchman, 1968). Instead of defining a bus simply as tires, engine, cabin with seats, and so on, we can examine the function of a bus and define it as a mechanical means of transporting groups of people from one place to another. We can then ask functional questions: Does a particular bus or bus company meet its function well and transport agency clients across the region, or is it failing to function effectively and efficiently? Does the bus system contribute to the community's well-being?

Talcott Parsons (1973) theorized that a social system only survives by dealing with four functional imperatives: adaptation, goal attainment, integration, and latency (pattern maintenance and tension management). His framework became known as the AGIL approach. Each social system exists in a physical and social environment, and must adapt to this environment. **Adaptation** refers to processes of gaining control over conditions in the environment, including resource generation and resource allocation. Private practitioners often join for-profit practices so that they can adapt to continually changing managed care policies and economic conditions. Each social system has certain purposes. A social system's **goal attainment** refers to systemic processes activated to satisfy needs, create desirable conditions, and pursue opportunities by organizing the activities of the member units into coordinated and purposeful action. The goals of the system must be defined, means of attempting to achieve these goals must be laid out, and then these goals must be pursued. A board of directors and the executive director of a social agency, for example, cooperate to develop the agency mission and facilitate goal-achieving processes. Social systems also need to coordinate, adjust, and regulate relationships among components within the system. **Integration** of the social system refers to the processes by which components of the system (subsystems) are adjusted to one another. Integration is similar to internal harmony and unity at the level of the individual system. The **latency** or pattern maintenance function refers to the system's processes for generating commitments to the system's distinctive values and principles of action so as to perpetuate preferred patterns of operation. Schools, universities, and religious organizations work to stimulate and channel the motivation of individuals and support the cultural beliefs and traditions that sustain this motivation.

Applied systems theorists suggest that social workers evaluate connections by asking what function—adaptation, goal attainment, integration, or latency—the connections fulfill. Functions, the consequences of the action or a part for the whole, may be functional, dysfunctional, or irrelevant. We have discussed and illustrated **functional** connections in the last paragraph. **Dysfunctional** connections are actions and processes of parts that are detrimental to the operation and maintenance of the whole system. **Nonfunctional** connections are those that have no identifiable consequences for the linked systems.

WHAT IS THE TYPICAL FOCAL SYSTEM?

Applied ecological theorists ask the social worker to use two lenses and focus on both the person and the environment. Applied systems theorists are more demanding. They mandate a simultaneous focus on multiple systems. Hartman's (1978) eco-map exemplifies this approach. The social worker directs attention to the client seeking help.

Simultaneously, the practitioner monitors related social systems, including friends, family members, the workplace, religious and recreational organizations, and the social welfare system. Any social system might request agency services and earn center place in the eco-map. However, Hartman, a family social worker, asserted that the family was the most typical client system.

The systems imagery of nesting also indicates the need for multifocal assessment and intervention. When a family seeks help, the worker alternates attention between the whole family; the systems nested within the family, such as the marital dyad and the individual members; and the systems within which the family is nested, including the community, informal and formal organizations, and society. The action of smaller systems is conditioned by bigger systems, and the smaller systems act back on or resist the elements of the larger nest. The social worker focusing only on the client system betrays this systems theory parts/whole logic.

HOW IS THE ENVIRONMENT CONCEPTUALIZED?

Environments contain social systems. Let's review definitions. A system is "a set of components and forces interacting among themselves and with an environment to produce some kind of holistic behavior which is often self-regulating and/or adaptive" (Buckley, 1998, p. 28). A **social system** is "a system composed of human beings and the products of their interaction over time" (Martin & O'Connor, 1989, p. 38). The products may include values, norms, roles, and patterns of interaction. Social systems have also been defined as "phenomena that include at least two people (spatiality) who associate with each other (organization) over time (constancy), who are set off from nonsystem members in some way (boundary), and whose association affects all members (mutual causality)" (Martin & O'Connor, 1989, p. 38).

Applied social systems theorists such as Parsons considered the society as the largest system (Lidz, 2000), but we might now view the world community of societies as the encompassing macro-level social environment. This environment is built, like an organism, from many parts. Rigney (2001) writes, "In an organism, cells combine to form tissues, tissues to form organs, and organs to form the organism as a whole. Similarly, in societies individuals combine to form associations based on shared characteristics, associations combine to form institutions, and institutions combine to constitute society as a whole" (p. 18). The environment includes social entities (actual groups or organizations) and social processes, including the continual processes of interaction among component parts, between the whole society and the parts, between different societies, and between societies and the world community and biosphere.

For practical reasons, the social worker and client must designate a focal system, the system of primary attention and information gathering. Assessment starts from the perspective of this system (Hearn, 1979). However, systems-oriented social workers attend to the entire client–environment matrix. *Suprasystem* is the designation for systems in which the client system is embedded, and *subsystem* is the designation for systems embedded in the client system. Comprehensive assessment, Buckley (1998) argued, requires a focus on the total matrix of the focal system: the suprasystems, the subsystems, and the environment as a whole.

Pincus and Minahan (1973) offer a useful typology of the systems central to the helping environment. The change agent system includes the social worker, social work group, or other helper employed for facilitating planned system change. The client system is the specific individual, group, or larger organization requesting or needing help, the expected beneficiary of the planned change effort. The action system is made up of individuals, groups, and larger organizations capable of working together to implement the plan necessary to achieve changes desired by the change agent and the client system. The target system includes the individual(s), group(s), or larger organization(s) that must be altered to achieve the desired results. This target system may or may not be the same as the client system.

IS PARTICULAR EMPHASIS GIVEN TO ANY SYSTEMS?

Applied systems theorists give theoretical and practical emphasis to more systems than most other theorists. Bronfenbrenner (1979) divided the environment into macro-level systems, including the society, communities, and organizations; meso-level systems, including a client's network of personal settings and the interactions among them; and micro-level systems, which are the individual, family, or group and its small, immediate, and personal environmental setting. All these systems and their influences on the client system merit attention.

Systems theorists also emphasize the embeddedness of smaller systems in ever larger systems. Theorists have offered several formulations of the embedded levels of a society. The placement in the environmental hierarchy may be determined by system size, complexity, and geographical dispersion. Becvar and Becvar (1996) focus on the organismic hierarchy: atoms, molecules, cells, tissues, organs and organ systems, nervous system, and person. Martin and O'Connor (1989) describe the components of the social hierarchy: persons, family and small groups, organizations, communities, nation-states, and the international arena of nation-states. Talcott Parsons (Lidz, 2000) provided an influential typology of societal systems, including the personality system, the cultural system, and the social system, composed of subsystems such as the economy, the polity, the societal communities (associations by class, status, ethnicity, or lifestyle), and the fiduciary or culture building systems generated by religion, family, kinship, and education institutions. Knowledge of each type of system, Parsons believed, is provided best by the associated academic discipline: psychology for the personality system, sociology for the social system, and anthropology for the cultural system. Encounters, temporary systems created when two persons interact, and associations such as professional organizations might be added to a social worker's inventory of relevant societal systems.

It is important to remember that systems theorists acknowledge that social groupings and human associations vary in their degree of "systemness." Groupings vary in degree of organization, the degree to which parts are arranged to form the whole. A social worker may be employed by a highly organized counseling unit on a military base, or a social worker may ally herself with an ad hoc, loosely organized set of supportive colleagues. Groupings vary, too, in the extent to which the organized arrangements become structured in stable and enduring ways (Rosenblatt, 1994). Some groupings, such as a military unit, may have lengthy histories (Anderson & Carter, 1990). Role and interaction patterns, attachment relationships, and authority and status hierarchies have almost become frozen. Such a structure becomes known for the consistent, repetitive, and predictable quality of its system action (Becvar & Becvar, 1996). Systems theorists often give primary attention to groupings characterized by high systemness (organization and enduring structure), but systems practitioners must serve groupings with low and high degrees of systemness.

HOW ARE RESOURCES AND THEIR FLOW CONCEPTUALIZED?

Applied social systems theorists conceptualize people and social systems as the major resources. Pincus and Minahan (1973) identified three types of resource systems: natural, formal, and societal. Natural resource systems include family, friends, neighbors, and coworkers who supply advice, emotional support, affection, and money. Formal resource systems are membership organizations and other official organizations such as labor unions, welfare rights groups, and associations for example, an association of parents of developmentally challenged children. These systems provide activities and services directly to the client system, and also help client system members negotiate to obtain resources from other systems. Societal resource systems are established by public mandate or voluntary social action and include hospitals, legal services, adoption agencies, and social security programs. These resource systems provide various resources to help citizens complete life tasks and maintain a satisfactory level of biopsychosocial functioning.

All social systems must deal with problems of resource allocation and ensure that system members have the resources necessary to help the system realize its goals. For Parsons, social systems differ in their control of the resources necessary to function effectively (Lidz, 2000). Potential resources might include particular kinds of tools, people who have been trained in special skill areas, and money.

Buckley, a noted systems theorist, and his colleagues (Baumgartner, Buckley, Burns, & Schuster, 1976) offer a detailed discussion of the resources available to social systems and the ways that social power influences resource acquisition. Material resources include weapons, tools, machines, land, goods, and money that system members can use to achieve system goals. Human resources are individuals and collections of people who can be controlled or used by the system. Nonmaterial or sociocultural resources include the social norms, values, and behavioral orientations that social systems can use to shape structures or actions. Those system members with great power or status typically have access to and control over these resources in ways that cannot be matched by less powerful systems or members. These influential members can also use the resources they control to change system structures so as to expand their power. For example, power elites may increase the bureaucratic features of an agency to benefit themselves and their allies who are in positions of command.

Resource flow is multidirectional; transfers from one system to another system, from a system's parts to the whole system, and from the system to the environment are common. However, the ease and quality of the resource flow depend on a critical system feature: the system boundary. A **boundary** may be physical or symbolic (Stein, 1974). My skin, for example, is the outer boundary of my body. Many organizations have a symbolic boundary, perhaps a set of sexist beliefs blocking access by talented women to positions of leadership. A system boundary separates its inside from the outside, and systems theorists offer the proposition that the transmission of information or other central resources occurs more easily within a bounded system than across the boundary. Flow across the boundary depends on the boundary's permeability.

All living systems require the transfer of some resources across their boundaries, but **closed systems** have relatively impermeable boundaries. These systems are not supportive of inflowing and outflowing energy and information (Martin & O'Connor, 1989). Such social systems aim for self-containment and minimal dependence on the environment for survival. Families are often used to illustrate boundary preferences (Kantor & Lehr, 1975). Here's a profile of a closed family system. The family has fixed and impermeable spatial boundaries, perhaps a high fence and a Doberman securing the property and a security system protecting the house. The family has a firm expectation that members will be faithful to the family and avoid alliances with outsiders. The family's authorities emphasize discipline and obedience, and restrict the physical movement of subordinates. Within the family, the male subgroup is reluctant to accept information and guidance from the female subsystem. Family subsystems operate in secrecy and with a zealous protection of privacy. The family has certainty about its convictions and clarity regarding proper beliefs; it rejects alien cultural or intellectual traditions.

Open systems are relatively receptive to energy and information flow in and out of the system. Energy and information cross system boundaries easily, and there is a continuous exchange of information with other systems and their environment (Martin & O'Connor, 1989). The open family system, for example, values mutual dependence and trusts neighbors. Spatial boundaries are very permeable. The front door is almost always unlocked, and the children's playmates visit regularly. The family gives members permission to explore relationship opportunities with outsiders. Divisions across age or gender are rare. Family subsystems operate openly, and privacy rights are flexible. The family is willing to negotiate with others about social and political convictions and expresses tolerance for diverse knowledge, values, and opinions.

When studying problems of resource flow between systems, the social worker should assess boundary permeability (Becvar & Becvar, 1996). Where are the boundaries? How permeable or porous are they? Are the boundaries clear and easy to detect? Do system members agree about the boundaries? Have boundaries changed recently?

What Descriptive Words Are Used?

Applied systems theorists use an unusual language, one developed by the integration of terms from biology, engineering, cybernetics, systems analysis, and other disciplines and occupations. From engineering and electronic technology, for example, the systems approach has borrowed terms such as *input, throughput, output, parameter, feedback, interface,* and *regulation* (Rigney, 2001). Applied systems theorists also like to create new and unusual theoretical concepts. *Morphostasis* and *morphogenesis* are two examples.

How Is Change Conceptualized?

Applied systems theorists are interested in changes in the complexity of system organization. Systems become more complex by processes of differentiation (dividing functions) and of specialization (assigning functions to certain parts).

For example, my social work department has recently added a graduate program. The department is growing to meet the new challenge by creating a new set of committees (curriculum and assessment committees, for example) and by assigning special duties such as program evaluation to these committees. The seasoned department members often comment on how complex department policies, procedures, and activities have become compared to the old days when three faculty members cooperated informally. Systems can grow from a low degree of organization (limited awareness of system dynamics and minimal capacity for collective action) to a higher degree of organization (extensive system awareness, a developed capacity for coordinated action, efficiency of output toward desired goal).

Systems differ in their orientation toward change (Rosenblatt, 1994). The two basic orientations, introduced earlier, are alternate preferences for stability or change, existing order or creative reordering (Becvar & Becvar, 1996). The morphogenesis orientation values change and growth, the continual and creative movement toward new system arrangements (new rules, interaction patterns) in relation to changes in internal and external environments. The morphostasis orientation values stability and tends to activate processes contributing to maintenance of system arrangements.

Applied systems theorists make another important distinction related to the ambitiousness of the planned change project. **First-order change** aims for changes in the surface manifestations of a system or system member problem. Family system members may agree, for example, to decrease or increase certain behaviors (bickering or negative criticism) but without agreeing to change overall system patterns. **Second-order change** aims for changes in basic system properties and dynamics (boundaries, degree of organization, and structural arrangements). For example, family members agree to examine how authority differences and gender differences structure family communication and then to improve the communication structure.

Systems-oriented assessment requires the worker to engage in extensive questioning and observing (Artinian, 1997). Buckley (1998) provides a framework to guide systemic assessment of a focal system. The worker would collect data about goal states the system seeks to achieve and their degree of clarity. The worker would learn about the parameters of the system's internal steady state. What are the minimum and maximum values tolerated on relevant variables? For example, what is the range of inequality acceptable in the United States? The worker would inquire into the state of the system (balanced or unbalanced) at important points in time, and the dominant orientation (morphogenesis or morphostasis). The social worker would assess the commitment or zeal of system members to work to achieve goal states. The worker would ask about the degree and quality of organization of the system's subsystems. Are system work teams well organized? The worker would explore the nature and quality of feedback to the system regarding activities geared toward goal achievement. The worker would also consider the quality of the use of feedback by the system's decision centers to initiate corrective action (adjust values, redefine goals, reorganize work via business and legislative procedures, for example) and to bring system activities closer to the stated goals.

Applied systems theorists and practitioners identify various relevant systemic interventions (Chetkow-Yanoov, 1992; Franklin & Jordan, 1999; Gordon, 1969; Pincus & Minahan, 1973). I will provide examples directed toward family social workers, but these interventions might be adapted to any social system. Feedback processes can be improved. A family decides to use monthly bank and credit card statements to revise its budget and alter spending patterns. Boundaries might be altered, established, strengthened, or loosened. A family agrees to open its home, adopt a child, and change boundary regulations to accommodate the new member and new support systems. The worker can help the system create new linkages to other systems and resources and support family member efforts to forge a partnership with a nearby child care center, for instance. The assignment of system functions can be changed. The father becomes ill, and the mother assumes functions associated with the role of primary breadwinner. System composition can be changed. The family might finally launch a 35-year-old son who has been reluctant to leave the comforts of home. The worker and client helping system can block dysfunctional patterns enacted by system members (the continual blaming of individuals without consideration for contradictory family system rules) and support functional patterns (family members conveying care and love to each other). The social worker can aid a client system in the management of people and resources to more effectively and efficiently achieve shared system goals. Systems-oriented social workers can also intervene to make the environment more conducive to the growth and development of a client system.

From the systems perspective, much of social work is boundary work (Hearn, 1979). Systems intervention can be targeted at boundary issues. Social workers can help client systems examine how they have established boundaries between the system and the environment and between internal subsystems. Social workers can pay special attention to what occurs at the boundary or interface of the client system and the environment, and can help clients change the degree of openness at this interface. Social workers can help client systems regulate the amount of information that comes across the system boundary to avoid the extremes of information overload or information deprivation. Social workers can help client systems expand their boundaries to incorporate new and stimulating ideas, people, or experiences into the system.

Systems theorists offer a comforting conception of client change, the notion of **equifinality**. This refers to "the achieving of identical results from different initial conditions" (Hearn, 1979, p. 337). Different client systems may begin with different psychosocial problems and participate in the helping process in different ways and at different paces. Yet these different client systems might achieve similar levels of social maturity, of responsibility, of effectiveness, or of satisfaction.

How Are Actual and Ideal Eco-Maps Contrasted?

Actual social systems vary in the state of the system, the properties and relations of system components at any point in time. The three major states are equilibrium, homeostasis, and steady state. A state of **equilibrium** is the state appropriate for mechanical systems, those closed systems that do not make use of external environment variety (Buckley, 1967). Inputs and outputs are in balance. Disturbances to the system state move it from the equilibrium point, but variations occur within a narrow range and automatically activate mechanisms to return to the equilibrium point. Furnaces, for example, are governed by fixed rules for how the machine operates and seek a constancy of outcomes. Despite any disturbance, the thermostat keeps the furnace operating to maintain a house temperature very close to the temperature set by its owner. **Homeostasis** is the state appropriate for living organisms (Buckley, 1967). The organism fights variety (wide ranges in noise, temperature, pressure on the body's surface, gravitational pull, and so on) and tries to maintain structures and processes within certain limits (Buckley, 1998). The limits are generally wider than those for mechanical systems, however. The organism has a fairly high level of organization compared to mechanical systems but, like a mechanical system, prefers a relatively constant set of system conditions (Walrond-Skinner, 1979). The organic system resists deviation from a set of operational parameters and maintains equilibrium by feedback processes and control systems.

Human systems may actually operate like machines or living organisms and seek equilibrium or homeostasis when not functioning naturally. However, human dyads, groups, and communities are goal-directed open systems ideally characterized by a **steady state** (Buckley, 1967). Social systems are complex and adaptive and thrive on environmental variety and disturbances. Disturbances are opportunities to generate new and creative organizational arrangements. As the environment changes, the organization changes. A steady state refers to this open interchange with the environment and continuous alteration of structure to adapt to changing conditions. Steady-state systems are always in flux and seek a moving equilibrium rather than the stationary equilibrium of machines (Davidson, 1983). Goals are continually adjusted (Martin & O'Connor, 1989). Organization is loose and flexible so that changes in direction are possible. The laws of equilibrium govern Monk, the obsessive-compulsive television detective who must maintain all aspects of his life in a narrow and rigid order. The laws of homeostasis govern Seinfeld, the television comedian who prefers a fairly stable and predictable routine and set of friends but can adjust to unexpected novelty. The laws of steady state govern Captain Archer, the television spaceship commander who constantly seeks new challenges and new environments. Social workers should help troubled clients and client systems move from states of equilibrium or homeostasis to the ideal steady state.

Mechanical and organic systems are characterized by **entropy,** the "tendency of an unattended system to move toward an unorganized state characterized by decreased interactions among its components, followed by decrease in usable energy" (Anderson & Carter, 1990, p. 13). The natural order is for bodies and things to wear out, decompose, and run down (Gordon, 1969; Norlin et al., 2003). Systems-oriented practitioners with much experience in clinical service in poor neighborhoods noted problems with energy loss and associated system disorganization. Minuchin and Montalvo (1967) observed during interaction with some of their clients that "families from the low socioeconomic population fluctuate between moments when members appear in relatively disconnected subsystems and other moments when these subsystems swiftly lose their boundaries and members mesh intensely into an undifferentiated whole. Moreover, a marked discontinuity of behavior among individual family members is evoked by different subgroupings" (1967, p. 880). Because of social and economic oppression and other extreme pressures from the external environment, these families could not maintain system vitality and the available energies of the systems were not distributed and expended in working order. Anderson and Carter (1990) described the factors contributing to system entropy and disorganization. The goals of a member clash with the goals of the whole system. System communication and feedback processes are interrupted or unclear and confusing. The energies and information available to the system are insufficient for meeting environmental or developmental challenges. The system members do not know how to organize to obtain energy and information from outside the system, or the larger systems deprive the focal client system of the energy and information it needs. Outside pressures related to discrimination or exploitation exert a disruptive influence on system organization.

Ideally, social systems can activate **negative entropy,** the tendency toward increasing complexity and order (Davidson, 1983). Social systems are unlike clocks that wind down, batteries that wear out, and bodies that age. Humans can find ways to rewind or reenergize their social systems. Social systems have access to energy and information that can be imported and organized (Hearn, 1979; Stein, 1974). Thus, entropy can be avoided and order increased. Social systems are also capable of **synergy,** "increasingly available energy within a system derived from heightened interaction among its components" (Anderson & Carter, 1990, p. 13). A perfect fit between a group of social workers, their team's task, and the team's culture and structure, for example, generates synergy. Many social systems that social workers serve are dysfunctional and entropic. System processes or subsystem activities are detrimental to the system's maintenance and survival (Chetkow-Yanoov, 1992). Social workers try to realize ideal conditions and increase the functionality of the parts and the energy of the whole system (Chetkow-Yanoov, 1992).

I will close this subsection by describing Buckley's (1998) characterization of ideal system properties and processes. Ideal systems are like political democracies. *Democracy* is a term for the "widespread participation of individuals and subgroups in the major decisions affecting themselves and society" (p. 22). Democratic action is oriented by the "basic goal of promoting the general public interest" (p. 259). Democracy from the viewpoint of systems theory focuses on an optimal way for organizing the set of structures and processes characterizing a whole system. Democracy is ideal as a form for maximizing the system's adaptation, comparing favorably to systems organized by antidemocratic principles such as tyranny (rule by dictator), oligarchy (rule by a few elite), and monarchy (rule by king). Democratic system processes increase the accurate and complete diffusion of information about the internal and external environment of the system. They increase the feedback to the system's decision centers from various subsystems. They increase the likelihood of future-sensitive decision making in important spheres of system activity. They increase a system's awareness of its own states and of the quality of its external relations. They increase the likelihood of curbing harmful system structures and processes. They increase the education of members in the ways that self-regulation through democratic procedures maximizes system member freedom. Democratic systems tend to meet the needs of members efficiently, to relate peacefully with other democratic neighbors, and to manage their environments effectively (Buckley, 1998). Most social systems do not realize their democratic potentials and operate as poor self-regulators and goal achievers. Yet social workers might use this systems theory appreciation for democracy, combined with that of critical theorists discussed in a later chapter, to inform their utopian aspirations.

How Are Issues of Diversity, Color, and Shading Addressed?

Applied systems theorists value societal diversity. Environmental variety is important to complex social systems. A culturally diverse community is like a large pool of behavior patterns, role relationships, and models of system organization. A social system can draw from this pool to further its self-regulation and adaptation (Buckley, 1998).

Applied systems theory offers a distinctive perspective on troubles associated with diversity. Bertalanffy (Davidson, 1983) articulated the systems critique of prejudice. Human beings are extremely complex and ever-changing living systems and cannot be reduced to isolated parts. Bigots may use one or two gender, racial, ethnic, or national traits to provoke hatred and violence against out-groups. Social workers should fight such simplification and try to replace the fallacy of prejudice with the scientifically based appreciation for the complexity of human and social systems. Rigney (2001) compares racism to malignant parts in the body. The diseased part becomes dysfunctional and eventually spreads and increases its negative impact. Social workers can act like doctors administering radiation, chemotherapy, or surgery to deal with the cancerous racism.

Parsons and other systems theorists conceptualize conflict between diverse groups, such as the protests by women and African Americans in the 1960s, in terms of functional imperatives (Holton, 1998; Lidz, 2000). The systems approach to such conflicts is still relevant. If certain membership groups are excluded from performing a social system's goal-setting function and these groups are not integrated into larger societal institutions, the smooth functioning and survival of the whole society is jeopardized. Democratic practices, including the extension of the rights of citizenship and the provision of opportunities to participate in political structures, are necessary to reintegrate the excluded members into the body politic. According to Lidz (2000), Talcott Parsons gave central importance to civil rights as the tool fostering integration of African Americans and other minority groups. Successful integration into the societal system depends on legal rights such as equal protection under the law, political rights including the right to vote and to influence the political process, and welfare rights such as the rights to equal educational opportunities, health care, and welfare support. These rights are necessary methods for combating the discrimination and deprivation blocking inclusion and participation in the modern economic system.

Norlin, Chess, Dale, and Smith (2003) also consider diversity issues from an applied systems perspective. They focus on the need to integrate parts for the sake of societal stability. Subcultural groups are subsystems in the larger culture. Members of the subsystems—the African American community in the United States, for instance—are integrated into their subculture because of shared values, beliefs, and norms. However, boundary dynamics block the efforts of these subcultural groups to integrate into the larger society or suprasystem. The dominant cultural group may try to compel adaptation by the minority culture's members to conventional cultural norms before allowing movement across boundaries. This protects the dominant institutions (such as banking centers and political organizations) from pressures to change. Some social systems within the dominant culture receive preferential treatment because they can more easily attain a steady state when members conform, speak the same language, validate the same identity, and interact in ways that are relatively stress free (consider a private and elite club restricted to white, upper-class, Protestant males).

Subcultural groups and their members have several strategies for coping with system problems. First, members of the subculture can decide to conform. They become integrated culturally, Americanized in our case. Historically, a few subcultural groups (Irish, Italian, and other immigrant groups) became eligible for inclusion in the larger society when they endorsed the American value system and abandoned the immigrant group values that diverged from the larger value orientation. Second, members of the subculture can choose to differentiate themselves completely from the dominant culture. Because they are not allowed to penetrate the boundaries established by the dominant culture, they choose not to conform to the practices and norms required by the sentries of this mainstream. They remain systems circling outside the walls. Finally, members of the subculture can attempt the difficult task of managing integration into the dominant culture without sacrificing their integration into the minority culture. Daily life presents the challenge of crossing boundaries frequently and participating in two incompatible social systems.

WHAT WOULD BE ADDED OR DELETED?

The original eco-map uses systems theory as its theoretical starting point. Therefore, the conventional eco-map and the applied systems theory eco-map are almost identical. Contemporary system theorists might make two changes. They might add an indicator of the permeability of each system's boundary. Perhaps dashed lines with the dashes widely separated but forming a circle could indicate great openness and dashed lines with minimal space between dashes could signify minimal openness. Social systems theorists such as Parsons also stress the importance of large-scale social systems for understanding people's actions. Therefore, they might add to the conventional eco-map major suprasystems such as the economy, the polity including governmental agencies at all levels, religious institutions, educational institutions, and social associations based on class structure, social status, ethnicity, race, and other solidarity ties (Lidz, 2000).

THE LIMITS OF APPLIED SYSTEMS THEORY: A SOCIAL WORK APPRAISAL

An evaluation of applied systems theory reveals some weakness and some strength. Check the concepts in bold in this chapter, and you will probably agree that systems theorists use a strange and inelegant language, one far removed from the everyday language of our clients. It is hard to imagine asking teenagers in a community center or elderly residents of a nursing home to report on their inputs, throughputs, and outputs. The terminology of applied systems theory is very broad and abstract, too, making it harder for evidence-based social workers to operationalize theoretical concepts, specify directives for particular helping situations in ways that can be replicated, make predictions about future states of the client system, and evaluate overall effectiveness.

Theory critics have also challenged the basic theoretical assumption that parts should not be separated from the whole. Phillips (1976), for instance, dislikes the practical implications of holism. He argues, "Borrowers, talkers, and husbands *can* be separated from their respective lenders, hearers, and wives, and can be meaningfully studied in isolation" (p. 55). Phillips asserts that systems theorists have not successfully refuted the analytic method. The woman separated from the role of wife has a socioeconomic status, physical features, intellectual qualities, and personality dispositions that can be assessed separately from her system participation. Social workers must and often do obtain useful assessment information about clients conceptualized as separate from their important social systems.

Some theory experts are wary also of the search for functionalist explanations for social arrangements and social organizations. Functional analysis requires that many preconditions be fulfilled, and its use is appropriate only when the family, group, or organization has the attributes of a real system. The systemness of a human grouping, the potency of system requirements, and the function of parts for the whole cannot be assumed. These system features must be empirically appraised (Buckley, 1967). Merton (1949) also has difficulty with functional analysis. For one, he cites the problem of circular reasoning. The assertion "Voodoo charms help group member survive against evil spells" when proven by the claim "The member is still alive, demonstrating that the voodoo charms fulfilled their function" is not adequate if judged by the standards of scientific thinking. A part's function and its contribution to the whole can be identified only by careful and difficult empirical study of the part in relation to other parts and to the whole. Merton (1949) also believed that some system functions are difficult to detect. He distinguished manifest functions and latent functions. **Manifest functions** are intended and readily recognized by system participants for their contribution to system adaptation. **Latent functions** are not intended or easily recognized. A society's harsh penal system functions manifestly to protect community members from dangerous predators. The system may function less obviously to frighten and to compel law-abiding citizens to conform to the behavioral standards set by the system's elite members. Finally, functional analysis has a complexity not always acknowledged by systems theorists. The system components (family members, for example) may perform multiple functions. They may frequently change the functions performed for the whole system, or they may experience great tension when performing functions because the system requires contradictory contributions (help the system adapt and reinforce system solidarity by showing only agreement with authority figures, for example).

Applied systems theorists often assume system harmony, a consensus on central system values, and the integration of parts, but these assumptions downplay the conflict common to many social systems and obscure the greater power and status of privileged system members (Lidz, 2003). Systems critics agree that parts influence each other reverberatively, but parts vary in their capacity to affect the other parts and the whole system. An alteration of the heart in a human body, for instance, has life-threatening effects, whereas damage to a toenail has negligible consequences for the system. Let's return to the social sphere. Domestic violence is not a simple system issue, critics contend, but a power discrepancy issue. Theory-minded practitioners must attend to the internal and external stresses, strains, and conflicts between parts of a system (Rigney, 2001) and how these are structured by the gender differences, racial differences, and power differences that structure the larger environment.

Finally, applied social systems theorists are prone to system determinism, the notion that system structures and processes are so powerful that there is little likelihood of personal choice by the system members (Monane, 1967). Members have been molded by the system in which they are embedded, and their actions are basically responses to the demands of the larger social systems. This view contrasts with the social work emphasis on the human capacity for self-determination despite system pressures. Social workers acknowledge system imperatives, but they also believe that people can act creatively and in defiance of a dominant system's ideology, values, and norms.

Applied social systems theory has much strength, too. The review in the chapter shows how the theoretical approach can help social workers understand comprehensively all the relevant and conditioning connections of the client system to other systems. Systems theory also offers social workers a sophisticated framework for assigning responsibility. Buckley (1998) taught, for example,

> Don't simply blame the individuals involved in policy decisions (although they must shoulder the moral and legal responsibilities); blame the sociocultural structure within which they are enmeshed. Search for the role pressures, the premiums and penalties that result from doing or not doing things in certain ways, the goals held out with associated carrots and sticks, and the tensions generated by the often incompatible demands of peers, family, sub- and super-ordinates, politicians, and national flag. (p. 257)

Bertalanffy (1969, p. 221) contributes the system principle, "Responsibility is always judged within a symbolic framework of values as accepted in a society under given circumstances." Last, applied social systems theory matches well with the generalist approach to social work. Social workers learn to work flexibly in different roles and different helping modalities with social groupings of different sizes using knowledge borrowed from diverse disciplines. Systems theory can help us handle this big job. Bertalanffy, the father of systems theory, was convinced of his theory's usefulness because "the educational demands of training 'scientific generalists' and of developing interdisciplinary 'basic principles' are precisely those general systems theory tries to fill" (p. 51).

OLSON'S CIRCUMPLEX TYPOLOGY: A MODEL FOR UNDERSTANDING MILITARY FAMILIES, FAMILY SYSTEMS FUNCTIONING, AND FAMILY LIFE CYCLE PRESSURES

Material for this case study was developed as part of the Virginia National Guard Family Research and Service Project (Forte, 1990; Green & Harris, 1989). Extensive questionnaires were administered to members of the Virginia Guard between November 1988 and January 1989; more than 75% of all Guard members completed them. The respondents in the study comprised a very large family data set. Their responses helped us learn about ways the military might support families, and about family system functioning and its relation to family life cycle changes. Here, I will focus on how this conceptual model might guide your use of the planned change process. The model makes significant use of David Olson's (1989, 1995) typology of family functioning. A typology is a systematic classification or categorization scheme.

THE SYSTEMS PERSPECTIVE ON FAMILY LIFE CYCLE CHALLENGES

General systems theory (Bertalanffy, 1969; Buckley, 1967) provides the underlying base for David Olson's Circumplex model of marital and family systems (Olson, 1989, 1995; Olson, Russell, & Sprenkle, 1983; Olson,

Sprenkle, & Russell, 1979). The Circumplex model identifies family cohesion, family adaptability, and family communication as the salient structures and processes that organize family interaction, whole family functioning, and family development. **Family cohesion** refers to the emotional bonding that family members have with one another. These family forces pull members together and serve as a counterbalance against forces pulling members away from the family. Circumplex scientists identified several indicators of cohesion, including permeable family boundaries, member interdependence, family members' shared use of time and space, family interests and recreation, and friendships outside the family. In the better functioning families, members are integrated into their families in ways that facilitate the fulfillment of personal needs and collective needs. Cohesion is categorized into four levels of functioning: disengaged, separated, connected, and enmeshed. Optimal family functioning reflects either a separated or a connected style of cohesion; problematic functioning reflects a disengaged style (the family members have little cohesion) or an enmeshed style (the family members are excessively close).

The second major family dimension, **family adaptability,** refers to the ability of the family system to change its power arrangements, role relationships, and relationship rules in response to situational and developmental stress. The optimally functioning family achieves a balance between morphogenesis, the tendencies toward growth and change, and morphostasis, the tendencies toward stability and maintaining current patterns. Family adaptability is operationalized by reference to the following aspects of family life: leadership, family discipline, role relationships, relationship rules, and negotiation styles. In the better functioning family, the governing process is democratic and participatory. Clear leadership, shared roles, and the flexible use of rules characterize the system. Overall family adaptability is categorized into four levels: rigid, structured, flexible, and chaotic. Optimal or balanced functioning is structured or flexible; problematic functioning is chaotic (characterized by a laissez-faire governance approach) or rigid (characterized by an authoritarian governance approach).

Family communication is the third major dimension in the Circumplex model. These are the processes through which members express and negotiate developmental issues related to cohesion and to adaptability and by which change on these two dimensions is facilitated. Optimal family communication requires that members use listening skills (empathy and attentive listening, for example), speaking skills (speaking for oneself and not for others, for example), and self-disclosure (sharing ideas and feelings about oneself and about family relationships). Positive family communication is also characterized by mutual respect and regard, and by family members' appreciation for the emotional aspects of communication (Olson, 1989).

Additional systems theory principles and concepts informed the Circumplex model and its use in understanding military families at different stages in the family life cycle (Buckley, 1967; Forte, 1990; Bertalanffy, 1969). The military family system is a patterned whole with interdependent components and a boundary, and it shares several characteristics with other social systems.

The concept of circular causality, for example, reflects the systems view that family group members are interrelated, so that a change in any member—the National Guard soldier, for example—reverberates and affects all members. Boundary maintenance, another common system characteristic, means that the family monitors its boundaries so as to establish an identity as a unit while fostering linkages with external groups. Military families must protect their boundaries or they will be overwhelmed by the Guard's culture and demands.

Another characteristic of the family as a system is its hierarchical organization. At the lowest level of the hierarchy are internal biological and psychological subsystems in the individual family member. Within the family, the individual member participates in a system of relationships or subsystems, such as the parent–child and the marital relationship. Our study examined the interrelationship of the individual subsystem (the Guard member), the marital subsystem (military member and husband or wife), and the whole family. Looking at the whole system, the family is viewed as a subsystem of larger systems. The military unit, the kinship group, the neighborhood, and the society are some examples of higher-level systems. Our study followed the U.S. invasion of Panama, for example, and this large-scale event had significant effects on military families.

Olson and his research team (Olson et al., 1979, 1983) developed a useful family typology based on the two basic dimensions of cohesion and adaptability. This Circumplex typology is illustrated by a display in which midpoints of the four levels of adaptability and the four levels of cohesion intersect at a right angle. The resulting matrix or family functioning map forms a classification scheme of 16 different cells. Each cell is a family type. These types can be grouped into three major categories of family functioning: balanced families, midrange families, and extreme families.

The four balanced types cluster at the center of the Circumplex display. Families that occupy this central zone are balanced on both adaptability and cohesion. In the Virginia Guard study, these were the families that maintained optimal family structures despite environmental stressors and developmental changes.

The eight midrange families radiate from the center. These families are balanced on only one of the major dimensions and function at an extreme level on the other. For example, some midrange Virginia Guard families were balanced on cohesion but rigid on the dimension of adaptability.

Finally, the four extreme types of families occupy the corner cells of the matrix. These families function out of the optimal or balanced zones on both adaptability and cohesion. For example, a military family that was very high in adaptability and very low in cohesion would be classified as the extreme type and characterized as chaotically disengaged.

According to Olson (1989), the two family system structures are curvilinear. Middle scores on the Circumplex measurement tool, FACES (Family Adaptability and Cohesion Evaluation Scale), are the best; very low or very high scores are bad. All families participate in a struggle to maintain a balance between the extremes of enmeshment and disengagement and between chaos and rigidity. Healthy families organize and operate to function mostly in the balanced or middle zones. Unhealthy or dysfunctional families have organizational problems and become stuck at the extreme ends of the cohesion and adaptability continuums.

FAMILY SYSTEM ASSESSMENT: JUDGING FAMILY STAGE, ADAPTABILITY, AND COHESION

Olson and his team have developed a variety of tools to assess family system functioning from the member perspective as an insider and from the social worker perspective as an outsider. In our study, the military members completed a version of the Family Adaptability and Cohesion Evaluation Scale (FACES IV) to summarize their subjective appraisal of family functioning (Green, Harris, Forte, & Robinson, 1991). The family and social worker can use FACES in other practice situations, and then talk about the family's type of family functioning, developmental challenges, and possible areas for improvement. Social workers can also use the Clinical Assessment Package and Clinical Rating Scale (Olson, 1989) to formulate professional judgments about family functioning.

Olson (1988) encourages helping professions to identify the family stage by using a framework created by the family developmental theorist Reuben Hill. Olson does not provide a nominal definition of family stage, but Hill conceived of family stages in relation to family development. **Family development,** he stated, "refers to the process of progressive structural differentiation and transformation over the family's history, to the active acquisition and selective discarding of roles by incumbents of family positions as they seek to meet the changing functional requisites for survival and as they adapt to recurring life stresses as a family system" (Hill & Mattessich, 1979, p. 174). A **family stage,** according to Hill, represents a modal pattern of family development that families experience. Each stage represents a distinctive structuring of the family's parts: persons, positions, and roles. His typology of family stages groups family systems into seven stages: young couples without children; families with preschoolers, newborn to 5 years; families with school-age children (ages 6–12); families with adolescents (ages 13–18); launching families, when the first adolescent has reached 19; empty nest families, when all the children have moved out of the home; and retired couples. These definitions were operationalized in our survey.

Family stage, family type, and family health are related, Olson (1988) suggests. For example, Olson offers the proposition that family cohesion will differ by family stage; specifically, families are likely to report high levels of cohesion at the two early family stages and lower levels at the launching stage. Therefore, social workers are advised to look for correlations between family functioning and family stage. Olson and collegial family scientists such as Falicov (1988) also note cultural and subcultural variations in how family systems develop across time. Moreover, many changes have occurred in the American family form since the creation of the family life cycle model. These changes reflect increases in divorce rates, stepfamilies, intimate homosexual unions, unwed mothers, childless marriages, and mothers' work time; as a result, many contemporary families develop in ways that vary from the traditional family life cycle scheme (Carter & McGoldrick, 1999). Contemporary assessment of family development must be carefully tailored to respect distinctive family system qualities.

Family System Intervention: Promoting Healthy Family Functioning

When working with military families or other family systems, the therapeutic goal is to move the client family from extremes of functioning on dimensions of adaptability and cohesion to midrange or balanced levels (Olson, 1989, 1995). On cohesion, the worker helps the family stabilize at the balanced levels of separateness or togetherness. On adaptability, the family and worker aim to reorganize the family system so that it operates in the structured or flexible areas. The worker and family cooperate also to improve family member communication skills because these tools are critical to moving the family from a dysfunctional to a functional location on the Circumplex matrix.

Social workers can help families negotiate change over time and across different situations. Families must change their structures of cohesion and adaptability and their communication processes in ways responsive to new social situations, to entry into or exit from a family life cycle stage, and to the emergent developmental needs of each family member at different family stages (Olson, 1995). Family counseling and education can help them make these transformations. Social workers should also be aware of the proposition posed by Circumplex family scientists: The greater the stress on the family system, the more likely it is that the family will move from healthy to midrange or to extreme levels of family functioning. Virginia Guard families, for instance, experienced the stresses of the periodic separation of family members from their families and of the need to manage both military and civilian careers. System resources also seemed most taxed for these military families during times when children were added to or leaving the family. Social workers can learn to anticipate likely challenges to the family steady state and help families to mobilize their system members and resources, to recover from stress-provoked unbalanced states, and to resume healthy family functioning and development.

Learning Activities

1. Examine your own family and its interaction with outside systems. How permeable or impermeable are your family's boundaries? What energy, information, or other resources are allowed to cross boundaries into the family? What is kept outside the family system? How are the boundaries protected from undesirable intrusion?

2. Think about the concept of cybernetic hierarchy. Jot down some notes on the ways that larger social systems have determined or influenced your value preferences, behavior patterns, and daily choices. Identify also the ways that you have resisted the controlling influence of the larger systems in which you are embedded.

3. Rate a community in which a client lives according to its functionality. How well do various community subsystems carry out the functions of economics, socialization, social control, mutual support, and social participation? Identify several dysfunctional community processes or subsystems, and comment on how these endanger community maintenance and growth.

4. Study a department in a social work agency or the social work department at your university. Use a systems approach to identify and describe inputs, conversion processes, and outputs. Report also on how well the decision centers or leaders use feedback to ensure high-quality cycles of these input-conversion-output processes. How has the system regained balance after a recent change in external or internal relationships?

5. Again, examine a department in a social work agency or the social work department at your university. How are the AGIL functions necessary to the system's survival performed: the use of resources to adapt to the larger environment; the setting of policies and objectives related to goal attainment; the socialization of members to accept agency values and maintain basic organizational patterns; and the overall integration of programs and personnel into the whole social system?

6. Using the applied systems approach, develop a five-year plan for a high school system, client's family household, or an urban community. Specify relevant systems (client, change agent, target, and action), system goals, the system activities necessary to achieve the goals, a test procedure for appraising progress toward goals, and a timetable.

7. Using Olson's Circumplex model of family functioning, reflect on your family of origin's functioning in terms of adaptability, cohesion, and communication. How well does your family function in these three areas? How has family system functioning changed over the past 10 years? What factors triggered the change? How does your family system change on the Circumplex variables during times of high stress? In what ways (related to adaptability, cohesion, and communication) is life in your family satisfying and frustrating? Explain and give examples.

8. Using Hill and Olson's characterization of family stages, identify one family stage that was very important to your family's development. Reflect on the challenges faced by your family in this stage, the impact of this challenge on you and other family members, and the changes the whole family system made to meet these challenges. Compare your family's movement through its history to Hill and Olson's seven-stage scheme. In what ways does the family stage approach accurately describe your family's development? What are some ways that your family varied from the scheme?

Additional Resources

Additional resources are available on the book companion website at **www.thomsonedu.com/ social_work/forte**. Resources include key terms, tutorial quizzes, links to related websites, and lists of additional resources for furthering your research.

APPLIED BIOLOGY

CHAPTER 6

Elizabeth DeLaney/IndexStock

INTRODUCTION

How would your life be different if you were seven feet tall? If you were born a male not a female, or a female rather than a male? If you couldn't remove the tattoo of a sailor with rippling muscles from your arm? If your skin color was four shades darker or lighter? If you weighed 100 pounds more, or less, than you weigh now? How would your thinking, feeling, and acting be different if you had inherited different genes? If your parents had transmitted genes to you increasing your vulnerability to alcoholism or mental illness or sickle cell anemia? If your genes limited the development of your brain? What would change for you and your family if you lost the use of a leg because of a car accident? If your child developed cancer? If your father became demented? How would your identity, social interaction, and role performances differ if you were blind, deaf, or mute? Could you live a productive and satisfying life if the local air quality were at the dangerous level five out of seven days every week of the year? If there were a 1 in 10 chance that the meat you purchased at the supermarket was tainted? If the noises of gunshots, fights, and car races penetrated your bedroom windows every night? What would be different for you if you could not take for granted that your body would function effectively and your environment would ensure you physical safety and a high quality of life?

Now, take the your answers to these questions and apply them to the lives of your social work clients. You have started to add the "bio" to your bio-psychosocial understanding of people and their environments. Social workers have only recently attempted to incorporate theories and research findings from the biological sciences into their professional knowledge base. In this chapter, I will review the two root metaphors that are implicit in many biologically oriented approaches to social work: images and ideas that characterize the client as an evolved animal and as a medical patient. I will summarize the basic assumptions of the evolutionary and biological perspectives on human behavior and the social environment, and I will translate evolutionary biological knowledge into ecosystem terms. Finally, I will present a social work model for helping alcohol abusers abstain from drinking. This integrative model makes use of biological, psychological, and social variables.

To start, I will discuss briefly the profession's ambivalence about using biological theories. Why have social workers lagged behind other scientifically minded practitioners in efforts to integrate insights from biology? Several obstacles to the incorporation of biological knowledge have been identified (Saleeby, 1985). First, politicians, military leaders, and social theorists have often hijacked the ideas of Charles Darwin to advance abhorrent social agendas. For the record, Charles Darwin was not a Social Darwinist. **Social Darwinism** is the name for a conservative social philosophy that justifies oppression by reference to the idea of "survival of the fittest" (Hofstadter, 1963). Herbert Spencer, one of the first sociologists, originated and promoted the use of the concept. Before the publication of Darwin's work, Spencer developed the idea as a theoretical extension of his classification and conceptualization of the evolution of societies (Turner, 2000). Social Darwinists believe that human society evolves only because of fierce competition between members and groups (Forte, 2001). The strong survive the competition, and the weak perish. Social Darwinists argue that this is good. The adaptive traits of the strong survivors are transmitted to the next generation, increasing the fitness of the society, its ability to meet environmental and reproductive challenges. Political leaders have used these ideas to categorize entire social groups—the economically dependent and the sexually different—as unfit. President Ronald Reagan, for example, persistently characterized welfare recipients in this way. Why waste resources on those who do not contribute to the evolution of the species? Leaders such as Adolph Hitler deemed Jews, homosexuals, and Gypsies as biologically inferior groups, thereby justifying the persecution, sterilization, and murder of members of these groups. Social theorists have also offered pseudoscientific explanations of public problems such as crime, school failures, and poverty using the logic of Social Darwinism. African Americans are more often implicated in these intractable problems, they say, not because of their often impoverished environments but because of inherited inadequacies. Since African Americans are less intelligent than Caucasians, the Social Darwinists suggest, they will succeed less frequently. Social programs are useless, Social Darwinists conclude, because they will not change these biological and determining differences.

Social work advocates of biological approaches have been discouraged in their efforts to further the use of this perspective for a second reason. Professional groups can be ranked by social status, and social workers always fall far below the status level of physicians, psychiatrists, and other occupations that apply biological knowledge (Saleeby, 1985, 1992). Some social workers have hoped that affiliation with higher status medical professionals might raise the profession's perceived value. However, this rarely happens. Social work psychotherapists, for instance, may adopt the study-diagnosis-treatment (SDT) model used by medical doctors. They may create clinic-like settings for serving their "patients," and seek lucrative reimbursement from managed health care systems. These therapists, however, have achieved only minor gains in their social status. Other leaders of our profession fear that social workers endorsing biomedical perspectives will be subordinated to doctors. Interdisciplinary teams dominated by doctors, for instance, use nurses to perform the ancillary, low-status tasks associated with healing. Biologically oriented social workers compete, often unsuccessfully, with these nurses for low-rank positions and resources in health care organizations.

Social workers might try to earn a role on such teams by demonstrating distinctive and necessary expertise: skills and knowledge in the realm of pyschosocial functioning, not biological processes. These social workers could differentiate their theoretical perspective from that of biomedical experts. They could propose holistic or humanistic approaches to assessment and intervention that differ from the SDT model, and they might assert and demonstrate that the use of posthospital psychosocial interventions in community settings achieves important personal and structural outcomes. Unfortunately, there has been little professional unity regarding the definition of social work, its similarities to and differences from biomedical work, or its equivalent value. Social workers have failed to develop a theoretical tradition incorporating the biological sciences that can compete with the dominant medical model.

Finally, social workers have been wary of the biological sciences because mastery of this knowledge requires great effort and time (Johnson et al., 1990). Social work educators have become adept at synthesizing and teaching knowledge acquired from psychology and the social sciences. Social work practitioners have numerous theories of psychosocial functioning at their disposal. Thousands of practice books have been written from the psychosocial perspective. Novice practitioners are socialized from their first class to attend to the cognitive, emotional, social, and cultural variables that influence and are influenced by person-in-environment transactions. Using the biological approach requires, in contrast, the mastery of new knowledge: knowledge of human biology, chemistry, physiology, neurology, genetics, and numerous other disciplines that illuminate the relations between biology and human behavior. Social work educators and practitioners have only recently begun to explore this new intellectual terrain. Ask yourself: What field settings are most challenging? Where must social work interns acquire extensive knowledge not commonly covered in the traditional curriculum? I think medical settings are the toughest. Students must familiarize themselves quickly with a massive and complex vocabulary used to diagnose patients. They must learn about assorted interventions, including hundreds of medications and their possible side effects or contraindications. They must learn to monitor and observe numerous symptoms and understand how these indicate deterioration or improvement. They must manage to cooperate with medical experts from numerous specializations. Educators, experienced practitioners, and field interns seem intimidated by the complexity of the biological sciences and the challenges of health settings, and often shy away from them. In this chapter, I urge you to muster your courage and begin to learn how clients can be understood not only as psyches, selves, spirits, and behavior patterns but also as bodies.

RELATED DIALECTS, ASSOCIATED SCHOOLS OF THOUGHT

Because social workers have not yet organized practical knowledge from the biological sciences, the profession lacks a commonly recognized term for this approach to practice. Here are several related names of theoretical frameworks. **Evolutionary theorists** explain human behavior and patterns of social organizations in terms of biological processes and structures as these have been shaped by natural selection (Forte, 2001). Evolutionary theorists take the long temporal view and consider changes in human bodies and capacities occurring over thousands of generations. **Evolutionary biologists** give special attention to genetics, genetic variations, and the processes of heredity. Social workers using such knowledge might help prospective parents assess the likelihood that an adopted child would have a genetic disorder. **Evolutionary psychologists** are more interested in the study of psychological characteristics and the relation between contemporary fears and phobias, mate selection preferences, sexual desires, inclinations toward jealousy, uses of language, personality traits, and behavior patterns and the adaptation by the human species in the distant past to ancestral environments. **Evolutionary sociologists,** including sociobiologists, attempt to unite biology and sociology by searching for the biological contributors to social behavior, patterns of social interaction, and major social institutions such as the economy, kinship, and religion. Currently, few, if any, social workers are building or applying theories of evolutionary biology, evolutionary psychology, or evolutionary sociology.

Many biological scientists and medical experts take a limited temporal perspective and study the human being as a biological system responding to contemporary or recent conditions in the physical environment. Social workers have referred to the resulting amalgam of biomedical assumptions about human life, knowledge from the biological sciences, and technologies for curing or managing diseases and injuries as the **medical model** (Miller, 1980). In the United States, medical science produces frequent advances in medical care. Recently, for example, innovators have developed a camera the size of a large pill. This can be swallowed and then guided through the digestive tract. The camera can detect hidden bleeding, ulcers, and tumors that were not accessible to doctors using the old 12-foot-tube method. Some social workers are familiarizing themselves with such remarkable new tools. Other social workers are making use of medical studies on the effects of drugs on persons with mental illness or other diseases. Some social workers are using medical classification systems to understand the physical conditions of their clients, and how these conditions limit psychosocial functioning. Social workers are also using medical knowledge about risk factors to screen and identify those persons vulnerable to diseases or other life-threatening problems.

The **biopsychosocial paradigm** is the name for a fairly new and comprehensive approach to social work practice that incorporates scientific knowledge about biological, psychological, social, cultural, economic, political, and ecological variables, and the interactions among these variables, into a unified understanding of human development and functioning in the environment (Johnson, 1999). The body, the mind, the social organization, and the culture are all essential building blocks, according to proponents of this approach, from which human action and social systems are constructed. The biopsychosocial paradigm requires interdisciplinary cooperation, and social workers, psychiatrists, nurses, physicians, and other professions are still learning how to articulate ways to blend biology, psychology, and the social sciences and to learn their counterparts' disciplinary languages. The biological approach to social work discussed in this chapter begins the task of adding theories about the "bio" to the traditional psychosocial paradigm (Johnson et al., 1990).

APPLIED BIOLOGY: EXEMPLARY MODELS

The scarcity of central figures identified with the biological approach to social work practice also attests to the underdevelopment of this framework. Nevertheless, two scientists and one social worker might inspire us.

CHARLES DARWIN

Charles Darwin (1809–1882) was the premier evolutionary biologist. He was born in England and studied ministry at Cambridge University. He became a naturalist who developed many of the major ideas of evolutionary theory (Darwin, 1892/1958). In 1831, Darwin sailed on a naval ship, the *H.M.S. Beagle,* and for five years he used the scientific procedures associated with botany, geology, and zoology on this ambitious data collection project. Darwin also began to analyze the fossil and geological record during his exploration of the Pacific coast of South America. The voyage helped transform Darwin from an aimless young man into an intellectual with great ambitions. Darwin's observations of slavery during his voyages led him also to criticize the practice of separating slave children from parents, condemn the institution of slavery, wish that England was the "first European nation which utterly abolishes it" (Darwin, 1892/1958, p. 145), and increase his estimation of the quality of the Negro character. These were not the sentiments of a Social Darwinist. During the voyage of the *Beagle,* Charles Darwin contracted a tropical illness that made him a semi-invalid for the remainder of his life.

After years of reading, collecting, conferring with animal breeders, and theorizing tentatively about human and animal origins, Charles Darwin published his major work, *The Origin of the Species* (1859/1996). Darwin's ideas about evolution included the concept of **natural selection.** He developed this concept to provide a theoretical explanation for the great variety among living beings. Traits useful to the survival of a **species** (organisms classified as members of the same category because of biological resemblance and ability to interbreed) in a particular environment are selected and transmitted to later generations. These traits increase the fitness of the species and the chances that members of that population will successfully reproduce and solve environmental problems. Those organisms with unfavorable variations of traits are eliminated in the struggle for life. The great diversity of life forms testifies to the variety of environments and the varied ways that living organisms have adapted to nature.

Darwin's book and his ideas were not well received at first. Darwin was aware that his theory of human evolution challenged biblical doctrine and would create trouble for himself, his family, and his wife. He did not publish it until 20 years after his worldwide voyage on the *Beagle* (Craig, 1980). In a sense, Darwin told his readers that our distant grandfathers and grandmothers were apelike creatures, that many aspects of human behavior were selected over eons of evolutionary time (rather than given to us by God), and that we should not be ashamed of these facts. This natural history of humankind was controversial then and continues to evoke passionate attacks. However, the scientific community has high regard for Darwin's innovative scholarship, and scientific evidence now clearly supports many of his theoretical claims about evolutionary processes.

Charles Darwin was a private man engaged in little public service. He rarely appeared in public, avoided social conversation, and rarely defended his scientific theories. He lived with his wife and children at a home in Downe, England. There, he followed a regimented routine of scientific study and research. His spare time was directed to plant experiments, gardening, and raising pigeons.

GREGOR MENDEL

Gregor Mendel (1822–1884) was one of the great biological scientists (Dunn, 2002; Orel, 1984). At an Augustinian monastery, Mendel taught himself science. He was an Austrian monk who first served as a substitute teacher and then, after failing his certification test, was sent by his abbot to the University of Vienna for studies in various nature sciences. Mendel later taught natural science in a technical high school. He never succeeded in passing the examination for a teacher's license. Mendel maintained an interest in botany, bee culture, and meteorology almost until his death.

In 1856, Mendel began his independent studies of the basic characteristics of pea plants. In a series of innovative experiments, Gregor Mendel crossed varieties of the plants and traced the differences in the resulting hybrids. He observed descendants that varied in plant tallness, blossom color, seed shape, flower position, pod form, and other features. Mendel theorized that the appearance of alternate plant characteristics across generations could be explained in terms of statistically predictable transmission of units of heredity. These units are now called **genes.** Mendel's first law or principle of segregation stated that the reproductive cells of a plant could contain either of two different traits, but not both. Heredity factors don't combine. His second law of independent assortment stated that plant characteristics are inherited independently of each other. Each member of the parent generation transmits only half of its heredity factors to each offspring (certain factors are dominant over other, recessive factors). Mendel proposed another law: Different offspring of the same parents receive different sets of heredity factors. Mendel used statistical analysis to document the patterned transmission of genetic information. His experiments, his mathematical data analysis, and his theorizing about heredity—specifically, his attempt to delineate the laws governing biological processes—were groundbreaking innovations.

The extensive research that Mendel conducted in his garden led to the science of genetics. His work also resulted in the discovery of the basic principles of inheritance, and to the naming of basic genetic concepts, including dominant traits, recessive traits, **genotype** (the genetic makeup of the living organism), and **phenotype** (the physical characteristics of the living organism). When Mendel was elected the abbot of his monastery in 1868, he had to shift much of his energy and time from scientific to administrative tasks. Gregor Johann Mendel was respected by his fellow monks and by the local townspeople. However, Mendel's scientific genius was not appreciated by the great scientists of his time, and he did not become famous until almost 20 years after his death.

HARRIETTE JOHNSON

Harriette Johnson (1980, 1999) has been one of the lone voices in the social work profession recommending the inclusion of biological science in our knowledge base. Her 1980 book summarized research from neuroanatomy, neurophysiology, neurology, nutritional science, and psychiatry to explain brain functioning and the other biological factors that cause assorted mental disorders. Later, she led a committee of social work educators (Johnson et al., 1990) that established the foundation for the biopsychosocial paradigm. They identified the relevance of biological knowledge to various fields of practice, including aging and substance abuse. They enumerated the social work functions (formal and informal screening, referral, collaboration, case monitoring, advocacy, and therapy) associated with the biological approach, and they suggested various strategies for integrating biological content into the social work curriculum.

More recently, Johnson (1999) has compiled the latest scientific findings and theories from researchers studying the brain; shown the relevance of this knowledge to understanding addiction, human development, and the major psychiatric disorders; and translated complex information about biological functioning and processes into concepts and images for use by social workers who are not medical specialists. The rapid development of biological knowledge and biomedical technologies (brain imaging, biochemical analysis, and electrophysiological measurement tools), Johnson also observed, presents a challenge and opportunity to social workers. Social workers should work to assimilate these scientific and technological advances, she advises, as part of a biological approach that integrates nature and nurture and that appreciates the biological and environmental influences on human behavior. Doing so will increase our ability to help a wider variety of clients dealing with a wider array of troubling conditions.

APPLIED BIOLOGY: ROOT METAPHORS

Two metaphors are implicit in the biological approaches to practice. One comes from evolutionary theorists and their long-term temporal view of adjustments by human populations to environments. The other comes from the more present-oriented temporal perspective of medical scientists and practitioners.

EVOLUTIONARY THEORY: THE ENVIRONMENT AS A JUNGLE

Men and women are like Neanderthals. Society is like a jungle. Some evolutionary theorists prefer this bloody and harsh conceptualization of the social environment. This characterization has been popularized in television game shows about "survivors" and "weakest links." Dangerous toothy predators are eager to eat humans. The environment is continually changing and frequently presents new threats and challenges. Resources are scarce, and different human tribes struggle and compete with each other to gain control over food and shelter. Those who most creatively adapt to environmental contingencies, including the evasion of predators and rivalries with other tribes, survive. The weak die young, and their children die soon after. The winners in the fight to the finish are rewarded with many descendants. Thus, the traits ensuring victory are encoded in genetic information and transmitted across generations. This increases the overall fitness of the winners' tribes. Violence and selfish behavior, in this metaphor, have been the hallmarks of past adaptations. Human beings have become kings of the jungle by their ruthlessness and cunning.

Darwin and other evolutionary theorists offer another image of life in the jungle (Forte, 2001). This comparison of humans to other species suggests that mutual aid and cooperation were the human traits essential to survival. These inclinations were selected for cross-generational transmission because they increased adaptation. Support not struggle characterized successful interaction within and across bands of early humans. Threats from predators and from rival groups required coordinated action. Successful tribal groups regulated competition, worked together to realize the strength in numbers, and collectively generated creative responses to environmental challenges. Resources might have even been abundant in some prehistoric environments, and selfish or violent members were considered a threat to group survival and wealth rather than a group asset. Group continuity was ensured by the isolation of those who committed antisocial acts. Access to food, eligibility for defense by the group, and reproductive advantages went, then, to cooperative and gregarious group members.

Twenty-first-century organizations are sometimes compared to the environmental niches of our ancient ancestors. We live in a concrete jungle. The social work agency is often stratified like bands of apes in the forest, and most organizational members accept their place in the hierarchy: men at the top, women at the bottom. The bosses act at times like dominant gorillas huffing, puffing, and displaying their power to injure subordinates. The workers, in contrast, act like submissive apes showing their willingness to yield by various displays of deference.

EVOLUTIONARY THEORY: THE PERSON AS ANIMAL

Evolutionary theorists think in terms of entire populations of living organisms or species. Humans are members of a distinctive animal species. We trace the emergence of our species-specific capacities for self-awareness and language back about 50,000 years. Darwinians use the image of the tree to characterize the branching from the main trunk of different species, including **Homo sapiens,** the species of modern human beings, across the evolutionary timeline (Leary, 1990). However, the anatomical foundation for these qualities evolved over tens of millions of years, and our distant ancestors during the early phase of this transformation were ancestors to modern chimpanzees and apes. There is continuity between humans and other animals.

In some ways, humans are still like the cave dwellers crudely depicted in movies about prehistoric times. We descended from the trees and began cooperative living in the savannas of Africa. There, our apelike anatomy slowly changed as the species adapted to the environment, and anatomical features similar to those of your family members (erect posture, sensitivity to touch, manual dexterity, and large, complex brains) spread widely. Although the physical environment has been transformed by human ingenuity and humans have created grooming aids and procedures resulting in modern bodies, many of the behavioral tendencies of our cave-dwelling and savannah-roaming ancestors persist today.

Humans resemble animals in basic adaptive characteristics. Evolutionary biologists assert that the elementary mammalian survival mechanisms of flight, fight, feed, fornicate, and startle (4FS), for instance, are still operative. However, they have been elaborated and are now driven by human emotion rather than animal instinct (Wentworth & Yardley, 1994). Evolutionary theorists maintain that contemporary dating and mating practices are like those of our not quite human forerunners (Toates, 2000). Men seek, consciously or unconsciously, women who appear capable of bearing many robust children. Men are inclined toward promiscuous sex, for this increases the likelihood that their genes will be transmitted to the next generation. Women aspire to join with partners who control many resources and can protect the family. Women are biologically wired to prefer monogamous relationships. Of course, culture influences behavioral tendencies. Therefore, the prehistoric patterns of dominance and sexual reproduction that persist today do not completely compel us (and some social theorists wonder if the facts even support these depictions of our inheritance). Evolutionary theorists make frequent comparisons between then and now, between chimpanzees and humans, and between cave dwellers and corporate executives.

EVOLUTIONARY THEORY: THE UNNECESSARY SOCIAL WORKER

Those who endorse the bleak portrait of humans competing violently with one another to survive see no role for the social worker (Stewart & Reynolds, 1985). Social Darwinists urge us to remember and appreciate that "biology is destiny." **Evolution** is an impersonal process of species change across eons, and individuals are helpless and passive. The process of natural selection is not guided, according to users of this jungle metaphor, by God, human design, or social work, but by biological mechanisms that operate like a "blind watchmaker" (Rigney, 2001). Humans are valuable only as bodily carriers of the species genes, not for autonomous and caring decision making. Vicious competition among humans best ensures the advancement of the whole population. Thus, attention to the losers of the competition is unnecessary. Biology is the prime cause of poverty, crime, and individual backwardness, and we cannot change basic human nature. Government programs and social workers only interfere in natural processes of change. Their efforts are ineffective, wasteful, and may even harm the society by keeping weak or inferior members in the gene pool. The only relevant and conceivable interventionist role would be that of "breeder," matching superior males with superior females to create the master race. Here, the social worker becomes like the owner of pure-bred dogs who controls the mating of her animals and purposefully selects the traits to be transmitted across generations.

The alternative depiction of humans cooperating to meet environmental challenges is a minority one. However, a few social group workers have used the image of "mutual aid worker" (Lee & Swanson, 1986) recommended by evolutionary theorists who recognize the limitations of the competition-for-survival metaphor. Social workers might advocate for this version of evolutionary biology, and begin to argue that a bioevolutionary account of human behavior has a place in it for sympathy, sacrifice, altruism, and social work.

MEDICAL MODEL: THE SOCIETY AS A MANAGED CARE SYSTEM

Medical experts are becoming very influential in the United States and Europe (Conrad & Schneider, 1992). The medical metaphor has been extended, and society has become in many ways like a hospital or managed care health system. All sorts of personal and public problems are now defined as diseases or illnesses. Restless children in boring and overcrowded classrooms are diagnosed with attention deficit disorder. Adults behaving in idiosyncratic ways or ways that are not easily comprehended by casual observation have one of hundreds of labels for mental illnesses attached to their condition. Gamblers, drinkers, fighters, overeaters, undereaters, and risk takers are understood as driven by their genes.

Newspapers regularly provide statistical evidence that most of the population suffers from some form of biological malady. Troubling public and personal conditions are increasingly diagnosed as medical problems by physicians, psychiatrists, and other medical experts. Very ill or dying persons are removed from natural settings and cared for in centralized medical facilities. The treatment of choice is a prescribed drug or surgery, and the site of choice for problem resolution is an agency or a health care institution. These may be hospitals, psychiatric facilities, clinics, or family care offices. Such health care settings are pervasive and are easily recognized as different from everyday settings. They are characterized by workers wearing interchangeable uniforms, by the same treatment regimes, by the same kinds of diagnostic and treatment tools, by similar furnishings, by comparable bureaucratic requirements, and by personnel with similar histories of professional socialization.

MEDICAL MODEL: THE PERSON AS PATIENT

Scientists and practitioners who take the short-term temporal perspective on biology compare the person to a biological system interacting with the environment. The medical metaphor (Miller, 1980) prevails in such depictions of the biological person. In the United States, for example, adherents to the medical model view the person as a patient. The label *patient* refers to a person waiting for medical treatment or receiving such medical services, and connotes weakness and dependence. The medical metaphor directs primary attention to diseases and other physical disorders. The patient exhibits symptoms that can only be interpreted accurately by a doctor or other expert in disease states. Diseases have a specific and identifiable cause, and the course of the disease is generally predictable. The locus of the disease is the patient's body, and treatment is directed to the disordered physical state, not to the larger environmental context. Treatment should be based on state-of-the-art empirical studies of efficacy. Patients have little say in any phase of the study-diagnosis-treatment process. *Compliance* rather than *participation* is the term for an effective patient response to treatment. Self-care or medication independent of medical oversight is discouraged. The patient is often treated as a machine, and the repair of damaged parts or inoperative mechanical systems proceeds with minimal if any attention to the person's feelings or thoughts.

MEDICAL MODEL: THE SOCIAL WORKER AS AUXILIARY TO MEDICAL PROFESSIONALS

The social worker is defined, according to the medical model, as an auxiliary to the medical professionals. In all health care settings, physicians have high status and social workers have low status. Physicians are most often male, social workers female. This reinforces the status differential. Physicians formalize the diagnosis, recommend the treatment, judge the efficacy of treatment, and make decisions related to physical deterioration. Social workers assist by identifying clients who are showing signs of a physical malady, by referring these clients to medical experts, by monitoring the client during the recovery process, and by guiding the discharge from the hospital. Social workers do not tell doctors what to do. Ideally, however, social workers contribute their assessment of the client as a whole person. Social workers assist also by engaging families in supporting the ill person, by preparing patients for reentry into the community, by offering bereavement services when loved ones die, by individualizing the designated patient so that his or her identity and relationship concerns are heard, and by educating patients to the dynamics of the recovery process.

Perhaps this discussion of the metaphorical base for the biomedical approach has understated the accomplishments of the medical approach to health sciences and overstated the pervasiveness of a profit-driven, corporate model of medicine. My discussion does not consider the newer or alternative approaches to health. New metaphors, for example, are associated with "holistic healing" and "wellness or health orientations." These alternatives are being developed as sensible ways to conceptualize the person, the environment, and the social worker. These new frameworks may resonate with social work values and principles better than the traditional medical model and may evoke greater professional interest in biological approaches to practice.

CORE ASSUMPTIONS OF APPLIED BIOLOGY

Evolutionary and biological theorists often hold the following assumptions.

BODY, MIND, AND CULTURE INFLUENCE HUMAN ACTION

The biological approach assumes that the body, the mind, and the culture influence human action in an interrelated way. Most advocates of the biological approach reject the separation of nature from nurture and of biology from the environment. The human organism cannot be understood apart from the environment, and the environment cannot be understood without understanding the biological features of human organisms. Your individuality, the distinctive way you are as a community member, emerged as a result of a complex sequence of transactions between your body's unique collection of genes, the particular environments in which you developed, and your personal choices (Riley, 1991). Averill (1990) cleverly summarizes this assumption: "humans are 'partly finished' at birth, with biological maturation completing one part and socialization the other" (p. 120).

Biopsychosocial theory users prefer multifactor models explaining human behavior and human development to single-factor models (Susman, 2001). Freud might explain mental abnormalities in terms of one main factor, intrapsychic conflict. A multifactor model, in contrast, would explain mental illness in terms of the interplay of genetic endowment, health history, social memberships, socialization experiences, life choices, organizational processes in the social environment, perceptions, expectations, stereotypes, and social norms (Piliavin & LePore, 1995). Other troubling conditions reported by social work clients, such as physical abnormalities, diseases, and developmental problems, are also caused or influenced by many different factors.

However, biological theorists still take sides in the **nature/nurture debate** by giving different weight to genes and the environment (Dodge, 2004). Johnson (1999) suggests that the essential ingredients for human action—body, mind, and culture—might be assumed to balance in three different ways. First, the influence might be mostly biological with fewer contributions from environmental factors. Some pervasive developmental disorders are thought to be fundamentally biological. Second, the influence might be mostly cultural with lesser contributions from biological factors. The posttraumatic stress disorders reported by Vietnam veterans after their combat experience may be accompanied by flashbacks, night sweats, waves of terror, and other painful bodily experiences, but it is caused primarily by lengthy physical exposure to the overwhelming environmental stressors associated with immersion in a total war. Third, the influence might be distributed fairly equally across biological, psychological, and sociological influence factors. Contemporary conceptions of alcohol addiction assume this pattern (Toates, 2000). The different ways that body, mind, and culture can be balanced will be elaborated further.

SOME BIOLOGICAL THEORISTS ASSUME THAT BIOLOGICAL INFLUENCES ARE STRONGEST

Some advocates of the biological approach assume that biological processes will have the strongest influence. Evolutionary theorists emphasize the determining influence of the distant past on human action. Our biology was patterned to fit with the physical and social environments of early humans. We are animals, with a physical form and a set of behavioral tendencies that have evolved from those of our primate ancestors who lived in a distinctive environment. This form and this set of tendencies influence our actions in contemporary environments, even though human settlements and ecological niches are different from those of our ancestors (Piliavin & LePore, 1995). The combination of form and dispositions inherited by all species members has been called human nature, the human biogram, or our species-specific capacities (Forte, 2001).

Evolutionary theorists trace human evolution over 35 million years up to the emergence 70,000 to 50,000 years ago of members of the species *Homo sapiens*, humans with symbol-making and symbol-using capacities. The most common ancestral environments, the environments of evolutionary adaptedness, were the savannas and woodlands of south central Africa. Prehumans had ventured down from the trees and organized in small bands as hunters and gatherers. Population density was low, but there were many predators and threats.

Body changes that contributed to success in this environment were selected for transmission to the next generations. These became the channels and bodily equipment necessary for the exercise of our species-specific adaptive capacities. Transformations included the growth of the brain's limbic system, with resulting increases in the ability to experience and emit numerous emotions; expansion in the size and organization of the neocortex, with resulting capacities for symbolization, cognitive storage and retrieval, and self-awareness; elaboration of the vocal tract, including control of lip and tongue muscles, which made possible vocalization (and the ability to refrain from screaming when near a predator); bipedalism, with an erect posture and a stance facing others supporting capacities for interpreting nonverbal communication and for expressing intent and emotion facially; and increased manual dexterity and sensitivity to touch, which facilitated the use of fingers to touch others and to use tools.

The evolved human body included mental and behavioral capacities especially suited for coordinated activity with others. I will describe these capacities in detail later. These adaptive traits are attributes and inclinations that all members of the human species share, although people vary in the degree to which they actualize their adaptive potentials. These capacities and our basic biological nature exert a powerful influence on many areas of contemporary social life, including mating and reproduction, child rearing, social organization and hierarchies, patterns of cooperation and competition, communication of emotions, ethnocentrism, and distinctions between in-group and out-group (Piliavin & LePore, 1995).

Biological scientists assume, too, that the more recent past influences human action. Riley (1991), for instance, indicated that "human beings carry with them chemically encoded information that makes each a member of the human species and each a unique individual. This information is shuffled, reshuffled, and changed by natural and unnatural events and through heredity influences the next generation of people" (p. 297). **Heredity** includes those characteristics or traits transmitted from one generation to the next, such as hair or eye color, blood type, and ear lobe shape. Heredity also includes **genetic predispositions.** These are biological traits that increase a person's susceptibility to environmental influences and, for example, the development of diseases such as hypertension, peptic ulcers, heart disease, and some forms of cancer. Even biological theorists who emphasize the power of genes accept that the development of a disease in persons with certain genes is probable but not automatic (Susman, 2001). Environmental and contextual factors may promote or prevent the expression of the inherited condition.

Membership in certain ethnic/racial groups or in communities from a particular geographic region brings with it a higher incidence of a particular **genetic disorder** (health problems associated with the genes) than is found in the general population. Persons from equatorial Africa, and less commonly the Mediterranean area, are prone, for example, to sickle cell anemia. The bodies of those with this condition have abnormally shaped blood cells that do not carry oxygen effectively. This results in reduced oxygen supply and episodes of severe pain, often requiring lifestyle restrictions. One in 12 persons of African descent in the United States carries the trait for sickle cell anemia (Riley, 1991).

Biological scientists have used adoption studies to identify the relative influence of genes on behavior. Which is more influential, shared heredity or shared environment? Researchers have examined how identical twins separated after birth and raised in different environments are alike and different. Research shows that separated siblings are often like each other in many ways despite growing up in different social environments. Studies of twins reared apart have shown genetic effects on income, personality, divorce, sexual behavior, smoking, selection of friends, and delinquent behavior (Udry, 1995). These findings support the assumption that biological variables are most useful in explaining human variation and human vulnerabilities. Please note that Hoffman (1985), a developmental psychologist, disagrees with the strong statements of the biological scientists using adoption studies. She claims that these studies have some methodological weaknesses. For example, the research design assumption that identical and fraternal twins have equally similar environments underestimates the likelihood that families react differently to twins who look alike compared to those with different appearances.

SOME BIOLOGICAL THEORISTS ASSUME THAT PSYCHOSOCIAL INFLUENCES ARE STRONGEST

Some advocates of the biological approach assume that in most cases, psychological and social processes have the strongest influence on human action (Susman, 2001). There is much evidence, for instance, that social groups differ in their responses to pain, symptom recognition, symptom interpretation, willingness to adopt the sick role, compliance with medical instructions, understanding of disease and medication, and patterns of health care usage (Kessler, House, Anspach, & Williams, 1995). Diseases and their interpretations exist in a cultural matrix, and social memberships related to ethnicity, class, and gender influence individual and social patterns of disease management. Women, for example, are more likely than men to monitor bodily sensations and to identify biologically based problems and seek help. There is evidence also that psychosocial traumas produce alterations in the body (Susman, 2001). For example, emotional stressors change hormone levels, primarily the hormone cortisol; these changes have been documented in infants, children, teenagers, and adults.

In the United States, different social classes have different health care opportunities. The poor tend to use health services as a last resort because the public and emergency health care services that they use are impersonal, highly alienating, low in quality, and very bureaucratic. Physicians also respond differently to patients based on their social memberships. Similar patient complaints evoke different diagnoses and treatment recommendations depending on the person's ethnicity and class. I worked, for example, with many adults discharged from state mental hospitals in the late 1970s. They were generally poor and usually people of color. They had been uniformly diagnosed as schizophrenic, but after release back to the community, it became clear that more of their troubles were related to poverty, low education, unusual physical appearance, or racism than to any mental disorder.

Many other biological processes are very strongly influenced by social memberships and culture. Families, for instance, affect many aspects of physical functioning and teach us how to channel various biological impulses. Family members teach us what impulses should be inhibited and what should be enacted. Such training can form physical habits and patterns that last a lifetime. Social groups influence our physical response to legal and illegal drugs. Novices are taught what it means to get "high" from marijuana and how to interpret the sensations associated with ecstasy. Without such lessons, a drug often has minimal impact on consciousness. Societies develop **appearance norms,** shared standards for judging physical appearance such as fat or thin, beautiful or ugly, and **appearance ideals,** social preferences regarding body stature, smells, skin colors, and hair textures. These norms and ideals affect our body image and body management, and they are implicated in physical disorders such as anorexia nervosa and bulimia. Finally, the criminal justice system in a given culture codifies acceptable bodily control procedures. Some of its agents are authorized to use physical punishment and threats of pain to obtain compliance from the citizenry. A person's health, sexual integrity, and life are jeopardized when his or her violation of law results in imprisonment.

Biological theorists committed to this assumption would agree with Kagan's (2003) summary of the scholarly trend: "contemporary scientists are more receptive to the suggestion that the meaning of most behavioral and biological reactions depends on the context" (p. 20).

SOME BIOLOGICAL THEORISTS ASSUME THE INTERRELATED INFLUENCE OF THREE PROCESSES

Some advocates of the biological approach assume that in most cases, biological, psychological, and social processes have relatively equivalent influence on human action. This holistic perspective assumes that "the functioning of the individual is consistently self-organized by the integration of psychological, biological, and social contextual processes" (Susman, 2001, p. 166). Our life chances are affected by both biological variables (vitality, hardiness, natural abilities) and societal reactions to our physical attributes (Piliavin & LePore, 1995). These physical features (height, body structure, facial features, hair, skin, eye color) have both an objective aspect and a subjective aspect. A blind person may be artistically talented yet not welcomed into educational settings for painters. A woman may be big, strong, fast, and tough, but she will never be employed by a national football team. Physically attractive people, whatever their actual capabilities, are perceived as special and thus receive preferential treatment in U.S. society. Physically attractive people earn more money, are promoted more often, are punished more leniently by juries, and are more likely to be divorced. Taller persons occupy higher status social positions and attain higher levels of education than shorter persons. Some bodily characteristics are stigmatized. **Stigma** refers to socially devalued characteristics. People with physical disabilities (blindness, spinal cord injury, amputation, or deforming scars) are stigmatized as inferior community members and discriminated against in employment, housing, transportation, and recreational activities.

Biological, psychological, and social processes influence illness behavior in an interrelated manner. Children at the Ronald McDonald Houses throughout the world suffer from various forms of cancer. Each disease has predictable symptoms, a likely course, and typical debilitating effects on the child's body. Yet the child's sense of self, her expectations that she can adapt to a changing body, and her positive thoughts and emotions can activate healing processes that curtail the disease's progression. Family members and friends also can rally, providing continuous supportive help and encouragement. The social agency provides food and housing, psychosocial programs, and financial support to minimize stressors that often diminish recuperative processes. The three dimensions—body, mind, and culture—can be interrelated in negative ways, too. Diseases and other biological disorders may impair cognitive or motor processes and restrict the person's ability to take on the roles and responsibilities necessary for capable participation in school, family, and community. The afflicted person may yield to despair and hopelessness. Community supports may be minimal.

Human growth and development are life processes that respond to biological, psychological, and social influences (Johnson, 1999). Human growth is the biopsychosocial process of adding new components to human physical structure, and development is the biopsychosocial process of improving the body components and their relations to each other (Ashford,

LeCroy, & Lortie, 2001). Biological and social scientists have learned that humans experience **critical periods** during the life cycle (Salkind, 1985). These are periods of growth when the developing person is most sensitive and receptive to opportunities for growth. After the period passes, the body has changed in ways such that mastery of relevant and basic psychosocial functions may not be possible. Wild or feral children deprived of interaction with other humans will not be able to learn language after the age of 10. Learning a second language must occur before adolescence if the learner is to speak fluently and without an accent. Capacities for social attachment, musical talent, emotional control, and other human functions develop best during the first five years of life.

Biology, psychology, and the social sciences all contribute to our understanding of failures in human development. Here is a vivid example. For many years, a cruel dictator ruled the country of Romania. He showed little interest in the well-being of the nation. Children abandoned by their parents were raised in large orphanages. Staffing was minimal, and there were no educational or developmental services for these children. These orphans spent the early years of their lives with inadequate diets, little physical contact, few intellectual challenges, and minimal social stimulation. American parents adopted some of these orphans in the 1990s, after the fall of the dictator. However, the combined effects of biological, psychological, and social injury were very great. No amount of loving care and nourishment could heal some of these orphans. The critical period had passed. Many had suffered irreparable damage, and their adoptive parents resigned themselves to the realization that their adopted children would never develop the capacities necessary for good social relationships and independent community life.

THE BIOLOGICAL MODEL OF HUMAN DEVELOPMENT

In this section, I will discuss the biological approach to human change across the life span. The section will include a profile of the exemplary scholar in this tradition; a review of the assumptions, metaphors, concepts, and propositions of the biological model; and a brief overview of its applications.

Arnold Gesell: Exemplary Role Model

Arnold Gesell (1880–1961) grew up in Alma, Wisconsin, and had a long and productive career (Ames, 1989). His town was situated on the banks of the Mississippi River, and as a child Gesell was fascinated by the cycle of the seasons. Gesell would later use similar imagery, "seasons and sequences," in characterizing the human life cycle (Craig, 1980, p. 21). He taught elementary school in New York City and lived in an East Side Social Settlement House before beginning his academic career. Gesell earned a doctorate in psychology and became a practicing psychologist, but to increase his knowledge of the biological processes essential to human development, he went to medical school at the age of 30 and earned a medical degree.

Arnold Gesell directed the Yale Clinic of Child Development for almost five decades. There, he engaged in extensive studies of the neurological and motor development of babies and children. His theorizing about child development was influenced by Darwin's theory of evolution but expanded our understanding of the relevance of various biological factors to patterns and rates of maturation (Salkind, 1985). He also pioneered many important methods for conducting developmental science. Gesell created one of the first tests of infant intelligence in 1941. He was one of the first researchers to make extensive use of photography and of "cinema records." For example, he studied five infants during their first year of life by filming their daily activity and then studied the same children again five years later (Salkind, 1985). Gesell and his colleagues also pioneered observation through one-way mirrors for research purposes and the use of co-twin research designs to study the relative influence of nature and nurture.

Gesell's work became the basis for a successful series of parent-oriented child development books written for the general public (Goldhaber, 2000). The series covered development from birth to early adolescence and outlined expected behaviors year by year while discouraging socialization agents from pushing children to develop faster than they are ready to develop (Salkind, 1985). He was considered an expert on babies and also influenced the thinking and work of Dr. Benjamin Spock. Arnold Gesell trained many researchers to collect data on child development in his clinic, and he and these researchers produced many influential reports. The Gesell Institute carries on his work today.

ASSUMPTIONS OF THE BIOLOGICAL MODEL

Adherents to the biological approach to human development like Arnold Gesell give the greatest causal power to a person's biological makeup (Clausen, 1986). One's sex, temperament, intelligence, appearance, body build (height, weight, and strength) energy level, physical integrity (or impairment), and maturational tendencies (early, on-time, or late) are biological givens that determine the life course. Genetic inputs to developmental processes are important. The child's first experiences with the environment in the womb, as affected by the mother's overall health, diet, drinking or smoking behavior, and exposure to physical trauma, are also important.

Clausen (1986) identifies some of the ways that biology influences development. A person's biological makeup sets the periods of readiness to advance developmentally. Biological makeup sets limits to the development of potential and the length of one's life. Brain maturation is slow in the early years of life, and this sets constraints on possibilities for behavior, feeling, and cognition; for example, limitations on the retrieval of past events and on empathy by infants are biologically based (Kagan, 2003). A person's biological makeup sets predispositions that direct a person to take advantage of certain opportunities—sports or academic pursuits, for instance—and that increase vulnerabilities to problems such as mental illness or substance abuse. Biological makeup also influences how others are likely to respond to us. When I worked with developmentally challenged adults, one of our Coffee House members struggled with the stigma of elephantitis, an abnormal enlargement of certain parts of the body. His head was considerably bigger than normal and very misshapen. Others avoided or feared him, even though he was a gentle and friendly person.

ROOT METAPHORS OF THE BIOLOGICAL MODEL

The scientists of Gesell's time were advancing the study of embryology, and used powerful microscopes to document how the embryo of any organism develops in a series of predictable steps organized in a clear sequence. This notion of the "sequential unfolding of structures" became a foundational metaphor for Gesell's conception of human development after birth (Craig, 1980, p. 21). Humans develop like the embryo according to an "inner timetable" that determines readiness to master new environmental challenges—the skills necessary to stand and walk, for example. Human capacities unfold according to a predefined genetic plan, "a plan that more closely resembles a blueprint than a rough sketch" (Goldhaber, 2000, p. 163). A plant or animal embryo grows in a predictable and orderly fashion, and all plants or animals of the same species follow this plan. Humans are the same, developmental biologists believe.

GESELL'S BIOLOGICAL MODEL OF HUMAN DEVELOPMENT

Developmental psychobiology (Goldhaber, 2000) is the approach to the science of human development that searches for tangible links between the maturation of biological structures and the development of functional capacities. Arnold Gesell was the premier theorist in this tradition. I will first define some of the concepts in his model of development and then present a set of propositions from the Gesell Institute.

Maturation is the mechanism by which genes direct the human developmental process according to an intrinsic, inborn schedule anchored in millions of years of biological evolution and regulated by human genes (Craig, 1980; Goldhaber, 2000; Salkind, 1985). Gesell gave special attention to changes in biological structures, especially the structure of the nervous system, and theorized that each growth step is only possible because of the previous step (Goldhaber, 2000). This maturational perspective assumes that development is orderly and sequential, that "physical structure must be present and developed before function can occur, and behavior is simply not possible if the necessary structures have not yet developed" (Salkind, 1985, p. 43). Changes in structures make possible the emergence of new developmental stages. Advances in the organization of the nervous system, for instance, are necessary precursors to cognitive and social advances. The lifetime pattern to development for a species is revealed as the organism matures (Salkind, 1985). Gesell and his colleagues worked industriously to observe and document the maturational pattern universal for the human organism.

Readiness refers to maturational growth that allows the human organism to take advantage of learning opportunities (Salkind, 1985). Readiness is rooted in the developing person's biological makeup and cannot be produced or accelerated by external agents (Gesell Institute, 2005).

All children develop through the same sequences, but children vary in how quickly they grow. A particular child's **rate of development** depends on the child's genetic background (Salkind, 1985). Gesell was not a complete biological determinist. He believed that developmental rates can be altered temporarily by environmental factors, such as malnutrition or illness, that reduce the quality of developmental outcomes. Rates of development can also be enhanced by enriching and meaningful experiences, enabling a child to grow more fully within a developmental stage (Gesell Institute, 2005). Gesell's colleagues summarized his position: "A favorable environment (home or otherwise) can, it appears, permit each individual to develop his most positive assets for living. An unfavorable environment may inhibit and depress his natural potentials. But no environment, good or bad, as far as we know can change him from one kind of individual to another" (Ilg & Ames, 1955, p. 44).

A **favorable environment,** then, is necessary to ensure the developing person's realization of his or her potentials as a human (remember the contrast to the environments of institutionalized children discussed earlier). However, Gesell was firm in his conviction that although favorable environments support and may modify the maturational forces, environmental factors do not change the norms or sequence of development (Goldhaber, 2000). Biological forces provide the essential energy and direction for human development (Salkind, 1985).

Though sequenced in universal ways, child development makes possible human individuality (Gesell Institute, 2005; Salkind, 1985). Gesell identified four developmental areas and argued that children differ in the interaction of these domains. *Neurological-motor growth* refers to locomotion and specific motor skills. *Adaptive behavior* refers to the child's ability to profit from past experience and apply learning to new situations. Adaptive behavior includes alertness, intelligence, and different forms of exploration. *Language development* refers to all forms of communication, and *personal-social behavior* refers to interactions with persons and with the environment. Gesell and his colleagues contended that each child is unique because heredity, developmental pace, health, and environmental influences contribute differentially to each child's progress in the four developmental domains (Gesell Institute, 2005).

Gesell's careful and extensive observations of developing children in scientific longitudinal studies resulted in the creation of a **developmental schedule,** expectations of what human beings can be expected to do at various ages. Achievement of a developmental milestone requires the demonstrated capacity to accomplish the major tasks associated with the milestone. Gesell and his team (Gesell, Ilg, Ames, & Bullis, 1977) documented normative patterns of growth for motor characteristics such as eye–hand coordination, personal hygiene, emotional expression, fear management, self-concept, sexual behavior, interpersonal relations, play and leisure time activity, school adjustment, ethical sense, and philosophical outlook toward time, space, death, and deity. This work resulted in the creation of widely used developmental norm charts and characterizations of the "typical day" of children at different ages (Goldhaber, 2000).

The Gesell Developmental Schedule is now called the Gesell Developmental Observation and Screening Tool. It requires observations by a trained examiner and measures a developing person's responses to standardized items and to situations, summarized as both qualitative and quantitative data. The results of a screening are formulated as a **developmental age** (which may differ from chronological age), defined as the composite of functional ability in physical, social, emotional, and intellectual domains. Each child screened is then compared to normative patterns for the same chronological age and given a **developmental quotient,** the portion of normal development present for the particular person at that age (Gesell Institute, 2005). These tools are used to identify areas of concern—for example, in relation to a developing person's ability to meet the school expectations established by educational curricula. Here's an illustration. The Gesell Institute (2005) uses more than 30 indicators of developmental readiness to observe and judge if a child should begin kindergarten. These indicators include the ability to stay comfortable away from parents for several hours, to express ideas and feelings to adults other than parents, to take care of toileting needs independently, to enter a new activity without fear, to listen to and follow directions, to hold a book upright, and to state one's full name and age to a teacher.

PROPOSITIONS FROM THE BIOLOGICAL MODEL

Gesell also developed a set of theoretical principles of development. The principle of *developmental direction* states that bodily organization and control advances from the body's center to periphery. The principle of *functional asymmetry* states that some behaviors go through a period of unbalanced or asymmetric development, resulting in a right or left hand preference, for example. The principle of *self-regulatory fluctuation* states that development progresses through periods of stability and instability (Craig, 1980; Salkind, 1985).

Developmental psychobiology propositions regarding the practical use of Gesell's theoretical concepts and principles will be more relevant to social workers. The Gesell Institute (2005) identifies a set of principles that can guide parents, educators, social workers, and others working for healthy development. I have reworded them slightly to follow the propositional form used in earlier chapters. First, the more that environments are arranged with attention to the person's developmental level, the better will be the person's learning. Second, the better the assessment of the child's individualized developmental pace and strategies, the better will be the planning of development-enhancing experiences. Third, the more careful the observation of a developing person's readiness for developmental growth, the more likely it is that the parent, teacher, or social worker will correctly time the presentation of challenging new content or activities.

CRITICAL COMMENTS

Critics have identified weaknesses in Gesell's theoretical model and research. The standards or age norms attached to his developmental schedule were based on too narrow a sample: middle-class children in a university community in New Haven, Connecticut (Craig, 1980). Gesell engaged in too little exploration of possible cultural differences in the predicted patterns of human development. His developmental psychobiology was child centered and would be more useful if extended to adulthood and later life. Finally, Gesell placed too much emphasis on the power of genetic determinants (Goldhaber, 2000). He doubted that training could modify biologically set characteristics, such as inborn athletic ability, and he gave too little credit to environmental influences, especially the cumulative effects of environmental experiences or training that do not show up immediately. For this reason, his model subtly discourages interventions directed at the environmental changes that might enhance human development (Salkind, 1985).

APPLICATIONS OF THE BIOLOGICAL MODEL OF HUMAN DEVELOPMENT

Gesell's child-centered model influenced parenting practices. He and his colleagues promoted the balancing of social expectations with maturational mechanisms (Craig, 1980). For example, newborn babies should be fed when they communicate cues indicating hunger cravings. Only as the child's control of the gastrointestinal tract, language mastery, time perspective, and overall capacity for self-regulation increase should he or she be expected to eat in accord with a family timetable rather than an inner timetable. Gesell's Developmental Schedule, its developmental behavior norms related to the four domains outlined above, and the developmental quotient derived from the schedule are still used by psychologists, pediatricians, and doctors to screen for developmental delay and to determine a child's readiness for entry into the formal education system (Goldhaber, 2000).

Arnold Gesell was very devoted to improvements in the child welfare system (Adoption History Project, 2005). He championed minimum standards for adoption and the involvement of professionals in the family formation process. He worked with the Child Welfare League of America and spoke on topics such as placement age, preplacement testing, clinical supervision in adoption, the confidentiality of adoption records, and parent–child matching. The Gesell Development Schedule was used to help social workers minimize underplacement (bright children to dull parents) and overplacement (dull children to bright parents). His arguments for the relevance of applied developmental psychobiology are still timely: "systematic psychoclinical examinations not only will reduce the wastes of error and miscarriage but will serve to reveal the children of normal and superior endowment beneath the concealment of neglect, of poverty, and of poor repute. Clinical safeguards cannot solve all the problems of child adoptions but they can steadily improve its methods and make them both more scientific and humane" (quoted in Adoption Project History, 2005, p. 2).

MAPPING THE BIOLOGICAL APPROACH

Figure 6.1 maps the ideas of evolutionary biologists onto a modified eco-map. This section translates the theoretical framework into answers to my basic eco-map and ecosystems questions. The eco-map display and discussion include concepts from both the evolutionary and biomedical traditions.

FIGURE 6.1
THE
BIOLOGICAL
VERSION OF
THE ECO-MAP

Source: Adapted with permission from *Family-Centered Social Work Practice* (p. 160) by A. Hartman & J. Laird, 1983. New York: The Free Press.

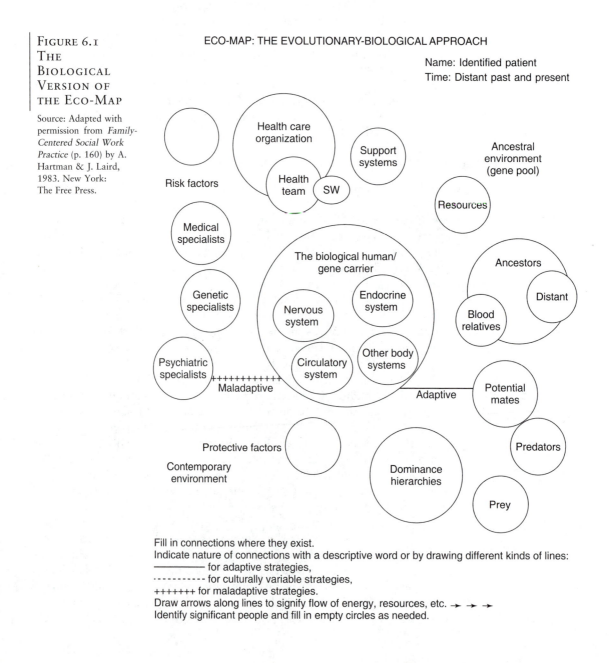

ECO-MAP: THE EVOLUTIONARY-BIOLOGICAL APPROACH

Name: Identified patient
Time: Distant past and present

Risk factors

Health care organization

Support systems

Ancestral environment (gene pool)

Health team SW

Resources

Medical specialists

The biological human/ gene carrier

Ancestors

Distant

Genetic specialists

Endocrine system

Nervous system

Blood relatives

Psychiatric specialists ++++++++++ Maladaptive

Circulatory system

Other body systems

Adaptive

Potential mates

Protective factors

Contemporary environment

Dominance hierarchies

Predators

Prey

Fill in connections where they exist.
Indicate nature of connections with a descriptive word or by drawing different kinds of lines:
———— for adaptive strategies,
----------- for culturally variable strategies,
++++++ for maladaptive strategies.
Draw arrows along lines to signify flow of energy, resources, etc. → → →
Identify significant people and fill in empty circles as needed.

How Are Connections Conceptualized?

Biological scientists often use the word **transactions** to characterize connections between the biological person and the environment (Johnson, 1980). The person is a living organism transacting across the body's boundaries. The continuation of the life process requires the intake of oxygen and nourishment from the outside world. As output, the energized organism acts in the immediate environment to satisfy needs and interests and to respond to challenges.

Environments change. The process of adjusting to these changing conditions and to the problems related to life challenges (finding food, securing shelter, mating, and avoiding predators, for example) is called **adaptation.** Adaptation is the active effort of the human species to achieve a pattern of optimal transactions, a goodness-of-fit with its environment, by competing and cooperating with other members of the species (and with members of other species) in response to pressing environmental contingencies (Riley, 1991). Human–environment transactions necessitate adaptive solutions to meet the challenges from the environment related to physical survival and the quality of life; to reproduction, including the maintenance of the population's size; and to the emotional, practical, and political complexities of human group life.

How Is the Quality of Connections Differentiated?

Evolutionary biologists assert that the responses of any organism to environmental challenges can increase or decrease its **fitness,** its suitability for life under particular contextual conditions.

Positive connections are adaptive. They enable the species to meet the challenges presented by environmental conditions, to enhance growth and development, and to accomplish life transitions successfully (Saleeby, 1992). Humans have adapted in many different ways. In general biological terms, adaptive strategies include effective methods for handling stress, optimal dietary and nutritional practices, mental activity, exercise, regular and adequate patterns of sleep, and lifestyle choices that use alcohol in moderation.

The evolved human body provides us with the species-specific capacities, discussed earlier, allowing flexible and creative psychosocial adaptation. **Emotionality** is one. Our large repertoire of emotions and ability to express and interpret these emotions, when used well, increase our survival chances by providing the means for constructing cohesive, energized, sympathetic, and well-regulated social participation.

Symbolic thought is another distinctive human capacity. Humans can retrieve memories, view themselves in social situations, visualize goals, and ponder alternative solutions to problems. These activities increase survival chances by freeing humans from stimulus–response chains and fostering creative responses to new predicaments.

Self-objectification or self-awareness is the human ability to conceive of the self as an object in the environment. This capacity enhances our survival chances by allowing us to integrate our actions with others, delay impulsive action, follow rules, play, and merge with social roles.

Symbolic communication includes the capacity to vocalize, to assign meaning to objects, to adhere to and create variation from grammar, and to present and interpret words, gestures, and meaningful objects. This set of capacities increases our survival chances by facilitating the transmission of cultural knowledge across generations and across local environments, by helping groups of people make sense of environmental challenges, and by enabling the formation of mutual aid societies. In summary, these species-specific capacities for sociality provide the foundation for adaptive responses. They increase human fitness by multiplying individual powers through cooperation with others, by regulating competition, by improving the use of intelligence for problem solving, by attracting and securing mates, and by strengthening human resilience in the face of stressful environments (Wentworth & Yardley, 1994).

Negative connections are maladaptive responses. Here, the species or individual member fails to meet the challenges presented by environmental conditions. Such failures may derive from several sources. First, the person may have failed to learn appropriate adaptive strategies during development. For example, children deprived of models of competent language use or exposed to television violence will have difficulty in situations requiring peaceful cooperation. Second, the person may use adaptive strategies with a physiological base linked to earlier ancestral environments. However, these strategies are not well matched to the demands or opportunities of the current environment. Certain behaviors that were adaptive for savannah dwellers 50,000 years ago—the consumption of fat and sugar, for example, in an environment where these substances were scarce and where quick energy bursts enabled flight from predators—can be maladaptive today. Excessive consumption of sweets and fatty foods results in obesity, and this impinges on movement and threatens our health. Third, the person may be acting adaptively, but as a nonconforming member of a population most of which is failing to adapt to changing environmental conditions. Thus, the larger community negates the individual's actions (Crawford, 1998). The purchaser of a high-mileage hybrid car will do little to preserve a pollution-free environment in a society where gas mileage is the 20th factor car buyers consider in vehicle selection. Finally, the person may succumb to biological disorders—genetic defects, brain damage, or disease—that make adaptive responses to the environment extremely difficult.

Tentative or ambiguous connections can be defined in biological theory as culturally variable response patterns. Such behaviors might be adaptive in certain social environments but not in others. Delayed child rearing and the use of birth control by women in information-oriented economies and societies that support female careers are adaptive. Societies organized around family-based farming, in contrast, would consider such choices maladaptive.

What Is the Typical Focal System?

Biologically oriented social workers and biomedical professionals typically give central attention to the individual. The individual is considered a biological system composed of many subsystems. Each subsystem has a different function, and all systems must operate in harmony for the biological person to achieve a degree of overall adaptation to the environment (Ashford et al., 2001; Gilson, 1999). The following is an abbreviated listing of some of the major subsystems in the evolved human body and possible adaptive challenges presented by their failure. The human nervous system includes the brain, spinal cord, and nerves It directs mental functions like thinking and planning, integrates sensory information, and makes language, the control of movement, and emotions possible. Brain injuries following a car accident, a fall, or poisoning, for instance, compromise adaptive capacities. The cardiovascular system is made up of the heart and the blood circulatory system. It is charged with maintaining the blood flow through the body. Adaptive challenges follow circulatory problems such as high blood pressure, blockage of arteries, or a heart attack. The respiratory system is organized around the lungs and handles the inhalation of oxygen and the exhalation of carbon dioxide. Problems such as bronchial asthma and attacks of shortness of breath can make an environmental adjustment very difficult. The endocrine system regulates the release of hormones into the bloodstream. These hormones arouse the body in response to perceived threat or crisis, play a part in normal body growth, and are important to body metabolism, learning, and memory. Diabetes mellitus is a condition related to problems with insulin production and utilization and can lead to blindness or infections. The musculoskeletal system includes the body's skeleton and all the muscles attached to the bones of the skeleton. It is charged with supporting the body and allowing it to move. Limb injury and problems associated with the overuse of certain muscle groups, as in repetitive motion disorders, can lessen chances for success in some work environments.

How Is the Environment Conceptualized?

Biological scientists are partial to general systems frameworks. The environment is conceptualized as consisting of the internal environment (the biological systems within the body) and the surrounding external environment: culture; economic, political, and other social institutions; and social organizations such as schools, agencies, and health care facilities. Although the internal and the external environments are separated by a boundary, the human skin, they are inseparable. Interaction between the internal and external environments is continual, optimally achieving a state of equilibrium. Disturbances in this equilibrium can arise from interior physiological events such as a vitamin deficiency, or they may be triggered by events external to the body such as a hurricane destroying one's community (Johnson, 1980). **Stress** is the indicator of a disturbance in the equilibrium achieved between organism and environment. Adaptive actions are those that respond effectively to the stress and restore equilibrium.

Social systems in the external environment can be divided into those conceptualized by evolutionary theorists, the ancestral environment, and those relevant to biomedical scientists, the contemporary environment. A bioevolutionary eco-map should include a circle indicating the continued influence of our species ancestors. Some contemporary social groups and persons have special valence for members of the human species because of our evolutionary inheritance. We are predisposed to respond alertly to social hierarchies, group structures characterized by patterns of dominance and subordination. Humans, like other primates, are sensitive to others' direct displays of physical superiority and of their ability to use violent methods skillfully. However, we are also sensitive to indirect and subtle displays of social status—information about another's reputation, for instance. In many modern societies, elite status in the social structure is more often obtained by the verbal assertion of honor and status and verbal threats of harmful action against others than by physical violence. The human sensitivity to hierarchy increases our ability to maintain social ties, avoid ostracism, obtain the benefits distributed by dominant leaders, and climb as high as possible given our attributes and the environmental opportunities.

Humans are also alert, bioevolutionary theorists claim, to possible sexual mates. We are predisposed to seek mates who display indicators of fitness. Do they appear biologically sound and good partners for the production of high-quality offspring? Females with prominent breasts (naturally or enhanced by clothing, cosmetics, or surgery) are more salient to men than those with unnoticeable breasts. Prospective partners attempt to advertise by their breasts that they are young, healthy, ready to reproduce, and able to nurse the young. I will leave to your imagination the bodily displays offered by males, and how these may act like the colorful plumage of male peacocks as sexual attractants to females.

The ancestral environment's influence is carried into the contemporary environment as the gene pool. Genetic scientists would include as part of a client's eco-map all of his or her blood relatives across at least three generations. These are our close ancestors, and we share many genes with them. Information about our genetic ancestors and their traits might help the social worker identify the likelihood of genetic disorders in desired offspring and the genetic vulnerabilities that might become activated in the adults.

A biologically oriented eco-map should include the health service organization with primary responsibility for care of the client. In this organization, the social worker often participates as a member of an interdisciplinary team charged with attending to the patient's biopsychosocial needs. The contemporary environment also includes numerous other health organizations and biomedical professionals that might assist in service delivery. Physicians, nurses, psychiatrists, medical geneticists, neurologists, allergists, learning disabilities specialists, nutritionists, endocrinologists, plastic surgeons, funeral directors, and epidemiologists are all potential allies.

Is Particular Emphasis Given to Any Systems?

Biological scientists tend to assume a public health perspective (Riley, 1991). Rather than emphasizing particular social systems, they search for factors that relate to the adaptive possibilities of the population. The environment includes both risk factors and protective factors. **Risk factors** or hazards are those substances, events, or variables that contribute to the occurrence of a problem, worsen the problem, increase the duration of the troubling condition, or lead to other adverse outcomes (Gilgun, 1996). These include toxic materials in workplaces, schools, and dwellings and toxic materials dispersed through the environment. Lead in paint, street drugs, workplace chemicals, adhesives, gasoline additives, industrial chemicals, solvents, medicines, and asbestos all negatively influence biological processes. Air and water pollution can damage environments and make them dangerous to humans. Some risk factors are substances that humans can but may not avoid, including alcohol, nicotine, HIV exposure, and ingestion of food that does not provide nourishment. Stressful life events and traumas related to physical or sexual abuse, violence, unmanageable and chronic work demands, and family responsibilities put a person at risk. Finally, a lack of control over one's environment and an involvement in interpersonal relationships characterized by high levels of hostility or mistrust jeopardize adaptations (Kessler et al., 1995).

Protective factors are those environment variables that contribute to the prevention of problem occurrence, lessen the severity of the troubling condition, or help the person recover faster from an adaptive challenge (Gilgun, 1996; Johnson, 1999). Social relationships and social support, for instance, are protective factors. They buffer the impact of stress on the body, reduce morality risk, and improve emotional adjustment to life crises such as widowhood or unemployment (Kessler et al., 1995). Social workers aim to improve a client system's adaptation to an environment by reducing risk factors and increasing protective factors.

How Are Resources and Their Flow Conceptualized?

Resources can be conceptualized broadly as things in the environment of limited supply that can be used to meet challenges provoked by events in the internal and external environment. Two kinds of resources receive attention in the biological approach. Knowledge of the human body, especially of diseases and their treatments, is a resource. This is often exchanged in a one-way manner from medical expert to patient. However, many sufferers from biological problems have also created support groups and share knowledge based on personal experience in a two-way, egalitarian, and symmetrical way. A second resource is medical technology. This resource includes the assorted tools that humans can use to adapt to changing biological or environmental circumstances. For example, **assistive devices** are those tools that enable a person with a physical disability to communicate, see, hear, or maneuver (Gilson, 1999). Such tools include motorized wheelchairs, visual and audible signal systems, voice-synthesized computer modules, talking software, and Braille printers. These tools can enhance the coping abilities of persons with body failures or weaknesses and allow successful participation in varied social roles.

WHAT DESCRIPTIVE WORDS ARE USED?

Biological scientists make use of a highly specialized, large, and complex language characterizing diseases, medications, genetics, and various biological processes. Each field of study in the biological sciences and each applied discipline has its own vocabulary. Social workers in settings that provide genetic services, for example, would need to expand their intellectual grasp to learn many concepts not covered in the typical social work curriculum (Riley, 1991). Terms associated with genetics that characterize features of the biological person include **deoxyribonucleic acid (DNA),** chromosomes, gametes, meiosis, alleles, homozygous, heterozygous, mutation, epistasis, pleiotropy, expressivity, and penetrance. Terms for genetic disorders and problems related to genetic transmission include Down syndrome, cri-du-chat syndrome, Klinefelter syndrome, Turner's syndrome, Tay-Sachs disease, and cystic fibrosis. Social workers, unfortunately, are at an early stage in developing strategies for mastering the terminology and theoretical principles common to the biological framework, and the many specialized languages used by expert theory users.

HOW IS CHANGE CONCEPTUALIZED?

Much of the biological conception of change has already been discussed in our review of the processes of adaptation to challenges presented by the internal and external environment. Here are some specific agendas for change. Social workers can work to change public policy, interactional patterns, and social values to enhance the human fit with the environment. An improvement in diet, a reduction in drug use, protection from exposure to toxins, elimination of many stressors, and the teaching of safe sex practices are some goals that we might work to accomplish with individuals, families, and groups. Social workers can support or lead social movements at the level of larger social systems that help people pressure corporations to refrain from profiting from the promotion of risky behaviors. Leaders of the antismoking movement, for example, have demonstrated how to influence national, state, and local laws and customs in ways that support health.

Many good summaries are available of the social work knowledge base and the helping roles associated with the biological approach (Johnson, 1980; Johnson et al., 1990). We need knowledge of the biological contributions to psychiatric disorders; the effects of psychoactive drugs (legal and illegal) on the brain; types of genetic disorders and their treatments; human sexuality, diseases related to sex, and safe sex practices; the symptoms of physical and mental deterioration; the biopsychosocial issues related to health and illness, aging, dying and death, disabilities, and other body failures; the difficulties of body maintenance and control, and the use of the body in relationships with others; and varied resources including support groups for persons attempting to cope with biologically based adaptive challenges.

The biologically oriented social worker has many possible roles. These roles include screening, participating with medical personnel in prenatal testing, newborn screening, and adult screening; referral for services such as genetic counseling or psychiatric assessment; advocating to ensure that the biological needs of all community members are addressed; brokering and linking to services for financial assistance, medical equipment, and respite care; educating, serving as teachers and prevention specialists who clarify information provided by health professions and translate medical terminology into information clients can understand; and case managing, monitoring and overseeing the health services offered to groups of clients.

How Are Actual and Ideal Eco-Maps Contrasted?

The environments of many social work clients are threatening and toxic. These environments may contribute to lifelong adaptive difficulties—for example, by failing to provide children with the sensory input, supportive relationships, and critical nutrients necessary for optimal development. Many environments lack accommodations such as ramps, elevators, electrically operated doors, and suitable public transportation that would enable people with physical challenges to travel widely and safely. Toxic substances and deadly viruses are too common in many environments.

Environments that are ideal for biological development are rich in objects, people, and situations that stimulate human capacities, offer experiences of pleasurable touch, and provide physical security. Enriched environments are especially important for infants. Gentle human touch from significant others, for instance, increases connections among nerve cells in the baby's brain and thus the quality of brain organization. Nurturing and stimulating play, talk, and interaction with others alter the brain structure in positive ways, facilitating intellectual and social advancement. Enriched environments are those with adequate medical insurance coverage and access to health care so that all community members, even poor citizens who experience biological breakdowns, can maintain their quality of life.

Neuhaus (1996) offers a bioevolutionary framework for appraising the quality of human environments. All humans share similar neural biological characteristics and possess common species-specific physiological and psychological needs. Transcultural needs include a need for shelter, a need to satisfy hunger and thirst, a need for extended care as an infant, a need for affiliation, a need for play, and a need for sexual activity. Failure to meet these common human needs by the species would mean the end of the human form. Public problem solvers and policy makers, then, should aim to create environments across the globe geared to fulfilling our common bioevolutionary human needs. The ideal environment is one that has social arrangements, policies, and conditions responsive to human nature and to the furtherance of adaptive fitness among all human populations.

How Are Issues of Diversity, Color, and Shading Addressed?

We have already discussed the approach to diversity of developmental biologists such as Arnold Gesell. Gesell argued for universal developmental milestones reflecting the shared characteristics of the human species, but he and his colleagues acknowledged that environmental and cultural factors may contribute to diverse rates of development (Gesell Institute, 2005). Regrettably, illustrations of possible cultural variations were not provided.

Two other illustrations of the biological perspective on diversity issues involve questions of race and disability. Social Darwinists argue that certain social groups are superior to others, and that social policy and programs for the inferior groups are useless. The research of contemporary geneticists and physical anthropologists, however, undermines the Social Darwinists' foundational theoretical assumption, that human species can be categorized into different racial groups. The Human Genome Diversity Project (http://www .stanford.edu/group/morrinst/hgdp.html), a collaborative worldwide interdisciplinary effort to document the genetic variation of the human species, for example, presents a substantial challenge. The project's scientists assert that each human being has about 100,000 genes. In almost all humans, almost all the body's genes are identical. An important variation is the presence of genes that increase susceptibility or resistance to disease. The genetic evidence, however, indicates no particular genes that make a person Caucasian or Zulu. Whatever their physical traits, behavior patterns, or cultural designation, members of different groups are biologically alike. Race is a cultural label, not a genetic category. In fact, people within a "racial group" are genetically more different from one another than the entire group is from other racial groups.

Physical anthropologists also question traditional biological theories of race. They argue that no categorizing principle accurately places all the billions of human beings into a small number of racial categories. Goodman (2000) provides several arguments against the concept of race. First, the traditional conceptualization of race assumes certain fixed and unchanging types of humans—Caucasian, Mongoloid, and Negroid, for example. Modern evolutionary theory documents that environments are continually changing, and consequently the characteristics and groupings of humans are continuously changing rather than fixed. Second, human genetic variation is continuous, not discrete. There is no clear way to designate where one race begins and another ends. Sharp boundaries are only in the eyes of the classifier and cannot be reliably drawn. Skin color, for instance, changes shade slowly from geographic place to place (my father's skin becomes dark olive-brown in the summer, a testament to his southern Italian origins not his "race"). Third, there is no way to classify people consistently and accurately by race. Race cannot be defined in a stable, universal way, and the salient cues used for classification change over time, setting, and circumstance. Moreover, human biological variation is too complex to be reduced to a simple racial categorization scheme. Efforts to identify race by skeletal and cranial characteristics such as skull size, for example, are little better than random assignment. Fourth, the argument that racial groups can be differentiated by their genetically based disease vulnerabilities is also questionable. African Americans in the United States, for instance, may experience hypertension more than European Americans, but the greater exposure to stressful situations and discriminatory treatment explain this pattern better than genetic variables. Physical anthropologists would complain about any eco-map that included social systems defined by racial membership.

As early as the end of the 1970s, the majority of textbooks in physical anthropology included statements arguing that races do not exist (Littlefield, Lieberman, & Reynolds, 1982). By the middle of the 1980s, the majority of members of three anthropology specialties dedicated to the incorporation of biological knowledge rejected race as a useful biological category (Begley, 1995). Brace (1995, 2005), an anthropologist expert on the subject of race, concludes that race does not assist biological scientists who seek to make sense of human physical variation. It is a biologically indefensible concept. The use of the concept and typologies of racial categories persist for nonscientific reasons. Brace (1995) argues that "the original creators of those labels occupied their dominant social positions by virtue of continuing political control, so the whole system of hierarchically arranged races—with their assumed differences in capacity—is simply the product of long-continued traditional political correctness" (p. 726). Physical anthropologists prefer grouping people—when scientific categorization is needed—by geographic origins. Traits such as skin shade, nose length and shape, and body type (long and thin versus short and squat) indicate a group's evolutionary adaptation to place-specific environmental conditions and climates (Brace, 1995). A system using multiple ethnic categories, with ethnicity defined as a combined heritage of dietary preferences, social customs, behavior patterns, and exposure to discrimination, would also be preferable to a category system based on a small number of racial groups (Begley, 1995).

How might physical disability be represented on an eco-map? Social workers take issue with the traditional biomedical approach to disability (Gilson, Depoy, & MacDuffie, 2002; Hiranandani, 2005; Pfeiffer, 2005). The medical model emphasizes biological normality. Disability is viewed as a deviation from the range of normal functioning and is compared to other illnesses and abnormal states like diseases and bodily dysfunctions. Evolutionary biologists would add that a wheelchair-bound or sight-impaired person faces a natural disadvantage when placed in competitive environments. A lack of fitness is assumed.

Several other tenets are associated with the biomedical conceptualization of disability. The problem is located within the individual person, not the larger environmental context. The deficit is unwanted, and the disabled person is assumed to be a tragic sufferer devastated by the medical dysfunction. The disabled person is cast into the "sick role" and excused from many of the social obligations of healthy persons. There are few social systems except health care systems in the ecosystem of the disabled person, and tenuous connections to the worlds of work and school are expected. The experience of temporary or permanent impairment is targeted for intervention. So, medical organizations become prominent. The disability should be properly diagnosed and cured or fixed, and medical experts recruit family members and friends to assist with the repair process. The disabled person is obligated to follow medical directives or be judged as noncompliant. Unfortunately, since some human impairments are not amenable to medical treatment, the disabled person stays "sick" or "abnormal" across the life span.

Social work theorists (Gilson et al., 2002; Hiranandani, 2005; Pfeiffer, 2005) seek a paradigm shift. Disability and reactions to disabled persons are cultural constructions. The meaning of the condition is socially created, and therefore conceptualizations of and attitudes toward this form of physical difference are malleable. These theorists promote an alternative theory of disability. Disability becomes one kind of social oppression, and the processes by which disabled persons meet discriminatory treatment in their social roles and social systems receive focal attention. Limited physical access, the curtailment of rights and privileges, and negative stereotypes are some of the social barriers that should be identified in clients' ecosystems and dismantled. The ways that persons defining themselves as disabled form subcultures organized around their common circumstances, similar concerns, and shared disadvantages also merit eco-map display and theoretical attention. Unstated or discriminatory assumptions guiding policy making and intervention procedures are suspect. A recognition that physical impairment need not evoke tragic responses, reduce the quality of life, or limit social engagement is required. Finally, Pfeiffer calls for a shift in root theoretical metaphors from abnormality to normality. This shift can be based on the observation that over time all human beings experience disability. Hiranandani (2005) outlines similar next steps for this shift in theorizing about disability: "social workers should endeavor to challenge extant notions of disability, to re-narrate disability, and to re-vision it as part of human experience and history" (p. 79).

WHAT WOULD BE ADDED OR DELETED?

Biologically oriented social workers might add historical information to the eco-map, perhaps as attachments to the standard eco-map. The worker and client, for instance, might create a health time line that records the physical events associated with discomforts, afflictions, and illnesses over the life course. Brief notations might also summarize the subjective meanings of these events; the attempted remedies for biological disorders; and the effects of these physical events on self-conceptions, daily routines, and patterns of social interaction.

The worker and the client might also develop a genetic history (Bernhardt & Rauch, 1993). This could be done in a form similar to the genogram, an assessment tool familiar to most social workers. The genetic history would attempt to identify dysfunctions or defects at the level of human cells and assess how these might contribute to current life difficulties or lead to future problems. Family members could use a genetic history to predict, for instance, the likelihood of a child's having a chromosome disorder that results in some form of mental retardation such as Down syndrome. Children affected by this syndrome have bodies characterized by large ears, large foreheads, highly arched palate, flat feet, and other deformities. The syndrome causes a delay in language acquisition, learning disabilities, and vulnerability to intestinal disorders. The risk increases significantly for mothers giving birth over age 35.

For a married couple, the genetic history should ideally summarize information from both partners and all their blood relatives over at least three generations (Ashford et al., 2001). Relevant information includes the country of origin and ethnicity of each grandparent. Detailed medical reports about incestuous relationships, miscarriages, alcoholism, mental disorders, cancer, birth defects, deformities, allergies, sensitivity to certain medications, exceptional abilities, and any other conditions with strong genetic components might be added to the history. Questions about the cause and age of death of parents, brothers, sisters, grandparents, uncles, and aunts should also be answered.

THE LIMITS OF APPLIED BIOLOGY: A SOCIAL WORK APPRAISAL

Social workers who intend to use the biological approach should heed several warnings. While Harriette Johnson (1999) takes a balanced and holistic approach to the interaction of biological, psychological, and sociological variables, many biological scientists and medical professionals overemphasize the biological dimension at the expense of psychosocial factors and human choice. Some evolutionary theorists, for instance, treat species-specific characteristics as compelling forces. They ignore the insights that humans have become capable of controlling many evolutionary processes, and that our capacity for culture making presents us opportunities and challenges unlike those faced by any of our ancestors. Some geneticists and other sociobiological scientists are prone to one-factor explanations. Claims such as "the gene for gambling has been discovered" or "homosexuality can be explained by a specific brain abnormality" revert to older and rejected approaches to knowledge building by separating nature from knowledge and by ignoring the complex interaction of genes, brains, biographical events, social context, and personal choice (Toates, 2000).

Biological approaches can also divert social workers away from the strengths and social justice perspectives that we value. If children have difficulty concentrating during classroom lectures only because of attention deficit disorders, then medication is the solution. Other factors that may be implicated in the attention problems of children in lower-class neighborhoods, such as overcrowding in classrooms, few books, minimally trained teachers, over-whelmed parents, and deteriorating school buildings, can be ignored.

The focus on disorder, disease, and abnormality common to contemporary physicians and psychiatrists tends to build on a language of pathology, disability, disease, and maladaptation. Such a weakness orientation ignores the strengths that persons bring to their transactions with the inner and outer environments. It also ignores the protective factors that might be subtly embedded in families, schools, and neighborhoods (Gilgun, 1996). Disease approaches offer few images, too, of optimal physical functioning, health, or wellness.

THE BIOLOGICAL APPROACH TO ALCOHOLISM

Social workers often help individuals, families, and groups affected by alcoholism, drug abuse, sex addiction, overeating, gambling, or other compulsive behaviors. Social workers are familiar with various psychosocial approaches to understanding and changing patterns of addiction. Yet social workers know that these approaches have only limited effectiveness. Johnson (1999) proposes that a biopsychosocial approach will increase our ability to help addicts refrain from alcohol use. Her conceptual model follows the convention of identifying the interrelated factors that cause addiction.

THE BIOLOGICAL THEORY'S PERSPECTIVE ON ALCOHOLISM

The following is a simple restatement of the biological components of Johnson's model (1999). Alcohol produces bodily sensations such as pleasure, excitement, and satisfaction. Repeated use of alcohol changes the biochemistry and circuitry of the brain. The limbic system is that portion of the brain that regulates the hunger and thirst drives, emotions, and arousal. This system assists in encoding experiences of pleasure or pain into memory. The mesolimbic dopamine pathway is a circuit carrying pleasure messages across the brain. Dopamine is a neurotransmitter, and the abundant dopamine created by drinking alcohol produces sensations of great pleasure. With the help of the brain's limbic system and the pleasure pathway, then, alcohol consumption results in the creation and storage of **privileged memories.** These intensely positive memories are easily evoked. Psychological and social cues in many interactional situations remind us of alcohol-generated euphoria. These memories are long lasting and may never decay entirely. Over time, these memories powerfully affect all the chronic user's emotional states and motivations.

Let me state some of Johnson's ideas about the biology of alcohol addiction in propositional form. First, the more chronic the use of alcohol, the greater and more lasting are the molecular changes in the brain. Specifically, alcohol increases the concentration of neurotransmitters such as GABA in the brain, causing relaxation. Alcohol increases dopamine, causing euphoria. Alcohol also changes the brain's pathways for pleasure in microanatomical ways and changes the pathways' chemical processes. Chronicity would be associated with extensive changes in these brain processes and mechanisms.

Second, the greater the changes in the pleasure pathway, the greater are the changes in the memory system. Memories of alcohol use and the associated pleasures become privileged and are easily recalled as highly desirable experiences. Third, the more privileged the memories associated with alcohol use, the more intense is the craving for alcohol. Fourth, the more privileged the memories, the more likely it is that the alcohol user will change his or her behavioral priorities. Obtaining and using alcohol becomes a goal ranked as very important by chronic alcoholics.

Chronic alcohol use can also lead to intense discomfort. The fifth proposition indicates that the more sudden and complete the withdrawal from alcohol by the chronic alcoholic, the more unpleasant will be the physical effects of withdrawal: tremors, hypertension, seizures, irritability, and hallucinations. The last proposition helps explain the difficulty of abstaining from alcohol use. The more privileged the memories associated with the pleasures of alcohol use (and the pains of withdrawal from use), the more likely it is that a recovering alcoholic will relapse (even after a lengthy period of abstinence).

THE BIOLOGICAL THEORY'S PERSPECTIVE ON ASSESSMENT

Johnson's biopsychosocial model (1999) recognizes that psychological and social factors are as relevant as biological variables. Psychological variables include psychosocial stress, and personal goals associated with experimentation or escape. Sociological variables include the availability of alcohol, peer pressure to use alcohol, a lack of behavioral alternatives for obtaining pleasure, and the widespread endorsement of community rituals and ceremonies that promote alcohol use. However, knowledgeable social workers must also consider biological variables, including the frequency of alcohol use, the amount of alcohol used, the chronicity of use (the length of time the person has been drinking), and the degree of addictiveness to alcohol. Additionally, biologically minded social workers need to appraise alcohol's effect on the body, and specifically on the brain. Comprehensive assessment of the problem drinker would consider all these factors.

THE BIOLOGICAL THEORY'S PERSPECTIVE ON INTERVENTION

Johnson's biopsychosocial model (1999) has important implications for practice with alcoholics. Effective remedies must consider all dimensions of human functioning. Psychosocial treatments can enable the person to take responsibility for his or her actions, and to use parts of the brain not changed by alcohol use to act against the brain parts that only want more alcohol. Rehabilitation counselors and peers might help the alcoholic learn to suppress or manage privileged memories by avoiding thoughts, emotions, and situations that cue these memories. However, psychosocial change does not undo the brain changes caused by continuous drinking. Biological remedies can increase the potency of the psychosocial remedies. Certain drugs, such as naltrexone, are called opioid blockers. A treatment team may recommend these drugs because they block the effects of opioid peptides, neurotransmitters like dopamine and GABA, reducing the craving for alcohol. Aversive agents such as disulfiram (Antabuse) can also be used. These agents make the person physically sick if he uses alcohol while on the medication and thus create privileged negative memories that connect drinking to unpleasant sensations rather than to euphoria. This deters drinking. Helping the whole person, Johnson might conclude, means changing the mind, the culture, and the body.

LEARNING ACTIVITIES

1. How would your life be different if you had been born a female instead of a male or a male instead of a female? Discuss the likely effects of this sex reversal on your health, your daily routines, your social interaction, your educational and work career, and your family.

2. Estimate the strength of the relationship between biological factors—sex, skin color, physical ability or disability, genetic dispositions to alcoholism or mental illness, physical appearance—and life opportunities and chances (for a long life, a good education, occupational success, protection from environmental hazards, and so on). For each biological factor that you correlate with life changes, decide if the relationship is strong, moderate, or weak. Discuss your reasoning and evidence for your estimates.

3. Carefully observe the behavior of an animal (dog, cat, or monkey) for some time. What similarities do you see between the animal's behavior patterns and your own behavior? What are the differences? How might your analysis of the continuities and discontinuities between animals and humans be useful for social work assessment and practice?

4. Consider the controversy associated with teaching evolutionary theory. What might opponents find objectionable? What do proponents mean when they claim that evolutionary theory has been validated by scientific evidence? Can you imagine a way of reconciling theological beliefs in a higher being or God with scientific confidence in the facts of evolution?

5. Recall a time in your life when you moved from one environment to another—for example, from your family home to a college dormitory. How did the two environments differ? What challenges did you face as you attempted to adapt to the new place? What adaptive strategies worked for you, and what strategies failed? How might your efforts to adapt to a new environmental context be like those of a client dealing with a forced or voluntary relocation?

6. Analyze one of your cravings (for alcohol, sweets, drugs, sex, gambling, or risky behavior) from a biological perspective. What rewards, psychosocial and physical, does the activity provide you? What occurs (or would occur) if you abstained from the activity for the next month? How has your biopsychosocial relation to the craving changed since you first noticed it?

7. Review your history of interaction with clients (or persons needing help) who vary from the cultural norms for physical appearance (height, weight, overall attractiveness, physical abnormality) or for the management of other bodily processes (vision, walking speed, smells, and so on). What stereotypes or expectations did these biological deviations evoke from you? How was your interaction affected?

8. Survey your campus or field internship agency. How well are persons with physical impairments accommodated? What improvements in attitudes, access, opportunities, rights, or treatment would you recommend?

9. Gather data about your family's genetic history. Identify your blood relatives over the past three generations. Make note of any diseases or impairments suffered by family members. Also note any cross-generational behavior patterns that might have a biological base. What evidence do you find in your history that genetic predispositions or vulnerabilities have been transmitted across generations?

10. Reflect on a personal craving. Separate out some of the psychological, social, and biological factors that increase your desire for coffee, soda, alcohol, or candy. How

does Johnson's idea of "privileged memories" help you understand the craving? Do you find yourself recalling at odd times, for example, the delicious taste of your favorite chocolate chip mint ice cream? Do such memories propel you to the refrigerator? What other lessons taken from Johnson's biopsychosocial model might help you understand and reduce the power of these cravings?

ADDITIONAL RESOURCES

Additional resources are available on the book companion website at **www.thomsonedu.com/social_work/forte.** Resources include key terms, tutorial quizzes, links to related websites, and lists of additional resources for furthering your research.

7 CHAPTER | APPLIED COGNITIVE SCIENCE

Jeff Greenberg/IndexStock

INTRODUCTION

A human being is an active, thinking organism. René Descartes, the French scientist and philosopher of the 16th century, defined human existence in terms of cognitive abilities with his famous statement "I think, therefore I am." We think about the objects in our environment and how we might act toward these objects (a barking dog, a lost child, a stranger approaching) before we act. When we start off on a hike, we think about the direction in which we are going to walk, think about the markers on the trail, and think about our destination. College students spend time thinking about classes, homework, friends, family, and leisurely weekends. Clients think about how they will pay their bills, deal with discrimination, and avoid the police. You have given some thought to what it means to become a social worker and what kind of social worker you will be. I am thinking about how best to write the sentences in this book.

Sometimes we think carefully, but sometimes we are sloppy in our thinking and use conventional categories and stereotypes to think about other people. Sometimes we think like scientists and systematically collect data, thoroughly analyze the data, and derive our conclusions using evidence and logic. Sometimes our minds are quiet and there is no thinking. We may cultivate this state for its meditative value, or we may dislike the inner silence. We reflect on our life experiences. We think with pride or shame about different past experiences. We think about what is going on in the present, and we contemplate the future. When we are in a tough situation, our thoughts may race through our minds as we consider various possible solutions to the problem.

Many scientists—including psychologists, social psychologists, sociologists, and some social workers—have formally studied human thinking abilities and processes. Cognitive psychologists have been most active in the development of a field focused on human cognition, including "structures of knowledge, the processes of knowledge creation, dissemination, and affirmation, the actual content of that knowledge and how social forces shape each of these aspects of cognition" (Howard, 1995, p. 91). In this chapter, I will use our theory mastery tools—exemplary models, metaphors, maps, and conceptual models—to introduce you to this theoretical perspective, and to some theoretical work supplementing cognitive science.

RELATED DIALECTS, ASSOCIATED SCHOOLS OF THOUGHT

Cognitive science is an umbrella term for scientific inquiry focused on cognitive processes, cognitive structures, and cognitive development (Cicourel, 1981). This theoretical tradition is not divided into major and competing schools. Variations are subtle and may be indicated by the word following *cognitive*. These terms reflect disciplinary allegiances and theoretical emphases— *cognitive psychology, cognitive sociology,* and *cognitive social psychology,* for example. Practice theories that apply cognitive science often use the inclusive term **cognitive therapy;** they share a focus on the alteration of thinking as the preferred method for changing feeling and behavior (Meddin, 1982). The major approaches to cognitive therapy include Ellis' rational emotive therapy and Beck's cognitive therapy. The *cognitive behavioral approach,* also called *cognitive behavior treatment* and *cognitive behavior therapy,* is a practice theory that blends assumptions, concepts, propositions, and models from the cognitive and behavioral schools of thought.

A few theorists and theory users identify their distinctiveness within the cognitive science tradition by placing an adjective before *cognition* or *cognitive. Social cognition theory,* for example, prioritizes the historical and environmental context of human thought; investigates how people make sense of themselves, other people, and events; and studies how such sense making is influenced by context (Howard, 1995, p. 91). *Social-cognitive theory* is another name for this perspective.

A few creative theorists have developed variations, or theoretical dialects, within the cognitive science language community. George Kelly, a psychologist, developed a framework called *personal construct theory* that compares the person to a scientist. Kelly and his followers studied how personal constructs or hypotheses are central to human perception and conduct, and how construals can be tested and revised in ways that enhance everyday problem solving. Jean Piaget's model of child development is also called *constructivism.* This term reflects his attempt to answer the question "How is knowledge built up?" and his conviction that the developing person is continually constructing and reconstructing his or her knowledge about the world. Piaget's biography and his conceptual model will be reviewed shortly.

APPLIED COGNITIVE SCIENCE: EXEMPLARY MODELS

The cognitive approach differs from some other schools of thought like the psychoanalytic tradition. The history of the psychoanalytic framework begins with Sigmund Freud, and the theoretical innovators building on Freud's work can be clearly identified as adding themes and variations on his original thoughts. The ancestry of the cognitive tradition is more complicated. Development theorists like Jean Piaget were influential and contributed greatly to our understanding of advances in intellectual capacities from childhood to adulthood. Theory users, especially practitioners, have been instrumental in preparing the knowledge base for application.

JEAN PIAGET

Jean Piaget (1986–1980) was a Swiss psychologist who pioneered the study of the development of intelligence (Brinquier, 1980; Evans, 1973; Ginsburg & Opper, 1969; Rosen, 1988). Piaget was very interested in nature as a child, and he enjoyed observing birds, fish, and animals in natural settings. He was considered a child prodigy. He published an article on an albino sparrow when he was only 10 years old, and several articles on mollusks in his early teens. At

15, Piaget turned down an offer to become the curator of the Geneva museum's mollusk collection. Piaget studied at several different universities. He spent most of his academic career as a professor of child psychology at the University of Geneva, but he is also known and respected as a zoologist, mathematician, and philosopher (Richmond, 1970).

In 1919, Jean Piaget began studies at the Sorbonne in Paris. During this period of his life, Piaget also developed and administered reading tests to schoolchildren at the Binet Laboratory. Unlike others who focused on students' correct answers, Piaget was fascinated by the wrong answers that children made. He noticed a correlation between the types of reasoning failures and the age of the child. Piaget extended this innovative slant on intelligence and learned much about child development by observing and talking with his own three children. He devised simple and flexible intellectual problems for his experiments, asked his three children to solve them, and then formed his notions of cognitive processes and advancement by analyzing their mistakes.

Jean Piaget codirected the Institute J.-J. Rousseau in Geneva from 1933 to 1971; served as the director of the International Bureau of Education from 1929 to 1967; and founded the International Center for the Study of Genetic Epistemology, an organization devoted to the interdisciplinary study of human learning processes. The center gathered together scholars from biology, psychology, mathematics, and many other disciplines. Deliberations and discussions at its yearly symposium were published in a series of monographs on a variety of subjects related to cognitive development.

Although Piaget had never passed an examination in psychology (Ginsburg & Opper, 1969), his research and scholarship became the foundational model in psychology for the conceptualization of cognitive development. Piaget published more than 60 books and 500 articles on child development and genetic epistemology over more than five decades. His work has inspired many psychologists, sociologists, educators, economists, philosophers, and social workers. For example, Hugh Rosen (1985, 1988a), a social worker, has formulated a "constructivist-developmental paradigm" that uses Piagetian ideas about the human construction of ways of knowing.

AARON BECK

Clinical psychologists such as Albert Ellis and Aaron Beck have also made influential contributions to the cognitive approach. They showed us that our beliefs and our thinking processes are central to explaining emotional and behavioral problems. Aaron Beck (1921–) was born in Providence, Rhode Island, the son of Russian Jewish immigrants. As a child, he almost died from an infection but recovered. His interests shifted, however, from athletics to reading. He graduated magna cum laude from Brown University in 1942, earned a doctorate in psychiatry from Yale University in 1946, and embarked on a career as a medical doctor (Aaron Beck Homepage, 2002). Beck served at the Cushing Veterans Administration Hospital and at the Valley Forge Army Hospital during the Korean War. In 1954, Aaron Beck joined the

Department of Psychiatry at the University of Pennsylvania. Initially, he used a psychoanalytic approach, but his search for empirical evidence did not support its efficacy with depressed patients. He created a new approach, called cognitive therapy, and demonstrated that it was effective with depression, anxiety disorders, panic disorders, drug abuse, eating disorders, and personality disorders.

Aaron Beck has designed and set up numerous inpatient programs, partial hospitalization programs, and outpatient programs that make use of his cognitive therapy model. He also founded the Beck Institute for Cognitive Therapy and Research in a suburb of Philadelphia. Aaron Beck's theories have even been used to help people suffering from severe psychiatric illnesses. Beck's research with Neil Rector at the University of Toronto demonstrated that patients diagnosed with schizophrenia showed greater improvement in response to a combination of drug treatment and cognitive therapy than in response to drug treatment alone. Beck is well known for his widely used assessment tools, including the Beck Depression Inventory and the Scale for Suicidal Ideation, and he has written 14 books and more than 300 articles. Beck has been married to his wife, Phyllis, for more than 50 years.

ALBERT ELLIS

Albert Ellis (1913–) is the father of the "rational emotive approach" to therapy and the grandfather of cognitive-behavioral therapy (Gregg, 2002). Ellis was raised in the Bronx, New York, and wanted to be a great American novelist when in his teens. The Great Depression undermined these plans, and Ellis went into the pants-matching business with his father. Ellis discovered while working as a businessman that he was sought out for advice on sexual matters. He decided to become a professional therapist. He returned to school and earned a doctoral degree in clinical psychology at Columbia University in 1947, and then participated in four years of psychoanalytic training at the Karen Horney Institute.

Working as a clinical psychologist, Ellis became frustrated with the slow progress and passive worker role associated with psychoanalysis. He developed his own approach, one outlining an active worker role and therapeutic tasks related to helping clients recognize their illogical ways of thinking and helping them replace irrationality with positive thinking. Ellis was convinced that many psychological problems were caused by self-defeating thoughts. Ellis also used advice and direct interpretation to accelerate client change. He incorporated ideas about logical thinking and the stoicism of philosophers such as Epictetus and Marcus Aurelius into his practice model. During his long career, Albert Ellis has worked at Rutgers University, New York University, the Northern New Jersey Mental Hygiene Clinic, the New Jersey Diagnostic Center, and the New Jersey Department of Institutions and Agencies. He is currently president of the Albert Ellis Institute, formerly the Institute for Rational-Emotive Therapy, in New York. The institute offers both a full-time training program for professional helpers and a mental health clinic.

Ellis published his first book on his rational emotive practice model in 1957. Rational emotive therapy met initially with much criticism but gained followers in the 1960s when many practitioners became dissatisfied with psychodynamic and behavioral frameworks. Ellis' ideas about "rational-emotive behavior therapy" (REBT) helped social workers such as Harold Werner (1965) create new cognitive approaches to practice theory. The Albert Ellis Institute (Gregg, 2002) reports that 12,000 psychologists, psychiatrists, and social workers now use rational emotive therapy.

SHARON BERLIN AND PAULA NURIUS

In the 1960s and 1970s, theorists, researchers, computer designers, and programmers increasingly compared the activities of the human mind to the operations of a computer. Promotion of the metaphor of human-as-information-processor led to great theoretical interest and much research in the "cognitive sciences." From this foundation, social psychologists interested in both the social context for mental development and cross-cultural variations in thinking styles are now building a "socio-cognitive" psychology (Howard, 1995). Social workers such as Sharon Berlin (1996, 2001) and Paula Nurius (1989, 1994) are using this knowledge base to advance a social and cognitive approach to practice by integrating psychological and sociological ideas about human information processing into their practice models.

Let me summarize my profile of exemplary scholars and practitioners briefly. The cognitive science approach to "human behavior and the environment" and to practice has many different parents. Social worker theorists and practitioners can learn from all of them.

APPLIED COGNITIVE SCIENCE: ROOT METAPHORS

You probably don't often think of yourself as a computer, and you certainly don't look at all your friends and see computers. Yet cognitive social scientists suggest that there is value to making the comparison (Hoffman, Cochran, & Nead, 1990).

THE PERSON AS COMPUTER

Cognitive scientists often compare human beings to computers. Flavell (1985), for example, summarizes this approach to cognition: "the human mind is conceptualized as a complex *system* of interacting processes which generate, code, transform, and otherwise manipulate information of diverse sorts" (p. 8). Sounds like a computer.

How is a person like a computer? Think of the notions of hardware and software. Your brain is a physical and neurological structure, and it operates like the hardware and central processing unit of a computer. Your brain attends to information in the external and internal environment. Then, your brain encodes and stores the sensory input (data bits) as representations of reality (information files) in your memory. Your brain accesses and retrieves this stored information when necessary (it searches folders for particular files). Your brain processes and uses the information that best serves its needs during a particular operation.

Computers are cybernetic. They include software that makes use of feedback to modify the machine's operation and to facilitate progress toward a goal. The central nervous system is like the computer feedback system. Our central nervous system regulates the physiological functions of the body and helps us maintain a physical steady state (Rigney, 2001). The "self" is also like a feedback system. Self-processes continuously check the relation between our actions and the reactions of others in the environment. The self directs us to change behavior so that we obtain confirmation for our prized self-images and conceptions.

Information processing by the computer follows a clearly defined sequence of computing activities. The computer encodes information entered by keyboard or microphone and stores it for ready use as sound, word, or picture files. These files are organized in folders with distinctive addresses on the computer's hard drive, or they are stored for eventual use on backup systems. Human eyes and ears might be compared to the computer keyboard and microphone. These bodily organs transform information from the external environment into a form that can be stored. These memory bits are filed in the brain's neural networks. Some psychosocial events have a transitory impact; they are like files in temporary folders that are soon discarded from a computer. Other events are significant; their memories are stored permanently as if on a human hard drive and backup system. We can retrieve and use these memories easily and quickly.

Human mental processes are similar to a computer's software operations. A software program is a set of instructions or algorithms that directs the computer to carry out tasks. We install software on our computers. The operating system is the special software that controls and directs all computer processes. Specific software applications make possible computer operations such as processing words, checking spelling and grammar, calculating numbers, analyzing statistical patterns, playing music, viewing pictures, and detecting "viruses." Computer operations will slow down if the number of active software applications exceeds the processing and memory capacities of the machine. Humans, too, have an executive controller (mind) regulating all information management processes. This is like the computer's operating system. Across the life course, each human acquires particular sets of instructions that help him or her adapt to the particulars of the environment. These are the rules and instructions taught to us by various agents of socialization. Each human "software package" activates different mental routines for processing environmental information and for responding to the information. We may forget (or uninstall) certain packages of mental software when we exit roles or social systems that required its use. Humans have performance limitations and will slow down or "crash" if compelled to process unmanageably large amounts of information or to multitask for extended periods of time.

A computer user must maintain his or her hardware and software for optimal use. Computer users might clean out caches, delete undesired "cookies," and restore administrative privileges and preferences periodically. The human also engages in regular activities to maintain his or her physical health, and perhaps to operate at an optimal mental and spiritual level.

THE SOCIAL ENVIRONMENT AS A NETWORK OF COMPUTERS

Let's extend the computer analogy to society or the environment. Computers may be networked in a society of artificial minds. Networking increases the power of each computer. It allows the quick distribution of information across individual computers, the downloading from a central server of new software or commands, and the cooperative efforts of many computers to carry out complex tasks. As you read this, for example, computers across the globe are assisting via the Internet in the SETI (Search for Extraterrestrial Intelligence) project. Networking poses risks to the society of computers. Computers that are linked by cables or radio signals are vulnerable to hackers and viruses. Computers with different operating systems—Apple, Linux, or Windows—may not be able to transfer files or work together on computational tasks. Network problems may follow the interfacing of incompatible systems.

Humans are joined, like computers, by social networks that share information. Social communication is like the digital signals transmitted across cables. Communication across human networks allows the exchange of news, of economic goods, and of affection. In social networks, people coordinate their "routines" and "subroutines" to interact effectively (Rigney, 2001). Together, people as members of networks can help each other realize ambitious projects and enjoy collective cultural pursuits that could not be realized or enjoyed individually.

Human networks also present risks to the network participants. People may pick up physical viruses or contaminating ideas when "hooked" to the social network. Groups from different cultures may not be able to understand each other or approach problems in compatible ways. Cultures may clash, and collaborative information processing may break down. Some people prefer isolation to the dangers of information exchange.

THE SOCIAL WORKER AS COMPUTER TECHNICIAN

If the client is like a computer, and the society or social agency is like a network of computers, then the social worker might be compared to a specialist in computer services at a university or social organization. Problems in human functioning can be diagnosed as caused by hardware or software deficiencies. Social workers use assessment tools just as computer technicians use diagnostic equipment and software.

Many clients experience hardware problems. The human mind afflicted by Alzheimer's disease, for instance, can no longer process information effectively.

Here, the social worker would recommend medical attention to limit the effects of the brain's (the hardware's) deterioration. Other interpersonal problems might be related to a loss of sight or hearing. The social worker, like the computer expert, can serve as a broker and obtain new devices, similar to the peripherals plugged into a computer (glasses or hearing aids, for instance, that minimize the effects of such losses).

Conceiving of problems in social functioning as software-related may be useful in expanding our social work imagination. A client who cannot seem to solve psychosocial problems related to work or love may need a new software package—job training, or a course in relationship skills. A client who continually irritates or antagonizes others may be operating with dated or limited software (instructions that make sense for a child but not for an adult). Such a client would benefit from a software upgrade (resocialization) to update the information-processing program. A client who experiences frequent mental breakdowns may be like the computer that crashes often. A social work assessment may indicate that the client does not have the memory or information capacities necessary for the task or that there is a conflict between two internalized sets of instructions. The worker can help clients recognize their limits, manage conflicting sets of instructions, and seek life challenges suitable for their information-processing capabilities.

Many terms familiar to computer scientists—*input, output, interface, feedback, network, glitches*—have been used by social scientists to explain human behavior in the social environment (Rigney, 2001). However, every analogy has limits, and human intelligence differs from artificial intelligence (Wolfe, 1993). Humans are unlike computers in many ways (Pribram, 1990). Humans, for example, can make sense of ambiguous and unexpected situations not imagined during our previous programming. Much human information processing is chaotic and out of our control. Humans can take initiative, think for themselves, use their intuition, and act to improve their information-processing abilities in creative ways. Humans can play, tell stories, and love, and humans can consider the surrounding context when thinking. Humans feel, and humans can use their emotions to increase their interpersonal sensitivity and skill. No matter how scientists progress in the realm of artificial intelligence, it will be a very long time before we have "stand-up comedian" computers that can make the whole room laugh, deal with hecklers, and keep the crowd entertained for an entire show. Social workers, too, are different from computer programmers in important ways. We do not program our clients. We do not expect our clients to adopt our directives for processing and using information. Instead, we encourage clients to write and execute their own programs of action.

CORE ASSUMPTIONS OF APPLIED COGNITIVE SCIENCE

Cognitive social scientists and social workers make several important assumptions about the person, human behavior, and the environment.

HUMAN ACTION DEPENDS ON THINKING

Advocates of the cognitive approach assume that human action depends on thinking. Simpler animals adapt to their environment by means of genetically based stimulus and response chains. When a lion smells and sees a wounded antelope, the lion automatically pursues this prey and then eats it. Human action is more complex. Cognitive scientists assume that unobservable information processing mediates between environmental stimuli and human behavior.

Aaron Beck (1976) compared the behaviorist, the psychodynamic, and the cognitive approaches. Behaviorists reject cognitive processes entirely. Behaviorists propose a simple stimulus–response model of human behavior; external events lead directly to conditioned responses. Psychodynamic theorists offer a more complex theory but one that also ignores the importance of thinking. Events arouse an unconscious impulse. Since the impulse is generally threatening to the person, the person tries to repress it and not think about it. Anxiety or guilt is the typical response to the intrapsychic conflict. Cognitive psychologists, Beck suggested, prefer a "stimulus-conscious thinking-response" model of human functioning. The person perceives and experiences an event or stimulus. Then, the person thinks about and makes sense of the event. The thoughts, images, and emotions that occur during this conscious appraisal process are critical to the response. People differ in their responses to an event, cognitive scientists argue, not primarily because of differences in conditioning or differences in unconscious psychodynamics. They differ because they can think differently about similar events.

People use their thinking powers to make sense of external stimuli. Who is that approaching a person, friend or foe? If we identify the person as a stranger approaching in a menacing way, rapid thinking precedes our response. We ask ourselves, "What should I do?" We use subvocal words, ideas, and images to think of alternative courses of action: running to a safe location, yelling for help, greeting the stranger and trying to evoke a friendly response, and so on. If we act to evade the threat by stepping into a crowded convenience store, for instance, our cognitive work may continue. We reflect on and evaluate our perceptions, emotional experiences, and behavioral responses. Self-talk at this point might include thoughts such as "That was a close one, I should avoid this block" or "I better pay more attention when walking alone."

Thinking, then, is like an inner conversation or internal communication (Beck, 1976). Children learn to internalize words and sequences of words that they have acquired during interaction with members of their primary groups. The child, for example, may use arguments voiced by her parents when deliberating silently about the right way to think and act, or the child may repeat subvocally his mother's directives for solving a problem. In threatening, novel, complex, or frustrating circumstances, the thinking abilities and instructions to oneself learned over the life course become essential tools for processing information and for directing action. The adult can intentionally activate these capacities and listen to the subvocal self-communication relevant to the task at hand. The power to conduct such rapid and reflective mental reviews of alternative ideas and action possibilities enables humans to adjust to environmental and social contingencies in ways unequaled by any other species.

Social workers use such thinking powers continually. The process recording, for instance, is a way that social work educators and supervisors help novice practitioners examine closely how they think and what they think when helping clients. Supervision requires that the novice practitioner examine and explain to an experienced practitioner how she thinks about helping challenges. Social workers also work regularly to help clients make better use of their thinking potentials.

COGNITIVE PROCESSES ARE SHAPED BY THE ENVIRONMENT

Advocates of the cognitive approach, especially cognitive social psychologists, assume that cognitive processes and structures are shaped by the environment. All humans have similar anatomies and similar brains; thus, certain cognitive processes and structures are basic to and universal for members of our species. Human beings are social animals, however, and we learn how to think, what to think, and what not to think during interactions with others in groups, organizations, and communities. Although capable of independent and novel thought, most community members have much in common with other members of their "thought communities" and thus tend to think like the others (Zeruvabel, 1999). A careful assessment can help us identify the environmental traces of culture, social class, history, and other social forces in the thinking processes of most of our clients.

Perceiving is an important mental process that involves attending to and focusing on some environmental stimuli rather than others. The objects that we recognize and think about in our environment depend on our socialization. Eskimos will see and recognize dozens of variations of snow, whereas Floridians might only recognize snow as a physical object different from rain. The concepts that humans have for various shades of skin color vary historically and culturally. If members of two different thought communities encounter the same brown-skinned male, one may see "black" and the other not notice skin color at all. Citizens of the United States attend to and recognize—probably more than members of any other culture—stimuli related to money and marketplace exchanges. Among aborigines in the outback of Australia, money and money matters will be less relevant, held in the background, or barely noticed. A person's location in a society's social stratification system also influences what that person perceives. Those in the working class, for instance, often attend closely to information from their superiors at work about the boss's thoughts, emotions, and intentions. Elite leaders, on the other hand, often perceive only dimly the emotional sensitivities and physical suffering of members of the working class and underclass.

Classifying or categorizing is another important mental process. People learn which criteria to use to determine if an object or event is a member of a particular category. We also learn to judge whether a member is a typical or atypical representative of a category (Lalljee, 1996). Rules for classifying are learned during our primary and secondary socialization and have a clear social basis. Social workers in mental health settings, for instance, learn a classification scheme for mental disorders that includes hundreds of categories. The educated social worker would probably diagnose a client's reports of conversations with spirits of dead ancestors as a hallucination and indicative of a mental disorder. Members of indigenous tribes in Africa, in contrast, might classify the same report as indicating a special talent and recruit the person for a role as spiritual leader. Communities also differ in the way that members classify "race" and ethnic groups.

Representing or assigning symbols to cultural objects is a mental process essential to effective communication. Yet this too is influenced by our social memberships. Contrast European societies with Muslim societies. The symbolic meanings attached to facial hair, short skirts, staring, God, death, and the United States differ dramatically. Subcultures, too, may differ from the larger culture in their central concepts and symbols. Imagine a concert that mixes adherents to the grunge subculture, with their appreciation for "moshing in the pit," and country western fans. We define (think about) social situations before we act, and we do so in socially patterned ways. Defining and symbolizing a situation as an "attack," for instance, will evoke a culturally specific set of thoughts and specific inclinations to act.

Remembering and the associated mental activities of storing, organizing, accessing, and retrieving memories are influenced by our social environment. Societies may have specific rules for remembering. Some outlaw public recall of certain historical events, such as the Japanese leaders who forbid civil remembrances of Japanese atrocities against the Chinese during World War II. Thought communities may battle over the correct version of history: America as discovered or America as conquered, for example. Cultures and subcultures vary, also, in the mnemonic devices that assist in building the "stocks of knowledge" important for maintaining group pride and solidarity. These often include narratives, rituals, and sites of remembrance distinctive to the culture.

Social work clients may think in idiosyncratic ways. They may think in ways that are universal and shared by all humans. Advocates of the cognitive approach teach us, however, that they often perceive, attend, attribute blame, conceptualize, classify, symbolize, infer, deduce, solve problems, relate means and ends, conceptualize time, take perspectives, and think like their associates in a particular shared web of social and mental affiliations (Zeruvabel, 1999).

CLIENT DIFFICULTIES ARE ESSENTIALLY COGNITIVE

Advocates of the cognitive science approach assume that many client difficulties (and the remedies to these difficulties) are essentially cognitive. Human action is the direct result of what people assume about others and the environment, believe about their identities and roles, and talk to themselves about in a social situation. Misconceptions about the social world (erroneous or negative self-beliefs and irrational self-talk), therefore, are likely to contribute to problematic or maladaptive action. Before a husband beats his wife, he generally engages in incorrect **attributions of blame.** He could blame himself for his problems with impulse control (internal attribution of blame). He could avoid assigning blame to anyone. However, he usually blames his wife and the family environment. He could believe that he can control his behavior, but he usually believes that his angry responses are compelled by his wife's inadequacies. After the violent and "impulsive" act, he judges his wife's behavior as the cause of his violence (external attribution of blame). The male batterer justifies his action by blaming his wife and absolving himself of responsibility—even when a more rational and aware assessment of the relationship dynamics would not result in partner blame or the postulate of uncontrollable behavior.

Beck (1976) demonstrated that many clients with relationship problems have allowed their thinking processes to become automatic and routinized. These clients stop listening to the subvocal conversations that contribute to troubling emotions and relationship conflicts. Cognitively oriented social workers assume that significant and lasting personal changes occur only when the client makes substantial cognitive changes. The worker, therefore, helps clients listen anew to their self-talk and identify, challenge, and change the automatic thoughts and distorted thinking processes that have resulted in problematic emotions, unsuccessful problem solving, and inappropriate behavior. Such social workers help clients become mindful of their thinking style, of the way that their beliefs govern their decisions and actions, and of the cognitive sources of their problems.

Ellis (1973) argued that many emotional disturbances and behavior problems have their roots in irrational thinking. Clients often hold irrational beliefs such as "It is a dire necessity to be loved and approved by every significant other," "One should be thoroughly competent in all possible respects to consider oneself worthwhile," and "Human unhappiness is caused by external events and people have no ability to control their emotional reactions." The rational emotive social worker shows the client how he or she accepts such irrational premises, and then uses various techniques, including didactic presentations, persuasion, and homework, to refute these illogical notions. Cognitive social workers follow Ellis' and Beck's work and assume that modifying the cognitive processes and content that produce unrealistic thinking and problems in living is the most economical and effective way to help clients.

PIAGET'S COGNITIVE MODEL OF HUMAN DEVELOPMENT

Advocates of the cognitive approach assume that the person develops his or her cognitive abilities over time. Piaget, for instance, proposed a series of distinctive periods and stages in human cognitive development (Rosen, 1988). In this section, I will discuss Piaget's approach to child development.

The section will include a review of the assumptions, metaphors, concepts, and propositions of his model, and a brief overview of its applications.

JEAN PIAGET: EXEMPLARY ROLE MODEL

You have met Jean Piaget earlier in the chapter. Since Piaget is considered one of the greatest and most influential developmental psychologists, his model of mental growth still merits study. Piaget's lifelong interest was **genetic epistemology.** Epistemology is a branch of philosophy concerned with the nature of knowledge. Genetic epistemology is the study of the nature of knowledge development in human organisms, "the processes by which bodies of knowledge grow historically and as internally organized systems" (Richmond, 1970, p. 1).

ASSUMPTIONS OF PIAGET'S MODEL OF COGNITIVE DEVELOPMENT

Piaget's approach is similar to Gesell's model of biological development. However, Piaget assumed the progressive advancement in a child's strategies of reasoning and knowing; each stage is better than the preceding one. Piaget assumed also that each stage is characterized by qualitatively different approaches to knowledge construction and use. Stages cannot be skipped, and the order of stages cannot be changed. Maturation of our intellectual functions and abilities occurs in a sequenced and predictable way across these distinct stages. The timetable is set by nature. The universal processes of cognitive development equip the developing person to understand concepts of time, space, causality, object permanence, means–end relationships, justice, and self–other interaction. The more complex and sophisticated thinking abilities of adulthood related to perspective taking, abstract problem solving, and moral deliberation are preceded by the step-by-step mastery of basic cognitive operations. Persons may vary, however, in how well they meet the stage-specific opportunities for intellectual growth, and not all people realize their full mental potential.

Piaget's approach assumes the interaction of nature and nurture. The working of the intellect as a knowledge producer and accumulator, for example, depends on a genetic heritage. Developing persons, however, are not determined by their biology. Family, schools, and the larger society all contribute to optimal growth.

Finally, Piaget's model of human development assumes that the developing person is an active learner. This inclination toward action rather than passivity is an inherent feature of the human brain. The smallest child assertively and enthusiastically explores the environment, and active participation and interchange with people and things in the environment stimulate intellectual development (Salkind, 1985). Infants make great intellectual progress, for instance, simply by independently crawling in, looking at, feeling, and tasting their homes (Crain, 1980). The developing person is a dynamic constructor of knowledge, and Piaget firmly asserted that the best understanding is the understanding that the child invents for herself. Crain (1980) summarized Piaget's theoretical position on human development as "an active construction process, in which children, through their own activities, build increasingly differentiated and comprehensive cognitive structures" (p. 77).

ROOT METAPHORS AND THE COGNITIVE MODEL OF HUMAN DEVELOPMENT

Several metaphors can help us grasp Piaget's conceptual model. The genetic epistemologist studies a child's development the way a molecular biologist studies cell division (Richmond, 1970). Because of the difficulty of differentiating the parts of a cell, the biologist uses a staining agent that increases the visibility of the borders of each part. Because of the difficulty of discerning the sequence of changes in a cell, the biologist photographs the cell as it changes and then uses an orderly examination of the photographs to clarify the pattern of changes. The work of developmental scientists is similar. Piaget used his innovative experimental situations as his staining agents. By challenging the developing person with an intellectual problem and asking questions to understand the child's thinking evoked by the experiments, he could begin to characterize each period and stage of cognitive development. By creating a series of experiments of increasing complexity and recording the changes in the developing person's ability to master experimental tasks, Piaget began to understand the overall pattern of cognitive development from birth to adolescence.

Human beings, like other living organisms, must adapt to their environments. The two modes of adaptation are **assimilation** and **accommodation.** Richmond (1970) illustrates Piaget's use of these concepts by comparing the developing person to an amoeba. The amoeba needs food to live and grow. The amoeba moves around, searches in its liquid environment, and takes in digestible substances. The ingested particles of food are transformed into new materials that fit into the amoeba's existing cell structure. This is assimilation. However, the shape and chemical nature of the ingested food particles affect the shape of the space that the amoeba must create and the type of juices necessary for digestion. Thus, the amoeba must make an accommodation to the qualities of the available food. The balancing of the amoeba's assimilative and accommodative actions is the way that the amoeba adapts to its environment.

Human learning is like the amoeba's digestive process. Children take in new experiences and fit them into existing experiences, mental structures, and beliefs. This is human assimilation, "the process by which the individual incorporates new experiences into already existing schemes or structures" (Salkind, 1985, p. 189). The intake of new experiences requires, however, the adjustment of the cognitive structures (models of the world) that had been built previously. This is human accommodation, "the process of modifying existing schemes to satisfy the requirements of new experience" (p. 190). The developing person balances assimilation and accommodation in a recurring process of **equilibration,** or self-regulation (Salkind, 1985). The better the balancing of these processes of assimilation and accommodation, the better is the person's adaptation to the environment at a given time. Richmond (1970) notes, however, that humans are unlike amoebas in an important way. Amoebas may change in size, or divide and increase in number. Humans however change both quantitatively (more knowledge) and qualitatively (intellectual powers expand and cognitive models of the world become more comprehensive and accurate).

Let me mix metaphors here. Return to our imagery of the person as being like an information-processing computer. New information is shaped to fit with the learner's existing knowledge (operating system plus software applications), and existing knowledge (the total configuration of software packages) is itself modified to accommodate the new information. The adaptive human continually balances assimilation and accommodation (just as a computer owner often balances decisions about the purchase of additional software with considerations of upgrades to the computer hardware so that it can better manage the new applications).

Piaget's Model of Cognitive Development

Here is a brief summary of Piaget's approach to cognitive development (Maier, 1978; Rosen, 1988). Let's begin with a more formal review of some of the major concepts.

Cognitive development is conceptualized as a "broad spontaneous process that results in the continual addition, modification, and reorganization of psychological structures" (Salkind, 1985, p. 185). Cognitive development is affected by the interaction of four variables: biological maturation, the genetically set timetable for new developmental possibilities; the developing person's physical experiences exploring the environment (explorations actualize cognitive potentials); the social transmission of knowledge from membership groups to the developing person (guided education); and the process of equilibration, the continual balancing of processes of assimilation and accommodation in response to changing environmental challenges (Thomas, 1999, 2001).

The concept of **cognitive stages** has already been discussed. Humans develop invariantly through a series of identifiable and qualitatively different levels of cognitive development. Each is characterized by a different form of mental organization, and with each new stage the developing person achieves a capacity for more complex intellectual functioning. The stage concept asserts that across the human life span, there are predictable patterns of thought and predictable likelihoods of solving different types of intellectual puzzles and problems (Crain, 1980).

The **schema** is the primary unit of cognitive organization, and schemes (or schemas) become organized as the cognitive structures necessary for adaptation (Salkind, 1985). Schemas are either patterns of physical action (sucking, grasping, backing a car out of the driveway) or patterns of mental action (solving a mathematical equation). When Piaget refers to the development of cognitive structures, he is referring to the expansion and reorganization of the person's collection of schemes.

Cognitive operations are actions that are internalized and performed mentally. These operations can also be carried out in the environment (Salkind, 1985). For example, the cognitive processes of addition and subtraction can be completed first in one's head and then on a piece of paper. As the cognitive structures of the developing person change, the person becomes capable of increasingly advanced cognitive operations. Cognitive operations emerge during the preschool years as children improve their ability to represent their experiences mentally and to act on those representations (Goldhaber, 2000).

Piaget divided life from birth to adulthood into four periods. Each period can be broken down into shorter and distinctive stages (Crain, 1980). Here I will refrain from making fine distinctions and summarize the characteristics of the four major periods.

SENSORIMOTOR PERIOD   The sensorimotor period extends from birth to about 2 years. The developing person knows the world by sensing it and acting toward objects in it. The child's sensory and motor experiences gain a focus and come under voluntary control. Reflexes including looking, grasping, sucking, and listening become the foundation for increases in intelligent movement and action. Recognition memory is apparent. Babies start to experiment with looking and then grabbing attractive objects in their environment. One important lesson that they learn from these experiments is **object permanence,** the recognition that toys, mothers, dogs, and other objects continue to exist even when not visible to the child. Babies develop dim understandings, too, of cause and effect, time, symbols, and space, and they start to use words and to develop a simple vocabulary. The infant also begins the lifelong process of freeing himself or herself from **egocentrism,** the inability to differentiate between self and other, internal and external, knower and known.

PREOPERATIONAL PERIOD   The preoperational or preconceptual period extends roughly from 2 years to 7 years. Children in this stage center their rudimentary thinking on observable appearances and perceptual cues. Play is one of the major means for learning about the properties of perceived objects, such as the properties of water splashed around a tub. Games of pretend help children learn about other people and social roles. Children imitate others and try to use sentences and other tools of language. Vocabularies expand significantly. For instance, children learn to understand their own names and the names of playmates, thus making consciousness of self and others possible. Piaget believed, however, that preoperational-stage children still think and speak mostly in egocentric ways. This is seen, for instance, in "childish talk," speech patterns not directed to the informational needs of the caretaker. Young children tend to process information from their own point of view, but eventually arguments with peers and demands for clarification or proof by socializing agents stimulate most children to begin to accommodate the perspectives of others in their own cognitive deliberations. Memory abilities also increase.

CONCRETE OPERATIONAL PERIOD   In the concrete operational period (7 to 11 years), children need not rely on sensorimotor manipulations or perceptual cues in their adaptive efforts. Instead, systematic conceptual thinking becomes possible. This may take the form of reasoning from evidence to conclusions, making inferences that go beyond observable information, judging quantities accurately, classifying objects and ideas, or recognizing the various phases in a sequence of activities. Children can grasp, for instance, that an amount of clay is conserved whether the clay is stretched into a long sausage shape or compressed into a wide pancake shape. Sociocognitive abilities develop also, and children increasingly "decenter" from their own perspective and consider the points of view of multiple others. Language capacities related to pronunciation, reading, writing, and vocabulary improve. However, thinking is still concrete, and children struggle to transcend the limitations of known reality. Few children at this stage can make use of a "what-if-it-were-true mentality" (Rosen, 1988a, p. 324).

FORMAL OPERATIONAL PERIOD   The last period of cognitive development, according to Piaget, is called the formal operational period and ranges from 12 years up. Formal thinking is scientific thinking. The developing person can use logical and scientific thinking with both physical objects and abstract ideas. Adolescents can think in terms of propositions relating two or more concepts ("if x, then y"), and they can do so even without physical indicators of the concepts. Adolescents can design and carry out experiments that test their working hypotheses in controlled conditions. At this period, thinking is not bound by time or place. Adolescents, for instance, can develop conceptions about events in the distant past or about future possibilities. They can combine ideas learned in very different places. Socially, adolescents develop capacities for accurate and deep perspective taking, and thus can participate effectively in collective thinking exercises with real and imagined partners. However, adolescents are vulnerable to the egocentric elevation of their ideas about ideal communities and to intolerance of those with different political and utopian conceptions.

In summary, as humans develop, they follow a fairly standard cognitive progression from ego-centered to decentered perspectives on events and situations. Thinking becomes less concrete and magical and more abstract and scientific, symbolic capacities expand, and cognitive operations multiply from the few achieved early in life to a wide range by adulthood.

CRITICAL COMMENTS

Piaget recognized that the particulars of a person's cognitive development were influenced by a society's language, its belief and value systems, its preferred forms of reasoning, and the types of relationships between members (Richmond, 1970). However, Piaget developed his theory based on research using small samples of children who were all products of European schools. Thus, he has minimized considerations of the impact of diversity and cultural variability on child development (Thomas, 1999).

Empirical evidence supports Piaget's conception of stage sequencing and stage characteristics, especially for the sensorimotor period and for scientific and mathematical reasoning in later stages (Crain, 1980). However, Crain adds that researchers have been puzzled by the finding that most middle-class American adults make only limited use of formal reasoning abilities.

Recent developmental psychologists and sociologists have refined Piaget's developmental theory (Forte, 2001). Here are several of their recommended modifications. First, young children may not be as "autistic" or "egocentric" as Piaget indicated. They may be capable of socially oriented thinking at a very early age, especially if they are exposed to rich and complex interactional learning environments. Second, the pace of cognitive development may not be restricted by or firmly linked to chronological age. Variations in factors such as opportunities for stimulating play, support for the development of language skills, and contact with significant others who promote thinking may result in accelerated mental development. Third, cognitive advancement may depend equally on the maturation of brain structures and on social experiences. Piaget preferred biological root metaphors and emphasized bodily changes as the primary causal factor. Recent researchers have shown, however, that cognitive advancement is intricately related to social advancement. Development-enhancing interactions (cooperative interaction with dissimilar others, social pressures to solve interpretive or technical problems, and social contradictions) may be even more important triggers of cognitive progress than physical maturation.

APPLICATIONS OF THE COGNITIVE MODEL OF HUMAN DEVELOPMENT

Piaget's model of cognitive development has been useful to educators (and school social workers) and social work counselors and therapists. I will begin by summarizing some educational applications and developmental propositions. Piaget (Ginsburg & Opper, 1969) was critical of traditional approaches to classroom education. The central goal of schools is not to teach facts or solutions to personal and public problems but "to promote the optimal development of thinking skills appropriate to each stage of mental growth" (Thomas, 1999, p. 35).

First, Piaget argued that teachers should provide opportunities for social interaction during efforts to solve intellectual puzzles. Classrooms should be noisy not quiet places. The discussion, deliberations, and arguments encouraged during interaction stimulate the exercise and development of cognitive abilities. Peer interaction also helps children grow from egocentric to decentered modes of thought. This theoretical proposition follows: A teaching approach emphasizing social interaction will result in greater learning than one that minimizes peer-to-peer talk, play, and problem solving.

Second, Piaget argued that the learning environment should support the activity of the child rather than center on verbal explanations from the teacher or written exposition from books. Children acquire knowledge through their actions, and thinking is considered to be action-based. Thus, a learning environment should be designed to encourage children to initiate and discover new things about themselves, others, and the world. Play was one of Piaget's favorite and recommended mediums for active self-discovery in ideal learning environments. This theoretical proposition follows: The more that children can actively control their learning and manipulate objects and ideas, the more that they will learn (Ginsburg & Opper, 1969).

Third, the Piagetian approach rejects the assumption that children at the same age should participate in lessons focused on the same material. Lessons should be planned and individualized with consideration of Piaget's schedule of cognitive development (Richmond, 1970). This theoretical proposition follows: The more the teacher understands and takes into account the stage-specific strengths and weaknesses of each child, the greater will be the learning (Ginsburg & Opper, 1969).

Fourth, Piaget believed that teachers should present situations, problems, and puzzles requiring children to adapt their past experiences and accommodate the old to the new (Richmond, 1970). Children must experience disequilibrium, an imbalance between their current cognitive structures and new information to be assimilated, in order to move to a new stage of development. Instructional strategies that make children aware of conflicts and inconsistencies in their thinking foster re-equilibration. This theoretical proposition follows: "When an experience is both familiar enough so that it may be assimilated without distortion into current cognitive structure, and novel enough so that it produces some degree of conflict, then interest and learning will be promoted" (Ginsburg & Opper, 1969, p. 231).

Allen Ivey (1986, 1991; Ivey, Ivey, Myers, & Sweeney, 2005) offers a comprehensive approach to helping work anchored in Piaget's developmental theory. The goal of this form of practice is helping the client system develop ideas and behaviors that are more effective in the world (Ivey, 1986, 1991). The assessment approach makes use of Piaget's periods of cognitive development but conceptualizes them as styles of cognitive problem solving (Ivey, 1986). This framework can help the practitioner understand client reactions to the helping process and client adaptive difficulties. For the sensorimotor style, the worker focuses on how the client sees, hears, and feels a problem through sensory-based data. The client profile for this style includes a short attention span, frequent bodily movement, the presentation of ideas in a random and disorganized manner, a priority to the here and now, some magical thinking, and immersion in basic elements of the environment. Ivey omits the preoperational period from his typology. For the concrete operations style, the worker focuses on how the client thinks about the concrete and specific details of a situation. The client profile for this style includes the tendency to provide concrete, linear, detailed descriptions of the self. Experiences with others, events, and emotions are described but not analyzed. Many client verbal responses are brief, or simple yes or no answers. For the formal operations style, the worker focuses on how well clients can think about their thinking and about their self-concept. The client profile includes the tendencies to use abstract thought, to talk about self and feelings from one's own perspective and from others' perspectives, to engage in abstract conversations, and to recognize patterns in one's own thoughts, feelings, and behaviors.

For each profile, Ivey (1986) has identified helping goals, worker tasks, and relevant assessment questions. He also offers a standardized cognitive developmental classification system to place clients within the typology. Ivey and his colleagues (2005) have offered additional tools, including case illustrations and potential developmental blocks for each profile, and a standardized developmental interview. Intervention from the developmental therapy point of view requires **perturbation,** another Piagetian concept. Ivey defines it as the challenging of client discrepancies or incongruities to upset the client's balance of assimilation and accommodation and thus open ways for the client to construct new knowledge and advance to the next stage of cognitive development.

Let's conclude this review of application highlights by suggesting that the assessment of cognitive development and functioning is critical to good practice but very hard to do well (Flavell, 1985). Coon (1989), for example, summarizes some of the dimensions that should be assessed when working with a child in the concrete operations period. These include the ability to demonstrate the following cognitive operations: **reversibility** (mentally undoing a series of actions); **decentering** (taking multiple perspectives on an object or person); **reciprocity** (recognizing that a change in one feature of a relationship is balanced by a change in another); **conservation** (understanding the conservation of mass, length, volume, and weight when nothing is added or taken away); the use of numbers (counting); **classification** (understanding category systems and the relationship between larger and smaller categories); **seriation** (arranging objects in an orderly series); **selective attention** (focusing on the relevant and ignoring the irrelevant aspects of a situation); **metamemory** (understanding how memory works); **metaphor use** (understanding that some words have both literal and nonliteral meanings); **communicative competence** (understanding complex sentences and the precise meaning and use of words); and the use of humor. Such a comprehensive assessment must make use of multiple measurement tools.

MAPPING APPLIED COGNITIVE SCIENCE

My translation of the cognitive approach into the ecosystems language draws from adherents to the cognitive developmental tradition such as Hugh Rosen (1985, 1988a) and from the work of cognitive psychologists, sociologists, and social workers, especially Paula Nurius (1989, 1994). Figure 7.1 displays the cognitive science version of the eco-map, and the rest of this section offers cognitive answers to our eco-map questions.

How Are Connections Conceptualized?

The cognitive approach conceptualizes the person as an information processor within a social and physical environment. The actor perceives informational cues, organizes and processes the information, and uses the information to

FIGURE 7.1
THE COGNITIVE
SCIENCE
VERSION OF
THE ECO-MAP

Source: Adapted with
permission from
*Family-Centered Social
Work Practice* (p. 160)
by A. Hartman &
J. Laird, 1983.
New York: The
Free Press.

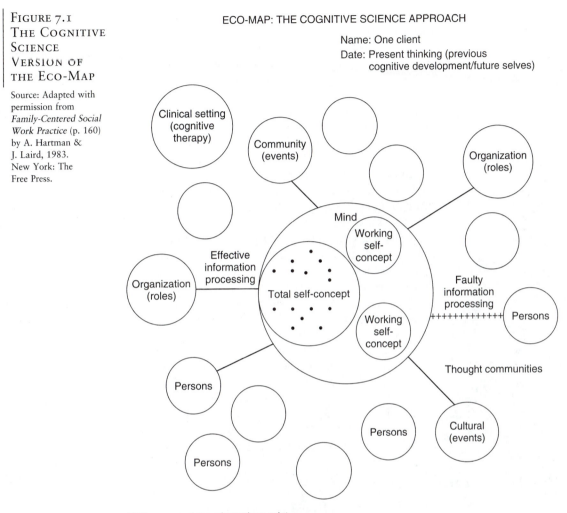

ECO-MAP: THE COGNITIVE SCIENCE APPROACH

Name: One client
Date: Present thinking (previous
cognitive development/future selves)

Fill in connections where they exist.
Indicate nature of connections with a descriptive word or by drawing different kinds of lines:
———————— for effective information processing ·········· for taken-for-granted
objects and events +++++++ for faulty information processing
Draw arrows along lines to signify flow of energy, resources, etc. ➺ ➺ ➺
Identify significant people and fill in empty circles as needed.

meet interaction and adaptive challenges. Informational processing of inputs from the environment are structured by schemas (mental representations usually as words or images). The stock of schemas that a person accumulates is built from the information he or she is exposed to orally, in writing, in pictures, and in gestures during interaction with others in the society. Cognitive social scientists would support the following general summary of the approach to linkages: Our understanding of who we are, what other people are like, how we should relate to others, and how we can and should participate in community and cultural events develops according to the information provided by our thought communities and the structures that we use to process that information. We are connected to others by our ways of knowing them.

Helping work with the bereaved illustrates the cognitive science approach to connections (Forte, Barrett, & Campbell, 1996; Malkinson, 2002). Our fundamental conceptions of self, others, and the environment are developed in relationships with significant others. When the death of a loved one occurs, our bonds of physical intimacy and our emotional attachments are severed. Cognitive theorists and practitioners assert, additionally, that our core cognitive structures are broken. Our beliefs about life and death may be challenged. Our assumptions about fairness and the predictability of events may be shattered. Our central self-conceptions and understandings of relationships—forged through interaction with the significant other—become questionable. Our hopes, visions, and dreams for the future become doubtful.

Grief work, cognitive therapists recommend, requires more than letting go of emotional cathexes or forming new attachments as advocated by psycho-dynamic practitioners. Grief work requires a process of cognitive reorganization. The bereaved person must find a way, often with the help of social workers and mutual aid groups, to understand and make cognitive sense of the loss and to grasp yet connect to a world devoid of the valued spouse, sibling, or friend.

The recovery of mental coherence may not be easy. The more sudden and traumatic the loss, the greater the impact on the bereaved person's belief system is, and the more difficult the task of cognitive reconstruction. Severe and long-lasting grief reactions may occur when extremely negative or unexpected cognitive evaluations of the self, the environment, and the future follow the loss. Many New Yorkers, for instance, struggle years after the September 11th attacks on the World Trade Center to process this information, to make sense of their lives, and to connect anew to other survivors and to their hometown.

How Is the Quality of Connections Differentiated?

Cognitive theorists would characterize positive connections as effective and accurate information processing. The cognitive schemas that structure such information processing would have the following qualities. First, the set of schemas would be elaborate. Each schema would hold much detail and be rich in information. By graduation from social work school, for instance, students have a clear, full, and specific set of ideas about the helping interview. Second, there would be a large number and a wide range of schemas stored in memory. Graduating social work students have memorized many ideas about interviewing skills, about adapting these skills to diverse clients, and about the steps involved in conducting an interview. Third, the schemas would be well developed. Our new social worker can explain completely and coherently each of his or her ideas about interviewing (the meaning of rephrasing and the cognitive content of the idea, confrontation). Fourth, the person who has many detailed autobiographical memories and much specific how-to knowledge, for example, will be able to process most information about social interaction well.

The student can recall numerous in-class role-plays and the final videotaped interview simulation and can use these memories to figure out how to help current clients. Fifth, the set of schemas would be functional; it would guide the person in searching for and collecting knowledge in ways useful for meeting environmental challenges. Functional schemas facilitate all the information management processes—perceiving, categorizing, remembering, symbol interpreting, symbol using, decision making, and acting—necessary to achieving relevant life goals. The student's theory of interviewing and repertoire of interviewing skills have become useful and versatile helping tools. Sixth, within the total set of schemas, positive schemas would be accessible. The new graduate has images of herself as a confident, competent, and caring interviewer. Finally, these schemas can easily be activated. The student easily draws self-schemas from the total self-concept (social work interviewer) into working self-concepts (intake interviewer or crisis interviewer) as he enacts different social roles. The frequency of activation of positive schemas strengthens the neurological pathways (physical connections), increasing the ease of accessing and using elaborated and functional schemas.

Positive information processing also means that the person processes information in accord with the highest standards of his or her thought community. In Western societies, for instance, we expect that information processing will meet the tenets of science and logic. Finally, optimal connections are those that occur between individuals who each process information accurately. The interactants can encode, transmit, and decode interaction information well because they have highly developed cognitive skills and because they share similar or compatible schemas about self, other, roles, and the situation.

Negative connections are defined in terms of faulty information processing. Such processing may involve distortions of reality and of self, the use of idiosyncratic or bizarre schemas, and limited skill in specific processing acts. The use of stereotyping when categorizing others, for example, indicates cognitive limitations and causes bad social connections. Faulty processing may indicate a developmental lag. The actor's level of information processing is not adequate for solving relationship and environmental problems. For example, childlike egocentric thinking may prevail even in adult clients. If these clients do not develop the capacity for understanding the viewpoints of their relationship partners, they are likely to experience painful social connections. Faulty processing may indicate that a client has taken a cognitively conservative stance toward intellectual development and seeks information and experiences comfort only at a preadult cognitive stage. Such a client refrains from searching for and using information that facilitates intellectual growth.

David Burns (1980), a student of Aaron Beck, identified some of the most common cognitive distortions associated with faulty information processing. These include all-or-nothing thinking, the tendency to evaluate personality qualities and social situations in terms of extreme categories (for example, self-evaluation as either a complete loser or complete winner); overgeneralization, the tendency to base conclusions on a very limited sample of observations (for example, the belief that all men are dangerous based on a few dates with two aggressive males); disqualifying the positive, the tendency to ignore or minimize the relevance of positive experiences while accentuating the importance of negative experiences; jumping to conclusions, the tendency to make decisions hastily without collecting all the facts (for example, mind readers assume others are rejecting them because of one critical statement, and fortune tellers make predictions of doom with limited evidence about probabilities); magnifying or minimizing, the tendency to give too much or too little importance to events, experiences, and errors; and personalizing, the tendency to attribute blame or credit to oneself arbitrarily.

Tenuous connections would be defined as those interactions in which minimal information processing occurs. These are habitual or ritualized encounters with taken-for-granted partners and places in the total environment. Few cognitive processes are activated, and the connected persons operate on automatic.

WHAT IS THE TYPICAL FOCAL SYSTEM?

Many practitioners committed to the cognitive approach are affiliated with a therapeutic framework that focuses on the mind of the individual client. Cognitive therapy attempts to change an individual's cognitive processes and **cognitive structures,** the person's relatively enduring and patterned ways of organizing information.

The focal system in the eco-map would be depicted as the mind and its schemas. Schemas are abstract representations of the distinctive features of an event, a person, or a cultural object. Schemas are essential mental tools in identifying and processing information. They serve the person the way an indexing system serves a library or a blueprint serves an architect (Nurius, 1989). Schematic representations may be in semantic form (words or other linguistic symbols) and operationalized as descriptors such as "empathic" or "resourceful." Schemas may also be stored in a form influenced by our senses, as images, sounds, or smells. Many schemas are learned in early childhood and become the core beliefs or assumptions that guide our actions. Once activated, these schemas strongly influence how their users organize incoming information.

Self-schemas are core organizing beliefs about the self. They often take the form of traits or qualities ("disliked" or "fat"). The set of self-schemas accumulated over time and across various socialization experiences is the total or global **self-concept.** From this large set of self-schemas, the person activates certain subsets depending on circumstances. Some schemas are relevant to challenges from the physical and social circumstances in the present moment. This subset is called the working self-concept. Since people participate in various social groups and situations (home, school, sports center), and each situation may require vastly different self- and role-conceptions, our minds have numerous working self-concepts.

There are several other important types of schemas. **Person schemas** are our beliefs about specific people and about types of people. They can lead to stereotyping. Some men's minds, for example, include schemas asserting that women are emotionally unstable. **Role schemas** are our beliefs about certain organizational positions and about the expected behaviors associated with these positions. Sexist men believe that administrative roles should be reserved for males. **Event schemas** are our beliefs about sequences of actions in familiar cultural events, like the script for a television show or movie. Event schemas include representations of various scenes and of the goals and actions of the actors in each scene. Patriarchal men at a military academy might conceive of graduation ceremonies scripted by men, led by men, and endorsed by high-status men. Each phase of these events, patriarchs might believe, should contribute to the transmission of information about male glory and valor.

Cognitive social workers try to change a client's mind, the interrelated set of schemas. Aaron Beck (1976) and others have directed the attention of practitioners to the major mental contributors to severe emotional problems. The cognitive triad of negative self-schemas ("I am defective and lack the qualities necessary to achieve happiness"), negative environmental schemas ("My situation presents me with insurmountable obstacles"), and negative event schemas about the future ("My difficulties will continue indefinitely") has been shown to result in depression. Changing the client's mood requires a change in these structured ways of constructing reality.

HOW IS THE ENVIRONMENT CONCEPTUALIZED?

Human beings create or construct the environment. What is the "environment"? Much of the environment, as indicated earlier, is taken for granted; it has yet to be conceptualized. Humans respond to certain stimuli habitually with minimal cognitive activity. Bike riding on the streets of one's neighborhood, for instance, requires little mental effort. Other aspects of the environment are ritualized and occur in patterned, predictable, and nonproblematic ways. Participation in a church service or an everyday greeting exchange requires minimal self-conscious or alert information processing. When we try to conceptualize the taken-for-granted—the various types of cloud formations in a clear sky, for instance—we discover that this takes effort and special training.

Cognitive scientists assert that the notion of "environment" varies. What "is" depends on the person's schemas or concepts for understanding the external world. People are active conceptualizers of the environment, and how we see and think about (notice, infer, interpret, evaluate, and predict) the environment and environmental stimuli is filtered through our cognitive structures.

There are hard and soft views of this notion that humans cognitively construct preferred versions of reality. Hard constructionists argue that there is no correct or "objective" version of reality. There are multiple realities or environments. Each person develops an individualized representation of the environment. This version may include schemas shared with other members of one's thought communities, but the conception of the environment is dominated by unique elements derived from one's special life experiences. Soft constructionists such as Sharon Berlin (1996), as well as early sociocognitive theorists such as George Herbert Mead (to be discussed in the chapter on symbolic interactionism), posit a "world-that-is-there"—an objective reality, independent of our cognitive constructions of it. I may define a prison wall in my own fashion as permeable, believe that a person can pass through it, and then imagine walking out of confinement. But this will have no observable effect on the actual walls of stone, the prison guards, the warden, my imprisonment, or the other obdurate aspects of the correctional environment. Thus, no matter what a client thinks, soft constructionists contend, there are other people, objects, and events in the external environment that limit the viability and efficacy of cognitive formulations.

Social workers can try to integrate both perspectives. Some aspects of the environment are negotiated and consensually constructed. One society agrees to conceptualize and recognize the indicators of "global warming"; another does not. Social workers need to be sensitive to variability in how the environment is conceived and to learn about different cognitive constructions of the environment and its elements. Yet social workers must acknowledge the constraints on conceptual possibilities presented by the realities of our body, our history, our social arrangements, and the physical world. Social work clients may not be able to change these obdurate features of their environment in significant ways, but with the help of social workers they can change the ways that they organize and use information about these environmental features. Social workers can also help clients modify old personal constructions and invent new cognitive constructions that meet pragmatic tests of goal achievement despite consensually agreed-upon physical and social constraints.

IS PARTICULAR EMPHASIS GIVEN TO ANY SYSTEMS?

The cognitive approach has been formulated primarily for use at the level of the person. Assessment, intervention, and evaluation of effectiveness are directed at the individual's cognitive processes, structures, and developmental capacities.

Application of the cognitive approach has been pioneered by those who identify themselves as therapists. Therapists traditionally serve one client at a time. The cognitive approach has been used less regularly for the education of families or groups of clients. However, didactic approaches are being proposed to help groups of clients identify the sociocognitive sources of problems.

Cognitive social psychologists would recommend also that practitioners pay attention to the **thought communities** in which clients learn to process information and build stocks of knowledge. This concept is defined formally as the groups, organizations, and societies that prefer particular ways of thinking and that judge the quality of a member's information processing according to collective standards. Clients may belong to many different thought communities, and these communities may socialize the clients and other members to distinctive patterns of "correct" thinking. These group influences on thinking should be considered during the assessment and intervention process.

How Are Resources and Their Flow Conceptualized?

The essential resources, for the cognitive social worker, are in the form of information. Resources include procedural or "knowing how" information. This information incorporates skills, instructions, and strategies for doing things. Resources also include general or "knowing about" information. This information incorporates knowledge about oneself and about the culture, including both knowledge shared with many others and personal knowledge generated during life experiences. Schemas or conceptions about possible selves, possible futures, and possible environments can also serve as informational resources transmitted between social systems and clients. All these resources can be used to enhance the thinking, feeling, and action of clients.

Cognitive social scientists endorse the notion of reciprocal intellectual influence. Information flow is a two-way process. Thought communities influence the person's style of information processing and the informational content of community members. Information processing and knowledge production by community members, especially by creative thinkers, in turn influences their thought communities and larger systems in the environment.

What Descriptive Words Are Used?

Some of the language of the cognitive sciences has been imported from the computer sciences and information technologies. Such terms were reviewed in the earlier discussion of root metaphors. Many descriptors used by cognitive practitioners are related to their conceptions of faulty information processing. Adjectives such as *irrational, illogical, distorted, problematic,* or *automatic* are commonly used. Nouns such as *misconception, error, discrepancy,* and *distortion* are frequently attached to clients and their relationship patterns. Phrases characterizing the faulty information-processing connections include *self-defeating thoughts, problematic automatic thinking, self-discrepancies,* and *irrational beliefs.* Cognitive theorists and practitioners, however, need to adopt the social work strengths perspective and create more descriptors to characterize optimal minds, ideal information processing, and wise thought communities.

How Is Change Conceptualized?

Cognitive practitioners would translate the social work maxim "Start where the client is" into the directive "Start with the client's mental representations of events, social organizations, other people, and his or her own behavior." An assessment requires the worker and client to collect data about the client's typical thought processes and level of cognitive development. **Self-monitoring,** listening to and observing the continuous flow of symbols and images in the mind, is one way to identify irrational beliefs, automatic thoughts, and other maladaptive patterns of processing and organizing informational cues (Beck,

1976). For example, the worker may help the client develop a log or journal in which he or she can record daily information about troubling situations and specific thoughts, especially **automatic thoughts** that "arise as if by reflex, without any apparent antecedent reflection or reasoning" (Beck, 1976, p. 90), that seem plausible to the client even though they seem unreasonable or implausible to other people. Beck gives the illustration of a physically healthy patient who thinks continually about developing a serious illness. Besides recording information about thoughts associated with these situations, the client writes down information about related feelings and behaviors.

Change starts with the initiation of metacognition, or "thinking about thinking." Structured thought monitoring can begin this process. Applied cognitive scientists conceive of change as largely a matter of transforming the client's beliefs and other thoughts about salient aspects of the problematic situation, not a matter of changing the situation.

Social workers might also use Ellis' (2005) A-B-C-D formula to guide the assessment and intervention. *A* refers to the *activating event* or *adversity* in the client system's life. *B* refers to the client's *beliefs* about the activating event or adversity. These beliefs are often unexamined, irrational, and self-defeating. *C* refers to the *consequences* that stem from the unrealistic interpretation of the activating event. Consequences may be troubling emotions or problematic behaviors. The social worker attempts to collect information and develop an assessment summarizing the disturbing event or adversity (internal or external, real or imagined, past, present or future). The worker then attempts to identify the irrational beliefs, looking and listening for dogmatic shoulds and musts, low frustration tolerance, and negative ratings of self and others. The social worker and client document the unhealthy negative emotions (anxiety, depression, shame, rage, jealousy, hurt, guilt) and the self-defeating behaviors for which the client system seeks help. A, B, and C are connected conceptually. Then, the worker begins the intervention, *D,* for *disputing* irrational beliefs. Ellis suggests that disputing involves posing tough questions about each belief to the client. What is the evidence for the belief? Is the belief logical? What have been the results of holding the belief? Is the situation as intolerable and awful as it could be?

Interventions for cognitive advancement can be at the personal or collective level. At the personal level, developmentally oriented social workers assume an educational role and help clients to achieve more adaptive information processing. Cognitive adaptation, as discussed earlier, is the balance of assimilation, the process of incorporating new bits of information into existing cognitive structures or schemas, and accommodation, the creation of a new schema or the modification of an old schema to enable processing information about objects or events that do not fit into existing cognitive structures (Rosen, 1988a). Workers can present clients with "development-enhancing experiences" such as those that provoke cognitive conflicts and challenge them to think in more advanced ways. Training in cognitive perspective taking helps clients decenter from their own problematic beliefs and use the perspectives of others to enrich their self- and social understanding.

Social workers uncomfortable with a developmental orientation can still use a variety of cognitive procedures to help the client test, change, correct, or restructure patterned ways of thinking that cause emotional or behavioral difficulties. These will be discussed in the section on our conceptual model at the end of the chapter.

Cognitive social workers can work at the collective level to create learning environments and educational models for groups, families, and communities that teach clients about common cognitive distortions; about how to monitor their thought processes; about processes for evaluating the quality or rationality of their thinking; and about using cognitive techniques to change emotional and behavioral patterns. Many social workers are developing such learning environments for men who think and act violently toward their partners and for substance abusers who desire to rethink their addiction to alcohol or drugs.

How Are Actual and Ideal Eco-Maps Contrasted?

Paula Nurius (1989) has developed the notion of **possible selves** to characterize the focal system in the ideal eco-map. Possible selves are conceptions of what we strive for and wish to become. They are characterizations of future-oriented parts of the total self-concept: positive representations of oneself in future states, social interactions, and anticipated environments. Possible selves can be desired ("become successful as a professional social worker"), optimistic, and positive. Possible selves can be feared and dreaded ("become an inept clerk in a department store"), pessimistic, and negative. Developing an ideal eco-map with a desired possible self at the center is a way to identify the "goals, aspirations, motives, fears, and threats that are stored in memory in the form of self schemata" (Nurius, 1989, p. 289). Workers can help clients create ideal eco-maps with hoped-for possible selves at the center. An effort should be made to include elaborate, vivid, compelling, accessible, and functional conceptions and images of the future self. These future schemas can set expectations for change and offer mental frameworks for evaluating the behaviors and events related to the change goals.

Nurius' notion of possible selves can be extended. We can help clients develop vivid, useful, and positive images and ideas about possible connections with others in the ecosystem; possible social systems, conceptualizing the characteristics of a desired family, community, or organization; and possible environments, representations of what the clients would like to see the total ecosystem become.

The ideal eco-map should also display information-processing connections characterized by scientific and logical thinking. Ideally, the client engages during transactions with others in the same practices as scientists. This mode of thinking and acting requires searching for empirical evidence that supports or challenges a belief; giving consideration to various interpretations and conceptual models for understanding the interrelation of elements in a troubling situation; testing questionable beliefs in behavioral experiments; drawing general conclusions about people or events only after sampling widely and repeatedly; monitoring emotional biases to believe or not believe something and exerting control over these biasing forces; recording data in a systematic way related to both the positive and negative consequences associated with endorsing certain beliefs; and accumulating empirically validated concepts, propositions, and frameworks for thinking and acting. Ideally, thought communities and social systems surrounding the focal client system also endorse and make use of scientific and critical thinking.

Actual eco-maps characterize the ways in which client systems fall short of the possibilities for self, relationship, social system qualities, and environment. Actual eco-maps would also detail the specific forms of faulty information processing that limit the focal system's efforts to make sense and to solve problems.

How Are Issues of Diversity, Color, and Shading Addressed?

We have already discussed several ways that cognitive scientists conceptualize diversity. For example, thought communities, the "churches, professions, political movements, generations, nations . . . to which we happen to belong" (Zerubavel, 1999, p. 9), influence both what we think and how we think. Members of different thought communities are likely to differ in their use of the major cognitive processes: perceiving, attending, classifying, representing, remembering, and reckoning time. An eco-map might include information about a focal system's important thought communities. We have also discussed how a person's self-schemas, person schemas, and event schemas may be based on stereotypes and perpetuate prejudicial or discriminatory behavior.

Social work clients often belong to vulnerable, oppressed, or hated groups. Social workers give special attention to stressful connections between our clients and the hateful or prejudicial groups threatening them harm. Cognitive scientists are also concerned about intergroup conflict and violence and have conducted extensive research on stereotyping. Kunda (2000) has reviewed many of the recent laboratory-derived empirical generalizations about the cognitive dynamics of stereotyping. I will report here on some of these important findings.

Kunda defines *stereotypes* as "cognitive structures that contain our knowledge, beliefs, and expectations about a social group" (2000, p. 315). He adds that definitions of stereotypes refer also to their lack of accuracy and degree of exaggeration. He then summarizes recent findings on the activation of stereotypes. Research indicates that stereotypes toward African Americans, for instance, are activated automatically and without awareness. Stereotypes about old people and about women are also activated automatically. This line of research shows that automatically activated stereotypes trigger negative thoughts, feelings, and behaviors toward the out-group member. Moreover, it suggests a self-fulfilling pattern. An African American interacting with a European American whose actions seem based on stereotypes would tend to act negatively toward that person—thus confirming the stereotype. Kunda reports also on individual differences in stereotype activation. People who are highly prejudiced toward a group (Blacks and West Indians in Britain, for example) automatically activate negative thoughts and negative feelings when reminded of the out-group. People who are less prejudiced show familiarity with the group stereotype but do not automatically activate negative thoughts and feelings when cued to think about the out-group.

Kunda summarizes several other interesting empirical findings. Stereotype activation requires effort. If a person has insufficient cognitive resources because he is mentally busy, for example, negative stereotypes are less likely to be activated. Kunda reasons that workplace hate crime may be infrequent because cognitive resources are directed to challenging mental tasks. Perhaps the opposite holds too. Too little mental activity frees energy for stereotype activation. This might help explain the correlation between membership in hate groups and unemployment. People also have the power to inhibit the activation of negative stereotypes. For example, when an African American praises a European American, the praised person demonstrates motivation to avoid stereotyping the one who did the praising. But stereotype inhibition also takes effort. If a person is tired, distracted, hurried, or in a bad mood, she is less likely to separate accurate judgments from stereotypical thinking about others.

Next, Kunda reports on some research-based findings about the applications of stereotypes. For example, when behaviors are ambiguous, the perceiver understands the behavior differently depending on the group membership of the behaving person. Members of ethnic minorities and poor persons walking through a department store are more likely than middle-class white shoppers to be stereotyped as shoplifters. Behavior is explained differently depending on the actor's group membership. The success of a man is often explained in terms of ability, but the success of a woman is more often explained by reference to luck and persistent effort. However, individuating information about a person deters the application of stereotypes. If we know about the behavior patterns, personality traits, or personality circumstances of a specific "housewife" or "construction worker," for instance, we tend to judge the person by the individuating information not by the stereotype. Study participants, Kunda reports, were also likely to apply a negative stereotype to a group member (Jewish woman or female professor) when doing so restored the participants' threatened self-esteem. Self-protection from bad grades, negative performance appraisals, and other damaging evaluations becomes the justification for stereotyping the evaluator.

Kunda also reports on research concerning the effects of stereotypes on the target. Members of stigmatized groups, including African Americans, Chicanos, and the facially disfigured, often buffer their selves from the impact of negative feedback by attributing it to stereotypical thinking by the judging person or group. Instead of accepting information about a personal inadequacy, they discredit the source of the information. **Stereotype threat,** "the fear that one will be reduced to the negative stereotype of one's group" (Kunda, 2000, p. 373), can undermine the performance of vulnerable groups. African Americans and women, for example, do not achieve at their level of potential in situations testing a domain in which they know that they are stereotyped as incompetent (African Americans tested for verbal ability, women tested for math ability). In contrast, when situational cues could be construed as irrelevant to a threatening stereotype, women and African Americans perform as well as European American males.

Finally, Kunda reports on efforts to reduce stereotype activation and application. Unfortunately, research shows that it is very difficult to change stereotypes through contact, such as cooperation in groups working to achieve common goals. When a person encounters someone who disconfirms a group stereotype (a wealthy African American, a respectful teenager, a gentle skinhead, a smart athlete), the person often dismisses the information as an atypical subtype and thus irrelevant to his or her conceptualization of the group's attributes. The person deals with the disconfirming evidence by cognitively "fencing off." These mental fences allow us to claim that "some of my best friends are _____" (fill in the disparaged group), yet maintain prejudicial and bigoted attitudes toward the whole category of people.

In summary, cognitive science has much to offer social workers about the contribution of stereotypes to stressful connections caused by faulty information processing and to the self-concept and self-esteem problems of members of disparaged and stereotyped groups.

WHAT WOULD BE ADDED OR DELETED?

Many cognitive scientists emphasize the present time frame and search for contemporary thinking-feeling-acting sequences. Beck (1976), for example, suggests that workers focus on conscious experience in the immediate present. However, developmental psychologists would add a retrospective eco-map to a full assessment, one that explores the client's cognitive development history. Sociocognitivist practitioners like Paula Nurius (1994) call for a prospective eco-map allowing a client to conceptualize a future self and future relationships. Cognitive scientists might also recommend the inclusion of important cultural events and clients' schemas about these events on the eco-map.

THE LIMITS OF APPLIED COGNITIVE SCIENCE: A SOCIAL WORK APPRAISAL

The cognitive approach has much to offer social work practitioners. Several cautions are worth mentioning, however, for those who adopt it as their theoretical base. We have already discussed the dangers of comparing clients to computers and thereby forgetting the qualities and capacities that contribute to "the human difference" (Wolfe, 1993). Several other reminders are in order.

Don't forget that the person is a biopsychosocial and spiritual whole. Cognitive social scientists give primacy to mental capacities and processes, which take priority over other aspects of human functioning. Some client problems, however, have biochemical or neurological sources rather than cognitive causes. Social workers helping addicted clients must be familiar with the physical cravings and withdrawal pains as well as with the beliefs supportive of drug abuse. Cognitive social scientists focus mainly on emotional disturbances, and some, like Ellis (Ellis & Harper, 1975), seem to suggest that emotionally tinged information processes are intrinsically "irrational" and inferior to logical or emotion-free information processing. Social workers know that emotions are not lesser capacities, that thinking and feeling cannot be easily separated except for analytic purposes, that high-quality information processing has both a cognitive and an emotional quality, and that attending to our emotions can increase our "reasonableness" and our ability to cope with challenges.

Don't forget the social context and diversity issues. The work of Piaget and many cognitive scientists tends to emphasize individual-level variables rather than social variables in explaining human failures and accomplishments (Forte, 2001). The notion of "rationality," for instance, is often defined in an individual (and circular) way as an individual's style of thinking. Rationality is that approach to information processing that accords with "objective" reality and that serves as an effective means for achieving desired ends. Many cognitive theorists and practitioners give only minimal attention to the group-based context for judging the rationality of a person's thinking processes. In-group conceptions of rationality vary. The standards of rationality learned by a European American upper-middle-class male professional psychologist may differ greatly from the standards internalized by members of a newly arriving immigrant group. Whole communities have engaged in apartheid or genocide and claimed the "reasonableness" of such destructive activity. The individual defying the group logic—even if cast as a lunatic on the fringe—may be more "rational" than the dominant community.

Additionally, cognitive social workers need to attend more to the notion that troubling ideas and faulty ways of information processing can be often traced to clients' families, peer groups, schools, and socialization contexts. Social workers might prod cognitive scientists to do more work to understand shared ways of thinking and the group processes that result in maladaptive thought patterns. Sometimes, change efforts might be more effectively directed at correcting faulty information processing at the level of the collective rather than the level of the person. Policies and programs that attack social organizations and movements promoting ideas supportive of racism, sexism, homophobia, hate, terror, and violence may do more social good than individual therapy for intolerant men and women.

Finally, some cognitive therapies may have limited utility in certain agency contexts. Work with clients at early stages of intellectual development may need to be more action or play oriented than cognitive (Beck, 1976). Additionally, clients who have limited capacity or motivation for monitoring and reflecting on their patterns of thinking may be reluctant to identify and restructure irrational beliefs or to use other cognitive techniques and procedures.

A COGNITIVE MODEL FOR HELPING NEGLECTFUL MOTHERS

Paula Nurius (1989, 1994), a social worker, has translated many ideas from the cognitive social sciences for use by practitioners. Instead of a midrange or grounded theory, she has developed a comprehensive model for social work practice (Brower & Nurius, 1993). Her causal model links negative cognitions and cognitive processes to troubles in child rearing, and she identifies the cognitive interventions that can effectively alter first information processing and then parenting behavior.

THE COGNITIVE PERSPECTIVE ON PROBLEMS IN SOCIAL FUNCTIONING

Nurius (1989, 1994) shares the cognitive approach's conception of the cognitive sources of client problems. Substantial and long-lasting changes in client behaviors can be accomplished only when there are changes in self-cognitions consistent with the desired behavioral changes. Negative, self-defeating thoughts, problematic automatic thinking, and irrational beliefs that mediate between stimulus and response must be altered if problems in social functioning are to be resolved. Nurius and her colleagues (Nurius, Lovell, & Edgar, 1988) have shown how to apply this theory to the problems of neglectful and abusive mothers.

THE COGNITIVE PERSPECTIVE ON ASSESSMENT

A **sociocognitive assessment** entails information gathering about the client's working self-concepts, especially those self-views activated in household settings. For example, abusive mothers often hold negative self-schemas and conceptualize themselves as "weak," "ineffectual," "inconsistent," "not very bright," and "out of control." These schemas are very accessible and easily evoked in parenting situations. The problems in social functioning faced by these mothers stem from these "damaged self-concepts." Additionally, the assessment includes consideration of a person's possible selves and, specifically, whether views of the future self are optimistic or pessimistic. Nurius et al. (1988) discovered that mothers who had trouble managing child-rearing crises typically reported negative possible selves ("It's just my nature," "I guess you are who you are and that's it"). Clients' visions of the future self included no conception of a possibility for improvement.

Nurius and her colleagues (1988) provided directives for assessment by practitioners. During group counseling with abusive and neglectful mothers, for instance, the worker should do an initial assessment of group members' ways of processing information. These are likely to be influential in later client processing of information about the self, others, and the group. The worker should assess members' self-schemas and role schemas as these relate to the group agenda (helping members with common parenting problems). Assessing members' working self-concepts and possible selves relevant to the parent role and gathering information about the anticipated implications of the group process for the clients' selves are also important.

A set of specific questions can be helpful in structuring this assessment process (Nurius, 1994). To what extent can the mother offer a clear and rich picture of possible alternative life goals? To what extent does the mother judge her self-views as harmonious or as discrepant? To what extent can the client articulate procedures that are useful in realizing the desired self-concept? Is the client mindful of information from the environment relevant to the self-concept and, if so, in what ways? How much awareness does the client show about the ways that the working self-concepts are activated from long-term memory?

The Cognitive Perspective on Intervention

The goals for intervention are elaborated with reference to the model's key notions of self-concept, possible selves, and negative self-views. Let's start with the client's working self-concept. Teaching the mothers about the idea of a "working self-concept" helps them understand that humans are naturally different and sometimes contradictory persons in different social situations. The practitioner also helps each mother to increase the salience or "accessibility" of positive and functional self-schemas (related to dedicated, effective, and nurturing parenting, for example) and to increase the "elaboration" of poorly defined but valued self-schemas so that these schemas might better compete with habitual, less adaptive self-views. In the area of hoped-for selves, the social worker helps the client practice, reinforce, and observe models of positive possible selves, and disconfirm existing negative selves or feared future selves. Potentially abusive mothers can learn, for instance, how not to conceive of themselves and what not to do with their children. According to this cognitive model, the strategy of conceiving of a positive possible self (and the negative self to avoid) helps mothers think about their strengths and potentials for change.

Finally, the social worker and client can collaborate in developing plans to challenge those negative and disconfirming self-perceptions and understandings that in certain parenting circumstances become simultaneous and painfully salient. Clear, meaningful, fully articulated, emotionally relevant, and achievable goals were developed for the mothers in Nurius' case study.

Following the cognitive model, the intervention strategies used in work with neglectful mothers included techniques familiar to many cognitive practitioners. Nurius described her use of such procedures.

In vivo rehearsal entails the mother's practice of self-concept elaboration in natural settings such as the home. The worker uses home visits to help the mother try her new cognitive and behavioral response patterns in difficult parenting situations.

Cognitive rehearsal during helping sessions entails brainstorming, visualizing, and observing models of detailed and efficacious possible selves. The mothers are helped to construct new possible selves characterized by elaborate conceptual detail and by a set of images related to effective parenting.

Rehearsal also involves planning strategies for invoking and sustaining these self-images and conceptions when relating to children.

Self-observation training requires teaching the mothers to monitor and record their patterns of self-referential thoughts as these relate to relationships with their children and to behavior in the household and other contexts. The mothers learn to pay special attention to self-statements indicating negative beliefs and schemas about the self. Journals with summaries of stimulus-cognition-behavior sequences noted during parenting and records of changes in these patterns are useful tools for facilitating change.

Cognitive restructuring requires monitoring and challenging conflictual or maladaptive self-thoughts. Specifically, the worker helps the mothers to disconfirm negative thoughts and to substitute images and words centering on the qualities and abilities of the hoped-for possible self.

Nurius and her team (1988) centered their intervention efforts on reducing the negative self-schemas of maltreating mothers. Evaluation data indicated that cognitive social work did reduce such negativity. The cognitively oriented social workers also helped their clients achieve associated positive increases in coping abilities and decreases in stress, family tension, and self-esteem concerns.

LEARNING ACTIVITIES

1. Compare the way you perceive, remember, classify, and think to a computer. What are some similarities? What are some differences?

2. Conduct a mini-study following Piaget's example. Watch a child in his or her natural setting playing with others or trying to solve a problem. Interview the child about his or her thinking. Try to identify the signs of the child's mental activity, and make a judgment about the child's stage or level of cognitive development.

3. Design a learning environment for 7- to 11-year-old children using Piaget's ideas and propositions about the optimal conditions for cognitive development. You might design a classroom setting, an activity center at a day care program, or an exhibition hall at a science museum. How does your planned environment differ from the settings in which your clients or your clients' children learn?

4. Create a list of some of your most important self-concepts. You might do this by completing the sentence "I am a person who ____"

with the qualities, attributes, characteristics, or social memberships that best describe who you are. Next, try to identify the ways that several of these self-conceptions influence your information processing, decision making, and action.

5. Construct an eco-map translated into the vocabulary of cognitive science. What are some of the self-conceptions that influence your emotional and behavioral reactions to social events? Characterize the quality of your thinking about your connections with other persons. Which different working self-concepts are activated in your information exchanges with different social systems?

6. Reflect on your important social memberships. How would you describe the "thought communities" that have influenced what you think and how you think? Identify the ways in which your thinking conforms to one of these communities. Identify some ways that you differ in your style of thinking from one of these communities.

7. Identify a troubling personal or interpersonal situation. Use the A-B-C-D formula developed by Albert Ellis to assess and change the situation. What is the activating event? What beliefs are associated with this event? What are the undesirable consequences of the event–belief sequence? Try disputing your irrational beliefs. Develop a change plan. How has this cognitive approach to self-change facilitated your understanding and improvement of the situation?

8. Think quickly about some group that is very different from you on a characteristic such as skin color, sexual orientation, generational cohort, religion, physical disability, nationality, or community type. Quickly list the common traits, attributes, and behavioral patterns of members of this group. Now examine your list carefully, slowly, and objectively. Solicit feedback, if possible, from a member of the group about the accuracy of your profile. Which items were stereotypes? How might the activation of these stereotypes cause prejudicial or discriminatory action toward group members?

9. Develop a possible self. Identify some of the major descriptors or schemas that are attached to this future you. Describe some images of the future self in action. Set one or two goals that specify the actions, attributes, and social circumstances that will help you become this possible self.

Additional Resources

Additional resources are available on the book companion website at **www.thomsonedu.com/social_work/forte**. Resources include key terms, tutorial quizzes, links to related websites, and lists of additional resources for furthering your research.

CHAPTER | APPLIED PSYCHODYNAMIC THEORY

BSIP Agency/IndexStock

INTRODUCTION

Have you sometimes felt overwhelmed by your impulses and passions? Do you wonder why certain situations consistently evoke strong feelings of anxiety? Have you noticed that when you return home to visit your parents you often feel the same powerlessness and dependency that you experienced decades ago? Have you tried to make sense of a confusing dream? Do you believe that you repeat the same mistakes that you have made many times earlier in your life? Did you ever regret what a casual joke revealed about your true feelings toward people or events? Have you been perplexed by apparent connections between physical symptoms such as headaches or stomach irritation and troubling relationship experiences? Would you like to end some of the inner battles between different parts of your self?

Applied psychodynamic theory may help you find answers to these questions and help you make some desired changes. It can guide your problem conceptualization, assessment formulation, and intervention planning with diverse clients. This tradition builds on the work of Freudians and classical psychoanalytic theorists. It incorporates the thinking of ego psychologists like Erik Erikson and object relations theorists like John Bowlby. The psychodynamic tradition has been reinvigorated by the contemporary theoretical advances of the self psychologists.

For almost 60 years of the 20th century, psychoanalysis and other variants on the psychodynamic tradition were the theories preferred by most social workers. In this chapter, I will use our theory mastery tools—exemplary models, metaphors, maps, and conceptual models—to introduce you to this school of thought. Special attention will be given to Erikson's ego psychological approach to human development and John Bowlby's attachment theory.

RELATED DIALECTS, ASSOCIATED SCHOOLS OF THOUGHT

Psychodynamic theory has many dialects. These variations from the language of psychodynamic theory can be understood by their degree of break from the core assumptions and root metaphors formulated by Sigmund Freud (Freud Loewenstein, 1985). There are four major schools of thought.

The **classical psychoanalysis** framework is the original language devised by Freud. The name now refers to "theories dealing with the psychic energy created by sexual and aggressive drives called upon by Freud to explain the mainsprings of human behavior" (Freud, 1992, p. 419). Priority is given to the powers of the id and to unconscious motivation. Most contemporary theorists and theory users refer to classical psychoanalysis only as a historical base.

Ego psychology is "a related set of theoretical concepts about human behavior that focuses on the origins, development, structure, and functioning of the executive arm of the personality—the ego—and its relationship to other aspects of the personality and to the external environment"

(Goldstein, 1984, p. xiv). Therapeutic intervention focuses on strengthening ego functions and overall ego functioning. Anna Freud, Heinz Hartmann, Erik Erikson, and Edith Jacobson were some of the prominent ego psychologists (Freud, 1992). Compared to classical psychoanalysis, theoretical emphasis shifts in this branch from id to ego and from unconscious processes to conscious processes.

Object relations theory prioritizes interpersonal relationships rather than instincts or ego functions. Object relations theorists study "the internal images or representations of the self and others (objects) that a person acquires in the course of development" (Goldstein, 2001, p. 7). Object relations theorists reject drive theory and prioritize interpersonal and sociocultural influences on human development. Clinicians using object relations theory attend to and help correct distortions in the process of developing capacities for mature relationships (Pearson, Treseder, & Yelloly, 1988). This dialect is sometimes called the British school of object relations because its major theorists—Melanie Klein, W. R. D. Fairbairn, D. W. Winnicott, Harry Guntrip, Wilfred Bion, and John Bowlby— were British or developed their most influential ideas in Great Britain. However, Harry Stack Sullivan, an American interpersonal psychiatrist, and other theorists, including Karen Horney, Erich Fromm, and Alfred Adler, also have ties to this branch of psychodynamic theory (Freud, 1992).

Self psychology, the most recent variation from Freud's original work, theorizes that the self is central to human development. Freud's assumptions about drives and about the personality's structure (id-ego-superego) are rejected (Goldstein, 2001). Heinz Kohut, the founder of this theoretical branch, shifted the theoretical focus to the unfolding of the potentials of the self and to the impact of the self/object environment on self-development, self-esteem management, and healthy narcissism. Paul Ornstein, Ernest Wolf, and Michael Basch are members of the community of self psychologists.

Otto Rank and Carl Jung are theorists influenced by Freud but not easily categorized. **Applied psychodynamic theory** will be used in this chapter as the inclusive term referring to "theories and therapeutic approaches which ultimately derive from Freud" (Pearson et al., 1988, p. 7).

APPLIED PSYCHODYNAMIC THEORY: EXEMPLARY MODELS

The psychodynamic theoretical perspective has a long and rich tradition with many branches and many great member theorists. All offshoots of the tradition, however, can be traced back to Sigmund Freud, who is considered one of the greatest social theorists (Craib, 1998).

SIGMUND FREUD

Sigmund Freud (1856–1939) grew up and then went to medical school in Vienna, Austria (Jones, 1955). He worked as the superintendent of a hospital. Later, he treated many different patients in his private practice, including patients suffering from hysteria and other forms of mental illness. Freud was dedicated from an early age to theory application. In his biography, Freud stated, "In my youth I felt an overpowering need to understand something of the riddles of the world in which we live and perhaps even contribute something to their solution" (Jones, 1955, p. 28). Freud made his living as a practicing therapist. He developed the psychoanalytic approach to practice, including the intervention methods of dream interpretation, free association, and transference analysis.

Freud became especially interested in problems that had a psychic origin. He coined the term *psychoanalysis* for his human behavior theories and his therapeutic approach (World Book, 2001). He theorized about the influence of unconscious forces on human behavior; the use of defense mechanisms to ward off anxiety and painful memories; the dynamic and conflictive interaction of id, ego, and superego; the ways patients resisted analysis; the stages of psychosexual development; the tension between society's civilizing influence and the individual's urges for gratification; and the basic causes of psychic disturbances. Some of his notions, such as those about the physical and psychological benefits of cocaine, the processes of sexual development, the prevalence of childhood trauma, and the inferiority of women, were very controversial. His theory of the person and society, however, is the "classic psychoanalytic perspective," and it has influenced many social work practitioners and educators.

Freud's theory use was sympathetic to social work causes and interests. Historical myth portrays Sigmund Freud as a therapist specializing in the treatment of wealthy and intellectually accomplished individuals. Recent historical research (Danto, 2005) documents that Sigmund Freud and his circle of analysts were also social activists who built free mental health clinics in different cities, including Berlin and Vienna. These clinics provided services to those in need regardless of gender, class, age, or occupation. The clinics were designed to facilitate both personal healing and social change. Danto links the development of child analysis, short-term therapy, crisis intervention, task-centered treatment, and clinical case presentations to these community-based clinics. Freud received awards for his social welfare work, and he valued social work. In 1926, Sigmund Freud joked about the need for an American follower who would train social workers in the psychoanalytic method and thus create a band of helpers to combat the neuroses of civilization (Pearson et al., 1988). Freud's gift to social work extended beyond his death. Sophie Freud, a granddaughter of Sigmund Freud, practiced as a social worker in the field of child welfare and child guidance, and spent 30 years as a social work educator at the Simmons College School of Social Work.

Freud differs from many other theorists in that he was an excellent writer. Lauzun (1965) characterizes his writing style as "clear, definite, dry, logical, outstandingly attuned to the thought to be expressed: a style in which all affirmations are clearly made and solidly supported; which is at once comprehensible to any cultivated reader; and which carries conviction to all save those who are systematically opposed to any new theory" (p. 14). After his initial discoveries, Freud attracted many followers. Alfred Adler, Carl Jung,

Otto Rank, and others expanded on some of his ideas and rejected others. Freud was considered by some to be arrogant, intolerant of challenge, and excessively certain of his insights. Great theorists like Carl Jung who differed from the master were eventually ejected from his inner circle. Nevertheless, Freud's theories about personality, psychopathology, and treatment were widely influential and eagerly absorbed by the humanities, psychology, sociology, social work, and other disciplines.

ERIK H. ERIKSON

Erik H. Erikson (1902–1994) championed an ego psychology revision of classical psychoanalysis (Roazen, 1976). Erik's biological father, a Dane, abandoned the family a few months before Erik was born. Erikson was later adopted by his Jewish stepfather, Dr. Theodor Homberger. A tall, blond, blue-eyed boy who was also Jewish, Erik was teased by both his Jewish and non-Jewish peers. With his wife and children, he left Vienna to escape the Nazis. The German-born Erikson rejected the family's last name, Homberger—perhaps, according to Roazen, because his children thought it would be confused in America with "hamburger." When he became a U.S. citizen, he renamed himself with a simpler name as Erik's son.

After studying art as a young man, Erikson was psychoanalyzed by Anna Freud and participated in intensive psychoanalytic training. He attended Harvard University and actually failed his first graduate psychology course. Although his later career demonstrated that he was an exceptional and multitalented theorist, practitioner, and educator, Erikson never earned a college degree (Crain, 1980). He worked for a time as the first child psychoanalyst in Boston. He conducted anthropological studies of Sioux Indians and Yurok Indians, and he learned how cultural groups vary in the social institutions they create to support members' ego development. He also traced the Indians' psychological problems to the destruction of their native and communal identity. Erikson valued interdisciplinary collaboration (Goldhaber, 2000; Smelser, 1996), and he learned across his career from contact with the work of biologists, psychologists, sociologists, anthropologists, and historians.

Erik Erikson invented modern psychohistory (Smelser, 1996) and used ego psychological ideas to write psychohistorical biographies of Martin Luther, Mohandas Gandhi, George Bernard Shaw, Maxim Gorky, and Adolf Hitler. His involvement in a series of longitudinal studies of children initiated at Berkeley in the 1930s stimulated his theorizing about normal human development (Goldhaber, 2000). Erikson's psychodynamic approach is especially attentive to the person's place in a matrix of social relations and to psychosocial development across the life cycle. Unlike Freud, Erikson argued, for example, that humans continue to develop beyond adolescence and can grow in vital and substantial ways even in old age. Erikson also theorized often about identity and the problems of identity, perhaps because of his own experiences as an immigrant to America (Smelser, 1996). He believed that **ego identity** represents the person's capacity to unify inner conflicts. Ego identity, which has personal and communal sources, allows the person to escape creatively and adaptively the constraints of childhood experiences.

Erikson assisted the U.S. government during World War II by analyzing German propaganda and the speeches of Adolf Hitler (Goldhaber, 2000). During the McCarthy hunt for communists, he made a decisive life change. Motivated by his commitment to behave in line with his true identity, Erik Erikson resigned from the University of California, Berkeley, rather than sign an oath asserting that he was a loyal citizen and not a member of the Communist party. Erikson was never a communist.

Erikson's ideas have been widely used by social workers, probably because he made greater use of social science ideas and of the notion of ego strengths than other followers of Freud. Erikson's psychosocial theory has contributed to theory-based approaches to childhood education, to therapy, and to social work practice because it is directed, in Erikson's words, to a "most specific problem: the strengthening and enriching of the ego" (cited in Roazen, 1976, p. 22). His psychosocial approach to development (Erikson, 1959/1980, 1968a) will be a major focus of this chapter.

FLORENCE HOLLIS

Florence Hollis (1907–1987) was a social work practitioner, educator, researcher, and theory developer. She translated many psychoanalytic ideas for practical use. Her theory-based approach to practice had roots in Freudian ideas about personality and practice but also assimilated concepts from newer theoretical frameworks such as systems theory and role theory (Hollis & Woods, 1981). Throughout her career, Hollis maintained close relationships with psychoanalysts committed to theory development. She theorized creatively but did so using a social work foundation to practice, a foundation acquired during leadership of the Family Society in Philadelphia and during her Depression era casework with families.

Her own approach systematically linked theory to practice. Hollis contributed, for example, a very influential typology of casework procedures that adapted psychodynamic practice theory for social work use. Her classification system included the treatment procedures of exploration, ventilation, pattern-dynamic reflection, developmental reflection, and person-situation reflection. Hollis published 30 books, including the classic *Casework: A Psychosocial Therapy,* and more than 40 articles on casework techniques, principles, and applications (Woods & Hollis, 2000).

Florence Hollis believed that abstract knowledge should be used by caseworkers to improve the lives of distressed clients. She balanced an interest in clinical practice with concern for inequitable political and social arrangements (Woods, 2000). She was troubled, for example, by drastic cutbacks in federal funding for social programs during the administration of President Reagan. Hollis spoke out about the hideous conditions experienced by the growing numbers of individuals and families left homeless as a result of Reagan's fiscal and social policies.

APPLIED PSYCHODYNAMIC THEORY: ROOT METAPHORS

Applied psychodynamic theorists are very creative in making use of the metaphorical imagination. Many different metaphors illuminate different aspects of the theoretical perspective. In this section, I will report on metaphors for the person, the society, and the social worker, beginning with metaphors relevant to Erikson's psychosocial model of human development.

THE PERSON AS MOUNTAIN CLIMBER (CAVE, BEAST, ENERGY USER)

To my knowledge, Erikson did not use this metaphor. However, he might have compared the client to a mountain climber. Each person proceeds up the mountain following a similar path or sequence of steps. These mountain climbers ideally master the skill and the knowledge necessary to ascend to one plateau after another. Some fail and get stuck on the mountain or even fall back down to an earlier place. Each successful advance up the mountain represents psychosocial growth and might be marked metaphorically by a certificate from a mountain-climbing association indicating advancement in the climber's overall level of mountain-climbing competence (acquisition of an additional basic strength). In Erikson's scheme, these might be the signs of recognition provided by the society's institutions such as the school or the workplace, and they indicate successful progress. Failures at the earlier stages cause psychological scars (Freud Loewenstein, 1985) that increase the likelihood of problems climbing to higher points on the mountain.

Psychodynamic theorists make many other comparisons. This tradition of studying human behavior has been referred to as "depth psychology" (Freud, 1992; Leary, 1990). The unconscious exists in the depths of the psyche. The person is like a buried city, an iceberg, or a land mass with vast underground caves. The most important aspects of the personality are unconscious and unseen, like the artifacts and buildings of ancient Troy or the dark crevices beneath the ground. Though much of the personality is unseen, the unconscious depths have great influence on what occurs above the land or waterline. In his theorizing, Freud engaged in explicit metaphorical thinking, comparing clients to archeological mounds. Much important information about the person and the society is buried. Earlier experiences are the first layers for the person on which later experiences are built. Understanding the present requires an excavation. The past persists in altered form in the present time. Erikson rejected Freud's conception of the personality as an archeological mound (Roazen, 1976) and believed that the past is like organic matter rather than dead stone. Therefore, the person can transform creatively the historical past for adaptive use in the present.

Psychodynamic theorists, especially id psychologists, have also likened the client to a wild man or beast (Freud, 1992). The client has sexual and aggressive instincts similar to those of the animals that continually seek expression for their urges. Freud, for example, compared the person to a runaway horse (id forces) with a small and relatively ineffective rider (ego) trying to slow it down (McReynolds, 1990; Roazen, 1976).

Adherents to psychodynamic approaches have used other metaphors. They conceive of the person as an energy user. Social work clients are like the operators of a massive dam transforming the latent power of water into electricity. Psychic energy, especially the energy generated by the id, is the major engine for power transformation. Psychic forces or pressures can build up like floodwater behind a dam. If this pressure is not released or discharged in a regulated fashion, the dam may break and the waters of the id will flow wildly in destructive and uncontrollable ways. The client who represses (dams up) repeatedly and forcefully all his hateful attitudes and angry emotions may experience their sudden and unanticipated release. Id energies become like tons of water breaking through a concrete barrier and flooding the nearby community. Ego psychologists like Erikson add to Freudian imagery of id energy the notion that the ego has its own capacities for energy production. The ego's energy makes self-preservation, love, and effective action in the environment possible.

Freud also used the metaphorical image of an unwanted party guest (Craib, 1998). Our unconscious includes desires, wishes, and ideas that we may choose not to invite into the conscious part of our psyche. However, after the unwanted guest is turned away, she sneaks around to the back door, slips in through a window, or comes down the chimney. The party's host might recognize the unwelcome intruder by monitoring for Freudian slips. These are unintentional but revealing verbal statements. On a visit to a field internship, I met an alumnus with the last name Bryant. In a conversation with our field instructor at the same agency, I referred incorrectly to our graduate as Anita Bryant, a noisy critic of homosexuality. What did this slip tell me about my unconscious associations to the chance encounter? Dreams may also show us how intruders from the unconscious have crashed our party. Psychoanalysts are interested in the clues that a dream provides to therapist and patient as both try to understand the patient's subconscious and unconscious desires and fears. These clues are often about erotic or aggressive inclinations driven from awareness. Dream analysis is the process of facilitating the safe expression and interpretation of these unconscious wishes. It is a therapeutic tool for increasing patient self-knowledge by integrating unwanted elements into the party.

THE SOCIAL ENVIRONMENT AS MOUNTAIN (DIG, CIRCUS)

Erik Erikson (1959/1980) developed a levels-by-stages model of human development (McCall, 1988). A stage is one interval in a series of temporal intervals, and a level is a distinctive form of psychosocial organization. Erikson did not use root metaphors with the flair of Freud. However, his theory might be grasped by comparing society to a mountain and psychosocial development to mountain climbing. A life cycle is the terrain of the mountain. Ascent to the mountaintop occurs in a step-by-step manner. There are various plateaus on the mountainside. Each corresponds to a life stage, and the path from one plateau to another presents different challenges and opportunities. The society provides social institutions and significant relations to assist each mountain climber. Each generation cultivates its own approach to mountain climbing, but Erikson argued that mountain-climbing knowledge and techniques are transmitted across generations. The cycle-of-life imagery suggests that the individual life cycle rounds itself out as a coherent experience and that generations are linked in a patterned way (Roazen, 1976). We start at the mountain's bottom and begin the long climb to our journey's end, but then the next generation begins the climb, again benefiting from our experience and wisdom.

Several other metaphorical conceptions of society are inherent in the psychodynamic tradition. Society is like the site of an archeological dig. Society is like a lake-and-dam complex. Society is like a large party. Let me elaborate on an additional comparison. Society is like a circus or horse stable where the energies of wild beasts are channeled into acceptable, civilized patterns of action. There is a never-ending conflict or tension between the beasts desiring to "go wild" and the animal trainers. The trainers are the civic leaders upholding cultural order. In the civilized society (and the successful circus), the members of the collective unite to restrain or restrict the human animal's urges for gratification, his or her instincts and passions (Jones, 1955). Complex society requires, in a way, that humans accept the same kind of misery that caged animals, unable to exercise their natural inclinations and powers, must endure.

THE SOCIAL WORKER AS GUIDE (SPELUNKER, ENGINEER, TAMER)

In Erikson's theoretical system, the social worker is like the experienced mountain guide who recommends the equipment, support systems, and techniques appropriate for each stage of the ascent. The social worker also helps clients with various climbing problems. The client may fear the climb and desire to return (or regress) to earlier stages in the climb and stop the upward movement. The client may need help rectifying deficiencies (core pathologies) acquired during earlier intervals of mountain climbing. The client may lack the support and resources (ego supports and social institutions) necessary for advancement to new levels of mountain-climbing proficiency. The social worker rallies significant relations to assist the mountain climber. At each stage, the worker helps the novice climber solve problems and resume progress to the summit.

Psychodynamic theorists also compare the helping professional to members of different kinds of occupations. Social workers are like expert party hosts. Social workers and therapists are like archeologists digging up one layer of historical sediment after another. The social work therapist as archeologist must dig down to the foundations at the work site and then determine their influence on the psychological and interpersonal constructions that followed. Social work therapists might also be compared to spelunkers, professional cave explorers, helping the patient descend to the depths of a cave and return with various treasures. Therapists lead the effort to explore the dark region of the unconscious and bring hidden aspects of the psyche to light so that these unconscious motivations, emotions, and relational patterns can be examined and revised.

The social work therapist is also like a member of a team of engineers assisting other power plant workers. The therapist-engineer monitors energy buildup, maintains an equilibrium of the forces seeking release and containment, checks and fortifies the structures constraining energy, finds safe ways to siphon off (by sublimation or displacement) portions of energy, and fosters a controlled discharge of energy to avoid explosions, implosions, or floods.

The social worker is like a circus tamer of unruly lions, tigers, and horses. She helps each client learn to control his or her id forces. Social workers need not use a whip, however. Instead, they employ psychological techniques to enable clients to internalize society's rules into the part of the psyche called the superego. The client's experience, once socialized and linked to guilt, becomes an inner whip discouraging the public expression of forbidden behavior. Tamed clients punish themselves, for example, when they feel like biting off the worker's head. Key psychodynamic concepts elaborate on this triad of beast, tamer, and circus. Concepts such as *instincts, aggression, sex drives,* and *unconscious desires* refer to humans' animal-like tendencies. Concepts such as *internalization, superego, repression,* and *suppression* refer to the mental procedures and apparatus for mastery of impulses. *Conflict* refers to the mental and social state of persons forced to comply with a restrictive social order.

Psychodynamic theorists have also been partial to medical metaphors (Averill, 1990) and liken the client to a patient, the practitioner to a medical doctor, client problems to pathologies or diseases of the mind, helping practice to treatment, and successful treatment to a cure. Some social workers still use such medical words and images to describe their clients and their helping work.

CORE ASSUMPTIONS OF APPLIED PSYCHODYNAMIC THEORY

In this section, I will review some of the basic assumptions that are derived from the psychodynamic approach's root metaphors.

HUMAN MENTAL LIFE IS CHARACTERIZED BY CONFLICT

Psychodynamic ego psychologists assume that human mental life is characterized by conflict. The psyche must regularly attempt to manage two or more tendencies to act, tendencies that are incompatible and hard to reconcile. **Psychodynamics** refers to the continually shifting relation of the inner processes (the interdependent components of the psyche—id, ego, superego) and outer processes (environmental constraints and opportunities) and the ways that the person manages the associated inner and outer conflicts. Psychodynamic theorists contend that people experience constant conflict with society, shown in the root metaphor of barely tamed beasts and the associated theoretical assumptions about primitive or uncivilized psychic forces clashing with civilizing societal pressures. Erikson and other ego psychologists were more optimistic than Freud and assumed that people can learn to master their conflicts and function with manageable amounts of inner and outer tension. Erikson's ego is a very capable horse rider.

EARLY LIFE EXPERIENCES HAVE GREAT FORMATIVE POWER

Psychodynamic ego psychologists assume that early life stage experiences have great formative power. Many adult problems have their source in early childhood experiences. Freud was pessimistic about our ability to overcome the determining power of these early traumas. Erikson (1963), in contrast, was optimistic. Although he believed that people might develop "core pathologies" if they failed to resolve earlier psychosocial crises, he also asserted that contemporary relationship experiences are important. Our origins shape us, but we can transcend their limiting power. With help from others, a person can return to earlier crises, correct past difficulties (to some extent), and develop new ego strengths. The social worker, for instance, can guide clients in a "life review" that considers past developmental successes and failures, plans remedial action, and results in constructive personality change. Despite a few missteps or accidents during the early stages of a mountain climb, the client can, with the help of others, regain her footing and continue the ascent.

OTHERS, ESPECIALLY CARETAKERS, INFLUENCE DEVELOPMENT

Psychodynamic ego psychologists assume that other people, especially early caretakers, have a great influence on psychosocial development. Erikson referred to the **radius of significant relations.** The concept of *significant* addresses the centrality of the other person to the biopsychosocial processes associated with development and identity formation. The concept of *radius* suggests that the maturing person enters relationships first with those in close proximity, such as parents, and increasingly to persons further from the household, including schoolmates, coworkers, and all humanity. How we develop, who we become, and what strengths we can use to meet challenges depends greatly on our interactions with significant people. Successful mountain climbers depend on others.

THE EGO HAS INTRINSIC CAPACITIES FOR ADAPTATION

Psychodynamic ego psychologists assume that the ego has intrinsic capacities for adaptation. The **ego** is the personality component that assists in moderating inner and outer conflict. The ego is essential for general adaptation and to meet the specific psychosocial crises associated with each step in the socially structured life cycle. All humans have ego potentials. Humans are like those mountain climbers who possess natural intuition and inborn wisdom about how to cope with rugged, steep, and rocky terrain. However, the development of these ego strengths depends on the successful mastery of biopsychological challenges with the help of other people and of social organizations.

ERIK ERIKSON'S PSYCHOSOCIAL MODEL OF HUMAN DEVELOPMENT

Erikson's psychosocial model of human development is known and used by many experienced social workers. In this section, I will review the model's basic assumptions, its root metaphors, its organization as a theoretical structure, its weaknesses, and its application.

ERIK ERIKSON: EXEMPLARY ROLE MODEL

Erikson has been introduced earlier. I recommend to the reader Erikson's reflections on his own psychosocial development (Erikson & Newton, 1973). He makes thoughtful connections, for example, between the historical time in which he grew up (Germany on the verge of Nazi control, the United States led by a progressive president, for example) and both his theoretical and psychological choices.

ASSUMPTIONS OF THE PSYCHOSOCIAL MODEL

Erik Erikson shared many of Freud's assumptions about human development (Goldhaber, 2000). Erikson accepted that the id, ego, and superego were the main components of the personality. Like Freud, he assumed that childhood stages were differentiated by the developing person's changing relationship to his or her body. Freud related growth to changes in the sensitivities of bodily parts and examined the oral stage, the anal stage, the phallic stage, and the genital stage. Erikson accepted this assumption. Erikson and Freud assumed also that developmental progress requires the resolution of stage-specific conflicts and that early developmental experiences have a substantial impact on later development.

Erikson, however, supplemented Freud's attention to psychosexual development with his theory of psychosocial development: the learning of psychological and social competencies associated with specific and socially structured stages (Goldhaber, 2000). Additionally, Erikson assumed cultural relativity. Human development occurs in a specific social and political context, and therefore the form and content of the life cycle varies across generations. In identifying the major determinants of development, Erikson added history to the Freudian variables of anatomy and personality (Erikson & Newton, 1973). Erikson saw possibilities for developing ego strengths where Freud saw pressures toward psychopathology. Finally, Erikson, unlike Freud, assumed that human development and work on identity are lifelong processes.

More than Freud, Erikson emphasized reciprocal relations not one-directional influences in his model of human development (Crain, 1980; Salkind, 1985). Development involves the interplay, for example, of biological maturation and changing social expectations Sexual urges increase in intensity during puberty, and specific others attempt to channel the developing person's expression of these desires. There is a two-way exchange between the developing person and the agents of socialization. A child's parents profoundly influence his or her development, but the developing child also influences the development of the parental adults. Finally, the realization of developmental possibilities for self-control or for identity consolidation, for example, depends on a supportive society, and the developing person may rebel and attempt to remake the social conditions affecting development. Erikson (1968b) noted, for example, how women's collective struggle for political and legal equality in the 1960s and the new social definitions of what a woman can and cannot be increased the likelihood that individual women could develop optimal identities.

ROOT METAPHORS OF THE PSYCHOSOCIAL MODEL

Borrowing from biological theories about embryos, Erikson (1963) used the term **epigenesis** to refer to the emergence of psychological parts or strengths according to an original and biologically based ground plan that naturally unfolds within nurturing environments (Freud, 1992). Erikson's model also uses the imagery of timing associated with embryology and the study of biological maturation (Goldhaber, 2000). He theorized that each ego strength has a time of emergence or ascendancy (the psychosocial stage). If the event (demand for identity consolidation, for example) occurs at the right time (adolescence) and with a supportive environment, successful psychosocial development is likely.

Erikson theorized that the emergence of all the parts or ego strengths results in the formation of a functioning and whole personality (Roazen, 1976). Supplement the mountain-climbing metaphor with images from the biology of tadpole/frog, insect, or plant development (McCall, 1988). All biological organisms develop into forms congruent with their genetic nature, but the development, health, vitality, and beauty of an organism can be modified by environmental factors.

Psychosocial stages are sequenced in a predictable fashion across the life span. The progression across stages engages the person in ever-widening social circles with others (family, school, work, religion, community). Person and society are interdependent. Stage-specific experiences provide individuals the opportunities to develop virtues and values necessary to communal life. Erikson's epigenetic outlook imagined, then, that all human life is characterized by patterned development through a normal sequence of stages at an identifiable rate structured by historical conditions: progression up the society's mountainside.

ERIK ERIKSON'S MODEL OF HUMAN DEVELOPMENT

Erikson identified eight **psychosocial crises** or crucial periods (Erikson, 1959/ 1980; Goldhaber, 2000; Hogan, 1976; Roazen, 1976). Each stage presents a specific life task. Each poses a particular dilemma or challenge for the community member. Each arouses psychic energies for meeting the challenge. Each can be a turning point when the person chooses to progress higher or to stop moving. At each stage, the person has both special opportunities to add an ego capacity and special vulnerabilities. The person can turn upward to greater realization of ego powers and accomplish the stage-specific task. Erikson referred to the result of such stage mastery as **basic strengths** or virtues. Or the person can avoid or fail to accomplish the stage-specific task and turn downward toward the false securities of childhood. Such failure leads to **basic ego weaknesses**, personality vulnerabilities caused by the stage's dangers.

The themes associated with the various psychosocial crises (trust, autonomy, initiative, and so on) emerge in various forms across the life span. Successful development requires the initial grappling with the themes but also coping anew and effectively every time the theme reemerges (Goldhaber, 2000). Erikson (1963) added to Freud's nuclear family–oriented model that there are various others in our radius of significant relations charged with helping us meet the challenges of each stage. The radius broadens across the life span, from the immediate family in childhood to friends, sex partners, colleagues, and rivals in adolescence, to the human community in old age (Goldhaber, 2000). Particular **societal institutions** such as the family, the law, the economy, and religion also provide frameworks for the guidance of development at each stage (Erikson, 1963).

The following is a very brief summary of the major challenge of each life stage.

Trust Versus Mistrust First is the oral-sensory stage. This stage presents the opportunity to develop a basic stance toward the world on a continuum of trust versus mistrust. Maternal persons, primarily, and other caretakers provide the feeding and caring that helps the newborn infant develop a basic sense of trust in others and build the ego strength of hope. Support and consistency are critical. Parental deficiencies or other causes of an infant's failure to meet the stage-specific challenge result in a basic sense of mistrust, an estrangement from others, a sense of doom, and a lack of faith. Such psychosocial vulnerabilities may trouble the person for the rest of his or her life. Organized religion is one of the important social institutions that can inspire caretakers as they help infants develop hope and faith.

Autonomy Versus Shame Second is the muscular-anal stage organized around the issue of autonomy versus shame and doubt. The challenge to find a balance between holding on and letting go occurs in early childhood. Both parents and other caretaking persons ideally aid young children to begin to develop their capacities for self-regulation and control of their behavior. Caretakers also start to help children emancipate themselves from total dependence on adults. When successful, the child acquires the ego strength of loving goodwill and the possibility for freedom of choice. Stage accomplishments result in self-certainty and minimize self-consciousness. If unsuccessful (parents are overprotective or do not allow limit testing), the developing person feels shame about difficulties with self-control and begins to doubt his or her own abilities to cope with the environment. Basic vulnerabilities of compulsion or impulsivity may form. In the community, the social institution of "law and order" guards the achievements of autonomy made at this stage.

INITIATIVE VERSUS GUILT Third is the locomotor-genital stage focused on initiative versus guilt. Society communicates through its agents that the developing person is expected to engage in increasingly more independent movement. The child moves more widely among the radius of significant relations. Playmates become important. Preschool is a common setting for development. Members of the family, especially siblings, present young children with the opportunity to experiment with self-chosen actions and, optimally, to develop a sense of initiative and the virtue of purposefulness. However, the development of conscience at this stage and an increase in fantasies of rebellion against one's parents may result in guilt and problems related to excessive guilt, including extreme conformity, excessive obedience, and the ego weakness of inhibition. The institution of economics is used and absorbed by the child who identifies with his parents' material aspirations.

INDUSTRY VERSUS INFERIORITY Fourth is the latency stage of industry versus inferiority. Associates in the neighborhood and at school start to engage latency-age children in work and craft activities. Teachers and peers become role models. Serious work is added to play routines, and children learn that recognition follows the production of things. Children learn how to participate in an apprenticeship and develop abilities for task identification. Their accomplishments should result in a sense of pride, competence, and efficiency. A sense of industry and the basic ego strength of competence ideally emerge. Psychosocial processes may go awry if children are provided few opportunities to work on projects and solve problems, or the worth of their efforts is repeatedly disparaged. The child may develop an inclination toward inferiority, work paralysis, and a sense of futility. The ego weakness of inertia is another undesirable outcome. Social institutions associated with a culture's technology are critical at this stage.

IDENTITY VERSUS IDENTITY DIFFUSION Fifth, identity versus identity diffusion is the major psychosocial dilemma of the puberty and adolescence stage. This stage offers a moratorium on identity development, a time for the person to try to synthesize earlier identifications. The developing person tries out various answers to the question "Who am I?" Peers, members of in-groups and out-groups, leaders, and other role models suggest ways to realize life aspirations. Successful teenagers learn how to try on different identities, integrate some childhood identities (and reject others), and acquire the capacity for fidelity to an identity (the stage's basic strength) and for loyalty to groups of others that affirm the cherished identity. The ego's failure to meet this stage's challenges results in confusion about one's ethnic, sexual, or work identity. The basic vulnerability of this stage is repudiation; the developing person demonstrates indifference to requests for commitment and allegiance or is defiant and embraces a negative identity. Social institutions that provide an ideology, the "unconscious set of values and assumptions underlying the religious, scientific, and political thought of a culture" (Hogan, 1976, p. 172), are critical at this stage. During Erikson's own lifetime, for example, the Peace Corps created by

President Kennedy was instrumental in directing the psychosocial development of many adolescents.

INTIMACY VERSUS ISOLATION   Sixth, the developing person deals with issues of intimacy and solidarity versus isolation in the stage of young adulthood. Friends, sex partners, and members of cooperative and competitive groups often challenge the person to learn how to affiliate with others without damaging the psyche. Teenagers begin to develop the capacity for love. Erotic relationships offer opportunities to learn mutuality, to learn to take chances with others, and to realize reciprocal sexual fulfillment. The basic strength of love grows. Ego failures at this stage contribute to urges for distance from others, to the avoidance of sexual intimacy, and to prejudice against those who seem foreign. Despair, low self-esteem, a sense of alienation are the correlates of the sense of isolation common to those who fail to meet this stage's challenges. The field of ethics is the social institution supportive of development at this life stage.

STAGNATION VERSUS GENERATIVITY   Seventh, the developing person faces the danger of stagnation but can realize the joys of generativity during the stage of adulthood. The person who can realize capacities for generativity (creative contributions to the next generation in the form of children, art, ideas, and products) and resist tendencies toward self-absorption will incorporate the ego strength of care. Such adults also develop a sense of responsibility to others. Ego interests expand, and the person devotes himself or herself to people and causes. All social institutions should reinforce the values necessary to the development of generativity and the success of generations. However, those with whom we learn, create art, and participate in scientific projects are especially important. Members of our shared households and extended family can contribute directly to successful resolution of this stage challenge. Developing adults who fail to become generative develop instead a sense of stagnation; the ego weakness at this stage is a preoccupation with one's own needs at the expense of the needs of others.

INTEGRITY VERSUS DESPAIR   Eighth, the essential ego strength for the person engaging the issues of the final stage of maturity is wisdom. In the tension between the attractions of ego integrity and despair or disgust with life, the healthy adult opts for integrity and conceives of his or her bonds to all humanity. Erikson (1968a) characterized ego integrity as the acceptance of one's life cycle and personal history, a sense of camaraderie with past and future generations, and the ability to defend oneself against physical or economic threats. For the successfully developing person, reviews of one's life evoke a sense of satisfaction and meaningfulness. The person who despairs often rejects the culture's notions of human finiteness and death and may indulge in sentiments of contempt and disdain (the ego weakness) toward other people and toward social organizations. The person seeks compensations for time lost. Wisdom comes to those elders who make use of the cultural knowledge and the capacities for judgment and understanding accumulated over a lifetime. Cultural institutions associated with economics, politics, philosophy, and religion provide resources to achieve integrity. Supportive societies offer meaningful roles to older persons, social opportunities to share their wisdom and serve as living examples of how to achieve developmental closure.

CRITICAL COMMENTS

Erikson's psychosocial model of human development is allotted a significant place in this chapter's presentation of applied psychodynamic theory. Critical perspectives on his model and rebuttals to these criticisms will be provided later in the final appraisal of the psychodynamic theory.

APPLICATIONS OF ERIKSON'S PSYCHOSOCIAL MODEL

Erikson's psychosocial model of human development is also a highly regarded social work practice model (Greene, 1991). Social workers use the model to assess a client's success in meeting developmental tasks, to develop a comprehensive developmental history, and to identify and understand current coping difficulties and ego strengths as these relate to unresolved psychosocial crises. Social workers use insight and ego support to facilitate clients' developmental processes, and social workers advocate for improvements in societal conditions and in social institutions for the sake of optimal human development.

Social workers have also developed specific tools for applying Erikson's model. Sherman (1987), for example, reported on the use of reminiscence groups. Here, elderly persons participate in a life review process and share with other group members memories associated with various stages of development. Photographs and other historical records are also shared. Sherman's research on the effectiveness for 104 members enrolled in these type of groups indicated improvements in life satisfaction, self-concept, and social relationships. As Erikson might have predicted, life review enhances generativity. Sophie Freud Loewenstein (1978) reported on her adaptation of Erikson's model. She teaches social work students how to provide life-transition group counseling. Students learn Erikson's approach to human behavior and the social environment, Bowlby's attachment theoretical approach to life transitions, the benefits of counseling people during stage transition–related crises, and particular counseling techniques that enhance group members' ego strengths.

JOHN BOWLBY'S ATTACHMENT THEORY AND ITS IMPLICATIONS FOR HUMAN DEVELOPMENT

John Bowlby has also developed a very important and useful theory. His attachment theory, a dialect or branch of the object relations language, "provides an explanation of the role of attachment across the life span and the transmission of attachment patterns across generations" (Stalker, 2001, p. 109). In this section, I will introduce you to Bowlby and his associates and report on the assumptions, metaphors, and concepts that constitute his attachment approach to applied psychodynamics. I will also summarize the critical reactions and areas for application.

JOHN BOWLBY: EXEMPLARY ROLE MODEL

In 1929, John Bowlby started his medical studies in London at the age of 22 (Holmes, 1993). He soon after entered the Institute of Psycho-Analysis and began a personal analysis. Bowlby earned his medical qualifications in 1933, trained for three more years in adult psychiatry, and then took a position at the London Child Guidance Clinic. At the clinic, Bowlby worked with two psychoanalytically trained social workers who introduced him to the idea of the transgenerational transmission of neurosis (Bowlby, 1988). He also aligned himself with an analytic society of British psychiatrists. His major paper for this society described some of his clinic cases and advocated for an assessment of the mothers of disturbed children that elucidated how the mothers' childhood difficulties interfered with their performance in the parenting role.

During World War II, John Bowlby served as an army psychiatrist. After the war, he accepted the task of organizing a Department of Children at the Tavistock Clinic. He began clinical services, counseled mothers and children together, supervised other workers, and chaired case conferences. John Bowlby was an innovator. He began to form cooperative linkages between local health workers, general practitioners, and social workers. Bowlby also organized a research team to study the effects of separation on children's personality development. James Robertson, a psychiatric social worker, was Bowlby's first research assistant (Bowlby, 1988). Robertson and Christoph Heinecke, another social worker, impressed Bowlby with their shared conviction that positive early family experiences were critical to healthy human development. Mary Ainsworth, a faculty member at the University of Toronto, also joined Bowlby's research team (Bretherton, 1992). She would become an innovative researcher and a cofounder of attachment theory. Many of Ainsworth's students published important studies on attachment-related topics.

In 1950, John Bowlby worked with the World Health Organization on a project investigating the ill effects on human development of prolonged institutional care and frequent changes of caretakers in early life. After conducting an extensive literature review on institutionalized children, he concluded that healthy development required that "the infant and young child should experience a warm, intimate and continuous relationship with his mother (or permanent mother substitute) in which both find satisfaction and enjoyment" (Bretherton, 1997, p. 34). He began searching for a theory to explain this proposition. Psychoanalytic theory could be enriched, Bowlby decided, by the infusion of ideas from ethology, a branch of evolutionary biology. Ethology is the study of animal behavior holistically and in natural conditions (Holmes, 1993). Bowlby was especially interested in the work of Konrad Lorenz on the following behavior of ducklings and goslings, and extended this ethological work to his theorizing about child development.

John Bowlby built his theory on his personal observations and clinical case studies but also on the work of theorists using other perspectives, including ethology, cybernetic systems theory, cognitive science, and developmental psychology (Bretherton, 1997). For the last 10 years of his life, Bowlby focused all his intellectual powers on the application of attachment theory by therapists (Bretherton, 1992).

ASSUMPTIONS OF ATTACHMENT THEORY

Bowlby (1988) identified his three major theoretical assumptions. First, intimate emotional bonds have a biologically based, primary status in human development. This assumption has two corollaries. The formation and the maintenance of human bonds are controlled by a feedback system within the human nervous system; for example, infants automatically respond to temporary separation from their mothers with emotions and behaviors designed to reestablish the homeostatic state of attachment. Additionally, the cybernetic system will operate efficiently only if the person builds mental working models of the self, of relationship partners, and of the interaction patterns that have developed with relationship partners.

Second, Bowlby (1988) assumed, as do most psychodynamic theorists, that early parent–child experiences have a powerful influence on later development. A child's mental health and personality development are deeply influenced by whether his or her relationships "are warm and harmonious; or tense, angry, and anxious; or else emotionally remote; or possibly non-existent" (p. 160). Bowlby asserted, for example, that "the pathway followed by each developing individual and the extent to which he or she becomes resilient to stressful life events is determined to a very significant degree by the pattern of attachment he or she develops during the early years" (p. 172).

Third, Bowlby (1988) rejected Erikson's assumption of universal and predictable stages and of possible stage fixation or regression to earlier stages of development. He postulated instead that humans can follow numerous different developmental pathways. Some pathways are compatible with healthy development; others are deviant and associated with developmental disorders and difficulties. Environmental factors, especially the quality of interaction with parents or parent substitutes, set developing persons down different pathways. However, Bowlby assumed that a course is not fixed—that if a developing person is treated in new ways, he or she may shift to more or less favorable pathways.

ROOT METAPHORS OF ATTACHMENT THEORY

Bowlby's imagery and comparisons came from his immersion in ethology. Human infants are like ducklings, goslings, and baby monkeys. Like ducklings following a mother duck, human beings of all ages, but especially children, have a biological need "to remain within easy access of a familiar individual known to be ready and willing to come to our aid in an emergency"

(Bowlby, 1988, p. 27). Picture ducklings racing to catch up with their mother as she moves toward the creek. Human infants have similar innate needs. Ethologists learned also that geese require close contact after birth. A goose isolated for a period of time from her mother and other geese will become very fearful, wary about approaching any adult geese, and unable to bond later with other geese. Infants forcefully separated from attachment figures develop comparable disorders. Bowlby (1988) also paid attention to the experimental research with infant monkeys. Monkeys that were deprived of any warmth and physical contact with the mother monkey during feeding invariably developed numerous relationship problems (Bowlby, 1998). Again, Bowlby saw parallels to human development.

The mother duck, goose, or monkey, Bowlby observed, is like a secure base or safe haven. When confident of the availability of this base, the infant animal explores confidently and actualizes its potentials. Bowlby (1988) transformed this image into a central construct in his attachment theory.

Bowlby (Holmes, 1993) made use of other metaphors in his theorizing and theory application. He argued, for instance, that a mother's love was as important to mental health as vitamins and proteins are to physical health. Bowlby also compared psychologically deprived children to physically infected persons and believed that the threat of social infection was as grave as the dangers of infection from carriers of typhoid.

Bowlby's Attachment Theory and Human Development

Bowlby, his colleagues, and their students have constructed attachment theory from a relatively small set of initial concepts. **Attachment** is an affectional bond, "a relatively long-enduring tie in which the partner is important as a unique individual, interchangeable with none other" (Ainsworth, 1991, p. 38). Attachment is characterized by "a need to maintain proximity, distress upon inexplicable separation, pleasure or joy upon reunion, and grief at loss" (p. 38). The need is strongest under certain specified conditions (Bowlby, 1988). These situations include prolonged separation from attachment figures, threat of abandonment by attachment figures, threat by attachment figures not to love the developing person, threat by attachment figures of intention to commit suicide, and parent's or sibling's illness or death, especially if the developing person feels responsible for these tragic outcomes. Threats to attachment evoke strong emotions, including jealousy, anger, anxiety, or panic (Bowlby, 1988).

The developing person attaches to a caretaker, according to Bowlby, in four distinctive **attachment phases** (Hazan, Gur-Yaish, & Campa, 2004). In the preattachment phase, from birth to about 2 months, the infant is interested in interaction and receptive to care without discrimination. In the attachment-in-the-making phase (2–6 months), the infant begins to preferentially signal and respond to certain individuals. In the clear-cut attachment phase (beginning at 6–7 months), the infant is capable of organized attachment behavior and begins to follow, seek comfort from, and react to separation from the attachment figure. By the goal-corrected partnership phase (about 36 months), the infant less urgently needs physical closeness to the attachment figure and can negotiate issues of separation and availability with caretakers.

Attachment theorists posit that security versus insecurity is the central human dilemma. A **secure base** is the physical and psychological experience provided by responsive caretakers that frees the infant to explore the physical and social environment. It is a base "to which he can return knowing for sure that he will be welcomed when he gets there, nourished physically and emotionally, comforted if distressed, reassured if frightened (Bowlby, 1988, p. 11). Secure bases are important to people across the life span. Attachment figures characterized as stable, predictable, constant, reliable, nurturing, responsive, intelligible, loving, and caring create secure bases (Marris, 1991). **Attachment behavior** is "any form of behavior that results in a person attaining or maintaining proximity to some other clearly identified individual who is conceived as better able to cope with the world" (Bowlby, 1988, p. 27). It is behavior with the aim of moving from an insecure location back to the secure base.

Mary Ainsworth, Bowlby's colleague, developed the **strange situation protocol,** a research procedure structured like a short drama to study infant behavior when a mother absents herself and then returns (Stalker, 2001). Examining videotapes of 12-month-old infants, Ainsworth and her team identified four **patterns of attachment** (Ainsworth, Blehar, Waters, & Wall, 1978). Bowlby (1988) and other attachment theorists (Holmes, 1993) have summarized the typology of child's attachment styles. Sable (1997), a social work expert on the use of attachment theory, has extended the typology to adult clients. Note that the terms *insecure* and *anxious* are used interchangeably by some attachment theorists.

The child with a **secure attachment** explores an unfamiliar playroom, returning to the mother frequently for reassurance. The mother's departure evokes protests and tears, but the returning mother can easily comfort the infant. The developing person is "confident that his parent (or parent figure) will be available, responsive, and helpful should he encounter adverse or frightening situations" (Bowlby, 1988, p. 123). This kind of child is often happy, demands little, and responds well to caretakers. Adults who grew up in responsive families have confidence in others and believe that comfort and help will be available during times of illness, injury, or distress (Sable, 1997). This type of adult trusts others, reaches out for care and assistance easily, forms satisfying relationships, and bounces back from emotional distress.

In the pattern of **insecure avoidant attachment,** the developing person expects to be rebuffed, not comforted or helped, when seeking support during an emergency. The child explores a room without consideration of the mother's presence and seems unaffected by the mother's departure or return, showing few signs of distress or joy. This kind of child keeps his or her distance from others, indulges a bad temper, and tends to bully other children. The child may give more attention to toys or other objects than to attachment figures (Bowlby, 1988; Holmes, 1993). Such children develop a tendency to live self-sufficiently and make do without others' love and support. Adults with this style lack all confidence in attachment figures (Sable, 1997). They tend to deny the need for support and defensively proclaim their self-sufficiency. They anticipate ridicule or rejection when seeking comfort. They are likely to inhibit their feelings and avoid information that might activate attachment behavior. Clinical manifestations include disordered mourning, alcoholism personality disorders, and psychosomatic symptoms.

In the pattern of **insecure ambivalent attachment,** also called insecure resistant attachment, the developing person is not certain that the parent, caretaker, or other attachment figure will be available and responsive when needed. Infants with this form of attachment are very distressed when separated from an attachment figure and not easily comforted after a reunion. They tend to whine, experience separation anxiety often, alternate between anger and clinging, and explore the environment reluctantly (Bowlby, 1988; Holmes, 1993). Adults who participated as children in disturbed families and fit into this category are uncertain that affectional figures are dependable (Sable, 1997). These adults tend to stay close to or vigilantly monitor protective people and places. They lack a secure base and are prone to separation anxiety at the prospect of a loss of support. They often appear overly dependent, demanding, and reluctant to try new activities and relationships. Clinical manifestations include agoraphobia, suicidal ideation and gestures, depression, and eating disorders.

The child with an **insecure disorganized attachment** displays a diverse set of conflicted and inconsistent behaviors in relation to changes in attachment possibilities, such as rising to meet the parent and then falling prone or approaching the caregiver with the head turned away (Bowlby, 1988). For the adult with this style, according to Sable (1997), feelings and memories related to affection and attachment are kept from awareness. These persons have difficulty talking about their attachment histories. They may become anxious or angry when pushed into relationships. Sable adds that this pattern is associated with borderline, histrionic, and narcissistic clinical conditions. Much additional research, Bowlby claims, supports the usefulness of this typology.

Internal working models are the developing person's inner representations of self and others. These are maps or models of the environment and of our relation to the environment (Holmes, 1993). The model has both cognitive and emotional components and is constructed from life experiences, especially the need to manage painful feelings. The insecure avoidant type of person, for example, develops a model of others as dangerous and approachable only with caution and of self as unworthy to be offered security. The task of therapy or counseling is to help persons with distorted and rigid internal models to develop more realistic and flexible models.

Much theory specification and empirical research have refined attachment theory. Let's direct our attention to theoretical propositions relevant to human development. Bretherton (1992) summarizes research-based propositions relating attachment patterns to various life stages. In infancy, there is a risk of insecure attachment if the child is placed in day care during the first year and the time spent in day care is extensive. For preschoolers, secure attachment is associated with emotionally open responsive behavior. In adulthood, a person's attachment style (secure, avoidant, or ambivalent) in romantic partnerships is related to experiences with the parent in the family of origin. For those in later life, the quality of protection by and care from their middle-aged children is related to earlier attachment patterns. There is also a relationship between close affectional attachments to pets and emotional and social well-being across all stages of the life cycle (Sable, 1995). Pets are likely to provide comfort and reduced feelings of loneliness during times of stress, for example.

Patterns of attachment are most likely to change during life-stage and family-life-cycle shifts. For example, the child's entry into school, the addition of a sibling to the family group, the preteen's experience of puberty, the adolescent's initiation of a sexual partnership, the beginning of a pregnancy, and the death of a family member often trigger adjustments to internal working models and attachment styles (Ainsworth, 1991). Attachment problems are often transmitted across generations. For example, Bowlby (1988) proposes that "a mother who, due to adverse experiences during childhood, grows up to be anxiously attached is prone to seek care from her child and thereby lead the child to become anxious, guilty, and perhaps phobic" (p. 37). Adverse experiences for the parent's generation, including neglect, frequent threats of being abandoned, and frequent threats of being beaten, are likely to damage members of the children's generation. Bowlby and his colleagues have transformed this proposition into testable form and have collected validating evidence.

Finally, Marris (1991) extends attachment theory to the macro arenas of public problems and social policy. He argues that there is a significant relationship between political and economic inequality and attachment difficulties. Specifically, Marris proposes that the poor are more likely than others to experience emotionally insecure childhoods, to experience sudden and traumatic losses in their dangerous and economically unstable neighborhoods, to experience continually changing life conditions, and to have weak and unreliable networks of supports, and are less likely to have the resources to change their circumstances and deal with predicaments. These manifestations of the inequitable distribution of uncertainty and unpredictability result in a higher incidence of attachment-related disorders among the poor.

CRITICAL COMMENTS

Attachment theory is highly regarded, many of its theoretical propositions are supported by a considerable amount of empirical evidence, and an extensive literature exists on the use of attachment theory for social work practice (Stalker, 2001). Attachment theory is not suited for all client issues, but it is emerging as the theory of choice for helping children separated from their parents or abused by caretakers and for helping persons of any age deal with loss and bereavement. Stalker calls, however, for the development of more specific guidelines and therapeutic techniques for the use of attachment theory.

Fonagy (1999) is impressed by the commonalities between Erikson's psychosocial model of development and Bowlby's attachment theory. Both theorists viewed development as a continuous process starting at birth. Both assumed a life span perspective. Both argued that individual and interactional factors are important but that cultural factors make possible the realization of developmental possibilities. Both Erikson and Bowlby believed that early life experiences accumulate and create patterns of trustfulness or attachment that influence later development. Both emphasized the quality of relationships with early caretakers as central to healthy development. Both Erikson and Bowlby added a sociological slant and asserted that the immediate social context and the larger environment condition the caregiving process.

Bowlby and Erikson differed in important ways, however (Fonagy, 1999). Bowlby placed greater importance than Erikson on the biological base of development and did not view problems with sexuality as central to psychopathology. Bowlby's focal unit was the relationship between the developing person and attachment figures, whereas the Eriksonian lens focused on individual development within a relationship or environmental context.

APPLICATIONS OF ATTACHMENT THEORY

Attachment theory has many areas for application, including nursing homes, foster care agencies, adoption programs, services to socially isolated persons, child abuse inquiries, residential corrections and prison work, family and parent–child education and therapy programs, divorce courts, military bases, and counseling centers dealing with loss caused by death, injury, or separation. Attachment theory may be used at the individual, family, group, or community level.

Bowlby (1988) directed practitioners who use attachment theory to follow these guidelines. Enact the role of providing conditions for the client's exploration of attachment figures and inner representational models and the restructuring of problematic attachments. Provide a secure base for the client's psychosocial explorations. Help the client examine how he or she brings attachment expectations and perceptions to the helping relationship. Help the client identify the unconscious biases he or she brings to contemporary intimate relationships. Help the client connect current difficulties to attachment disappointments experienced during childhood or adolescence. Free the client from old and stereotypical models of relationships to significant people, and free the client to imagine and pursue more suitable models and relationships.

Social workers might use the "adult attachment interview" as an assessment tool to identify an adult client's stance toward earlier attachment experiences (Holmes, 1993). Social workers might also assess attachment behavior provoked by the loss of cherished persons, places, pets, objects, or beliefs. Social workers can provide supportive interventions that help young mothers form high-quality attachments to their infants, creating the foundational conditions for optimal development (Freud, 1992). Many client problems, including depression and anxiety, are caused by the frustration of the need to be close to other people, especially attachment figures (Stalker, 2001). Attachment theory can help with such problems. Social workers can also use attachment theory to guide individual therapy with clients with many different mental health problems and family therapy with families dealing with relationship issues (McMillen, 1992).

MAPPING APPLIED PSYCHODYNAMIC THEORY

Figure 8.1 translates psychoanalytic ego psychology into eco-map terms. In this section, I will elaborate on these translations. The eco-map and its ecosystems concepts serve as a universal translator. Social workers might translate psychodynamic concepts, propositions, and conceptual models by answering my ecosystems translation questions.

FIGURE 8.1
ERICKSON'S EGO
PSYCHOLOGICAL
VERSION OF
THE ECO-MAP

Source: Adapted with permission from *Family-Centered Social Work Practice* (p. 160) by A. Hartman & J. Laird, 1983. New York: The Free Press.

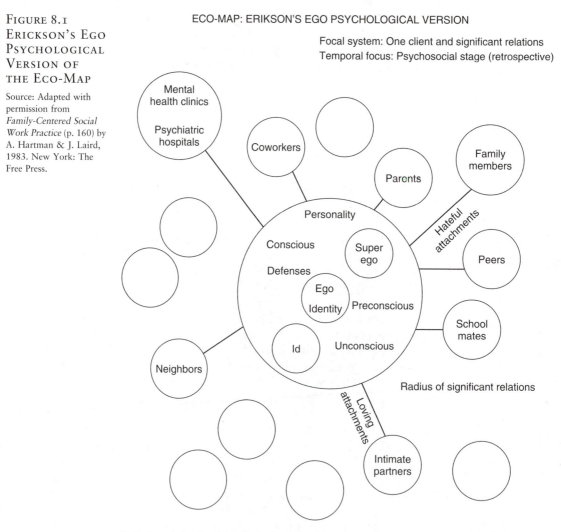

ECO-MAP: ERICKSON'S EGO PSYCHOLOGICAL VERSION

Focal system: One client and significant relations
Temporal focus: Psychosocial stage (retrospective)

Indicate nature of emotional attachments with a descriptive word or by drawing different kinds of lines: ———— for ego supportive relationships ·········· for ambivalent relationships +++++++ for ego destructive relationships
Draw arrows along lines to signify flow of ego supports, gratifications.
Identify significant caretakers and others and fill in empty circles as needed.

How Are Connections Conceptualized?

Psychodynamic theorists assert that connections are emotional, invisible, and psychic. Meaningful social bonds or connections are conceptualized as emotional attachments to other persons. Emotional attachments are commonly forged with those in our early lives who gratify our drives for contact comfort, for self-assertion (aggression), and for sensual pleasure. At later stages, we develop attachments to those who assist us in meeting stage-specific challenges. These connections are characterized by intense emotional bonds (cathexes) and by their contribution to personal health or trauma. They are very influential on our psychic functioning. Childhood connections are often internalized and influence us as adults. For example, our connections with family members are often used as models for later identifications.

The **internalization** of representations of attachment figures is the major mean of psychosocial development. We identify with persons who most "affect" us. We then incorporate their attributes, their bodily characteristics, their values, and their approach to role performances. We internalize these social relationship experiences. Internalized attachments are both to those we love and to those we hate. The internalizations of our attachments are established often without our conscious awareness or rational deliberation. Our emotional attachments can become the psychic foundation for personal growth and self-fulfillment or for aggression and despair.

How Is the Quality of Connections Differentiated?

Connections can be loving, hateful, or indifferent, secure or insecure, based in reality or based in fantasy. The quality of an attachment depends on the emotional valence.

Loving and good attachments are those that help us gratify our needs for comforting contact, for sensual pleasure, for security, and for self-assertion. Mutuality is a feature of these relationships. Mutual and loving attachments are characterized by interdependency and efforts by each to help the other develop ego strengths. Good connections are based on a realistic appraisal of self and of social reality. Good connections contribute to a basic sense of security. Those with whom we have loving attachments support our ego as we try to cope with psychic and social challenges.

Hateful and negative attachments are those with punitive, harsh, and uncaring others who frustrate our efforts for gratification and security. Our bonds are insecure; therefore, we fear abandonment or rejection by others. The other in hateful attachments is seen as a threat to the ego. Hateful attachments in adulthood may reflect infantile fantasies about bad mothers or bad parents. Bad attachments may increase our propensity for **transference**, the perception of a contemporary relationship partner in terms of the emotions, desires, and beliefs developed in a childhood relationship. Hateful attachments undermine our efforts to accomplish stage-specific developmental tasks.

Indifferent connections would be to those others with whom we interact regularly but with little emotional attachment. Most impersonal relationships in modern societies are of this sort, and many have minimal impact on the person's psyche or psychosocial development. However, the child in an eco-system characterized entirely by indifferent connections will have great difficulty developing the ego strengths or virtues identified by Erikson. Psychodynamic theorists also focus on ambivalent connections. These attachments include elements of both love and hate.

What Is the Typical Focal System?

The typical client for the psychodynamic social worker is an individual. The worker may also focus on a couple or a family, with special attention to the influence of these micro systems on individual psychodynamics.

Therapeutic attention is given to the three parts of the client's personality: id, ego, superego (Turner, 2002). The notion of **id** refers to our organic or biologically rooted drives: our passions, appetites, core motivations, and other impulses associated with our unsocialized and animal nature. Sexual drives include the need for affection, love, and physical contact. Aggressive drives are also central to the id. The concept of **superego** refers to internalized moral principles: the prescriptions and prohibitions acquired as a family member and as a member of the larger sociocultural community. The superego is the part of the personality that censors antisocial thoughts and desires and that blocks inappropriate impulses. The superego includes the conscience, the internalization of group expectations, and the ego ideal, the internalization of group goals (Turner, 2002). The **ego** is the organizing and synthesizing aspect of the psyche with responsibility for mediating between impulses and demands, testing reality, and determining what works. **Ego functions** are adaptive mental processes such as perception, memory, anticipation, judgment, and deliberation. Ego processes generate perceptions of relevant and acceptable ways to con-summate id impulses. The healthy ego regulates the timing, method, and form of impulse expression to promote productive, responsible, and satisfying social relations.

The social worker focuses on varying levels of individual consciousness. Degrees of consciousness include unconscious, preconscious, and conscious. The **unconscious** refers to behavior that occurs without self-communication and is not subject to social control. Psychodynamic theorists believe that much of what we do has causes and meanings that are hidden or unconscious. The **preconscious** includes impulses and inclinations that influence our actions and remain outside our awareness until we question them. Then, preconscious elements can be reflected on consciously. **Consciousness** refers to those sensa-tions, feelings, ideas, and impulses that are readily available for consideration or study.

The psychodynamic social worker focuses on an individual's **ego defenses.** Anxiety is the emotional signal that the person may not be able to manage the conflict between urges and inclinations and social conventions, or may not be able to meet the demands of others in the community. Anxiety and other negative emotions, especially those associated with perceived threats to the self (Turner, 2002), trigger defensive processes. Ego defenses, Swanson (1985) adds, are strategies for developing "an account of one's conduct that will enable one to live equably with oneself and others despite being self-condemned and at least, implicitly, socially condemned for deviant tendencies" (p. 339). They are the methods used to manage internal and external conflicts such as those between personal desires and the standards of our partners in collective ventures. Sometimes they can help us solve intrapsychic and interpersonal problems in ways unlikely to damage social relations.

Psychodynamic theorists generally differentiate adaptive and maladaptive defense mechanisms. Swanson (1985, 1988) suggests that good (adaptive) defenses respond to the challenging relationship strain, build on the grounds of community feeling offered by the relevant social relationship or organization, and deal with the relationship disruptions caused by deviant impulses and acts. They help the person resolve the conflict, build solidarity, and remedy disruptions caused by deviant impulses and acts. Bad (maladaptive) defenses result in damaged relationships and unresolved conflicts.

Psychodynamic theorists identify various ego defenses. Repression, for instance, is the exclusion from awareness of unacceptable impulses that clash with the ego and social ideals. Projection involves charging others with faults to minimize awareness of one's own failings. Displacement is the expression of a deviant impulse toward a target that is not socially prohibited. You are angry with your boss, for example, but yell at your children instead. Table 8.1 provides definitions of these and other common defensive processes.

	Defense	Purpose
TABLE 8.1 SWANSON'S ANALYSIS OF SELECTED SELF-DEFENSES	Displacement	Indirect expression of deviant impulse toward a substitute target that is not socially prohibited
	Projection	Charging others with faults greater than one's own to inhibit their accusations or to trivialize one's own failings
	Rationalization	Demonstrate that one's behavior is justified by reasons so that the behavior does not call into question one's solidarity with others
	Reaction formation	Substitutes acceptable desire realized in "good behavior" for deviant impulse deemed destructive of social relationships
	Regression	Appeal for others to view expression of deviant desires as affirmation of person's basic dependency and demand for care from others
	Repression	Prevents unacceptable impulse from influencing behavior by excluding it from awareness and focusing on socially proper standards
	Undoing	Positive action designed to right a wrong the person has committed and buttress claim that prior actions are not representative

Source: Based on Swanson, 1985, 1988.

How Is the Environment Conceptualized?

Psychodynamic theorists refer to the environment as the outer world, social reality, or civilization, in contrast to the inner world or psychic reality. Psychodynamic theorists tend to offer two characterizations of the environment. First, the relation between person and environment is not harmonious. The environment or civilization constricts the person; it does not allow the fulfillment of many of our wishes and dreams. The parents are the first social agents to frustrate our bodily urges, but assorted other authority figures soon join in subduing us in the name of the collective morality. The willful and drive-ridden id is at odds with the agents of civilization committed to taming and domesticating it. Usually the civilization prevails, leaving the person with a residue of discontent. Humans experience a continuous tension between polarities, including liberty versus order, rebellion versus submission, and gratification versus renunciation. Ambivalence about the benefits of civilized social life is a common human sentiment.

Second, psychodynamic theorists assert that a person transforms the objective environment into a personal and subjective psychic reality. This personalized version of reality may correctly and accurately map the actual environment, or it may correspond poorly with how others experience the same environment. When I worked at a community mental health center, for example, certain clients who had been discharged from a state institution joined us. At times, these clients responded with urgency and conviction to sounds, images, and people in the clubhouse living room that could not be perceived by anyone else.

Is Particular Emphasis Given to Any Systems?

Psychodynamic theorists emphasize the individual, the family, and parent–child relations within the family system. Ego psychologists give less attention to the community, formal organizations, society, and the global community of societies. Erik Erikson was an exception. He did value the social sciences and was interested in the influence of social institutions and historical processes on life stage behavior. He recommended an ego psychology that considered mezzo-level and macro-level social systems as part of the person-in-environment configuration. Erikson was concerned especially with questions about how the needs, capacities, and experiences of members of different generations are coordinated in a society (Hogan, 1976). Child-rearing practices are a critical element, for example, of the contribution by one generation to the next. An eco-map developed by Erik Erikson would probably include information about the influence of these institutional configurations and the **historical moment** on the focal client system. It might also show how the previous generation structured opportunities faced by the client system and how the client system's strengths and weaknesses will in turn affect the next generation. John Bowlby would single out attachment figures for special attention.

How Are Resources and Their Flow Conceptualized?

Psychodynamic theory posits that the major resources necessary for the optimal relation of personality to the outer reality are psychosocial in nature. **Ego support** is one of the most valuable psychological resources available in the environment. Ego support during adolescence, for example, confirms the identity of young members and provides guidance in the development of a life plan. Woods and Hollis (2000) report on Hollis' typology of specific actions and how these can be treated as resources necessary for the support of others' ego. **Sustainment** includes demonstrating interest in the other and communicating confidence in the other's ability to mobilize ego strengths. It also includes reassurance when the other is anxious or guilty, especially because of the reemergence of troubling childhood memories. **Exploration** and **ventilation** are actions that invite the other to describe emotionally charged events and then to express difficult or repressed emotions. **Person situation reflections** are actions designed to help others develop insight into the causes of their behavior, their patterns of moral judgment on self and others, and their feelings about particular relationships. **Pattern dynamic reflections** invite others to learn about the psychodynamic sources of psychological and relationship patterns and about the repeated and predictable methods they use to distort reality. **Developmental reflections** challenge the other to examine the experiences during psychosocial development that have been internalized and that influence current thinking, feeling, and action. If Wood and Hollis used theoretical propositions, they might conclude that those clients in relationships characterized by the frequent and bidirectional sharing of these psychosocial resources are likely to develop strong egos and master intrapsychic and interpersonal challenges.

What Descriptive Words Are Used?

Classic psychoanalytic theorists have developed a collection of descriptors that focus on personal and interpersonal failures and pathologies. A theory-specific diagnostic terminology is used often, for example, to refer to disordered personalities. Words such as *borderline, hysteric, narcissism, neurosis, obsessive compulsive,* and *schizophrenia* are often attached to the client (the typical focal system). Distortions and disturbances in connections or social relationships are also characterized in a distinctive psychoanalytic vocabulary (*oedipal complex, penis envy, womb envy, projection, transference, countertransference,* and so on). Finally, problematic features of psychosocial development are characterized by terms such as *regression* or *fixation* (in eco-map terms, the person reverts in the present to the version of reality identified in an eco-map of an early life stage). Ego psychologists and object relations theorists are starting to conceptualize systems and connections in a language of strengths. However, the language of abnormality, pathology, deficit, and disorder still prevails in this perspective.

How Is Change Conceptualized?

Since disturbances in interpersonal relationships are the chief cause of unmanageable inner conflicts, the worker must help the client change the internalized effects of destructive past relationships. The worker should also work to help create a social environment characterized in the present by ego supportive relationships. The worker's creation of a therapeutic relationship with the client is often the starting point for the process of personal and social change.

Several specific goals for psychosocial change follow. The worker provides new experiences, or **corrective emotional experiences,** that help the client in a variety of ways. These therapeutic experiences can increase openness to and awareness of the influence of previous life stages and unconscious processes on psychosocial functioning. Awareness of repressed episodes in one's psychosocial development might be increased. Thus, the worker helps free the person from the determining influence of the unconscious so that the person's actions are chosen rather than compelled. Therapists also aim to help the person increase his or her awareness of earlier identifications and attachments, especially those with destructive powers. The therapist and client can then work to mitigate the negative influences. Psychosocial therapists try to strengthen the client's ego so that it can tolerate intrapsychic and interpersonal conflict and reconcile personal impulses and community demands. Finally, ego psychologically oriented social workers can use therapeutic approaches such as the life review to strengthen the conflict-free aspects of the personality so that the client can participate fruitfully in love and work relations.

How Are Actual and Ideal Eco-Maps Contrasted?

Ideal ecosystem conditions are conceptualized at the personal and social level. At the personal level, ego psychologists aim to bring about psychological harmony. Mental health requires the realization of repressed aspects of the self and results in the replacement of internal division with harmony and solidarity. The mentally disordered person is subject to intrapsychic conflicts that interfere with the ability to interpret others and social events in a consensually valid way. Reality is distorted, and the intentions of others are misunderstood. As a result of these incorrect appraisals, the mentally disordered person has a hard time cooperating with others and succeeding in social role performances. Psychological transformation requires the development of a degree of ego synthesis and strength. The healthy person can organize herself and her social relations in line with the reality principle, thus acknowledging and taking account of present physical and social realities.

Psychological health is also associated with the basic **ego strengths** or virtues acquired at each life stage: hope, will, purpose, competence, fidelity, love, care, and wisdom. The healthy person develops these capacities and makes conflict-free and habitual use of the ego strength appropriate to his or her life stage.

At the social level, Erikson (1959/1980) and other ego psychologists contrast actual and common social arrangements with social or generational harmony. The older generation commits itself, in the ideal ecosystem, to creating an environment supportive of the developmental needs of the next generation. Rites of passage are socially structured and legitimized so that all community members are supported during their transitions from one life stage to the next. Social groups, organizations, and institutions provide the supports that enable each member to develop a firm and efficacious ego identity—a sense of personal continuity despite changes in changing social conditions. Ego identity is the integration of earlier life identifications and self-representations. Each person's ego identity is built during conditions of generational harmony in a distinctive way yet in concordance with the expectations of important others.

Optimal social relationships, then, have personal and social consequences. They are those relationships in which the person can consummate id impulses, but in ways that also demonstrate the person's commitment to cultural standards and ideals and use of stage-specific ego strengths (Turner, 2002). Personal needs and communal needs are reconciled in the ideal ecosystem.

HOW ARE ISSUES OF DIVERSITY, COLOR, AND SHADING ADDRESSED?

Psychodynamic theorists have had some problems with diversity issues. Classical psychoanalysts might display spirituality, sexual orientation, gender, and social class membership in ways offensive to members of diverse and oppressed groups. Contemporary ego psychologists and object relations theorists are rejecting these traditional conceptions and replacing them with more affirmative ideas.

Freud, for example, viewed religious pursuits in many different but almost exclusively negative ways. He characterized religion as infantile, as a universal and obsessive ritual, as a social neurosis, as a disguised attempt to work out problems with the mother and father, as an illusion offering protection from our sense of infantile helplessness, as a mass delusion, and as a quest for the bliss of the baby fused with his or her mother (Freud Museum, 2005). St. Clair (1994), an object relations theorist, more objectively suggests that our representations of God are formed like the representations of parents developed in childhood, and that adult spirituality is influenced by early development. Erikson (1968a) rejects Freud's position calling "religion as such childish or religious behavior as such regressive" (p. 106). In contrast, he theorizes that religion "is the oldest and has been the most lasting institution to serve the ritual restoration of trust in the form of faith" (p. 106). He adds that religion provides a world image infusing community members with a vital and shared reverence for life. Erikson might add a client's religious organization to the eco-map as a source of strength, defense against evil, and personal restoration.

The traditional theoretical conceptualization of homosexuality has been equally obnoxious. It characterizes the homosexual orientation as reflecting "arrested, immature, narcissistic, and undifferentiated object relations"

(Goldstein, 2001, p. 51). Endleman (1981) summarizes other classical psycho-analytic views toward homosexuality in a series of generalizations. He writes that "there are likely to be pathogenic processes involved in the formation of the homosexual object choice," that "it [homosexuality] is commonly associated with disorders of a neurotic character disorder, or psychotic variety, or with disorders of impulse control, of addiction, or of narcissism, or a borderline character organization," and that "interpersonal relations of many kinds, not only those involved in sexual partnerships, may be difficult, strained, abrasive, full of dominance-submission struggles, and frequently hatred disguised as 'love' " (p. 273). Newer theoretical conceptualizations assert that the object relations and self-structures of gays and lesbians follow from alternative but potentially positive and affirming developmental experiences (Goldstein, 2001). Social workers have easily adapted Erikson's model of human development and ideas about middle adulthood to expand the meaning of generativity to gays. Gays may not have children, but they pass their gifts on to the next generation through productive career activities and creative involvement in volunteer service and hobbies, and by teaching younger gay persons about identity issues and their resolution (Cornett & Hudson, 1987).

Psychodynamic theory has been charged with disparaging women. Freud and Erikson held the theoretical assumption that anatomy is destiny, that human development and possibilities are determined differentially for males and females by their bodies (Roazen, 1976). Typically, the result of the difference was the inherent weakness of women and their incompleteness as persons. Classical psychoanalysts argued that "the development of hetero-sexuality and maternality in the girl are a secondary product of her sense of failed masculinity" (Chodorow, 1990, p. 116). They conceptualized **penis envy** as a little girl's tendency to react to the absence of a penis with shame and envy (Freud Loewenstein, 1985). They argued that women are suited biologically only for roles as mothers and wives (Pearson et al., 1988) and that the vaginal orgasm is critical to female maturity; the clitoris doesn't matter (Freud, 2005). Erikson (1975) disparaged the women's liberation movement as "a moralistic projection of erstwhile negative self-images upon men as representing evil oppressors and exploiters" (p. 241). He complained that its leaders were too volatile and sharp.

Contemporary psychodynamic theorists assert that learned behavior, not biological programming, makes the critical difference in role performance (Roazen, 1976). Theorists at the Stone Center for Developmental Services and Studies at Wellesley College in Massachusetts built on object relations theory and self psychology to create an influential model of female development called self-in-relation theory (Goldstein, 2001). These theorists posit that females develop in different but not inferior ways. Females thrive on enhanced connections with other people, not on the differentiation of the self and separation from objects in the environment. Females' psychosocial problems are often caused by developmental experiences characterized by nonrespon-sive relationships and disconnection. Feminist object relations theorists reject Freud's essentialist arguments (gender is determined by biological essences, for example). They theorize instead about how gender identity, awareness of genital differences, and gender-based inclinations toward subordination emerge as part of gender role learning during experiences of self with others in a context of male-dominated hierarchy and cultural negative valuation (Chodorow, 1990).

Early psychodynamic theorists simply ignored people of color and gave negligible theoretical attention to racism and discrimination. Erikson (1968a) began to rectify this omission. He suggested that members of vulnerable groups are prone to identify problems not because of ego defects but because of cultural conflict, negative and internalized societal attitudes toward group members, and developmental experiences that were not growth enhancing but stigmatized, excluded, or oppressed people of color (Goldstein, 2001). Sophie Freud argues for the extension of psychodynamic theory. **Projective identification,** the process of assigning "split-off and disowned parts of the self to an intimate other" (Freud, 1992, p. 422), for example, is a concept useful for explaining the social processes of racism and homophobia. Members of a group in power project their undesired impulses onto a weaker and vulnerable group. The less powerful group is condemned, persecuted, and oppressed for its alleged despicable attributes, while members of the projecting powerful group remain blameless for their disowned inclinations.

Classical psychodynamic theorists were also inattentive to issues of social class and oppression. They located the source of all biopsychosocial problems in the individual, a theoretical approach implicitly excusing unjust and destructive social arrangements. Sigmund Freud, for example, gave no place in his theory for the concepts of class or class conflict, and he did not incorporate any observations about the systematic oppression of certain groups into his psychosexual stage model or his characterization of social life (Smelser, 1996). Since Freud, a group of psychodynamic theorists including Erich Fromm, Herbert Marcuse, Norman O. Brown, and Louis Althussser have attempted to merge Freud's theoretical perspective with the critical perspective of Karl Marx to identify the consequences of capitalism on psychic operations and family life (O'Neill, 2001).

Late in his career, Erik Erikson participated in a multi-day conversation with Huey Newton, a black revolutionary and leader of the Black Panther Party, and attempted to correct his earlier theoretical efforts. Erikson (Erikson & Newton, 1973) explained that he had developed his model of human development during the presidency of Franklin Roosevelt, an era when the United States was moving in an antiracist direction and was liberating other peoples from fascist rulers. He still regretted that he "had largely overlooked the fate of the black citizenry who were kept in their place so as to constitute what slaves always meant besides cheap labor—the inferior identity to be superior to" (p. 54). He sketched the preliminary draft of a radical ego psychological model of oppression. He explained the dynamics of prejudice in terms of defensive processes allowing the "normal majority" to "overlook in themselves vulnerabilities and conflicts" that are driven into the groups subjected to this form of "enforced inferiority" (Erikson & Newton, 1975,

p. 51). Oppressors develop a core identity as a **pseudospecies.** Group members imagine themselves as the human species, the "real people," characterize others as less than human, and cultivate hatred and fear of the inferior others. For example, the leaders of the British Empire believed that they were specially chosen by God, and used this identity to justify exploitation in their colonies. Erikson theorized that a main task for colonized or oppressed groups is the psychic transformation of negative identities into positive ones. Building on Marx's ideas, he argued that the oppressed group suffers from "class unconsciousness" and must become aware of "the collective image of reality" that is "daily enforced by the media serving those in power" (p. 52). Erikson did not endorse violent social action, but he applauded Newton's efforts to "create a set of new images for black and white people" (p. 79) and interpreted the militant defiance of the Black Panthers positively. In Erikson's approach to empowerment movements, "armed love" is the demonstration that "one can really love only if one knows that one could and would defend one's dignity, for only two people of equal dignity can love each other" (p. 110). Militant minorities are necessary to shake up the old self-images protected by the oppressive majority.

WHAT WOULD BE ADDED OR DELETED?

Ego psychologists like Erik Erikson give special attention to the notion of **generation** and to the person's ability to master challenges associated with each phase of the **life cycle.** Ego psychologists would probably recommend the use of retrospective eco-maps. A life history or **life review** completed by the social worker and client might involve the creation of multiple eco-maps. One eco-map might characterize the present psychosocial situation; others might depict the psychological, social, and historical circumstances associated with earlier life stages. Erikson was also attuned to the influence of large-scale historical and cultural forces on life cycle progressions. He might recommend that an eco-map be supplemented by a psychohistorical study, an attempt to understand a client's intrapsychic conflicts and identity issues in light of the common problems and opportunities of the historical period and society.

Psychodynamic theory users might not include the social welfare system as an eco-map circle. Their work tends to be done in mental health settings. The circle for psychosocial services would be best represented as the location for a therapeutic relationship between client and worker. Typical locations include the mental health clinic, the psychiatric hospital, the psychosocial clubhouse, and the for-profit therapy center.

THE LIMITS OF APPLIED PSYCHODYNAMIC THEORY: A SOCIAL WORK APPRAISAL

Psychodynamic theory is an important and influential theoretical approach with a long history and with many concepts that have become part of the professional social work vocabulary. Erik Erikson advanced the psychodynamic theoretical approach in many ways (Hogan, 1976). He rejected Freud's notion that later life stages are determined by events in early childhood. He showed that people grow and change across the "eight stages of man." Erikson incorporated sociological and anthropological insights into the study of psychodynamics, breaking with the individualistic biases of earlier psychoanalytic theorists. He valued the analysis of the personal unconscious but also encouraged analysis of the sociological unconscious. Erikson shifted attention from the id and from human pathologies to the ego, ego strengths, and ego possibilities. He was more interested in the way that social arrangements can support ego development than in the damaging effects of the civilizing process. Erikson (1968a) developed a "total configurational approach—somatic, historical, individual" (p. 248), anticipating social work's shift to holistic theories of the biological, psychological, and social influences on human behavior. Critical reflection on psychodynamic theory and Erikson's work alerts us to several drawbacks to the theoretical tradition. These are related to social work interest in theory attentive to diversity, justice, and science.

Erikson assumed that development occurs in universal and equivalent ways. Societies and cultural groups in the world of the 21st century vary greatly, however, in how they structure members' progression from birth to death. Societies may also vary in the conception of each stage, in the stage-specific tasks, in the chronological ages that begin and end life stages, and in the particular virtues or ego strengths that are promoted during important life stages. Ego psychologists assume greater universality to their theory than would be supported by anthropological research.

Additionally, Erikson's model of the life cycle has a conservative tone and may need a critical edge. Social institutions are generally considered beneficial rather than harmful. The ideal life cycle is characterized by heterosexuality, marriage, child rearing, and quiet resignation by the aged to their impending death. Girls envy boys and their penises. Social patterns are relevant to individual dysfunction, but primary attention is given to the personality and its malfunctioning psychodynamics. Psychotherapy, not social change, is the intervention of choice. Social workers committed to social justice differ with psychodynamic therapists and argue that many personal troubles are exacerbated by unfair policies and inequitable social arrangements. The analysis of psychodynamics and the review of life stage resolutions should be supplemented by socioanalysis. Conformity to the expectations of a society's standard setters must be supplemented by rebellion against those whose standards and actions contribute to bigotry, privilege, and suffering.

Finally, psychodynamic theorists have made insufficient progress, critics contend, in testing their ideas or in showing how to establish the effectiveness of psychodynamic practice. Sophie Freud (2005) traces the lack of interest in scientific advance to Sigmund Freud's dogmatic certainty about his ideas and his pattern of casting critics of psychodynamic theory as villains. The theoretical framework needs revision, including a loud rejection of ideas of questionable validity like "instincts" or "psychic energy," a dismissal of outdated

Freudian theories about women's subordinate position to men, and total abandonment of a root metaphor comparing human to hydraulic mechanical systems. Some theory defenders assert that psychodynamic theorists search for interpretations, not scientific explanations, and should not be judged by the empirical standard of knowledge permitting behavioral prediction and control (Pearson et al., 1988). Other advocates of the newer approaches to psychoanalysis are beginning to test empirically and revise psychodynamic concepts and propositions (Eagle, 1984). Vaillant and Milofsky (1980), for example, conducted a major study of 486 adult men and found empirical support for three hypotheses derived from Erikson's life cycle model. Greater efforts to produce case exemplars of psychodynamic effectiveness supported by research evidence would also benefit the profession.

A PSYCHODYNAMIC MODEL OF CORRECTIVE EMOTIONAL EXPERIENCE

In this section, I will summarize a midrange theory from the psychodynamic theoretical tradition that might be useful for assessment of and assistance to clients attempting to manage intense grief. Scheff (1985, 1987) developed this approach to therapeutic catharsis. Table 8.2 summarizes the concepts used in this theoretical model.

TABLE 8.2 SCHEFF'S MODEL OF CATHARSIS: EMOTIONS, CORRECTIVE EXPERIENCES, AND PSYCHOSOCIAL FUNCTIONING

Major Constructs	Concepts
Coarse emotions	Grief, rage, fear, boredom
Emotional distress	Emotion with physical tension
Emotional response cycle (adaptive)	Environmental event evokes emotion Arousal of cognition, feelings, body Physical climax Diminution of feelings and tension
Influences on cycle	Biological inheritance Psychological (participation-observation) Social norms (emotion experience-display)
Continuum of distances	Overdistanced, aesthetic distance, underdistanced
Rituals of release	Evocation of distress Balanced distance Discharge (in supportive and challenging context)
Psychosocial functioning	Degree of physical relaxation Heightened sensitivity to self and others Clarity of thought Pleasurable feelings Creative action

Source: Based on Scheff, 1985, 1987.

Catharsis refers to the elimination of psychic distress associated with loss, failure, or other traumatic experiences by emotional expression. Catharsis restores the person's sense of competency and worth and frees the person to act in an unconflicted way. Problems related to failure to master life stage challenges might be remedied by catharsis. Humans are vulnerable across the life stage, for example, to psychic disruptions when they do not manage well the coarse emotions, primarily grief, rage, and fear. These emotions are universal and require the activation of a particular biopsychosocial sequence for relief.

The client who experiences the severing of an emotional attachment—the death of a loved one, for instance—may work through the grief response cycle associated with this loss successfully or unsuccessfully. The grief response cycle is affected by three processes that, in optimal circumstances, become part of an integrated sequence that is carried to completion.

First, the biological process refers to basic human nature and the genetically based inclinations discussed by Freud. The loss of a valued other creates biopsychological tension that normally results in catharsis. The loss by death of an emotionally significant other evokes specifically the arousal of cognitions and feelings related to woe and sadness and the associated physical tension. The biological process culminates in a physical climax, a release of bodily tension in a socially acceptable form such as deep sobbing and weeping.

Second, the psychological process focuses on the degree of consciousness and participation in the emotional processes. The id represents the powerful impulses associated with the loss, and the superego represents the judgments about the appropriateness of acting on such impulses. When in the id phase, we participate fully and spontaneously in the grief process. During the superego phase, we step back and watch the process from the perspective of important others and internalized norms. Optimal catharsis requires an ego with the strength to shuttle back and forth between the id and the superego, between a participant role and the role of observer. The grieving person uses his or her ego to achieve an aesthetic distance like that of a drama critic, neither too close to nor too far from the action.

Scheff (1987) identified different degrees of emotional distance during the psychological processes that accompany the grief response cycle. In the **overdistanced emotional state,** the psyche is influenced completely by superego processes. The participation occurs only in the observer role and from a great psychological distance. A high degree of repression of deviant or dangerous impulses is common. In the **underdistanced emotional state,** the psyche is influenced completely by id processes. Full involvement in the participant role follows. Repressed impulses and emotions emerge and are acted on without consideration for consequences. **Aesthetic distance** is the optimal psychological distance. Here, the ego directs movement back and forth between the id and the superego. Neither dominates. The ego shifts repeatedly between the roles of participant and observer. The ego also regulates consciousness, alternating between high repression and no repression depending on the ego's capacity to cope with the experience.

Third, the community or sociocultural process is also important. Communities and cultural groups vary in their conventions regarding the expression of emotion, the social norms for emotional display, and the rituals for emotional release. In optimal circumstances, community life is governed by emotional norms supportive of the full experience of grief-related emotions and the public display of grief. Ideally, the community also provides public rituals for the shared expression of emotions and release of tensions. The ideal community or support group structures these rituals with sensitivity to the needs of members at different life stages.

Scheff (1987) notes that there are maladaptive approaches to the emotional response cycle. These include delaying movement through the sequence, interrupting the sequence, or avoiding all phases of the sequence. Traumatic events present a challenge. However difficult, humans can participate in the emotional response cycle with aesthetic distance and develop ego strengths that enable "working through" the blend of suffering and reflection on the suffering. Or human beings can defend so strongly against the powerful impulses associated with loss that the biopsychosocial tensions and psychological conflicts continue as wounds that influence all later psychic functioning and interpersonal interaction.

A PSYCHODYNAMIC ATTACHMENT THEORY MODEL FOR GRIEF WORK

A related model for psychodynamic grief work merits attention. Psychodynamic theorists emphasize the biological and emotional aspects of human connections. Early psychoanalytic theorists explained bonds in terms of cathexis, energy attached to a person or object. Weinstein and Platt (1973), for example, reviewed this approach and suggested that "at the conscious level cathexis appears as an emotional attachment to, or feeling for, some object" (p. 42). Freud's successors, especially John Bowlby (1988), used the new term *attachment* to refer to bonds between a person and important others, and the term *attachment behavior* to refer to intense and insistent inclinations to be with those to whom we are attached and the actions taken to end separation (Marris, 1996). Marris (1982, 1991, 1996) began the work of translating these concepts into a language suitable for practitioners aiding adults challenged by the death of a loved one.

THE PSYCHODYNAMIC ATTACHMENT PERSPECTIVE ON BEREAVEMENT PROBLEMS

Mapping a person–environment configuration involves searching with the client for his or her major attachment relationships. These unique and indispensable relationships in the life space are those with people to whom the client has attached special meaning. Marris (1991) defined **meaning** as "an organization of experience which enables us to identify those events which matter to us, relate them to previous experiences, and determine how we should respond to them" (p. 78). The client's set of attachment figures becomes crucial to his or her overall structure of meaning and well-being.

Lofland (1982, 1985) further developed the implications of this psychodynamic approach to social bonds. In the terms of eco-maps, she characterized the connections between clients and attachment others in a psychosocial way. Attachments, she argued, take seven forms. We develop bonds with role partners as we come to see them enact complementary roles. We develop bonds with those we define as available to help us with mundane daily tasks. We develop connections to those confirming our cherished images and conceptions of self, to those supporting our assumptions about social reality, and to those joining with us in creating useful myths and narratives. Attachments are like threads of connectedness, and we are tied to those who link us to members of a social network. Finally, we become attached to those with whom we construct a vision of a shared future.

Lofland (1982, 1985) switched from the metaphor of attachments as strings tying us to others. Attachments are also like eggs; we can spread our eggs across many baskets or place them all in one basket. Cultural, historical, and personal factors, Lofland added, influence whether we develop a full set of meaningful attachments with multiple others or with a single other.

People, Marris (1991) argued, have a conservative impulse to protect the predictable order of attachments and meanings that they have established. Separation from attachment figures, or the loss of significant others to death, threatens this order and weakens one's resistance to uncertainty by severing the meaningful bonds between the client and these others. In this psychodynamic attachment perspective, **grief** is the socially shaped emotional response to the disruption or disintegration of the person's set of central meanings about loved ones and about self in relationships. Severed attachments cause damage to a person's structure of meanings about self and central social memberships.

The nature of self and social connectedness is dramatically altered by the death of a significant other. Successful grieving essentially entails recovering from an assault on personal and social meanings. The grief work that practitioners provide to the bereaved, then, should be "a socially structured interactional process which helps the bereaved achieve continuity and coherence by forming a new sense of self and significant memberships" (Forte, Barrett, & Campbell, 1996, p. 46).

THE PSYCHODYNAMIC ATTACHMENT PERSPECTIVE ON ASSESSMENT

Our research team refined several assessment tools to use in such grief work. The perceived social network, the level of significance of the person who died, the bereaved person's specific relationship connections, and the overall pattern of social connectedness can be measured by a modified Social Network Map (SNM) and Social Network Grid (SNG). These self-report measures, developed by Tracy and Whittaker (1993), use a graphic approach like the eco-map to assess the structure and functions of a personal social network. The network map requires respondents to identify attachment figures in seven domains: household, extended family, work or school, church, friends, neighbors, and formal services. After generating a list of attachment others and placing them on the map as a visual aid, respondents can be asked to rate cards representing each of these attachment others. The seven types of attachment can be assessed: role partnership, mundane assistance, linkage to a network of others, self-confirmation, comforting myths, reality validation, and shared futures. The interviewees in our study used the card sort technique to rate each significant other on the quality of the seven threads of connectedness (1 represented low intensity or frequency and 3 represented high intensity or frequency). Group members completed the Social Network Map and Grid twice: first, retrospectively, for their ecosystem and social network before the loss of the loved one, and then, currently, for their social network while in the bereavement group.

THE PSYCHODYNAMIC ATTACHMENT PERSPECTIVE ON INTERVENTION

The social workers used these assessments to engage clients in mutual aid groups, to help them cope with the assault on their meaning systems and begin the search for new human connections and new meanings. The bereavement mutual support group evaluated was offered through the medical social work department at a large Southeastern private hospital. This service was directed toward family members of hospital patients who had died as a result of illness or accident. Approximately four weeks after the death of a patient, a sympathy card informed family members about the bereavement service. The open-ended group met twice a month. The group had been offered continuously for three years, and group members chose how long they would stay involved in the service. After a dinner provided by the hospital, members typically engaged in a 60-minute mutual aid discussion group. The group that I assisted was co-led by a social work director with more than 10 years of experience in health social work and a second-year graduate-level social work student.

Members who reported the most serious destruction of their network of attachments received the most group and worker attention. The group helped members in a variety of ways. Corrective emotional experiences were used so that members could learn to convey support and concern to each other about their losses; to create a set of new and valuable attachments; to express and cope with emotions such as anxiety, anger, and loneliness; to provide each other feedback on their grief management; and to educate peers and collaterals about the psychological and social dynamics involved in adjusting to the loss of a significant other. The social workers also facilitated emotional ventilation, member disclosure, mutual advice giving, ego support, and common concern discussion related to member-selected topics.

Our small-scale study offered some empirical evidence for the assertion that social workers can facilitate the grieving process using a conceptual model based in a psychodynamic attachment theory of grief work. After shared grief work, group members on average had formed social connections equivalent to those while the loved one was alive. Group work–facilitated connectedness was associated with reductions in remembered grief, present grief, and total grief. Members spoke almost unanimously of the group's usefulness in creating a supportive and meaningful network of new attachment figures. The bereaved began the search for new attachments and meanings, and through the help of transitional relationships to group members, this search resulted in a renewed certainty about self, a new acceptance of the death, and insights into how to lead a life despite the dissolution of a crucial social membership.

LEARNING ACTIVITIES

1. Analyze a recent dream or Freudian slip. What does this message from the unconscious tell you about your personality and your relationship to other people or the environment?

2. Identify a challenging or conflict-ridden situation that you have faced in the past five years. What psychological defense processes did you use to deal with the situation? In what ways was your use of defenses effective (facilitated coping) or ineffective (hindered coping)?

3. Recall an early childhood relationship with your mother or father or another important caretaker. In what ways do the memories, images, or words associated with this person emerge in your consciousness? How does your past experience affect your current social relationships and psychological functioning?

4. Referring to Erikson's life stage model of psychosocial development, identify an important psychosocial stage in your life. Discuss the persons and organizations important to you during this stage. Describe how well you met the stage-related challenge. Identify current ego strengths or weaknesses that you can trace back to your psychosocial experiences during this life stage.

5. Try out Ainsworth and Bowlby's typology of patterns of attachment. How would you categorize your own style? A friend's style? A client's style? Check your classification decisions with a fellow student, family member, or agency worker. Comment on the inter-rater reliability or lack of reliability.

6. Collect information and assess the environment of a member of a poor, stigmatized, or oppressed group. What are the opportunities for secure attachments? What are the obstacles to secure attachments? How might attachment theory explain member and group problems in this environment?

7. React critically to the generalizations made by classical psychodynamic theorists about diverse members: Religion is a neurosis. Homosexuality is often the result of pathogenic developmental processes. Women's biological difference from men conditions their psychology and relationships. What evidence might you use to support or reject these generalizations? What alternative explanations might you offer for spiritual practices, alternative sexual orientations, and gender-based identity and interaction patterns?

8. Construct an eco-map translated into psychodynamic terms. What are some inner or outer conflicts that you are trying to cope with? Describe your radius of significant relations and their contribution to coping (or not coping) with these conflicts. Characterize the qualities of connections with these others (ego supportive or ego destructive).

What psychodynamic changes (relation of id-ego-superego processes) would you like to make?

9. Identify a loss in your own life. Using Scheff's theory of coarse emotions, identify how you coped with the experience. In what ways might you have changed the physical, psychological, and social dimensions of your grief management to achieve a healthier resolution of the loss?

ADDITIONAL RESOURCES

Additional resources are available on the book companion website at **www.thomsonedu.com/ social_work/forte.** Resources include key terms, tutorial quizzes, links to related websites, and lists of additional resources for furthering your research.

APPLIED BEHAVIORISM

CHAPTER 9

Jacob Halaska/IndexStock

INTRODUCTION

Hamlet, prince of Denmark, pondered, according to William Shakespeare, the existential question, "To be or not to be?" After the murder of his father, Hamlet ruminates continuously but hesitates to take action. He wants more evidence of the evil deed. He remains indecisive even after learning the identity of the person who poisoned his father. His inner struggles are so lengthy, persistent, and troubling that Hamlet is taken for a madman. Finally, Hamlet chooses to answer his own query by becoming an avenging agent. His delay has tragic consequences. Both Hamlet and the murderer Claudius die in the final sword fight.

Behaviorists recommend consideration of a simpler question, "To behave or not to behave?" The foul behavior of Claudius merits punishment. Other princes would not delay in demanding justice, and other princes could serve as models for justice-seeking behavior. Hamlet's behavioral restraint is condemned in the castle as insanity and earns him no tangible or social rewards. His behavior will be rewarded only by the members of the royal court, by his subjects, and by the ghost of his father (Hamlet's standards for conduct) if he takes appropriate and effective action.

In this chapter, I will use our theory mastery tools—exemplary models, metaphors, maps, and conceptual models—to introduce you to the applied behaviorism school of thought. I will give special attention to Albert Bandura's influential social learning theory of human development.

RELATED DIALECTS, ASSOCIATED SCHOOLS OF THOUGHT

Behaviorism is the theoretical tradition within the social sciences that promotes the study of animal and human behavior. John Watson (1924/1970) defined behaviorism as "a natural science that takes the whole field of human adjustments as its own" (p. 11). Watson added that behaviorism is "intrinsically interested in what the whole animal will do from morning to night and from night to morning," and "it is the business of behavioristic psychology to be able to predict and to control human activity" (p. 11). **Social behaviorism** is a sociological approach to human conduct pioneered by the first symbolic interactionists. George Herbert Mead, for example, used the term *social behaviorism* in one of his lectures about the interactionist approach to social psychology. He wrote, "Our behaviorism is a social behaviorism" (Mead, 1934, p. 6).

Behavioral schools of thought vary in the importance given to the human mind and cognitive processes. **Radical behaviorism,** championed by B. F. Skinner, is defined, according to Bruce Thyer (1988), as "an attempt to account for human behavior without recourse to mental events within the person" (p. 124). **Social learning theory** is a variation of the behaviorist tradition developed by Albert Bandura (1977b). Bandura differs from the radical behaviorists because he assumes that an adequate theory of how humans learn complex human behavior must consider cognitive events. This perspective, he suggests, "approaches the explanation of human behavior in terms of a continuous reciprocal interaction between cognitive, behavioral, and environmental determinants" (p. vii). Special attention is given to social factors, especially learning by modeling others. Client problems, in Bandura's (1967) view, are problems in social learning. Clients learn abnormal or ineffective behaviors for coping with environmental demands. Later in his career, Bandura referred to his approach as *social cognitive theory,* and this term has been adopted by many other theorists and theory users (Evans, 1989).

Applied behaviorism provides a set of concepts, methods, and principles for understanding and solving personal and collective problems. Applied behaviorism has been called *behavior modification, behavior therapy, applied behavior analysis,* and *behavioral social work.* Gambrill (1994), for example, defines **applied behavior analysis** as an empirical approach in which "the principles of behavior form the basis of contingency management (rearranging the relationships between behavior and the environment to attain socially valid outcomes)" (p. 32). Miller (2002) characterizes **behavior modification** as "the application of principles of operant conditioning to naturally occurring undesirable behaviors such as temper tantrums" (p. 175). Gambrill notes that terms such as *behavior modification, applied behavior analysis,* and *behavior therapy* are often used synonymously.

As discussed in the cognitive science chapter, there have been many attempts recently to integrate the two theoretical approaches, cognitive science and behaviorism. Practitioners who use tools from both these traditions generally identify themselves as cognitive behaviorists.

APPLIED BEHAVIORISM: EXEMPLARY MODELS

A genogram for the family of contemporary behaviorists would show a clear line of descent. The following reports on the tradition's grandparents and parents.

IVAN PAVLOV

Ivan Pavlov (1849–1936), a Russian physiologist, was the son of a poor village priest educated at a theological seminary (Hogan & Smither, 2001). Fortunately, he won a government scholarship and attended the University of St. Petersburg. He became a professor with a lifelong interest in physiology. His research into the physiology of digestion led to his study of the digestive processes of salivating dogs, and the creation of the science of conditioned reflexes. Pavlov's insightful work was so exceptional that he won the Nobel Prize for physiology in 1904.

Pavlov discovered that various neutral stimuli—a metronome sound, a buzzer, a light flash, or a touch on the collar—could be paired with the presentation of food to a dog. These new stimuli were called **conditioned stimuli;** because food automatically evoked salivation (an ordinary animal reflex or **unconditioned response**), the food was called an **unconditioned stimulus.** Eventually, the dog would salivate in response to the external agent. For example, Pavlov could ring a bell and the dog would salivate, even in the absence of food. Pavlov called this a **conditional reflex.** Learning was, Pavlov asserted, the creation of associations between stimuli and responses. Pavlov's research became the basis for the behavioral approach to learning by conditioning.

Pavlov dedicated much of his energy to reform of the scientific establishment in the Soviet Union (Nobelprize.org, 2005). His international stature earned him political favor and funding from political leaders. Pavlov's institutions for the study of physiology became world centers of scientific knowledge, and he nurtured a large group of distinguished students and followers who continued to develop his ideas. The Pavlov Institute of Physiology of the Russian Academy of Sciences, founded by Pavlov in 1925, is still an active research organization. The Institute supports more than 300 researchers working in 32 different laboratories. Members of the Institute build on Pavlov's heritage in their studies of physiology, higher nervous activity, the functioning of sensory and visceral systems in humans and animals, and adaptation.

Pavlov's study of conditioned reflexes was the scientific breakthrough that made behaviorism possible, and his work still helps us understand the development of fears and aversions. For example, I worked when I was a teenager in my grandfather's Italian restaurant. One night I was in a hurry and dipped my glass into the shrimp container instead of the water jar. I gulped down the briny shrimp liquid and soon became very, very sick. A negative association was formed between shrimp and illness, and I have never eaten shrimp since. The Psi Café (2005) provides a humorous story demonstrating the application of Pavlov's ideas about conditioned reflexes. One summer, a student at the Massachusetts Institute of Technology went to the Harvard University football field every day. He wore a black and white striped shirt, and he walked up and down the field for 15 minutes throwing birdseed while blowing a whistle. He then left. At summer's end, the Harvard community readied for the season's first home football game. A referee walked onto the field and blew his whistle. The birds responded to the sound and crowded the grounds. The game had to be delayed for a half hour until the field was cleared. Incidentally, the Psi Café claims that the student wrote his thesis on this application of classical conditioning theory and graduated.

JOHN WATSON

John Broadus Watson (1878–1958) transformed the study of conditioning into one of the most influential approaches to psychology. He is known as the father of behaviorism, the experimental study of human behavior.

Watson was born in rural South Carolina to a large and poor family, and his mother urged him to become a clergyman (Hogan & Smither, 2001). Instead, he took classes in psychology at undergraduate and graduate schools.

Watson eventually studied under John Dewey and George Herbert Mead at the University of Chicago and earned his Ph.D. in 1903. His topic was "The Psychical Development of the White Rat." However, Watson rejected Dewey's complex model of human conduct and had scorn for researchers who showed interest in the unseen mental correlates of behavior. He argued that psychology should model itself after natural sciences like chemistry and physics, with no place for subjectivity or introspection in the discipline.

John Watson was strongly influenced by Pavlov's research into conditioned reflexes. Watson built his theoretical framework on a commitment to studying only observable behavior. Arguing that humans and animals learn according to the same laws of behavior, he engaged in extensive research on animal behavior, on trial-and-error learning, and on the conditioning of emotional reactions in children. In one controversial experiment, Watson worked with a boy called Little Albert (Simpson, 2000). Albert was a healthy 9-month-old baby with no natural fear of rats, rabbits, dogs, or monkeys, but Albert was afraid of loud noises. Watson put a rat near the boy and then hit a steel bar with a hammer, creating a loud unpleasant sound. After several such sessions, Albert was conditioned and began to cry at the sight of the white rat. Watson had shown that humans could be conditioned to fear arbitrary objects. Albert's mother, by the way, removed her son from the study soon after, before his fear of rats had been deconditioned.

John Watson gave great importance to the shaping influence of the environment and asserted that most of a child's behavior was conditioned. Watson was so confident in his behavioral technology that he claimed that he could take any child and train him for any type of career specialty that he selected. Watson (1924/1970) also asserted that adult developmental problems could be explained best by reference to habit systems acquired in early life. Watson fashioned himself as a public expert on psychological issues, but his views were controversial (Simpson, 2000). He predicted the demise of monogamy. He advocated the outlawing of religion as an inefficient form of social control. He advised that parents refrain from hugging and kissing their children, and he complained that family life destroyed children's independence and individuality. He recommended instead that children be raised by a rotating collection of parents and nurses.

Watson's academic career at Johns Hopkins University ended because of a sex scandal involving a research assistant. Watson shifted his career interests to the New York advertising industry, where he showed advertisers how to use behavioral psychology to condition customers to buy fast food, vehicles, deodorant, and hundreds of other commercial products. He became a vice president of one of the largest advertising agencies in the country.

B. F. SKINNER

Burrhus Frederic Skinner (1904–1990) is probably one of the most influential psychologists of all time (Hogan & Smither, 2001). Skinner was born in a small railroad town in Pennsylvania (Skinner, 1967). He began a career as a novelist but gave up on this and went to Harvard. There, he studied industriously and developed skills that aided him as a professor, first at the University of Minnesota and then at Indiana University. During World War II, Skinner helped train pigeons to serve as guidance systems for missiles. In 1948, he wrote a novel about a utopian community called *Walden Two*. This book described social life organized on behavioral principles. His work inspired social pioneers who in 1967 created a cooperative community in Virginia called Twin Oaks. They modeled their mini-society on Skinner's fictional community, and it continues successfully today (Sinclair, 2001).

Unlike Pavlov and Watson, who studied the antecedents of behavior, Skinner focused on the relation of consequences to behavior. Studying rats and pigeons, Skinner discovered that he could shape the behavior of these experimental subjects by rewarding successive approximations to a desired behavior until the creature performed perfectly. He developed so-called Skinner boxes for use in his animal laboratory. These boxes for controlling an animal's movements included a mechanism designed to automatically dispense rewards when the animal pushed a lever or button. Skinner even placed his second child in a version of this device during her infancy.

Like Watson, Skinner condemned social scientists and practitioners who gave credence to concepts like "psyche" or "mind" and to therapeutic techniques like "introspection." He preferred to focus on forces external to the subject. Skinner concentrated on the learning that occurs because of what happens after a person responds to a stimulus. For Skinner, "Behavior is a function of its consequences" (Hogan & Smither, 2001, p. 227). A behavior pattern can be shaped by changing the positive and negative reinforcements that occur after the behavior. Follow a child's response to the calling of its name with a gentle caress (a reinforcement), and the child is likely to learn to respond to such calls (turn toward the parent). Skinner used the term *operant conditioning* for his method of shaping or modifying behavior by changing the relationship between a response and its consequences.

Skinner's eldest daughter has documented some of the ways her father applied his ideas (Vargas, 2005). B. F. Skinner extended his behavioral theory to policy and public problem-solving topics. He appeared on various television programs to discuss the implications of his science of behavior for social life. He proposed, for instance, that the use of behavior modification procedures could improve families and the whole society. His book *Walden Two* specified how a community might be planned in accordance with behavioral principles to foster cooperation, communal child rearing, job sharing, member happiness, and opportunities for leisure. His practical applications included a teaching machine that provides feedback to the learner after each attempted solution to a problem; and programmed instruction, a structured way of educating that sequences the presentation of information in small steps and maximizes the likelihood of correct answers. Skinner's approach to teaching has been applied successfully by educators working with autistic children.

Skinner took informed positions on practical matters (Vargas, 2005). He argued that the use of punishment by change agents such as prison guards was an ineffective method of behavioral control. Positive reinforcement, he advised, would more effectively produce desired and lasting change. Token economies, a procedure derived from Skinner's theory, is an alternative to punitive systems. In token economies, the teacher, counselor, or social worker provides rewards for behavior in accordance with established rules in the form of tokens such as chips, stars, or notes. Token economies are used in many group homes for juveniles, in psychiatric institutions, and in school classrooms. In his book *Beyond Freedom and Dignity* (1971), Skinner contended that the concepts "free will" and "individual autonomy" were obsolete. He believed that human behavior was better explained by genetics and environmentally determined learning histories than by personal feelings or beliefs. Behavioral technologies should guide social change. Therefore, a society needs problem-solving specialists who direct their efforts toward redesigning the environmental contingencies that control behavior. Skinner's proposal for bypassing "the autonomous inner man" (p. 205) in favor of the scientific design of culture evoked many negative reactions.

BRUCE THYER

There is no record indicating that the great behavioral theorists—Pavlov, Watson, Skinner—engaged in social work or in other human service projects. However, social work has a champion of behaviorism, Bruce Thyer. Professor Thyer teaches at the University of Georgia, Athens, Social Work Program. He has written numerous books and articles on the behavioral approach to human development, to public problems, and to social work practice. He founded and edits the social work journal, *Research for Social Work Practice*. This journal reports on the effectiveness of interventions using behavioral and other theoretical frameworks. Professor Thyer has also written about behavioral and social learning approaches to social work education, and he has summarized much of the empirical evidence showing how various applications of behavioral principles effectively solve numerous client problems.

APPLIED BEHAVIORISM: ROOT METAPHORS

Behavioral social scientists and practitioners assume that useful comparisons can be made between the behavior of humans and the behavior of animals in captivity, especially in laboratories.

THE PERSON AS ANIMAL

Behaviorists assume that social work clients are similar, at least in some important ways, to rats, pigeons, dogs, and monkeys. Members of all these species adapt to the environment through similar basic learning processes, including classical conditioning and operant conditioning. Members of the higher species—dogs, monkeys, and humans—are also capable of observational learning. Even a complex human activity like speech, according to the behaviorists, is not essentially different from animal vocalization. A child learns to talk in ways that can be explained by the same behavioral principles that apply to animal learning. Children are "rats with language" (Miller, 2002, p. 169).

Many behaviorists model themselves after scientists who specialize in animal studies. They believe that exclusive attention should be given to the public and observable aspects of the behavior of human animals. Concepts such as *mind, mental states, inner experience,* and *consciousness,* referring to private and unobservable phenomena, should be avoided. Scientific exploration of these concepts has been fruitless, according to these behaviorists, and introspection is not a valid research method. If your dog nips at the hand of a neighborhood child, you do not attempt to understand and analyze the dog's semiconscious motivation. Instead, you identify the observable provocation that led to the bite. You teach the child to be more careful, and you punish the dog firmly and repeatedly so that nipping behavior ceases.

Behaviorists think that humans are like animals in other ways too. Animals learn to respond quickly and adaptively to various environmental cues and challenges. Humans also must respond to the environment or perish. The metaphor of extinction is applied to animals and humans. Animal species that fail to adapt become extinct; likewise, the learned responses of humans that are not followed by positive and favorable consequences are extinguished (Smith, 1990). Animal and human actions are determined by environmental causes. Freedom, self-control, and self-direction are not concepts that radical behaviorists like Skinner would endorse (Leary, 1990).

In summary, many behaviorists prefer a parsimonious theory. Simple explanations are better than complex explanations and complicated theories. Thyer (1992) argues "to the extent that animal models are similar to human behavior, it seems more parsimonious to ascribe the human phenomena to processes similar to those employed in animal behavior rather than postulating the existence of complex cognitive events" (p. 412). We can explain most types of human activity in terms of the same mechanisms that explain the activity of other animals. Radical behaviorists, including Watson, Skinner, and Thyer, strongly endorse this metaphorical characterization of human beings as animals. But Albert Bandura and the cognitive behaviorists differ from their colleagues and suggest that there are significant differences between humans and animals. Behavioral theorists should examine these differences, and behavioral practitioners should attend to mental processes, they argue.

THE SOCIETY AS A LABORATORY

Although humans may be like animals, behaviorists do not conceive of the environment as a jungle or animal habitat. Ideally, society is like a psychology department's laboratory. Here all the conditions that affect learning can be controlled. Variables related to lighting, temperature, noise level, crowding, the nature and quantity of stimuli, the type and quantity of consequences, and so on can be manipulated to create an optimal learning environment. In this artificial society, laboratory scientists can make judgments about desirable behavior; conduct carefully structured experiments to determine what reinforcements, punishments, and models produce the desired behavior; and carefully monitor the results of these experiments. In this way, they can build a scientific knowledge base necessary for shaping behaviors. Animal experimentation in the lab leads to social experimentation by policy makers and problem-solving professionals. The empirically based tools of behaviorism can be applied until all participants in the societal laboratory act as expected.

Society includes laboratories, and the laboratories include mazes (Smith, 1990). Humans are like rats with a sense of the desired end state: getting the cheese, for the rat; becoming successful, for many Americans. There are many alternate routes to the end state. Societal leaders, the equivalent of laboratory scientists, offer incentives at various choice points. In this way, they direct us to the tunnels in the maze that will bring us to their preferred endpoints. Smart rats find efficient paths from the entrance of the maze to the final reward. Dumb rats wander, and turn left or right with no global understanding of the maze. The final reward is attained only after long and difficult effort.

The behaviorist, like the laboratory scientist, takes a position of distance from the behavioral events in the laboratory. Emotional involvement with laboratory guinea pigs (or human clients?) is discouraged. The behaviorist tries to influence the learning process in a detached and objective manner. B. F. Skinner imagined a society organized according to the behavioral tenets he used in laboratory research. In this characterization, the ideal society (Walden Two) would be engineered and governed by a master behaviorist.

THE SOCIAL WORKER AS BEHAVIORAL ENGINEER

Behaviorists would liken the social worker to a laboratory psychologist. A psychologist assembles the pigeons, dogs, and monkeys in the artificial laboratory society and then manipulates conditions and stimulus–response sequences to change animal behavior. A behavioral social worker also attempts to create a controlled learning environment. The worker may assemble a group of clients in a carefully designed meeting room and offer a structured educational program through the local mental health clinic, for example. Both the psychologist and the behavioral social worker assume complete authority. They analyze the **contingencies** (predictable relationships between stimuli, behavior, and environmental consequences) maintaining the problematic behavior, establish behavioral goals, control learning conditions, implement the behavioral technologies to achieve those goals, and report in a scientific journal on the results of the experiment. The special knowledge of behavioral theory and of the techniques for behavioral modification justifies the assumption of authority.

Behaviorists such as Skinner also use the notion of shaping behavior. Here, the social worker is implicitly compared to an artist who shapes and transforms a piece of clay, the client (Smith, 1990). The clay is inert and formless and gains value only when manipulated by the artist. Clients who lack access to social workers will be shaped haphazardly by the contingencies in their environments.

Some critics of the "rats and reinforcement" root metaphors of the traditional behavioral approach (including some contemporary behaviorists) reject this authoritarian conception of the social worker role (Hoffman, Cochran, & Nead, 1990). Humans have a right to dignified treatment, as do animals. Behavioral social workers should not be engineers, control agents, potters, or technologists. Behavioral social workers should be partners with their clients, share their knowledge, and develop agreements about behavioral change strategies that fully involve clients in the helping process.

CORE ASSUMPTIONS OF APPLIED BEHAVIORISM

Most applied behaviorists share the following assumptions, which are important to behavioral theory and to behavioral practice.

UNDERSTANDING, CONTROLLING, AND PREDICTING BEHAVIOR ARE PRIORITIES

Behaviorists assume that theoretical attention should go to understanding, controlling, and predicting human behavior. Behaviorists prefer a division of labor between social scientists and practitioners. If mental states exist, then these states—free will or inner representations, for example—should be studied by philosophers or psychoanalysts. If the environment includes more than reinforcers, punishers, and models—large-scale patterns and social structures that influence human behavior, for instance—then these should be studied by anthropologists and sociologists. Behaviorists want a different job. They restrict their theoretical inquiry and helping work to observing and changing the behavior of individuals.

Behaviorists are most interested in the question "What is the person doing?" McPhail (1991), for example, took a behavioral approach in his study of social movements and crowd activity. Instead of examining unseen variables such as collective hypnosis or group catharsis, McPhail catalogued the forms of observable and collective behavior of the actors. Separate individuals become a crowd or a social movement by doing things (behaving) together. Such coordinated behaviors include collective vocalization (behaviors such as crying at funerals or booing at political events); collective verbalization (praying, singing, or pledging with others); collective gesture making (raising a clenched fist); collective vertical locomotion (standing, sitting, or kneeling together); collective horizontal locomotion (lining up, or surging with others); and collective manipulation (clapping, throwing objects, waving flags or banners). Building on this typology of basic crowd behaviors, McPhail used a social behaviorist strategy to analyze the complex social forms that were built from two or more basic behaviors.

Some contemporary behaviorists are extending their theory's range. They use behavioral concepts and principles to study covert (unseen or private) behavior, behavior that occurs under the skin. They argue that phenomena related to the "self" should be studied as a type of behavior. People learn to use words to describe themselves as social objects. A person, for example, might be taught and rewarded for labeling herself as a Christian or an Asian. A person learns in many different social environments, and different audiences may reward different behaviors and different self-designations. The same person might be rewarded as a funny comedian by her peers and as a serious student by her classmates. The person also learns how to use self-describing behavior privately and silently, and the person learns to monitor inner experience because others ask, "What are you thinking or feeling now?" These friends and associates reinforce sensible, socially acceptable reports on this inner behavior. Social cognitive theorists and cognitive behaviorists are interested in such study of private self-talk.

HUMAN BEHAVIOR IS LEARNED

Behaviorists assume that human behavior is learned behavior. Almost everything that humans do, according to the behaviorists, can be explained by reference to the three forms of learning identified by the tradition's founding fathers: classical conditioning, operant conditioning, and observational learning.

Classical or respondent conditioning is the fundamental learning mechanism identified by Pavlov and studied by Watson. **Classical conditioning** involves the pairing of a neutral stimulus like Pavlov's metronome sound with an unconditioned stimulus like food, producing an automatic or innate reflex such as salivation (the unconditioned response). After repeated pairings or trials, the neutral stimulus becomes conditioned and evokes the unconditioned response from the animal or human. My dog, Atticus, for instance, automatically initiates a set of territorial defense behaviors when she sees or hears a potential threat at the boundaries of my house. After some conditioning, not all of it intentional, she has learned to respond to the doorbell as a signal of threat at the house front and to respond to the word "squirrel" as a signal of threat in the backyard.

Classical conditioning focuses on the antecedents of a behavioral response. **Operant conditioning** focuses on what follows the behavioral response, the consequences of a behavior. Skinner advanced the study of operant conditioning. **Reinforcers** are those consequences that increase the likelihood of a behavioral response. **Punishments** are consequences or aversive stimuli that weaken the behavioral response or decrease the likelihood that it will occur. My dog has learned to sit, lie down, bark, stand on two legs, and jump to receive treats. She has learned to refrain from nipping guests because nipping results in a smack on the butt with a broom.

The third major learning mechanism is **observational learning.** Albert Bandura (1977b) systematized the study of how humans can learn even when they do not directly experience a reinforcement or punishment. Humans and some animals learn by observing the behavior of models. If the model is punished, the observer participates vicariously in the lesson and learns not to act in the way that resulted in punishment. If the observed behavior seems rewarding, the observer may imitate it. My dog, for instance, learned the odious behavior of eating horse manure by watching my nephew's dog, Merlin.

Behaviorists acknowledge that biological factors contribute to human behavior. Genetic variables may be related to the capacity for intelligent behavior, for instance. However, behaviorists would start with explanations based on learning principles and learning opportunities (rewards for studying, competent teachers, models of academic skills). Then, biological variables might be considered. Behaviorists assume that if members of two different cultural groups differ in their school performance, the differences in their learning histories are probably more relevant than ethnically based genetic variations.

Basic Learning Processes Are Universal

Behaviorists assume that the basic learning processes are universal (Thyer, 1994). Learning by conditioning, learning by consequences, and learning by observing the behaviors of others are human adaptive capacities developed during our long evolution as a species. These three basic learning mechanisms operate in the same manner for all humans. They operate in the same manner across different cultures and environments. They operate in the same fashion across the life span of each individual, and they have operated in a similar way across the history of our species.

Contemporary behavioral social workers have tempered this claim of universal learning processes with an appreciation for cultural diversity. Cultural groups vary in what they identify as rewarding and punishing. They vary in their judgments about acceptable or desirable outcomes, and they vary in the tools and practices used in changing behavior. Lowery and Mattaini (1999), for example, offer a culturally oriented behavior analysis of the Pueblo people, a Native American group. Among other cultural practices, these Native Americans have developed a culture of "shared power." They prefer community reinforcement to coercive forms of behavioral control. They prefer to reinforce (or punish) behavior in direct face-to-face encounters rather than by abstract rules and indirect contingency systems. They aim to reduce self-oriented behaviors that reinforce the individual rather than the collective. They consider the consequences of behavioral decisions across multiple generations and attempt to minimize the negative consequences for anyone influenced by a decision. And they learn to report their observations of the behaviors of other community members in nonpunitive, honest ways. This package of learning strategies and behavioral preferences, Lowery and Mattaini suggest, is unique to this culture. The applied behaviorism perspective on diversity will be reviewed further in the eco-map translations section.

THE BEST PRACTICE IS SCIENTIFIC

Behaviorists assume that the best social work practice is characterized by a commitment to the scientific standards of logical positivism. Social work practice should be empirical. The scientific standards of laboratory research are extended to helping work. Behavioral practitioners should collect data about the observable behavior of clients. Behavior assessment requires the use of valid and reliable measurement tools. Since environmental consequences are the causes of behavioral problems, social workers should use problem analysis to identify objectively the behavioral contingencies determining client action. Goals for behavior change should be operationalized—stated in observable, specific, realistic, and measurable form. Behavioral social workers should choose intervention procedures whose effectiveness has been demonstrated scientifically. It is irresponsible and unethical, behaviorists argue, to use untested or ineffective procedures when scientifically sound behavioral methods are available. Client progress should be monitored systematically and scientifically, and practitioners should be able to respond to the question "What were the observable indicators of successful intervention?" Behaviorists recommend the use of single system research designs for this purpose, and through social work journals share their studies of practice effectiveness in detailed ways allowing replication. Practice evaluation is mandated in this approach. Worker and client decisions to vary from the contracted behavioral program should be based first on careful examination of data regarding the treatment process and only then on hunches or feelings.

Advocates of the behavioral approach conclude that a practitioner's choice of a theoretical framework and model for practice should be evidence based. Behaviorists have accumulated the most scientific evidence establishing the utility of their approach, they argue, making behavioral social work superior to models like psychosocial therapy that are not supported by evidence.

THE SOCIAL LEARNING THEORY OF HUMAN DEVELOPMENT

The concept of a *model* is central to the models, metaphors, and maps approach to learning theories introduced in this book. Albert Bandura has significantly increased our understanding of how developing persons learn from exemplary models and also from deviant models. After presenting a profile of Bandura, I will review the basic assumptions of social learning theory, its root metaphors, its organization as a theoretical structure, its theoretical gaps, and its application.

ALBERT BANDURA: EXEMPLARY ROLE MODEL

Another behavioral theorist who has been very influential is Albert Bandura. He was born in 1925 in Canada and is still teaching. His parents were Polish immigrants (Hogan & Smither, 2001) and proud of Bandura's distinguished career. Bandura earned numerous honors and awards for his research and scholarship and served as president of the American Psychological Association in 1974.

Bandura studied human learning. He wanted specifically to provide a theoretical explanation for novel behavior, a form of learning not explained by Skinner's radical behaviorism (Goldhaber, 2000). He and his colleague Richard Walters proved, for example, that children learn new behaviors by watching others even when there are no reinforcements. Bandura concluded that cognitive factors are critical to human development and that most human behavior is learned by observation of others. Humans do learn from the consequences of trial and error, but, more frequently, we increase our behavioral competencies by modeling. We can observe others and learn vicariously by noting how these models are rewarded or punished and by figuring out the rules that govern the model's style of behaving. Bandura and his colleagues also pioneered theoretical explanations relating observational learning, especially the modeling of parental behavior, to adolescent aggression (Goldhaber, 2000).

Unlike earlier behaviorists, Bandura (1977a) was not opposed to including covert or unseen processes in his theories of human behavior. He referred to his approach as *cognitive social learning theory*. In a sense, he fashioned a bridge between the work of the early behaviorists and the theoretical innovations of the cognitive scientists. Bandura argued, for example, that human motivation is greatly affected by beliefs about self-efficacy. He accumulated much research evidence supporting the following proposition: The person who believes himself to have little power and minimal ability to influence events and change patterns will be unlikely to persevere when facing environmental obstacles.

Albert Bandura was also one of the first theorists committed to what is known today as *evidence-based practice*. He asserted the strong conviction that "a responsible Clinical Psychology should be founded on a reliable knowledge base. We should not be subjecting people to treatments and then, some years later, trying to figure out what effects they have. We should test treatments before we embark on widespread applications" (Evans, 1989, p. 3).

ASSUMPTIONS OF THE SOCIAL LEARNING THEORY

Applied behaviorists assume that an individual's development is best understood in terms of that person's learning history (Thyer, 1992). Behavioral analysts collect data on the history of transactions between the client and his or her environment. Human development is considered the increase of behaviors in a total repertoire of behaviors. Images and ideas about the addition or accumulation across life of classically conditioned, operantly conditioned, and modeled responses are more important than ideas about biopsychosocial development (Miller, 2002). The child first learns simple behaviors and on such a foundation adds complex behaviors. The various learning processes are relevant. Behavioral advancement occurs because of classical conditioning. The child learns to cease forward movement near the stove by associating the sight of the stove with intense physical pain. Through operant learning experiences (praise, gentle caresses, and other reinforcers from caretakers), the child learns to share toys, to play cooperatively, to use new words, to touch others gently, to work on projects, and to sit quietly in class. The child also learns to alter her behavior by following the instructions or rules taught by parents and teachers. Finally, the child learns a new behavior demonstrated by models and then rehearses the behavior until the imitation is exact. An older sibling, for example, may show her sister the various behaviors necessary to ride a bike and then coach the sister until she can ride a bike safely.

Albert Bandura rejected the radical behaviorist assumption that cognitive processes have no causal influence on feelings or behavior (Evans, 1989). His social learning theory accepted the assumptions about classical and operant conditioning but assumed that humans also have the capacity for creative and intentional thought. People use cognitions to generate novel patterns of behavior that cannot be explained by the radical behaviorists. Cognitive factors also influence how the person perceives, interprets, values, and reacts to environmental stimuli (Bandura, 1983).

Bandura and the other behaviorists reject stage models like those of Piaget and Erikson. Behaviorists dislike the focus of these models on sequenced changes across distinguishable stages in unseen aspects of the mind or personality (Thyer, 1992). Behaviorists think that development is gradual, depends on everyday life learning opportunities, continues for life, and cannot be divided into clearly differentiated stages. The social learning mechanisms identified by Bandura, for example, have equal relevance across the entire human life span (Goldhaber, 2000). If there are commonalities in the psychosocial development of members of a culture, these can be explained by similarities in the culture's sequencing of learning experiences, not by stage-related unfolding of inner potentials. Social learning theorists tend to focus on learners' differences, not commonalities, especially differences in their learning environments. Social learning theorists also assume greater variability in the set of behaviors persons can acquire across the life span than does Erikson or Piaget (Miller, 2002).

Behaviorists trace current behavioral problems to earlier learning experiences. They contend that the behavioral model is better supported by scientific evidence than the cognitive and psychosocial hierarchical stage approaches. Behaviorists and social learning theorists focus on quantitative changes—the accumulation of skills, habits, strategies, and other behaviors into a growing repertoire of behaviors. They do not accept the assumption of transformations of underlying structures during shifts to qualitatively different stages of development (Salkind, 1985). Bandura reverses Piaget's causal logic (Crain, 1980). For Piaget, cognitive development across stages determines which models the developing person will imitate and what the developing person will learn. For Bandura, the models a developing person is exposed to and the observational learning from these models determine cognitive structures.

ROOT METAPHORS OF THE SOCIAL LEARNING THEORY

Imagery and ideas associated with models are at the core of social learning theory (Gecas, Calonico, & Thomas, 1974). Think of fashion models displaying the latest outfits and "beautiful" behavior. Think of the heroes and heroines that children choose to emulate. Think of the bad influences and models that parents admonish children to avoid. Social learners watch and imitate models of desired behavior in the environment. Social learners acquire the behaviors and attitudes of these models. Certain conditions make it easier or harder to model the exemplar. Great Britain has recently implemented a policy requiring the use of "ugly" male models when alcohol is being advertised. They hope that this will decrease imitation, and ultimately problem drinking. For social learning, watching the experiences of models (parents, peers, television celebrities, computer game personalities) is one of the most effective teachers (Salkind, 1985).

Bandura (1983) identifies another root metaphor of social learning theory. He rejects the radical behaviorist comparison of the person to a fully automatic camera triggered by environmental stimuli. If a person were like an automatic camera, his or her responses to the environment would be completely predictable and very rigid. The person could not easily adjust to varying situational demands and circumstances. Bandura prefers the image of "a semiautomatic camera system in which, to achieve desired results the photographer must select a lens of appropriate focal length, decide on whether or not to use certain filters, and set shutter speeds and lens openings based on judgments of light and movement conditions" (p. 15). The social learner, like the semiautomatic camera, is flexible and can bypass preset operating parameters. The social learner can make cognitive judgments to assess environmental events and potential behavioral models, to make comparisons between events and models using internalized standards, and to select the optimal reactions. The semiautomatic camera produces better pictures. The semiautomatic social learner produces more adaptive environmental responses.

BANDURA'S SOCIAL LEARNING THEORY OF HUMAN DEVELOPMENT

The central construct in Bandura's theory of human development is observational learning. Observational learning, or learning by modeling, is a social process during which "observers acquire mainly symbolic representations of the modeled activities which serve as guides for appropriate performances" (Bandura, 1977b, p. 24). Observational learning frees the learner to learn without first trying out the behavior and without trial-and-error processes followed by direct reinforcement (Crain, 1980).

Bandura's perspective on modeling still gives importance to the consequences of behavior, but he conceptualizes the functions of consequences such as reinforcements in a new way (Bandura, 1977b; Salkind, 1985). First, consequences have a **reinforcing function.** In this classical behavioral view, reinforcement following the enactment of a modeled behavior automatically strengthens the behavioral response. Bandura, however, identifies two additional functions. Consequences have an **informative function.** Observing a model receive rewards or punishments, for example, provides the social learner with information about the likely effects of his or her own actions. Effective observers learn what to expect after various behaviors and become better at predicting what behaviors will increase chances for success. This has implications for social work practice. Learning programs will be more effective if participants are told first what behaviors will be rewarded. Explain what behavior is necessary to earn reinforcements, show the model, and then provide instructions to the client on what to do. Consequences also have a **motivational function.** Observers learn to anticipate certain benefits from particular behaviors in specific situations. Because of the incentives, social learners begin to direct their behavior toward receiving these consequences. For example, the student watches a peer gain approval from a prestigious teacher by presenting a report. The student's motivation to earn similar praise is increased.

Learning through modeling involves several component activities (Bandura, 1977b; Salkind, 1985). I will explain and illustrate these components with reference to gender development (Franklin, 1988). How do adolescent males learn to behave the way they do, to become a "guy"? Bandura believes that observational learning is central to learning to be a male or a female (Goldhaber, 2000). Let's use the example of a boy learning to ask a girl (or boy) to dance at a high school party or a mad hot ballroom.

Attentional processes are important. The modeled event and its elements must be observed, and the learner must pay attention to the behavior sequence. Young males start to pay close attention to the relevant behaviors of older males in social interaction with females at a dance. Males who seem engaging and influential, the cool guys, receive the most attention. Those learners who fail to pay attention will not progress from being a "geek" to being a "guy."

Retention processes are important. The modeled event and its elements must be retained in memory. Young males learn to remember the male behaviors of their models by coding them in the form of symbolic representations using images and words. Effective learners engage in mental rehearsal, the use of cognitive symbols to try out in one's imagination and memorize the observed problem-solving strategy or creative action. Those with memory problems forget how to act as they approach a potential dance partner.

Motor reproduction processes are important. A social learner must possess the ability to physically perform the modeled event, including all the discrete behaviors that constitute the entire social act. The imitated behaviors need not replicate exactly the model's actions but only approximate the set of behaviors in a way suitable to the social learner's needs and interaction style (Salkind, 1985). Young males begin to physically reproduce the males' behaviors when approaching and asking for a dance: the walk, the hand gestures, the eye contact, the words of an invitation. They do this by initiating a behavior, monitoring their performance of the behavior, and refining the performance based on feedback. A male in a wheelchair might have difficulty learning to ask for a dance if he can only observe but not physically reproduce the "moves" of physically able exemplars.

Motivational processes are important. The social learner must anticipate rewards for modeling the observed behavior. Young males are likely to adopt the male's behaviors that are seen as achieving valuable outcomes—a smile and a "yes" from the female dance partner. They will have little motivation to adopt behaviors that are punished or not rewarded. **Vicarious learning** can be the major source of motivation (Bandura, 1977b). The social learner observes the model, notes whether he is rewarded or punished for the behavior, and imitates the rewarded behavior without receiving any direct reward. Bandura noted that learning new behaviors is often more dependent on observing the consequences to a model's responses than on direct reward or punishment (Goldhaber, 2000). The social learner observes one model receive the reward of a smile and a dance and imitates this behavior while forgetting the model who earned a glare and a rejection from his potential partner. Direct reinforcement is another source of motivation. This concept is the same as reinforcement in the traditional stimulus–response theoretical framework. Observational learning is followed by direct reinforcement. The social learner imitates his older friend in asking for a dance, and the admired friend later praises him for his behavior.

Social learners prefer certain models. Bandura (1977b) reported that the following characteristics of models are important: high status or prestige, competence, and high power. Observers make judgments about these characteristics by using cues such as appearance, speech, style, age, symbols of success, and signs of expertise. Bandura adds that the similarity between the observer and the model may be relevant. Thomas (1999) identifies another important characteristic: the degree of a model's success as indicated by positive consequences following his or her behaviors.

Bandura (1977b, 1999) and his interpreters have identified several types of modeling. In **abstract modeling,** the learner observes the person performing various responses and deduces the rule or principle common to the entire set of behavioral responses. Children, Bandura suggests, learn grammar such as passive construction—for example, "The rabbit was chased into its hole"—by observing other language users. Once the underlying rule is extracted from the modeled events, the social learner can generate new behaviors that are similar but go beyond the observed behavior to fit similar circumstances. The developing person learns to form new sentences using passive construction. In **creative modeling,** the observer combines aspects of the behavior of various models into a new amalgam that differs from the individual sources (Bandura, 1977b). Bandura illustrates this form of observational learning by discussing the creative genius Beethoven, who adopted the musical form of his predecessors but added greater emotionality.

There are different kinds of models, too. Social learners may imitate personal or **live models.** Just as important are **symbolic models,** including characters presented in books, cartoons, movies, television shows, video games, or other media formats. Such models can influence the learning of a large portion of a society (Bandura, 1999; Goldhaber, 2000). New technologies permit a single model to transmit new ways of behaving to vast numbers of people in numerous localities across the globe. Remember the controversy over

Janet Jackson's wardrobe malfunction at the Superbowl football game. Political leaders were concerned about the potential influence of this negative model on millions of television watchers. New technologies also increase significantly the number and variety of models available to members of a society.

Models can have different effects on the observer (Goldhaber, 2000). The model might elicit novel responses from the social learner. My dog learned to enjoy horse dung after observing my nephew's dog dining at the beach. Janet Jackson fans might experiment with novel forms of exposing their bodies after watching her performance. The model might inhibit or disinhibit previously acquired behaviors. A girl who had been casual about her choice of clothing might note how Jackson was punished and inhibit exhibitionist behaviors. The model might elicit similar but not identical forms of behavior. Music celebrities competing with Janet Jackson try out variations on her theme of "shocking" but attention-getting concert behavior.

CRITICAL COMMENTS

Albert Bandura's theory of social learning is highly regarded (Goldhaber, 2000). His emphasis on the social sources of human learning corresponds to social work's appreciation for the influence of the social environment. Bandura's work fruitfully expands the classical and operant learning foundation of applied behaviorism to include cognitive factors. Bandura and his colleagues have been commended for validating social learning tenets with an extensive series of carefully designed and rigorous experiments (Crain, 1980). Developmental theorists, however, criticize Bandura for not explaining how cognitive processes change as the person develops and how these changes affect observational learning (Miller, 2002). Miller also recommends that investigators into social learning processes give greater attention to social structural and ecological factors such as urbanization, a community's demographic profile, and gender norms.

APPLICATIONS OF BANDURA'S SOCIAL LEARNING THEORY

Social learning theory has great practical value. Bandura extended his ideas about symbolic modeling to the policy realm (Evans, 1989). He advocated for the reform of television at various congressional hearings. He urged development of more television programming (such as *Sesame Street*) illustrating rewards for constructive behavior and a reduction in programming that relies on action, noise, and violent behavior. Bandura applauded public broadcasting as one of the best means to improve offerings.

Bandura's mastery modeling programs have been widely used for skill development. For instance, mastery modeling has been used in the training of organization supervisors (Evans, 1989). First, videotapes present trainees with models dealing with typical social situations. Then, trainees translate their new knowledge into behavioral strategies and skills. Practice occurs in simulated and safe conditions, using role-plays followed by informative feedback. Finally, trainees are given weekly performance tasks to complete on the job. They report back to the group on successes and observe models perform skills in areas that are still challenging.

Social learning theory has been applied to the successful treatment of persons with phobias and other fears and inhibitions (Bandura, 1977b). The therapist models coping with a threatening activity; then the client enacts the modeled conduct until he or she can perform it without difficulty.

SELECTIVE PROPOSITIONS FROM APPLIED BEHAVIORISM: REINFORCEMENT SCHEDULES

Would you rather be paid for 10 therapeutic sessions with your clients or be paid at the completion of 40 hours of work no matter how many clients you served? Your choice tells me about your preferred reinforcement schedule. A **reinforcement schedule** specifies how frequently and under what conditions a person's behavioral responses are reinforced (Sundel & Sundel, 1999). The **fixed ratio reinforcement schedule** specifies the exact number of responses (or sessions with clients) that must be performed before reinforcement will be earned. One managed care organization may require that a clinical social worker conduct 5 sessions before being financially reimbursed. Another organization may require 15 clinical sessions. The **fixed interval reinforcement schedule,** in contrast, specifies the amount of time that must pass before the response is rewarded. Imagine that you work on a flexible 40-hour schedule from Monday through Friday and that your paycheck is available early Monday morning. This is a fixed interval pay arrangement. After clocking in for 40 hours of work, you find that your check is waiting for you when you arrive at the agency, and you begin to work again.

Sundel and Sundel (1999) propose that different reinforcement schedules evoke different patterns or rates of response. The following propositions are derived from this behavioral approach to labor. Social workers subject to a fixed ratio reinforcement schedule are likely to work at a high and consistent rate with few breaks until completing the ratio (10 helping sessions). Then they are likely to pause and relax for a brief time after the reinforcement (their reimbursement check). Let's consider another example of the fixed interval reinforcement schedule. The social work field interns at my social work program have 16 weeks to complete 224 hours of fieldwork. Students are encouraged to complete 16 hours per week in the field but can make some adjustments in their internship schedules for health or personal reasons. The behavioral theory proposes that students on this fixed interval schedule will generally perform fewer weekly hours at the beginning of the semester, more in the middle, and increase their weekly field hours toward the semester's end to meet the final deadline. After completion of the 224 hours and receipt of the reinforcement (a grade), the students are likely to take a pause and relax until the second semester starts. A few students may find the field experience so rewarding independent of the grade that they continue to work during the holiday break. These behavioral propositions indicate that the type of reinforcement schedule influences both the rate of behavioral response and the pause or cessation of behavior after reinforcement.

MAPPING APPLIED BEHAVIORISM

Figure 9.1 represents the translation of behavioral social work into eco-systems terms. In the following section, I will elaborate on the behavioral version of an eco-map and ecosystems practice.

FIGURE 9.1
THE
BEHAVIORAL
THEORY
VERSION OF
THE ECO-MAP

Source: Adapted with permission from *Family-Centered Social Work Practice* (p. 160) by A. Hartman & J. Laird, 1983. New York: The Free Press.

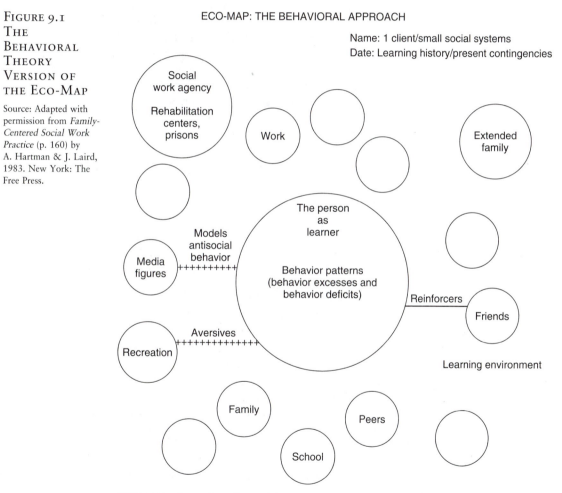

ECO-MAP: THE BEHAVIORAL APPROACH

Name: 1 client/small social systems
Date: Learning history/present contingencies

Fill in connections where they exist.
Indicate nature of connections with a descriptive word or by drawing different kinds of lines:
——————— for reinforcing and positive models
- - - - - - - - - - for weak reinforcers or aversives
+++++++ for aversives and negative models
Draw arrows along lines to signify flow of reinforcers, punishers, modeling, etc. ➝ ➝ ➝
Identify significant people and fill in empty circles as needed.

How Are Connections Conceptualized?

Behaviorists conceive of connections as the "exchange of contingencies" (Mattaini, 1990). Contingencies include the interrelated set of responses targeted for change, antecedents to the behavioral response, and consequences following the behavioral response. How we behave is contingent on (depends on) antecedents, stimuli, and consequences. We are linked to the people, groups, and organizations in the environment responding to our behavior with reinforcers or aversives. We also are linked to those in the environment whom we select as models. Reinforcers are the objects, activities, and events in our environment that increase our behavior. These may include money, praise, gentle caresses, public recognition, or food. **Aversives** are the objects, activities, and events that we try to avoid. They are unpleasant, painful, or irritating. Aversives may include blows to our body, loud noise, condemnation by others, and conflict during social interaction. These are likely to decrease the preceding behavior. **Models** are persons living or dead, real or imagined, that we observe, hear, or read about in our environment. They are persons that we admire or respect. Models provide examples of behavior that we imitate. A behavioral analysis translated into eco-systems terms would identify behavioral problems reported by the focal system and then map the entire network of contingencies. This would be the collection of people and groups that exchange reinforcers and aversives with us, and that serve as models for us or imitate our behavior.

How Is the Quality of Connections Differentiated?

Behaviorists might begin any consideration of the quality of connections by identifying the target behavior and making a judgment about the appropriateness, social acceptability, or desirability of that behavior. For example, social workers serve clients who physically abuse their children. This behavior is widely condemned as unacceptable in our society.

Positive connections, from the behavioral perspective, would be those contingencies that increase desired behaviors and decrease undesirable, socially unacceptable behaviors. An abusive parent, for example, might create a connection with members of a mandated parent education group. This group (and the court system) provides new instructions or rules about parenting, offers models of acceptable child-rearing behaviors, reinforces peaceful disciplinary procedures, and uses verbal condemnation to punish unacceptable hitting behavior.

Negative connections would be those contingencies that decrease the likelihood of desirable behaviors and increase antisocial or unacceptable behaviors. For example, the abusive parent may have some neighborhood associates who also abuse children. These peers might praise the mother for beating her daughter. They might act as daily models for forceful and bullying interactions with children. They might provide parenting instructions such as "Spare the rod and spoil the child," and they might berate and mock (punish) the mother when she uses gentle and nonaversive parenting techniques in public.

Tenuous connections would be those contingencies that have little strength in shaping or changing the targeted behavior toward or away from the desired quantities or qualities. A distant aunt's recommendations about ideal parenting might have little force, for example.

WHAT IS THE TYPICAL FOCAL SYSTEM?

The behaving person is the focal unit for behaviorist social workers. Unlike some other theoretical traditions, however, the inner experience (personality or mind or psyche) would not generally be broken into component parts and depicted in the center circle. Instead, behaviorists characterize the person in terms of his or her total repertoire of behaviors: what the person does in numerous social situations (school, peer groups, family, and so on). Behaviorists often characterize this repertoire in terms of behavior excesses or behavior deficits (Baldwin & Baldwin, 1998). **Behavior excesses** are behavior patterns such as overeating, drinking excessively, dominating conversations, displaying anger daily and intensely, and nonstop monitoring of one's overt and covert behavior. Behavior excesses may contribute to assorted problems in living. **Behavior deficits** refer to the absence of behaviors and of the associated thoughts and feelings necessary for meeting environmental challenges. Behavior deficits might include social skill deficiencies (communication, assertion, study, or relationship skills), self-care limitations (dressing, feeding, and hygiene), self-monitoring and self-control deficits, and gaps in the set of behaviors (abilities to reinforce one's action) necessary for personal change. Behaviorist social workers would help clients learn to decrease excesses and to develop or improve the adaptive behaviors that are missing.

HOW IS THE ENVIRONMENT CONCEPTUALIZED?

The environment, for the behaviorists, includes all those antecedents and consequences that influence a person's behavior. For cognitively oriented behaviorists, this includes the internal environment (private and unseen events) as well as the external environment (public, observable events). Baldwin and Baldwin (1998) compare the environment to a "stimulus collage." The environmental collage includes **primary reinforcers,** such as food, water, moderate temperature, rest, physical contact, sex, and drugs that are reinforcing for all human beings because of the biology that we have developed during species evolution. The environment also includes **primary punishers,** such as extreme temperatures and environmental conditions, blows to the body, poisons, burns and stings, and certain odors and tastes that are aversive and that humans automatically try to avoid. The environment also includes **secondary reinforcers** and **secondary punishers.** These are actions, objects, and events that we come to value or avoid because of what we learn as members of society rather than because of biological factors. Culture rather than nature establishes these experiences as reinforcing or punishing.

Human environments also include, according to the behaviorists, assorted antecedents that influence behavior. These are the behavioral models already discussed. The environment also includes **prompts** that help us start or stop a behavior. These can be words, signs, physical gestures, or other kinds of stimuli. For example, there are two switches on the side of my kitchen sink. One operates a light, and the other operates the sink's garbage disposal unit. I put a small note to remind me not to activate the garbage disposer accidentally. Social work students playing the role of helper in a simulation may receive subtle prompts (a whispered word or empathic facial expression) from their fellow students reminding them to listen actively or to reflect feelings.

Environments also include **instructions** or rules. These are guidelines for behavior summarized in verbal form. These rules often communicate information about important contingencies (antecedents, behavior, and consequences) in shorthand. A residential program for nonviolent criminal offenders might convey this rule to all newcomers: "If you use any illegal substance during your weekend pass, then you will lose the privilege of leaving the facility for two months."

Some of the stimuli in a stimulus collage influence human behavior in an automatic way. However, people can learn to discriminate between different stimuli in the environment and respond differently depending on the stimuli. Social work students, for example, learn to differentiate between various emotional expressions of clients. Skillful discriminators will be able to tailor their helping responses to the displayed emotion of each client.

Albert Bandura (1999) provides a useful typology of environments. The organizing principle for his categorization scheme is the environment's responsiveness to intentional human behavior. The *imposed physical and sociostructural environment* is the total environment in which human agents behave. People are thrust into this environment by birth and circumstance. The rewarding and punishing aspects of this type of environment exist only as potentials; we have some limited control over how we think about and react to it. A migrant laborer must live in the camp but can alter his feelings about this imposed environment from positive to negative. The *selected environment* is that aspect of the total environment that people selectively activate. By their behavior, human agents select associates including role models, competencies worth developing, preferred activities, and preferred settings for performing these activities. Such selections create an actual and experienced environment situated in the imposed environment. The migrant laborer might associate with exemplary workers and participate in support activities offered at the local community center. Finally, Bandura identifies the *constructed environment*. Here human influence is greatest, and actors can to some extent shape their own destinies. People think and act creatively to generate new institutions and new social environments. The migrant laborer may enact leadership behaviors and persuade a local priest to offer a Sunday service at the camp. Success in the construction process is conditioned by the interplay of personal factors, behavioral choices, and the structural and cultural features of the total environment.

IS PARTICULAR EMPHASIS GIVEN TO ANY SYSTEMS?

Generally, behaviorists are interested in those agents in the larger environment that directly control the behavior of others. These agents are the persons, groups, organizations that reinforce or punish us in observable and regular ways. Behaviorists give primary attention to individuals who control our behavior.

Even when behaviorists give attention to groups and communities, they prioritize attention to individual members of the social systems. Some behaviorists, however, do give focal attention, at times, to mid-level social systems: couples, groups, families, or organizations. Couples, for example, might be helped to analyze their behavioral patterns and develop **behavioral contracts** involving agreements to increase the exchange of reinforcements. Groups might agree on behavioral goals and then provide opportunities for demonstrating, coaching, rehearsing, and reinforcing desired behaviors. Organizations might be redesigned with the help of behavioral social workers to provide a new system of reinforcements. Schools for developmentally challenged adults, for instance, often institute **token economies.** Tokens such as chips or stars are presented for performance of desired behaviors, and students can exchange these tokens at the end of the day for desired food or prizes.

The service-providing system identified by behaviorists often has a correctional or rehabilitative function. Behaviorists commonly work in prisons, group homes, boot camps, and community-based correctional agencies. In some of these settings, however, practitioners use a "behavioral" approach (the use of harsh and degrading punishment, for example) that would not be endorsed by most applied behaviorists.

Behaviorists are less likely than those affiliated with some other theoretical frameworks (symbolic interactionism or structural functionalism, for example) to consider group and organizational processes and dynamics other than those related to the three basic learning mechanisms. Behaviorists only minimally attend to large-scale social systems such as a society's culture, economy, or political order. Changes in global conditions are a low priority, too. Behaviorists often leave these factors in the background as indirect influences on behavioral patterns.

HOW ARE RESOURCES AND THEIR FLOW CONCEPTUALIZED?

All the activities, people, objects, and events that can be associated with a behavior as punishers or reinforcers are potential resources. All the people who can enact socially desirable behaviors and might be used as models of behavior patterns are potential resources. Those conditions and supports, such as transportation to a workplace, money, or educational materials, that make it possible for people to enter and use a learning environment are also potential resources.

Behaviorists assume a transactional or bidirectional flow of such resources. Every person is capable of punishing, reinforcing, or demonstrating behaviors to others. Likewise, each person might be the recipient of punishment, reinforcement, or a behavioral demonstration. Optimal transactions occur when interactants agree to exchange mutually beneficial contingencies.

WHAT DESCRIPTIVE WORDS ARE USED?

Behaviorists often use a language developed by psychologists engaged in laboratory research. I have discussed some of the ways that connections might be characterized (punishing, reinforcing, or neutral, for example). Behaviorists describe the antecedent aspect of a learned response in several ways (Baldwin & Baldwin, 1998). Stimuli may vary in complexity, from simple and familiar to novel, surprising, or ambiguous. Stimuli may differ in intensity, from low (soft, dim, gentle) to high (loud, bright, harsh). Stimuli may vary in meaningfulness. Certain stimuli may have little meaning to the person. Americans do not typically respond to the German word *Schadenfreude,* but Germans readily understand it as glee in a neighbor's misfortune. Other stimuli are very meaningful. Think of an American's likely response to the phrase "stock market crash." Behaviorists characterize the strength of a response in a particular way (Sundel & Sundel, 1999). Connections or contingencies may result in responses that vary by rate (how frequently they occur), duration (how long they last), or intensity (measured in various ways).

Behaviorists do not use a concept like *social system.* They prefer less complex concepts like *network of contingencies* or *patterns of behavior.* Thus, the theory does not include a set of descriptors to characterize social systems.

HOW IS CHANGE CONCEPTUALIZED?

For behaviorists, the change process is systematic and scientific. The following is a brief summary of the major steps. After intake, the worker conducts a behavioral assessment. This involves gathering data about the client's learning history and the client's contemporary configuration of environmental rewards, punishments, and models. Assessment tools might include interviews, observations, role-plays, and behavioral checklists, but each tool should be well established and validated. Peers, family, and other system members who are involved in the relevant behavioral contingencies might contribute information. Problem analysis would require identifying the specific contingencies (antecedents and consequences) that maintain the problematic behavior or increase the difficulty of learning new behaviors. Problem analysis would also involve identifying the characteristics of the problematic behavior (strength, rate, duration, intensity). Goal setting would be in behavioral terms, specifying the desired behaviors in measurable form. Resources and obstacles relevant to goal attainment would be identified. Intervention would consist of providing new learning experiences and/or rearranging the environment to promote appropriate and adaptive behaviors. Behaviorists have tested and refined many intervention procedures. Assertiveness training, model presentation, positive reinforcement, discrimination training, systematic desensitization, thought stopping, shaping, and negative reinforcement are just a few of the possible methods (Gambrill, 1994).

The social worker is the expert. The worker would select the procedures best matched with the problem and develop a behavioral contract. Those individuals and organizations in the ecosystem controlling reinforcements, punishments, and models would agree, ideally, to be part of the change plan. The behavioral change program is implemented, and the social worker helps the client make the desired change and plan to maintain these changes in the natural environment. Systematic and scientific evaluation of each phase of the behavioral change process would help the worker and client document that the problem has been resolved, as indicated by the timely achievement of the desired behavioral change. Throughout the planned change process, the social worker acts as a highly skilled behavioral engineer with mastery of the varied technologies for changing behavior.

One of my practice-oriented research projects evaluated a behavioral approach to the change process (Forte, 1997, 1999). In the spring of 1993, many in the United States were considering a revision of the concept of government and a new understanding of the nation's obligation to its poor and undervalued members. During this time, two representatives of Home Base, a local agency coordinating regional efforts to help the homeless, invited themselves to my undergraduate social work class. They spoke eloquently for 50 minutes, documenting the dramatic increase in the number of homeless in our area, the inability of service providers to meet client needs, and their troubled feelings about moving possessions of the newly homeless to a storage facility. Many of my social work students were receptive to their plea. Together, several of my students and I decided to recruit other volunteers. We designed a one-year pilot project involving Christopher Newport University students and area agencies serving the homeless and christened it CREW-VA (Creative Response Empowering Worthwhile Volunteer Activity). We hoped to change students' commitment to service by fostering behavioral habits of helping.

Several steps in our socialization-for-altruism program used behavioral ideas. Students were placed in agencies that agreed to serve as learning laboratories. Students could accept an individual weekly placement at one of the local organizations serving the homeless, including a soup kitchen, two shelters, and an information and referral center, or they could participate in one of the special group events developed to provide services to the homeless. These included a three-day "Coats for Kids" drive, two days of home building with Habitat for Humanity, and a Christmas dinner and party for 15 families residing in a shelter.

Social workers and teachers provided various structured learning activities that modeled the behaviors and skills necessary for successful membership as a volunteer. In the social agency, additional modeling activities included the typical agency orientation and demonstration processes by which the students were taught appropriate volunteer behaviors. In a weekly one-hour seminar, we made use of a variety of other observational learning strategies. For example, there was a series of presentations on topics such as the extent of area homelessness, economic contributors to homelessness, city housing policies, types of homelessness, types of service agencies, needs of homeless subgroups including the mentally ill, substance abusers, and HIV-infected persons, legal advocacy, philanthropic and civic responses to homelessness, and pathways off the streets. These didactic presentations were given by carefully picked regional and state experts who modeled adept and committed service to this population. The three social work faculty members facilitating the service seminar did so as volunteers, and also demonstrated their way of serving at each class. Additionally, senior social work students demonstrated various helping behaviors during several group activities. Class members were coached until they felt comfortable trying out these behaviors in their agencies.

We used shaping activities to present the novice volunteers with reinforcements and gentle persuasion. For example, a service reward structure was established. Students were asked several times to affirm their intentions to serve and report on their experiments with a service identity. Public praise from teachers and peers was provided during such conversations. Volunteer activities at special events were recorded and displayed prominently on the campus, resulting in positive recognition. Coat-drive photos were presented in the local paper, and videotape footage of home-building efforts appeared on the TV news. Students also earned one credit for participation in the seminar. Many students were acknowledged by the volunteer service coordinators in their agencies and invited to participate in volunteer appreciation events. The CREW-VA service-learning project concluded by certifying 20 students as "bona fide" volunteers.

Program evaluation at the end of the project indicated that we were successful in teaching habits of helping. The project modeled and shaped student behavior so that substantial service was provided in a variety of social agencies over many hours to numerous homeless adults and children. During the semester, 1463 homeless beneficiaries received more than 1800 hours of free service. Students reported that volunteering had become part of their behavioral repertoire. Many students ranked the volunteer role as one of their most salient or important memberships. Considering that the six other roles competing for salience included those related to family, religion, work, and ethnicity, the finding that 40% of the students rated volunteering in their top three memberships is noteworthy. No student viewed the volunteer role as only a rank of six or seven. Eighteen of 20 students stated that they were very likely or somewhat likely to perform volunteer behaviors in the next six months. The two others made a point of telling the social work faculty that they found volunteering rewarding but as graduating seniors they were compelled to work and pay debts. Seventeen students planned to volunteer 14 or more hours over the coming year, with a mean expected amount of service for all 20 students of 75 hours—better than an hour of service per week. Finally, 16 of the students estimated that there was a stronger than 75% probability that they would volunteer soon; the modal response on this variable was 100% (n = 10).

HOW ARE ACTUAL AND IDEAL ECO-MAPS CONTRASTED?

The ideal eco-map would describe environmental conditions that support desired and socially appropriate behaviors. Good work at the workplace would result in praise, bonuses, and promotions. Classes would include stimulation that elicits the attention of each student and would reinforce models of diligent, creative, and cooperative academic problem solving. All of those in the environment with influence over our behavior would refrain from the use of punishment as much as possible.

Punishment has many disadvantages as a behavioral control procedure (Sundel & Sundel, 1999). It has less effect when the punisher's surveillance stops. It evokes aggression from the person punished. It signals that the punisher is someone to be avoided. It may suppress both inappropriate and appropriate behavior. It can serve as a model for the use of aversive techniques. It is often ineffective, especially if it is not administered immediately after the targeted behavior or if it is perceived as unfair (administered in different ways to different people for the same behavior).

In the ideal ecosystem, the client would have knowledge of all the contingencies influencing her behavior. The client would also have a sense of **self-efficacy,** the perception that she has the power to avoid aversives and increase reinforcements to achieve behavioral goals. The client would see herself as able to select models who exemplify socially desirable behavior, who are reinforced in public for their exemplary action, and who are similar in some ways to the client. Besides the perception of efficacy, clients would have the real power, in the ideal eco-map, to influence their environment in positive ways.

I will briefly elaborate on Bandura's (1977a, 1986) efficacy theory of empowerment as a tool to create ideal ecosystems. Bandura discusses efficacy at both the individual and collective level. At the level of the person, Bandura (1983) defines perceived self-efficacy as "judgments about how well one can organize and execute courses of action required to deal with prospective situations" (p. 23). A person with high **efficacy expectations** appraises his competence or efficacy and concludes that he can perform a particular behavior successfully. High self-efficacy translates, Bandura argued, into accomplishments, motivation, personal well-being, and increased control over life events (Evans, 1989).

Bandura (1977a) also theorized about **outcome expectations,** or what Gecas (1989), an expert on self-efficacy, calls *system responsiveness:* the person's appraisal of the environment and of the likelihood that a given behavior will lead to a desired outcome. People may feel hopeless and believe that behaviors aimed to improve conditions are futile, either because of low efficacy expectations or because of low outcome expectations, perceptions of an unresponsive social system. People may even have knowledge of their capabilities and a high sense of self-efficacy but anticipate that the environment will undermine attempts at effective behavior. Children of color in poor urban school systems, for example, might possess the motivation to achieve academically and possess good learning skills and attitudes but become discouraged because of social constraints such as lack of textbooks and computers, poor quality of teachers, scorn from peers directed at academic achievers, and distractions related to deteriorating school buildings and unsafe streets.

At the group level, Bandura (1986) theorized about **collective efficacy,** group members' shared beliefs about the group's ability to engage in concerted and successful political action. Collective efficacy helps sustain group members' commitment to a social change project; the opposite, collective powerlessness, leads to political inaction or apathy (Gecas, 1989). Groups whose members believe in the collective's efficacy are characterized by a greater investment in social change efforts, greater persistence in the face of obstacles and setbacks, and greater accomplishments than groups with lower collective efficacy.

Social workers can use Bandura's efficacy theory to work toward ideal ecosystems. Bandura explicitly referred to the application of his theory to practice as an "empowerment model," stating "if you really want to help people you provide them with the competencies, build a strong self-belief, and create opportunities for them to exercise these competencies" and "we empower people with the coping skills and a strong sense of coping efficacy" (Evans, 1989, p. 16). Ozer and Bandura (1990) provide an empowerment approach for teaching women who have been physically or sexually assaulted as an illustration of the theory's application. Women were given an opportunity to acquire the self-defense knowledge, skills, and efficacy beliefs necessary for protecting themselves. The key component of the empowerment work was mastery modeling. Members observed skilled models and practiced defense and escape behaviors in simulated assaults until mastery was achieved.

Social workers must carefully make the distinction between efficacy expectations and outcome expectations during the assessment of powerless clients. Recommended interventions will vary depending on the obstacle to social change. If the obstacle is efficacy-based futility, then the worker must help the client develop his or her set of competencies and expectations of personal effectiveness. Bandura (1977b) outlines several methods for increasing efficacy. Performance accomplishments are a very dependable source of efficacy. Successful mastery experiences increase clients' sense of efficacy. Vicarious experiences, observing others perform challenging or threatening activities successfully, can be used to increase efficacy. Verbal persuasion is another method. Here, the worker helps clients obtain information from others about their capabilities and helps clients yield to the arguments of others that the clients can cope successfully. Finally, workers can use emotional arousal. Clients tend to infer their capabilities from their emotional states. Fear and anxiety are associated with low efficacy. Workers can teach clients not to become overwhelmed by aversive emotional arousal and to persist in their judgments that success is possible.

If the obstacle is outcome-based futility, then the social worker must work to change group and environmental contingencies so that clients will increase their instrumentality—the likelihood that their behaviors will trigger rewards from the relevant groups, organizations, or institutions. Social workers can increase the freedom of members of oppressed groups, according to Bandura (1977b), by group interventions that provide skills, confident beliefs, and capacities for self-regulation. Group members will then have a wider range of behavioral options at their disposal for meeting environmental challenges and constraints. Social workers can help groups with a high degree of collective political efficacy use their efficacy-based tools to work together to solve public problems associated with poor schools, inadequate health services, self-destructive and risky behaviors, and the proliferation of nuclear weapons (Miller, 2002).

Contemporary social learning theorists would add a psychological component to the center circle. The ideal eco-map would depict as the focal system a client who has developed the array of behaviors necessary for self-efficacy, self-monitoring, self-reinforcing, self-management, self-control, and self-change (Baldwin & Baldwin, 1998). These behaviors would include the skills necessary for observing and learning from others, acquiring and remembering rules and instructions, eliciting and initiating helpful verbal prompts, using reinforcements and punishments to modify covert and overt behavior, and acting efficaciously in a variety of social situations.

How Are Issues of Diversity, Color, and Shading Addressed?

John Watson prioritized environmental influences on behavior.

> Give me a dozen healthy infants, well-formed, and my own specified world to bring them up in and I'll guarantee to take any one at random and train him to become any type of specialist I might select—doctor, lawyer, artist, merchant-chief, and yes, even beggar-man and thief, regardless of his talents, penchants, tendencies, abilities, vocations, and race of his ancestors. (1924/1970, p. 104)

This famous quote summarizes his rejection of theorists who claimed that tendencies to criminal and immoral behavior were inherited. Scientific claims for the genetic basis of different behavioral potentials of groups were wrong. Moreover, they were immoral because the claims excused families, schools, and societies from responsibility for their inadequate methods of training the young.

Applied behaviorists have continued in the tradition of John Watson. Differences between people and between human groups are best explained by differences in learning environments. Behaviorists consider differential consequences. People evoke different reactions from others in the social environment because of their physical characteristics, including age, sex, race, physical size and attractiveness, and their social characteristics, such as prestige, power, and status (Bandura, 1983). These differential reactions then shape the personality. For example, Bandura suggests that a person in a high position in an organizational hierarchy is more likely than a person of low social status to evoke deferential responses to his or her leadership behavior.

These differential social reactions influence behavioral inclinations and self-concept patterns.

Behaviorists study specific differences in consequences, such as differential reinforcement and modeling. In the 1970s, Ronald Akers and his behaviorist colleagues (Akers, 1977, 1996; Akers, Krohn, Lanza-Kaduce, & Radosevich, 1979) slightly altered Sutherland's differential association theory of deviant behavior to make its use of behaviorist learning principles explicit. Akers drew from Skinner's work on operant learning and Bandura's work on imitative learning to theorize about "differential reinforcement," the process by which "we learn that some behavior is appropriate, approved, and likely to be rewarded in some situations and not in others" (1977, p. 51). Three processes of social reinforcement are central to becoming deviant. Initially, delinquent acts are learned through vicarious reinforcement, the observation of models rewarded or punished for their actions. The social learner may associate with parents who fail to behave as law-abiding citizens, with deviant peers, or with deviant members of socializing institutions such as group homes or schools. Models can be real or imaginary persons, and the social learner may also turn to models available in the mass media. Delinquent acts are then sustained through direct reinforcement, self-reinforcement, or vicarious reinforcement. The person likely to act deviant is the one who has received from others, given to him- or herself, or observed in others positive consequences following deviant acts. Reinforcement varies, however, depending on which actions are rewarded or punished. Thus, in contrast to the delinquent, the person whose deviant actions have been followed by punishment or by the removal of rewards will soon opt for conforming behaviors.

Turning to Sutherland's notion of definitions of behavior as acceptable or unacceptable, Akers (1977) proposed that these too could be explained in behavioral terms. He wrote that definitions are "verbal behavior (overt and subvocal) which can be reinforced" (p. 51). Definitions can be viewed as a type of social stimulus called a *discriminative stimulus*. The definition of an anticipated act—whether verbalized or thought about—becomes a cue that signals the actor to expect that a reinforcement or a punishment will follow the contemplated act. For example, the child who has repeatedly heard "lying is not right" and has been sanctioned for lying will use this verbalization in a later situation as a cue to refrain from the undesirable behavior. In summary, Akers specified the learning mechanisms essential to the creation of deviant behavior patterns. Variations in inclinations toward deviant definitions of behavior and toward behavior orientations (deviant or prosocial) are explained by variations in social learners' learning environments.

Behaviorists consider differences in patterns of association. With whom is the social learner likely to interact? Involvement in social networks is structured in the United States by race (Heimer, 1996), gender (Heimer, 1995, 1996), age, type of community, family wealth, neighborhood stability, and other variables influencing one's social location (Heimer & Matsueda, 1994). Heimer (1995) offered an example of how network involvement relates to behavioral patterns. Our social networks powerfully influence our definitions of the law and the reinforcements likely for breaking the law (positive peer reactions or enhanced esteem). Different sources of reinforcement have different ideas, for example, about what to reinforce and about how to reinforce behavior. Our society is characterized by extensive age segregation of social networks. The daily activities of youth rarely bring them into contact with adult models. Adolescents are directed to choose associates who are similar in age and in behavior patterns (Bandura, 1977b). As a result, they are likely to adopt the standards and activities common to these peers even if these are at odds with the law-abiding practices of adults. Heimer and Matsueda (1994) added that certain youth may live in communities characterized by high delinquency rates, broken families, much mobility, physical deterioration, and other forms of social disorganization. Pro-law social networks and effective behavior control efforts are often minimal in such communities. Big Brothers or Sisters and other positive models are also scarce.

Patterns of association with symbolic others also differ among groups. African Americans and women are exposed in the mass media to many stereotypical depictions of minority group members (Crain, 1980). Opportunities for symbolic modeling are limited to the set of models available in the dominant media outlets. Activists try to improve learning opportunities for their constituent groups by advocating for positive models—women and African Americans as doctors, scientists, political leaders, and judges, for example.

How would applied behaviorists conceptualize cultural differences? Thomas (2001) summarized the research on differences between countries and cultures from a social learning perspective. His literature survey included comparisons between East and West Germans, Chinese and Americans, Japanese and Americans, Germans and Americans, and European Americans and African Americans. He noted wide variability in learning environments across cultures, including differences in the types of behavior approved and admired, the degree of approval for certain behaviors, the appropriate consequences for approved and disapproved behavior, the ratio of positive to negative consequences, the use of corporal punishment as a preferred consequence, the kinds of people who exemplify admired behavior, the behaviors suggestive of social competence, and cultural beliefs about the emotions that should be experienced in relation to the public demonstration of personally efficacious behavior (pride, joy, guilt, or shame).

Culture-based differences in learning environments produce differences in behavior orientations. Thomas (1999) illustrated this point by summarizing the research on differences in the behaviors encouraged in males and females. Some countries (Japan, Germany, the United States) reward conventional displays of "masculinity" and "femininity." Masculinity includes assertive behaviors, tough behaviors, and behaviors geared toward the attainment of material success; femininity includes modest behaviors, tender behaviors, and behaviors geared toward improving the quality of relationships and life. These countries reward men who are masculine and women who are feminine. Some countries, however (the Nordic countries, Costa Rica, France, Thailand), reward both males and females when they engage in behaviors associated with femininity. Culture-based differences are manifest also in specific behavior preferences. Men are rewarded for dominance behaviors and for displays of superiority over women in India, Iran, and the Apache culture in the Southwestern United States. Different gender-based leisure-time activities and toy usage are rewarded in Haiti, Hong Kong, Japan, and Peru. In Hong Kong, for example, boys are rewarded for playing with toy cars and weapons; girls are shown how to play with dolls, stuffed animals, and cooking utensils and are rewarded for such play activities. Cultural differences are also evident in rewards for academic achievement, with interesting results. In Finland, intellectual activities by females are rewarded, and more than 50% of university graduates are women.

Thyer (1994) summarizes the behaviorist stance toward diversity: "cultural differences are not intrinsic to people but to the different environments in which they live and from which they learn" (p. 135). Applied behaviorists would not approve of grouping people on the eco-map by age, race, sex, or sexual orientation and using such groupings to make behavioral predictions. Grouping should be by characteristics of the group members' learning histories. Let's return to the example of antisocial behavior. Applied behaviorists would note that the prevalence of prisons, jails, and correctional institutions in the eco-maps of male, lower-class people of color does not indicate genetically based dispositions toward crime. Instead, socially structured differences in associations, in reinforcements and punishments, and in models better explain such group differences in deviant behavior.

WHAT WOULD BE ADDED OR DELETED?

The behavioral version of the eco-map will have a great similarity to the conventional eco-map. Mattaini (1990), for example, developed a behavioral eco-map that looked like Hartman's original eco-map. The behaviorists add specific detail (reinforcers, aversives, models) to the characterization of connections and ask social workers to operationalize all variables that emerge during assessment. Albert Bandura would recommend inclusion of the symbolic models important to the client system.

Large circles surrounding the focal system circle might be omitted. Some behaviorists see the large-scale social system as simply the aggregation of the behaviors of all the members of the system. They recommend against using complex and unnecessary theoretical concepts like culture or structure. The systems theory notion of boundary, for example, has no clear equivalent in the behavioral vocabulary. Technically, then, the line around social systems suggesting that groups of people have distinctive insides and outsides makes no sense to behaviorists.

Behaviorists might request a retrospective eco-map so that a client's learning history could be mapped. Behaviorists require scientific evaluation of all practice. They might recommend, therefore, the addition of a series of behavioral eco-maps, one for each measurement period established as part of a single system design. Evidence for changes in contingencies related to problematic client behavior could be easily displayed and shared.

THE LIMITS OF APPLIED BEHAVIORISM: A SOCIAL WORK APPRAISAL

I have reviewed earlier in the chapter some of the limitations of the behavioral approach to social work. Applied behaviorists may not adequately consider cultural differences in learning content and processes. Behaviorists who follow Skinner often underestimate the degree to which clients use higher mental processes. Several other criticisms of the tradition can be offered.

Behaviorism's root metaphor likens humans to animal. However, are humans more like animals or angels? Behaviorists stress the similarities between humans and other animals, especially in the ways we learn. Those learning processes and patterns that are common to humans and animals interest behaviorists. However, other theoretical frameworks, such as cognitive psychology and symbolic interactionism, focus on the distinctive capabilities of humans, qualities that emerged during human evolution and set us apart. These include our capacities for abstract thinking, for goal setting and choosing, and for communicating through complex social symbols. Adopting the behaviorist root metaphor would dispose workers to characterize humans in terms of qualities that have been found in rats, pigeons, monkeys, and other non-humans. Reinforcement schedules, positive and negative behavioral control, conditioned stimuli, and operant learning may be concepts appropriate to understanding lower animals. These animals behave automatically and in identifiable ways in response to varying external conditions. Humans are different. We are not passively shaped by external rewards and punishments. Humans interpret, choose, and actively respond to stimuli according to our values and our objectives. Humans have a degree of freedom from inevitable stimulus–response linkages. Our evolutionary heritage makes possible intelligence, the conscious consideration by inner imagery and conversation of alternative courses of action and the likely utility of these alternatives in solving current problems. Intelligent humans, unlike other animals, can replace automatic responses with delayed response. We can make probabilistic forecasts about the likely results of various action scenarios.

Many social workers, I suspect, assume that clients have special capacities, and most social workers prefer that theorists not mistake clients for animals. Responding to such criticisms, Albert Bandura (1999) has made some progress in integrating conceptions of the human capacity for symbolization and human agency into the behavioral theoretical edifice. Social workers might apply his theory to practice as an alternative to Skinner's radical behaviorism.

Behaviorism's root metaphor of practitioners as expert lab scientists leaves little place for the self-determination and self-direction that are central to the social work value and ethical system. Skinner and many of his successors adhered to a deterministic view of human behavior. Skinner commented once that "personal exemption from a complete determinism is revoked as a scientific analysis progresses" and "all behavior is determined, directly or indirectly by consequences" (cited in Baldwin, 1988, p. 122). Thyer (1988) views determinism favorably as a key assumption of behaviorism. His behavioral approach to social work "contends most emphatically that all human behavior has potentially identifiable causes located within the past and present environment of the individual" (p. 128). Such statements are in clear contrast to social workers' emphasis on the contribution of deliberation, choice, and planning to human behavior. Humans have the capacity for self-conditioning. We can teach ourselves to use a stimulus intentionally as a prompt—a word, gesture, picture, or physical directive that calls out a desired response. In an effort to increase my appreciative behaviors, for example, I might remind myself to "be thankful" before entering a social event and then reward myself after voicing gratitude. Social workers are realists and accept the possibility that some aspects of human activity are determined, and some clients are more vulnerable to conditioning than others. For example, biological necessities and the prior environmental reinforcement of particular impulses may determine the inclinations that emerge as a person prepares to act. However, many social workers would reject the claims that there are inevitable, direct, and easily identified determinants of all human activity and that the social worker is the best judge of these determinants.

Some versions of behaviorism fail to meet social work's standard of social justice. Katovich (1987) suggested that behaviorism harbors a political philosophy that supports oppressors. People are treated as captives of their learning history who can gain behavioral flexibility only with the aid of expert and authoritarian behavioral engineers. Social scientists and practitioners become oligarchs with a monopoly on knowledge of psychosocial change. Behaviorist tenets have supported the bureaucratic and elitist impulses of social control agents and have often become an extension of the government's apparatus for using power. I worked in a community correction agency, for example, where residential workers prided themselves on their use of "behavioral" approaches like group punishment for a rule violation by one offender, public humiliation, and the continuous removal of privileges for slight infractions. The behavioral imagery of control may also explain the prevalence of this approach in prisons, mental hospitals, income maintenance programs, and substance abuse agencies. Large-scale behavioral conditioning and manipulation technologies developed by behaviorally oriented media experts and marketing gurus have made conditioning quite effective. Such conditioning at the societal level has turned some citizens into a mass of lemmings, conformists who have forsaken their decision-making powers and have become the overweight, overmedicated, oversexed, and overstocked consumers desired by these salesmen. Behavioral procedures can be used in ways that dehumanize; such use will not produce thoughtful and collaborative-minded citizens, meaningful social communication, or societies based on mutual understanding. Many social workers prefer to conceive of the knowledge-building process as a partnership between social work scientists and community members.

Many social workers support the creation of egalitarian helping groups and communities where members are creative and innovative constructors of their own destinies and social order is accomplished by cooperative and mutually respectful collective action. Science and practice, these critics might suggest, are more justly advanced by theoretical approaches other than applied behaviorism.

A MODEL OF BEHAVIORAL TREATMENT FOR SUBSTANCE ABUSERS

Drawing from the behaviorist tradition, Munson and Schmitt (1996) suggested that behaviorists might assess behavioral patterns in a comprehensive way by using naturalistic inquiry. This research method studies problematic sequences of behaviors or stimulus–response chains in the everyday social contexts where they occur. This method is sympathetic also to the merging of cognitive and behaviorist approaches, and thus data about the client's perspective on his or her behavior are also collected. Slightly translating behaviorist concepts, the researchers attempted to learn about substance-using "triggers." Behaviorists refer to these as discriminative stimuli, antecedents that control the performance of a behavioral response (Sundel & Sundel, 1999). The following model summarizes the themes that emerged from their qualitative data analysis.

THE BEHAVIORAL PERSPECTIVE ON SUBSTANCE ABUSE PROBLEMS

Substance abuse is conceptualized as a chain of contingencies. For substance abusers, stimuli or triggers include occasions and settings where cognitive and emotional reminders of past drug experiences are activated. These triggers, in turn, lead to covert behavioral responses—substance-using self-statements and observations about the thoughts and feelings generated by the triggers. Although these covert responses cannot be seen, they are important links in the chain. The next link in the behavioral chain is the overt behavioral response to these private events. The response of drinking alcohol or using cocaine, for instance, often follows substance-using thoughts. The substance use has become a primary reinforcer that supports the entire chain. Secondary reinforcements such as praise from peers increase the strength of the chain's links.

THE BEHAVIORAL PERSPECTIVE ON ASSESSMENT

Using assessment tools such as substance-use journals, interviews, and behavioral observations, the researchers collected data from 47 adolescent participants in a residential drug treatment center. Nine types of drug-related triggers common to those in the treatment context were identified. "Direct use triggers" included seeing a beer bottle, smelling pot, or watching cocaine use by others; "contextual use triggers" were places and activities associated with past substance use, such as a bowling alley, swimming hole, or Fourth of July celebration; "symbolic triggers" included beer signs and sweatshirts with the word *Bud* on it; "pretend triggers" were imitations of some aspect of a prior drug experience, such as the person faking smoking marijuana; "mass media triggers" included television or magazine advertisements, film scenes of substance abuse, and music glamorizing use; "interaction triggers" included hearing "war stories" of previous drug use during talks with peers; "treatment-related triggers" included educational videos, role-plays, journals, and talks with staff that centered on substance use; "cognitive triggers" included random thoughts about previous drinking or dreams about user friends; "emotional triggers" were anger, depression, boredom, happiness, and other emotions that evoked drug use memories or urges. Social workers helping substance abusers should collect information about the triggers most relevant to their clients.

Munson and Schmitt (1996) then offered a social behaviorist analysis of the environment and the features of these stimuli. They noted that the triggers were omnipresent in the society and the treatment center. They resided both covertly in problem users' thoughts and overtly in the surrounding environment. Triggers could be understood temporally as reminding substance users of previous experiences while potentially moving the client to future use. Triggers are generally interpreted by the client rather than responded to automatically. They provoke critical moments in the behavioral chain. Thus, practitioners can identify triggers and use them as a therapeutic focal point for behavioral change.

The Behavioral Perspective on Intervention

Munson and Schmitt (1996) offered a temporal framework for understanding problematic drug-using chains of behavior. This contrasts somewhat with the more straightforward linear sequences (past learning history conditions present behavior) of the radical behaviorists. First, substance-related thoughts and feelings prompt problem users to enter the future in their minds. The clients experience a desire to be in drug-using situations and to use drugs soon. Second, the substance-use triggers call out the past by reminding problem users of past drug experiences. Third, clients learn, under ideal therapeutic situations, to resist the past and not allow triggers to intrude into the present or future. Fourth, some substance-using thoughts and feelings situate the client in the present in a way that reinforces substance use. Clients may relive the experience of using, for example, and experience again the physiological effects associated with past drug use. Clients may use objects in the immediate environment, such as a cigarette, to pretend that they are using drugs and enjoy this image. Fifth, Munson and Schmitt discussed "extinction" in temporal fashion. Successful clients disconnect memories and feelings of past drug-related experiences from former triggers. Sobriety entails reconstructing the past so that there is an "absence of drug-using memory." Environmental stimuli no longer elicit the conditioned substance-using response.

The treatment center's behavioral program attempted to break the chain of stimulus–response units. Specifically, clients were helped to change the antecedent conditions that initiated the chain reaction. For example, the environment was changed in a way that reduced the presence of discriminant stimuli. Commercial-free radio and television were provided. Group sharing of drug "war stories" was punished. Clients were sometimes restricted to the treatment center, thus helping them to avoid public situations that encourage using behaviors.

Other recommendations for intervention flow from this behavioral model. Clients might be helped to break the link between covert pro-drug-using behavior (thoughts, memories, images, and feelings) and overt using activity. They might be reinforced for substituting a response of "resisting drug use" after the substance-using thought occurs. Such behaviors might include engaging in treatment-related activities such as attending an Alcoholics Anonymous meeting, talking with staff, seeking the support of nonstaff others for help in fighting pro-drug-use feelings and thoughts, or engaging in nontreatment behaviors such as walking or praying because these behaviors are not compatible with substance use.

Clients can also be helped to change the consequences of substance-using responses. Following worker instructions, they might think about the negative consequences of use. Plans can be developed so that lapses in sobriety are followed with punishment, or the worker and clients might increase the reinforcers for substance-resisting behaviors such as commendations for progress toward a "sober self."

LEARNING ACTIVITIES

1. Develop a list of potential reinforcers. These are things, activities, and the behaviors of others that provide you pleasure. Create a list of aversives, also. These are things, activities, and behaviors of others that are unpleasant or annoying. How might you increase the reinforcers and reduce the aversives in your environment?

2. Identify a person you might use as a model of effective and responsible social work practice. Carefully observe this person in a helping situation. Make note of several verbal and nonverbal behaviors that the model displays. Develop a plan for rehearsing or role-playing these behaviors until you can perform them comfortably.

3. Who are the contemporary symbolic models emulated by some of your clients (or friends)? Make an effort to learn about several of these models. Attempt to answer the following questions: Why was each

model chosen? What behaviors are clients imitating? In what ways are clients learning acceptable and socially appropriate behaviors from their models? In what ways are clients learning unacceptable or lawbreaking behavior from the models? How might you encourage your clients to pick prosocial models and to reject deviant models?

4. Trace how you learned to become a man or a woman. What behaviors were you taught to associate with masculinity and femininity? Who taught you about gender-appropriate behavior? What rewards and punishments were used during these lessons? What models did you emulate? What changes would you recommend in the social learning process for today's boys and girls?

5. Identify a behavior that you would like to change. Briefly describe the situation or problem area. Clearly and fully specify the target behavior. Make your description empirical

(describe behavior that can be observed or heard), and report on what you would like to do differently. Note the beginning and end of the target behavior. Indicate how you want to change the rate (frequency in a given time period), duration, or intensity of the target behavior. Comment on how the behavioral change relates to the problem situation.

6. Assess your sense of self-efficacy. In what situations do you most fully believe in your efficacy? In what situations do you have doubts about your ability to act efficaciously? What are some of the correlates (emotional, cognitive, and behavioral) for you of low self-efficacy? How might your self-efficacy differ if you had been raised in a community characterized by poverty, prevalent attitudes of hopelessness, distant and nonresponsive political leaders, and numerous uncontrollable threats to your safety and health?

7. Construct an eco-map translated into the vocabulary of the behavioral approach. What are some of the behavioral patterns that characterize your transactions with others in the learning environment? Which people are the sources of reinforcers, aversives, or models? Characterize specific connections with some of these people as reinforcing, punishing, modeling desired behaviors, or modeling undesired behaviors. What contingencies (related antecedents, behaviors, and consequences) would you like to change?

8. Think about your ideal eco-map, and develop a behavioral self-change plan. Select an area for improvement. Develop a strategy for collecting data about the problem or challenge (target behaviors, possible controlling antecedents, negative consequences for self or others, possible reinforcers). Set a goal in precise and measurable terms. Identify one or two relevant behavior change techniques. Show how you will monitor and judge the effectiveness of your behavioral change program.

ADDITIONAL RESOURCES

Additional resources are available on the book companion website at **www.thomsonedu.com/ social_work/forte.** Resources include key terms, tutorial quizzes, links to related websites, and lists of additional resources for furthering your research.

APPLIED SYMBOLIC INTERACTIONISM

CHAPTER 10

Shelly Harrison/IndexStock

INTRODUCTION

Applied symbolic interactionism, interactionist social work, was conceived sometime in the 20-year period from 1890 to 1910 (Forte, 2003). This was a time of great innovation and productive scholarship by academics at the University of Chicago such as John Dewey and George Herbert Mead. Social workers were making their mark, too. During this period, Jane Addams started serving the poor and immigrants of Chicago in community centers. She and her friend Ellen Starr founded Hull House in 1899. They soon began to provide basic social work services to about 2000 people per day. Addams and the other Hull House workers offered groups to help new citizens, advocated to improve working and living conditions, and lobbied for humane laws and policies. Her work inspired many interactionist theorists, social group workers, community organizers, and social work leaders. Most social workers have forgotten, however, that her closest colleagues were professors who taught pragmatism and interactionism (Forte, 2004a, 2004b).

Dewey, Mead, and Addams were close friends, professional collaborators, and partners in many service and social action projects. They shared a commitment to the philosophy of **pragmatism** (Forte, 2003). Pragmatists assert that the best knowledge helps community members solve problems of living together, and facilitates the construction of democratic and caring social organizations. Pragmatist philosophers insist also that human beings are active agents, not passive respondents; that truth is to be tested by the practical consequences of the asserted beliefs; and that members of social groups together create useful stories to characterize reality. Pragmatists posit that numerous different groups and organizations produce many different versions of reality. Dewey, Mead, and Addams were great pragmatists. Jane Addams was a practitioner with an interest in scholarship and a commitment to applied pragmatism. Dewey and Mead were scholars interested in service and respected for their intellectual pragmatism. Each member of the triad believed passionately in the pragmatist tenet that theory and practice should not be separated. All three founding figures were committed to thinking and doing, to the university and the agency, and to social science and social work.

RELATED DIALECTS, ASSOCIATED SCHOOLS OF THOUGHT

The official formalization of a sociological version of pragmatism occurred at the University of Chicago. The naming of the tradition *symbolic interactionism* is credited to Herbert Blumer in 1937 (Forte, 2001; Shalin, 2000). Some refer to the theoretical tradition as the *Chicago school of sociology*, but very important variations on the tradition are linked to schools in Berkeley, California and in Iowa. For the past two decades, interactionists have emphasized commonalities across distinct schools of thought, and all applied theorists refer to the dominant and shared interactionist language rather than to dialects. Therefore,

I will not pursue the differences among Chicago, Iowa, and Berkeley approaches to the theoretical perspective.

Unfortunately, there is no complete history of the partnerships between symbolic interactionists and social workers, nor is there any consensus regarding the best name for the use of symbolic interactionism as a practice theory. *Applied interactionism, applied* or *social pragmatism*, the *membership perspective*, and *interactionist social work* are all contenders for the title. In the 1960s, social work theorists also developed *socialization approaches* to practice that drew heavily from interactionism (Forte, 2004a, 2004b). Contemporary social workers often refer to *constructivism* or *social constructionist* approaches to social work. These have much similarity to applied symbolic interactionism (Forte, 2003). In this chapter, I will refer to the tradition as *applied symbolic interactionism* and use our theory translating tools to demonstrate the tradition's contemporary utility.

APPLIED SYMBOLIC INTERACTIONISM: EXEMPLARY MODELS

As my first paragraphs suggest and recent historians of the social sciences (Deegan, 1988; Shalin, 2000) have documented, applied symbolic interactionism has identifiable parents.

JOHN DEWEY

John Dewey (1859–1952) made major contributions to the specification of a problem-solving method that might be called "intelligent social reconstruction" (Campbell, 1992). This is a pragmatic framework for cooperative, rational, and creative inquiry by civic groups committed to improving social arrangements. Dewey rejected forcefully the separation of ideas from practice. He believed that the intellectual's job demands the use of research and writing skills to ameliorate troublesome conditions, that social philosophers should examine the real social needs of societal members, that theorists should direct their imagination and inquiry to possibilities for betterment (Stuhr, 1998). Among other theoretical contributions, Dewey provided an interactionist conception of knowledge, a person-connected-to-environment theory of human behavior, an approach to personal habits that emphasized their social sources, and a "teach the whole child" framework for progressive education (Petras, 1968a).

John Dewey believed passionately that life in a democratic society requires that all community members develop habits of social usefulness and service. Dewey found personally that his engagement with the urban difficulties faced by Chicagoans and identified by social workers stimulated theory development (Feffer, 1993). He worked with Jane Addams to attack corruption, challenge power holders, and remedy the educational troubles of Chicagoans. Dewey and Addams collaborated also to improve conditions for workers and for new immigrants. Dewey and Addams read each other's books, and, according to his daughter, Dewey deepened his faith in the centrality of democratic processes to education because of his contact with Addams and other Hull House members (Dewey, 1951). John Dewey was a hardworking member of the Hull House Board of Trustees (Deegan, 1988). He was impressed by the settlement house model and hoped to see schools staffed by residential social workers carrying out settlement-like educational, social, and recreational programs (Davis, 1967).

Besides his civic engagement with Hull House, Dewey was president of the League for Industrial Democracy, the League for Independent Political Action, and the People's Lobby. He consistently worked to reform the Chicago school system (Dykhuzien, 1973). He also believed that the extremes created by capitalism were damaging American democracy (Denzin, 1994), and he called urgently for a fundamental redistribution of financial wealth as a way to aid those devastated by the Great Depression (Campbell, 1992).

George Herbert Mead

George Herbert Mead (1863–1931) was a scholar of great distinction and a dedicated, versatile practitioner. He contributed in widely recognized ways to interactionist sociology and developed a powerful theory of progressive social change. Smith (1931), a student of Mead, reported that Mead's life concern was "amelioration through understanding" (p. 369). Mead gave secondary importance to his theoretical work on the social self. He advanced concepts relevant to practice, including the working hypothesis, international-mindedness, narrow versus larger selves, the universal human society, the democratic assumption, intelligent social reconstruction, and institutionalizing the revolution (Forte, 2001). Each of these concepts illuminates aspects of the planned change process.

Mead wrote more than 80 articles and reviews dealing with topics of interest to social workers: sympathy, the school system, war and peace, conscientious objection, truancy, punitive justice, vocational training, social settlements, moral problem solving, labor–management tensions, economic inequality, human rights, international relations, and philanthropy. Mead's lifelong interest in service began with his exposure to the Social Gospel movement and to activists in Oberlin, Ohio, a town that had earlier provided an Underground Railroad station and one of the first colleges to admit African Americans (Shalin, 2000).

For Mead, there was no gap between theory and praxis (Deegan, 1988). He even considered a career as a Christian social worker before accepting academic employment. Mead served on numerous committees and boards, many of them composed of members from different professions, including the University of Chicago Social Settlement Board of Trustees, the Immigrant's Protective League, the Chicago City Club, the Child Welfare Committee, and the Illinois Progressive Party. He translated abstract ideas into terms that various groups could understand, lecturing frequently at Hull House, at the Chicago School of Civics and Philanthropy, at the City Club, and at the National Conference on Social Work. Mead also joined collective movements that broadcasted the needs and rights of laborers, immigrants, and women, and he collaborated with settlement workers in empirically studying community conditions. His academic contributions at the University of Chicago included successful efforts to break down disciplinary walls between philosophers, teachers, sociologists, and social workers.

Mead worked closely with social workers. In 1910, he chaired a subcommittee with Sophonisha Breckinridge, a social worker, and Anna Nicholes, the head of Northwestern's Neighborhood House, charged with finding a way to end a garment worker strike (Deegan, 1988). He worked with Graham Taylor, a social work leader, on various community projects. Taylor praised Mead as an expert and catalyst in the social settlement and city club movements. Mead served as the doctoral chair for Jessie Taft, a social worker. Blessed with abundant energy, he engaged in scholarship with lasting effect while also doing much social work, including raising funds for a school for the deaf and speech impaired, assisting in labor arbitration, marching for women's suffrage, advocating school reform on behalf of truants and teachers, and orchestrating a massive survey of the stockyards district.

Mead (1918) imagined and tried to realize a vision of the ideal society: one that paid workers the wages necessary for adequate housing and a good standard of living; ensured safe and healthful living conditions for everyone, including the economically weak; provided socially necessary education; offered opportunities for political influence; demanded a government that distributed wealth produced by community members toward the community's welfare; and pursued foreign policies that universalized democracy and compassion.

JANE ADDAMS

We know now that Jane Addams (1860–1935) was the "founding mother" of symbolic interactionism (Deegan, 1988). She was also an exemplary model of the politically active and scholarly social worker. Although inspired and assisted by others, Addams essentially developed "settlement house theory," a theory that powerfully influenced social group workers and community organizers. She taught as a visiting lecturer at the University of Chicago Extension School and lectured at the Chicago School of Civics and Philanthropy. She was a charter member of the American Sociological Society and addressed the group on four occasions. Addams published five articles in the *American Journal of Sociology.* Major social theorists reviewed her books favorably. Mead (1907), for example, viewed Addams' book *The Newer Ideals of Peace* as "the expression of enlightened social intelligence in sympathetic contact with men, women and children" (p. 128). He praised her for revealing the reality of life as experienced by immigrants, workers in industrial factories, and poor city dwellers, a reality hidden from academics by their "academic and political abstractions" (p. 128). A research study that she edited, *Hull-House Maps and Papers,* was published in 1895 and later emulated by Chicago School sociologists (Shalin, 1990).

Hull House, administered by Jane Addams, was a center designed for creative problem solving. It became the center at which reformers, politicians, and academics would meet to discuss pressing public problems (Bulmer, 1984). Here are just a few of many Hull House innovations: the first citizen preparation classes; the first group work school; the first "little theater" in the United States; the first settlement with male and female residents; and the first Chicago investigations of sanitation, cocaine distribution, midwifery, infant mortality, and children's reading. Jane Addams transformed Hull House into a place where civic and academic leaders could observe and learn about the problems of the underclass. Reformers, politicians, and academics met there as equals; identified the social processes retarding community growth; and conceived of theories, techniques, and programs for advancing positive social processes.

With Dewey and Mead, Jane Addams recommended an approach to social work practice that related social theory to specific practical situations (Ross, 1998). She scorned "the men of substantial scholarship [who] were content to leave to the charlatan the teaching of those things which deeply concern the welfare of mankind" (Addams, 1910/1990, p. 247). The settlement actualized in daily practice, for instance, the interpretive tenets of symbolic interactionism. Settlement workers learned to create ways to improve two-way communication (symbolic interaction) between Chicago's marginal and established members. These applied interactionists interpreted American institutions, customs, and norms to settlement house members who came from other social worlds and who were bewildered by Chicago. Furthermore, settlement workers interpreted the experiences of the settlement members, experiences alien to the mainstream, in ways that the privileged and fortunate members of Chicago could understand and accept (Ross, 1998).

Jane Addams and the other Chicago practitioners grappled, like George Herbert Mead, with tough problems (Feffer, 1993). Each week thousands of needy people sought services from Hull House, the community center established by Addams and supported by Chicago sociologists. These needy persons belonged to many cultural groups, spoke various languages, told diverse life stories, and possessed only rudimentary understandings of the knowledge required of citizens. The practice scene was turbulent. Industrialists and laborers battled repeatedly. Revolutionaries and radicals called for violent action. Business and political leaders often evaded their responsibility to the poor. Addams and her colleagues attempted to mediate between dissenting groups and find common values and interests.

HANS FALCK

Professor Hans Falck (1988) is the preeminent translator of symbolic interactionism into terms for use by social workers. He started from the pragmatist and interactionist assumption that the self and the society are indivisible, and he proposed that clients are members, not separate individuals. Membership behavior is the client's active reconciliation of demands from one's contemporary membership groups, demands from those unseen and historical membership groups related to family and peers, and demands from one's self as these relate to life interests and concerns. Interactionist social work, Falck proposed, is the rendering of professional aid to clients in the management of membership. Practitioners work with members to solve membership problems and to help membership organizations realize their potentials for full, satisfying, and democratic participation. Notice how closely this formulation accords with that of the great symbolic interactionist Anselm Strauss (1977), who wrote of "the complete therapist, were he to have a sociological understanding of the patient as a member of a variety of interacting groups" (p. 297). Change the word *therapist* to *social worker* (and *he* to *he or she*), and this quote becomes a guiding motto for Falck's membership model of social work.

APPLIED SYMBOLIC INTERACTIONISM: ROOT METAPHORS

Symbolic interactionists have made use of many different metaphors to help them develop their theories (Forte, 2001). Images from and comparisons to the arts abound. Face-to-face interaction is like a dance routine, fluid yet intricately coordinated. We dance or interact well with some but poorly with others. Group interaction is like playing jazz music. Members of a jazz ensemble often improvise, but they do so with an appreciation for jazz conventions, for the performance setting, and for the rest of the band.

The essence of symbolic interaction, like the essence of art, is its representative quality (Skidmore, 1975). People, like artists, attempt to emphasize or clarify meanings about a self, a relationship, a situation, and an environment that may be obscure or not fully appreciated. Artists use paints, film, sound, language, or other mediums; but people primarily use language. A successful interaction, like the interpretation of a work of art, depends on an accurate understanding of the other's creative acts and intentions. Social life has also been compared to theater. A social worker, for example, performs differently and plays different roles in front of different audiences. Social workers make up their faces and pick out the clothing or costumes that are consistent with the professional images they wish to project. Social workers enlist the help of many others to carry out social programs. These people are like the caterers, decorators, actors, extras, stage crew, and costume designers in a theatrical production. They help social workers successfully "stage" a fund-raising event or a volunteer recognition ceremony.

Interactionist researchers are like Impressionist painters. They aim to provide accurate portrayals of social scenes and relationships. However, the objective and clean perception sought by behaviorists and other positivist social scientists is neither possible nor interesting to symbolic interactionists (Forte, 2001). Instead, interactionists scan the human landscape and look for the subtle, complex, messy, or hard-to-see features. They offer creative interpretations of these landscapes, portraits that capture the character, contour, colors, and context of people doing things together every day. Understanding these metaphors may help you make sense of interactionist theory and research.

THE PERSON AS MEMBER

The central metaphor of symbolic interactionism, the metaphor with greatest relevance to social work, is the one identified by Hans Falck (1988). Symbolic interactionists assume that human beings are members. Most people have memberships in at least four kinds of groups. First, we are members of the same species. Because of this membership, we develop special and basic capacities for participating in human groups. These include abilities for self-awareness, for thinking, for communicating with symbols, and for understanding what others are communicating. Next, we are born into memberships in **primary groups** like the family, and we join other primary groups of friends and schoolmates. These groups socialize us so that we are prepared to use our special capacities to participate responsibly and effectively in the various membership organizations deemed important in our society. Then, we are recruited or drafted into many **secondary groups** after childhood. Secondary group socialization is a process by which "membership coaches" (teachers, mentors, employers, and social workers, for example) help us to develop advanced capacities or membership competencies. These allow us to join sports groups, work groups, civic groups, and professional groups. Social work students, for example, experience a transformation process from novices or absolute beginners to apprentices to full-fledged members of the social work profession (and, hopefully, to a national social work membership association). Finally, we have memberships in **tertiary groups.** These are the categories of people, and the large-scale institutions, in which face-to-face interaction never occurs. Western society, for example, groups people by gender, race, age, and sexual orientation. You will never meet all the others in your racial category. Yet your experiences as a member of society, and as a member of primary and secondary groups, are strongly influenced by your tertiary memberships. Women and African Americans, for example, have a harder time securing membership in the club known as the United States Senate than European American men.

The membership metaphor suggests that human beings are never alone. We share companionship in face-to-face ways with other members of our groups. These are our seen memberships. We also interact indirectly or vicariously in large-scale membership organizations by watching our favorite baseball team as one of the fans or by logging on to a website for followers of a particular musical group. We talk to unseen members silently, in our mind when no one is present. Even a modern Robinson Crusoe alone on a barren island as in *Castaway* will create an imaginary friend out of a volleyball to form a membership group of two, and thus lessen the agony of isolation.

THE ENVIRONMENT AS SOCIAL CLUBHOUSE

Symbolic interactionists are fond of metaphors related to communication, social conversation, and places for conversation. If a person is like a member, then society can be compared to a large collection of membership clubs. Each club has its distinctive language or set of symbols. Members of the baseball club understand terms such as *strike, double play,* and *world series,* as well as the numerous gestures used by umpires, players, and fans. Members of the social work club learn an entirely different language. When members of my home state, New Jersey, meet each other for the first time in a foreign location, instead of asking "Where are you from?" they are likely to ask "What exit?" All respondents know to identify the exit marker and highway that situates them in the state's web of roads.

Society can be characterized as the mass of members involved in thousands of conversations about hundreds of current public issues. The society is a great web of communication, a giant multipurpose clubhouse. The media—newspapers, radio, television, and magazines—are the major forums for conversations within and across membership groups. Mass media can help to foster a sense of common membership in the very large club of the United States, for example. A society's conversations take shape over time, and the society develops a culture. Culture is like a collection of stories and conversations that have been continuously told or written, revised and improved, and retold by the society's members. Favorite cultural stories and conversations guide community members as they try to solve environmental problems, interpret ambiguous circumstances, choose personal and social identities, and participate in social organizations.

In the interactional realm, conversations between members of different clubs in a society are complicated because each club develops its own culture— a unique set of symbols, dictionaries, topics of conversation, and stories. Members of different clubs do not share the same language or use the same symbols as members of other clubs. Communication between clubs can become difficult, and conversation often breaks down. Think about the clubs organized around social class in our society. The children of the elite in a large high school tend to form their own in-group. They use the same phrases, wear clothes from the same designers, drive the same type of expensive vehicles, understand the same party games, drink the same beers and wines, and share similar aspirations. The Mexican American and Asian American students from the working class are the out-group. Their "inferior" club doesn't use the special codes and interaction patterns cultivated by the in-group. In-group members judge them as awkward and inarticulate, and reject them.

Not all conversations between members are public, face-to-face, or two-way. The self, for interactionists, is likened to a private conversational forum, an internalized society or clubhouse. This self is formed through repeated dialogues with caretakers and influential others. We have invited, in metaphorical terms, numerous seen and unseen members to become part of our club. The self's inner life, then, is a continuation of the important talks, arguments, and discussions with the members of the many other groups to which we belong.

THE SOCIAL WORKER AS GROUP WORKER

The interactionist metaphor for social worker is group worker, club worker, or membership manager (Falck, 1988). Community centers, the modern version of settlement houses, are places for participation in various recreational, educational, and civic clubs. The worker learns to serve each of these clubs. She is a communication expert who works to learn the central meanings that constitute the life of each club. She familiarizes herself with the club's history and the roles, rules, routines, and vocabularies that the club has created to facilitate interaction. With these understandings, the worker can help each club set goals, make decisions, maintain discipline, recruit new members, socialize members into the ways of the club, work through relationship conflicts and misunderstandings, offer beneficial programs, and follow the guidelines of the larger agency. For the new members of any club, the social worker uses various communication techniques to help these novices become competent and responsible participants. The club worker also helps each club understand its place in the larger agency and in society. Therefore, the worker helps clubs communicate with each other, resolve conflicts with other clubs, elect and send representatives to community center councils, select and carry out service projects, find ways to share resources, and advocate for improvement of agency and societal conditions.

Think of the social work commitment to working respectfully with diverse groups. From the symbolic interactionist perspective, this means that we develop skills and attitudes that allow us to gain acceptance and convey acceptance to multiple membership groups. Some of you will become adept at communicating and serving members of the military. Some will excel in conversing with recently arrived immigrants from other nations. Some will refine your talents for grasping the life experiences of the homeless or the urban poor. All of you will become membership translators like Jane Addams who can teach the larger society about the meanings and needs of those members of oppressed, unfortunate, or invisible membership groups.

CORE ASSUMPTIONS OF APPLIED SYMBOLIC INTERACTIONISM

There are three basic interactionist assumptions (Blumer, 1969). First, humans act toward objects on the basis of the meanings of these objects. Objects are tangible things, abstract ideas, and cultural events in the environment that can be represented by symbols. Native American Indians, for example, define the mountains in the southwestern United States as "sacred places" and act worshipfully in these places. Representatives of the U.S. government define the same mountains as potential "repositories" for radioactive waste and hope to dig into vast sections of these mountains. Second, meanings emerge through interaction between people. The young tribal member learned during interaction with his elders that the mountains had a sacred meaning. Third, meanings are used and modified through an interpretive process, and this facilitates transactions with the environment. Conversations between tribal leaders and government scientists or politicians include communication designed to create new meanings: ways to symbolize the rocks, hills, and canyons that respect tradition yet serve disposal needs. If they are successful, transactions between members of the two groups, and between humans and the mountain range, will proceed with minimal social and environmental damage. Other interactionist assumptions amplify or elaborate on these core tenets.

APPRECIATE THE DIALECTICS OF SELF AND SOCIETY, SCIENCE AND PRACTICE

Applied symbolic interactionists assume a dialectical approach to self, society, science, and practice. Interactionists renounce the dualistic conceptions common to many theories; they show interest in individual and collectivity, organism and environment, subject and object, agency and structure, reform and science, freedom and constraint, subjectivism and objectivism, knower and known, micro and macro, nature and nurture, idealism and realism, psychology and sociology, change and stability, particular and universal, conservative and radical, socialism and capitalism, science and sympathy, sociology and social work. Rather than endorsing one aspect of a dichotomy, interactionists seek synthesis. Interactionists emphasize neither "this" nor "that" but "both."

Falck (1988), for instance, rejected the common division of social philosophies into two categories: individualism and collectivism. He offers an antidualistic notion, the "individuality–group effect." His focus on members as symbolic interactors, rather than on individuals or on societies, avoids breaking the link between individual and society. The member, for Falck and other interactionists, is both a subject and an object of social activity. The member is both a producer of society, a free agent who influences social processes, and a product of society, a responder caught in the necessities of the social historical drama. The member has both individual characteristics and characteristics shared with important groups. The boundaries between the member as a physical being and the surrounding environment are permeable. A fetus removed prematurely from the womb will perish. A person severing all links to membership groups and trying to end all communication with others will become inhuman.

THE PERSON IS ACTIVE AND SOCIALLY SELF-DETERMINING

Applied symbolic interactionists conceive of persons as active and, with others' help, capable of determining the course of their lives. This emphasis on personal agency differentiates interactionism from psychoanalytic, behavioral, and social structural theories that assume a person is passively subjected to internal or external forces. Psychoanalytic theorists assume that much of human behavior is motivated by unconscious drives and needs. Interactionists give central importance to consciousness and to the human capacity to make sense of and thereby control the taken-for-granted or semiconscious meanings we experience. Behaviorists propose a simple stimulus–response model and compare humans to animals. Interactionists counter with a stimulus–self-communication–response model. As humans, we have the capacity to resist the call for action of an external stimulus and to delay our response sequence long enough to deliberate silently or talk to ourselves about alternative courses of action. Thus, we can free ourselves from the determining power of environmental antecedents and consequences. Social structuralists assume that human action is governed by norms imposed by large-size social systems or by the society's distribution of material and symbolic goods. Interactionists argue that our capacities for symbolization and for creative group action give us power to shape any reality. Even some of the weakened Jews in Nazi concentration camps, for example, deprived of adequate food, shelter, and hygiene and commanded by threat of death to yield to constant humiliation, found ways to resist overtly or covertly. The genocidal system could not force them to abandon the search for meaning, dignity, and defiant action.

Pragmatism is one base for this image of a person who learns to direct him- or herself by acting to achieve practical ends. Social life is a world of human activity, and membership groups are organized around the continuous doing, constructing, creating, building, forging, coordinating, and adjusting of the members. Interactionists prefer verbs (*selfing* and *minding*) to nouns (*self* and *mind*). They give special attention to the thousands of ways that people act together to expand their capacities, to respond in novel ways to environmental challenges, and to realize their aspirations.

Focus on the Distinctively Human

Applied symbolic interactionists focus on the distinctively human. Interactionists recognize the contribution of other schools of thought to explaining the continuities between human and nonhuman activity. In some ways, we are like the rats, pigeons, dogs, and monkeys studied in behaviorist laboratories. Yet symbolic interactionists give special emphasis to the unique symbol-making and behavioral capacities of human beings. You will never see dogs who keep humans as pets, monkeys who set up scientific centers for studying human beings, or pigeons who collect pictures of scantily clad celebrities in the pigeon society. These activities all require symbolic interaction.

During evolution, humans became qualitatively differentiated as a species from other species. Humans developed the capacity to share symbols and to store these symbols as a complex language. Thereby, humans became able, to some extent, to change nature and to influence evolution. In the early phases of the life course, the infant interacts with significant caretakers and actualizes its species-specific capacity for language. In ways more complex than that of other animals, infants learn to become self-punishing and self-reinforcing, and thus to take charge of their relations with the environment. Our ability to absorb and manipulate abstract symbols in the form of words, gestures, or physical objects allows us to understand highly nuanced, situated meanings; to use remembered pasts and imagined futures in our deliberations; and to evaluate alternative responses before acting. Unlike other creatures (possibly excepting the most sophisticated, humanlike chimpanzees), humans can reflexively view themselves as an object from others' perspectives (self-awareness) and use such reflections to choose actions (self-control). Unlike even the chimps, we can refer to ourselves by our many names, and we can share verbally our sense of personal and group history.

Human Beings Are Fundamentally Social

Applied symbolic interactionists conceive of human beings as fundamentally social. Symbolic interactionism has had a long-standing concern with how participation in social groups leads to the emergence of consciousness, of the mind, of cultural objects and practices, of selves, and of patterns of human conduct. Interactionists notice that *communication, common,* and *community* are words that share many letters and meanings. By communicating, we develop understandings that we share in common with other interactants, and the repetition of this process results in the creation of a community. Many Americans and members of Western societies tend to see the person as an autonomous moral actor, free from situational pressures and related only by choice. Even social workers attuned to social contingencies are prone to this social philosophy. Sometimes, we elevate the value of self-determination to the highest good and forget that the best choices are mutually determined by the client, his family, his friends, and his community. Interactionists reject the "individualistic fallacy" and prefer a theoretical language of relationship. Let me restate that in social work terms. Interactionists prefer a membership perspective. A person is embedded in a social and cultural milieu, and his or her behavior is a response to transactions with others who share common memberships in this milieu. The person cannot be separated from the relational matrix. Our genes bear the physical stamp of our biological heritage. Our dreams, our memories, our emotional displays, our hopes and disappointments, our illness trajectories, our systems of categorization, our drug experiences, our artistic creations, our vocabularies, our motivations, our identities, and our perspectives all bear the stamp of our salient social memberships and of our daily transactions with others. Interactionists promote the value of social self-determination.

Social Arrangements Are Negotiated and Negotiable

Applied symbolic interactionists conceive of social arrangements as negotiated and negotiable rather than immutable. Complementing the image of the person as active and self-determining, interactionists suggest that our social orders are negotiated agreements. We talk together with members of our important groups until we arrive at a consensus. At the dyadic level, people continually negotiate the terms by which they will align their actions. Two lovers, for example, give and take until they arrive at a reasonable mesh of their different sexual styles. Larger social systems, social organizations and institutions, represent complex and continually negotiated agreements about collective purposes, roles, rules, and decision-making procedures. For example, your social agency probably has a mission statement, an organizational chart, and a set of organizational policies. Agency board members, administrators, social workers, and clients (hopefully) developed these documents during many long and complex periods of group deliberation.

In everyday interaction, knowledge of the human agents involved in negotiations of some arrangements may have faded. For instance, the authors of organizational structures endorsing special privilege for the administrators or male workers are long forgotten by most. In everyday interaction, people may differ considerably in the symbolic and material resources they bring to the negotiating table. Cleaning men and women and groundskeepers at my university, for instance, have little power and are invisible to most decision makers. Organizational members may act during everyday interaction as if policies and other agreements are set in concrete, never to be challenged or revised. Although these stubborn and powerful realities cannot be ignored except at a severe price, interactionist social workers focus on how humans can engage in daily life in ways that confront, negotiate, rethink, and remake the agreements out of which social structures, social institutions, and social selves have been constructed.

Human Action Is Multidimensional

Applied symbolic interactionists explain human action in multidimensional and holistic terms. Interactionists reject approaches to theory building or practice that oversimplify or distort human experience. Simplistic, linear models of cause and effect are replaced with models that acknowledge the fluid, complex, and unpredictable aspects of personal and social change. Interactionists think of cause, for example, as a unique and complex set of self and social interactional processes involving very large numbers of conditions and factors. Human behavior cannot be completely understood by reducing it to aggressive and sexual inclinations or to reinforcement and punishment. Interactionists advise an appreciation for the complexity of "interactional fields," and recommend attention during problem assessment to interacting historical, ecological, social, psychological, and biological processes. Humans are integrated and active members or components of these complex and dynamic fields. Moreover, because humans are capable of novel and self-chosen action, interactionists recommend awareness of the change processes deliberately initiated by actors in a given context. Humans constantly surprise each other, and clients regularly act in unexpected ways. The interactionist, therefore, assumes a humble posture in the face of a somewhat mysterious, uncertain, and ever-changing pluralistic universe.

Human activity has a unity not always acknowledged by noninteractionist theorists. A person's experience cannot be broken into inner and outer parts, for example, because inner, mental dynamics are part of an outer, observable social process. An individual act cannot be dissected independently of social activity, and a social act cannot be understood simply in terms of its constituent behaviors. The jazz musician "swings" as a member of a "swinging" combo. Both solo and collective action are elements of a larger social and cultural context. For classroom lectures, teachers may treat cognition, emotion, and behavior as separate things, but human experience actually has an organic quality. Behavior is a coordinated system of acts, with inseparable sensory, cognitive, affective, and motivational (and spiritual) aspects. The interactionist and membership perspectives endorse a holistic approach to explanation.

SCIENTIFIC INQUIRY REQUIRES PARTICIPANT OBSERVATION

Applied symbolic interactionists assume that the best scientific inquiry complements their framework's assumptions about members and membership organizations. The distinctive character of human conduct and of membership organizations necessitates, for interactionists, a special scientific methodology, or at least a modification of conventional research methods. The interactionist researcher holds that social circumstances are always changing; that reality is interpreted; that humans are capable of self-communication and thus unpredictable, not determined; and that social roles are dynamic and creative. These convictions necessitate an approach to inquiry and strategies different from those used for the study of inarticulate aspects of the physical world. "Respect the nature of the empirical world, and organize a methodological stance to reflect that respect" is my paraphrase of Herbert Blumer's (1969) influential position on scientific methodology. Thus, interactionists have taken the lead in developing participant-observation strategies of inquiry from which concepts sensitive to the lived experience of those studied emerge. Understanding the meanings of people in their everyday symbolic environments is the primary research goal, and the researcher should be integrally and actively involved with these people during the discovery process. Interactionist researchers try to gain acceptance as group members (recognizing that they are a bit different from other members) and then immerse themselves in and empathize with the participants in a community. A successful interactionist inquiry would be similar to the mastery of a new foreign language and culture.

HAVE FAITH IN THE POSSIBILITY OF HUMAN BETTERMENT

Applied symbolic interactionists have faith in the possibility of human betterment. Addams, Mead, and Dewey were neither blindly optimistic nor paralyzed by pessimism. Instead, each took a melioristic stance. This means that they shared the belief that the specific conditions that exist at one moment, be they comparatively bad or comparatively good, can always be bettered. The early interactionists were committed to democratic social activism, to reform of corrupt and inefficient practices, and to the improvement of social membership conditions for all societal members. Interactionists believe that humans, like other living organisms, continually attempt to solve problems related to their adjustment to the environment. Through conscious, deliberate, and intelligent collective effort, humans can make this problem solving more rational. We can interrupt the flow of problematic actions, reflect together on circumstances, and expand the range of possibilities in the situation under inquiry. The application of the interactionist method of "intelligent social reconstruction" provides practical solutions to practical problems of human membership.

Science is the major tool for social amelioration. For pragmatists and interactionists, theory and research must serve the ends of practitioners. Knowledge should be useful and aid people who hurt, groups that suffer, and advocates trying to change mercenary organizations. Whatever the constraints, interactionists believe that we can inquire together about troubling conditions, can develop working hypotheses about how to make improvements, and can follow the inquiry with provisional and flexible efforts to improve the quality of social membership for all.

THE INTERACTIONIST APPROACH TO HUMAN DEVELOPMENT

In this section, I will introduce you to the interactionist approach to human development. This approach synthesizes the scholarship of numerous theorists, including Cooley, Mead, and Cahill, and it builds creatively on the root metaphor of "person as member."

EXEMPLARY ROLE MODELS

The interactionist approach to human development expands on the Cooley–Mead heritage. Charles Horton Cooley (1864–1929) contributed the concepts *primary group* and *looking glass self* to interactionist thinking about socialization. Cooley also acknowledged that his conception of primary groups, now a classic, was influenced by contact with settlement house workers, and by their observations of delinquent gangs (Chaiklin, 1975). For Cooley, the primary group was characterized by spatial proximity (members live in the same household, for example), small number of members, face-to-face interaction, long duration or permanent bonds, and intimacy (Gandhi, 1978). Participation in such groups is fundamental to psychosocial development, especially of the person's self-conception, values, and social nature. Cooley's image of the **looking glass self** captures his conviction that the person's identity is a reflection of the judgments and reactions of others. The developing person imagines how he or she is seen by others, infers the favorability of the appraisal, and accrues sentiments of pride or shame depending on the character of the reflection. For example, a young boy uses his father as a mirror. He decides that Dad is regularly displeased with his youthful demeanor and conduct. The boy begins to import the father's negative judgments into the self, with an accompanying sense of inferiority.

Cooley also developed the idea of *sympathetic introspection* for research methodologists and practitioners. According to his nephew, Cooley recommended this process of imagining imaginations as a way to challenge social theorists and researchers to "project themselves into people's minds and interpret the world as those people did" (Angell, 1968, p. 5). This is similar to the core social work skill of "tuning in." Healy (1972) confirms this parallel and suggests that Cooley's sympathetic introspection method contributed to the repertoire of case history techniques used by social workers at child guidance clinics.

Cooley's orientation toward human development had several other noteworthy characteristics. He was committed to "diversitarianism," the assertion of "the beneficence of variety, diversity, dissimilarity, or heterogeneity" (Hinkle, 1967, p. 15). Cooley also emphasized the importance of emotion to self processes and human development, a theme and emphasis shared by all social workers. In his efforts to master social knowledge and prepare for teaching sociology, Cooley considered Jane Addams to be one of the "accredited authors" and studied her work (Cooley, 1930, p. 5). Cooley valued the theory–practice linkage. He wrote of appointments to his university that "particularly notable was the appointment, in 1916, of Arthur Evans Woods to an instructorship with the understanding that he was to develop social work courses and to cooperate in every way practicable with the social workers of the state" (p. 14). Cooley also wrote extensively on social change. He took the position that successful social reform required attention to a society's primary groups and to the influence of these group memberships on the developing person's ideals and social consciousness (Petras, 1968b).

You have already met George Herbert Mead. Mead (1934) also theorized about the emergence of the self and the development of cognitive abilities (Callero, 1985–1986; Miller, 1973). Mead viewed human development as the increased integration of multiple social perspectives and the use of these perspectives to guide action. He argued that social interaction contributed in critical ways to self-development, mental development, and moral development.

According to Mead, the developing person progresses through three levels: the presymbolic level, the play level, and the game level. At the **presymbolic level,** human conduct is evoked by immediate stimuli in impulsive or habitual ways. The developing person has minimal capacities for perspective taking, for self-consciousness, and for moral problem solving. From a diversity perspective, the infant or the developmentally challenged adult is ego-centered. This is a preparatory period for participation in human groups and communities. The ability to understand and use significant symbols, especially words, will herald the shift from infancy to a new level (Goodman, 1985). Natural sounds become babble. Through interaction with caretakers, babble becomes "mama" or "dawgie." Rudimentary language use follows.

At the **play level,** the growing mastery of language accelerates the developmental process. Human conduct tends to be compulsive. Human action is dictated by one's playmates and intimate others. Customary patterns are preferred. There is some perspective taking, but the developing person takes the perspective of a single other at a time (Goodman, 1985). The child, for example, begins to consider the perspective of a parent or an imaginary playmate. The developing person follows the rules of his or her primary groups but with little awareness of how social roles are intertwined or of conflict between different systems of rules. From a diversity perspective, the child or the adult who has not advanced beyond this level is ethnocentric.

At the **game level,** the developing person broadens his or her social engagement. Mead (1934) emphasized the importance of organized games to psychosocial development. As an illustration, he commented on how children playing on a baseball team become adept when they learn to consider each team role, the relationship of each role to the network of roles, and the rules of the sport. The developing person becomes capable of relating to two generalized others: a generalized sense of the whole team and a generalized sense of the baseball league. Human action in the game stage is based on the awareness of conflicting views and the values of the self–society relationship. The developing person extends knowledge from playing games and begins to grasp his or her location in the social structure (Goodman, 1985). The creative discovery of new alternatives is possible. Perspective taking becomes increasingly complex and extensive. The person gains an appreciation of diversity within the unity of generalized others and a capacity for complex moral problem solving. From a diversity perspective, the developing person or adult has become polycentric.

ASSUMPTIONS OF THE INTERACTIONIST APPROACH TO HUMAN DEVELOPMENT

Applied symbolic interactionists assume that the fundamental stimulant of human development is the "episode of interaction" (Foote, 1957). A child and mother coordinate their acts. One episode of such interaction conditions the next episode, and the child and mother construct a patterned way of relating. Development is the cumulative biopsychosocial product of successive outcomes of episodes of social interaction (between the child and mother, father, other significant influences, and so on). The life span is a lengthy series of episodes of interaction, and the person's life is the ordering of this series in response to personal preferences, social constraints and opportunities, and change events. Interactionists also assume that socialization is primarily a matter of developing the cognitive, emotional, and behavioral capacities for effective and responsible membership in primary, secondary, and tertiary groups (Goodman, 1985).

ROOT METAPHORS OF THE INTERACTIONIST APPROACH TO HUMAN DEVELOPMENT

Instead of stages, Mead's (1934) interactionist approach is built on the metaphor of levels. This root metaphor suggests that there is nothing inevitable about movement from one level to another, that progress to higher levels entails effort, that advancement involves the self interacting with significant others and social structures, that actors can move up or down in the complexity of their conduct, and that the same actor may shift from one level to another in a short amount of time.

The metaphor of membership is important to the interactionist approach also. Cahill (1980, 1983, 1986a, 1986b, 1989, 1994) has outlined an interactionist approach to development. He compared socialization to the recruitment processes used by groups and organizations to attract, orient, train, and govern new members. Cahill studied preparation related to gender. Members of a society need assorted competencies—those related to determining the other's sex by "examination of sex-identificatory displays" and those related to the evaluation and guidance of one's behavior in terms of "the culture's gender ideals" (1986a, p. 166). Gender socialization entails mastering the complex knowledge and intricate skills related to a culture's gender codes. The acquisition of such knowledge and competency makes possible the "interactional achievement of normally sexed identities" (1986a, p. 166). Gender socialization, Cahill maintained, is preparation for "bona-fide societal membership" (1980, p. 164). Cahill (1986a) referred to it as "a process whereby societal initiates are recruited into self-regulated participation in the interactional achievement of normally sexed identities" (p. 167). Using this metaphor, interactionists like Cahill are suggesting that society prepares developing persons for its preferred clubs. Heterosexuals are those accepted into our biggest and most favored club, but male heterosexuals are usually the owners and managers of the club. Homosexuals aren't allowed into the big club, so they create their own clubs. Bisexuals try to maintain membership in two clubs, and transvestites yearn to tailor their appearance to the standards of a club to which they do not officially belong.

THE INTERACTIONIST APPROACH TO HUMAN DEVELOPMENT

Symbolic interactionism has been the theory of choice for understanding human socialization. Attentive to both the Cooley–Mead heritage and feminist streams of thought, Cahill's (1980, 1983, 1986b) recruitment approach to gender socialization builds on the core tenets of the interactionist framework. First, gender identity, like other identities, emerges during naturally occurring episodes of interactions and social experiences. Field research, consequently, is the research method of choice for studying socialization. Second, gender socialization is primarily a process of language acquisition. The initiate learns the culture's gender-oriented vocabulary, grammatical rules, language practices, and preferred gestures. These facilitate self-identification, other identification, gendered action, and gendered interaction. For instance, the label *male* or *female* (with its accompanying social meanings) is one of the key influences on the course of socialization. Third, gender socialization occurs as initiates take the perspectives of significant others (How does Dad want me to act as a boy?) and of the generalized community (Why is the Catholic Church so hostile to gay males?), especially as these responses are sex-differentiated, and then internalize these perspectives. Even biological inclinations considered different for males and females (the mother's disposition to nurture her child) can be suppressed, strengthened, or elaborated through this interaction process. Fourth, the developing person is an active participant in his or her gender development. Socialization is not a one-way process from socializing agent to passive recipient. A child interprets others' responses to his or her gender identity and actively seeks gender-identity-confirming transactions with others in the social environment. Fifth, gender socialization occurs in a social and historical context. Available models (heroes and villains, "real" boys and "perfect" girls) shape the process by the ways in which they accentuate or downplay gender. Physical environments and the sex-differentiated designs of the meanings of these environments (colors and objects in boys' versus girls' bedrooms, for example) also shape the socialization process.

A summary of the central macro structures, interactional processes, and personal outcomes identified by Cahill in his model of gender socialization follows. Macro influences include media images of boys and girls and men and women and cultural standards regarding appearance, masculinity, and femininity. Interactional processes include social labeling, instruction from socializing agents, playful experiments with fashion and toys, and reflected appraisals from significant others. Possible personal outcomes include skill at appearance management, coherent or confused gender identity, and preferences for "masculine" or "feminine" behaviors.

By expanding the interactionist theory of self-formation, Cahill differentiated his model from other approaches to gender socialization (Cahill, 1983). Despite behaviorist claims, Cahill showed that gender development is not simply a matter of behavioral reinforcement. Labeling by self and by others is critical, for example. Despite Freudian claims, Cahill demonstrated that gender development is not a "biographic drama resulting from universalistic reactions to anatomical characteristics" (p. 9). Despite the claims of cognitive scientists like Piaget, Cahill indicated that gender is not the structuring of gender performances by cross-cultural criteria related to anatomy. The interactionist approach to gender socialization, Cahill concluded, involves the developing person's "construction of social worlds around sexual classification" (p. 10). It traces the deepening mastery of capacities necessary to interact in specific social situations and groups; to reference the particular gender ideals of one's social groups; and to use culturally specific tools, such as dress, hairstyle, and manner, toward the end of confirming individualized gender meanings.

The process of gender recruitment can be divided into distinctive levels, each characterized by the initiate's degree of agency, the characteristic social activities, and the major socialization procedures of that level (Cahill, 1986a).

ACQUIESCENT PARTICIPATION   This level begins at birth. The person is passive and cannot resist his or her recruiters. The primary group makes the preliminary sex identification. The infant's anatomical appearance and rudimentary actions elicit responses from caretakers and other family members. The family typically views the social world as divided into two sex categories, males and females, and thus behaviorally conditions sex-appropriate behavior (Cahill, 1994). Repeatedly, family members pattern the behavior of the new group member in a sex-differentiated way (let boys cry some but soothe distressed girls, for example). By investing the body and action with socially shared meanings, the family also begins to define the infant's "essential nature" as male or female. Sex-designating terms and sex-differentiated physical environments and objects are used as tools for such investments of meaning.

UNWITTING PARTICIPATION   As infants become more active, they become unwitting participants in the interactional achievement of a sex identity. Significant others make finer judgments about the infant's inherent masculinity or femininity. Behavioral conditioning of the infant's actions in line with cultural expectations continues. Treatment by caretakers differs according to the infant's sex, with somewhat predictable effects. Boys should be independent, so touching and clinging behaviors are discouraged. Girls should be sociable, so close contact with Mom is rewarded. Language acquisition becomes the critical socialization procedure (Cahill, 1986b). The infant begins to learn language basics, including the critical role of gender terms in interaction across many situations and how to engage in basic perspective taking to appraise others' expectations. For instance, most children begin to associate the sex-specific labels used by others with their own self-conceptions.

EXPLORATORY PARTICIPATION   Children now start to use their group's verbal labels and to view the social world as others describe it. They begin to master cultural knowledge about appearance symbols (hairstyle, accessories, jewelry, makeup, body adornments) and to risk exploring alternative ways of participating in their groups as a boy or a girl. Observation of real and imagined models of gendered action, direct instruction from peers and parents, social play, tentative selection of dress and objects, and the acquisition of additional labels for self- and other identification result in tentative and temporary commitments to socially approved gender identities. The male tries to dress into the social identity of "big boy." The female may try "dressing out" of the identity of "dainty girl" by costuming herself as Batman or Superman (Cahill, 1989). Trial efforts to cross gender boundaries are often punished, and usually result in the insight that environments include male and female territories and each environment has different objects, activities, and rules (Cahill, 1994). Recruiting agents continue to respond to the child's sex category and try to channel gender identity explorations along culturally accepted grooves.

APPRENTICE PARTICIPATION   During the preadolescence period, boys and girls make their first entry into the disciplined system of gender-governed interaction characterizing their primary and secondary social groups. While participating in cohesive and small peer groups, often segregated by sex, preteens construct microcosms of the larger social world. The preteens seek status in these mini-cultures through negotiations about the acceptability of their presented gender identities. Game playing is fairly sophisticated. The developing person's use of the community's gender language is refined. By rehearsing the verbal and nonverbal display of masculinity and femininity, preteens can refine their performances so that established gender displays become habitual, smooth, and apparently "natural." Many boys in the United States incorporate the meanings necessary for the aggressive pranks, dirty talk, and sports activity common to their culture. Girls attempt to master the skills of appearance management, empathy, and sociability prevalent in their culture (Cahill, 1994). Firmer and more permanent commitments to gender and related social identities are made.

BONA FIDE PARTICIPATION Following the bodily changes associated with puberty, the recruit embraces his or her gender identity. Concurrently, he or she is increasingly trusted to act in conformity with gender ideals, and to conform without the support of or interference from others. Repeated enactment of varied social identities in various social circumstances enhances gender membership skills. Impulses contrary to one's gender ideal are stifled. Appearance management in line with gender standards becomes easy. The bona fide member can readily announce her "femaleness" and distance herself from "maleness," for example (Cahill, 1989). Verification by gatekeepers of their confidence in the recruit's competence to achieve a normally sexed identity completes the training period.

CRITICAL COMMENTS

Schwalbe (1992) has offered a very similar interactionist model of gender socialization that nicely complements Cahill's model. Schwalbe referred to gender socialization as the process of "gendering the self." During interaction, the child learns to "gender self as a subject" (I see myself and act as a male), to "gender self as an object" (I understand how society divides people including me into males and females), and to evaluate his or her competence and moral worth by gender-specific standards. Eventually, external demands become internal compulsions. Cahill's and Schwalbe's approaches are important. They balance the interactionist assumption of personal agency with the recognition that many of our most salient memberships are patterned by our membership organizations. Switching back to Cahill's metaphor, both these interactionist approaches illustrate that our induction into a gender club started before we had any choice in the matter, has effects permeating all our other membership activities, and becomes so automatic that rejecting the club's bylaws seems very difficult.

The interactionist conception of levels of membership from unwitting participation to bona fide participation seems useful also for understanding memberships other than gender, such as social class, ethnicity, and physical ability or disability. To my knowledge, however, it has not yet been extended to or researched in other areas of social life.

APPLICATIONS OF THE INTERACTIONIST APPROACH TO HUMAN DEVELOPMENT

It is difficult to provide illustrations of the practical application of interactionist approaches to human development. Concepts such as the primary group, reflected appraisals, perspective taking, and the play and game stage of development have been incorporated (sometimes in diluted form) into the social work knowledge base (Forte, 2004a, 2004b). Yet interactionist theorists, researchers, and practitioners have failed to show how a membership slant on human development might guide any phase of the planned change process.

LABELING THEORY, SOCIAL JUSTICE, AND THE SELF: SELECTED PROPOSITIONS

How would your life be changed if you were called a psychotic, a delinquent, a welfare fraud, or a faggot? What if the label stuck, and your friends and neighbors all treated you as what you had been labeled? Are labels fairly attached? The interactionist labeling perspective helps us answer questions like these, both for ourselves and for our clients.

The labeling perspective is an important approach to understanding deviance. It shifts attention away from the personality of the actor to the reactions by the community to which the member belongs. An act condemned in one society may be widely praised in another. Therefore, to understand deviance we should study context-specific social norms and social processes. The middle-range theory uses the concepts of *social act, label, self-concept, societal reaction, deviance,* and *hierarchy of credibility.*

Social acts are given meaning through social interaction. The meanings attached publicly to social acts are called **labels.** Psychiatric social workers, for example, attach diagnostic labels to patterns of action exhibited by hospital patients. Our **self-concept** is the collection of labels or meanings that we have constructed about our self during interaction with others and during self-interaction.

Community members, especially those associated with social control organizations such as the court system, react to the social actions of others. These are called **societal reactions.** These label givers may define an act as deviant, a violation of important norms and customs; they may attach meanings that indicate it is socially acceptable; or they may ignore it. The **labeling** process involves a social interaction organized around the matching of a label to a behavior or set of behaviors. In the United States, for instance, hundreds of different observable behaviors are treated as symptoms indicative of physical or mental illness. The Diagnostic Statistical Manual collects all such labels used by professionals when diagnosing such symptoms. A particular diagnostic label is attached to a person in specific interaction circumstances, such as those associated with involuntary commitment procedures.

Labeling occurs, then, in a particular historical and situational context. What gets labeled varies. Who will be labeled depends more on social status and power than on the activity labeled. A **hierarchy of credibility** determines which labels stick. Community members who do the labeling are differentially valued. The determination of a judge in Salem, Massachusetts, several hundred years ago that a local farmer's wife was a "witch," for example, was judged as credible by many in the town. The claims of the low-status family members and friends that none of the wife's acts involved witchery were not believed. Lawmakers and rule enforcers are given special power for creating and attaching labels. They are considered credible. Minority group members have less credibility. Even African American professors at elite universities such as Princeton have had a hard time fighting state troopers on the New Jersey Turnpike trying to brand them as dangerous drivers or drug couriers.

The way others label us, and then treat us according to these labels, affects our self-concept. Imagine children secretly applying a paper to the back of a schoolmate, "Kick me—I'm a doofus," and then laughing and taunting the newly defined "doofus." The victim of the prank starts to wonder about his image and place in the group. The act of labeling, then, may persuade the labeled to identify himself as deviant. Negative labels increase the power of the deviant identity, and the likelihood that the person labeled will start a pattern of deviant behavior.

Social workers are often employed by organizations that assign labels to children or adults. A few propositions from the labeling perspective suggest that we should do so with consideration for the social reactions to various acts. First, those labeled as deviant by important others and treated differently because of this label are likely to modify their set of self-conceptions to include the idea of being deviant. A teenage girl labeled a "troublemaker" by one teacher because of a few acts of clowning in class (primary deviance), and then treated as "trouble" by a widening set of teachers, may accept this label. Second, those who internalize negative labels are likely to act in ways fulfilling the expectations of others for deviance. "I guess I must be a bad girl," the student begins to think, and then responds to invitations to participate in acts of deviance regarded as very criminal (secondary deviance). Thus, a labeling process intended to correct unacceptable behavior may contribute to a deviant career. Third, members of low-status groups are more likely to be labeled deviant by official organizations than members of high-status groups. Stereotypes influence the process. Poor adolescents of color in central city areas who smoke crack cocaine are caught, labeled as dangerous drug dealers, and given lengthy prison sentences. White teenagers in suburban neighborhoods who use cocaine in a refined powder form are labeled as experimenters and warned to be careful. In summary, labeling theorists warn us that the classification of members by their actions often perpetuates social injustice and restricts the chances of those labeled for future positive membership experiences. Label with care. Sticks and stones may hurt the bones of clients; labels can kill them.

MAPPING APPLIED SYMBOLIC INTERACTIONISM

Figure 10.1 presents an interactionist version of the eco-map. The remainder of this section translates and summarizes interactionist conceptions of eco-map components and processes.

HOW ARE CONNECTIONS CONCEPTUALIZED?

Humans connect to each other by symbolic interaction. A **symbol** is a sound, image, or action that serves interactants in various useful ways by representing some tangible or intangible object in the environment. The word *adoption,* for instance, is an essential symbol that social workers and childless families use

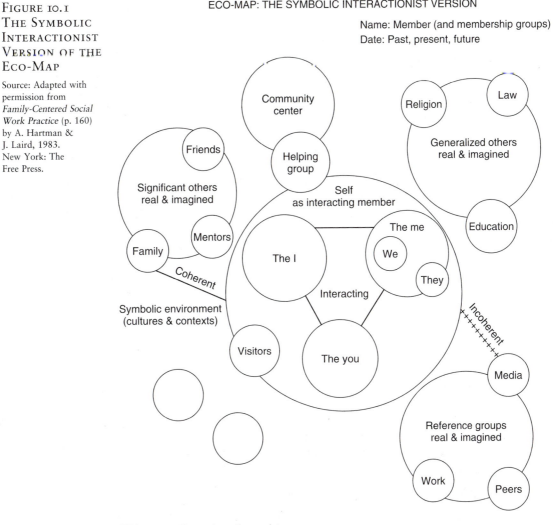

FIGURE 10.1
THE SYMBOLIC
INTERACTIONIST
VERSION OF THE
ECO-MAP

Source: Adapted with
permission from
*Family-Centered Social
Work Practice* (p. 160)
by A. Hartman &
J. Laird, 1983.
New York: The
Free Press.

ECO-MAP: THE SYMBOLIC INTERACTIONIST VERSION

Name: Member (and membership groups)
Date: Past, present, future

Community center

Religion   Law

Generalized others real & imagined

Friends

Helping group

Significant others real & imagined

Self as interacting member

The me

Education

We

Mentors

They

The I

Family

Coherent

Interacting

Incoherent

Symbolic environment (cultures & contexts)

Visitors

The you

Media

Reference groups real & imagined

Work   Peers

Fill in connections where they exist.
Indicate nature of connections with a descriptive word or by drawing different kinds of lines:
——————— for successful communication - - - - - - - - - - for mixed communication
+++++++ for unsuccessful communication
Draw arrows along lines to signify flow of energy, resources, etc. ➤ ➤ ➤
Identify significant people and fill in empty circles as needed.

when working together. Symbols can be linguistic. These are called **discursive symbols.** Interactants use words, phrases, sentences, or combinations of words to communicate with each other. The "coming out" stories of those declaring an alternative sexual orientation are shared in words. **Expressive symbols** are the facial and bodily expressions used to exhibit particular emotional states, desires, and planned actions. Traffic police use varied expressions and gestures to direct car drivers at a very busy interaction. **Appearance symbols** help members communicate their mood, values, and attitudes through hairstyle, face painting, body tattooing, choice of attire, and bodily ornaments. **Significant symbols** are those symbols that evoke similar responses (images, thoughts, and action tendencies) from multiple members of an interacting group.

Interaction occurs when two or more people act in ways that take account of each other. When interacting, communicators construct a coordinated line of action in a particular social situation by considering each other's perspectives. An interaction may be symbolic (each interactant interprets the communication of the other) or nonsymbolic (occurring automatically and without any conscious thought). Symbolic interaction often involves the transmission of **relationship messages** (linguistic, expressive, and appearance symbols about the desired form and content of the relationship) and **task messages** (verbal and nonverbal information about the problems or concerns at hand).

The social patterns and structures common to an ecosystem are built up, according to interactionists, by symbolic interaction. Some of this predates the current generation. The symbolic interactions of our parents, their parents, and earlier generations all might be influential during a current family social event. Even intertwined systems of meaning with long histories must be maintained and changed through contemporary processes of symbolic interaction.

How Is the Quality of Connections Differentiated?

Communication is never perfect. Human communication can lead to consensus (an agreement about meanings) or to conflict. Consensus can vary from complete understanding and confirmation of presented symbols to minimal understanding and confirmation.

Positive connections are episodes of coherent and constructive communication. **Coherence** refers to the ability of each interactant to present and interpret meanings accurately. **Accuracy** is attributing meanings to others' words, demeanor, and behaviors close enough to the intended message to allow coordinated action. The speaker, if asked, would respond, "Yes, you seem to understand what I am trying to communicate." Successful communication helps interactants do things together. Understanding does not need to be perfect; minor errors in the mutual grasping of meanings may be tolerable. Effective interactants select symbols from cultural dictionaries significant to each other. They are clear. They communicate verbal messages that are congruent with their nonverbal messages. They alternate between the roles of listener and speaker. They share responsibility for mutual meaning making, and their communication enables them to mesh their lines of action so that they accomplish social business and satisfy personal and collective goals.

Negative connections are those characterized by incoherent and destructive social communication. The singer Screaming Jay Hawkins often included in his songs strings of bizarre sounds and half words like "grr gobbly woh yrrr" that made sense to no one. Interactants may find one another's communication incoherent when they come from different social worlds and do not share a set of significant symbols and perspectives on life. Members of youth cultures often use slang and gestures that are incomprehensible to parents and other elders. Meaning making may be impossible when one of the interactants uses an idiosyncratic code, one not even shared by a subculture. Persons are often diagnosed as "mentally disordered" when they use phrases and images that cannot be interpreted by others in the community.

Negative connections also include those in which symbolic interaction results in damaging effects on the social process or the social group. An interactant such as an unscrupulous salesperson may use refined communication skills to manipulate and deceive a customer; or the interactants may differ in power and status, allowing those in a superior position to impose their interpretations on subordinates. The Bible offers the vivid story of the Tower of Babel. God punishes the haughty and overambitious builders, causing them all to speak different languages. Construction halts, and the people, unable to understand each other, scatter across the world. Many personal and collective problems identified by social workers, such as mental disorder, delinquency, criminal behavior, interpersonal violence, exploitation, and substance abuse, can be explained, at least to some extent, by reference to ineffective, irresponsible, or immoral communication.

Tenuous connections might be defined by interactionists as somewhere on the continuum between coherent and incoherent communication. Mutual understanding and coordinated action may be possible, but only with great effort to clarify ambiguous meanings; to negotiate consensual conceptions of situations, roles, identities, events, and objects; or to equalize the distribution of power so that all perspectives are considered.

WHAT IS THE TYPICAL FOCAL SYSTEM?

For interactionists, the focal system is at least a member. All members bring to the social work agency their **unseen memberships,** actualized in inner conversations, and their **seen memberships,** real-life others who may be used as references during worker–client interaction. Interactionist workers also focus on collectivities or membership organizations. Interactionist workers never help "individuals" (Falck, 1988).

The person as a member is like a miniature society. Interactionists use the concept *self.* Subvocal conversations occur in an **inner forum,** the psychological space in which members of the internal society participate with the overall self in defining, interpreting, arguing, clarifying, reminding, and other types of intrapersonal interaction. Interactionists use pronouns such as *I, you, me,* and *them* to represent the important cultural memberships and identities that have become part of the self. Using the first-person pronoun *I* as the subject of a sentence is the grammatical way to signal the singular personhood of the speaker. The word attaches the speaker to a specific body situated in an actual place with accountability for the words and actions emanating from the body. The pronoun *I* references also the "nowness" of the speaker's communication, and the aspect of self that is the active doer or knower. To tell one's mother "I am coming home on Saturday" can signify to her in one short word varied membership information: one's title (son), relationship history (enduring bonds with recent separation), rights (to plan a visit without asking permission), and qualities (dutiful). The *I* is the core member in the society of the self. This member has been characterized by interactionists as spontaneous, as unpredictable, as impulsive, and as the source of our autonomous action. The *I* is the thinker of thoughts, the sense of self or personal identity that differentiates between that which is me and that which is not-me. The *I* is that aspect of the self with the power to endow internalized others with a specific voice, to initiate inner conversations, and to use others as allies in problem solving.

Using the word *me* conforms to the grammatical rule that sets the self as a sentence's object. The pronoun *me* is closely related to the word *mine*, which signifies all that a person possesses, material and symbolic goods alike. The person referring to *me* refers to the objectified aspects of the self that have been created and determined in past memberships during interpersonal and intrapsychic interaction. The pronoun *me* is singular, but it might be converted to the clumsier plural form *mes* to indicate that this member of the self can be differentiated into subparts. In the society of the self, the *me* is the member that can be represented to self or others. The *me* is the components of the self aggregating what the person has become so far, including our internalized morality, our social labels, and our traits. The *me* is the socially sensitive and interpersonally responsive contributor to inner deliberations. It is the internalization and inner representation of the perspectives of all those important membership experiences in our life, the voices that endorse or reject our spontaneous inclinations to act. The *me* incorporates experiences with significant others and role partners. These have become settled and permanent members of the inner forum and have often lost their distinctive voices. So, the critical words of a specific parent or teacher earlier in life are experienced as a disembodied and anonymous contribution to the inner dialogue.

The *me* incorporates also the "voices of the community" or generalized others. These are composite conceptions of social collectives, the internalized norms and perspectives of an entire group or institution. During socialization, we can internalize the perspectives of larger official and impersonal institutions such as the criminal justice system. We can create representations of these imagined entities. Social workers, for example, learn to give consideration in their thoughts to the hypothetical and amorphous group of clients referred to by labels such as the oppressed, the disenfranchised, or the undervalued. Our generalized others provide answers to silent questions we ask when coordinating our actions with others in a membership group or society. What are this group's or community's rules for verbal and nonverbal communication and its rules of conduct? How can I best play my part and help the entire collective?

The *me* might be further differentiated into *we* and *they*. Our silent reference to the set of others who affirm our inclinations and with whom we identify would probably be by use of the pronoun *us* or *we*. *We* is the pronoun used for speaking of more than one familiar person and group. *We* signals our sense of shared fate, of collective identity, of a willingness to sacrifice. The living and dead social theorists and social workers associated with the social work tradition may become a *we* for readers of this book. In public conversation, *they* is the pronoun used to refer to those people and groups that are strange, surprising, or different in terms of sex, race, nationality, or some other social membership. In inner dialogue, the person might refer, then, to others and communities as *they* or *them* when the others' expectations conflict with the self's impulses, desires, or values.

The *you* is the appropriate pronoun for addressing a thought or feeling to a second person or group. Its use indicates grammatically our effort to take the standpoint of particular real or imagined others to whom we address our words: "I have some idea about how *you* view my decision." Its use can also signify the attributes and identities of the other: "Mom, I hope *you* (excellent, health-oriented cook) will feed me when I visit." The pronoun *you* commonly refers to a singular other, but a phrase from the southern United States, *you-all,* shows that it can point to multiple others. As a member of the self's inner forum, the pronoun *you* may represent a distinctive other imagined to be present in an inner conversation. A practitioner might query, "What would you do, Jane Addams, if you were in my shoes?" The pronoun *you* may also refer to our conception of a future self. Children, for example, mumble words to themselves to the effect "Don't do that or you will get in trouble." The concept *you* has similarities to the sociocognitive notion of the "possible self" presented in the chapter on cognitive science. This is a mental representation of what the practitioner would like to become or would like to avoid becoming. During intrapersonal communication, the person sometimes makes this representation explicit and addresses the self in the second person, asking, for example, "What will you become, Jim, if you choose that line of action?"

How Is the Environment Conceptualized?

Interactionists emphasize the symbolic aspects of the physical and social environment. We do not know the environment in a direct way. All knowledge of the environment is acquired through the medium of symbols. The following sports story reveals the interactionist perspective. Three baseball umpires swap opinions about the purpose of their job. The first says, "Some are balls and some are strikes, and I call them as they is." The second umpire says, "Some are balls and some are strikes, and I call them as I sees them." And the third umpire (an interactionist) remarks, "Some are balls and some are strikes, but they ain't nothing until I call them" (Anderson, 1979).

The realm in which we live has no inherent meaning, nor any meaning that preexists humans. Men and women endow events, people, objects, and social organizations with meaning using their culture's definitional procedures and vocabularies. Humans do not experience a "raw physical reality," but rather interpret the environment in accord with socially derived meanings. These meanings are encoded in and then transmitted through language. Most of us take for granted our culture's conceptions of the environment. We are like goldfish living in our customary bowl of water, but the water we are immersed in is language. Interactionists are not complete idealists. The environment can affect us even if we do not notice or interpret the effect. Carbon monoxide will kill us if we are trapped in a garage, irrespective of our success in labeling the car's fumes. Nonetheless, interactionists advise practitioners that the goal of understanding clients' transactions with the environment requires us to make sense of how the client interprets the environment and his or her action options.

As indicated earlier, the environment includes multiple social worlds or language communities. These vary in the ways that self, roles, time, space, objects, norms, and social situations are commonly symbolized. Members of each social world tend to share similar vocabularies for describing motives and emotions, similar interaction patterns (wedding rituals or potluck dinners, for example), similar stories, and similar jargons. Interactants are influenced by and influence every level of membership organization that constitutes their entire ecosystem. We are embedded in our relationships, social groups, organizations, institutions, social worlds, and society. Human environments also include various media technologies and formats. Social interaction is structured, patterned, constrained, or liberated depending on the environment's dominant technology. For instance, symbolic interaction between face-to-face interactants offers different possibilities and challenges than symbolic interaction across the World Wide Web among members of virtual communities.

Is Particular Emphasis Given to Any Systems?

Interactionists give the priority to those persons and groups that are invested with meaning by the client. These range from the small to the large, from the personal and intimate to the impersonal and remote. Primary groups often predominate early in life. They include our caretakers, members of our friendship groups, and others with whom we interact in ways that form many of our central or core meanings about life, others, and self. Throughout life, we find **significant others**, persons with whom we develop important symbolic bonds or connections. Significant others validate or confirm our prized sense of self. They understand us in special ways. They are our role partners in valued life projects. They influence our conceptions of self and our self-esteem. They become internalized and join our inner forum.

Reference groups include any group whose perspective is used as a frame of reference for our action in a particular interactional field. The reference group often provides standards that help us judge the appropriateness of our actions. They become like an invisible audience reviewing our performances. Social work students and faculty members, hopefully, will choose to use the National Association of Social Work as a reference group and attempt to act in accord with this group's ethical guidelines and directives for practice. Today, many people use mass media personages and groups as points of reference.

Generalized others provide perspectives and vocabularies representing the synthesis of multiple members of a large social organization or institution. The American institution of Little League baseball, for instance, becomes a generalized other for many young boys and some girls. The Catholic Church is an important generalized other for me, and for my family. New members learn through communication the goals shared by all members of the institution, the rules and values of the large social aggregate, and the habitual ways of doing things. The legal system, religious institutions, and the political-economic order are often internalized as generalized others.

How Are Resources and Their Flow Conceptualized?

Interactionists attend to the transfer of meanings between communicators. **Meanings** are representations of objects in the environment. Meanings often have multiple dimensions, including cognitive, affective, and behavioral aspects. For you, *teacher* may mean "an expert who passes on social work knowledge." The word may evoke friendly and respectful feelings toward a favorite teacher, and you may experience an impulse to behave studiously after talking about this teacher. Your peers, however, may give different meanings to *teacher*.

The flow of meaning can be two-way, or **symmetrical**. Interactionists often refer to this as a **dialogue**. During dialogue, all parties to the exchange of meanings are perceived as open and responsive to the others' communication. Perspective taking is reciprocal. Attention is given to each interactant. Linguistic symbols are selected from a common set of meanings (a shared culture) as much as possible. When not possible, interactants attempt to broaden their sociocultural understanding by learning about different others. Interaction partners express appreciation for the others' communicative purposes, and they communicate as equals.

The flow of meaning can also be **asymmetrical.** The mutuality of dialogue can be contrasted to a monologue. In public monologues, a speaker, often more powerful or dominant than the listener, indulges in long passages of speech. Extensive one-sided reporting on the powerful person's feelings, ideas, experiences, and points of view is normative, and little attention is given to the sensitivities or opinions of the subordinate interaction partner. In these one-way transfers of meaning, the powerful person may compel by force, or the threat of force, the other's compliance. Social workers must take care. Typically, they have the power to refuse services to clients, to judge a client as ineligible, or to attach a negative label to the client. Social workers committed to egalitarian communication refrain from using their position or their professional expertise to impose meanings on the client. Social workers should try instead to negotiate symmetrically the assessment formulation, goals, and intervention strategies.

Interactionists consider symbolic resources as important as tangible resources. Words, images, stories, roles, information, gestures, and behavior signaling rebellion or deference can all be used to advance personal and collective interests, to facilitate social action, to mobilize or inspire others to resist oppressors, and to fight for social justice. The leaders of social movements—for example, the Jewish resistance fighters in Warsaw, Poland, during the Nazi invasion—can use symbolic resources effectively in a battle against enemies with vastly more material resources. Symbols associated with Jewish tradition and with personal honor united thousands of Jews in a creative and daring response to the extermination efforts of the Nazis. Those social workers and social work clients who have symbolic dexterity, the ability to manipulate symbols, have powerful tools.

Symbols that serve as resources have several qualities (Schudson, 1989). One is **force,** a vividness that captures the attention of the audience like images of the collapse of the World Trade Center. **Resonance** deals with salience to the audience. The U.S. flag was a resonant symbol for those participants at the 2001 World Series. Such symbols are in line with community interests and cultural frameworks. Symbols with high **resolution** are those that clearly specify and direct social action. The president of the United States once displayed a dollar bill and asked American children to help children in Afghanistan by sending a gift of one dollar. **Institutionalized** symbols can be used as resources. These are representations of cultural objects displayed and reinforced over time in various social institutions. A moment of silence or prayer has been institutionalized as a common symbolic practice at school meetings, media events, worship services, and sporting events.

WHAT DESCRIPTIVE WORDS ARE USED?

Connections between systems might be labeled as *symmetrical* or *asymmetrical,* or as dominated by *symbolic* or *nonsymbolic* interaction. Social systems in the environment are characterized in terms used by the members themselves. Interactionists prefer the ethnographic approach to depicting membership groups and are wary of concepts generated without grounding in the lived experiences of group members. An interactionist researcher, therefore, might observe and interview members of a social work agency to learn the collective identities (formal and informal) that members attach to the organization as well as the perceived qualities, characteristics, and other meanings associated with these identities. Interactionists also prefer descriptors reflective of their conviction that membership organizations are dynamic and continually changing rather than static. System patterns are characterized, for example, in terms of generic social processes related to member recruiting, socializing, regulating, participating, and exiting.

HOW IS CHANGE CONCEPTUALIZED?

Interactionists attempt to change communication processes at the intrapersonal, interpersonal, and cultural level. The assessment of a member would be based on data about the member's ability to use symbols, to take the perspectives of others, and to engage in coherent and constructive interaction with the particular and collective others that the other deems significant, and the person's awareness of his or her patterns of symbolic interaction in a variety of membership settings. Intervention would aim for changes in systems of meaning.

Kiecolt (2000) discusses self-concept change at the intrapersonal level. The self-concept is the total set of identities (*I*'s, *me*'s, and *you*'s) and qualities. Many of these are derived from our roles in important membership groups. Self-concept change involves change in the meanings associated with a particular role identity (social worker); changes in the perceived functionality of an identity (what can be accomplished through the social worker role); changes in the identity's representation (the images presented to self and others of the role identity); and changes in the interconnectedness across identities (degree of sharing of representations across different social worker, citizen, and family identities). Self-concept change can include the addition of new role identities (as activist social worker) to the inner forum; the reordering of the ranking of varied role identities in a hierarchy of identities (social worker becomes more important than athlete); or an increase or decrease in the importance of a quality or attribute associated with a particular identity (empathy becomes a valued quality linked to the social work identity).

The social worker, for interactionists, is a caring, skilled, and human communicator with facility in a variety of helping roles. The competent interactionist social worker can take the perspective of many different clients in a deep and empathic way; can communicate an understanding of the others' perspectives; can regulate his or her helping actions by anticipating sensitively the likely responses of others; can help clients and colleagues take each other's perspectives; can help clients learn to communicate understanding and empathy to their significant others; can help others monitor and learn from their self-interaction; and can facilitate reciprocal and caring communication that helps members work well together to solve practical problems. At the interpersonal level, the competent social worker can understand various membership organizations and challenges as seen by various members. The worker can translate agency requirements and helping jargon into symbols the client can understand, and can translate the client's perspectives to others in the agency and to community members who may lack sympathy for the client's predicament. To summarize, the applied symbolic interactionist is a persistent and versatile interpreter, asking questions like "What perspective is the other using?" "What might that communication mean?" and "How might I interpret or redirect communication between participants so that they can better understand each other and achieve communal ends?"

HOW ARE ACTUAL AND IDEAL ECO-MAPS CONTRASTED?

Let's start with the focal system or member. Inner life is governed by the **individuality-groupness effect.** The person is one and many simultaneously. The *I*, the *me*, and the *you* are not separate psychic entities but discriminated aspects of the total self. Healthy persons have a dialogical relation between and among these unseen members of the self (Perinbanayagam, 2000). Through their interaction, the actor can attach meanings to objects and events, and because of their interaction, the person can create a composite or whole self integrating those perspectives internalized during contact with the external world and those perspectives generated creatively within the inner forum. Ideally, the person achieves a balance among the *I,* the *me,* and the *you.* For the immature self, conversations center on the perspective of one member of the inner forum. In the *I-centric self,* the acts of the individual will be creative and spontaneous but insensitive to the influence and demands of the others. In the *me-centric self,* the person's acts indicate a machinelike suppression of creativity and spontaneity and a rigid or absolute conformity to social and cultural standards. In the *you-centric self,* the person imagines future possibilities to the detriment of contemporary realities. Becoming trumps being, resulting in too little acting and too much dreaming. Personal and professional growth can be thought of not as the maturation of one self, but as an achievement of unity within diversity. Growth is an increase in the overall quality of the organization and relatedness of multiple members of the self. Growth can also be thought of as a continuous temporal integration and reintegration of past selves (*me*), present self (*I*), and future selves (*you*). Personal growth occurs because of the purposeful, coherent, and productive communication among the members of the inner forum.

Interactionists also have some particular notions about the characteristics of ideal membership organizations (Forte, 2003; Schwalbe, 1988a; Shalin, 2000). These organizations are committed to democratic principles and procedures. Policies and patterns that will help all members realize their potentialities for symbolic interaction are institutionalized. Power is distributed equally, and all members of the organization participate in free and open communication. Deliberations continue until actions that creatively synthesize divergent perspectives and interests in moral ways emerge. Therapy and social movement work are not polar opposites for interactionists. Personal reconstruction should contribute to social reconstruction, and social reconstruction must foster personal reconstruction.

The progressive reformers who founded symbolic interactionism did not advocate revolution. They preferred locally tailored and modest reform efforts and were wary of utopian schemes. General conceptions of the ideal ecosystem must be melded to particular circumstances and specific problems. Yet interactionists engage often in discussions about the desired effects of ideal membership organizations and contexts. In communities characterized by optimal interactional processes, each member would possess an enlarged social self, one that has incorporated the viewpoints of multiple others. This ideal is contrasted to those communities in which many members have narrow selves. The **narrow self** is one limited to using the perspectives of one or a few others. Each member with an **enlarged self** would possess fully developed role-taking abilities, the capacity to discern accurately and deeply the cognitive, emotional, and motivational tendencies of a wide range of fellow citizens. Each member would also have strong role-taking propensities, or inclinations to use role-taking abilities in many social situations. Role taking would be moral and used to understand and cooperate with others, not to achieve strategic advantage. Each member would understand and commit to the principle of **sociality.** This is the view that the interdependence of community members is essential to mutual survival and social growth and that such interdependence should be fostered. Each member would be able to take the viewpoint of the whole community (the generalized other) during deliberations over technical, interpretive, and moral problems. The task of perfecting the social process would spread widely. Mead and Addams had international aspirations for their vision of membership improvement. They imagined and worked for the universalizing of empathy, of social intelligence, and of democracy so that across the globe people could achieve a high degree of sympathetic understanding, mutual identification, tolerance of diversity, and commitment to collaborative need fulfillment.

How Are Issues of Diversity, Color, and Shading Addressed?

Applied symbolic interactionists are very attuned to diversity factors. Interactionist social workers conceive of modern society as a "multiverse" rather than a "universe." A modern society such as the United States is characterized not only by territorial diversity and heterogeneity of social structures but also by the proliferation of systems of meaning and of orderly systems of interaction. William James (1907/1958), a pragmatist psychologist and contributor to early interactionism, rejected the idea of one reality or a single universe. He preferred to think of a "pluralistic universe." In interactionist terminology, then, we might say that a society is composed of multiple symbolic universes or social worlds rather than just one. Each of these worlds has members using a distinctive language, a special perspective on social life, and a unique pattern of communication with other social worlds. Think of a large Catholic for-profit hospital with a social work unit. In a sense, the doctors, the nurses, the priests and nuns, the administrators, and the social workers all belong to different social worlds within the hospital. Each social world is its own subculture or club. Each social world has a distinctive set of significant symbols, its own argot or special shorthand for talking with insiders, its own preferred nonverbal gestures, its own vocabularies of emotions and motives, and its own cherished stories. Social workers often need years to understand adequately the medical culture that comes readily to trained doctors.

Interactionists have a long history of theoretical concern with diversity. Mead (1929/1964) stated this position firmly when he wrote that "society is the interaction of these selves and an interaction that is only possible if out of their diversity unity arises. We are infinitely different from each other, but our differences make social interaction possible. Society is unity in diversity" (p. 359). Shalin (1986) claimed that "the project of interactionist sociology . . . is an inquiry into the pluralistic social universe brought into being by various collectivities, each one creating a separate environment of meaningful objects that distinguish its members from those inhabiting different social worlds" (p. 12). Wiley (1994) theorized using an interactionist lens that human nature is characterized by both commonality and difference. Universally, humans share an evolutionary heritage equipping us with capacities for reflection and self-awareness. Yet human identities—semiotic representations of the qualities of self—are enormously varied because of the diverse historical, cultural, and social circumstances influencing the group construction of such identities. Additionally, important interactionists such as Park, Thomas, Hughes, and Blumer and their more recent successors have developed a diversity-sensitive literature (Lal, 1995). They have examined issues related to ethnic and racial identity, racial prejudice, ethnic community life, appropriate characterizations of various membership groups, and the collective symbolic processes that support or suppress respect for diversity.

Historically, interactionists have demonstrated a nuanced appreciation for cultural pluralism in their theory-based policy and practice recommendations (Carey, 1975). In the early part of the 20th century, Park and Thomas, for example, opposed Americanization programs requiring repudiation of all ties to immigrant culture. Other interactionists worked closely with settlement house and ethnic group leaders. Herbert Blumer was a courageous and socially engaged scholar, one who was not intimidated by his adversaries. When teaching at the University of Missouri around 1925, Blumer lectured that scientific evidence did not support claims of racial superiority nor the claims of a pure race. Threats from local Ku Klux Klan members did not scare him into resigning or retracting his views (Lofland, 1980).

Interactionists would warn social workers that coordinating the interests, interaction styles, and inventory of symbols of members from different social worlds or membership clubs is a challenging task. These social clubs may be in conflict, coexistence, symbiosis, or harmony with one another. Most members of a modern society, interactionists add, are attempting to manage membership in many groups and social worlds. Symbolic interactionists attend with special interest to the dilemmas that occur when multiple memberships challenge people to deal with contradictory behavioral expectations, disparate perspectives for viewing social phenomena, differing codes of communication, and competition for identification and loyalty.

Symbolic interactionists are also interested in finding ways to promote unity, mutual tolerance, and action for the common good amid global diversity and suspicion. At the recent turn of the century, countries throughout the world were experiencing murder and mayhem in the name of tribal and cultural differences. The interactionist approach, according to Seidman (1996), is "respectful of differences, comfortable with ambiguity and uncertainty, and oriented toward inventiveness and temporary agreements" and, therefore, seems today to be "especially appropriate, encouraging civil, peaceful modes of managing daily collective life" (p. 758). George Herbert Mead was a dedicated internationalist. Other interactionists followed his example. Blumer's (1990) sociological work in Brazil, Chang's (2000) use of interactionism to understand changes in China's class structure, and Sjoberg's (1996) articulation of the global ramifications of the human rights movement continued this commitment to theory building across national boundaries. Mead (1934) explicitly called for a global awareness. "We are struggling now," he wrote, "to get a certain amount of international mindedness. We are realizing ourselves as members of a larger community. The vivid nationalism of the present period should in the end call out the international attitude of the larger community" (p. 325). Mead theorized about the potential utility of global processes, including the increase in worldwide economic interdependence; the dispersion of symbolic systems like science, logic, and religious missionary work; the cooperative interaction among members of the global community; and the development of a "generalized other," referring to all humankind (Aboulafia, 1995). Change agents might harness these processes to hasten the transformation of narrow and parochial selves into larger selves and to unite earthlings. Mead imagined that such forces could foster a world community more and more capable of peaceful conflict resolution, democratic decision making, sympathetic support of distressed global neighbors, and the celebration of similarities amid disparate perspectives. Practitioners interested in pluralistic societies, in the global social scene, and in the earth's ecology can learn much from Mead's international-mindedness and from the interactionist approach to diversity.

What Would Be Added or Deleted?

Interactionists might recommend several changes to the eco-map. The effective social worker, for instance, develops a dual membership and participates in both the agency life and the helping group created with clients. The social worker could depict this by overlapping circles. Additionally, interactionists give importance to the human capacity for time shifting. People can use symbols and imagination to shift to a historical perspective or to a future perspective on their current predicaments. Interactionists would prefer, then, a retrospective eco-map that adds assessment data collected from life histories, autobiographies, diaries, and artifacts of the client's earlier experiences; a contemporary eco-map including membership data collected by participant observation, interviews, and focus group discussions; and a prospective eco-map that characterizes the member's projection of self into a desired future situation. Interactionists might also recommend placing the focal system visually in the larger global network of societies.

THE LIMITS OF APPLIED SYMBOLIC INTERACTIONISM: A SOCIAL WORK APPRAISAL

Critics of the interactionist approach have charged that interactionists pay too little attention to the large-scale social structure and social systems that constrain communication and action. These critics view interactionists as naive and insufficiently alert to the indicators of social inequality and social injustice that undermine attempts at reciprocal perspective taking and cooperation. Interactionists have tried to rectify such oversights and are doing much work useful to practitioners in these areas.

More seriously, interactionists have failed to develop a standardized and scientific vocabulary of many key concepts, including self, identity, and social reconstruction. Concepts are rarely operationalized with consideration for validity and reliability. Thus, the perspective is hard to teach to social workers and inadequate for social workers committed to evidence-based practice.

Moreover, most interactionists have forgotten the pragmatist directive to use knowledge for solving public problems. Case studies by interactionist social workers are extremely rare. Interactionists offer us too few examples of the application and evaluation of interactionist concepts and theories for the effective improvement of membership conditions.

Finally, the literature on applied symbolic interactionism is large but has not been integrated carefully into the profession's knowledge base (Forte, 2002a, 2004a, 2004b). Social work practice theorists often fail to trace ideas and principles to the interactionist heritage. Theorists and theory users in allied disciplines such as sociology and psychology show minimal interest in the application of interactionism, especially with vulnerable and oppressed populations.

AN INTERACTIONIST MODEL FOR WORK WITH THE CHRONICALLY DEPRESSED

David Karp is an interactionist sociologist and a teacher. He has suffered from depression for 20 years. Karp (1996) decided to use his familiarity with this affective disorder to study others who reported long-term problems with depression and to advance an interactionist approach to assessment and group intervention with these troubled persons. For one of his inquiries, he was a participant and observer for two years in a support group offered at a mental hospital in the Boston area. The following discussion summarizes his qualitative and grounded approach.

THE INTERACTIONIST PERSPECTIVE ON CHRONIC DEPRESSION

About 120 different members attended the group over this time. The group helped members of various ages, educational levels, religions, and occupations. Men and women, whites and blacks, participated. The members shared several commonalities. All had experienced hospitalizations in mental health facilities. All had been officially labeled with a diagnosis of clinical depression, and all reported that depression had negatively effected their interaction in family groups and work organizations.

Karp (1996) argued that symbolic interactionism is an ideal theoretical perspective for understanding the subjective experience of depression. The physical sensations, thoughts, images, feelings, and reactions associated with emotional disorders are complex communications that often lack clear meaning. The signs of depression must be carefully interpreted by the sufferer, her significant others, and her professional helpers before a definition of clinical depression is established. Moreover, the causes and the features indicating depression are ambiguous, and our culture does not provide a consensual vocabulary for appraising and coping with depression. In our society, *depression* means different things to different groups. Medical doctors, psychologists, spiritual counselors, and laypersons do not use the same symbols, images, or theories to characterize the condition, but humans have a strong urge to make sense of social life and of unclear or confusing events or experiences. Moreover, the signs of depression are "ineffable"—hard to describe, hard to define, and hard to communicate.

Karp (1996) bolstered his interactionist analysis with an attempt to identify some of the societal changes and community arrangements that may contribute to increased reports of depression. He referred to dialectics, the interaction of social historical processes with psychological processes that results in depression. Several features of membership in Western societies have contributed to increased reports of affective disorder. These include a cultural preoccupation with the inner life of members and with personal therapy and medication as remedies for malfunctions; the spread of the ideology of individualism, a worldview that explains life difficulties as personal failings rather than as caused by institutional contradictions and inhospitable membership arrangements; a loosening of social connections that bind members to their communities, and specifically to the workplace, to intimate others, to place communities, and to society. Without such connections, many members experience isolation and loneliness, and the medicalization of their emotional pain and unhappiness. Problems of living are increasingly labeled as diseases, diagnosed by medical experts, and treated by medications.

THE INTERACTIONIST PERSPECTIVE ON ASSESSMENT

Help from others can be very beneficial with the "problem of sense making." Karp (1996) suggested that to cope successfully support group members need to resolve four interpretive dilemmas: What are the appropriate labels to attach to this difficulty, and from whom does one obtain a useful label or diagnosis? To what extent is the sufferer responsible for causing the emotional disorder and for remedying it? How much should sufferers rely on medical experts for interpreting and relieving the problem? What meaning might group members attach to the recommended treatments for depression, especially psychoactive drugs? Social workers might work to assess each client's way of responding to these dilemmas.

Unfortunately, Karp's model does not include specific guidelines for collecting information or for arriving at an interactionist assessment. He implies that the worker should obtain a history of the changing and multiple meanings that each group member has assigned to depression, and the meanings associated with the depressed person's answers to each of the four dilemmas. He might also recommend the exploration of critical interaction experiences with significant others, doctors, pharmacists, employers, peers, and other relevant people.

THE INTERACTIONIST PERSPECTIVE ON INTERVENTION

A mutual aid group was the intervention reported on by Karp (1996). The group of 15 to 25 members participated in a common concern, topic-oriented group familiar to social group workers. Although the group leaders had special training, they also shared the affective disorder identified by other members. Leadership was rotated. Group sessions included "testimonies," "story swaps," and "problem-solving conversations." Group members selected discussion topics, either responding to critical needs of a troubled member or addressing topics related to the four interpretive dilemmas. Group talk was a collective examination of cultural meanings attached to depression and a search for new meanings. The discussion often resulted in a consideration of various ways to symbolize the issue under consideration. The group focused on commonalities, and members attempted to arrive at a consensual understanding of each dilemma and of possible interaction coping strategies. However, the group accepted that each member was entitled to develop his or her own unique interpretation, even if it failed to correspond with the consensual views.

The supportive group assisted each member in resolving his or her interpretive dilemmas. Group members addressed the issue of labeling. Mental illness is a negative label. Those so labeled are often blamed for their failings and stigmatized as meriting degradation. Sufferers of affective disorder know this and struggle with questions about keeping their symptoms private or announcing them publicly. Group members helped each other name and talk about their complex feelings and experiences in a safe setting. Fellow sufferers were unlikely to react negatively to the label "depressed person." Such group discussion offered a remedy to the isolation and despair that comes from hiding one's emotional vulnerabilities. The group also provided more positive interpretations of and labels for the condition than those used by critical workers, family members, or neighbors.

Group members addressed the issue of responsibility. Members discussed, for instance, the dominant interpretive framework in society. In the United States, medical experts cast depressed persons as "victims" of a biochemical illness needing treatment. This was an attractive identity to some sufferers because it lessened the sense of responsibility for their troubles. The downside, however, is the sense of passivity and helplessness associated with being a victim. Group talk helped members navigate between the rhetoric of physical determinism and submission to the disease and the rhetoric of personal power and control over one's painful experiences.

The support group helped members talk about their use of experts. The group gave much attention to relationships with doctors, and many members reviewed their histories while complaining about misdiagnosis and contradictory diagnoses. The members often reported on their efforts to find "Doctor Right." Members also shared their anger and frustration about poor advice from experts and the insensitivity of some helpers. However, members also indicated that they valued the sense of clarity that medical experts offered.

Defining the troubling condition as an illness suggested specific treatments that would alleviate suffering. The group helped many members find a balance between relying on the expertise of medical professionals and becoming allies with other sufferers to develop layperson expertise. The group also helped members advocate for egalitarian interaction with their doctors and for relationships characterized by open communication and mutual participation in the assessment and intervention selection processes.

Karp (1996) showed how the group helped members explore the multiple meaning of recommended treatments. All group members had used psychotropic medications at one point for their affective disorder. The group gave frequent attention to the collective evaluation and interpretation of drugs and their effectiveness. Members reported too on their drug management strategies, including dosage levels, side effects, and interactions among multiple medications. After much deliberation, the group arrived at some consensus. Chronically depressed persons should not self-medicate; expert and peer help should be sought in this area. Group members also explored alternative coping strategies, including spiritual practices and the mobilization of support from family and friends.

Interactionist group work helped members clarify their sensations, thoughts, and moods; develop a self-affirming vocabulary for talking about their condition; and create a sense-making framework for interpreting responsibility, mental illness labels, experts, and medications. Individual sufferers learned that they were members of a community of sufferers, that they might collectively better understand and manage their membership experiences, and that they could find meaning and dignity with each other despite dehumanizing societal pressures.

LEARNING ACTIVITIES

1. What are some group experiences that have had great influence on you? Identify and describe two or three of the social groups or organizations that made these experiences possible. In what ways did your membership in the groups influence your sense of identity and your behavioral patterns?

2. Emotions may seem like a basic and universal feature of social life. Interactionists suggest that emotional experience varies by group membership. Report here on some of the ways that you describe and label your emotional states, display your emotions to your interactional partners, and try to cope with emotional difficulties. Then contrast your approach to emotions with that of members of a group very different from yours (a different generation such as your grandparents, a military unit, or a different nationality—people you know from Italy or China or some other country).

3. Using Cahill's approach to gender socialization, analyze how children are socialized in your family or a client family. What different meanings are attached to boys and to girls? How do significant others interact differently with boys and girls? How are the family environments designed differently to accommodate boys and girls? What effects of gender-based socialization practices have you experienced or observed? How might socialization processes be improved?

4. When I was dubbed "Doctor" Forte after receiving a Ph.D. in Social Work, my life changed in many ways. What labels have been attached to you so far? Pick one, and analyze why you were labeled. Who labeled you? How did your interaction with others change after being labeled? How did your self-concept and behavior change?

5. Which persons have become significant to you? Why? Which groups do you use as a reference? How do the standards and expectations of these groups influence your perspective on social work, life, and your behavior? What institutions or large organizations are part of your generalized others?

6. Construct an interactionist eco-map. Analyze specifically the interplay between your social memberships or public interaction and your inner forum, your set of internalized memberships. Monitor your private and silent self-interaction, and pick one episode of self-talk. In what ways does your inner dialogue include the voices of past memberships (the *me*), the voices of future or possible memberships (the *you*), and the voices of your distinctive self (the *I*)?

7. Debate the following statement: "Personal problems and relationship difficulties are too often defined as medical diseases." What evidence for and against this statement can you present? What are some positive and negative implications of the medicalization of problems?

ADDITIONAL RESOURCES

Additional resources are available on the book companion website at **www.thomsonedu.com/ social_work/forte**. Resources include key terms, tutorial quizzes, links to related websites, and lists of additional resources for furthering your research.

APPLIED SOCIAL ROLE THEORY

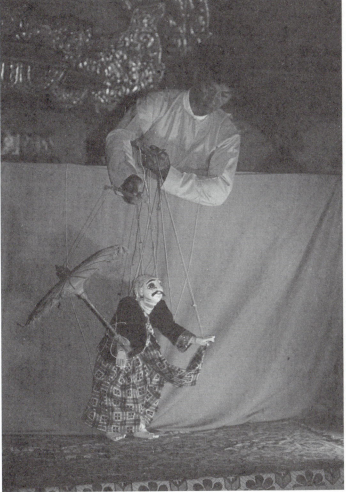

CHAPTER 11

Ernest Manewal/IndexStock

INTRODUCTION

The social role theory has ancient origins. The concept of *role* is derived from the Latin word that Romans used to describe a wooden roll. Sheets of parchment were fastened to this roll. Prompters helped the theatrical actors of the time learn their parts by reading the playwright's words from these rotating sheets (Biddle & Thomas, 1966). The practice continues today, but prompters use cue cards instead to help late-night talk show hosts and comedians play their parts.

Social role theorists liken human behavior to the dramatic action of performers. Kollock and O'Brien (1994) summarize the theoretical perspective as follows: "We behave differently in front of different people, we pick out clothing that is consistent with the image we wish to project. We enlist the help of friends, caterers, decorators, in helping us successfully 'stage' a dinner for a friend, a birthday party for a relative, or a rush party for a sorority or fraternity" (p. 127). The theory's imagery, Sarbin (1984) suggests, "is that of human beings, actors, who try to solve their identity and existential problems in a world of other people, things, and symbols, not unlike actors in the theater" (p. 23).

Actors enact established roles, modify conventional roles, or create new roles to solve problems and meet challenges. Social workers and social work clients do the same. Actors use various dramatic techniques to improve their performances. People do the same thing in everyday life (Goffman, 1959). Our clients use impression management techniques to present ideal self-images. They use face-saving techniques to avoid embarrassment when they stumble during leisure time or professional performances. They use masking techniques to hide their true feelings, beliefs, or identities from enemies (and sometimes social workers) or to present false identities. They use ritualized acting to convey respect and deference to powerful persons in the human services organization; they use performance tricks to withhold secrets and other information that might undermine the credibility of their claims to sincerely desire help. Many social roles that people enact can be compared to the positions or roles found in the world of the theater: actor, director, supporting player, audience member, producer, and stagehand.

In this chapter, I will show how concepts inspired by the drama-turgical perspective, such as *role, role enactment, role playing, role taking, altercasting, coaching, stage, performance, presentation of self, actor, psychodrama,* and *persona* (Thomas & Biddle, 1966), can be applied to understanding and helping people with troubles. Several exemplary models will be introduced. The metaphor of social life as drama will be used to conceptualize the client, the social worker, and the social organization. Role theory concepts and propositions will be displayed on an eco-map and translated into ecosystem terms. Finally, I will outline a conceptual model of the application of role theory to the problem of recruiting volunteers to serve homeless persons.

RELATED DIALECTS, ASSOCIATED SCHOOLS OF THOUGHT

Two major traditions or schools of thought have contributed to the development of social role theory. The **structural approach** originated in the work of Ralph Linton and was developed by Talcott Parsons, Robert Merton, and other sociologists. The interactionist or **processual approach** grew from the creative scholarship of George Herbert Mead and was embellished by Florian Znaniecki, Robert Park, Ralph Turner, and other theorists and researchers. Each approach makes different use of the theatrical metaphor.

The structural tradition conceives of social life as being like a drama school that believes actors should perform in response to the explicit and detailed directives provided in the script. The processual tradition characterizes the drama school of life as one in which most acting is improvisational, where actors invent their characters in relation to themes and broadly sketched story lines. Structuralists give primary attention to the social positions that constitute formal social organizations and the roles associated with each position. Structuralists focus in the theatrical sense on the standard parts in the classic and well-known plays staged by established Broadway producers. Interactionist role theorists give greater emphasis to the creative aspect of human behavior. The most interesting and lifelike plays, for the interactionists, are experimental and off Broadway. According to the structuralists, actors earn fine reviews when they conform to standard expectations about the performance and when they subordinate personal inclinations for the sake of the whole play. For interactionists, actors merit accolades when they use communication abilities such as **role taking** (imagining the situation from the other's perspective) and **role making** (creatively collaborating with others to find meanings that enable coordinated action) to pull off fresh and spontaneous performances.

This chapter will incorporate elements from both traditions as well as the ideas of Jacob Moreno and Erving Goffman, whose dramaturgical perspectives cannot be easily classified as solely structural or interactionist. Theorists, researchers, and practitioners who have applied role theory to practice problems are also resources for this chapter.

APPLIED SOCIAL ROLE THEORY: EXEMPLARY MODELS

ROBERT LINTON

One of the most important social scientists in the lineage of role theory was Robert Linton (1893–1915). Linton, an American anthropologist, taught at several prestigious universities, including Columbia and Yale. He conducted archeological and cultural studies in East Africa, Guatemala, New Mexico, Madagascar, and the South Pacific.

Linton made the important conceptual distinction between **status,** the collection of rights and duties associated with an organizational position, and **role,** the dynamic aspect of status—the use of the rights and duties during social interaction (Hardy & Conway, 1988). Later, role theorists used Linton's ideas to analyze organizational structure as a network of interrelated positions with their associated roles (Biddle & Thomas, 1966). This has relevance to you as a field intern. When social work students begin a field placement, they learn the positions that constitute the agency structure. Over the next several months, students learn how agency employees enact the roles for each position. Linton also differentiated between two kinds of roles: **ascribed roles,** such as the sex role that is determined by a person's physical anatomy; and **achieved roles,** such as an occupational role or the role of college graduate. A person assumes the second kind of role by effort and accomplishment (Sarbin & Allen, 1968).

GEORGE HERBERT MEAD

George Herbert Mead (1863–1931), the founder of symbolic interactionism, also contributed much to role theory. He was a philosopher at the University of Chicago. Mead is now appreciated for his work as both a scholar and a practitioner (Shalin, 2000). Many of his courses focused on the relationship between self and society and influenced the generation of sociologists known as the Chicago school. George Herbert Mead was probably the first person to use the concept *role* as part of a theoretical framework (Sarbin, 1984). Mead wanted to explain how community members worked together to achieve shared objectives. Cooperative social interaction, he argued, required reciprocal role taking. People must place themselves imaginatively in the other person's shoes or roles, and use the other's perspective to judge and guide their own contribution to the stream of action. Thus, role taking makes cooperation possible. Cooperation among a multitude of actors and groups makes society possible. Role taking has other important functions (Biddle, 1979). Role taking makes the self possible (the self is constituted mainly of the imported perspectives of significant role partners), and it is essential to the process of socialization (socializing agents challenge novices to learn acceptable membership behavior by taking the role of competent members).

Mead postulated that the social self emerges and develops through interaction with important role partners. The self is composed of the many different role perspectives that the person has imported into his or her mind while communicating with these significant and generalized others. George Herbert Mead is a wonderful model of the use of role theories for practical purposes (Hardy & Conway, 1988). He collaborated with Jane Addams and other Chicago area social workers in social roles such as activist, researcher, board member, political reformer, and teacher. He worked to improve conditions for workers, immigrants, women, and other client groups so that these members could enact satisfying, effective, and valued community roles.

ERVING GOFFMAN

Erving Goffman (1922–1982) received his master's and doctorate degrees from the University of Chicago, where he studied with many great sociologists (Fine & Manning, 2000). His book *The Presentation of Self in Everyday Life* (1959) is a masterful development of the theatrical metaphor as a framework for understanding human behavior. Goffman elaborated on the theatrical metaphor for social life, elucidating such concepts as performance, front and back stage, and impression management (Franklin, 1982). His work is central to this dramaturgical perspective on role theory.

Erving Goffman is not an easy theorist to categorize. He preferred not to be labeled as a member of any school of thought, which he considered to be clubs that fragmented sociology (Verhoeven, 1993). Goffman wrote on many topics of importance to social workers and other human service practitioners. For instance, he examined **total institutions** such as mental asylums, prisons, and military bases and how those in the role of "inmate" struggle to maintain their honor and value despite continual humiliation and degradation. Goffman also analyzed the various types of **stigma** (physical deformities, character blemishes, and contaminated social memberships) attached to certain actors. He showed how the stigmatized try to adjust to interaction with "normals" in a quest for social acceptance. When challenged by feminists in the mid-1970s, Goffman abandoned some of his sexist inclinations and wrote extensively on gender, gender inequality, interactional manifestations of gender inequality, and depictions of gender ideals in the media (West, 1996). Goffman became interested, for example, in media representations of gender ideals for masculinity and femininity. He reported on the various subtle ways that advertisers use male and female images to subordinate women to men. In many of their role performances, women must overcome these cultural stereotypes if they intend to succeed.

Unfortunately for scholarly practitioners, Goffman did not balance his prolific scholarship with public service or a proservice stance. Other than a term as president of the American Sociological Association (Lofland, 1984), no other civic commitments have been recorded. Gary Marx (1984), a student of Erving Goffman, criticized Goffman's approach to social welfare for several reasons. Goffman did not supplement his incisive social criticism with any suggestions for reform. He avoided all political controversy, and he failed to refrain from caricatures of interventionists. Nor did Goffman extend his remarkable sympathy for the underdog to the administrators and other social work operatives working in large organizations. When challenged by a black student who asked Goffman about the practical use of his ideas for changing conditions, Goffman stated in a curious fury, "I'm not in that business" (cited in Marx, 1984, p. 657). Though Erving Goffman did not consider himself a practitioner, he did document his appreciation for Moreno's psychodrama approach to role theory (Gosnell, 1974), and his body of work shows a concern for the plight of discredited, marginalized, and oppressed people. Goffman's moral outrage at attacks on the self and his nuanced depiction of the microprocesses by which actors seek to enlarge their liberties might serve as a base for practitioners committed to client empowerment.

JACOB MORENO

Jacob Moreno (1889–1974) was born in Romania and became a doctor in Vienna. He moved to the United States in 1925. Moreno pioneered the application of role theory. In 1912, he organized one of the first self-help groups, an organization for prostitutes exploited and harassed by government officials (Blatner & Blatner, 1988). He also invented a wire recorder for taping and playing back process recordings of interactions with his clients. During his long career, Moreno provided services to refugees, prostitutes, prisoners, persons with mental illness, and delinquent adolescents.

Moreno is best known for his contribution to the technology of the planned change process, especially the creation of psychodrama and sociodrama (Biddle & Thomas, 1966). Experimenting with these new intervention methods, Moreno learned how to use the techniques of role play and role reversal in small groups for psychiatric patients and in groups of citizens committed to solving sociocultural problems such as the hostility between racial groups. **Psychodrama** uses the roles, situations, and scripts presented by the client (rather than by a playwright) and invites clients to "act out" their problems. Through this playing of vital roles, Moreno gave group members a safe way to realize their potential for spontaneity and vitality and to learn how to perform a role more effectively and responsibly. At Saint Elizabeth's Hospital in Washington, D.C., for example, the first psychodrama stage in a large facility for those with mental illness was constructed according to Moreno's design. Many patients received treatment on this stage. Influential mental health professionals, encounter group leaders, and social workers have acknowledged Moreno's important contributions to modern approaches to individual and group therapy (Blatner, 1996).

HELEN HARRIS PERLMAN

Helen Harris Perlman is one of the most distinguished social work professors. She taught at the University of Chicago School of Social Service Administration. She developed a very influential problem-solving model of practice organized around the four P's (person, problem, professional, and process). In her book *Persona: Social Role and Personality* (1968), Perlman recommended role theory to the social work profession. She wrote:

> Among the many notions, ideas, and findings that sociology and social psychology and their sister sciences poured forth, the concept of role, it seemed to me, held most ready usefulness for me and fellow caseworkers—and for other professional helpers too—in our job of understanding the individual person's psychosocial problems to the end of improving the adequacy of his social functioning and of his sense of well-being. (p. 5)

Perlman also taught that the social work intake process was one of inducing the applicant to play the role of client. She demonstrated role theory's utility by using its concepts and propositions to explain adult change, personality dynamics, workplace relationships, marriage, parenthood, and clients' psychosocial problems.

APPLIED SOCIAL ROLE THEORY: ROOT METAPHORS

What are the implications of the dramaturgical metaphor? Turner (1998) suggests that the metaphor permits many useful comparisons:

> Just as players have a clearly defined part to play, so actors in society occupy clear positions; just as players must follow a written script, so actors in society must follow norms; just as players must obey the orders of a director, so actors in society must conform to the dictates of those with power or those of importance; just as players must react to each other's performances on the stage, so members of society must mutually adjust their responses to one another; just as players respond to an audience, so actors in society take the role of various audiences or "generalized others"; and just as players with varying abilities and capacities bring to each role their unique interpretations, so actors with varying self-conceptions and role-playing skills have their own styles of interaction. (pp. 383–384)

The primary comparisons of relevance to practitioners are those of people to actors, social organizations to theaters, and social workers to directors.

THE PERSON AS ACTOR

People, like stage performers, may participate in their social situations as protagonists, auxiliaries, antagonists, or members of a chorus (Hare, 1985). Let's relate this metaphor to social work clients. The client is like the protagonist in a theatrical production (Hare, 1985). The client reports to the social worker his images, themes, plots, and scripts and how these are related to role performance problems. Everyday life has presented clients with unmanageable performance problems. These problems come to the client's attention in the same ways that actors learn of acting difficulties. The client reflects on the enactment of a role and experiences dissatisfaction with the quality of his performances, or the audiences who observe and judge client performances present negative reviews. Reviewers—judges, probation workers, psychiatrists, and teachers—may have decided, for example, that the client is playing the part of villain or fool, or is performing the role of responsible and effective citizen poorly (Hare, 1985).

As in the worlds of theater and psychodrama, auxiliaries in the client's world help the protagonist stage and put on life shows. For clients, these auxiliaries may be family members, friends, coworkers, or community associates. These auxiliaries contribute in varying ways to the career of the protagonist. They may support everyday role performances as the husband does for his wife. During role playing in a helping group, the auxiliary may enact the roles complementary to the role practiced by the protagonist. Members may play the roles of employer, parent, spouse, child, or doctor so that the protagonist has a lifelike simulation (Schaffer & Galinsky, 1974). Thus, auxiliaries can help clients learn to enact their parts in effective ways and to win the applause of relevant audiences.

Clients as protagonists often face antagonists. These are persons in the client's social world taking roles in opposition to the client's role. Clients may need social work help in advocating for their rights or in mediating conflicts with these antagonists. A chorus may support the client's performance in everyday life and in the social agency. In theatrical productions such as musicals, the chorus sings words that underscore important aspects of the dramatic activity (Hare, 1985). The chorus in social work–sponsored mutual aid groups may serve a similar function. Seasoned members of the group—a group supporting a substance-free life, for example—can cheer, encourage, or fortify by their words and movements the new client as she performs on center stage.

Clients are like actors, too, in that they vary in their awareness and command of acting technique. Goffman (1959) offered the concept **expressions given** to refer to the posture, body movements, facial changes, and voice tone deliberately chosen by an actor to provide coactors and audience information that illuminates the part. **Expressions given off** are unintended gestures—information communicated by words, deeds, or appearance without awareness of control. A client may monitor the expressions given while performing a role, or the client may act with limited or faulty awareness. Clients may also vary in their beliefs about a performance. Some are sincere, believing in the parts that they are playing. Some clients are insincere and perform despite holding convictions contrary to the observed performance. These clients try to deceive workers. Goffman (1959) offers other useful comparisons. Clients, like actors, may stay "in character" while performing important social roles; or clients may behave like actors who repeatedly and intentionally offer "asides" on their performances out of character; or clients may relax their guard and communicate "out of character" because of carelessness or arrogance. For example, an "ideal" prisoner participating in a work release may let slip words indicating hatred, violent rage, and contempt for the rehabilitation process. The correctional social worker walking in hearing range is alerted to a major discrepancy between the "mask," the public performance, and the "persona," the private personality of the inmate.

THE SOCIAL ENVIRONMENT AS A THEATER

From the perspective of dramaturgical role theory, a society and the social organizations providing social work services can be compared to a theater company that operates a theater house. My comparison will elaborate this dramaturgical image of agencies. The president of the board of directors is like the producer. She is responsible for obtaining the resources necessary for successful agency productions. The executive director is like the playwright, suggesting the inspiring ideas, plots, and scripts that will guide the performances of agency cast members. Program administrators and professional team leaders are the directors who teach, coach, and reward the direct service social workers. Social work service providers are the essential cast members. They are the actors trained in the arts and sciences. They make possible outstanding helping performances. Clients are the other essential actors. The social workers and clients act together to pull off the shows that bring credit (or infamy) to the theater company. Their joint performances evoke positive or negative reviews from various audiences, including family members and friends, community members, politicians, workers in allied organizations, and funding providers. The secretaries, janitors, security guards, and groundskeepers are the stagehands, maintaining the theater and supporting indirectly the onstage performances.

Each social organization providing human services offers a setting or stage for enacting roles critical to the helping process. The building housing the agency is like a theater. The observable features of the stage set the conditions for the kind of helping work that can take place. A worker's office, for example, is like the set. In a correctional agency where I worked, my office was a small cubicle in close proximity to a dozen similar cubicles. Voices carried from one office to another; as a result, clients were often reluctant to play their parts in an open and unreserved way. The scenery in social organizations varies, but many workers try to personalize their offices. A worker may decorate her stage with various props to support professional performances: diplomas and certificates, books, awards, and photographs.

Each helping process completed in the organization is like the performance of a play. People apply for the role of clients, learn the role, take the agency service stage, enact with the social workers the themes and scripts suitable for their life problems, take bows for their hard work right before the curtain falls at the final session, and use the postperformance period to review the quality of the performance and the improvements in client performance off the agency stage and on everyday life stages. Later in this chapter, I will continue the comparison of a human service organization to a theater and discuss further the importance of the offstage and outside regions to organizational activity.

THE SOCIAL WORKER AS DIRECTOR

If we extend the theatrical metaphor to the practitioner, the social worker is the director. He or she organizes the resources for the dramatic helping action, makes the problem-solving play happen, warms up the client, encourages the client to perform well, ensures that roles are enacted effectively, oversees the performances of all cast members (client, coworkers, family members, and support staff) during the engagement, responds to issues presented by audience members who judge the client's performance, facilitates the experience of catharsis or therapeutic emotional release (for clients and for auxiliaries), and helps clients gain insight into their performance and the entire play (Hare, 1985; Shaffer & Galinsky, 1974).

The helping process, like a theatrical production, occurs in a series of scenes or meetings. In the preparatory scenes, the worker imagines how best to organize the setting, script elements, acts, actors, and dramatic climaxes in ways that will evoke cathartic and appreciative responses from his or her clients (Sarbin, 1984). The social worker uses the beginning or contracting scenes to educate the applicant to the part of client and to the helper's part. Agreeing to follow these scripts (and to discuss when improvisation is appropriate) increases the likelihood of a successful joint performance. The essential scenes occur during the middle or work phase. The social worker directs the planned and spontaneous action of the client (or client group) to help bring about a **catharsis** for the client and audience members—a special emotional experience (like that special effect that theater-, movie-, and concertgoers experience) that frees the actor or observer from emotional constraints and intellectual banalities (Gosnell, 1974). The social worker as director helps clients experience new meanings and understandings about how they have been playing their parts (Hare, Blumberg, & Kressel, 2001). The director brings clients who veer from the script back to a suitable and responsive reading of the lines (Goffman, 1959). The social worker should not be an authoritarian director, however. The change-process show is best directed by a social worker seeking continuous creative input from the client. The final or ending phase scenes involve a review of the completion of agreed-upon tasks and of all the performances. In the best circumstances, tensions and conflicts in the dramatic plots that constitute the client's life script have been resolved (Hare, 1985). Ideally, reviews from external audiences confirm the worker's and client's opinions about the quality of their performances.

Generalist social workers are versatile directors. They direct two-person plays (the dyadic helping relationship), multiperson plays (group and family work), and multi-organization plays (community organizing and social advocacy). The social worker even directs one-person plays when she processes a helping session in the solitude of the office, alternating in the internal conversation between the roles of actor recreating the performance and audience reviewing the performance.

Many duties of a social worker are like the duties of a director of a play (Hare, 1985). The social worker often works with agency administrators to visualize the ideal stage setting for therapeutic performances, and helps design the appropriate stage or client meeting room. The social worker attempts to assess and understand the style of each client/actor and their relationships to the other actors in their everyday life casts. The social worker uses this information to help the cast enhance the overall quality of their social productions. The social worker may perform the roles of both director and playwright. The playwright provides a "commanding image," a special insight into and interpretation of the dramatic possibilities in the play. Social workers "lend a vision" to clients, groups, and communities who cannot imagine participating in a rewarding play. When clients have limited intellectual power or are disoriented by mental or physical illness, the worker may take charge of the details of the helping play, including the scenes, the organization of scenes into acts, the script, and the blocking of the dramatic action (Hare, 1985). When clients are full participants in the helping process, they can share the directing and playwriting functions with the worker. The social worker closely monitors client performances. He or she finds the themes present in the client's target problems, observes the plot that the client is enacting, and helps the client write a new plot or story for her life. Social workers also help clients change the inner monologues that interfere with their public role enactment. The social worker using the group method prepares the actors for their performances in front of a supportive audience. The worker may coach the actors during these performances. Finally, the social worker as an enthusiastic director spreads the word to the public about the special accomplishments of his or her performers.

CORE ASSUMPTIONS OF APPLIED SOCIAL ROLE THEORY

The social role theory includes a set of basic assumptions about the person, the environment, and transactions between the person and the environment. I will review four assumptions, explaining each, when possible, using comparisons to acting and the theater.

HUMAN BEHAVIOR IS PATTERNED AND MEANINGFUL

First, social role theorists assume that much human behavior is patterned and meaningful to the particular organizational and group members who observe it (Biddle, 1979). What would social life be without patterns? Imagine a play in which the actors speak gibberish, one actor begins playing Hamlet but then takes the character of Homer Simpson, the actors leave the stage after 10 minutes and never return, and the actors use real bullets instead of blanks to dramatize a violent encounter. Weird!

Instead, people generally enact roles in ways similar to the way other community members enact the role and reminiscent of how they acted the part in the past. Roles are patterns of action that can be identified by competent members of the society (Callero, 1986). Patterned behavior has several features. It is recognizable, distinguishable, and predictable. A social worker conducting a home visit can recognize when a woman is enacting the mothering role with her children. The set of behaviors associated with mothering forms one gestalt (Turner, 1978). One role is distinguishable from another, and the social work observer can tell the difference between the woman acting as mother with a child, picking up the phone and assuming the wife role, and acting as a client by questioning the worker. An actor's commitment to enact a role indicates that her behavior will become somewhat predictable. During the home visit, for example, the woman becomes the host to the guest social worker. Her actions follow a familiar social script for the host role. The woman welcomes the worker, takes the worker's coat, and offers the worker a seat and a glass of water.

Roles are like the tangible objects that we see in the physical environment. They are recognized by community members, accepted as real, and used to accomplish goals (Callero, 1994). We can imagine the response of an animal if we were to kick it. Also, we can imagine how a coactor in a particular role will respond.

Several cues help us anticipate the pattern associated with a role. First, community members attach the same name or title to the role. The title of a role, such as doctor or social worker, summarizes the cultural information about how the actor is expected to fulfill that role (Lopata, 1994). Second, a particular configuration of costume, gestures, and spoken lines is associated with each role. A successful interaction requires that we identify the other's role by observing these physical, verbal, nonverbal, and contextual cues and placing the other in the role. Then, we can better anticipate the other's likely actions. Interaction problems occur as a result of misattribution. For example, once a psychology professor made a cursory examination of my presentation of self and assumed that I was a professor and peer. He prepared to allow me many privileges and resources and to treat me as an equal on a research project. His action and attitudes toward me changed abruptly when I informed him that I sought his cooperation, but in the role of doctoral student.

Roles have a historical and cultural base. The pattern for each role in the society has recorded and contemporary models. Members have learned what to expect of various role incumbents (Lopata, 1994). Experienced adult community members in the United States, for example, have direct or vicarious knowledge of hundreds of social roles. They have observed representations of many social roles in television shows, movies, plays, and video games. Because of this common cultural experience, actors in this society share conceptions of the appropriate and convincing patterns of behavior for many roles. They have also learned how role models adjust their role performances to a wide variety of social situations. Let's relate this to the theater. Hare and Blumberg (1988) suggest that an actual stage performance is based on the text. Actors bring to the theater (and to everyday life), however, a pre-text: cultural knowledge about the roles, scripts, and staging appropriate to the performance. This influences the ways that they interpret and perform the text on the social stage. Therefore, actors do not need to master a new pattern of behavior role for each performance or social encounter. They can adapt the patterns that are customary and use these patterns in situation-specific and creative ways while respecting the cultural text for the performance.

PERFORMANCES ARE INFLUENCED BY CONTEXTUAL FACTORS

Second, social role theorists assume that performances occur in and are influenced by the social and ecological context. People are expected to play certain parts in certain ways at certain times and under identifiable social and ecological conditions. Performances appropriate to one role on a particular stage may seem incomprehensible or unacceptable in another role. This assumption becomes most apparent when the role behaviors expected in a social context are breached.

At the mental health clubhouse where I worked, for example, we attempted to create an agency context that reinforced the values of tolerance, peacefulness, and responsible behavior. Our orientation process, our posted rules of conduct, and our gentle reminders to rule breakers earned the agency the reputation as a "cool place." One client, however, defied all the contextual cues and responded frequently to peer criticism with loud, dramatic outbursts. He declared his outrage. He gestured that he was likely to become violent, and he echoed lines of flamboyant gangsters and villains from the popular culture. This client behavior might be appropriate in the context of a music video or a gang den, but it was not responsive or acceptable in the context of a community living room serving fragile persons with chronic mental disorders. The staff chastised the client for "going Hollywood," and challenged him to either end this kind of performance or continue it on a stage outside the agency.

Social contexts vary in the degree to which they compel compliance from role enactors. In some organizational contexts, actors are expected to follow clear, detailed, and explicit scripts. Other organizations have looser scripts in which action sequences are neither specified nor totally controlled. The social worker, for instance, after leaving a job on a tightly scripted military base, will find that the scripts for worker and client role enactments in the community center allow much room for creative interpretation.

The Social Role Is the Dynamic Aspect of the Social Position

Third, many social role theorists assume that a social role is the dynamic aspect of **social position.** A position can be filled by different sets of persons, but all must take into account the identity, rank, job description, and communication channels inherent in the position as they enact their positional roles (Biddle, 1979). Fifty different men and women assigned to the same position of executive director, but serving in 50 different United Way agencies, will enact their roles in similar ways. The performances of the executives will certainly share more commonalities than will the performances of any one executive and all the secretaries in the same agency.

Many organizations and groups that social workers work in and serve are **chart organizations.** These social systems possess charts depicting the organizational structure as an interrelated set of social positions with different titles for each category of actors in the organization (Stryker & Statham, 1985). Social roles played in systems (a family, kinship network, formal organization, or neighborhood) characterized by chart positions have clear rules for membership in the position (only a licensed clinical social worker can enact the role of supervisor in many for-profit mental health agencies, for example) and a proper sphere of activity for each role (Lopata, 1994). At my college, for instance, faculty members are located on the organizational chart in a position above support staff (secretary, computer technicians) but below administrators (president, provost, dean of student affairs). An applicant must have a doctoral degree to achieve a faculty position. Three roles are attached to the position: teacher, scholar, and server (as student adviser, committee member, and community consultant). Faculty members are expected to perform well in all three roles, with special weight given to the teaching role, if they expect to be retained and promoted.

The organizational chart shows, too, that a social position exists within a set of positions. Also, roles are relational (Blatner & Blatner, 1988). The notion of role implies the concept of counter-role: son *and* father, social worker *and* client, and leader *and* followers (Sarbin & Allen, 1968). The faculty position, in the example from my college, is related to the student position. A faculty member can enact the adviser role only with the cooperation of an advisee or student in the major.

Here is one last note on the assumption of a positional base for most social roles. An organizational chart is like the playbill for a theater production listing all the actors, their parts, and information on how each is qualified for his or her part. Social organizations are unlike theaters in one way. Their playbills are often out of date and inaccurate. Last-minute changes in the cast are not included. Members do not always have the listed qualifications. Actors may have greater authority and directing power than the director or producer. Actors may play their parts in the total production in creative and deviant ways not hinted at by the playbill.

PERSONS ARE AWARE OF ROLES AND RESPOND TO EXPECTATIONS

Fourth, social role theorists assume that persons are often aware of social roles, and to some extent they are influenced by others' expectations for their performance of the role (Biddle, 1979). In the theater, actors working together during rehearsals expect each other to practice lines and listen to suggestions for improvement, and they recognize that each actor is entitled to fair pay and to bask in the applause. Likewise, **role expectations** can be defined in everyday life as "the rights and privileges, the duties and obligations, of any occupant of a social position in relation to persons occupying other positions in the social structure" (Sarbin & Allen, 1968, p. 497). **Duties** are the explicit or implicit demands communicated to an actor about how she or he should enact a role. The rights of the social role include both those resources that must be supplied to the actor so she can perform her duties and the obligations of others toward the actor. Rights include the permission or authorization to carry forth the role duties. Social workers, for example, have the right to obtain (but not to divulge indiscriminately) confidential knowledge about their clients. Duties are the activities deemed necessary by the role occupant and counterparts to fulfill the role's purpose. Social workers have the duty to warn others in a timely and intelligent way of a client's stated intentions to commit acts of violence. Lopata (1994) offers another example and suggests that mothers are expected universally to care for the welfare of their children.

Actors expect certain behaviors from persons enacting a social role and organize their performances with that person because of these expectations (Stryker & Statham, 1985). Seasoned acting troupes excel because they know deeply what to expect of all cast members. Members of a social work committee expect the designated leader to convene and run the meetings. The committee secretary is expected to keep the minutes, and all committee members are expected to attend and share the workload. Committee members also share the right of taking some credit for the team's accomplishments. Actors expect not only that role occupants will perform certain acts but that they will perform them in specified ways. The stage performer who speaks his lines in a mumbled, droning voice will disappoint all. Expectations can vary in their specificity and rigidity. Some organizations (like Broadway production companies) may clearly communicate role expectations as part of a formal employment contract and job description, but other organizations (like off-off-Broadway experimental theater groups) allow much negotiation between the person enacting the social role and the social circle of role partners (Lopata, 1994).

APPLIED SOCIAL ROLE THEORY AND HUMAN DEVELOPMENT

Exemplary Role Model

The creation and refinement of the applied social role approach to various facets of human development has been a collective effort. No one useful theorist or scholarly practitioner has emerged as the tradition's exemplar or champion. This section will make reference to the theoretical work of many different contributors.

Assumptions of Social Role Theory Related to Human Development

Social role theorists assume that people must be socialized for role performances. Because socialization experiences differ, people vary in their effectiveness in playing roles and in the satisfactions of performing (Biddle, 1979). **Socialization** is the interactional process whereby socializing agents help socializees acquire the knowledge, skills, and dispositions necessary for competent and responsible performance of social roles (Hardy & Conway, 1988). Socialization is similar to the process that prepares new and talented actors for dramatic performances. Actors in both the theater and everyday life are taught the **scripts** necessary to play a part. Actors work hard to learn the lines, expressions, and costuming necessary to give a credible performance. Actors observe role models. They practice and rehearse. They try new roles on stage with receptive audiences before performing in front of tough critics.

Social role theorists make some additional assumptions about human development (Clausen, 1986). They make temporal assumptions. Socialization is a lifelong process, and role theory is relevant to infants, teenagers, adults, and older persons. A society structures a person's development from birth to death in terms of the roles that the person performs and the societal norms for the appropriate timing of role entry and exit. My life, for example, changed in major ways when I entered a social work doctoral program, and I succeeded even though the program director believed that I had waited too late in my life for this career transition. Role theorists make assumptions about sequencing. A person's life is given order by the phases in relationships and commitments associated with different roles. A newlywed couple will face a fairly predictable series of challenges following the decision to adopt a child, for example. However, role theorists do not assume an automatic correspondence between role sequences and the stages of development conceptualized by cognitive and psychodynamic theorists. In some war zones in Africa, children assume the adult responsibilities and privileges of "soldier" despite their limited cognitive, moral, and social development. Moreover, role sequences may vary greatly across societies, communities, and individuals. The newlywed couple might decide to parent before finishing high school, or after exiting the school role but before entering work roles, or soon after establishing occupational careers, or even late in life near retirement.

ROOT METAPHORS AND THE SOCIAL ROLE APPROACH TO HUMAN DEVELOPMENT

The social role theory approach to human development can be explained as an elaboration of the root metaphor of "person as actor." There are several types of role socialization. The preparation for a role performance is called **anticipatory socialization,** "the process of learning such phenomena as norms, values, attitudes, and subtle dimensions of a role before being in a social situation where it is appropriate actually to behave in that role" (Burr, Leigh, Day, & Constantine, 1979, p. 84). Social work students, for example, serve as interns for hundreds of hours and receive extensive preparation before they are judged ready for performances as paid and autonomous social workers. **Professional socialization** is the carefully orchestrated preparation through a formal education process by which a novice acquires the professional competencies and professional self-identities necessary for a career as a professional performer. This might be comparable to the extensive training provided to actors who specialize in the plays of William Shakespeare. Roles are learned, and can be relearned if necessary (Blatner & Blatner, 1988). **Resocialization** refers to the processes by which socialization agents help the actor relearn or better learn how to perform a role. This occurs usually after a string of performance failures with the accompanying negative judgments of family members, peers, coworkers, and agents of social control.

People are socialized to perform parts of varying duration: relatively short role careers, longer institutional careers, and very lengthy phases of the life course. This is like the theatrical notion of the "run" of a play (Goffman, 1974). Some actors perform a part for one night, and the play closes. Some perform plays for a limited run—six weeks, for instance—and some play the same part for a record-breaking run of a decade. Much socialization of clients is for time-limited runs.

Perlman (1968) uses the role metaphor to explain the process by which an "applicant" makes the transition from petitioner or candidate for services to the role of client. As newcomers to an agency, novices must come to terms with the expectations and perspectives associated with the client role. The social worker plays an active part in this **role induction process.** The worker and the newcomer negotiate "payment" and other terms of services. The worker elicits the client's expectations for the client and worker roles. The worker educates and confers with the client to develop clear, complimentary, and consensual expectations. The worker and client specify their understanding of the different roles in the helping process by creating a contract. Novice clients learn the skills and dispositions necessary for identifying, explaining, and working on the problems that brought them to the agency. Optimally, clients become intensively involved in the role of help user, and eventually the client exits the role. All this may occur in a time sequence ranging from hours to months. Successfully socialized clients take their new role-based self-definitions, attitudes, and competencies from the agency stage to relationships outside the agency.

The socialization process can be organized in longer sequences. A **career**, for example, is conceptualized as a sequence of related roles, often arranged in a hierarchy of prestige and power, through which actors move in a more or less predictable and ordered way (Barley, 1989). Perhaps you have a favorite film actor or actress (Russell Crowe or Halle Berry, for instance), and you have followed this performer's career. Careers are found in social institutions related to the educational system, the workplace, the family, and religious organizations. Generally, the actor is socialized to adjust his or her self-conception, manner of self-presentation, interaction partners, and interaction patterns during each transition through a career phase. Social work students, for instance, may move through a long educational career differentiated into new social work major, baccalaureate-level social work student, master's-level social work student, social worker in supervision for licensing, and doctoral-level social work student. The specific requirements for enacting the student role become progressively more difficult. Great effort and many resources are invested in training across a career, and the actor must learn to perform increasingly difficult parts with knowledge, skill, and confidence.

Socialization is essentially a role-learning process, and life is a continuous process of socialization to new roles and the unlearning of old roles. A person's **life course** is the sum of his or her history of interrelated careers: family, student, worker, community member, and so on (Clausen, 1986). At your retirement party, as you reflect with your friends and your families about your life, you will probably consider how you moved into and out of different social work parts, how you took jobs with different organizations or performing companies, how you dealt with positive and negative reviews of your work, and how your sense of identity changed with the transitions from one to the next (Wells & Stryker, 1992). Your personal chorus of friends and family will likely offer some encouragement as you contemplate new social roles suitable to the postwork phase of your life.

THE SOCIAL ROLE APPROACH TO ROLE TRANSITIONS AND SELF PROCESSES

Social role theorists have extended their theoretical approach to two important topics: role transitions across the life course, and the relationship of socialization experiences to self processes. Work in each area will be discussed next.

THE SOCIAL ROLE MODEL OF ROLE TRANSITIONS   Social role theorists have developed a potent model of **role transitions**. A person's life course is organized by role acquisitions and role losses. Social workers often help clients exit stigmatized roles such as school dropout, delinquent, welfare recipient, prisoner, prostitute, or substance abuser. Transitions into and out of roles are often normative. The transitions are triggered by institutional scripts: the shift from worker to nonworker triggered by retirement; the shift from active parenthood following the departure of children from the home; the shift to widow or widower in old age triggered by the death of a spouse (Clausen, 1986). Some transitions are nonnormative and triggered by extraordinary and unexpected events. In September 2005, Hurricane Katrina abruptly cast many residents of New Orleans out of the roles of homeowner, worker, city resident, and pet owner.

Transitions can be either "on-time" or "off-time" (George, 1983, 1993). Many transitions are governed by social timetables, and their timing can be predicted. On-time transitions accord with commonly shared expectations about the age of the person entering the new role. Off-time transitions are atypical, innovative, and contrary to cultural expectations and schedules. For example, the 85-year-old grandmother in a rural community who decides to begin a new work career or to marry varies from "appropriate" conduct.

Role theorists propose that identifiable factors influence the ease of transition from one role to another (Allen & van de Vliert, 1984; Burr et al., 1979; White, 2005). A role transition is defined as "the addition or deletion of a role from one's role set," and ease of transition is defined conceptually as "the degree to which there is freedom from difficulty in activating or terminating a role and the availability of resources to begin or exit from a role" (Burr et al., 1979, p. 84).

Let's use the example of a young woman's transition into the role of mother to illustrate the model's theoretical propositions. I will begin with the positive causal relationships. The greater the anticipatory socialization for the role transition, the greater will be the ease of transition. Expected role changes are easier to deal with than unexpected changes. For example, if the local community center begins preparing pregnant clients early and ensures that each receives prenatal courses, parenting training, and instruction in securing babysitting assistance, the clients are more likely to succeed in managing their new role demands. The clearer and more defined the transition procedures, the greater will be the likelihood of an easy transition. For example, the pregnant woman who understands the detailed procedures associated with giving birth and with care of the newborn will manage the first experiences of the mothering role better than the woman who has a confused grasp. The more the transition into the new role facilitates the role performer's attainment of important personal goals, the greater will be the probability of a smooth transition. White (2005) offers the illustration of the pregnant woman who has longed for a child, dreamed of being a mother, and sought to create her own family, and suggests this orientation should facilitate the transition. Finally, the longer the socially endorsed period of transition from one role to another, the greater will be the likelihood of a smooth adjustment to the new role.

Social role theorists also propose some negative causal relationships in their model of role transitions (Burr et al., 1979; White, 2005). The greater the role strain resulting from the addition of a new role, for example, the harder the transition will be. The young adult balancing both a work role and a student role and facing childbirth and child rearing with minimal support from others is likely to experience great difficulty with the transition to the mother role. Finally, the less the social norms associated with a new role resemble familiar social norms, the greater will be the difficulty of adjusting to the new role. The new mother may have never before accommodated herself to norms with the complexity or urgency of the mother role. She may never have had to answer to so many others judging the quality of her role performance. Therefore, the transition is likely to be very challenging.

We have identified the causal factors that influence the ease of a role transition. Allen and van de Vliert (1984) add "consequences" to the role theory model of transitions. Negative consequences resulting from difficult role transitions (and the role strain associated with the transition) include a reduction in psychological well-being or a deterioration in physical health. Almost all my peers participating in the long and painful transition from doctoral student to doctor of social work experienced health problems, including migraine headaches, stomach ulcers, and back pain. Positive consequences resulting from a successful transition can include the strengthening of one's self-identity and the fortification of one's social network. Many survivors of the doctoral-program transition process, for instance, emerged with a solid and prized identity as a social work scholar or researcher and a cohesive and proud family–peer network. Professors van de Vliert and Allen (1984) also provide a review of strategies and intervention techniques for minimizing the negative consequences of role transitions and maximizing the likelihood of positive consequences. Their review is organized as guidelines for altering each phase of the role transition process: the antecedent or causal factors, the ease (or strain) of the transition, and the consequences of the transition. The suggestions for theory use by these role theorists are very similar to those developed independently by Naomi Golan (1981) and discussed later in this section.

THEORETICAL PROPOSITIONS: SOCIALIZATION AND THE SELF   Actors are affected by the parts they play. A role that calls for the expression of grief and extensive weeping will leave the actor emotionally exhausted. Typecasting as a villain may change an actor's conception of himself. Socialization into social roles, whether brief, moderately long, or decades in duration, also affect everyday role players in many ways. Several effects that have been discovered can be presented in propositional form (Wells & Stryker, 1992). First, the more roles we learn to play, the greater will be the number of role-related identities that we accumulate. Second, the content of our identities is changed in accordance with the roles we learn. Third, socialization agents and significant others influence our sense of the importance of the particular roles that we play, and our identities in these roles, by the prestige and support they offer for certain performances. Fourth, our sense of self-efficacy and our self-esteem are bolstered when we learn to play challenging roles effectively and to accept the positive regard of our role partners.

CRITICAL COMMENTS

Several criticisms have been directed at the social role theory approach to human development. White (2005), for example, notes that role theorists have not yet identified how socialization across role transitions varies by historical period, by the age of the actor, and by social cohort. How, for example, did the transition to motherhood differ for my mother, who became a mother as a teenager soon after World War II, and my sister, who became a mother in her mid-30s in 1988? Hansen (1988) reports on an unresolved argument between role theorists from the two different theoretical schools. They debate whether role transitions are best explained by regularities in a society's structure and norms or by the choices and actions that emerge when actors coordinate their performances. Did you enter the college role, for example, as a result of common expectations for all persons in similar positions (by age, class, race, and so on) in the social structure? Or did you enter the college role following thoughtful deliberations with family and peer group members leading to a personal decision? If both structure and process are important to explaining role transitions, what is the relative weight of each factor, and how might these weights change under different circumstances? We might add that White and Burr and his colleagues have not taken the next step and subjected their model of role transitions to a comprehensive empirical validation.

APPLICATIONS OF THE SOCIAL ROLE APPROACH TO HUMAN DEVELOPMENT

There are several important applications of the role theory approach. Golan (1981) has developed a comprehensive social work practice theory built on the foundation of the role transition model. She defines and classifies transitions. She identifies the common transitions experienced by social work clients at various stages of the life course, and she provides case illustrations of the management of typical transitions. Golan also identifies the various resources that the social worker and client system might mobilize to ease the transition. These include the worker's self, the natural helping system of caring friends and neighbors, the family, mutual help groups and associations, structured educational programs, and voluntary and professional service organizations.

Golan provides a set of recommendations for role-based interventions. The practitioner should assess the interplay of personality, role, and environment. The practitioner should prioritize the present and near-future time frames. The practitioner should use appropriate educational and interpretive techniques to help clients deal with role transitions and specific adjustment problems, including personal difficulties. These include difficulties in meeting new role expectations, differences between the client and important others about the expectations from the setting of the new role, ambiguities about role expectations, and value clashes. The practitioner should agree explicitly with clients on the role transition tasks and use a short-term approach to help with the accomplishment of these tasks. The practitioner should help clients explore and obtain the resources and supplies necessary for new role performances. The practitioner should help clients deal with the role strain particular to the transition period and develop increasing competence until role performances meet public norms and pressures are manageable. The practitioner should emphasize preventive interventions to enhance the management of upcoming transitions.

Ashforth (2000) has developed a theory- and research-based application of the role transition model. His book provides a comprehensive treatment of the processes of transitioning across the life course into and out of the roles embedded in formal organizations. He argues that contemporary human development is shaped primarily by organizational memberships. The life course includes encounters from birth to death with day care, school, religious, correctional, military, workplace, managed care, funeral, and many other formal organizations. Ashforth also outlines the individual competencies necessary to manage the role transitions commonly experienced by members of Western industrialized nations, as well as the transition bridges (comforting identity narratives and routines) and transition roles like "trainee" that organizations can develop to ease transitioning processes.

Finally, George (1983) directs practitioners to the self-help literature. Theory users have written widely on strategies for managing role transitions. Applications relevant to social workers helping older persons, for example, include written guidance on how to cope with widowhood and on how to make the best of retirement. George also directs practitioners to call for assistance from the client's informal support networks.

MAPPING APPLIED SOCIAL ROLE THEORY

Many of the key concepts from social role theory are displayed on the eco-map in Figure 11.1. The translation of role terms into ecosystems terminology and a discussion of how role theorists might conceptualize key elements of a role version of the eco-map follow.

HOW ARE CONNECTIONS CONCEPTUALIZED?

Social role theorists conceptualize connections as **expectations.** These are the demands and rights recognized by two actors as they use social roles to coordinate their performances. Expectations have a structural dimension—that is, they become a compelling and enduring element of our social organizations and groups. Expectations have an interactional dimension—that is, they must be communicated by word, gesture, deed, or object. Expectations also have a psychological dimension—that is, they are the definitions, anticipation, or understandings of what an actor is likely to do and should do when performing

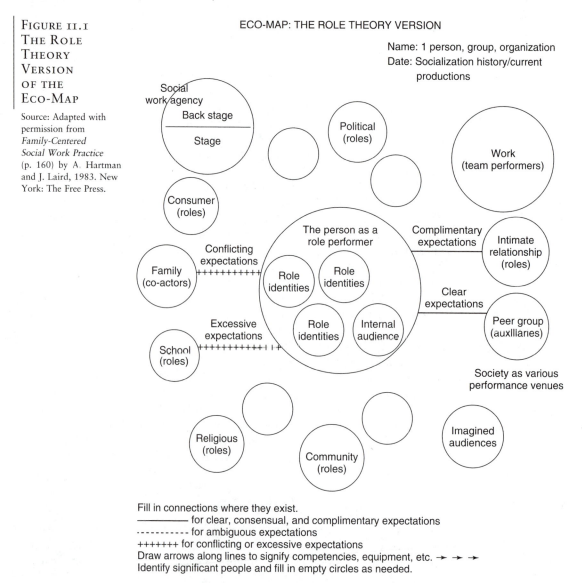

FIGURE II.I
THE ROLE
THEORY
VERSION
OF THE
ECO-MAP

Source: Adapted with
permission from
*Family-Centered
Social Work Practice*
(p. 160) by A. Hartman
and J. Laird, 1983. New
York: The Free Press.

ECO-MAP: THE ROLE THEORY VERSION

Name: 1 person, group, organization
Date: Socialization history/current
productions

a counter-role. The ecosystem, then, might be characterized as all the connections that an actor has to real and imagined others because he or she responds to their expectations.

HOW IS THE QUALITY OF CONNECTIONS DIFFERENTIATED?

Positive connections are those characterized by the three C's: consensus, clarity, and complementarity. Actors will report positive connections when there is a consensus about the relevant role expectations. **Consensus** refers to "how much the role expectations of two or more individuals agree or disagree" (Burr et al., 1979, p. 59). Consensus may range from a high degree of agreement about expectations (positive connections) to little agreement (negative connections). Field students often report positive connections to their field placement agency when they and the field instructor agree that the primary expectations associated with the field intern role are to learn, and that students should not be expected to do agency clerical work.

Positive connections are characterized by **clarity** of role expectations. Clear expectations are unambiguous or obvious, and the actor can identify with little difficulty what she should do and what she shouldn't do (Burr et al., 1979). Our social work program, for instance, asks the field interns and field instructors to write down the student's job description and learning contract. This ensures that expectations are clear.

Positive connections are characterized by role **complementarity.** Two roles work well together. The coordinated action of two or more actors makes possible the accomplishment of specific tasks (Biddle, 1979). The expectations and behaviors of each actor in the joint performance fit together harmoniously (Turner, 2002). The absence of one of the roles would make the accomplishment unlikely or difficult. People in complementary roles verify or validate each other's performance. Each actor has an assurance that his or her psychosocial needs will be met. Biddle gives the example of a smoothly operating criminal trial where there is complementarity between the roles of judge, jury member, defendant, and attorney.

Negative connections would be characterized by low consensus—actors quarrel about the expectations appropriate to their role performances; little clarity—expectations are hazy, ambiguous, uncertain, and vague (Sarbin & Allen, 1968); and discordance—the role performers act at cross-purposes (Turner, 2002).

Negative connections, according to social role theorists, cause various psychosocial problems. **Role strain** refers to "the stress generated within a person when he or she either cannot comply or has difficulty complying with the expectations of a role or set of roles" (Burr et al., 1979, p. 57). Hardy and Conway (1988) and Hage and Powell (1992) offer useful summaries of the various types of role strain. The major role difficulties that they discuss include the following.

Role ambiguity occurs when the cues and feedback from an actor's role partners are not sufficient to understand the partners' intentions and desires. These unclear role expectations might be compared to careless coaching from a theatrical director. Ambiguity causes performance problems.

Role conflict occurs when there are varied and incompatible expectations for role performance. Two acting partners recommend different scripts for the client's performance, for example. There may also be disagreements about the person's obligations in the role. There are two types of role conflict. **Intrarole conflict** occurs when the expectations associated with one social position or role by two or more relevant others are contradictory (Sarbin & Allen, 1968). For example, a dying client may have conflicting expectations of the social worker. The client wants the worker to be a supportive friend and ease pain, but simultaneously wants the worker to report honestly the anticipated course of the disease. The role of mother may be defined differently by the woman acting it, by her husband, and by her children. **Interrole conflict** occurs when expectations associated with various roles that an actor simultaneously enacts are incompatible with one another (Davis, 1986). For example, a social worker plays both counseling and custodial roles in a prison. The expectations for these two roles are contradictory or mutually exclusive. When counseling, the social worker is expected by her peers and the professional association to treat all prisoners with dignity and to help them realize their potentials. However, when the worker is monitoring activity room participation, she is expected by the prison warden and guards to humiliate and punish prisoners and thus (theoretically) ensure their compliance.

Role incompetence occurs when the actor lacks the knowledge, skill, and level of commitment necessary for a successful role performance. He or she is underqualified and cannot meet others' expectations.

Role incongruity occurs when there is a poor fit between the actor's values and self-conceptions and the requirements of the role. In the theater, the director asks you to play a villain when you only feel suited to play saints. Students selecting a field placement are often advised to take care to check the fit between their self-views and the likely expectations of the field instructor. One student accepted a placement in a hospice and found that the expectations that she deal regularly with dying clients clashed with her fear of death and her fragile sense of self.

A **role overload** occurs when role demands exceed the actor's personal capacities, as when a stage performer does six shows a week and is physically and emotionally exhausted. There may be insufficient time to meet all demands. The demands may seem excessive in number or too complex. Too many people may be making demands on the actor, and each considers his or her demands to be the highest priority. **Burnout** is the word social workers use to refer to an overload, especially of our emotional capacities. The burned-out social worker feels that he does not have the physical, mental, or emotional energy to perform his work role productively and convincingly. A role overload is possible, also, when a person attempts to enact multiple roles. A person makes commitments to perform, for example, as a social work student, a wife, a mother, a worker, a church leader, and an athlete, and then feels overwhelmed.

A **role underload** occurs when role expectations are minimal, and the role does not fully utilize the actor's talents. Tasks are too easy to complete, and boredom results.

What Is the Typical Focal System?

Social role theorists simultaneously give focal attention to three units: the person, the role, and the social organization. Role enactment is the bridge between the individual and the organization (Hare & Blumberg, 1988).

Goffman (1959) summarizes the contribution of each unit to this triad. The person manages impressions and stages with varying degrees of awareness to achieve goals. The person brings the physical equipment (a body), the intellectual capabilities, and the emotional dispositions necessary for a role performance. The person identifies with his roles and experiences enhancement or damage to self-esteem and emotional tranquility or embarrassment, dishonor, loss of face, degradation, disrespect, and so on depending on how his performance is received. The person's self and situational conceptions must be negotiated through role relationships in ways that build a consensus among actors or teams of actors (or lead to the breakdown of communication and the halting of lines of action). Large social organizations teach roles to members and provide many of the resources that make role performances possible. They also provide the stages, role conceptions, dramatic formulas, and performance rules essential to good acting. Successful performances by organizational members deepen the legitimacy and reputation of the organization, whereas performance disruptions or failures discredit the organization.

Since the social role theory view of the person differs greatly from the conception of other theoretical frameworks, some elaboration is required. The person is made up of the roles that he or she plays. These are transformed into role identities and are organized into a salience hierarchy with the identities ranked according to the person's commitment to each (Stryker & Statham, 1985). **Role identities** are the meanings attached to self in a role, internalized designations that summarize how we understand our performance in a part ("jealous husband" or "hardworking and socially concerned social worker"). **Salience** is the degree of importance that a role identity has in the person's overall sense of self. In the entire set or cluster of roles, a person gives different importance to each. This hierarchy helps the person make decisions about which role to enact in the face of competing expectations. My conceptions of myself as a social worker, for example, are very important parts of who I am. The **hierarchy of salience** is the probability of various identities' coming into play in a particular social situation or across situations. In a crisis (and in many other circumstances), my identity as a social worker is more likely to be activated than my identity as an avid music collector. Those identities that are characterized by a high level of commitment are generally ranked high in the salience hierarchy (Stryker & Statham, 1985).

Commitment to role identities grows in several ways. If extensive and intensive social relationships to other persons depend on my enacting a social role with a particular identity, my commitment to that role identity increases. If there are few cognitive or socioemotional costs and many benefits associated with a role, then my commitment to the role identity increases.

Here is one last example of role identity processes. While in school, students begin to form an identity as a social worker. If after graduation you discover that many clients, coworkers, and friends regard positively, count on, and support your performances as a caring and responsible social worker, you will probably develop a high commitment to this role and its meanings. In a neighborhood dispute over group homes for persons with chronic mental disorders, where you might assert either your professional identity or your local identity as a homeowner, the more salient social work identity will be activated.

The person, social role theorists assert, also has an inner audience or *me*. The *me* is made up of all the significant others and groups that a person has internalized during his or her lifetime. These become a set of imagined audiences reviewing our best and worst performances. The *me* observes, cues, encourages, criticizes, applauds, and reinforces the acting person just as flesh and blood audience members react to a performer on stage (Hare & Blumberg, 1988). The *me* includes our reference groups, who are like unseen but always present drama critics.

How Is the Environment Conceptualized?

In this section, I will elaborate on my discussion of the theatrical metaphor and the comparison of the social organization to a theater company. The social environment is like a collection of theater companies (Hare, 1985). Each social organization—formal organizations like the university and less formal organizations like an assemblage for a volunteer recognition event—involve show people. The participants in the organization take the roles of directors, protagonists and antagonists, auxiliary role players, and audience members. All interaction among actors is dramatic and occurs on stages with the sets, props, and costumes particular to each organization.

Social organizations differ in the degree of preparation for performances that members receive. Undergraduate social work students are coached and rehearsed for years, whereas partygoers obtain only brief and minimal direction. Organizations differ, too, in the permanency of the acting roles. The social work field intern role may be limited to a nine-month partnership between agency and school, whereas all United Way agencies have permanent leadership positions and incumbents who typically enact the executive role for many years. Organizations differ in the actors' concern for the reaction of audience members. In workplaces, new field interns are continuously monitoring their performances and gauging likely reviews from field instructor, field liaison, and agency workers. In the household, family members may act on their impulses with little effort to achieve praise or avoid the condemnation of their kin.

The physical environment can be compared to the theater building (Hare, 1985; Hare et al., 2001). The organization includes two different territories or regions: the stage and the backstage. The **stage** is where the actors perform in view of the audience. Stage designers give careful consideration to the use of lighting, physical layout, props, scenery, decorations, furniture, and other permanent fixtures to enhance the quality of the performances. Some human service organizations have many different stages; the social worker knows that she must perform different roles when in her office, the family therapy room, the staff conference room, or the residential facility.

Activity in the **backstage** area is not easily visible to audience members. Barriers allow for behavior that would not be acceptable to non–cast members.

Here, actors prepare for their performances, and auxiliary personnel assist by operating special effects equipment, applying makeup, preparing the costumes, and handling the props. Actors can relax in the backstage area and laugh at the audience or mock their critics. The classroom is a stage, and students are performers to an audience of one, the professor. Students perform their roles in one way on the classroom stage and in another way in the hall outside the classroom. Embarrassment follows if students are discovered acting backstage in ways that contradict their onstage performance—for instance, by making fun of a professor that they defer to in the classroom.

There is also the territory outside the social organization or theater. The people here have not bought tickets and thus are not yet involved with the theater company's production as either actors or audience members (Goffman, 1959). Many human service organization workers must also work outside the theater. Agency leaders are like producers who venture into the community to seek funding for new agency productions. Public relations specialists publicize agency events to neighbors and possible clients like the hawkers selling tickets on the street.

Several other concepts developed by social role theorists such as Robert Merton (Hage & Powell, 1992) describe important elements of the environment. The **role set** is the list of companion roles with which a position in a social organization is linked. The position of faculty member is part of a set; it is linked to other social positions, including students, secretaries, faculty colleagues (people in the same role in the organization), and administrators. The **person set** is a term for all those particular people with whom a position occupant enacts role relationships. For example, in my faculty position I have role relationships each semester with about 100 different students, 10 full-time faculty and five or six adjunct faculty members, one secretary, one assistant to the secretary, and several administrators (two department chairs and two deans). **Role networks** are the chains of social roles that are linked through the direct or indirect communication of reciprocal expectations, through social exchange, and through cooperative action. These are the accumulation of a large number of role sets into an extended and integrated social structure. Professors, program directors, and students of social work programs in my state, for example, are linked through a consortium of a dozen schools that meets twice yearly. This network potentially connects any member to thousands of network members playing complementary roles.

IS PARTICULAR EMPHASIS GIVEN TO ANY SYSTEMS?

The audience is essential to drama. Hare (1985) writes that "an audience is crucial for a theatrical experience . . . there is no play until it is performed" and "there is no performance unless there is an audience" (p. 54). In everyday life, too, actors are especially concerned about the impressions they give to audience members (I feel sick today. What will my students think about my lecture?) or to imagined judges (My lecture is not quite up to the standard set by my colleagues). Social psychologists have conventionally referred to unseen but important audiences as **reference groups.** These are groups to whom the actor turns for reviews—the reviews that matter. Everyday life has some differences from life in the theater. Audiences need not be seated in an actual theater to influence the actor's performance. Teenage delinquents, for instance, may consider the likely reviews from physically distant gang members when they encounter a rival gang.

The social worker assessing the person-in-environment configuration by using a role theory perspective would give special attention to the client's major social connections and the resulting role sets, person sets, and role networks. The worker studies how well the client uses social roles to organize his or her own behavior and to understand and coordinate his or her performances with others. The worker also seeks to identify client role difficulties related to particular connections or expectations. The social worker would look for mismatches between the client's personality and the plays in which she has been cast. The lack of congruence between the client's self-conception and the role often appears in performance problems. The social worker reviews the client's role history like a talent agency reviewing an actor's stage experience. The worker might ask: Who have been the influential acting coaches and directors in the client's past? How well have they socialized the client to perform various roles and to succeed in different social settings? What is the relation of earlier role learning to present performance difficulties? How are clichés, bad acting habits, and antiquated theories about acting undermining the quality of current enactments? The social worker will want to watch the client during acting tryouts and discover the expressions given off without awareness (Goffman, 1959), especially those expressions that trouble coactors. The social worker serves as an acting coach and assesses the client's competency to perform various roles and the client's specific needs for additional instruction, training, and practice in acting technique.

HOW ARE RESOURCES AND THEIR FLOW CONCEPTUALIZED?

Social role theorists discuss resources in various ways. Resources include personal attributes and achievements such as educational attainment, life experience, social status, cultural knowledge, interpersonal skills, motivation, and vitality. With these resources, the actor on everyday stages has the psychosocial equipment necessary for performing a role. These resources are valuable to both the role performer and the team with which the actor performs (Hardy & Conway, 1988). Social role theorists give special attention to interpersonal skills as resources for enriching public performances. Social intelligence and competencies, including the ability for affective role taking and empathy across varied social situations, become resources that increase the actor's versatility and ingenuity. Social intelligence and competencies specific to a particular role are resources that will help the actor earn accolades for her performance. Think of the highly developed crisis management skills that some exceptional social workers bring to their work in hospital emergency units. **Rhetorical skills,** the abilities to persuade by writing and speaking to an audience to gain acceptance for one's arguments or dramatic assertions, are also important resources (Sarbin, 1984).

Social role theorists have mixed opinions about whether some social roles serve as resources enriching other role performances. **Multiple role involvement** refers to circumstances requiring the actor to shift frequently from one stage and performance to another (Marks & Leslie, 2000). Doubters assert that multiple role involvement restricts opportunities and impairs the performance of each role. Energy supplies are scarce and easily exhausted. Human energy and potentials cannot be easily expanded to satisfy audiences to our multiple acting jobs. A person who enacts multiple roles must meet insurmountable challenges. Time, energy, money, commitments, and other resources must be divided and spread widely. Since these are limited, the actor will experience much role strain.

Optimists propose that there are benefits to multiple role involvement. The person enacting multiple roles also has special opportunities. In this model, energy and other resources are not in finite supply. Participation in numerous role relationships and the likely negotiation of duties and rights with varied others tend to increase one's capacity for role taking and thus for complex thinking (Lopata, 1994). Membership in many groups also increases the pool of role network resources, symbolic and material, that a person may call upon when facing a challenge in any particular role. Ego gratification, status security, personal rights, and validation of competencies may all increase for the actor because of his participation in rich and extensive role networks. The experience of enacting multiple roles also prepares the person for acting well in unexpected or challenging scenes.

WHAT DESCRIPTIVE WORDS ARE USED?

The social role theory is dominated by concepts that have their origin in the theater. At the level of the individual system, common concepts include the *actor*, the *role player*, or the *performer*. Dramaturgical role theorists use words such as *director, playwright, auxiliary, antagonist*, and *protagonist* to refer to members of a psychodrama. The *producer* and *stagehand* are other possible designations. At the level of the social system, social role theorists refer to the *performing team*, the *role set*, the *chorus*, and the *audience*. The vocabulary for social connections often involves the addition of a second term to the theatrical concept of role. Terms used to describe connecting processes include *role playing, role making, role taking, role reversing*, and *role enacting*. *Role expectations* are communicated. A person makes a *transition* from one role to another. A difficulty in performing is called a *role strain*, and the self is *presented*. Concepts for intervention make use of the theatrical metaphor. Words such as *coaching, improvising*, and *rehearsing* are widely used. Psychodrama makes explicit use of theater terms such as the *warm-up*, the *monologue*, the *soliloquy*, and the *monodrama*. Many additional concepts used by role theorists draw on the theater, including *auditions, costumes, props, scenes, scripts*, and *stage* (*onstage* and *backstage*). A few important role theory concepts such as *social norm* and *social position* have less clear roots.

How Is Change Conceptualized?

Conceptions and images of the planned change process incorporate dramaturgical ideas. For example, Kiecolt's (1994) model of psychosocial change uses role theory and can be summarized by reference to acting and theatrical processes. Why does a person decide to change? Problems related to our role performances are the major causes. First, unfavorable reflected appraisals evoke the urge to change. In dramaturgical terms, these are our perceptions of negative reviews from important audiences. Second, lower self-perceived competence evokes the urge to change. These are our perceptions that our performance does not meet the evaluative standards of an audience that we use as a reference group. Third, unfavorable social comparisons evoke the urge to change. These are the perceptions that our performances compare poorly to those of other actors in similar roles and social situations. Continued acting problems in these areas lessen the esteem, sense of efficacy, and feelings of authenticity that are critical to meeting performance challenges. Such changes in self-processes tend to evoke the inclination to change the self–environment relationship. A change by clients, social role theorists such as Perlman (1968) would add, involves a change in the reference groups or audiences for whom one performs.

PLANNED CHANGE TECHNIQUES Practitioners who apply social role theory use planned change techniques that are similar to acting techniques. These include the following:

Coaching The social worker as director helps the member begin enacting a new role just as an acting coach helps a novice by providing comfort through supportive physical touch, verbal encouragement, and insights into the acting process.

Mirroring The social worker as director mimics the person's tone of voice, body language, statements, or other actions to show the client the strengths or limitations of her performance (Hare, 1985).

Rehearsal The social worker as director helps the client use a fantasy process of trying out lines of action in one's mind before a performance (Hage & Powell, 1992) and an interactional process of practicing the lines for an upcoming performance in a safe and supportive setting.

Role Bargaining The social worker as director helps the client bargain with role partners over the role definitions and expectations related to an important performance (Stryker & Statham, 1985).

Role Clarification The social worker as director helps the client obtain information that makes explicit the expectations for a particular role and the goals, beliefs, and feelings associated by significant others with the role (Meleis,

1988). The social worker helps the client ask, for example, "What exactly do you expect of me in this role?"

Role Learning   The social worker as director helps the client learn a new script: the verbal and gestural responses appropriate to a performance. The actor may be encouraged to observe others who have performed the role in a convincing or distinguished way. The actor rehearses and practices the performance with help from the director and coactors. The social worker may prompt and remind the actor of his lines during the performance (Sarbin & Allen, 1968).

Role Making   The social worker as director helps the client use interpersonal communication capacities to negotiate with others a creative role in situations where cultural frameworks provide only minimal scripts (Turner, 1998). Clients become able to cue each other by word, gesture, clothing, or possessions about their claims on the new role. Reciprocal validation of these claims results in successful cooperation. This is like the work of a stage director who helps improvisational actors use their acting equipment—facial expressions, tone of voice, gestures, costume, and makeup—to communicate with each other as they construct new characters.

Role Playing   The social worker as director helps the client participate in an intentional and experimental performance of a role in a safe and structured therapeutic situation. The client attempts to authenticate a real-life challenge without the risky and totally committed involvement of real life because the director reserves the right to halt performance as needed (Blatner & Blatner, 1988). The social worker encourages the actor to "play" in the role and discover creative and new ways to enact it and to solve performance problems. This is especially useful for clients who have problems because they perform in habitual, stereotypical ways in their social dramas.

Role Reversal   The social worker as director asks the client to take both the perspective and the physical position in a group of another person to better understand the other person's thoughts, emotions, and action tendencies (Hare, 1985).

Role Taking   The social worker as director helps the client to understand and anticipate the other's behavior by viewing it in the context of the role that the other is enacting (Hardy & Conway, 1988). The client can learn to use cognitive role taking to grasp the way the role partner is thinking, or affective role taking to grasp the way the role partner is feeling. The social worker also makes frequent use of cognitive and affective role taking to imagine and to extrapolate the client's feelings, thoughts, and action tendencies as these relate to the helping process and the worker–client role relationship (Blatner & Blatner, 1988).

Soliloquy   The social worker as director asks the client to voice his thoughts and feelings to an audience or cast members (other than a current antagonist) while enacting a particular role (Hare, 1985). The client is helped to think aloud, especially after a troubling social interaction, and thus learns to examine the feelings and attitudes associated with a role performance.

STRATEGIES FOR COPING WITH ROLE STRAIN   The social worker as director can also help the client select techniques to deal with role strain (Lopata, 1994). The client can learn to compartmentalize and deal with each demand separately. The client can learn to delegate duties to auxiliary actors. The client can learn to negotiate and change duties, rights, or the norms used for judging the quality of the role enactment. The client can learn to avoid a troublesome or demanding role partner. The client can learn how to leave a stressful role. The client can learn to use the social worker as a mediator to resolve conflicts between members of the person set.

The job of the social worker incorporates some of the social roles found in a theater company. Social workers and their clients can work like stage designers to change the stage design. The design of the stage expresses the qualities of the play enacted on the stage and influences how audiences understand and judge the performance. A family that creates a home characterized by broken windows, doors that do not lock, animal feces on the floor, and scattered garbage may be communicating that in their family drama little value is given to the children's safety or health. The child protective workers who visit such homes are likely to present a critical review and facilitate changes in the staging and performance of the parent roles.

Social workers, like theatrical directors, can help clients improve the quality of their solo or group performances. Social workers may use the group directing methods associated with psychodrama to help a client enact scenes that dramatize her problems, identify lines and scripts that might improve the role performance, enlist additional clients to rehearse, and use coaching as her problem is revealed on the group's stage (Hare & Blumberg, 1988).

HOW ARE ACTUAL AND IDEAL ECO-MAPS CONTRASTED?

Helen Harris Perlman (1968) referred to three major difficulties that characterize troubled person–ecosystem configurations: deficiencies, disturbances, and discrepancies. **Deficiencies** are those difficulties that limit a client's capacity to enact important social roles. These may include deficiencies in material goods (the money, furniture, books, and other items that parents need to support their children in the student role). Deficiencies may be personal. Some clients lack the intellectual, emotional, or physical capacities necessary for successful performances in the work role. Clients may be unprepared for a challenging role assignment. Because of inadequate prior socialization, for example, a client may lack knowledge of the behaviors, sentiments, and beliefs necessary for a role enactment.

Disturbances or disorders are the intrapsychic constrictions, distortions, or vulnerabilities that interfere with a person's attempts to meet role obligations or to assert the rights necessary for role enactment. Perlman (1968) refers to the psychiatric conditions that often limit an actor's capacity for playing life roles.

Clients with chronic and intense social anxiety, for instance, may even be reluctant to apply for public social positions.

Discrepancies are difficulties that exist within the role definition or because of how the roles are related to each other. The various types of role strain discussed earlier illustrate some of the most common discrepancies. Perlman (1968) points out that the careful social worker will differentiate between performance problems caused by disturbances and those caused by discrepancies. Discrepancies point to the interaction and social structural factors that complicate social functioning and remove the onus of failure from the actor.

An actual eco-map of the client–environment configuration may reveal some other role problems. The person may choose (or be compelled) to enact high-risk roles. Performance in these roles may be hazardous to his or her physical health, mental health, or community reputation. Despite awareness of the potential negative consequences of continued performance of the role, the client refuses to exit the role (Meleis, 1988). One of my community corrections clients refused to refrain from drug dealing and from selling customers laundry detergent instead of cocaine. He was eventually murdered.

The ideal eco-map and person–environment relationships might be described by social role theorists at both the group and the individual level. Deficiencies, disturbances, and discrepancies will be removed. Goffman (1959) studied, additionally, how teams of actors—members of a committee, an activity group for elderly residents, colleagues in a social work department—achieve a high level of quality in their group performances. A **team** is a group of role performers who work together to stage and present an "actable idea" or dramatic routine to an audience. Effective teamwork requires team solidarity resulting from a working consensus and from collective displays of dramaturgical discipline, loyalty, and circumspection. A **working consensus** is an agreement about the definition of the situation, the appropriate lines, and the expectations for each performer. **Discipline** requires that each member manage her words, face, voice, and body language in a way that shows involvement in the part. The disciplined team has members who remember their lines, suppress spontaneous impulses and feelings that would evoke negative reviews, and work hard to polish their performances. **Loyalty** requires that members refrain from revealing the secrets of the rest of the cast when performing. Nor do loyal members denounce or undermine the team by revealing unflattering information about the other actors during public performances. **Circumspection** requires that members show care and insight into their decisions about how best to stage a performance, how to select the ideal audiences for the show, how to prepare for the performance and for unexpected problems, how to adapt the performance to the particular circumstances, and how to manage adeptly the length of the performance. Ideal eco-maps include teams of successful social organizations—teams that often display a high degree of discipline, loyalty, and circumspection.

Ideally, each member of the eco-system role network will perform his or her role well. Sarbin and Allen (1968) offer the following criteria for optimal role performance. First, it is appropriate. The actor has selected the role suitable for the social context in which the performance is presented, and role partners agree that the performance has been correctly applied to the social situation. Second, it is proper. The actor enacts the role in accordance with social norms so that the performance will not be judged as bad, deviant, or criminal. Specifically, the performance meets the evaluation criterion for propriety used by the audience. Finally, the performance is convincing. The actor performs the role so that the audience judges the performer as legitimate and able to play this part, and as motivated to enact the role. Our role models often provide examples of appropriate, proper, and convincing role players. For example, Martin Luther King Jr. stands out in my mind for his performances as an advocate for oppressed Americans.

How Are Issues of Diversity, Color, and Shading Addressed?

Role theorists offer several distinctive perspectives on human diversity. Callero (1986, 1994) has amplified the role theory conceptualization of *role* to account for cultural variability. Callero (1986) suggests that a role "represents a pattern of social actions classified, identified, and shared in the same way by all members of a particular culture or subculture" (p. 350). Callero expands on the symbolic interactionist notion of *significant symbol* and argues that a role is a specific type of object that achieves significance in a culture. Members of a culture share a language with a common vocabulary. Members also share an inventory of social roles. Like other cultural objects, roles are selected by members of the society or subsociety from a total pool of available cultural objects and used to accomplish practical goals. The role of "mayor" can be used as a tool to solve urban problems in the United States, for example. Like other significant symbols, roles are distinguishable cultural objects that are relatively stable and widely shared. They are not private or idiosyncratic. An empirical study could demonstrate, for instance, that a role such as mayor exists as a cognitive representation available to all the members of a given Eastern Maryland community.

Callero (1994) points out that the roles available for use and that the ways actors can use available roles are culturally patterned. Four factors condition role use: a culture's endorsement of a role, a culture's evaluation of the role, social accessibility to the role, and situational contingencies. First, cultures vary in the roles supported or blessed. Certain roles may be named privately or in a subculture but not recognized by the larger society. Endorsement for the folk healer role of "curandero" is low in non-Spanish cultures. Other roles are easily accepted and validated widely in the focal society (the United States, for instance), such as the role of "priest." Second, roles differ in how they are evaluated by the culture and its members. In mainstream American culture, evaluation can range from the very negative, contemptuous evaluations of roles such as prostitute, child molester, or felon to the prestigious, positive appraisals associated with the roles of athlete, film entertainer, and entrepreneur. Third, the degree of social accessibility to social roles varies for different cultural groups. For some roles, many restrictions, obvious or implicit, impede entry into the role and use of the role. An actor's physical characteristics, ethnic and racial background, gender, level of education, social skills, work competencies, language, and other membership qualities may interfere with access to roles. In the United States, for example, few women of any background and few men of Mexican descent have attained the role of senator or corporate executive. Fourth, roles vary in their degree of situational contingency. Some are highly dependent on situational factors and can be enacted only under specific circumstances in particular cultural settings. Callero provides the example of "nudist." Others are fairly independent of cultural situations and can be used successfully across various situations and circumstances. Callero gives the example of age-related roles such as infant or senior citizen. Callero proposes that a role analysis attuned to diversity issues might identify different cultures' or subcultures' inventory of roles and then characterize each role in terms of cultural endorsement, cultural evaluation, accessibility for different groups, and anchorage in situations.

Role theorists have documented a variety of cross-cultural differences in roles (Thomas, 1999). Cultures can differ in beliefs about the proper ways to perform a role. For example, American students are expected to demonstrate independent thinking and to interact actively with teachers, whereas students from Korean backgrounds learn to treat teachers as authority figures and to relate to teachers in a passive and deferential manner. Cultures differ in the prestige attached to particular roles. Medical doctors are highly regarded and rewarded in the United States but not in Russia, where many physicians are women. Cultures vary in the costumes required for certain role performances. Some cultures in the Middle East require female teachers to wear long robes that cover most of the body, whereas North American female teachers can wear short skirts. Thomas advises that social workers use role theory as a guide during encounters with role performers from other cultures. First, social workers should attempt to identify the similarities and differences between the role practices of members of the social workers' original culture and members of the new culture. Second, social workers should participate in training so that they can perform relevant roles in the manner preferred in the new culture. Third, social workers should apply their cultural lessons in enacting roles during their helping encounters with members of the new culture.

Let's expand on Callero's notion of differential access to rewarding and powerful roles (Clausen, 1986). Social role theorists consider issues of inequality critical in some social contexts. People are often assigned to roles not as distinctive and individual beings but as members of cultural categories organized by gender, ethnicity, race, sexual orientation, and social class (Turner, 2002). In certain social contexts, these categorical memberships will powerfully influence acting possibilities and chances for success. For example, in many U.S. communities, there is limited access to highly valued and powerful roles and careers for gays and Arab Americans. It is as if there were a "casting call" for the high-paying parts in an exciting production, but auditions were restricted to those in a few membership categories. When the minority member obtains an audition, no amount of talent, hard work, or vitality ever seems to land a role. Social scripts differ, in certain social contexts, depending on the actor's memberships. This impedes access. Additional expectations and tougher lines and scenes are required of female or physically challenged performers. After obtaining access, members of certain groups face new obstacles. Some communities and subcultures respond differently to a man who enacts the executive director role than to a woman. Followers are more likely to wonder if they can expect the woman to act tough enough to ensure the agency's growth in the competitive and political human services arena. Therefore, the woman must act, onstage and offstage, during show time and overtime, for bosses and employees, as a ruthless, cunning, and controlled corporate tiger.

To obtain access to desired roles, sometimes members from undervalued backgrounds attempt to "pass" and assume an identity allowing them to enact a role from which they would normally be prohibited (Goffman, 1963). African Americans might attempt to pass as European Americans. Physically challenged persons might attempt to pass as fully functioning role performers. For years, President Franklin D. Roosevelt hid his polio-related infirmities from the American public. The Jewish person might attempt to pass as a Christian. The process of passing is complex. A young woman who wants to date another woman in a homophobic community might attempt to pass as a boyfriend. Adjusting her physical appearance, her wardrobe, and her behavior, she might work hard and approximate the performance made by actual males in the boyfriend role. However, the woman attempting to pass is in constant danger. The actor might slip and reveal her true social identity. The actor might be recognized by someone who knows her personal history, and this observer can disclose the discrepancy between the actor's claims to the role and actual qualifications (or blackmail the pretend role-player). Members from socially disvalued groups who attempt to pass also often suffer because of the psychological complexities of managing attachments to two different and incompatible groups.

Impression management is a role theoretical concept referring to the methods actors use to attempt to control the impressions others have of the actors' role performances and to make favorable impressions (Rosenfeld, Giacalone, & Riordan, 1994). Women, members of minority groups, and immigrants may not need to pass by assuming a false identity in order to succeed in social organizations. However, they may need to carefully modify their customary impression management behaviors to succeed in workplaces and other organizations traditionally dominated by European American males. Poor and oppressed clients may feel compelled to manage impressions and stage shows insincerely, not because they want to deceive or manipulate their bosses and other superiors but to survive. Giacalone and Beard (1994) refer to their study of managers who work in international companies. They suggest that individuals entering an organization with a foreign cultural orientation must prepare carefully. Such individuals should participate in an anticipatory socialization experience that teaches the role content for making good impressions from the new cultural point of view. They must learn the cultural-specific procedures for gaining credit for their performances and for protecting against a negative reputation for mistakes. They should also participate in anticipatory socialization to learn how to use appropriately the new culture's symbols in relation to food, dress, and social traditions. Effective and responsible job performance requires impression management sensitivity.

Members of vulnerable or powerless groups often have limited access to the resources necessary for successful performances (Clausen, 1986). Role theorists recognize that the resources necessary for role performances may be either tangible or intangible. Clients may have performance difficulties because of the ways that their cultural or class origins limit available resources and because of differences in educational attainment, social skills, and desirable talents. As indicated earlier, differences in organizational selection and reward processes may also handicap certain groups. Migrant workers from Mexico, for example, may lack the vocabulary, the accent, the clothing, the automobile, and the skills of manipulation required for sales work in a U.S. shopping mall. Hurricane Katrina shed light on the relationship between inequality and role success. Many residents of New Orleans did not own cars, and therefore they were not able to enact the role of evacuee. After the storm's devastation, many lacked basic supplies such as food, water, and mattresses and were cast by the media as "looters" rather than "survivors" when they took necessities from abandoned stores.

WHAT WOULD BE ADDED OR DELETED?

In the discussion so far, I have alluded to a special group that social role theorists would include in their eco-maps. These are the audiences for the client's performances. Audiences can be specific others, groups, and organizations. They are the people whose opinions matter (Hardy & Conway, 1988). Audiences can be seen or unseen groups. Audiences can be real or imagined. Audiences serve several important functions for the actor. The audience often supplies the norms or rules of conduct for the performance. Boos and jeers signal that the actor has veered from acceptable behavior, for example. The audience provides standards or comparison points by which a person can judge whether she is receiving equitable compensation for a performance. A battered woman may use a support group as an audience, and the group members may indicate that she receives too little support, respect, and appreciation from her husband. The audience may include members whom the client uses as a model and whose performances can be emulated. Students often internalize images of their field instructors and use the supervisor as an imaginary audience and an exemplar.

THE LIMITS OF APPLIED SOCIAL ROLE THEORY: A SOCIAL WORK APPRAISAL

In this chapter, I have tried to show that the theatrical metaphor can help practitioners understand and use social role theory. Mead, Moreno, Linton, Goffman, and Perlman were introduced as role models who have developed and applied this theory. Major role concepts were displayed on an eco-map, and key concepts and propositions of role theory were translated into ecosystem terms.

I will conclude this section by reviewing some of the differences between everyday life and life in the theater (Goffman, 1959, 1974). Social interaction in everyday life is often more unpredictable than stage interaction. Our clients do not follow expected scripts, and often surprise us by their bizarre or unorthodox performances of standard roles. The spatial boundaries for social interaction in everyday life are often less delineated than they are onstage. For example, clients in a support group do not face an audience when talking to each other in everyday life. In real life, clients do not often take center stage. Nor do most clients hold the focus of an audience for long. Clients in real life are rarely afforded the opportunity for lengthy and grand speeches. Other clients either interrupt or ignore the most important pronouncements. In real life, clients must perform some roles with very little rehearsal.

The social role theory does not provide a holistic understanding of the person. It guides us in our assessment of only some of the parts clients play, those with relevance to our own roles and positions in social work agencies. A comprehensive practice approach based on role theory would need to be supplemented to provide knowledge of the whole client as a biopsychosocial and spiritual being.

The dramaturgical perspective is most useful in helping us understand the actions of clients intending to transmit an impression to some onlooker (Hare & Blumberg, 1988). However, some everyday activities such as housekeeping tasks are primarily goal-oriented without concern for an audience. These performances may have few dramatic qualities. Finally, people at times require material goods—food, shelter, clothing, and medicines, for example—with an urgency that has little to do with how these resources are dramatized, packaged, or symbolized. The role theory rarely attends to this social justice issue. Dramaturgical role theory is an important but imperfect theoretical perspective.

AN APPLIED ROLE THEORY MODEL FOR PROMOTING ALTRUISM AND COMMUNITY SERVICE

As part of the National Service movement stimulated by President Clinton, the Virginia Campus Outreach Opportunity League (VACOOL) offered to fund innovative efforts to engage students in service learning. In Chapter 9, I referred to the response by Christopher Newport University, a campus service learning project, to illustrate the behavioral approach to the change process. Applied role theory was another theoretical foundation for the project. The following discussion of this theoretical hybrid identifies the causal factors necessary to create service role identities and increase service activity.

THE APPLIED SOCIAL ROLE PERSPECTIVE ON COMMUNITY PROBLEMS

During this time, two representatives of Home Base, a Newport News agency coordinating regional efforts to help the homeless, invited themselves to my undergraduate social work class. They spoke eloquently for 50 minutes, documenting the dramatic increases in the homeless in our area, the inability of service providers to meet client needs, and their troubled feelings about moving possessions of the newly homeless to a storage facility. The social work faculty agreed to design and implement a one-year pilot project involving Christopher Newport University (CNU) students and area agencies serving the homeless. We received funding from VACOOL for this pilot project. We hoped to increase student commitment to service roles, to aid service providers in helping the homeless, and to start a campus-wide service learning center. In the dramaturgical sense, we believed that a call to service could recruit more actors to perform caring and compassionate work for vulnerable groups. This project was informed by behavioral theory, but social role theory served as the primary conceptual inspiration (Forte, 1997).

THE APPLIED SOCIAL ROLE PERSPECTIVE ON ASSESSMENT

Work by previous researchers using the role theory perspective suggested that we focus on four social systems in the environment (Forte, 1997). First, we should encourage leaders in the university community to communicate widely the university's expectations that students participate in service activities. Second, we should support the development of role networks: families, peer groups, and work groups that would communicate expectations that their student members participate in service activities. Third, we should encourage specific and significant others, especially friends and volunteer supervisors, to convey that the students should participate in service activities. Fourth, we should help each student in our service program create a connection to a new social system—a human services agency, school, or church at which they could volunteer on a regular basis.

We hoped to help students enter a role relationship with a social agency and connect to the volunteer role based on expectations that were clear, complementary, and agreed upon by the student and the agency volunteer coordinator. We aimed also to provide each student with new connections to homeless persons and intended that these be characterized by accurate role taking—students would grasp cognitively the feelings, beliefs, attitudes, and needs of the clients they served; expansive role taking—students would become able to understand and serve a wider range of people, even those very different in social class, age, race, and manner from the student; and empathic role taking—students would connect to clients in ways characterized by empathy, a feeling with and sympathizing for the plight of the homeless person.

Several of our program's objectives were directed toward change in the student actors. These included role identity development so that students would begin to internalize images, conceptions, and behavior tendencies similar to those who volunteer regularly, and different from those who never serve others; positive changes in the salience of the volunteer role—that is, after a semester, the volunteer role would rise in rank and importance compared to the other roles in the students' role hierarchy (family, work, religious, and political); greater **role–person merger,** meaning that students would begin to incorporate the meanings and actions associated with the volunteer role into their overall self-conception as "an important part of who I am" and anticipate a sense of loss if they were not able to volunteer; and an increased behavioral commitment to the volunteer role as indicated by public pledges to serve additional hours during the summer.

THE APPLIED SOCIAL ROLE PERSPECTIVE ON INTERVENTION

The major component of the CREW-VA project to be described here is the Spring 1994 role theory–based service learning seminar. Socialization was conceptualized as the transformation of a novice role actor into a bona fide team performer. The socialization activities central to this transformation of members were recruiting, placing, showing, shaping, certifying, and internalizing.

Recruiting for CREW-VA was done with the help of student assistants. Officers of the student government, leaders of student organizations, and representatives of campus fraternities and sororities were invited to assist in the project. Incoming students at the summer orientation and advising session were introduced to the project. Flyers announcing service opportunities were displayed throughout the campus on a biweekly basis. My two assistants, costumed as homeless women and burdened with bags containing their possessions, twice paraded around campus asking students to help the homeless. The school newspaper offered two feature articles on volunteer efforts to address homelessness. Recruits were asked to bring their friends. Finally, students enrolled in a new Introduction to Volunteer Services course were encouraged to meet the class's service requirements through service to the homeless.

Placing took two forms. Students could accept an individual weekly placement at one of the area organizations serving the homeless. These included a soup kitchen, two shelters, and the information and referral center. Students completed an experience and interest inventory and were then matched with a role assignment appropriate for their comfort and skill level. Or students could participate in one of the special team events developed to serve the homeless. These included a three-day Coats for Kids drive, two days of home building with Habitat for Humanity, and a Christmas dinner and party for 15 families residing in a shelter. Various team roles could be chosen.

Showing activities are those that provide the knowledge and skills necessary for successful performance as a volunteer. In the social agency, these were the typical orientation and modeling processes by which the students were taught agency service functions. A variety of role-training strategies were used in the seminar. A series of didactic presentations included discussions on topics such as the extent of area homelessness, economic contributors to homelessness, city housing policies, types of homelessness, types of service agencies, needs of homeless subgroups, legal advocacy, philanthropic and civic responses to homelessness, and pathways off the streets. These didactic presentations were by experts who also modeled adept and committed service to this population. The three social work faculty members facilitating the service seminar were also doing so as volunteers, another demonstration of the service orientation. Additionally, during group discussion, seminar facilitators intentionally aided members in developing a vocabulary of concepts related to helping roles.

Shaping activities apply rewards and punishments for role performances of novice actors. The emphasis was on reward and gentle persuasion. Volunteers were guided to take the role of and put themselves in the shoes of the homeless. Sociodrama activities focused on "Where would you sleep tonight if you were in a place without money or friends?" A panel discussion with three homeless women and a simulation of a homeless client seeking benefits from an overworked and uncaring bureaucrat were some of the empathy-building exercises. A proservice reward structure was also established. Students were asked several times to affirm publicly their commitment to serve in the volunteer role and to report on their experiments with a service role identity. Public praise was provided during such conversations. Volunteer activity at special events was recorded and displayed prominently. Successful role performances were advertised. For example, coat drive photos were presented in the local paper, and videotape footage of home building efforts appeared on the local news.

Certifying consists of the ongoing evaluation of a novice's progress and final certification of readiness to perform the role independently. Initially, volunteers were asked to complete monthly reports of their volunteer activity and to participate in monthly evaluation and support meetings. Many students found this role demand too time-consuming. As a more realistic certification process, our two interns conducted brief monthly phone conversations with the volunteers to assess progress, to solve service-related problems, and to offer support. Additionally, volunteers were certified by agency social workers and volunteer coordinators. Incidentally, many students were accepted in the role of regular volunteer after completion of the service learning seminar.

As the primary strategy for internalizing the knowledge, competencies, and rewards associated with the volunteer role presented in the seminar and in the service setting, volunteers maintained a journal. Students recorded important service experiences and reflected privately and publicly on these role experiences. The public consolidation of role learning occurred at monthly reflection-on-service group discussions led by a campus service learning coordinator. Several seminar sessions included student reports on their subjective reactions to their performances in the volunteer role. Our pilot project was successful (Forte, 1997), and we managed to assemble a large and enthusiastic cast of students dedicated to serving the homeless.

LEARNING ACTIVITIES

1. Identify two or three of the most important or salient roles that you enact. Review the pattern of action appropriate to each role, the social context in which you perform the role, and how you learned to play the role.

2. Complete an analysis of a social agency that you have visited or of your field internship agency. Become familiar with the organizational chart, including the major social positions that constitute the organization and the lines of authority and communication between position holders. Identify, if possible, the specific features and roles for the following positions: direct service social worker, field instructor, and client. What are the requirements for entry into these positions, and what are some of the different expectations associated with each position?

3. Think about a social work agency or a human services organization that you have visited. Identify the stage-setting elements that a client might observe when seeking services at this place. What costumes did the workers wear? Were there clear indications of which regions were onstage and which regions were offstage? What props were used to communicate agency values and preferences? How were furnishings, decorations, and other objects used in the setting? How did these staging devices seem to influence the roles that workers and clients played in the agency?

4. Trace your career so far as a family member, a student, or a worker. Identify the important role transitions that you experienced. What were the particular challenges that you faced as you moved into each role? What personal strengths and social supports helped you cope with the challenges of each transition? Reflect on a time when you chose not to make a transition and enter a role. How would your career have been different if you had chosen instead to attempt the transitioning process?

5. What are some of the challenges that you have faced while in college or graduate school? Focus on one challenge caused by role difficulties. What type or types of role strain were involved? How did you cope with the role difficulty?

6. List some roles that you enact regularly—work roles, family roles, community roles, friendship roles, student roles, and other kinds of roles. Rank these roles in order of importance to your overall sense of who you are. Think about the most important or salient role, and identify the interaction and emotional experiences and commitments that contributed to its high rank.

7. Reflect on a culture or subculture different from mainstream urban American culture (the culture of rural Ireland or the culture of the hip-hop community in the United States, for instance). Identify some of the roles that are important in this culture and the patterns of action associated with each role. Report on the evaluation of each role by cultural members. Note who in the culture or subculture has access to each role and who has difficulty gaining the right to use the role. In what specific cultural settings and in how many settings might you observe the enactment of each role?

8. Evaluate the quality of your performance as a team member in terms of discipline, loyalty, and circumspection and as an individual role player using the standards of appropriate, proper, and convincing conduct. Identify several ways that your team could work better together and several ways that you could better enact an important role as a team member.

ADDITIONAL RESOURCES

Additional resources are available on the book companion website at **www.thomsonedu.com/ social_work/forte.** Resources include key terms, tutorial quizzes, links to related websites, and lists of additional resources for furthering your research.

APPLIED ECONOMIC THEORY

INTRODUCTION

The word *economy* is derived from a Greek term meaning "skilled in household management." Ancient Greeks were interested in how family members managed their property and resources. Today, the concept has a broader definition. Lewis and Widerquist (2001), for example, characterize **economics** as "the study of how humans decide to use available resources to satisfy their wants" (p. 2). Contemporary economic theorists pay careful attention to the dynamics of production and distribution in the family, but also to exchange processes in larger human organizations. Economics offers "a framework for analysis of the dynamics of economic processes, providing guidance for economic planning and decision making and for predicting the results of market activities and/or economic policies" (Prigoff, 2000, p. xi).

Social work textbooks that survey theoretical frameworks and provide knowledge of human behavior and the social environment have rarely included economic and exchange theories (Pearman, 1973). However, these theories are very important. Carl Couch (1989) reminded theory users that "members of all societies must extract the necessities of life—food, clothing, and shelter—from their environment to survive" (p. 193). Couch (1979) valued economic theories also because these theories recognize that "we do have bodies that demand food if we are to survive, that we are flesh and blood organisms with needs and wants that can only be satisfied by entering in commerce with others" (p. 396). Many people throughout the world deal with situations characterized by scarcity. Economic theories can help social workers understand how decisions about the allocation and provision of goods and services cause such scarcity.

In this chapter, I will show how the economic theoretical perspective can be applied to understanding and helping people with troubles. Several role models who advanced this approach will be introduced. The root metaphor of "social life as marketplace activity" will be elaborated and extended to the economic theory's images of the client, the social worker, and the social organization. Economic theory's concepts and propositions will be displayed on an eco-map and translated into ecosystem terms. A model outlining how economic theory might be applied to the problem of enlisting cyber-allies in a "Save Our Social Work Program" campaign will be outlined. Much of the chapter uses concepts and examples from the neoclassical approach to economics, but some of the work of institutional economists challenging neoclassical assumptions and the work of sociologists applying exchange and rational choice approaches to topics of concern to social workers will also be reviewed.

RELATED DIALECTS, ASSOCIATED SCHOOLS OF ECONOMIC THOUGHT

Economists may engage in either of two kinds of economic theorizing (Lewis & Widerquist, 2001). **Microeconomics** is the study of small-size markets for particular goods and particular services and the study of the relation of various economic actors to these markets. Microeconomists are interested in family economies and in social work businesses. For example, they might study the factors influencing the price of a therapy session charged by a clinical social worker. **Macroeconomics** is the study of the economy as a whole, including topics such as the economy's total output of goods and services, the level and causes of unemployment, and the overall rate of inflation. Macroeconomists might compare different types of economies, including their economic productivity and total yearly spending for social services. The **social exchange theory** is a middle-range theory grounded in the economic framework. There are microeconomic and macroeconomic versions of exchange theory. Both versions address specifically the transfer of material and symbolic goods by exchange processes and mechanisms, and people's calculations about the profitability of exchanges.

The field of economics has a long history and includes many different schools of thought (Lewis & Widerquist, 2001; Prigoff, 2000). I will first review some of these major variants or schools and then introduce several exemplary economic theorists.

Classic economics began with the work of Adam Smith and was further developed by David Ricardo, who studied the distribution of income among landowners, workers, and capitalists. Thomas Malthus, another important classical theorist, argued that rapid increases in population and limited land resulted in more people than could be fed and paid well and thus precluded raising a society's standard of living. The neoclassical school builds on the work of the classic economists and has become the dominant approach in the field. **Institutional economics** focuses on how individual and collective economic processes occur as part of larger social and cultural patterns. Institutionalists challenge the assumptions of classical economics that people are rational calculators primarily motivated by economic self-interest and that laissez-faire government policies result in economic well-being for all. **Keynesian economics** expands on the work of John Keynes, discussed later in this section, and focuses on planned government spending and taxation to stabilize the economy during recessions. The Marxist school will be discussed in the chapter on critical theory. Newer approaches to the economic framework, including monetarism, rational choice theory, and socioeconomics, amplify or revise the theories of these major schools of economic thought.

Classical and neoclassical economic theories are related to the philosophy of utilitarianism. **Utility** is the enjoyment or use that a consumer obtains from a good that she consumes (Lewis & Widerquist, 2001). **Utilitarianism** is the philosophical doctrine asserting that the value of a decision, policy, or social arrangement depends on the usefulness or goodness of the results of the decision. Human **hedonism**, a basic feature of human nature, is the desire to obtain pleasure and avoid pain. Hedonism helps us rationally determine the utility of various courses of action. A utilitarian is a person who endorses the philosophy of utilitarianism, and acts after making judgments about the relative utility or pleasure of possible behaviors. Utilitarian political leaders and social workers try to reconcile individual and group interests by applying the criterion of usefulness and then choosing the public program or policy that will bring about the most useful or pleasure-producing result for the greatest number of community members—even if a minority suffer because of this decision. Utilitarian policy makers often argue that the ends justify the means.

APPLIED ECONOMIC THEORY: EXEMPLARY ROLE MODELS

Several theorists and several scholarly practitioners were exemplary economic thinkers.

ADAM SMITH

Adam Smith (1723–1790) is the founder of modern economics (Grolier Encyclopedia, 1999). Smith, a Scottish social philosopher, laid the foundations for the laissez-faire approach to economic policy. It is important to understand that Smith developed his ideas in a society almost completely controlled by the state, one inhospitable to the private investor and entrepreneur (Prigoff, 2000). The British Crown had established state monopolies, and it discouraged competition. Smith attributed Britain's economic and public problems to state rulers. In his book, *An Inquiry into the Nature and Causes of the Wealth of Nations* (1776), he asserted that the government and its agents should not interfere—except for limited reasons, including defense, justice, and select public works—in a nation's economic processes. When individuals pursue their self-interests, and meet in the marketplace as buyers and sellers, then a desirable pattern of economic activity develops. This results in social harmony and progress. Naturally coordinated and voluntary trade is like an "invisible hand," and it provides for social needs better than any heavy-handed policies instituted by a state, crown, or government.

Smith's conception of capitalist society was based on a complex conception of human sentiments and conduct (Khalil, 1990). Adam Smith postulated that humans are motivated to advance their personal interests *and* to achieve a degree of positive self-regard. The human capacity for sympathy activated as an internal and "impartial spectator" compels us to consider the reactions of others to our profit-seeking action, thereby enabling us to both profit and maintain our positive self-image. Adam Smith conceived of community members who compete against one another, but who also try to create institutions that affirm the virtue of their competitors. Smith preferred a conception of people as citizens channeling their self-interested action toward a moral and common good. Much of Smith's career was directed toward the teaching, writing, and service associated with an educator's life.

JOHN MAYNARD KEYNES

One of the most important economic theorists is John Maynard Keynes (1883–1946). Keynes was born into an elite family in Cambridge, England.

After graduating from Cambridge University, he worked as a civil servant, a professor, a treasury economist during World War I, an editor of an academic journal, and a journalist (Encyclopedia Britannica, 2002). The Great Depression stimulated Keynes to write his monumental treatise, *The General Theory of Employment, Interest, and Money* (1936). During the Depression, millions of willing workers could not find employment. In his book, Keynes rejected the claim of neoclassical economists that the unemployed were responsible for their predicament because they were unwilling to work for lower wages. Additionally, he argued that recovery in a market economy would not occur unless the total or aggregate demand for goods and services increased. Because workers were limited during a depression by their meager incomes and were not able to increase their spending, alternative stimuli were needed. Here, Keynes differed with the laissez-faire theorists, who opposed all government intervention. He proposed specifically that the government should spend for public works and for subsidies to afflicted groups—even though such spending created a budget deficit. This fiscal policy would increase the aggregate demand and encourage business managers to resume production and hire more workers. Thus, the implementation of his recommended policy would stabilize the economy.

An energetic scholar, Keynes published many books and essays on economic policy. His views of the relation of government to the economy coincide with those of some social workers. These social workers believe that activist government can foster economic development beneficial to the whole population, especially the vulnerable sectors of citizens barely able to meet their basic needs for food, clothing, shelter, and work (Prigoff, 2000). Keynes stayed active in public service throughout his life. In 1944, for example, he helped to create the International Monetary Fund and the World Bank. Unfortunately, the economic principles adopted by these agencies came to reflect the views of orthodox economists more than of Keynes.

JANE ADDAMS

Several social workers have achieved acclaim for their application of economic theory. Jane Addams (1860–1935) was a founder of the famous Hull House social settlement in Chicago's Near West Side. Chapter 10 documents her contribution to the formation of the symbolic interactionist school. Jane Addams was also an economic reformer who lived with the poor, advocated for the investment of public funds in the neighborhoods of recently arrived immigrants and other poor Chicagoans, and fought for economic justice (Lundblad, 1995). She challenged the powerful businessmen who controlled the meat packing, railroad, and garment industries to act with a greater sense of social responsibility and to abandon their "gospel of wealth," a philosophy based on classical economic principles and used to justify the gap between the poor and the rich (Pottick, 1988). Her 1902 book, *Democracy and Social Ethics* (1902/1920), analyzed the cultures of the working class and middle class and the social problems that the class division aggravated by industrialism caused.

Addams' accomplishments were many (Addams, 1910/1990). She supported trade unions, offered Hull House as a meeting place for workers, created the Labor Museum for the display of immigrant crafts and skills, offered labor leaders advice about conflict mediation strategies, criticized the factory system, and advocated for striking workers. Addams was vice president of the National Woman's Trade Union League. She demanded that business leaders support workers' democratic participation in business and community policy making. She campaigned for laws governing child labor, mandating factory inspections, limiting women's working hours, guaranteeing workplace safety, and recognizing labor unions. Addams reacted negatively to the self-righteous and controlling attitude of rich philanthropists. In the economically unified society that Addams imagined, philanthropy would not be a one-way transfer. Transactions would be based on the interdependence of the classes and the social value of reciprocity. The giving and receiving roles would be interchangeable. While the rich contributed the money that funded Hull House social programs, they in turn would receive valuable social lessons. Hull House residents offered a culture, a set of creative ideas, and an industriousness that could benefit and advance the elite and the whole community.

Addams complemented her practice activities with many scholarly contributions (Deegan, 1988). *Hull House Maps and Papers* (1895/1970), the culmination of an extensive project profiling the economic, social, and geographic features of her community, served as a model of action research. Addams taught courses at the Chicago School of Civics and Philanthropy (later the University of Chicago School of Social Service Administration), but in ways that inventively wove "social thought and activism into a nexus of praxis" (Deegan, p. 75). Jane Addams wrote extensively on public problems associated with economic inequality such as prostitution, poor housing, inadequate wages, dangerous work conditions, political corruption, poor city sanitation, delinquency, and the hopelessness of the elderly poor. She offered a radical and confrontational model of social work practice, one organized around the extension of democratic processes to political governance, to social intercourse, and to economic structures, and one that extended the right to participate in economic decision making to the poor and powerless members of society.

HARRY LLOYD HOPKINS

Harry Lloyd Hopkins (1890–1946) was another social worker known for using economic principles and processes to achieve social work goals. Hopkins had once lived in a New York Settlement House, so he had intimate familiarity with the difficulties associated with poverty. He championed the application of Keynesian economic theory to the problem of economic recovery and, as an influential adviser to President Franklin Delano Roosevelt, helped develop the New Deal approach. Between 1933 and 1940, Hopkins headed three different federal departments (World Book, 1999). He served on at least a half dozen other committees or councils devoted to the use of government resources to solve economic problems. Using the logic of Keynes, Hopkins and Roosevelt assumed that government spending would stimulate the national economy. Together they obtained political support for the expenditure of $9 billion in public relief and found ways to supply jobs to 8 million Americans. Roosevelt, with Hopkins' assistance, pushed legislation that authorized investment in public works projects resulting in the construction of parks, schools, low-income housing, and public buildings. Their policies and programs rescued the U.S. economy from a major disaster (Prigoff, 2000).

APPLIED ECONOMIC THEORY: ROOT METAPHORS

Economic theorizers make extensive and creative use of three root metaphors. The social environment is compared to a marketplace where buyers and sellers can conduct business. The person or client is considered a consumer using rational calculations to make financially sound purchases, and the social worker is like a financial consultant.

THE SOCIAL ENVIRONMENT AS A MARKETPLACE

Economic theorists compare society to a marketplace. Complex societies can be compared to a set of multiple and interrelated markets. First, I will discuss economic markets. A **market** is "a place where buyers and sellers come together to make exchanges" (Lewis & Widerquist, 2001, p. 25). It is the cultural context for the sale and purchase of goods and services. The market can be a physical place like the grocery store in your neighborhood, or it can be a virtual place like eBay, a website that facilitates exchanges between people all over the globe. Markets are the social organizations that make economic transactions practical. Many contemporary societies include markets for clothing, for automobiles, and for entertainment. There are labor markets, housing markets, health care markets, markets for assorted goods, and farmers markets. Community members sometimes create their own markets. My nephew and his network of friends have created an informal market so they can buy, sell, and trade *Pokemon* playing cards with each other.

Society is imagined to be a marketplace. A society's members interact for economic and noneconomic purposes as do buyers and sellers in conventional markets. Members of contemporary societies or their social organizations become connected by their exchange relationships. Such patterned giving and taking generally structures other forms of interaction. Members alternate between the roles of "buyer," an actor who tries to find the best sellers of desired goods and services, and "seller," an actor who tries to find the best buyers for his or her products and services. In contemporary societies, markets are competitive. Community members like business administrators strive to realize competitive advantage over their counterparts. Modern societies are also characterized by cash economies. Members prefer to use money as the universal medium for exchange transactions. Successful markets develop standardized procedures for determining weight, value, and price per pound in a grocery produce aisle, for instance. Community members also seek to standardize the process of judging costs and benefits in nonmonetary decisions.

Social policies and social work organizations can be understood by reference to the market metaphor. Some political reformers have used the economic framework to suggest, for instance, that welfare recipients are like other consumers who make rational calculations about the most profitable line of action in a given market (Lewis & Widerquist, 2001; Rigney, 2001). Poorly designed social welfare policies provide clients incentives to become dependent on government programs and to work less. Welfare recipients are acting rationally in these welfare systems when they have children to receive benefits. However, such systems offer disincentives to seek employment and to create mutual help family structures. Markets for social welfare benefits and services in a society that stigmatizes and humiliates the poor create other exchange problems. Welfare recipients may calculate that their social status is a scarce resource, and decide that the welfare worker's request that they give up status and dignity to receive financial or social aid is too great a price (Foa, 1973). These clients may drop out of this welfare market and become more vulnerable to homelessness, crime, or suicide.

In a case study, Handelman (1976) used the economic metaphor to understand agency operations. He showed that clients bring resources to an agency and look for opportunities to invest in the agency. When the agency and the client negotiate terms for a fair exchange, a relationship is established. He also discovered that the pattern of socioeconomic transactions between agency workers and client structures the client's career. Clients who give what the worker expects and exact few unexpected costs in time, effort, or emotion complete the casework process successfully. Clients who fail to invest in the helping process or seem to make irrational calculations about the client–worker relationship are often ejected from the agency marketplace and told to shop elsewhere.

Some social work organizations are designed as bureaucracies funded by the government and protected in some ways from marketplace competition (Lewis & Widerquist, 2001). Other social work organizations and organizations that host social workers are organized by market principles like profit-oriented enterprises. However, both types of agency can be compared to economic markets. The social work organization offers services to customers shopping in a health, mental health, or social services market. When the organization's practitioners work hard and creatively, and the organization responds to the preferences and wants of potential customers, then it can "sell" its services. When the organization is not responsive to client demand, or squanders its resources, then competing agencies can steal customers by indicating that clients can obtain services at a better price. The administrators and employees of organizations that do not foster "profitable" relationships with clients are fired or sanctioned, and the survival of an organization with many costs is jeopardized as would be the survival of an inefficient business.

The Person as Buyer and Seller

According to economic theorists, people are like calculating machines (Lewis & Widerquist, 2001) or actuaries who continuously weigh the risks, the potential gains, and the desirable insurance premiums associated with various possible investments. Human action follows **calculations** or judgments about the "expected benefit or detriment attributed to an object relative to the individual's needs"(Abbot, Brown, & Crosbie, 1973, p. 505). These calculations are motivated by the universal urge to advance self-interests, and people calculate with the intention of maximizing **profit**—the rewards gained minus the costs incurred during an exchange (Rigney, 2001). Humans as calculators are constantly assigning value to their transactions with the environment and completing cost–benefit analyses of these transactions.

The social work client can be compared to the financial investor who attempts to calculate strategically, and enrich his or her overall personal economy, by making wise investment decisions based on these calculations. Capital resources must be allocated among the alternative organizational opportunities available for personal realization in a way that, on balance, will bring the most profit. Reflecting on past investments and projecting possible future returns, the client uses a subjective cost–reward calculus to decide which organizations best value his or her self. To the extent possible, investments are made in the organizations that confirm prized personal and social identities. McCall and Simmons (1982) summarized this metaphorical position by stating that people's personal economies require "skillful and caring investment of self in managing the demands and opportunities of the various relationships to conserve, maintain or enrich our resources" (p. 213). Careless expenditure of psychosocial resources brings bankruptcy. A wise investment brings the wealth of power, status, or security.

Rigney (2001), also using the economic metaphor, suggested that the client is a consumer who organizes her life like an investment portfolio. The client considers how best to use her limited time, money, emotional energy, and material goods. The client then makes commitments to, or invests in, those activities, relationships, and organizations that bring the best return for the investment. The client attempts to sever negotiations and bargaining with those relationship partners or organizations that bring a meager profit or are too costly. Here, the client acts like the investor who sells undesirable stock or withdraws savings from a low-interest account. Economic considerations by the client also include calculations of **opportunity costs**. These are the opportunities the person loses by making choice A rather than choice B. Opportunity costs accrue when resources might have been invested elsewhere at a higher rate of return. The person asks herself, "Am I profiting less from choice A than choice B?" If a client considers, for example, investing four or five years in a college education, she will consider not only the likely long-term profitability of such a choice but also the lost opportunities for time with family, leisure time activities, and advancement as a practitioner.

The calculating person is also like an accountant adding up revenue and expenses and making monthly tallies of his financial state. Many people like to build up a long-term fund of confidence and goodwill from others by publicly recognized and appreciated acts of contribution and competence. This fund can be drawn on between successes (Collins, 1993). The person's mental spreadsheets are used for further decision making. Kollock (1996) proposed that actors use two different accounting systems to monitor exchanges and to judge if a partner's line of credit is too far extended. When using the **loose accounting system,** the calculating accountant is generous and allows credit to friends and relatives with few restrictions. The books can remain unbalanced. Precise tallies of the other's contribution in goods and services to the relationship are not maintained. Additional credit is available so that the other can overdraw on his or her line of account when necessary. Relaxed accounting leaves its user vulnerable, however, to exploitation. In contrast, the **restrictive accounting system** personifies stinginess. Credit is not easily given. The calculating accountant expects that the relationship books be kept constantly in balance. Debts must be repaid quickly, and often in kind. Careful and exact track is kept of each person's contribution to the exchange system. Restrictive accounting leaves its user vulnerable to recrimination and charges of intolerance.

Clients, like all people, can be compared to calculators, investors, accountants, and economists. Such metaphors help us understand how clients differ from one another, and how most clients differ from privileged members of a society. Clients vary in the availability of resources (labor, money, mutual aid networks, social competencies) that they can use for investment purposes. These resource constraints affect the financial strategies and choices of many clients, and the likely return on their investments. Clients vary in the opportunities that they have to invest successfully in various social organizations and economic ventures. A few have many investment opportunities, but most clients have limited access to moneymaking schemes. Clients vary in the likely payoffs that they can expect from their economic and noneconomic investments. Most cannot expect or demand high rates of return, and many settle for meager remuneration. Clients also vary widely in their investment knowledge and skill. Many social work clients have limited ability to calculate all the costs and benefits from a contemplated transaction, to predict likely future payoffs, or to invest wisely.

THE SOCIAL WORKER AS BUSINESS CONSULTANT

Although economic theorists do not often characterize the social worker by using marketplace metaphors and imagery, such comparisons are implicit to the theoretical framework. The social worker is like a business consultant. The social worker has a general expertise in **cost–benefit analysis.** For instance, the economically oriented social worker can make sophisticated calculations of the estimated social and economic benefits of a policy, program, or client action minus the estimated social and economic costs. In this way, the social worker can identify the likely net benefits or profit from a proposed course of action (Lewis & Widerquist, 2001).

The social worker uses business expertise in both micro-level and macro-level practice. When working with individuals, couples, or groups, the worker challenges the client system to calculate the likely costs and benefits of various decisions. These may include decisions about having a child, optimal family size, premarital sex, divorcing a spouse, staying with a violent partner, fleeing the correctional system, care arrangements for an elderly relative, engaging in unprotected sex, or using drugs. With the worker's counsel, the client can then make a rational choice and avoid choices with hidden or long-term costs.

Social workers act like businesspeople when serving communities, organizations, or societies. **Externalities** are costs not included in the costs of production or in corporate ledgers. The government or community pays these costs (Prigoff, 2000). Economically savvy social workers may join with public interest groups to alert local residents about the undeclared costs to the community of a corporate activity, and then advocate until the corporation becomes fiscally and socially accountable to the public and liable for its externalities (Prigoff, 2000). Social workers use economic analysis to help administrators of social work organizations and universities identify all the revenues and all the expenditures associated with serving their clients or educating their students (Cournoyer, Powers, Johnson, & Bennett, 2000). Such financial information enhances the organization's decision-making and planning processes, and ensures the program's accountability, effectiveness, and growth. Macro-level social workers are like business advisers when they help societal policy makers fully consider the consequences associated with proposed public legislation. These include the health costs, the social costs, and the environmental costs (Prigoff, 2000). Social workers report to legislators about the potential benefits of public investments in prenatal health care, early child care, nutrition programs, or summer jobs for youth.

Social workers are businesspeople when they engage in **social marketing.** This is an approach to the change process that segments the market by lifestyle or some other marketing principle, focuses on a "target market," prioritizes the needs of "customers" in this market segment, conducts research into the specifics of customer needs, and then crafts programs to address the needs, wants, and perceptions of the selected customer segments (Andreasen, 1995). Social work programs can market behavior change related to quitting smoking or drug use, increasing recycling, losing weight, switching to a low-cholesterol diet, getting vaccinations, or driving under the speed limit.

Social workers may also act as responsible business leaders and contribute to global economic change. Twenty-first-century capitalist economies tend to exploit their weaker partners in the world market, often contributing to unemployment and poverty (Wagner, 1997). **Globalization** refers to "the integration of markets, information, technology, and cultures" across the planet Earth (Stoesz, Guzzetta, & Lusk, 1999, p. 251). Social workers can monitor the various costs of economic globalization and advocate for the economic rights of the least fortunate members of societies around the world.

Candace Clark (1987, 1997) is one of the few economic sociologists explicitly using the marketplace root metaphor to characterize social workers. Let me review her framework for understanding the allocation of sympathy. There are similarities, she argued between a monetary economy and a socioemotional economy. First, both money and emotions are valuable yet scarce resources. We portion out our sympathy with care. To act with sympathy, a person must take another person's perspective, empathize with the other's plight, and show concern for the other's misery. This takes time and effort similar to that needed for making investment decisions. Second, societies typically develop patterns for distributing both financial goods like money and emotional goods like sympathy. Third, individuals have inclinations toward frugality, and prefer not to exhaust through indiscriminate giving their limited supplies of either money or prosocial emotions, whether love, gratitude, attentiveness, or sympathy. Fourth, people follow societal or group patterns for exchanging items with both monetary and emotional value. A society's principles guiding the exchange of items with monetary value and the exchange of behaviors with socioemotional value can be identified. These principles help us decide what monetary and socioemotional resources we should give to and take from others to be considered good people, who owes what to whom, how exchanges of material and symbolic gifts should be handled, who has collected too many resources, and who has too few.

Using this theoretical foundation, Clark (1997) has developed the idea of **sympathy margin,** and this concept can help us characterize the social work role. Bankers may extend a line of financial credit to good clients. Community members may extend a line of social credit to those clients experiencing bad luck or other misfortune. A client's sympathy credit rating, however, is negotiable and continually adjusted. In certain circumstances (exposure to a traumatic natural disaster such as a flood or hurricane), clients can overdraw their credit limits and receive massive expressions of sympathy and concern from friends, family, and associates. In some circumstances (repeated choices to engage in self-destructive drinking or drug using despite challenges from peers), the client may cash in all his or her credit. There is no longer a sympathy margin. Previous sympathizers now feel free to display indifference rather than concern. In other circumstances (a heartfelt and articulate communication of gratitude from a client recovering from an illness), the client can replenish his or her line of credit. Sympathizers feel a renewed openness to sympathizing. In a final set of circumstances, the recipient of sympathy endeavors to repay the kindness and to clear up all debts owed to the sympathizer.

Clark (1997) characterized social workers as **sympathy brokers,** professionals who aim to create "large sympathy margins for all clients, indeed, for all humanity" (p. 186). By participating in professional socialization processes, social workers strengthen their inclinations to advocate for concern and sympathy for the society's underdogs. Nonsympathetic social work students are screened out of the profession; callous persons, stingy in their allotments of sympathy, would not be considered fit for a social work career. Social workers can approach the job of sympathy broker in different ways. Many social workers are "sympathy overinvestors." They advocate for offers of extensive credit even to those who have little social value, have contributed to their own difficulties, or do not follow sympathy distribution rules. Social workers also can be "sympathy underinvestors." These professionals husband their emotional resources and resist inclinations to feel and display sympathy.

Sympathy brokers can learn to attend both to a society's distribution of economic resources and to its distribution of socioemotional resources like empathy, sympathy, and compassion. Many social work clients cannot mobilize sympathy on their own behalf, so social workers learn to step in. As entrepreneurs of sympathy, social workers try to stretch a society's "sympathy logic" (Clark, 1997). Generic sympathy-generating efforts might involve impressing the public with the sympathy worthiness of those affected by particular social problems, describing the "character" of the unfortunate in sympathetic terms, justifying the allocation of sympathy to victims of circumstances and systemic inequities, and pressing for an expanded base for giving sympathy. Practitioners can intervene in specific ways to create sympathy margins for the homeless and other undervalued groups. Specific strategies inspired by Clark's work (Forte, 2002b) might include increasing the social value of those without homes, educating the public about the particular and human biographies of the homeless, aiding the homeless in enacting public roles in ways that evoke sympathy, generating a sense of debt among the domiciled and a desire to act on their sense of obligation to the less fortunate, and building a strong community so solutions that are both sympathetic to the homeless and attentive to the socioeconomic concerns of various community stakeholders can be generated.

CORE ASSUMPTIONS OF APPLIED ECONOMIC THEORY

The economic framework includes a set of basic assumptions about the person, the environment, and the transactions between the person and the environment. I will review four assumptions and explain each by using, when possible, comparisons to buying, selling, and the marketplace.

MARKETS OPERATE ACCORDING TO CERTAIN RULES

Economic theorists assume that markets have certain characteristics and operate according to certain rules (Lewis & Widerquist, 2001). Markets are open and competitive. There are no **monopolies**. Each buyer and each seller has limited influence over the price of goods in the market. No one buyer or seller is so large, powerful, or unscrupulous that he or she can set prices in a nonnegotiable way. In an automobile market, for example, there is not one car dealer in a region, Ralph Spoilsport, who controls so many cars that his dealership can charge exorbitant prices while car buyers can find nowhere else to shop for better-priced cars.

In the markets imagined by theorists, conditions of complete information prevail. Information flows freely to all participants in marketplace activities. There is no "insider" information. Every buyer and seller knows all that he or she needs to know about the prices of products, their quality, and all factors related to their possible purchase. Transactions follow these informed decisions. The automobile shopper, for instance, knows what the car dealer paid for the car on the lot, and the customer can discover the standard amount of profit for car dealers in that region.

Theoretically, markets do not establish barriers that impede commerce between willing buyers and sellers. Anyone can enter and engage in a marketplace transaction. Anyone can exit the market and choose not to participate in an exchange. Sales do not occur in inaccessible places. Markets do not prohibit members of certain social categories from buying or selling. Ralph Spoilsport, our imaginary car dealer, would not set up a barrier to screen out African Americans or women. He would not instruct salespersons to collude and strategically steer away all buyers who come to the dealership informed with precise pricing information obtained from *Consumer Reports*.

In theoretical markets, property rights are protected. Men with guns cannot use force to take over a company, a house, or a collection of prized possessions. Moreover, there is a degree of basic trust between buyers and sellers. Trade is not coerced, or subject to fraud and deception. Trust allows the car shopper, for example, to authorize an agent of the Automobile Association of America to locate a desirable car. Trust fortifies the hope that a car dealer is "reputable" and is selling a quality vehicle, not a lemon. Trust helps the seller believe the buyer's pledge to pay for the car over an agreed-upon loan period.

GOVERNMENT POLICIES INFLUENCE THE ECONOMY

Economic theorists generally assume that there is an optimal degree of regulation of the economy by agents of the government. Economists often divide economies into three types. The notion of an **unregulated economy,** or pure capitalism, refers to market arrangements under which "exchanges between buyers and sellers in markets determine all economic decisions" (Lewis & Widerquist, 2001, p. 6). Government regulators do not make decisions for the community about what can be sold or how selling should be organized. Market participants are free from regulation. Government interference in economic processes is minimal. If a seller wants to sell debris from a fallen space shuttle and there are people who want to buy the remains of the shuttle and of its astronauts, so be it.

The concept **centrally planned economy** refers to "an economy in which a government makes all economic decisions" (Lewis & Widerquist, 2001, p. 6). In some socialist societies, for example, political leaders and government bureaucrats use government planning, social legislation, and economic regulations to influence economic processes toward the end of an equitable distribution of wealth (Rigney, 2001). Mechanisms of exchange such as cooperatives and participatory ownership replace competitive market activity in these economies (Lie, 1997).

In a **mixed economy,** there is a role for government as, for example, the social entity responsible for social security, labor safety, and aid to the poor. Equally, there is a role for the market in the form of the vigorous competition that minimizes inefficiencies in resource distribution. Free market capitalism and socialist planning are both valued. The government regulates economic processes to protect the property rights of buyers and sellers. The government functions also to curtail abuses by businesspeople, and to provide for the public goods and the defense systems not provided by the marketplace (Prigoff, 2000; Rigney, 2001).

Classical and neoclassical economists assume that the unregulated economy is ideal. Markets free from government regulation bring ever-increasing prosperity to the society's members. Smith's "invisible hand" operates as a protective process. Greedy producers and sellers looking for unfair advantages are eventually undersold by market-oriented competitors. Market consumers benefit from the free and unencumbered competition. State interference in the production or allocation of resources, these economists assume, only decreases efficiency and causes avoidable economic and social problems.

UNREGULATED MARKETS PRODUCE THE BEST SOCIAL OUTCOMES

Economic theorists assume that when economies are characterized by unregulated or minimally regulated market conditions, outcomes for the society are socially optimal. Open, competitive, and free markets provide the most options and benefits to buyers and sellers (Prigoff, 2000). If a seller raises prices higher than a market standard, for example, then buyers can seek substitutes from others willing to sell at a standard price. This confidence in markets can be traced to Smith's theory of market self-regulation. Adam Smith argued that when each actor pursues his or her unique interests, the adjustments necessary to mutual profit taking, though unintended, result in an orderly economy and society. Dyadic and small group exchanges under free market conditions lead in aggregate to a more complex and better economic system than that found in socialist societies. Market institutions work "to harmonize private interests and public welfare" (Knight & Johnson, 1999, p. 578) and to maximize benefits for investors, sellers, and consumers.

These economic self-regulating processes are characterized in terms of the interaction of supply and demand (Lewis & Widerquist, 2001; Lie, 1997). The **supply** is the quantity and the price of a good or a service that producers are willing to sell. The **demand** is the quantity and the price of a good or service that consumers are willing to buy. **Equilibrium** is the point at which the quantity demanded and the quantity supplied become equal. Free markets tend to stabilize, economists assume, and both consumers and firms creating consumables are satisfied by the marketplace exchanges. Consumers can purchase all they want of something and do so at an acceptable price, and producers can sell all they want at an acceptable price. For example, reflect on the introduction of the Apple iMac G4 with an LCD display in 2002. Demand for this computer was quite high at first, partly because production problems had limited the supply. Apple took advantage of this high demand and increased the price of each iMac by $100. Many shoppers did not want to pay the new price, and a balance of supply and demand was soon achieved.

When the conditions for a free market are met, the invisible hand operates, and the allocation of resources available to the society is efficient, then prosperity follows. An optimal quantity of goods and services is available for all participants in the marketplace economy. Efficient markets result in flexibility in allocation and provisioning, the rapid flow of resources, motivated manufacturers and service providers, productive labor, constraints on greedy producers, consumer autonomy, and, eventually, material abundance and economic security.

MARKET LOGIC OPERATES IN OTHER SPHERES OF HUMAN LIFE

Economic theorists assume that marketplace principles and logic operate in almost all spheres of human activity. Economic theorists extend the metaphor, imagery, and reasoning of markets to many forms of social interaction and to many settings for human activity. For instance, we go to the market not only to obtain consumable items, stock in corporations, and jobs but also to find intimate partners. When we enter the dating or marriage scene, we market ourselves as a worthy mate and use our physical appearance, clothing, possessions, and personality traits as inducements to potential partners to buy our product. Successful dating can be characterized as a pair of buyers and sellers agreeing to purchase each other's offerings of intimacy. Repeatedly rewarding exchanges between the intimates often lead to marriage. Marriage can be defined economically as the formal creation of an economic unit bound by a contractual agreement on the exchange arrangements related to labor division, wealth production, child rearing, sexual interaction, and leisure time. Some mate seekers have troubles when shopping. A single, female, African American social work professional may enter the dating market in her community seeking a same-race mate. She may find a limited supply of available African American men. The demand for these eligible men from other African American women and from women of other racial and ethnic backgrounds may also be great. The professional soon discovers that market conditions require her to pay dearly for her preferred type of partner or to settle for a less desirable partner.

Economists assume that humans act as rational calculators not only when buying and selling goods and services but also when interacting with friends, family members, coworkers, and neighbors (Rigney, 2001). Turner (1991) proposed that such **rational decision making** includes the following components: "reviewing viable options, reviewing events that may occur, arranging information and choice in chronological order, evaluating the consequences of alternative courses of action, judging the chances that uncertain events will occur, and choosing actions with minimax outcomes" (p. 84).

Rational calculations flavor many private and public behaviors. Will a social work client help an elderly parent? Clarke (2001) conducted a study of 218 nursing home residents in Canada. Based on extensive interviews and observations, he concluded that considerations of physical and emotional costs, reciprocity, obligation, and profitable exchanges were central to the thinking of adult children with ill elderly parents. Why did some non-Jewish Europeans help Jews evade the Nazi soldiers? Opp (1997) reviewed the extensive research literature on those who helped their Jewish neighbors during the World War II Holocaust. Opp concluded that even this prosocial activity followed rational calculation and was motivated by the rescuers' desires to advance their interests. Benefits from helping included positive regard from family and friends, the satisfaction of complying with religious and work-based norms of service, financial and material rewards, and feelings of pride in resisting the Nazi regime. Rescuers generally calculated also that they had the money, space, knowledge, and skills to achieve successful and profitable results despite the risks and costs.

THE ECONOMIC APPROACH TO DEVELOPMENT

Economic theorists have not developed a distinctive conceptual framework for understanding human development. They are interested in development, but at the level of the economy and the society, not at the level of the individual. In this section, I will review the traditional classical/neoclassical perspective on economic development.

EXEMPLARY ROLE MODELS

Economics is a science committed to cumulative knowledge building. Many contributors have lent their intellectual powers to the construction of contemporary economics. The traditional approach to economic development represents a synthesis of conversations and arguments stimulated by many different theorists. These include British political philosophers Thomas Hobbes, John Locke, and David Hume; classical economists such as Adam Smith, Jeremy Bentham, David Ricardo, and John Stuart Mill; neoclassical economists including Carl Menger, Alfred Marshall, and J. B. Clark; rebel economist John Maynard Keynes; and neoliberal economists such as Milton Friedman and Deepak Lal (Peet, 1999).

ASSUMPTIONS OF THE ECONOMIC APPROACH TO DEVELOPMENT

This approach to economic development rests on the same assumptions endorsed by classical and neoclassical theorists used to conceptualize general economic processes. Certain factors contribute to the achievement by an economy of a dynamic equilibrium (Stoesz et al., 1999). These include minimally regulated markets; limits to state interference with the economy in the form of tariffs, excessive taxation, coercion of economic actors, corruption, trade regulations, or government monopolies; a high quality of information about products, prices, buyers, and sellers; and the economic rationality of those involved in transactions. Traditional economic theorists assume that the ideal economic development policies will maximize the influence of these factors.

Economic theorists also assume that economic growth is the engine for all societal development and human progress. Improvements in the overall efficiency of an economy result in improvements in the general welfare. Increased economic productivity and increased trade, for example, stimulate a nation's development (Parpart, Connelly, & Barriteau, 2000). Here's the logic of this assumption. As a society becomes richer because of economic growth, the leaders of the society will divert an increasing portion of the excess resources to meet its social needs related to child welfare, education, health, housing, and protection from hazards. Economic policy makers use a related image. The growth for rich people theoretically "trickles down" to benefit the poor people. Unfortunately, the fact that wealth rarely trickles down has not challenged economists to revise this assumption.

Traditional economic theorists also assume the universality of their theoretical premises. Neoclassical economic concepts and propositions apply across cultures and historical periods (Peet, 1999). Therefore, policies toward economic development based on this framework are sensible tools for transforming the modes of thinking, valuing, and exchanging for members of societies with diverse cultural backgrounds and varied environmental characteristics.

ROOT METAPHORS OF THE ECONOMIC APPROACH

Although economic theorists do not theorize about individual development, they still use the "stages of development" metaphor (Connelly, Li, MacDonald, & Parpart, 2000). The imagery for this root metaphor is taken from the developmental sciences. The fully developed organism has certain well-defined and predictable characteristics. If the plant, animal, or human lacks the characteristics of full development, then it is judged to be undeveloped or underdeveloped. This imagery is extended to societies in several different ways.

Some economist theorists use a continuum to characterize societies as underdeveloped (or less developed), developing, and developed. This conception of economic development was popular during the post–World War II period and was used "to describe the process through which countries and societies outside North America and Europe (many of them former colonial territories) were to be transformed into modern, developed nations from what their colonizers saw as backward, primitive, underdeveloped societies" (Reddock, 2000, p. 24). Advancement to an industrialized, modern, urbanized society was considered a linear path. Connelly and her colleagues (2000) comment on the limits of this root metaphor. In the realm of economic development, societies do not all follow a linear path. Some advance. Some resist the economic promises offered by purveyors of global capitalism. Some travel on a roller coaster. Leaders of a society may set a straight course, yet deindustrialization, material dislocation, or economic restructuring can divert the society from this path.

Other economic theorists use the imagery of center and periphery. The United States and European economies are at the center of the globe's economic development (Connelly et al., 2000). Pakistan, Malaysia, and Zimbabwe are far from the center. The greater the physical and psychological distance of nations from the technology, economic theories and policies, and modernization tools of the central economies, the slower their economic development will be. Critics of classical and neoclassical economic theorists, such as Marxist economists, accept the imagery of center and periphery but reverse the conclusion. Economies in the Southern Hemisphere—the nations of Latin America and the Caribbean, for example—have become dependent on the exploitative and dominant powers at the center of the global economy. Economic development will accelerate only when the peripheral economies severe their ties with the center and pursue economic policies of self-reliance.

Some economic theorists used the imagery of ranking as competitors to compare different nations' stages of development. This imagery was prevalent during the era of communist competition with capitalism (Stoesz et al., 1999). Three ranks, also called worlds, are used to classify nations. The First World referred to the industrial nations of the capitalist West such as the United States. These are the highly developed capitalist economies. The Second World referred to the socialist economies of the communist nations constructed as alternatives to market-dominated societies. The Soviet Union was the exemplar. The Third World referred to nations that had been colonies of the First World but achieved independence through liberation or revolution. First and Second World nations competed to influence the underdeveloped Third World nations and their choice of approach to economic advancement. This metaphor lost favor and utility following the fall of the Berlin Wall in 1989 and the subsequent collapse of the Soviet Union.

THE TRADITIONAL ECONOMIC APPROACH TO DEVELOPMENT

Let me begin defining some concepts important to understanding the classical/neoclassical approach to economic development. **Economic growth** refers to an increased capacity to produce goods and services at lower cost for a larger number of members of the economy (Stoesz et al., 1999). This is often measured as increases in the value of all the goods and services produced by an economy, the **gross national product,** divided by number of persons in the region or society. The resulting number represents per capita income (Peet, 1999). **Development** means "improvement in a complex of linked natural, economic, social, cultural, and political conditions" of a society (Peet, 1999, p. 1). **Developmentalism** is "the belief in the viability and desirability of this kind of economic progress" (Peet, 1999, p. 1). **Human development** is an alternative way of conceptualizing development promoted by the United Nations. The United Nations' human development index (HDI) expands the focus for assessment of development to include the expansion of people's choices, especially in the areas of knowledge, nutrition, health, political and cultural freedom, and leisure (Peet, 1999). The index measures longevity, adult literacy, years of schooling, and income sufficiency of members of a country.

The goal for traditional economic theorists is economic growth. Other forms of development will follow. Theoretical emphases follow from the foundational premise that the market is the best arbiter of decision making (Peet, 1999; Stoesz et al., 1999). Factors that free the power of the market must be protected. Several additional and specific economic interventions will stimulate growth. Worker productivity should be enhanced through increased division of labor, mechanization, specialization, and improved technologies so that workers can produce more with the same inputs. As labor becomes divided and specialized, laborers refine the skills and qualities essential to achieving and then maintaining high levels of productivity. The allocation of labor and other resources should become increasingly efficient. Goods and services are allocated in the market via price mechanisms reflecting consumer preferences, supply, and demand. Because of advances in productivity and efficiency, greater wealth is produced, and more participants in the economy have an abundant supply of material goods and money. The increases in output also generate greater self-sufficiency for the economy and free the nation from dependence on any other particular trading partner. Commerce should be increased, and national markets should be opened to international competition. This attracts foreign investment, increases capital savings, and improves the ratio between capital and labor. Competition also increases the quality of available goods and services and lowers their cost. Economic growth should be based on increased saving and investment, especially in technological improvements to further expand labor output and worker productivity. The integration of technological improvements into the society should be coordinated through free market processes.

For traditional economic theorists, economic development is the responsibility of private companies first. Private nongovernmental organizations and development agencies can assist. Governments fall last in the assumption of leadership responsibility (Reddock, 2000; Stoesz et al., 1999). The elite businesspeople and technocrats of private corporations lead economic developmental projects (Peet, 1999). Economics is the master science directing policy makers, and many theory-based national policies are recommended (Peet, 1999; Reddock, 2000; Stoesz et al., 1999). Economic developmentalists should reduce budget deficits by freezing public sector employment, cutting back on public sector investment, removing public sector subsidies (such as those given to farmers), and reforming the tax system. Developmentalists should promote the private sector by deregulation, by contracting for public services, and by selling state enterprises. Developmentalists should expand export-oriented manufacturing. Developmentalists should open local markets to greater domestic and foreign competition by various means, including the removal of price controls and supports for local industries and encouragement of exports. Developmentalists should rationalize public sector institutions by reducing state services, making social services more cost effective, and reforming civil service systems. Classical and neoclassical theorists advocating for the economic development of nations across the globe chant the slogan: more privatization, greater trade liberalization, and less government interference.

CRITICAL COMMENTS

Unfortunately, the economic policies derived from classical and neoclassical economic theory often fail to achieve the predicted results. There are three major strands of criticism. For critical and Marxist theorists, the evidence shows that pro-capitalist, free market policies are usually imposed on developing nations, and the implementation of these policies has the effect of reducing a country's standard of living in areas such as nutritional levels, access to social supports, and employment rates (Reddock, 2000). In the name of modernizing Third World nations, economic developers from First World nations have extracted raw materials, drained social resources, and taken control of institutions away from the local inhabitants of many poor countries. Such exploitation has resulted in the dependence of the peripheral societies in Africa, for example, on economies at the center like those of Europe (Peet, 1999). These societies were not developed but actively exploited by foreign economic interventionists. Critical and Marxist theorists cast doubt on the assumption that economic growth is associated with the advancement of human development and the elimination of poverty. They are concerned with the problem of "distorted development," a situation in which the benefits of economic progress fail to reach many members of the population (Stoesz et al., 1999). Critical and Marxist theorists focus on the goals of wealth redistribution (Stoesz et al., 1999) and the realization of human potentials, especially by societal members "whose life chances are restricted (or even eliminated) by the constant pressure of overwhelming need" (Peet, 1999, p. 12). These theory users support investment in human development to supplement investment in economic development (Prigoff, 2000). They advocate for social services that provide "safety nets" for at-risk sectors of the labor pool, regulations that safeguard workers' health, fair wages that allow workers to escape poverty, and economic assessments that consider not only the potential profits of business enterprises but also their impact on individuals, families, and communities. Just development is characterized not only by economic growth but also by equity, democracy, and social justice (Peet, 1999). Just development also requires the radical democratization of a society's economic, political, legal, and other institutions.

Ecological theorists do not believe that traditional economic theories and policies create sustainable economies. Matsuoka and McGregor (1994) provide a social work case study demonstrating this point. Hawaii has suffered the results of many large-scale economic development projects initiated by transnational corporations. In the past several hundred years, these corporations have aggressively pursued the establishment of large-scale plantations for growing pineapples and sugarcane, the logging of thousands of acres of rain forest, and the creation of resorts and tourist attractions. This "economic progress" has had severely negative impacts on Hawaii's ecology and the vitality of indigenous cultures. Roughly one-half of the original 140 native bird species in the Hawaiian island chain have become extinct. In 1993, experts predicted that 103 Hawaiian plant species would be added to the list of endangered species. Many sites that were once critical to traditional cultural activities have been transformed for corporate uses. The natural resources that allowed indigenous groups to subsist by gathering, fishing, and hunting have been depleted. Besides ecological and cultural destruction, the introduction of capitalist economic principles has produced the opposite of the promised trickle-down effects. In the early 1990s, almost 20 percent of Hawaiians fell in the lowest income bracket, the highest proportion among all Islander ethnic groups. Ecological theorists like Matsuoka and McGregor warn that economic developers generally proceed with minimal consideration for the environmental consequences of their business ventures. Traditional notions of economic development have supported projects and policies that have undermined the health, longevity, customs, community cohesion, family life, spirituality, traditional lifestyles, and ties to the natural environment of Hawaiians. Ecological theorists prefer conceptualizations of economic progress committed to the reproduction of resources for the benefit of both current and successor generations (Prigoff, 2000). Economies organized by simpler and more harmonious lifestyles are also recommended as an alternative to the promotion of ceaseless consumption as the stimulant of growth.

Feminist theorists also take issue with the assumptions, concepts, propositions, and midrange theories of classical and neoclassical economists. Feminists characterize capitalism as "a patriarchal, class system, a type of society operated in the interests of a male elite, based on the profit motive to the exclusion of everything else" (Peet, 1999, p. 197). Capitalist policies have many unexamined consequences for women in societies around the globe (Connelly et al., 2000; Reddock, 2000). The reduction of an economy's public sector and social services, for example, shifts responsibility for health care, for education, and for the care of the vulnerable, the sick, and the elderly to women who are already burdened by unpaid work. Capitalist policies and practices also perpetuate the subordination of women to men. Household labor, for example, is less valued than work outside the home. Women are pressured to do certain types of work such as reproduction and child care, and restricted from other employment opportunities such as political or corporate leadership. Women generally are restricted in their access to an economy's resources and benefits—for example, land ownership, education, and even food and clean water in some nations. Women are provided fewer protections against violence. Women are exploited in many workplace settings such as factories where the demands for work are great but the pay is minimal. Traditional economic development policies favor men and integrate women into the economy only in marginal or exploitative ways.

A commitment to gender-sensitive approaches to economics requires new theorizing about the developmental process (Connelly et al., 2000; Barriteau, 2000; McClean, 2000). Theoretical emphasis must be given to the unequal power relations that characterize men's and women's influence over economic decisions. Women should be included as full participants in policy making, and allowed to take an equal place with men in identifying practical needs and the best economic strategies for meeting these needs. Policies promoting comparable wages for comparable work, similar employment opportunities, and participation in legislative projects are recommended. For feminists, people-centered development efforts give greater priority to immediate community needs related to family survival, health, food, water, medical treatment, and the education of children than to the artificial needs associated with military competition to build great arsenals, projects to increase the wealth of the very rich, or vanity spending on public works by wasteful politicians. Feminists seek a change in the attitudes and values of mostly male economic theorists, economic decision makers, and operatives of governmental and nongovernmental economic agencies. Feminist philosophy and morality-oriented theoretical frameworks must be added to conventional economic thinking.

INNOVATIVE APPLICATIONS OF THE ECONOMIC APPROACH TO DEVELOPMENT

Classical and neoclassical economic theory, the brains behind the engine of modern economic development, has worked to advance the standard of living for members of countless economies. However, critics caution that development has not been uniform. Wagner (1997), a social worker committed to economic theory, observes "more countries are experiencing the unsettling paradox that the process of economic globalization and rapid industrial expansion has increased general prosperity but also created growing numbers of unemployed and poor people" (p. 55). Many adult men and women and many children die every day despite abundance. Critics call for reformulation of the purpose of economic development. Stoesz, Guzzetta, and Lusk (1999), for example, offer applied economists a new purpose statement: "to enhance the human condition in a sustainable manner respective of individual rights and cultural practices" (p. 264). Critics also recommend creative and alternative approaches to economic development. McClean (2000), a feminist economist, commends Women's World Banking, "a nonprofit financial institution created in 1979 to provide poor female entrepreneurs access to financing, market information, and training" (p. 180). She also cites the Self-Employed Women's Association, a union committed to the advancement of the interests of 40,000 of India's poorest working women, as an exemplar. Additional innovative applications of economic theory to the development of economies and societies will be discussed in the next section in response to the eco-map translation question about change processes.

MAPPING APPLIED ECONOMIC THEORY

In this section I discuss many of the key concepts from economic theory displayed on the eco-map in Figure 12.1. Included are a translation of economic terms into ecosystems terminology and a discussion of how ecosystems

FIGURE 12.1
THE ECONOMIC
THEORY
VERSION OF
THE ECO-MAP

Source: Adapted with
permission from
*Family-Centered Social
Work Practice* (p. 160)
by A. Hartman and
J. Laird, 1983. New
York: The Free Press.

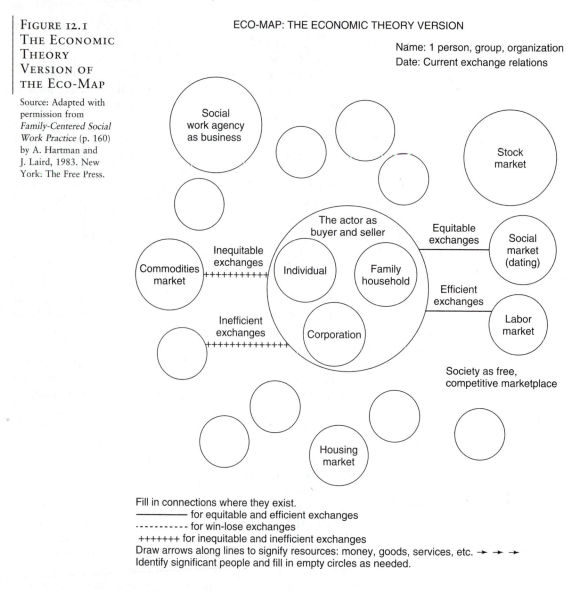

ECO-MAP: THE ECONOMIC THEORY VERSION

Name: 1 person, group, organization
Date: Current exchange relations

Social work agency as business

Stock market

The actor as buyer and seller

Equitable exchanges

Social market (dating)

Inequitable exchanges
++++++++++

Commodities market

Individual

Family household

Efficient exchanges

Labor market

Inefficient exchanges
+++++++++++++

Corporation

Society as free, competitive marketplace

Housing market

Fill in connections where they exist.
——————— for equitable and efficient exchanges
- - - - - - - - - for win-lose exchanges
+++++++ for inequitable and inefficient exchanges
Draw arrows along lines to signify resources: money, goods, services, etc. → → →
Identify significant people and fill in empty circles as needed.

theorists might conceptualize key elements of an economic theory version of the eco-map.

HOW ARE CONNECTIONS CONCEPTUALIZED?

Connections are characterized as exchanges between buyers and sellers. The concept of **exchange** refers to the patterned transference of material items like animals, food, or books and of immaterial items like status, power, and helping services (Kapferer, 1976). People, groups, and societies connect by exchanges involving the transfer of goods. **Goods** are material or immaterial items that people find valuable, useful, or desirable, whereas **resources** are defined as items that can be used to produce other goods (Lewis & Widerquist, 2001). Clients, for example, may exchange money, volunteer labor, or tangible gifts with the expectation that social workers will reciprocate by providing concrete or counseling services.

Exchange connections have at least five defining characteristics (Couch, 1989). First, they are constructed when two people or groups decide to interact for acquiring a good or service in exchange for another. The interactants bring interests that are different but compatible. The interactants can be physically copresent, or they can conduct the exchange in a way mediated by a phone, a computer, or another technology. Second, exchange relationships require that interactants establish congruent identities. Common commerce-related identities adopted during an exchange are buyer and seller, owner and nonowner. Third, exchange relationships necessitate, at least momentarily, that each person attends to the other's welfare while pursuing his or her personal interests. Common objectives and a context of mutual benefit must be generated as participants attempt to understand and negotiate with each other. Fourth, exchange relationships are organized by cost–benefit calculations. Appraisals of what A will sacrifice and gain, what B will sacrifice and gain, and of the differences in profit for A and B are inevitable. Fifth, exchanges involve a temporal component; that is, members complete the exchange or fail to complete the exchange after determining the specifics of their shared future. Each must answer the question "Can a future benefit be anticipated from a here-and-now exchange?"

How Is the Quality of Connections Differentiated?

Exchanges are often judged by two standards: **efficiency** and **equity.** Marketplace exchanges are efficient when producers can produce large quantities of goods at low cost and consumers purchase these goods (Prigoff, 2000). Exchanges are positive or efficient when the benefits and costs are weighed for all exchange partners and when the benefits to all members of the exchange system outweigh the costs. Inefficient or negative exchanges occur when a producer produces goods at a very high cost for each unit and marketplace processes do not provide alternative places for consumers to purchase these goods.

Using the standard of equity requires normative judgments about the desirable distribution of resources (Lewis & Widerquist, 2001). Calculations about what each actor is contributing to an exchange and what each actor is taking from the exchange, about the perceived worth of the actions performed, and about the parity of two sets of actions result in the determination of equity or inequity (Walster, Walster, & Berscheid, 1978). Equitable or positive connections are characterized by a fair pattern of distribution of resources, a balance in give and take, and a proportionality in what each contributes and what each receives.

Equitable systems are characterized by **distributive justice.** Each participant feels that the transaction was a fair and just exchange. No one profited at the other's expense. After negative or inequitable exchanges, one of the actors feels shortchanged. The dissatisfied person may have problems with the speed of the exchange or problems with the amount of goods or services exchanged (Berg, Piner, & Frank, 1993). Participants connected inequitably often have different exchange experiences. One exchange partner feels underbenefited and views himself or herself as receiving less or contributing more compared to the other partner. One exchange partner feels overbenefited and views himself or herself (if calculations are honestly made) as receiving more or contributing less compared to the other partner. Incquitable connections may be documented by empirical evidence, or they may be perceived subjectively as a sense of being exploited, victimized, or cheated. These perceptions may persist even when an impartial judge would not support such a claim.

Besides efficiency and equity, there are several other ways to characterize an exchange-based connection. Clark (1997) reported on three prevailing and general standards for judging the quality of a social exchange. The "principle of complementary role requirements" dictates that people give to each other when they are so obligated by social roles. Mothers owe love and loyalty to children, and children owe love and appreciation to mothers. The "reciprocity principle" directs members of a community to give to those entitled to a return. One exchange partner provides benefits to the other because the other has provided benefits to him or her in the past. A therapist offers concern, and the client pays the bill. The "beneficence principle" dictates that societal members give to others in need, whatever the status of the needy person and whatever the abilities or inclinations of the giver. One exchange partner gives benefits to the other because the other needs the particular resource, and benefits are provided to recipients regardless of their contributions to the exchange. The beneficence principle can operate at the level of the society (Stolte, 1987) and govern the redistribution of resources. Resources are taken from participants in the economy who have resource advantages and privilege and given to those members who have suffered an economic disadvantage, have fewer resources, and cannot meet their subsistence needs. Positive exchange connections thus might be efficient, equitable, complementary, reciprocal, or beneficial.

What Is the Typical Focal System?

Economic theorists would place the exchange agent or transactor at the center of an eco-map. The focal system, however, might be any social entity involved in economic decision making and exchanges—an individual, a family household, a corporation, a social service agency, a government bureaucracy, or an international association (Lewis & Widerquist, 2001).

Economists give primary attention to firms. A **firm** is a social organization with certain characteristics. These include a primary goal of maximizing profits; a specialized knowledge or expertise (for example, in the provision of therapeutic services to substance abusers); a voluntary contract system binding various equity holders (directors, administrators, stockholders) and employees who have no ownership of the collective enterprise; and a legal authorization from courts and legislators to conduct business. Examples of firms include local businesses, corporations, and partnerships of social work private practitioners.

The firm is similar to an individual exchange agent. Such an economic organization can act like an individual and make rational calculations about how to pursue its goals in ways that maximize benefits, minimize costs, and increase the probability of commercial success. The firm may be the focal client system for an economically oriented social worker. A social worker providing services to a for-profit cooperative of private practitioners might help this firm raise capital; gauge its financial performance by reviewing the ratio of current assets to current liabilities; engage in financial forecasting; develop a long-term plan related to entering new markets for potential clients; manage its accounts receivable; collect fees from delinquent clients; and secure loans for acquiring computers or leasing new office space.

How Is the Environment Conceptualized?

In the earlier section on metaphors, I discussed how economic theorists conceptualize the environment as a market or a set of interrelated markets. A market is a social invention that makes possible the exchange of goods and services between buyers and sellers. Marketplaces enable these agents to enter into contact with one another, either directly in a particular physical place or indirectly through mediating brokers or institutions. Markets in the original sense were physical places. Imagine stalls constructed by farmers in ancient Greece. Meats and vegetables from around the region could be brought and displayed in one location to interested buyers. In modern markets, standardized items such as copy machines or vehicles might be sold. Unique goods or services might also be exchanged. Modern markets are not limited to place and may exist as global networks connected by computers.

Systems in the environment include buyers and sellers, individual and corporate actors. Economist theorists might add to an eco-map the groups of systems composed of advertisers and their associated packagers, salespersons, and marketing experts. These participants in the marketplace work to brand or differentiate certain products as meriting attention and to stimulate the purchase of these commodities by assigning meanings to them that resonate with the potential buyers (Carruthers & Babb, 2000). In capitalist societies, the dreams, fantasies, identities, and needs of many citizens are constructed from the images and appeals designed by advertisers.

Is Particular Emphasis Given to Any Systems?

Corporations dominate contemporary environments. These organizations have special influence over a society's economic, political, and social processes (Prigoff, 2000). Corporations can gain a competitive advantage over small or local businesses by using economies of scale. Unit costs for a product decrease when very large numbers of the product can be produced. The new Wal-Mart in my sister's community of Ashland, Virginia, has put many local merchants out of business. Wal-Mart has so many customers that it can sell hardware, televisions, office supplies, food, and other goods at very low prices. Corporations also have the clout to use strategies such as short-term price cuts, mergers with other corporations, favoritism to certain product brands, and price agreements to gain a controlling share of the market. Large corporations like Microsoft or General Motors can pressure the suppliers of parts and the distributors of their products to create a conglomerate. The formation of a conglomerate makes it more difficult for competitors to enter the market or compete successfully. In an earlier section comparing social workers to business consultants, I discussed how corporations externalize the costs of their production. Often, corporations do this in partnership with political leaders, military leaders, or other elite decision makers. Workers, consumers, and citizens, for example, are forced to pay for the health care costs generated by cigarette smokers with cancer. Cigarette manufacturers need not include these costs in the prices of their products.

Social workers who use the economic theory should demand that economic theorists and policy makers also pay attention to at-risk populations in the environment. These are groups of people who lack a minimal income, who have few employment opportunities, who fall through the inadequate health "safety net," or who are indigent and destitute (Prigoff, 2000). These groups are too often excluded from the decision-making processes in a market economy because they lack the income and the wealth to influence corporate and political decision makers.

HOW ARE RESOURCES AND THEIR FLOW CONCEPTUALIZED?

Resources are tangible and intangible things that can be exchanged or used to increase the value of other goods and services. Conventionally, economists view a society's **currency,** coins and paper bills designated as having an agreed-upon value and used as a medium of exchange, as a resource. Social workers and social psychologists, however, have expanded the economic conception of resources. Specht (1988), a social work theorist, summarized Foa's (1973) work on defining and categorizing resources. Resources are "valued responses" exchanged by two or more people. Resources are exchanged to attain other resources and to help exchange partners achieve their goals. There are several types of economic resources. Money, conceptualized as a coin, currency, or token assigned a standard unit of value, is an important resource. Goods or commodities that can be exchanged, including tangible objects, materials, or products such as cars, food, and books, are resources. Services—activities provided by the labor of one person for the body, psyche, or belongings of another person—are a form of resources. Foa believed that exchange partners also deal in interpersonal resources. These resources have been less often examined by classical economists. Interpersonal resources include love, the expression of warmth and regard; status, an expression of evaluation that conveys prestige or esteem; and information, advice, and other kinds of instruction.

Foa (1973) offered a useful scheme for differentiating resources. Resources may vary on a concrete–symbolic dimension. A **concrete resource** is a tangible physical resource such as a pocketful of $10 bills. A **symbolic resource** is an abstract and intangible resource. A person cannot touch the resource, but it is important in exchange relationships. A telephone call from a loved one and the knowledge obtained from a college education are symbolic resources. Some resources have both concrete and symbolic aspects. A credit card can be presented physically to a merchant, but its design and color symbolize the credit available to the cardholder. Resources may also vary on a particularistic–universalistic dimension. **Particularistic resources** are those tied to a particular person, object, or exchange situation. These relate to resource situations where the specific person involved makes a difference. An individualized way of expressing caring by a social worker may be highly valued by the client recipient. The concept of **universalistic resources** refers to resource situations like the exchange of money. Here, it doesn't matter who gives or receives the resource. Information from a local United Way about emergency services may be standardized and valuable regardless of the hot-line worker providing the information.

Foa's economic theory of resources, Specht (1988) concluded, can help social workers understand their transactions with clients, coworkers, and others. Kerson's (1978) paper on social work and gift exchanges is also helpful. Social workers participate in complex exchange relationships and engage in the exchange of various kinds of resources: concrete services and goods like food baskets and winter coats as well as symbolic resources like information and counseling. Several useful propositions follow from Foa's and Kerson's ideas about allocating and using resources in exchange relationships. First, exchanges of currency and goods are clearer and more straightforward than exchanges of interpersonal resources. Generally, social workers prefer to be paid in dollars rather than in gestures of appreciation. Second, exchanges are likely to be more effective and satisfying when similar types of resources are exchanged. Universalistic resources are best exchanged for other universalistic resources—money for professional services, for example. Particularistic resources are best exchanged for particularistic resources—parental care for gratitude. Exchanges are more likely to break down when unlike or mixed resources are transferred. The offering of money and gifts for love often leaves both exchange partners dissatisfied. Third, the propriety of using certain types of resources is frequently established by the organizational context for the exchange. Agency-based social workers are expected to offer services and to accept gratitude and the agreed-upon payment for these services. Social workers who instead accept personal and particularized gifts, such as massages or engraved jewelry, are likely to be sanctioned by their employers and by their national association. Fourth, humans need both economic and interpersonal resources to grow and develop. Market-oriented solutions to public problems that rely only on the provision of money or goods are not adequate remedies. The homeless, for instance, want interpersonal resources like esteem and respect as well as financial grants and temporary shelter.

Economic theorists conceptualize the direction of exchanges by the symmetry of the transaction. Exchanges may be symmetrical and involve equals. Resources are transferred to and from each exchange partner. Exchanges may also be asymmetrical and involve one participant with a monopoly over services or goods. The resource-rich employer in an exploitative economy, for instance, might take the labor, sweat, and tears from resource-poor employees and offer almost nothing in return.

What Descriptive Words Are Used?

The vocabulary of the economic theory should seem familiar to most readers of this book. Many of the framework's concepts and descriptive adjectives are also used to characterize economic processes and conditions by social work administrators, by columnists in newspapers, by television and radio reporters, and by financial consultants offering advice to the public. Words for economic processes include *calculate, evaluate, bargain, budget, negotiate, distribute, trade,* and *invest.* Economic resources are referred to by terms like *assets, capital, commodities, goods,* and *services.* Words for economic organizations include *market, exchange network,* and *economy* (including *household economy, underground economy,* and *global economy*). Exchange partners might be called *consumers, buyers, customers, suppliers, sellers,* or *traders.* The quality of an exchange might be judged by descriptors such as *equitable, inequitable, efficient, inefficient, productive, profitable, costly, risky,* or *exploitative.* Note how many of these terms were familiar to you before reading this chapter.

How Is Change Conceptualized?

A change is equivalent to economic development (Prigoff, 2000). Economic development occurs by means of income-generating and income-saving projects that increase the capacity of a community or society to provide economic security (food, water, clothing, shelter) to all its members. Social workers prefer economic development approaches that also foster **reciprocity,** in which exchanges are not organized solely around monetary transactions but also around culturally assumed roles. Reciprocal exchanges are based on the value of mutual support rather than individual gain. They build community members' financial and human assets, including their financial holdings, talents, skills, and dispositions to cooperate.

Prigoff (2000) reviewed some of the strategies that social workers might use when working for economic development. Community cooperatives focus on providing goods and services at a reasonable price rather than maximizing profits, on allocating benefits proportional to use of the cooperative not the amount of capital invested, on democratic decision making by members of the cooperative, and on a limited financial return on member investment in the cooperative. Credit unions cultivate saving and the ownership of assets. They offer affordable banking and credit services such as credit cards, home rehabilitation loans, check-cashing privileges, and personal loans. Food cooperatives, farmer cooperatives, and employee-owned companies might also be developed by teams of social workers and citizens.

Financial institutions committed to fostering economic progress in economically disadvantaged neighborhoods can promote economic and community development. Community development banks provide loans for mortgages, for home improvement, for commercial businesses, for college tuition, and for social agency programs. They make available resources that could not be obtained from conventional banks, credit organizations, and mortgage companies.

Affordable housing strategies include the creation of shared housing arrangements such as communes or multifamily homes owned by an extended family and the construction of housing for those with low or moderate incomes. Habitat for Humanity works to build homes for the poor.

Local exchange trading systems (LETS) promote economic development. In such systems, members earn hourly time credit for helping others in the community or for participating in community projects. Members bank these credits, which they can later exchange for rewards including college credits, computers, or specialized services. Micro enterprises are small businesses often operated by low-income people and meeting local needs.

How Are Actual and Ideal Eco-Maps Contrasted?

A social worker's clients often live in a physical and social environment where the "invisible hand" has not operated to bring them prosperity and security (Prigoff, 2000). Free trade may benefit corporations by facilitating the unrestricted flow of capital. Actual eco-maps would often indicate, however, that free trade means a weakening of regulations that protect the worker's health, ensure workplace safety, and increase job security. Sometimes, free trade undermines efforts to protect the environment of many clients and potential clients. Sometimes, free trade contributes to labor markets that allow employment discrimination, enabling corporate policy makers to actualize their racist or class prejudices by relocating their companies. Competition does not always work as well as "invisible hand" theorists might pretend. Clients' eco-maps are often dominated by corporations, for example, and these corporations control politicians and raise and lower prices despite the exchange preferences of numerous other buyers and sellers. Witness the difficulties of elderly Americans who seek affordable and fairly priced drugs from pharmaceutical companies that value profit over social responsibility.

A middle-range theory called power-dependency theory, developed by Richard Emerson and his successors, better models the economic connections of most clients than does classical economic theory (Emerson, 1962; Cook & Whitmeyer, 2000). In brief, Emerson postulated that economic differences lead to power differences, which lead to dependencies. When an exchange partner (a nation, an employer, a family member, a government bureaucrat, a supervisor) has resources that the other perceives as valuable and necessary, and when there are no alternative or potential partners perceived as possessing these resources and available for a trade, then there are predictable relationship results. The resource-rich partner gains power over the resource-poor partner and can influence the latter's behavior and decisions. Additionally, the trading partner without resources becomes dependent on the partner with resources. Here are a macro- and a micro-level example. The United States currently depends on the oil-producing states in the Middle East to provide most of our energy resources. Critics of U.S. energy policy would like us to decrease our dependency on oil, and thus lessen the influence of a state like Saudi Arabia over our collective action. Some women in intimate relationships become dependent on their husbands for economic, social, and psychological resources (Forte, Franks, Forte, & Rigsby, 1996). Violent men often exploit the power associated with this control over essential resources, and assault and humiliate their dependent wives. The women see no viable alternatives and yield to the abuse. This has disastrous effects on their self-esteem, coping ability, and emotions. The eco-maps of many social work clients, I suggest, would portray problematic economic dependencies on corporations, bosses, landlords, welfare workers, and intimates.

Many economists assume conditions of **scarcity** in the client ecosystem. There are not enough goods available for every conceivable use without sacrificing something else. For example, there are limits on the land available for houses (Lewis & Widerquist, 2001). Therefore, policy makers must consider costs and benefits and make choices with costs to certain social groups. The ideal eco-map is based on the assumption of prosperity rather than scarcity. Humans have reached a level of technological, social, and economic development allowing the possibility of **abundance**, where more goods are available than the collective needs and where goods can be consumed without sacrificing something else of value (Lewis & Widerquist, 2001). The ideal eco-map would depict client connections to resource providers that enable them to meet their needs for food, clothing, health care, and housing. The ideal eco-map would include systems that provide opportunities for the client to benefit from societal abundance: opportunities for training and education, child care, affordable housing, transportation, youth programs, health insurance and health care, realistic job placement, and a living wage. The ideal eco-map would depict an economic and social environment that is just, nurturing, and sustaining. Prosperous economies and visionary leaders should tap our economic genius for the "production and distribution of a nurturing, healthy, rewarding, and sustainable quality standard of living for all people" (Prigoff, 2000, p. 243). Social workers can advocate for such changes.

Prosperous and just economies would not be controlled by a few corporations. Bruyn (1977, 1991), for example, proposed that democratic self-governance might lead to social policies that create ideal ecosystems. Policy makers guided by this idea would aim to increase participation at all economic levels (the household economy, the workplace, corporations, the societal and global marketplace) and to foster communication among all constituents of the economy (the estranged producers, workers, and consumers, for instance). Fifty-percent worker representation on corporate boards is a policy that might help a society to achieve these ends. Offering an optimistic slant on personal and economic development, Bruyn (1991) contended also that "as people's roles become linked through their relations with others in various roles in trade associations and the wider market economy, they will grow in their own capacity to identify with others and will thus assume responsibility for their place in the larger economic order" (p. 61).

HOW ARE ISSUES OF DIVERSITY, COLOR, AND SHADING ADDRESSED?

Economic theorists have tended to give minimum attention to issues of diversity. Bartlett (1996) reports, for example, on studies of the major textbooks in the field. In the mid-1980s, women were mentioned less than 1 percent of the time in 22 books. In the mid-1990s, the economic topic of "the influx of married women into the workforce" was mentioned in only one of nine leading textbooks, and topics related to people of color were covered rarely or with insensitivity. About the Los Angeles riots, one economist wrote, "Black resentment was certainly understandable but it was also perverse" (Bartlett, 1996, p. 141).

Nonetheless, economic theorists can contribute to our understanding of diversity. Thomas (1999) documents the ways that **exchange norms,** expectations about fair transactions, vary across cultural groups. Referring to the anthropological literature, he reports that the Sioux Indian group condemned the "hoarder" as a tribal member lacking confidence in the abundance of food and the generosity of peers. The Yurok respected tribal members who could amass property for personal use, and the Kwakiutl Indians expected their wealthiest leaders to confirm their social status by ceremonially giving away large portions of their property. The kinds of items exchanged also vary across cultural groups. Material goods, social opportunities, sexual favors, diligent labor, cheerful dispositions, and public prestige may all be traded. The inhabitants of the islands near Papua, New Guinea, give food, shell necklaces, and other valued objects to earn honor and fame from the gift recipients. Thomas adds that communication difficulties may occur when members of different cultural groups engage in exchanges. At his university, Chinese and Japanese graduate students confused their American professors, for example, by giving valued objects such as Oriental art pieces, culinary delicacies, and fancy leather belts as gestures of gratitude. These professors desired only the student's excellent performance in the subject area. Eco-map analysts should therefore learn about the preferred items for exchange and the exchange norms of social systems linked to the focal client system.

Cultural and other membership groups affirm their distinctive identities in many economic ways. Zelizer (1999) documents how "the same physically indistinguishable dollar became a wage, a bonus, a tip, a gift, an allowance, or charity" (p. 196) depending on the cultural preferences of different religious, ethnic, racial, gender, and age groups. Cultural groups also supplement the official currency with local means of exchange, including tokens, coupons, money orders, trading stamps, cigarettes, or alcohol. Groups may differentiate themselves by selecting credit cards identifying their affinities and endorsements. My card is a National Association of Social Workers Visa card. Groups may maintain their sense of cultural particularity by the foods they purchase, by the distinctive ways that they use goods to adorn their homes, by the special items that they purchase for group rituals. Major corporations recognize this and design and market some of their products to accommodate diverse tastes and preferences. Zelizer concludes that economic processes (creation of a national currency and the consolidation of a standardized consumer culture, for example) can unite members of a society such as the United States, but economic processes can also expand the options for those societal groups determined to celebrate their differences.

Economic theorists analyze the objective and subjective conditions impeding the social progress and personal development of members of poor communities. William Julius Wilson (1995) has become expert on the negative impact of the departure of manufacturers from many U.S. cities. He identified a group of extremely poor and segregated African American neighborhoods characterized by minimal opportunities for employment. Such neighborhoods experienced assorted problems of social organization. For example, family members were not able to organize daily routines and interaction in relationship to the structure provided by a work schedule. Neighborhood joblessness and social disorganization were associated with crime, gang violence, drug trafficking, idleness, public drinking, and family violence. Weak labor force attachments also led to a high sense of futility and a low sense of self-efficacy. Neighborhoods experiencing the most psychosocial difficulties were those in which negative economic conditions (poverty, welfare dependency, and joblessness) were concentrated. Objective deprivation causes group and individual problems for vulnerable or oppressed populations identified on a worker's eco-map.

Economic theorists add that the subjective sense of one's own deprivation compared to others, or **relative deprivation,** also has a negative impact (Corning, 2000). Relative deprivation follows "the perception by an individual of particular events as disproportionately negatively affecting oneself as a member of a stigmatized group in comparison with a non-stigmatized or less stigmatized group" (Corning, p. 464). For example, the person experiences a discrepancy between the social goods of his or her affiliation group (residents in a poor African American neighborhood) and the social goods of another group (the residents of a wealthy white neighborhood located immediately across the city's main street). The person's subjective assessment of her or his deprived status in an ecosystem compared to other, nondeprived groups can cause anger, resentment, and aggressive political action. Corning relates this topic to the college setting. Many female college students observing their male counterparts experience relative deprivation because of their disproportionate vulnerability to violence and victimization, differential standards of physical attractiveness, and disadvantaged career development processes and supports. The psychological, emotional, and behavioral patterns of these women are strongly influenced by this perceived deprivation.

WHAT WOULD BE ADDED OR DELETED?

Economic eco-maps include buyers, sellers, commercial organizations, and markets. Economic theorists are interested, also, in the commodities or consumer goods that constitute modern environments. Our houses, garages, and yards are storage areas filled with valued things, including furniture, clothes, shoes, jewelry, compact discs, paintings, and toys. We surround ourselves with both goods that sustain us and goods that serve as symbolic embellishments of our sense of self (Carruthers & Babb, 2000). Some objects (vegetarian food items or military paraphernalia) help clients create desirable impressions on others in their reference groups. Some objects (designer jeans or $100 sneakers) reflect the status striving of clients. Some objects (new computers and technological devices) may communicate the client's attachment to social values, or they may indicate a client's admiration for certain celebrities from sports, films, movies, or television who promote the objects. Many marketplace exchanges and consumption activities are driven more by the cultural meanings of products than by their functional utility. Economically minded social workers should add the highly significant objects possessed by clients to the eco-map.

THE LIMITS OF APPLIED ECONOMIC THEORY: A SOCIAL WORK APPRAISAL

In this chapter, I have tried to demonstrate the value of economic theory. Market-oriented economies, the prevalent form of economy in most modern societies, depend on exchange relationships. Social workers and their clients are participants in economic processes and subject to various forms of exchange: buying, selling, trading, sharing, gift giving, theft, and taxation (Couch, 1989). Such exchanges result in patterned arrangements for the distribution of goods and services, and these arrangements influence workers' and clients' efforts to satisfy their material and psychosocial needs. Social workers will better understand economic theory by learning its root metaphors: society as marketplace, client as buyer and seller, and social worker as business consultant and sympathy broker. Social workers can better apply economic theory if they translate the framework's central concepts into the profession's language, the ecosystems theory. Critics of economic theory have noted, however, several limitations to the classical and neoclassical versions of economic theory.

First, the economic assumption that societies are like marketplaces, and that these markets are free, competitive, information-rich, and almost universal (Rigney, 2001), is undermined by empirical investigations into the operation of real markets in particular societies at particular historical periods. Economies differ greatly across societies depending on the political, social, and cultural practices of each society. Economic theory describes the experiences of men in a capitalist society dominated by a male ruling elite. The economic model of social structure, in the view of critics of conventional economics (Forte, 2001), does not characterize well all communities, all societies, or all historical periods. Deviant cases challenge theoretical assumptions and tenets. The Vikings, for instance, stimulated a regional transfer of goods by theft. Some Mennonite communities forsake health insurance, agreeing that everyone's financial resources will be available to any member in dire need.

Inequalities related to knowledge, power, and status are found in all markets. Economic theorists forget that a person's economic action is supported or constrained by his or her place in a society's power and status hierarchies and by common cultural scripts (Smelser & Swedberg, 1994). Markets can be dominated by monopolies. One firm sells a unique product and has acquired great power and wealth. This firm can prevent other, less powerful companies from entering the market and selling an acceptable substitute at lower prices. Consumers who, under these conditions, have minimal influence on market processes are forced to purchase products at very high prices. Microsoft, a computer software giant, has repeatedly faced charges of monopolistic practices. Initial differences in the distribution of goods, services, and property (or rights to acquire property) at the start of marketplace processes also influence all later deals in ways not predicted by "invisible hand" theorists (Lewis & Widerquist, 2001). Some transactors—those privileged by birth, for example—enter the marketplace with advantages of wealth, knowledge, position, and connections that enable them to compete for favorable exchanges more effectively than others. This system ensures that the rich prevail in marketplace activities, and the poor become poorer. Real markets are also characterized by uncertainty or imperfect information. Consumers of health services are not medical experts; they lack the knowledge necessary to make wise decisions about which services or medications to purchase and which doctors to hire. Moreover, doctors' records and reputations may be protected from public inquiry, thus making it very hard to determine the quality of a medical service provider.

Second, the assumption of economic theorists that the client is a rational and calculating consumer who behaves like an economist in most spheres of activity is suspect. People are not fully aware of the processes involved in their choices. They are often propelled by nonrational forces, including habit, addiction, erroneous belief, and emotion. Turner (1991) identified several weaknesses in the typical depiction of rational calculation offered by utilitarian economists. First, these economic theorists neglect the creative use of imagination by which actors identify "non-obvious yet plausible action options" (p. 90). Second, these theorists often treat decision making as if it occurs autonomously, whereas most social workers recognize that all psychosocial processes reflect social memberships, societal institutions, and the social-environmental context. Third, Turner argued that economic theorists cynically assume that rational choice is designed to advance self-interest. However, people can act rationally in pursuit of altruistic and idealistic goals. Humans do not always act for profit or to advance their self-interest; self-sacrifice plays a major role in family life, community service, and military combat. Fourth, many economic theorists minimize the politics of interaction. For them, action directly follows a self-interested rational choice. Social workers know that clients and community members often act because of their emotional responses to symbols, and these meaning–response associations can be manipulated for political purposes. Sometimes people abandon rationality totally and decide to uncritically follow charismatic leaders. Fifth, many economic researchers assume, according to Turner, that human goals can be precisely identified in most circumstances. However, goals have a subjective component and may be hard for outsiders to pinpoint. Actors may proceed without clear goals. They may keep their goals private. They may deceive others about their goals, and they may change goals while interacting.

There is another problem in assuming that economic and rational reasoning can be extended to most spheres and stages of human thinking and acting. Money differs from other exchangeable resources. Money as a currency can be measured with some degree of precision (Rigney, 2001), but other resources like love or status that are exchanged cannot be readily translated into a common and accepted measurement standard. Thus, calculations of the profitability of noneconomic exchanges are more complex and arbitrary than for economic trades. Unlike bankers, social workers and clients lack a conversion table or a common metric for easily judging value and for comparing costs and benefits (Collins, 1993). How can clients make sure calculations when facing choices involving money versus honor; or money versus vengeance; or wages versus the meaninglessness, gratification, or pride associated with work; or money versus gifts? Moreover, market regulations do not govern the exchange of resources other than goods, services, and money. A volunteer who receives less gratitude than he feels he deserves for helping Habitat for Humanity cannot appeal to a market regulator with this claim and obtain a clear arbitration.

Many economic theories lack a psychosocial developmental perspective on economic calculating and decision-making processes. Economists focus on short-term encounters, spot markets, and one-time purchases or trades, not on the development of long-term exchange relationships or the lifetime socialization processes related to buying and selling. During a lifetime, for example, some people develop interaction patterns based on mutual dependence and group solidarity. Their calculations are less influenced by considerations of short-term gain than by images of making a collective and enduring contribution to their membership groups.

Third, the assumption that social workers are best compared to the agents of capitalism, and that social workers will bring prosperity to their agencies and clients by applying economic wisdom and logic, has problems. Social workers should not naively trust theorists who assert that free markets automatically result in a socially optimal allocation of resources and thus in an ideal society. Referring to the collective, economic theorists assume that as individuals calculate to advance their interests while minimizing their costs, "the greatest good for the greatest number emerges" and "the broader social outcome, though unanticipated by any set of individuals, nonetheless, results in the common good" (Sjoberg & Vaughan, 1993, p. 125). Individual valuation leads to a desirable collective valuation.

John Dewey, a philosopher and colleague of Jane Addams, doubted the economists who claimed that community members would be served well by this "invisible hand" (Stuhr, 1997). Any theory glorifying the pursuit of private interest and assuming that unregulated economic forces benefit all, Dewey suggested, falsely separates processes of self-advancement from processes of democratic community development. Dewey argued that what actually happens because of economic processes depends on the perception and communication of consequences, upon foresight, and on the use of knowledge of likely consequences to guide planned change endeavors. Social workers, Dewey might have added, should take an advocacy role, contributing to the equitable distribution of knowledge about the consequences of economic decisions while promoting an informed and lively sense of shared interest.

Contemporary critics would extend Dewey's critique (Lewis & Widerquist, 2001). Social workers should help communities learn about and solve problems of externalities. Negative externalities include pollution not paid for by car manufacturers or operators of industrial plants and health care costs for cigarette smokers not paid for by tobacco companies. When all collective decisions are made by calculations about the most profitable way to purchase or sell goods and services, even political decisions become like commodities that can be bought and sold (Prigoff, 2000). Profits are reduced when transactors anticipate and pay for externalities, so they buy politicians' votes to avoid such expenses. Social workers should help communities solve **free rider** problems. These occur when public goods are made available to everyone. Libraries, community swimming pools, parks, and many social services are made possible by taxes collected from the general populace. An individual may underreport income, cheat on taxes, and yet still use these public goods. In the economic sense, this person obtains a free ride instead of a paid ride. Lewis and Widerquist suggest also that social workers should address problems of economic discrimination, the refusal of some consumers to purchase goods and services from certain groups of sellers not because of price disagreements and not because of the worker's inability to be productive. Market exchanges are not always free. Instead, the membership characteristics—nationality, race, gender, sexual orientation, or religion—of some market participants limit their buying and selling power. Many labor markets, for example, include employers with a taste for differential treatment and racially selective hiring.

Social workers should be more than entrepreneurs and financial consultants. The interests of buyers and sellers do not always harmonize in economic markets. When the economic logic extends its influence into all spheres of social life, community members begin to think of each other as commodities to be used and consumed rather than as humans to be valued and respected regardless of their economic worth. The science of economics is not value-free, and an unregulated market will not protect the interests of many social work clients or magically better the human condition. Social workers should work purposefully with clients and economically minded professionals to promote the values necessary to the continuation of human life, the health of all community members, the overall quality of social membership, and economic prosperity.

APPLIED ECONOMIC THEORY: A MODEL FOR SAVING A SOCIAL WORK PROGRAM

Peter Kollock and his associates (Kollock & Smith, 1996; Kollock, 1998a, 1998b, 1999) have recently pursued a line of scientific inquiry that blends sociological and economic concepts. Kollock's theoretical ideas and guidelines became conceptual tools that helped me lead a fight to save an undergraduate social work program (Forte, 2005). This case study offers a narrative of how taken-for-granted skills with tools for computer-mediated communication became a pragmatic tool for influencing the cost–benefit ratio associated with program termination. The elements of the story are organized in a form developed by researchers committed to qualitative research as a processual or step-by-step report.

THE ECONOMIC PERSPECTIVE ON COMMUNITY ORGANIZING

Kollock's (1998a, 1998b, 1999; Kollock & Smith, 1996) work identifies the features of successful online communities, and it has direct relevance for practitioners. Only a brief summary is possible here. Computer-mediated communities provide new opportunities and challenges to those interested in constructing trusting, cooperative, and potent social groups. Kollock's social exchange theory suggests that community builders can help create "virtual" social action groups if they define group boundaries (who can and who cannot use the collective resources available online), provide incentives for contributing to the public good, develop group rules for the use of net resources, create systems for sanctioning "free riders" and others who overuse scarce resources, and offer methods for low-cost conflict resolution. Kollock reported that community builders must also find ways to encourage online interaction, to enable interactants to identify each other, to discourage deception, and to provide information about all interactants' reputations and trustworthiness.

Kollock and his colleagues (Kollock & Smith, 1996) documented how several practitioners have made wonderful use of these economic principles to lead successful mutual aid projects. In 1996, computer-savvy activists in California used the "virtual world" to enlist and organize 20,000 volunteers, who then entered the real world of local schools and wired them to the Internet. Kollock and Smith provided several other illustrations of practitioners who used an online interaction to quickly, cheaply, and effectively mobilize and coordinate social action.

Kollock's conceptual model for mobilizing allies helped us save our social work program. Here's the story. A social work program at a public university is a "public good." It provides valuable services to students, social agencies, families, clients, and community members (Lewis & Widerquist, 2001). Some pay the tuition for this public good. Others provide field instruction to obtain benefits. Some gain because of their proximity to the university. The following application of Kollock's exchange approach is reported in more detail in my case narrative of a "Save Our Program" Campaign (Forte, 2005).

On a Tuesday in early April 2000, the chief administrator of my university announced his intention to meet with the faculty the next day. The next day, he announced that his vision of an economically tight university would require a "disciplined and focused" examination of several programs, including social work and nursing at the undergraduate level as well as our few graduate programs. These "may have to go" if they are not judged "central to the mission" and "cost-effective," he warned. The nursing program was explicitly characterized as too expensive. Termination of the program would "free up six faculty positions" for other uses. The administrator added that a speedy decision was important, and stated that the fate of the programs must be determined by the fall Board of Visitors meeting.

THE ECONOMIC PERSPECTIVE ON ASSESSMENT

Our social work faculty had an emotional and career investment in our 20-year-old program. We wanted to protect our investment, and we needed to mobilize supporters quickly at minimal cost to the program, the university, and the supporters. We hoped to discourage "free riding," the use of program resources without reciprocating with help during this crisis. We also needed to demonstrate to the administration that elimination of the social work program would be more costly than beneficial to the university. The relevant social systems included the faculty of three fighting for their jobs and their program; the administration, which conceived of the college as a $50-million-a-year business with more than 500 employees and 5,000 customers/students; and the community network of alumni, field placement supervisors, social workers, and friends of the program who would lose much if the program were terminated.

Important assessment questions included the following: Was the social work program more beneficial than costly to the university and community? Could all the concrete and symbolic benefits of the program be documented? Would potential allies make the decision that the time and effort needed to fight for the program were worth it? Could faculty advocates afford the time and work taken from teaching, scholarship, and service necessary for a potentially long battle? Could program advocates and allies increase the costs attached to administrative termination actions? Could the faculty advocates avoid any hidden or long-term costs to their reputations or to student careers resulting from resistance to the administrator? Could the program advocates and allies identify a series of community organizing and advocacy options and select the one with the greatest likelihood of success at the lowest cost? With my colleagues, I appraised the community, the university, the program, the student body, and our own personalities, and we answered "yes" to each of these assessment questions.

The faculty decided to transform our tenuous or inactive connections with many potential allies into strong connections. Connections were based economically on the pool of student interns that provided valuable social work services to internship sites and on the workers that the program prepared for the labor market. Psycho-economic linkages included the social status that advisory board members, field instructors, and employers derived from their affiliation with the social work program and from the sense of solidarity to other social workers in the university-generated network. Friends of the program also received advice, a way to advertise positions, invitations to special events, library usage, and other perks because of their connections to the university.

THE ECONOMIC PERSPECTIVE ON INTERVENTION

The members of the "Save Our Program" campaign agreed to try to evoke a public declaration from the chief administrator that, at best, he would rescind his request for a discontinuance review and, at least, he would support a faculty-led, by-the-book, one-year review process. The group also made a commitment to conduct ourselves in a consistently professional and civil manner so as not to raise hidden costs of the program if we were perceived as damaging the university's reputation. Kollock's (1999) economic model for fostering cooperation among members of virtual communities alerted us to the networking possibilities of computer-based communication. He documented how the Internet can drastically reduce the costs associated with producing public goods (such as saving a program), especially compared to the investment of time, effort, and emotion necessary for conventional face-to-face community organizing or letter-writing campaigns. New tools for Internet use (Netscape Communicator 4.7 browser and messenger) were used to supplement voice mail and snail mail requests for support. These tools allowed fast and effortlessly computerized communication with widely dispersed allies; the creation of address cards for the individual and group members of a rapidly expanding network; message dissemination at any time of the day; multiple e-mail mailings with one mouse click; censorship-foiling tactics (a planned shift, if necessary, to home-based Internet service providers, for example); and the easy use of e-mail reply, forward, save, and print procedures. More important, the Internet allowed extensive community organizing with a manageable expenditure of our faculty's time and money, and the time and energy of our allies.

The blending of online, voice-to-voice, and face-to-face organizing made a difference. My tally of e-mails shows that in only one week we had enlisted the help of more than 45 cyber allies. These included a college program administrator, four faculty members, three current social work majors and nonmajors, 12 members of a local social service agency, three sets of parents, six community practitioners and agency directors, 13 alumni, and two faculty members from other colleges. Many others probably communicated with the administration, but without sending me a copy of their correspondence. Each had responded to our electronic request for help by writing to the chief administrator about the program's positive features. Noting the administrator's commitment to the courtesy of responding to all letters, we believe that he suspected the start of an avalanche. Proceeding with the plan to review and terminate the social work program would have been very costly to him. Costs would have included time, effort, expenses associated with mailings, and losses of community goodwill. There would have been opportunity costs, too. A battle with allies of the social work program would have diverted the administrator's attention from his higher priority goals of student recruitment and expansion of residential housing facilities. He recalculated, changed his mind, and endorsed the program's continuation.

LEARNING ACTIVITIES

1. Answer the following questions: What does money mean to you? How much do you want, and why? Do you speak openly with your family members about the meaning of money? If so, how does your family resolve differences about money meanings? If not, what are some of your family's secrets and taboos about money?

2. Analyze the region in which you live from an economic perspective. How well do agents in your regional marketplace distribute goods, services, and other resources? Are there certain neighborhoods or groups of people who do not have full access to these? What resources do they lack?

3. Develop a social marketing plan directed at client behaviors that increase their risk for legal, mental, or physical health problems (unprotected sex, cigarette smoking, violence, or gambling). What message will you communicate? How will you communicate this message?

4. Learn about the budget of a local agency or of your social work program. What are the sources of revenue? How much income is generated from each source? What are the major personnel costs and nonpersonnel costs? Interview an administrator, and learn how he or she uses budget information to help the agency or program achieve its goals.

5. Take a market approach to finding a social work job. How might you best market yourself to a potential employer? What assets can you offer to the agency? How might you respond to questions about liabilities or costs that you might bring to the organization? What bargaining strategies might you use to help sell yourself to the members of the hiring committee?

6. Think about your relationship with your spouse, lover, or roommate, and pick one important area of the relationship: decision making about finances, holidays, or purchases; intimacy or sexuality; household labor; or relationship maintenance. How equitable are the exchanges in this area? Are you overbenefited or underbenefited? Are you economically dependent? What changes would make the relationship more equitable?

7. Think globally. What is your understanding of the distribution of the earth's resources across the network of nations? How have processes of globalization positively or negatively changed this distribution? How does daily life differ for people in the poorest countries compared to people in the richest countries? What are the possible roles for social workers during this time of global changes?

8. Collect information about the economic situation of several client groups. Is there evidence of objective and subjective deprivation? What is the impact of such deprivation on the biopsychosocial functioning of members of the client group? How might

objective and subjective deprivation negatively affect the life chances of members of the client group compared to members of economically privileged groups?

9. Take a tour of your living space with the eyes of an economist. Select for consideration several objects in your home that you have purchased in the last five years. How did you obtain them? What do they symbolize to you and your friends? What societal values, group memberships, or other factors influenced your choice of each item?

ADDITIONAL RESOURCES

Additional resources are available on the book companion website at **www.thomsonedu.com/social_work/forte.** Resources include key terms, tutorial quizzes, links to related websites, and lists of additional resources for furthering your research.

13 CHAPTER | APPLIED CRITICAL THEORY

INTRODUCTION

The critical theorists merge the classical Marxist approach to social theory with newer empowerment theories. Critical theorists and practitioners pose tough questions (Throssell, 1975). Why does the United States, with roughly 6 percent of the world's population, use 55 percent of world resources? How can such a wealthy nation leave more than 40 million people in poverty? Why is the infant mortality rate of black Australians (Aborigines) in the Northern Territory 81 per 1000 people, compared to a figure for all Australians of 19 per 1000? With what logic does a doctor in a capitalist system justify refusing life-saving emergency treatment or discontinuing necessary treatments if fees cannot be paid? What policies and procedures have resulted in an American penal system that locks up more than 7 percent of all adult citizens for felonies? This critical questioning by critical theorists serves as the catalyst for change projects aimed at fundamental personal and social transformation (Morgaine, 1992).

This chapter uses my models, metaphors, and maps approach to explain this theoretical language and to present the essential ingredients of the critical approach to conceptualizing and furthering social justice. Two exemplary practice-minded scholars, Jurgen Habermas and C. Wright Mills, are profiled. Bertha Capen Reynolds will be presented as a scholarly social work practitioner with a distinctive commitment to applied critical theory. Critical theory's root metaphors—society as contested meanings, client as politically active citizen, and practitioner as an advocate for ideal speech situations—will be reviewed and related to the metaphors used by traditional Marxists. The critical theory will also be translated into eco-map terms. A critical theory approach to understanding and influencing the relationships among community inequity, public deliberations about policy and problems, and cooperative social action will be conceptually modeled. I hope to show that critical theory offers a set of tools that social workers can use for promoting social, political, and economic equality.

Critical theory is also known as an **emancipatory theory,** a broad category of inquiry intended to raise the consciousness of people about oppression and to help them become emancipated from their subjugation (Burr, 1995). The critical tradition offers explanations of destructive social arrangements and myths, as well as the self-defeating beliefs and actions of people subjected to these unfair arrangements. Social workers aligned with the critical tradition examine how societal patterns and preferences often undermine the provision of social services and welfare (Langan & Lee, 1989). Empowerment theories used by feminist, Afrocentric, and "queer" social workers include a critical component.

Critical theory in the broad sense refers to a variety of theoretical perspectives committed to social criticism and radical change (Pease, Allan, & Briskman, 2003). In the narrow sense, it refers to a school of thought generated by members of the Frankfurt School in Germany. Critical theory will be used in both ways in this chapter, but special attention will be given to the efforts by Jurgen Habermas and his followers to join the intellectual tradition initiated by

Karl Marx with the Frankfurt tradition of examining critically the influence of the mass media. These theorists worked at the University of Frankfurt. Its Institute of Social Research was founded in 1923. The major Frankfurt School scholars were Theodor Adorno, Max Horkheimer, Herbert Marcuse, and Habermas. These scholars developed substantial critiques of capitalist **ideology** (the dominant political orientation) and culture (Feagin & Vera, 2001). Jurgen Habermas stands out as a major critical theorist, and much of this chapter will focus on his theoretical and practical contributions to social theory.

Critical theorists share many theoretical commitments. They take a critical stance toward communication—for example, the manipulation of the press to serve the interests of the rich. They challenge social forms such as slavery and indentured servitude that impede human development. They investigate the values and meanings sustaining inequality in social institutions. Critical theorists also look behind the masks and facades used during face-to-face encounters to avoid egalitarian and authentic interaction. Some theorists blame victims for their problems. Critical theorists trace personal troubles to biographies shaped by political, economic, and social injustice (Hansen, 1976; Musolf, 1995). Critical researchers use critical theory and methods to deepen the public's understanding of group ideologies and control processes (Thomas, 1993), to make members aware of the social sources of their predicaments, to suggest how suffering can be alleviated, and to make authority relations problematic (Visano, 1988, p. 240). Critical practitioners study the interrelationship of history, political economy, power, interaction, meaning, and self processes.

Critical theorists, researchers, and practitioners are unlike professionals who create theories for the sake of theorizing. For them, scholarship and theory application occur in the service of practice efforts to promote radical democracy and self-realization (Denzin, 1992). Theorizing must have a political and practical intent, critical theorists (Mullahy, 1997) assert, and social theorists must engage in criticism not to identify the sources of injustice while accepting the status quo but to contribute to social change and to the reduction of the destructive consequences of unjust social arrangements. Critical theorists try to create a special kind of knowledge, theories to change the world (Feagin & Vera, 2001, p. 201).

RELATED DIALECTS, ASSOCIATED SCHOOLS OF THOUGHT

A convention of critical theorists might include Marxists, neo-Marxists, scholars associated with the Frankfurt School, feminists, and others. If asked their primary theoretical allegiance, convention members might identify various approaches. Some would describe themselves as conflict theorists. **Conflict theory** is concerned with the prevalence and processes of struggle and competition in human social life. Some might call themselves liberation theorists and trace their inspiration to **liberation theology,** a conceptual approach developed by Catholic activists to promote progressive change in Central and South American postcolonial countries (Feagin & Vera, 2001). A few would prefer the label of **progressive theorists** to indicate that they recognize the prevalence of conflict and contention between social classes but reject the revolutionary, violent change strategies preferred by the Marxists, instead trying to conceive of strategies that stimulate cooperation among contending groups toward the shared end of social progress (Galper, 1975). Another group would call themselves **radical theorists** because they aim to theorize in ways that change society at its roots rather than gradually reform it (Tilman, 1984). Radicals seek a profound transformation of the political and economic structure of society and the construction of a profoundly different future (Galper, 1975).

Newer members of this society of critical theorists have chosen the name **structural theorists.** They focus their critiques on the relation of oppressive structural arrangements in a society to the troubles of its members (Mullahy, 1997). For structural theorists, problems are an inherent aspect of societies that are ordered or structured in unjust ways. They are not caused primarily by the personal characteristics of individuals. Guests at the convention of critical theorists might also include political social work theorists, empowerment theorists, feminist theorists, strengths theorists, Afrocentric theorists, and queer theorists.

APPLIED CRITICAL THEORY: EXEMPLARY MODELS

In this book, I have argued that many ideas and theories become part of the professional knowledge base only because of the creative thinking and acting of exemplars, great or key figures in the history of theorizing about human behavior and the social environment (HBSE). These exemplars can serve us in the way that our heroes do. Jay Haley (1969), for instance, a family therapist, used Jesus as a role model. Haley showed how Jesus' life exemplified the use of ideas and tactics to bring about revolutionary social change. When facing professional challenges, Haley could converse imaginatively with Jesus and use the lessons taught in the New Testament. In a sense, then, Jesus was a critical theorist. Jurgen Habermas, C. Wright Mills, and Bertha Capen Reynolds are contemporary heroes in this tradition.

JURGEN HABERMAS

Jurgen Habermas (1929–) was born in the small town of Gummersbach, Germany (Outhwaite, 2000) and grew up during the time of the Hitler Youth. His life work was shaped by his horror of the crimes of the Third Reich and his deeply felt awareness of the dangers of fascism and totalitarianism. Habermas has been judged one of the essential contemporary philosophers and social theorists. However, his interests extended beyond philosophy in an interdisciplinary way to include political theory, sociology, social psychology, linguistics, and legal theory.

Habermas was an important member of the **Frankfurt School of critical theory,** a collection of social theorists and philosophers working at the University of Frankfurt's Institute of Social Research (Stephens, 1994). This institute dedicated its talents and energies to diagnosing and solving public problems. Habermas and several other theorists at the institute, including Theodore Adorno and Max Horkheimer, were strongly influenced by the Marxist theoretical tradition (Outhwaite, 1994).

As a theorist, Habermas is committed to a critical emancipatory perspective yet familiar with and appreciative of the American traditions of pragmatism and interactionism. For instance, he commented on his high regard for the work of John Dewey and George Herbert Mead, "I have for a long time identified myself with the radical democratic mentality which is present in the best American traditions and articulated in American pragmatism" (Habermas, 1985, p. 198).

Habermas uses the concept of crisis as an alternative to the Marxist concepts of class struggle and revolution. Habermas is critical of modern society and its crises of legitimacy. His concept of **crisis** refers to the failure of modern society to meet the needs of its members and to the frequent manipulation of community members by their institutional leaders. States and corporations manipulate the public sphere, according to Habermas, by using publicity to gain political and financial advantage (Outhwaite, 1998). Habermas, however, believes in the liberating potential of social interaction and the ability of citizens to fight for participatory government. Clear communication is the essential ingredient of successful political and social life. Community members respond to their society's crisis by communicating with each other, deliberating about possible social change strategies, agreeing on the preferred change plans, and working to address social problems. Habermas developed these ideas in his two-volume book, *The Theory of Communicative Action,* first published in 1981.

Habermas has been more than a theorist. He is a public intellectual, actively involved in his society's debates and social movements (Stephens, 1994). Habermas was one of four professors who founded the Socialist German Student Alliance (Horster, 1992). He engaged student radicals in the 1968 student actions, unlike most of his colleagues who ignored this movement. But Habermas challenged the student leaders to plan responsible protest actions. Habermas also influenced political activists. In the late 1980s, his writings inspired a leader of the Polish Solidarity movement and others opposed to state communism in Eastern Europe. In 1992, Habermas also wrote articles directed to a general audience, voicing his opposition to right-wing attacks on foreign workers and immigrants. His articles influenced many German political party leaders and journalists. He has also strongly criticized German revisionist historians who attempted to minimize the horrors of Nazi concentration camps. Habermas has been sympathetic to the Greens, the environmental party, and he does not qualify his strong support for the welfare state.

Habermas blends a critical perspective with an appreciation for the centrality of symbolic interaction. He shares Dewey's and Mead's commitment to champion democratic principles and processes (Stephens, 1994). Critical-interactionist theories can be used to guide practitioners who advocate for reasonable discussion and debate about public policies and problems, who call for active participation by citizens in political parties and in government processes, and who fight for an expansion of the scope of free speech and for economic decision making that considers the interests of the whole community (Forte, 2001). Social work community organizers, politicians, educators, and leaders can learn much from Habermas.

C. WRIGHT MILLS

C. Wright Mills (1916–1962) was an angry and radical sociologist, a maverick, and an outsider (Cuzzort & King, 1989; Tilman, 1984) who wrote many scathing criticisms of American culture, of the powerful who control America, and of the citizenry's insensitivity to atrocities and war. He was born in Waco, Texas, and worked as a professor at Columbia University for most of his career. Mills was angered by social oppression, by political manipulation, by detached and ineffective intellectuals, by the Cold War, and by U.S. policy in Latin America. Although appreciative of Karl Marx, Mills extended his criticism to the Soviet Union; while a guest at an official Soviet dinner, he chastised its surprised leaders for censoring the works of Leon Trotsky (Tilman, 2004). His anger and confrontational style damaged his interpersonal relationships, and his adult life was characterized by failed affairs and marriages, conflict-ridden exchanges with colleagues, and the development of a negative consensus among his peers about his obnoxious personality (Horowitz, 1983).

C. Wright Mills did not consider himself a Marxist or label himself a critical theorist, but he considered Karl Marx one of the most astute students of the society that modern civilization has produced (Tilman, 1984). He shared Marx's conviction that society was divided sharply between the powerful groups and the powerless groups. Mills' book *The Power Elite* (1956) characterizes the political economy of the United States as one controlled by corporate chieftains. These executives, warlords, and political directors manipulate social processes in hidden ways to escape the accountability necessary to a democracy (Tilman, 2004). Mills argued that power was becoming increasingly centralized in this relatively small social network, and he was especially concerned about the dangers posed if this unaccountable and secretive elite gained control of weapons of mass destruction (Gitlin, 2004).

Mills (1959) pioneered the concept of **sociological imagination,** an outlook or perspective on society that enables its possessor to understand the large historical scene in terms of its meaning to the inner life and the external career of a variety of individuals. This imagination links personal troubles and joys (private experiences of the person and his or her significant others) to public issues and policies (events associated with social problems, large-scale organizations, social institutions) and to historical forces. In many ways, Mills' idea of the applied sociological imagination equals social work. When we use an eco-map to understand a client's personal problems by placing the client in a social context, or when we analyze the relationship between public policies and programs and the daily difficulties and struggles of vulnerable or oppressed clients, we are thinking like a critical theorist. Schwartz (1969), an important social work scholar, recommended the use of the sociological imagination to conceive of the social agency as an arena for the conversion of private troubles into public issues (p. 38). Mills' advice, "know that many personal troubles cannot be solved merely as troubles, but must be understood in terms of public issues" (1959, p. 226), is central to the creed of politically active social workers.

Mills wrote about many topics, including social stratification and power, the disintegration of the pride and style of craftsmanship, the insecurities and passivity of the middle class, the role of the intellectual, the immigration of Puerto Ricans to New York, the manipulation of community members, and the resulting mass apathy and political impotence. Mills was committed to **praxis,** the integration of theory and practical action (Tilman, 1984, 2004). He supplemented his work on scholarly books and articles by writing pamphlets such as *The Causes of World War III* for a general audience. He harshly criticized his sociological colleagues and called on public intellectuals to become social activists. Mills cut out parts of the *New York Times* every day and filed these illustrations of current events and public problems for use in grounding his sociological analyses (Becker, 1994). He also influenced the student movements of the 1960s. Students for a Democratic Society (SDS), for example, incorporated Mills' ideas about democracy into their 1962 Port Huron statement of basic principles (Gitlin, 2004).

Mills offered remedies for the powerlessness of most members of American society. His practical prescriptions resemble those of radical democrats like Dewey, Mead, and Habermas. Mills advocated for a participatory democracy. If a policy would affect members in any sphere of social activity, then those members should participate in the deliberations, decisions, and administrative activities associated with the policy. Mills promoted specific policies that would increase the responsibility of the power elite to the electorate and major economic changes that would result in worker ownership and control of industries.

BERTHA CAPEN REYNOLDS

Bertha Capen Reynolds (1885–1978) grew up in a Massachusetts farm family challenged by economic hard times, the death of two children, then the death of her father to tuberculosis, and social isolation (Hartman, 1986). Her first teaching job was in a high school department in Atlanta, where she was struck by the unjust and exploitative conditions experienced by black community members.

Reynolds returned to school and graduated from the Smith College School for Social Work (Hartman, 1986). She returned to Smith College in 1925 as a social work educator and became the school's associate director. In the 1930s, she began to integrate Marxist theory with the Freudian approach she had already learned. She believed that the works of Karl Marx and Frederick Engels should become the key to a science of society and were invaluable aids in the struggle for democracy (Reynolds, 1938/1992). Reynolds accepted the Marxist position that major changes in the political and economic institutions of most societies were necessary. She saw in the socialist countries inspired by Marxism a useful alternative to capitalist systems. Reynolds (1963) believed in the radical political activists in these countries, and she applauded them for attempting to institutionalize universal education, universal health and welfare services, universal arming of the people for military defense, and universal equality of status for women and minority groups. An idealist, Reynolds believed that social work in the United States could make similar major structural changes and the country could become an exemplar of the commitment to democratic principles and processes.

Bertha Capen Reynolds' professional ideas and interests became more radical as she matured. She decided, for instance, that social workers could change bad working conditions, reduce crushing caseloads, and increase low wages only by organizing and unionizing (Cullen, 1980). Therefore, she worked to unionize social workers and to challenge the elite leaders of social welfare organizations. She recognized that powerful and organized interest groups with much money had to be resisted even when these groups were sponsors of the welfare system (Leighninger, 1986). The integrity of social work was at stake. Coalitions with labor groups and other political allies were required. Reynolds (1951) articulated the critical theory conviction that "social work can defend its standards only if it realizes the organized nature of the opposition to it, why these interests are opposed, and where its own allies are to be found" (p. 166).

Reynolds also believed that it was a mistake not to connect casework to the labor movement and to the small groups relevant to most clients' daily lives. Therapy and social action should not be separated. Reynolds became convinced that social workers had been used as "unwitting instruments of social control, to regulate behavior, to maintain the status quo, and to forestall needed and fundamental social change" (Hartman, 1986, p. 87). Reynolds argued that the social work interest in professionalism often perpetuated the distinctions between social classes and failed the most disadvantaged clients (Kaplan, 2002). Reynolds preferred a conception of social workers and clients as equals, a conception that challenged social workers to recognize that their primary allegiance was to the poor and powerless even if they were paid by members of the ruling class (Cullen, 1980). Reynolds also fought for an inclusive rather than a selective social work profession, a profession that embraced a broad membership including relatively untrained and unskilled practitioners (Leighninger, 1986).

Reynolds' radicalism was not warmly received. She was fired from her college position in 1938 and was blacklisted by many employers, including the American Red Cross, during the 1940s and 1950s. She directed her critical and organizational talents to activities as a public critic, an active member of the Social Service Employees Union, a political activist, an advocate for workers and oppressed groups, a contributor to *Social Work Today*, a left-wing journal, and a public speaker on issues of justice, civil rights, and peace (Cullen, 1980; Kaplan, 2002).

Late in her career, Reynolds obtained a job as a casework supervisor in the United Seamen's Services, a program serving merchant seamen and their families in the National Maritime Union from 1943 to 1947. Reynolds (1951, 1963) appreciated the union's philosophy of help. This approach emphasized the use of mutual aid processes, the right of members to obtain services and loans, the involvement of members in program policy making, the refusal to demean seamen seeking help, the cultivation of workers' mentality as union brothers, the accountability of service providers to elected representatives, and the expectation that seamen would act responsibly to their groups. Reynolds built on this foundation and created one of the first theories of radical and short-term casework. She outlined this model of practice in *Social Work and Social Living* (1951).

APPLIED CRITICAL THEORY: ROOT METAPHORS

In this section, I will use theoretical root metaphors to describe some of the implicit assumptions and foundational beliefs of critical theorists.

THE SOCIAL ENVIRONMENT AS FACTORY AND PUBLIC FORUM

Critical theory merges the metaphors of older Marxist traditions with contemporary theorizing about society, the person, and the practitioner. Traditional conflict theorists like the Marxists see all social processes as marked by contention. Society is like a battleground where warring groups fight for territory, wealth, and prestige. Marxist theorists also used images related to the factory systems that became commonplace in industrial nations at the end of the 19th century. The battleground became the factory floor. Society was compared to a dismal and dangerous industrial workplace. Capitalists controlled the factory, exempted themselves from the hazards of unregulated work, exploited the workers, and took all the profit. Capitalists used the police or hired thugs to beat rebellious employees into submission. Workers struggled in unsafe and demanding workplaces, labored for 12 hours or more per day, lost any sense of pride in their work, and lived or died because of the whims of the factory owner. Children as well as adults were losers in the economic battle and compelled to work for cruel masters. Marxists might have imagined social workers as the labor organizers who helped workers fight for better working conditions and more pay.

Critical theorists build on images of contention between social groups by focusing on conversational contests. A society is like a conversation, one that started centuries ago, now involves thousands or millions of people, and eventually will talk about numerous different topics. However, these conversations are not friendly. Combatants no longer use guns, clubs, and fists. Now the battle is fought with words and images. Society is compared to a public forum where contending groups argue over definitions of reality and public meanings. The conversation is seen in many ways as a one-sided debate. The powerless are weak like the factory workers and either blocked at the doorway to the debate hall or permitted entry but not allowed the resources—the microphones, clear speaking voices, good arguments, and debate skills—necessary to argue with the powerful. The elite control the conversation and the outcomes of the public arguments in ways similar to the control of the factory supplies, work conditions, and products by capitalists. Both capitalist factory owners and elite opinion shapers share a determination to maintain their wealth, interests, and privileges. Social conflict has moved, critical theorists suggest, from the factory floors and offices of industrial giants to the newspapers, radio stations, films, web blogs, and other media of mass communication.

Humans are not destined to divide into groups and fight each other. Critical theorists such as Habermas (2001) offer an alternative vision of society as a responsible and caring public forum. A society can be like a town meeting held in some New England villages several centuries ago. The forum is open and inclusive; all community members are allowed entry. There are clear and fair rules for argumentation, and the referees monitor rule compliance impartially. New ideas and arguments can be contributed. All participants in the debates of an ideal society are fully informed. Decisions are made by consensus based on consideration of the merits of the alternative arguments. Concerns about the good of the whole community are heard in every debate. Might does not make right; truth does. The expansion of the metaphor of society as public forum by Habermas and his followers into a theory of political problem solving will be presented at the end of this chapter.

The Person as Combatant and Debater

Traditional conflict theorists conceive of the person as a combatant in one of two armies: the army of the privileged or the army of underdogs. In the factory system, the owners of the factory building, equipment, and supplies were called the capitalists. They were the privileged. Generally, they lived lives of luxury and indulgence. However, most members of the factory system were workers. They were like dogs under the heels of sadistic owners. The lives of workers were short and brutish, and they had to fight against the capitalists to fulfill their basic needs and to receive dignified treatment. Capitalists could manipulate the courts, corrupt politicians, misuse the press, and hire mercenaries to enforce their desires. Workers could only organize and protest as a unified group. Strikes, walkouts, and job actions were their weapons. Almost all social work clients are like the workers in the factory system and underdogs in the battle for justice. The privileged control most of the machinery for combat and so prevail in many struggles.

The metaphorical imagination of critical theorists adds the conception of the human species as capable communicators. Members of the species can interact with each other using words, gestures, and actions. Humans are the best conversationalists on the globe. Critical theorists, like the earlier conflict theorists, often divide communities into two groups. Societal members are conceptualized as elite and powerful symbol users who manipulate language and control public discourse or as voiceless or muted symbol users who must fight to participate in community deliberations, decision-making processes, and problem-solving action. Only a few powerful societal members control the public discourse of millions. Most powerless members of the language community follow commands but don't give commands. The powerless must use the vocabularies of the elite but cannot create or challenge these vocabularies. The powerless often listen to public debates without recognizing that the ultimate decision was preordained by the powerful participants. A few of the powerless develop strong voices, offer new arguments and stories, and learn to speak up even when silence is ordered. The powerful make special efforts to stifle these voices of dissent.

Social work clients are generally those with silenced voices and diminished communicative power. Clients are characterized as unwelcome participants in the public debates and the conversations held in government buildings, corporate headquarters, and media vehicles. Clients are generally ignored, misunderstood, or told to shut up. Clients often adopt the perspectives (words, explanations, opinions, and judgments) of the privileged and come to engage in private conversations or self-talk characterized by self-blame, acceptance of the present state, and passive resignation to their exclusion from the conversations that matter.

THE SOCIAL WORKER AS STRATEGIST AND CRITIC

Early conflict theorists likened practitioners to revolutionaries, labor organizers, and saboteurs of unjust factory practices. Social work strategies might help those without power win battles for power, privilege, and prestige. Workers are still dying in factories from poisons and dangerous machines. Rather than providing individual counseling to workers one at a time, the critical theorist imagines the social worker as a Norma Rae strategizing and fighting for safe, healthy work conditions in the factory so all will benefit.

Critical theorists might compare practitioners to strategists and advocates who try to help the underdogs defy the odds, win some battles, and obtain a share of a society's resources. However, critical theorists such as Habermas prefer communication metaphors. Social workers are compared to public critics and communication experts who assess the gap between the rules of debate in public forums and advocate for the conditions necessary for ideal speech.

Let's use our metaphorical imagination to think of the social worker as a public critic. Social workers are like art or theater critics (Bohman, 2001). All have strong convictions about what is true, right, or beautiful and are willing to present arguments and opinion statements elaborating on their positions. However, social workers give critical attention not to entertaining performances but to the society's recurrent problems of social coordination and cooperation, especially as they hurt the weak and vulnerable members. Additionally, social workers use standards of excellence in public problem solving and service provision rather than standards related to art, theater, film, or dance. Critical theorists might add that social workers use their faculties for social criticism to comment on both the subjects of public conversation (prescription drug costs, the resumption of a military draft, global warming, or national tax policy) and the policies and procedures governing the conversation. The social work critic engages in acts of criticism and evaluative remarks about the systematic distortions that render public deliberations undemocratic. The critic speaks up courageously even when there is a risk of censure or retaliation. The critic poses alternatives and correctives to his or her audience with the desire of transforming undesirable speech situations into inclusive, fair, cooperative public debate. The social work critic hopes to increase audience members' self- and public awareness, sense of citizenship, and devotion to communal mutual aid.

Let's now use our metaphorical imagination to think of the social worker as a communication expert. The social worker is like the interpreter or translator who helps people who lack facility in the dominant language gain access to public forums. For instance, the social worker helps members of language communities (working-class Hispanic or African American groups) that are outside the mainstream join in and influence national, state, and local conversations about social welfare policies. The social worker is like the referee or impartial umpire at a town meeting or public forum who requires all participants in the debate to honor the rules of fair argumentation and who challenges the loudest debaters when they try to manipulate or distort the communication process. Social workers are like mechanical amplifiers when they transform weak, soft voices into resonant and sonorous sounds. They are like the debate coaches who help powerless participants prepare good reasons for their positions. They are the speech trainers who prepare those considered by the elite to have speech impediments in the competencies essential to articulate and forceful elocution. Social workers are the noisemakers yelling and shouting that the powerful must listen to and address concerns about human needs even when these are at odds with the priorities of profit (Farris & Marsh, 1982). Social work critics and communication experts are the allies who convince the powerless to monitor their self-talk and refrain from self-denigration and from justification of exploitation.

CORE ASSUMPTIONS OF APPLIED CRITICAL THEORY

Critical theorists begin with a set of theoretical assumptions that would be endorsed to different degrees by adherents to various emancipatory theories.

A STRUCTURAL ANALYSIS OF PROBLEMS IS PREFERRED

Problems are caused by processes generated by economic, political, and social structures, not by personal failings. Critical theorists look to a society's institutions and other large-scale structures like the economy, the political order, and the social welfare system to find the sources of dysfunctional group processes, troubled relationships, and identity disorders (Mullahy, 1997; Reisch & Andrews, 2001). Critical theorists reject the assumption that problems are caused mainly by faulty personality development, negative family experiences, or biological malfunctions (Cloward & Piven, 1975). The proponents of capitalism and individualism may preach these victim-blaming explanations enthusiastically, but these false theories distort the damaging impact of inequitable structures. Bertha Capen Reynolds (1963) exemplified this structural assumption when she argued, "Social workers deal largely with disadvantaged people whose difficulties . . . run back to conditions much more widespread than can be attributed to the mistakes of individuals alone" (p. 263). Critical theorists assume also that social structures shape what is perceived as reality, how morality is established, which problems community members discuss, and even the ways discussions and deliberations about reality, morality, and public problems are conducted.

CONFLICT, NOT CONSENSUS AND COOPERATION, CHARACTERIZES SOCIAL LIFE

Critical theorists offer a bleak picture of the common patterns of interaction. Competition, contention, the pursuit of individual gain, manipulation, deception, and coercion typify social interaction. **Cooperative activity,** collective action driven by the quest for common interests, mutual aid, and consensus, is rare (Mullahy, 1997). Conflict and contention are especially common to **capitalism,** defined by critical theorists as a socioeconomic system based on the production of profit, in which workers do not own the means of production and nonworkers do, and in which labor offers its services to the highest bidder in the marketplace (Farris & Marsh, 1982).

Critical theorists assume that conflict is manifest currently in the media of communication and the forums for public deliberation. Fights for interpretations of reality and for the construction of social problems are legion. Groups battle for definitional victories. Is marijuana use a danger to the entire society or a body- and mind-altering process akin to that sought by prescription drug users? Does legalized gambling provide a responsible form of family entertainment or an opportunity for corporate and individual crime? Was the U.S. war against Iraq initiated to liberate an oppressed people or to maximize oil profits and to revenge insults?

Bertha Capen Reynolds (1951) offered insightful observations supporting this core assumption of what she called *society in conflict.* She complained that welfare legislation designed to prevent human misery was opposed by well-financed lobbies, federal low-cost housing programs were undermined by real estate interests, a system of costly and ill-distributed medical care was supported by medical societies, and a surplus of unemployed labor was manipulated for the profit of powerful groups. Those committed to constructive social work must fight the interest groups opposed to cooperative and fair policy solutions, she concluded.

Societies Divide into Two Major Groups

Societies are divided into two major groups, and membership is assigned to these groups based on people's location in the social hierarchy. One group has a disproportionate control of society's resources, such as material goods, power, wealth, social status, and means of communication. Membership in this **privileged group** in the United States was restricted for much of the country's history, with some exceptions, to males of English ancestry who endorsed Protestant religious beliefs. The other group, the group to which many social work clients belong, is resource poor. Political influence is minimal for the **underprivileged groups.** A financial catastrophe is one missed paycheck or one serious illness away. High status and positive public regard within the community of the have-nots is a rare or fleeting experience. Motivation and skills for public debate and influential communication are also underdeveloped. Bertha Capen Reynolds (1938/1992) noted that United States–style capitalism had created a two-group society. Great wealth, political influence, and control of the media characterized a ruling minority. This oligarchy had even succeeded in turning many of the middle-class members against the poorest social members.

Critical theorists assert that these social divisions and disparities in material and symbolic resources are the major sources of societal conflict (Mullahy, 1997; Tilman, 1984). The privileged group members create culture, institutions, laws, and media for the distribution of ideas that favor them. They use their privileges to transform state institutions into instruments of oppression. The privileged group members work together to extend their **domination,** which Gil (1998) defines as "the *means* to enforce exploitation toward the *end* of attaining and maintaining privileged conditions of living relative to some other groups" (p. 10). Victory for those with privilege means subordination, hardship, silenced voices, and ignored arguments for the vanquished. The subordination of the oppressed by the oppressor, or **oppression,** defined as "a mode of human relations involving domination and exploitation—economic, social, and psychological" now describes "interaction between individuals, between social groups and classes within and beyond societies; and, globally, between entire societies" (Gil, p. 10).

Social Workers Should Empower Oppressed Groups

The social work profession has a special responsibility to protect members of oppressed groups from exploitation by dominant individuals, groups, and organizations and to empower these oppressed peoples so that they can protect themselves. The professional mission of social workers, critical theorists assume, should be to fight injustice in all its forms. **Injustice** refers to "coercively established and maintained inequalities, discrimination, and dehumanizing, development-inhibiting conditions of living (e.g., slavery, serfdom, and exploitative wage labor; unemployment, poverty, starvation, and homelessness; inadequate health care and education), imposed by dominant social groups, classes, and peoples upon dominated and exploited groups, classes, and peoples" (Gil, 1998, p. 10). Social workers also should fight for **justice,** "the absence of exploitation-enforcing domination" (p. 10). Social workers, then, are not neutral. They must take sides and become champions for the underdogs, the oppressed, the marginalized, and the impoverished populations subject to domination by the privileged elite.

Critical theorists recognize that in capitalist societies, this approach to social work creates many contradictions. However, these contradictions can be criticized, analyzed, and resolved. Here are some contradictions faced by social workers. Social workers often affirm their commitment to client needs but find themselves defending indefensible agency and government policies and budgetary decisions to keep their jobs (Reynolds, 1963). Social workers create programs to serve people with problems caused by the exploitation or indifference of the powerful, but these programs depend on financing from those same uncaring elite groups (Reynolds, 1963). Social workers design organizations to help clients but watch as these organizations shift their mission to one of controlling, stigmatizing, and co-opting these clients (Reisch & Andrews, 2001). Social workers learn to empower, yet they also find themselves dominating and interfering in many aspects of their clients' lives, including child-rearing preferences, housing choices, alcohol use, and recreational activities (Reisch & Andrews, 2001). Social workers encourage clients to advocate for themselves in lawful ways but deal with the likelihood that those who do so may be vilified as evildoers or as unpatriotic and harassed or subjected to government surveillance (Reynolds, 1963). Social workers aim to treat clients as partners in the helping process and respect the clients' life experiences, yet the same social workers take pride in their professional status, claim greater expertise about client problems than the clients living these problems, and impose "informed" ideas about best solutions.

Social workers have the potential to recognize the contradictions inherent in the profession, in welfare organizations, and in many practice approaches. Bertha Capen Reynolds (1951) posed the challenge well:

> The real choice before us as social workers is whether *we* are to be passive or active. Shall we let the existing forms of social work, full of contradictions as they are, shape us to their mold? Shall we be content to give with one hand and withhold with the other, to build up and tear down at the same time the strength of a person's life? Or shall we become conscious of our own part in making a profession which stands forthrightly for human well-being, including the right to be an active citizen? (p. 175)

Cloward and Piven (1975) propose that social workers break with the professional doctrine that the institutions in which social workers are employed have benign motives. They advocate a critique of institutional practices based on using our common sense and humanity to look at what agencies actually do. Social workers may find government health programs organized for expansion and profit, housing programs controlled by construction and real estate businesses, public schools designed to convince the poor to blame themselves for their failures, welfare institutions created to force the poor into dangerous and low-wage work, and prisons and mental hospitals serving to exile and stigmatize those overwhelmed by the stresses of lower-class life. Critical theorists argue, however, that social workers need not resign themselves to doing society's dirty jobs. We can recognize that social work is a political activity, expand our power, and willfully oppose unjust social arrangements, programs, and policies.

The Countersystem Method Best Guides Inquiry and Practice

Critical theorists use the **countersystem** method for social inquiry, research, and practice. The concept of a countersystem is like that of a counterculture. In the 1960s, hippies created a counterculture, a community supportive of values and lifestyles opposed to those of the dominant capitalist and individualistic culture. Countersystem analysis requires that social workers abandon thought patterns and methods of inquiry imposed by dominant groups (the logical positivist paradigm of science, for example). Countersystem analysis requires thinking by contrast (Lyng, 2002). The critical researcher attempts to transcend her culture-bound sense of reality and question negatively all aspects of current structures and practices. What if we rejected, for example, the notion that the pursuit of profit should be a society's central value? Countersystem analysts imagine a counterset of arrangements (Feagin & Vera, 2001) and a wide range of alternative futures. What if our health care system or mental health institutions were organized with human need not profit as the central value? Countersystem analysts may look for standards external to the existing inequitable social order. These standards serve as a reference point for a critical examination of the focal system. How might the principles and ideals set in Scandinavian and Canadian hospitals, clinics, and medical offices illuminate the problems with U.S. health care? Or countersystem analysts might develop a vision of ideal communities and persons, and then identify the ways that existing conditions diverge from the ideal. Habermas wondered, for example, what the ideal speech situation might look and sound like. He then proposed that critical theorists and practitioners measure the gap between this hypothetical model of communication and the public deliberations that characterize relevant groups, organizations, and societies (Bartlett, 2000).

Countersystem practice is the implementation of these visions of better futures and fairer societies. Social workers might take on the job of building countersystems either outside or inside current social organizations (Leonard, 1975) and use these as a power base for developing critical perspectives for long-term efforts to change radically all oppressive social arrangements. Social workers can develop or support, for example, alternative social service organizations that counter the actions and premises of mainstream agencies. I worked at a New Age Settlement House created as an alternative to the traditional mental health system. We provided caring aid to many deinstitutionalized and abandoned adults (Forte, 1988). A social work director might reject the bureaucratic or managed care model of service delivery and organize her agency to actualize worker participation, community control, mutual aid, and shared decision making (Mullahy, 1997). Leaders of the social work profession might recognize the need to develop meanings, symbols, and definitions about social workers contrary to those promoted by the dominant media industries (Denzin, 1992). Such a blitz might show the public that social workers cannot be stereotyped as bleeding hearts who indulge clients and who indiscriminately support self-serving tax and spend policies, but as rebels with a legitimate cause.

Galper (1975) provides one useful summary of countersystem analysis and practice. He describes it as "creative and imaginative work to develop affirmative visions of a humanized society and strategies for social reconstruction aimed toward the goal of transforming society so every person is afforded maximum opportunity to enrich his or her spiritual, psychological, physical, and intellectual well-being" (p. 14).

THE CRITICAL-FEMINIST APPROACH TO HUMAN DEVELOPMENT

Feminist theorists have constructed an important variation on critical theory. In this section, I will introduce you to the ingredients of the critical-feminist approach to human development, including the exemplary role model in this tradition, the core assumptions and root metaphors, the conceptual model, critical reactions, and practical applications.

CAROL GILLIGAN: EXEMPLARY ROLE MODEL

Carol Gilligan was born in 1936 and is still actively teaching and theorizing. Considered one of the pioneers of American feminist theory (Facing History, 2005; Qin & Comstock, 2005), Gilligan taught at Harvard for more than 30 years. Early in her career at Harvard, she collaborated with renowned ego psychologist Erik Erikson, and she worked as a research assistant to Lawrence Kohlberg, a prominent theorist in the area of moral development. Gilligan noticed that Erikson and Kohlberg had created developmental theories inspired by and reflective of their experiences as men. In her own research, Gilligan began to interview and listen to the life experiences and struggles of many different girls and women. She realized that the traditional theories of human development, those of Freud, Erikson, and Kohlberg, were rooted in the lives of privileged white men and did not accurately represent the female point of view. This insight inspired her lifelong project of enriching developmental psychology by incorporating knowledge appreciative of the female voice.

In 1982, Gilligan published *In a Different Voice: Psychological Theory and Women's Development*, a landmark study showing how the inclusion of knowledge about women's life transformations changes our understanding of development. Men's experiences should not be the sole standard for explaining and judging human behavior. Gilligan challenged the assumption of many development theorists that women were inferior to men in their capacities for asserting interests, for clarifying self-identities, and for moral reasoning.

Gilligan showed how theorists who listen to women speaking in their own right and with their own integrity might challenge male-dominated theoretical discourse by drawing attention to aspects of human experience that previously were distorted, dismissed, or silenced.

Gilligan's studies of women's psychology, girls' development, adolescence, ethical decision-making processes, and conflict resolution have earned her a reputation as a major contributor to gender studies and to the feminist slant on diversity (Qin & Comstock, 2005). For example, Gilligan (1987) investigated the real-life moral reasoning of pregnant women who were considering an abortion. She discovered that, contrary to the conventional notion that independent judgment is essential to ethical problem solving, women were embedded in social relationships and made moral decisions by balancing care for others with care for the self. Men and women speak in different voices. Men prefer an ethics and language of rights and justice; women prefer an ethics and language of needs and care. Gilligan learned that the different female voice was a relational voice.

Carol Gilligan has authored and coauthored numerous books and publications, and her research and theoretical work have influenced educators, clinical psychologists, development theorists, social workers, and scholars of moral theory. Her book *In a Different Voice,* for example, stimulated many educational, artistic, and cultural projects designed to encourage girls' voices and build on females' strengths. Primary and secondary schools throughout the country developed girl-friendly curricula and teaching methods designed to help girls resist the conventions of femininity that hindered their intellectual and psychosocial development—behavior norms that required girls to be nice, to silence honest opinions, and to suppress parts of their authentic personalities. Gilligan's work also lent support to scholars interested in studying differences in the way men and women communicate. Gilligan is known for cofounding the voice-centered relational method, a distinctive accomplishment of the Harvard Project on Women's Psychology and Girls' Development. Her recent interest has been in developing the Listening Guide Method. This is a voice-centered, relational approach to understanding the social world. The method studies people's voice and resonance as they describe important relationship experiences. In developing this approach, Gilligan and her colleagues collaborated with voice teachers who were expert in theater work.

ASSUMPTIONS OF THE CRITICAL-FEMINIST APPROACH TO HUMAN DEVELOPMENT

You may have heard the feminist slogan "The personal is political." This slogan captures an important theoretical assumption. Individual experiences can be understood only by reference to the political context, as well as the social, cultural, and economic context, of the developing person. Gilligan (1982) recommends this assumptive position to critical-feminist theorists' interest in human development. She advises theorists to prioritize "the contextual nature of developmental truths" (p. 174).

Some critical theorists differ with feminist theorists in the choice of the central membership category. Critical theorists emphasize social class. Feminist theorists assume that gender is the central membership category. Social class, race, and sexual orientation are important social memberships that powerfully influence life chances, but gender is the primary and inescapable membership. Critical or radical feminists argue that "women's oppression is the first, most widespread, and deepest oppression" (Rosser & Miller, 2000, p. 21). From birth, the child is cast into the world of males or the world of females. Through the primary socialization process, each person is "engendered" (Wood, 1994), and most people incorporate the expected behavioral characteristics, rules for physical display, and gender ideals of the larger society. Even those who rebel against gender stereotypes do so within the vocabularies, repertoires of images, and sets of cultural roles constructed by a society to differentiate the two genders. Agents of socialization use "the myths of essential feminine nature" (Ferguson, 1980, p. 145) to channel developing girls into preferred gender paths. For example, the "mothering instinct," the claimed propensity of women for the intuitive, emotive, and caring behavior necessary to nurture others, is a powerful tool of social control. This tool is used strategically by men to argue that women are biologically directed toward some roles while inherently incapable of sterling performance in other roles. It is advantageous for men to convince developing women, for example, that women are "destined" to be inept at roles associated with politics, commerce, warfare, and religion. By using such "essentialistic" logic, men can perpetuate gender inequality and maintain their own privileges.

Critical-feminists like Gilligan assume that the experiences of marginal groups have been neglected in theory development. Much theory points, instead, to the standpoints and voices of adult males of European ancestry. When minority members turn to social theory for depictions of their own life, they make a frustrating discovery. They find that as women and members of other marginal groups they must deal with a disparity between their own experiences and the concepts and models provided by the official forms of social knowledge. Feminists assume specifically that "women, women's experiences, and women's values have been ignored, trivialized or persecuted throughout history" (Seigfried, 1996, p. 143). Feminists warn that theoretical analysis should bring in "those whose experiences have been excluded in the past" (Seigfried, p. 161) and emphasize that theory should validate the experiences and perspectives of girls and women.

Let's review once more the importance of this assumption to developmental theorists. Critical-feminists assume that traditional theories of human development are based on an observational bias more attuned to masculine images and standards than to images and standards relevant to women (Gilligan, 1982). Gilligan leveled this charge against Freud's theory of psychosexual development, Piaget's theory of cognitive development, Erikson's theory of psychosocial development, and Kohlberg's theory of moral development. Each male theorist failed to affirm the centrality of connection and relationship to female development and, instead, assumed that the male values (autonomy, individuation, and hierarchy) apply equally to males and females. Gilligan offered a detailed feminist critique of the limitations of each of these theories and concluded with the conviction, "only when life-cycle theorists divide their attention and begin to live with women as they have lived with men will their vision encompass the experience of both sexes and their theories become correspondingly more fertile" (Gilligan, 1982, p. 23).

ROOT METAPHORS AND THE CRITICAL-FEMINIST APPROACH TO HUMAN DEVELOPMENT

Two metaphors serve as foundations for critical-feminists: voice and marginality. Gilligan (1982) popularized the comparison to speaking with her identification of women's different voice. Gilligan (1987) believed that feminist theories of moral development include the care perspective common to women and thus "may facilitate women's ability to speak about their experiences and perceptions and may foster the ability of others to listen and understand" (p. 32). Reinharz (1994) reviewed research on "oppressed" women, including studies of wives of corporate executives. She learned that women often elaborated on the root metaphor of voice and used phrases to describe their situations such as "having no voice" and "not being heard," "losing one's voice" and "being silenced," and "wanting a voice." She proposed a useful definition of **voice** as "the ability, the means, and the right to express oneself, one's mind, and one's will" (p. 180). She urged women to act on their desires to develop a strong and clear voice. Dorothy Smith (1974, 1996), an important feminist theorist, has also advocated for theoretical and political attention to the female voice. Smith encouraged women to speak from experience. Such speaking emanates from "the site of consciousness in an individual's own living" but accepts that speakers are always "embedded and active in social relations and organization" (Smith, 1996, p. 172). Smith recognizes that experience is not easily translated into language. There are two types of experience: experience that cannot be spoken of directly, and experience as spoken. Creative moments will occur in a community, Smith added, when women make the "transition between what is lived and what is spoken" (p. 184). Let's relate the root metaphor of voice to human development: Growth is a process by which women learn to listen to their own voice, to express this voice confidently in relationships with others, and to fight against those who would mock or silence this special voice.

Feminist theorists also make use of comparisons and images associated with the idea of marginality. For example, hooks (1984) conceives of oppressors who are at the center of economic, political, and social power. In contrast, women and members of other oppressed groups are at the edges or margins of this power. The greater the distance one is from the center, the more difficult is the effort to secure and use resources for self-protection and for advancement. Along similar lines, Deegan (1994) asserts that in a sexist society the marginality of women makes them "the quintessential other" (p. 67). Deegan claims that women must face an "unresolvable experiential difference" (p. 62).

Women are marginal in a way unlike that of immigrants. Immigrants have some anchorage in two worlds, but women cannot return to a home world. Women don't belong to a separate society "with its own language, national structure, and identity" (p. 62). Moreover, women cannot escape systematic discrimination because the female social world is always and everywhere subservient to the male world. Lacking the male self, the male body, and the male way of being, women are forever experiencing themselves as strangers in their own society. Women's marginality defines them as "others," not to be celebrated, but as "others to be exploited" (p. 65). The marginality of female immigrants and those of color only multiplies the vulnerability and estrangement of these women.

THE CRITICAL-FEMINIST MODEL OF HUMAN DEVELOPMENT

Critical-feminist theorists have expanded Gilligan's insight that female development differs in significant ways from the development of men. I will use four theoretical constructs to describe the model: oppressive contexts, asymmetrical interaction, internalization of subordination, and constricted coping options (Forte, Franks, Forte, & Rigsby, 1996).

OPPRESSIVE CONTEXTS AND DEVELOPMENT   Females develop in oppressive social contexts. Oppression is "a state of asymmetric power relations characterized by domination, subordination, and resistance, where the dominating people exercise their power by restricting access to material resources and by implanting in the subordinated people self-depreciating views about themselves" (Prilleltensky & Gonick, 1994, p. 153). Oppression means "the absence of choices" (hooks, 1984, p. 5). The characteristics of oppressive social context include large status and power differences between women and men (women have less status and power); structural and personal dependence by women on the resources provided by men; and a lack of access to supportive others and to alternative perspectives for use in developing noncompliant definitions of the situation (Forte et al., 1996).

Oppression pervades the larger societal context as well as specific contexts and settings for human development (Comstock, 2005). Many societies are patriarchal contexts. **Patriarchy** is a concept referring to the rule of fathers. In patriarchal societies, positions of authority in the society and in the family are reserved for men, and societal resources including authority, power, and wealth are passed from father to son. Women are prohibited from exercising authority. When I was growing up, for example, my grandfather and father ruled over the extended family during Sunday dinners. They set the time for the meal, called all to the table, dominated the conversation, and retired for after-dinner drinks and manly talk after the meal. The women cooked, served, cleaned, and kept quiet.

The cultural symbols in patriarchal and sexist societies reinforce men's favored position (Mackie, 1987). These symbols permeate advertising, advice books, etiquette manuals, birthday cards, children's stories, fairy tales, films, television shows, video and computer games, and rock, rap, and country music.

In fairy tales considered classic in the United States, for example, females are symbolized in unflattering ways as passive and sleepy beauties waiting for charming princes. In advertising, images of obedient, nurturing wives, images of superwomen pursuing work interests but without ignoring family obligations, and images of scantily clad beautiful women adorning the sales object are common. Video and computer games often portray women as the voluptuous conquests of violent men or the admirers and imitators of these male aggressors.

The cultural norms in patriarchal and sexist societies reinforce men's favored position and impede women seeking equal authority (Benson, 1991; West & Fenstermaker, 1993). Such norms are justified by claims about the "essential" characteristics of females. Women should embrace motherhood and realizing their purposes by filling the role of mother. Women should do all the household labor such as cleaning, cooking, and clothes washing. Women should assume greater responsibility for parenting duties than men. Women should accept that they are best suited for lower-paying, care-oriented jobs like stewardess, social worker, and teacher. Women should defer to men in problem-solving conversations and follow men's lead. Women should passively serve as objects for men's sexual use. The prevalent social and political theories in patriarchal societies also reinforce men's favored positions. Gilligan (1982) rejected traditional sexist theories of human development because they provided rationalizations for the continuation of men's domination over and oppression of women.

Oppressive beliefs, values, and attitudes are embedded also in specific contexts. The mass media in the United States, for instance, promote a conception of the ideal woman as thin, youthful, and sexy. Developing girls learn that their bodies are to be evaluated and obsessed over by male voyeurs and that in most cases their natural physical appearance will be deficient (Benson, 1991). Mackie (1987) located a "tyranny of beauty" in the economic industries associated with cosmetics, fashion, and weight loss. Female body parts are sexualized, she proposed, in accordance with masculine standards, and female value is made dependent on physical attractiveness. Neighborhoods, parking lots, and other public settings are sites of oppression. The fear of sexual harassment, psychological intimidation, sexual abuse, sexual assault, and rape is a constant for many women.

The family is a site for oppression (Comstock, 2005). Here many women are trained to defer to the needs and desires of their fathers and brothers. The acceptance of financial and social dependence on father and then husband is encouraged. Developing females are taught to keep their own appetites for food, sex, power, equality, and career advancement in check. Many girls are brainwashed to believe that their aspirations should be limited to the enactment of the role of mother. In the household, the father and then the husband can demand obedience and retaliate with the support of the community for a female member's defiant assertion.

Let me summarize. Oppressive societal contexts and daily contexts create a condition of permanent inequality, and every aspect of a woman's development is affected by this gender-based inequality.

ASYMMETRICAL INTERACTION AND DEVELOPMENT Oppressive societal and social contexts condition face-to-face interaction. Men have the power and status to remain imperceptive to the needs and interests of less powerful girls and women (Forte et al., 1996). In contrast, women must cultivate their capacities for interpersonal sensitivity and perspective taking as a counterbalance to the greater power of men. Using the root metaphor of voice, we might say that men have the power to silence female speakers and women lack the power to demand to be heard. In sexist societies, women's voices are not listened to, are marginalized, or are misunderstood when women attempt to communicate with male family members, policy makers, scholars, and researchers (Prilleltensky & Gonick, 1994).

Reinharz (1994) reviews the substantial research documenting asymmetric interaction. Girls have shared accounts of significant bodily experiences, and they report feeling ignored or discounted by examining male physicians. Adolescent female students in a mostly minority public high school identified a "push toward silence" from their teachers. In research on the interaction experiences of attorneys, 50 percent of female attorneys reported being cut off by judges while speaking, compared to 6 percent of the male attorneys. In my own review of the research on conversational advantages exercised by men when interacting with women (Forte, 2001), this pattern of asymmetric interaction was widely supported. In cross-sex interaction, men have been found to talk more, talk longer, violate rules of turn-taking more often, control the topic of conversation more, use conversation-dominating strategies more, and interrupt more frequently than women.

There are some additional indicators of asymmetric interaction. Men often use devaluing forms of speech in interacting with women. These include addressing women only by their marital status, verbal harassment, the use of stereotypical labels, and reference to physical attributes as in "Hey, Blondie" or "My Beauty" (Reinharz, 1994). The language that men use in interacting with women (or talking about women with their buddies) includes many words that depreciate women. Mackie (1987) reports, for example, that the English language has more than 200 negative words to describe sexually promiscuous females but only a few, mostly positive phrases for describing sexually promiscuous males. Men also use nonverbal communication to dominate women. Staring, touching as a gesture of control, and crowding women's personal space are examples.

Across the life span, then, women are subject to interactions during which they are treated as invisible and interactions during which their voices are barely heard or are silenced (Comstock, 2005). Some developing women lose their own "voice." They may even disassociate from girlfriends, mothers, and other women as they strive to become like men and to be liked by men. To develop their full potentials, some women learn to reject the explicit and implicit messages absorbed during interaction with fathers, brothers, boyfriends, male teachers, bosses, and others and to begin to trust their own developmental experiences and those messages from caring female mentors.

THE INTERNALIZATION OF SUBORDINATION AND DEVELOPMENT Critical-feminists theorize that women comply with the demands of their oppressors not only because of coercive external conditions (the threat of a beating or economic dependency on a man's money, for example) but also because of inner constraints. During the developmental process, many women import sexist ideology and gender inequality into their own personalities. Because of this **internalization of subordination,** England and Browne (1992) suggest, "Women carry normative values, preferences, cognitive beliefs, or behavioral proclivities across situations" (p. 99). Women are cast into subordinate positions and internalize at various points in their development parts of the oppressive hierarchy. At an early age, many girls internalize a model of female development emphasizing deficiencies and inferiority to males, and this contributes to trouble identifying and valuing their own strengths (Comstock, 2005). From youth, many women are socially trained to be blind to indicators of their worth other than those associated with physical appearance (Benson, 1991). As girls mature, internalized social standards regarding the importance of using looks to increase the likelihood of obtaining meaningful work, financial security, or social acceptance impair their free action. Some women cope with oppression and subordination by internalizing the negative judgments of men and assuming a stance toward the self of hatred or doubt. Girls and teenagers may accept dominant sex role stereotypes and limit their role aspirations to those deemed "feminine" (Comstock, 2005). Finally, developing women may internalize societal commands to suppress personal impulses to express anger or competitiveness and struggle instead to display behavior that fits with normative social images and expectations (O'Brien, 1998). Many women participate in intersecting oppressive systems, and the impact of the internalization of subordination is especially damaging because these women must deal with internalized racism, internalized homophobia, or internalized class prejudices (Comstock, 2005).

COPING OPTIONS AND DEVELOPMENT The internalization of oppressive gender norms, preferences, beliefs, and habits inhibits women's ability to use effective and flexible coping responses. Feminist-oriented theorists and researchers have extended the Marxist notion of alienation to document the negative impact of alienation from self, interaction, and social organizations on coping activity. Reese (1997) defines **alienation** as a separation of the social self "from fulfilling activities, autonomous interaction and solidarity relationships" (p. 75).

Arlie Hochschild (1983) drew on critical theory and feminism in her study of a modern form of alienation from self that is common to the service industries. She dubbed this "alienated emotional labor." In exploring the work of female flight attendants, Hochschild discovered that airlines train attendants to suppress any feeling of irritation or anger toward passengers. No matter what attendants feel, they must act in a reassuring and friendly way, and act so under all circumstances. Thus, the attendants' emotional style becomes part of the service offered by the organization. Unfortunately, the requirements of emotional labor, such as the constant maintenance of an artificially produced "professional smile," separate workers from the emotional aspects of the self. Accurate reading of one's emotional states is crucial to effective coping. Hochschild expected that the emotional labor done by social workers could result in similar alienation from the self.

Alienation affects social interaction and community participation. Previously internalized norms, values, and behaviors, especially those maintaining one's inferiority and relationship subordination, must be challenged. However, the interaction partners endorsing and often justifying these perspectives and reality constructions resist challenge. Many men actively oppose the liberation of the females in their sphere of influence. Girls and women under such influence can become alienated from interaction experiences and from contact with social organizations providing alternative perspectives on the dominant political-economic reality. They may comply with their oppressors and limit their daily interaction to a narrow social network. Consequently, they never develop the social base for questioning internalized and core beliefs necessary to empowering coping choices.

In the course of a woman's development under oppressive circumstances, other coping problems may emerge. Comstock (2005), a critical-feminist theorist, contends that many adolescent and adult women's self-destructive behaviors, "such as chronic dieting, anorexia, bulimia, substance abuse, and other forms of self-mutilation including plastic surgery" (p. 116), indicate failed attempts to cope with social devaluation. In a study of domestic violence, my colleagues and I (Forte et al., 1996) documented that battered women experienced more troubling emotions than nonbattered women. Moreover, troubling emotions such as shame, guilt, anxiety, confusion, doubt, and depression were associated with self-perceived coping difficulties. Internalized subordination also tends to block some women's imaginative powers, lessening their ability to identify problem-solving alternatives except those that serve men's interests and desires (Benson, 1991).

Despite the pervasive influence of patriarchy and sexism, some women liberate themselves from the damaging impact of oppressive social situations. They develop flexible and potent coping capacities, capacities for caring relationships, personal and social power, and the ability to direct their own lives (Gilligan, 1982). We will discuss the process of liberation in the section on theory application.

CRITICAL COMMENTS

The critical-feminist model of development challenges developmental theorists to understand human development in its social and historical context (Scholnik & Miller, 2000). This context is often characterized by inequalities related to gender, social class, race, ethnicity, and sexual orientation. Traditional developmental theorists discovered how human development progresses within biological and psychological parameters. Feminists add depth to the notion of developmental constraints by voicing the ways that oppressive social contexts also limit growth possibilities.

Feminists present a valuable critique of models of development that fail to consider women's experiences, perspectives, and voices. However, critical-feminist theorists have yet to provide a comprehensive and detailed alternative mapping of male and female biopsychosocial development across the life span. Also, feminists, like most critical theorists, divide the world into two groups, the oppressor and the oppressed, and then theorize on behalf of the oppressed. How does feminist developmental theory apply to cultures and subcultures that divide gender into more than two categories? What can this theoretical perspective tells us about the development of boys and men subject to oppressive contexts? Compared to women, what are the similar and different development paths and processes for members of other oppressed and vulnerable groups such as African Americans, the poor, and homosexuals? The critical-feminist developmental model has the vitality and potential of a young theory. As the tradition matures, theorists will deepen the explanatory and predictive power of the feminist model and begin to answer these and other unanswered theoretical questions.

APPLICATIONS OF THE CRITICAL-FEMINIST MODEL OF HUMAN DEVELOPMENT

The critical-feminist model informs practical approaches to the consciousness raising and liberation of oppressed women and of members of other oppressed groups. Here I will discuss briefly this application of theory to the end of human empowerment.

Oppressed people must develop a critical awareness of the social and political conditions maintaining their oppression and associated exploitation and marginalization (Prilleltensky & Gonick, 1994; Reinharz, 1994). Social workers can help. The purpose of liberation-oriented practice theory is to remove the internal barriers (internalization of subordination) and the external barriers (political and material inequality) obstructing the full development of women. Social workers also aim to support women's quest for self-fulfillment across the life span and to create supportive communities that make possible a dignified life of individuals living together in the absence of domination, with reciprocity of interaction, and committed to equality of rights. The process of helping is guided by feminist principles. Listen to the voices and stories of women. Democratically include those persons oppressed because of gender in setting change goals, in selecting methods of change, and in deciding how to evaluate practice. Allow oppressed clients to "tell it like it is" even when that challenges social work expectations, and appreciate the diversity of stories told by those who have been oppressed. Finally, the content of all helping actions must be grounded in the historical and environmental specifics of oppressive situations.

Ferguson (1980) developed a critical feminist approach to liberation. Her insights can be added to the practice framework detailed above. Power entails the control of definitions of reality. Liberation from dominators requires asserting one's own definitions. This entails shuttling between compassion (appreciating and emotionally affirming the perspective of others, even oppressors) and freedom (projecting and asserting one's own experiences, perspectives, and preferences into social relationships). Oppressed women may be compassionate and attuned to others' needs to the degree that their freedom is endangered. So, the assertion of autonomy must be promoted. Specifically, practitioners can aid these clients in identifying alternative reference groups, exploring relationship perspectives that increase autonomy, developing their own perspectives and definitions of reality, and asserting their right to actualize these definitions even if doing so undermines the oppressor's version of the relationship. Practitioners should also join the fight for the legal equality and economic independence necessary to increase the possibility that oppressed women will achieve the power necessary to influence reality-defining processes.

As indicated in the biography of Carol Gilligan, her theoretical work on women's development has also stimulated many applications. I will add one more here. Gilligan's work (1982) has become the foundation for gender-sensitive approaches to moral education, one that considers the "feminine voice" and the "centrality of the concepts of responsibility and care in women's construction of the moral domain" (p. 105).

MAPPING APPLIED CRITICAL THEORY

The section begins with Figure 13.1, a critical theory version of the eco-map. The eco-map is presented as a metatheoretical tool that translates critical theory propositions and vocabulary into the ecosystems language familiar to social workers. The critical theory conceptions of person–environment connections (distorted or authentic communication), of the environment (a public forum for work on social problems), of salient systems (media, corporations, military, and political systems), of optimal ecosystem arrangements (ideal speech situation), and of the change process (intelligent social reconstruction) are reviewed.

How Are Connections Conceptualized?

Community members are connected to each other, according to critical theorists, because of civic-minded communication. Experiences of collective deliberation, decision, and action by members of families, peer groups, neighborhood associations, political parties, legal systems, and public problem-solving enterprises create a linguistic bond (Bartlett, 2000; Habermas, 1981/1984). As members of human associations, we must talk together about how to regulate our common life, how to solve problems, and how to deal with the direct and indirect consequences of environmental and social processes.

How Is the Quality of Connections Differentiated?

Critical theorists might identify three kinds of connections. Strong connections are deliberations characterized by **authentic communication** and symmetrical relations (Bohman, 2000). Such communication connections support the participation of all members of the collective. Citizens connected strongly arrive at mutual understanding by speaking in accord with **validity claims.**

FIGURE 13.1
THE CRITICAL
THEORY
VERSION OF
THE ECO-MAP

Source: Adapted with permission from *Family-Centered Social Work Practice* (p. 160) by A. Hartman and J. Laird, 1983. New York: The Free Press.

ECO-MAP: A CRITICAL THEORY VERSION

Name: _____
Date: Present

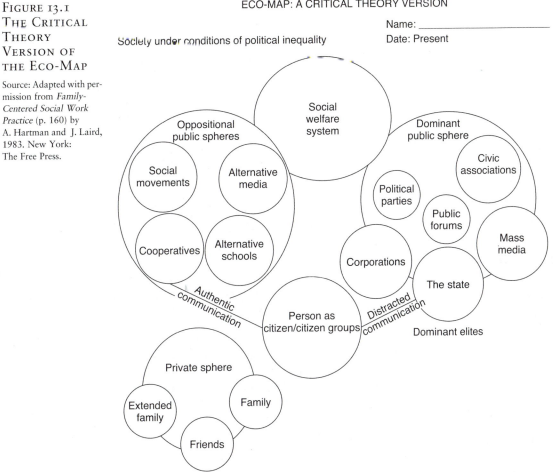

Fill in connections where they exist.
Indicate nature of connections with a descriptive word or by drawing different kinds of lines:
———————— for ideal and symmetrical communicative action
- - - - - - - - - - for restricted access to participation in deliberation
+++++++ for systematically distorted and asymmetrical communicative action
Draw arrows along lines to signify flow of political and semantic resources ➤ ➤ ➤

These include truth (what I say is factual), moral correctness (I have the moral right to my social identity and I am communicating in an ethically responsible way), and sincerity (I am who I say I am and I mean what I am saying). Honoring these claims is necessary to coordinated and legitimate social action. Such communication is the foundation for group living. Critical theorists also conceive of strong connections as deliberations guided by democratic values and principles, such as the right of free and equal citizens to influence policies that matter.

Stressful connections are deliberations characterized by **distorted communication** and asymmetrical relations. Speakers voice words and sentences (presented reasons, declarations, statements, arguments, and so on) that violate the necessary conditions of successful communication, but these utterances or reasons are influential nevertheless (Bohman, 2000). Generally, distorted communication occurs when there are asymmetries in the power of the two speakers, and one speaker can use his or her greater power to bypass the constraints necessary for successful communication or to restrict the access and participation of other speakers. Such a misuse of communication uses the compliance arrived at by this distorted process to maintain inequality. Organizational leaders, for example, may make repeated and empty promises to organizational members, knowing that the subordinate members lack the means to withdraw from their obligations to listen to such inauthentic speech or to call the leaders liars. Critical theorists conceive of stressful connections as those guided by capitalist ideology, the use of ideas, symbols, and language to reproduce relations of inequality and domination.

Tenuous connections are those in which persons with limited social power and communicative capacity have difficulty obtaining access to deliberations about public policies and problems. Wealthy corporations may avoid deliberations about contested topics such as the planned takeover of a local electric utility company. They may do this by threatening to withdraw their investment in the community if community leaders voice dissent or demand an open discussion (Bohman, 2000). Members of the political elite may place restrictions on speakers, topics, and themes. For example, Ralph Nader was not allowed to participate in televised debates during his presidential campaign in 2000; thus, all those interested in participating in his pro-environment and pro-consumer conversations were excluded from the deliberations with Nader about the next president.

What Is the Typical Focal System?

Critical theorists would place citizens in the center of the eco-map. A democracy depends on its citizens. Individual citizens and groups of citizens can be assessed in terms of their mastery of the communication capacities necessary for public deliberation: competencies in the use of speech and action, the ability to produce valid utterances and reasons for their claims, the ability to distinguish between the valid and invalid expressions of others, and the discernment necessary to appraise the reasons of others (Bohman, 2000). The problems addressed by social work often reflect the failures of both the society and its members to develop these citizenship potentials.

Bertha Capen Reynolds (1951) placed citizens at the center of her model of social work, too. She argued that a government has the responsibility to ensure opportunities to all citizens for a healthy and socially useful life, and all citizens have the concurrent responsibility to ensure that community needs are met and democracy is protected. A central service of social workers, then, is to "build up and maintain the full sense of citizenship in the people with whom they work" (p. 50).

Social workers should help clients become useful, active participants in democratic processes who are well informed and are committed to staying informed. These ideal citizens participate regularly in public forums and contribute to political deliberations and decisions that increase the common good.

How Is the Environment Conceptualized?

The environment is conceptualized as intersecting spheres of influence. According to Habermas (1962/1989), the **public sphere** began appearing around 1700 in Europe. This sphere consisted of organizations of information and public debate, such as newspapers and journals, and the public places and institutions that fostered discussion of social and political issues. These included parliaments, political clubs, literary salons, public assemblies, pubs, coffee houses, and meeting halls (Kellner, 2000, p. 263). It is the place where private individuals meet each other as public citizens. The public sphere became a new place in the social environment, one where individual and group members of a nation could talk about their needs and perspectives, identify common concerns, organize to resist oppression, and attempt to influence public policy making and problem solving. In this critical theory conception of the environment, the public sphere mediated between two other domains: the **private sphere** of the family and workplace and the domain of the state or government (Kellner, 2000).

The dominant public sphere has been controlled, many critical theorists assert, by white, property-owning males. Those who control the public sphere exclude persons of other categories, such as women, the working class, and people of color, from full participation and from voicing their concerns. However, the environment also includes alternative or **oppositional public spheres** (Kellner, 2000). These are public spaces where groups excluded from the dominant public sphere can develop innovative cultures and participate safely in political discussion and debate. These serve as the preparatory schools and staging grounds for citizens who want to organize and challenge nondemocratic institutions. Jane Addams, her social work colleagues, her academic partners from the Chicago school of sociology, and other Hull House members created an alternative public sphere. At the settlement house, men and women created various forums for communication and civic groups. These citizens deliberated, decided, and acted to change Chicago and promote progressive policies and practices related to housing, health, education, welfare, workplace conditions, voting, the law, and public arts.

In contemporary countersystem or oppositional public spheres, citizens develop alternative media such as progressive presses, Internet discussion lists, web-based bulletin boards, and talk radio stations to foster lively debate (Kellner, 2000). Public television and radio broadcasting have become part of an oppositional public sphere in some societies and communities. Activists and public intellectuals committed to oppositional public spheres may create alternative schools that prepare students to serve their communities as informed and engaged citizens. These function outside the dominant political and institutional systems and serve as new sites of information, discussion, contestation, political struggle, and organization (Kellner, p. 279). Feminists have created **consciousness-raising groups,** safe places for women to increase their understanding of the interaction of personal, social, and political forces in their lives and to find ways to resist male domination. Community activists have started people's health centers, food co-ops, communal living agreements, and mental health clubhouses that operate in contrast to conventional organizations.

Bertha Capen Reynolds (1938/1992) tried to foster an oppositional sphere for the social work profession. She urged social workers to join with rank-and-file labor groups and to form countermovements for democracy. Allies in such movements could participate in discussion groups to criticize social welfare organizations that treated clients (and social workers) like animals herded into unsanitary factory buildings. These alliances, she hoped, would contribute to the development and implementation of higher standards for decent working conditions for all workers, acceptable workloads, job security, and optimal training.

Is Particular Emphasis Given to Any Systems?

Critical theorists give special emphasis to several social systems that are especially influential in contemporary capitalist societies (Kellner, 2000). These include the **power elite,** the leaders of military, industrial, corporate, and political organizations, and the **culture industries,** the loosely connected set of organizations and people who labor together to provide the cultural productions and performances available to the public as film, television programming, music, and Internet content (Cuzzort & King, 1989). Critical theorists ask questions like the following: How do these select groups use a society's cultural representations and public deliberations to maintain their power and privilege? How do these groups compel or trick others to accept their versions of reality? What groups have been excluded from public forums by these elite members and cultural industries? What specific strategies of manipulation and deception have been used to intimidate and silence dissenters? How can power controlled by the elite be redistributed widely, and how can the cultural industries be challenged to provide truthful, responsible, and community-enhancing cultural products?

How Are Resources and Their Flow Conceptualized?

Critical theorists place importance on resources as conceived conventionally by political theorists and economic theorists. These include political power, social status, and wealth. Those with resource advantages can use these advantages to force or coerce cooperation. They need not labor toward the end of collective inquiry and deliberation.

Critical theorists also give great importance to semantic or communication resources. These are the tools essential to effective argumentation. These **communication resources** include preferred and publicly accepted styles of public communication, pools of reasons for public arguments, and media and technologies for mass communication (Bohman, 2000).

Certain groups have greater control over these symbol-making resources. The control of these means of communication is comparable to the Marxist understanding of capitalists' control over the means of production in a factory system. For example, in 2004 several media giants used their control of radio stations and movie houses to suppress criticism by Howard Stern and Michael Moore of President Bush. Similar efforts ended the practice by newspapers and television stations of showing images of the coffins of dead soldiers. This decreased the possibilities for producing alternative symbols, stories, and pictures of the Iraq war and the consequences of Bush's international and national policies.

WHAT DESCRIPTIVE WORDS ARE USED?

Critical theorists use words and concepts associated with democratic theory, such as *deliberation, popular sovereignty, egalitarian, rights, liberties, consensus, compromise, representation, majority rule, politics,* and *the public.* They also make frequent use of words associated with pragmatic theories of communication, such as *speech act, utterance, meaning, assertion, claims, linguistic codes, communication style,* and *reasons.* Many of their theoretical writings include concepts that trace their heritage to Marxist theories and conflict theories. These include *conflict, power, inequality, interest, critique, alienation, oppression, social class, praxis, privilege, false consciousness, revolution,* and *dialectics.*

HOW IS CHANGE CONCEPTUALIZED?

Critical theorists like Habermas are interested in institutionalizing nonviolent revolution rather than encouraging violent revolution. This requires the creation and cultivation of oppositional public spheres, the furthering of democratic processes, and the enhancement of the community's intelligence (ability to deliberate, decide, and act with rational consideration of multiple perspectives) for personal and social reconstruction projects.

The role of social worker, for the critical theorists, is that of a social critic (Bohman, 1997, 2000). The social worker grounded in a critical theory approach encourages community members to examine and reflect on the conditions of communication, to identify and challenge those who impose limitations or restrictions on forums for public discourse, and to fight to make public forums inclusive of a wider range of community groups and a wider range of topics. Cloward and Piven (1975) add that social workers should engage in resistance. They argue that "if we believe that the maintenance of wealth and power in the United States depends partly upon the exploitation, isolation, and stigmatization of the victims of capitalism by the agency of the welfare state, then our role is to resist these processes" (p. xlviii).

Change methods recommended by critical theorists include class-oriented confrontational politics (see Tilman, 2004); political or emancipatory education of the oppressed, raising their critical capacities and consciousness (Leonard, 1975) and helping them see the connections between their experience and problems and the dominant ideologies and material conditions in society (Pease et al., 2003); the mobilization of oppressed groups and client groups; consciousness-raising group work (Galper, 1975); labor union work and community organizing; the democratization of social agencies; and the creation of alternative organizations.

How Are Actual and Ideal Eco-Maps Contrasted?

Critical theorists would anticipate that examination of the eco-maps of many social work clients would not reveal happy and prosperous lives, egalitarian families and groups, or active engagement in ideal and democratic communities. The public sphere has been taken over by the power elite, state capitalism, the culture industries, and big corporations. Consequently, most citizens have retreated into the private sphere and now participate in society only as consumers of goods, services, and spectacle (Kellner, 2000). Passivity and a focus on private interests and concerns have replaced dedication to democratic participation and public service for the common good. A culture of acquisitive individualism has crowded out impulses toward mutual aid and collective problem solving.

Critical theorists are idealists, however, and they have developed a detailed picture of the desirable and preferred ecosystem. Their approach characterizes both the ideal community and the ideal citizen. Habermas referred to the defining feature of optimal social systems as the ideal speech situation. His ideas can be extended to community life. Leaders of the **ideal community** endeavor constantly to provide the conditions for effective member participation. This includes the development of social institutions governed by democratic and humanistic laws and rules. Habermas and other theorists of radical democracy also recommend society-wide norms of freedom, such as freedom of speech and assembly; norms of equality, including the right of all to participate in political debate and decision making; and norms of publicity, the openness of all political and social processes to scrutiny and consideration by citizens (Bohman, 2000; Kellner, 2000). Norms at the local level are important also. The ideal community provides deliberative forums where participants make commitments to abide by rules of turn taking, restraint from interruption, and consensual topic change (Bohman, 2000).

The ideal community is based on principles of radical democracy, universal compassion, and mutual recognition and respect. Ideal communities are modeled after **mutual help groups**, in which families and neighbors share resources and alternate in roles of giver and taker. Visions of the ideal community have also been inspired by trade unions and the efforts of labor leaders to create a community of interest of all workers, transcending differences of color or creed (Reynolds, 1951, 1963), a place where norms of cooperation rather than exploitation are operative. Reynolds adds that the ideal community is built on the same principles as good casework: compassion, mutual respect, and cooperation (Reynolds, 1963).

Critical theorists offer, too, a detailed characterization of the ideal citizen. The ideal citizen has fully developed **communicative capacities** (Kellner, 2000). These include the ability to understand others' speech, to argue, to reach consensus, and to take public action. The ideal citizen has advanced role-taking abilities and propensities, and thus can take the perspective of multiple others during public debates. The ideal citizen actively seeks information about public affairs, knows how to assess and appraise this information critically, and uses information adeptly when participating in democratic discussion and deliberation.

Critical theorists, like social workers, use a dual lens that keeps both environment and person always in focus. For Habermas (1992), the ideal community is a deliberative democracy, a collectivity using processes of public deliberation such as reflection, argumentation, public reasoning, and consensus building to develop active, rational, and moral citizens. Ideally, citizens strive mightily to preserve the integrity of these democratic processes and to solve problems cooperatively.

How Are Issues of Diversity, Color, and Shading Addressed?

Critical theorists are most interested in the differences in a social group's relation to privilege (status, power, wealth, enhanced life chances, and protections from risk). Persons of certain groups are more likely to lack privilege and face oppressive systems (O'Brien, 1998). Membership in certain ethnic and racial groups, such as the African American and Mexican American groups, is associated with limited access to opportunities for meaningful, safe, and steady employment and to high-quality education. Members of these groups must contend with systems of racism. Societies are stratified economically, and members of certain classes, the working class and the very poor, have limited access to wealth, health care, and nurturing physical and social environments. Members of these classes must contend with systems of exploitation. Women differ systematically from men. Generally, women live with fewer privileges, greater threats to liberties, and more obstacles to the pursuit of happiness. Women must contend with systems of patriarchy. Persons of certain sexual orientations are likely to be underprivileged. Homosexuals face discrimination because of sexual orientation. They are not allowed the validation and legal benefits that heterosexuals receive for marriage. Homosexuals must contend with systems of homophobia.

Critical theorists also use the imagery of intersecting social systems or categories of oppression (West & Fenstermaker, 1995). There are many possible sources of devaluation. Many members of unjust societies experience oppression from multiple directions. Imagine the different life chances for the working-class, African American lesbian and for Bill Gates, the European American, male, heterosexual, wealthy executive of Microsoft.

Critical theorists argue that other theorists seriously underestimate the extremely hostile environments experienced by many women, people of color, minorities, and those with different sexual orientations (Seigfried, 1993, 1998). Because of the "extent and depth of misogyny, racism, homophobia, and classism in personal habits and societal institutions" (p. 194), Seigfried suggests, there are few possibilities for changing adverse physical, economic, and social conditions, at least not for oppressed societal members. Moreover, the powerful, typically men, are not as honorable or as amenable to community change efforts as other theorists believe. The oppressors often mask their inclinations to expand power, skillfully use others' interests and needs as leverage for manipulation, and "stubbornly persist in suppressing others" (p. 199), whether by subtle or overt use of force. For women, for example, patriarchy is a major system of discrimination and exploitation, and the men invested in this system cling tenaciously to their privileges. Social workers must note this during the assessment process.

Critical theorists show special interest in the **politics of difference**, "social movements that make a political claim that groups suffer oppression or disadvantage on account of cultural or structural social positions with which they are associated" (Young, 1997, p. 383). Victims of oppression often organize to confront the privileged groups who exclude the oppressed groups from public discourse and policy making. Gay Republicans, for example, continue the difficult fight to be heard by leaders of their political party. Legal immigrants on the Eastern Shore of Maryland and their advocates attempt to influence the state legislature so that their health and educational needs are no longer ignored. Critical theorists assert that group differences can become resources that enrich democratic communication. Public forums benefit from a plurality of perspectives because deliberators must consider what are just solutions rather than what solutions advance the interests of select groups. Public forums benefit when marginalized perspectives are included because the privileged participants are forced to recognize that their experiences and preferences are partial and rooted in blindness to others' perspectives. Participants in public forums where diverse perspectives are shared increase their knowledge of social life as experienced by persons at different locations in the hierarchy. Differences by social class, race, ethnicity, sexual orientation, and other categorical memberships are resources that can increase the wisdom brought to democratic problem solving.

Candace West and her colleagues (Fenstermaker, West, & Zimmerman, 1991; West & Fenstermaker, 1993, 1995; West & Zimmerman, 1987) have integrated critical, feminist, and ethnomethodological theories to offer new conception of gender and diversity. Their approach focuses on "the dynamics of human interaction" and on the "institutional structures that emerge from and are maintained by such interaction" (Fenstermaker et al., p. 291). Instead of thinking of a person as being masculine or feminine, this approach invites us to consider how interactants "do gender" (or race or class) collectively.

Gender, then, is the definitional agreement about the identities of each interacting person accomplished during the interaction process. A few important lessons about gender, power, and inequality have emerged from theorizing about gender as a situated social accomplishment. First, to the extent that members of a privileged group (men) can assert that certain ways of interacting are natural for women, sex category membership can be used to legitimate or to discredit women's actions. Such tactics will maintain and protect the status quo. Uncontested statements like "It is only natural for women to do domestic chores, to do the bulk of the parenting, to do jobs associated with service" are best seen as political ploys. Second, women who routinely and predictably interact in accord with these norms of "natural" female behavior (and internalize them) perpetuate their own subordination. The woman who conducts herself in defiance of these expectations finds herself accountable to determined coalitions of men. Third, the "doing gender" perspective suggests that social change entails challenging social organizations and groups that differentiate persons according to sex category. At the macro level, pro-woman movements can weaken the institutional and cultural laws, policies, practices, and understandings dictating that there are natural or appropriate ways for males or females to act. Pro-woman movements might also provide images, vocabularies, gestures, and emotional support so that, at the micro level, gender rebels have tools they can use to reject social norms and to explore innovative ways for coordinating multiperson action. We need to learn to treat people like people instead of treating women like women or like men. Critical feminists would add that we need social institutions that make possible such gender-free social interaction.

Critical-feminist theorists add gender to the eco-map, and some invite us to think also about the differences experienced by men. A male supremacist society is one "where a vastly greater share of political and economic power is in the hands of men," where "men largely control the resources that are used to propagate cultural values," where "greater value is given to things male and masculine" (Schwalbe, 1996, p. 69), and where those equipped at birth with penises receive special treatment. Schwalbe (1996) believes that many men in Western societies develop a "masculinist self." They view themselves as "rational, tough, indomitable, ambitious, competitive, in control, able to get a job done, and ardently heterosexual" (p. 18). Other highly valued meanings associated with the masculine self include "competitive striving, heroic self-sufficiency, the ability to dominate, and the denial of tender feelings" (p. 57). In male-dominated societies, a man succeeds when he can "signify these qualities in a style befitting his ethnicity and social class" (p. 18).

Such male supremacist identity meanings, according to Schwalbe (1992), become central in men's overall self-concept, and this centrality perpetuates gender inequality. For one, males often internalize masculine meanings because they learn that males are privileged in relation to females and they learn that by habitually acting in masculine ways the fruits of such differential valuations can be earned. Second, men come to evaluate the self in terms of masculine standards, with problematic consequences. Inclinations to compete are perpetuated; impulses to understand, negotiate with, and validate the feelings of women are inhibited. Inclinations to produce and to achieve foster a relentless focus on goal achieving, whatever the means. Inclinations to view self as more worthy than others can result in the repression of emotions necessary to moral behavior. Third, the person with a masculine self is unlikely to develop propensities to take the perspective of women in an empathic rather than manipulative way. So, such men don't identify with women. They don't see any interdependence with women, and they remain insensitive to women's emotional and physical pain, rarely asking "How might she perceive, think about, and feel in relation to this situation?" Last, men who internalize the masculine self make reference to a social order that takes male supremacy for granted. Men's experience of the social world becomes defined as the universal social reality, with little awareness of how such thinking silences or devalues women.

In summary, critical theorists encourage social workers to locate clients and others in the client's eco-system in a social hierarchy arranged by gender, class, race, ethnicity, and sexual orientation. Note also whether the clients and relevant others are oppressors or oppressed persons in this social hierarchy, and the implications of oppression for all members of the community.

What Would Be Added or Deleted?

Critical theorists urge social workers to give attention to several social systems not found on conventional eco-maps or on eco-maps specific to other theoretical frameworks. Their eco-map would include a circle for the dominant elite and a circle for the mass media (Kellner, 2000). The map would specify the members of the political, economic, and military elite who pursue their private interests by staging displays, managing discourse, and manipulating public opinion rather than by promoting rational debate and consensus building. The circle for the mass media would specify the giant corporations and the television stations, the press, the websites, and the radio stations that they control. Eco-map analysis could then consider the damaging impact of these media conglomerates and how the mass media have become increasingly influential and capable of molding public opinion in ways that bypass democratic participation. These operatives of the mass media seek little feedback from citizens, and their media outlets rarely encourage rational deliberation or action. Critical analysts might also give special attention to the media leaders who have transformed news, public affairs, and information into forms of entertainment.

THE LIMITS OF APPLIED CRITICAL THEORY: A SOCIAL WORK APPRAISAL

Critical theorists minimize the contributions of capitalism to societal development. Many capitalist economies are very productive systems with beneficial effects. These include an elevated standard of living, promotion of innovation, reduction in the mistreatment of groups differing by race, ethnicity, or sexual orientation (because all are potential customers), and flexible adaptation to changing environmental and technological conditions. Vast injustice and despotism are possible outcomes, however, when collective action is not taken to reconcile profit seekers' interests with community interests. This does not justify a thorough rejection of capitalism nor the blaming of capitalists for all the difficulties a society faces in its attempts to achieve prosperity and realize democratic ideals.

Social workers may have ethical doubts about the change methods recommended by some critical theorists. Marxists and critical theorists like Herbert Marcuse theorized that qualitative change in social arrangements requires sudden, discontinuous, and revolutionary action by a vanguard able to identify clearly the sources of their oppression. Capitalist societies must be destroyed in a violent revolution initiated by those excluded from the benefits of such a system. Social workers attempt, in contrast, to balance likely effectiveness with ethical considerations in selecting the best means to achieve social goals. Class violence and militant politics are not the only means of achieving fundamental social change. Many social workers prefer educational, socialization, policy advocacy, and social action approaches that foster social integration rather than social division, that build on an optimistic and strengths-oriented understanding of people, and that protect the rights and freedoms of community members. Social work designed to encourage cooperative activities among members of family, neighborhood, and voluntary associations, to support community-level organizing, and to initiate policy reform will instill the democratic values and communal bonds necessary to social advancement more responsibly and effectively than political revolution.

Critical and conflict theorists tend to make a false and simplistic division of society into two major groups. They assume that society is organized into these groups according to people's positions in economic production as buyers or sellers of labor. Those who own the means of production, the capitalist class, try to take advantage of the working class, those who work in the factories, corporations, and businesses owned by the capitalists. One's perspective is inextricably linked to one's position as a privileged or a nonprivileged group member. Societies are actually composed of multiple overlapping social communities, interest groups, and categories. A society's members vary in their identifications with particular groups or classes and in their balancing of multiple memberships. Those with great wealth and power are capable of empathizing with the lowly and often do. Critical theorists encourage a class consciousness and an allegiance to class interests that can undermine efforts toward rational and respectful deliberations and cooperative problem solving on behalf of the greater whole. Social workers prefer a vision of a complex, pluralistic society composed of ever shifting associations and of social members looking to identify common interests. The rich and the poor need not be irreconcilable enemies. Constructive conflict resolution and public accommodation of the interests of diverse social groups are possible.

Social workers have faith in the possibilities of self-determination and human betterment. This contrasts with critical social theorists, especially the structuralists, who emphasize the constraining force of large-scale social institutions and organizations. Historical processes and public policies contribute to client troubles, as Mills asserted, but not in a deterministic manner. Social workers desire theories that show how every client has the power to choose creatively a direction contrary to the dictates of elite leaders or guardians of entrenched structures.

THE APPLIED CRITICAL THEORY MODEL OF JUSTICE WORK

In the last section, I present a conceptual and causal model that elucidates the critical theory approach to justice work. This incorporates the theorizing of Jurgen Habermas and his interpreters and successors, especially James Bohman. It characterizes the community features (varied groups' locations in the social stratification system), the capacities and conditions (rules and rights) necessary for effective participation in the public sphere, and the characteristics of public deliberation (ideal speech processes) that influence the quality of public problem solving. Figure 13.2 provides a visual summary of the variables identified in this model and their relationships to one another.

Habermas begins with two theoretical assumptions. First, he assumes that communication is the central human process. This differs from the Marxists,

FIGURE 13.2
DEMOCRATIC
DELIBERATION
IN THE PUBLIC
SPHERE:
HABERMAS'
MODEL OF
POWER
INEQUALITY,
COMMUNICA-
TION, AND
POLITICAL
PROBLEM
SOLVING

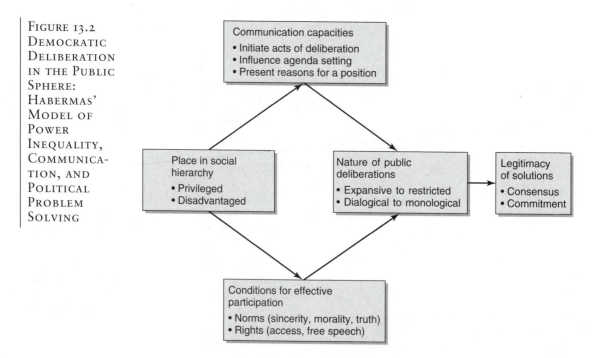

who give the primacy to labor. Communication, especially the type of communication guided by social norms (members experience a sense of obligation to meet each other's expectations during symbolic interaction), is indispensable to effective public problem solving (Habermas, 1981/1989). Next, Habermas assumes that democracy is the ideal form of human association. **Democracy** is both a "specific set of institutions which assure citizens self-rule via procedural mechanisms that, at the very least, provide equal access to political influence" and "a structure of communication among free and equal citizens" (Bohman, 2000, p. 12). Habermas (1997) uses these assumptions about communication and democracy in his countersystem analysis of the radical democratic ideal. Democratic deliberation is based on a process of reaching reasoned agreement among free and equal citizens (Bohman, 1997, p. 321). Governmental and other major institutions are constrained by reasons and arguments. Habermas hypothesizes also that when contending groups can participate in ideal democratic deliberations, each is more likely to grant legitimacy to political authority, contribute to problem solving, and comply with policy decisions even if one of the contenders loses a debate.

CRITICAL PROBLEM FORMULATION AND ASSESSMENT: THE SOCIAL HIERARCHY

Habermas uses his model of the ideal speech situation to investigate the real barriers to realizing democracy. Social structural factors are relevant (Bohman, 1996). In ideal circumstances, community groups have equal standing in the society. There are no significant differences in access to or control of resources, including cultural resources (knowledge and information), material resources (the money to pay for an ad campaign, finance a political campaign, or take time from work to engage in deliberations), and deliberative resources (familiarity with the official language, communication style, and frameworks used for political discourse).

In contemporary societies, Habermas (1997) and Bohman (2000) suggest, groups are located at different strata in the political and social hierarchy. A group's place influences its communicative capacities, its ability to wield rights and norms, and its approach to public deliberations. Resource-rich group members can use their wealth, status, and power to act undemocratically. The powerful can use intimidation and coercive tactics bolstered by threats of state violence and claims of privileged position to avoid public debate, to control the agenda of public problems, to bring discussion to a halt prematurely, or to force settlement on one interpretation or decision unacceptable to other groups. Corporations that bypass deliberation and threaten to relocate and remove their resources from a community if their wishes are not fulfilled exemplify the evasion of democratic responsibility (Bohman, 2000).

Those lower in the social hierarchy are subjected to both economic poverty and political poverty. They lack the money and power to capture the public's attention, to pursue their grievances in public forums, or to contest unjust decisions. Their reasons and arguments are easily ignored, and thus resource-poor groups are vulnerable to the intended and unintended negative consequences of the dictates of elite policy makers and problem solvers (Bohman, 1996). Critical social workers should assess the location in the social hierarchy of contending groups and the likely consequences of these differences in location.

CRITICAL PROBLEM FORMULATION AND ASSESSMENT: COMMUNICATION CONDITIONS

The communication capacities of societal members and the conditions governing deliberations bear on the quality of public problem solving. Communication capacities are defined as the knowledge, skills, and dispositions necessary for the full and effective use of political rights and liberties (Bohman, 1996). Members must possess these capacities if they are to engage competently in a complex and temporally extended activity of public deliberation (Bohman, 1997, p. 337). Members must have current and wide-ranging information, including a large pool of reasons to bring to a debate and to influence the agenda-setting and problem-solving processes (Habermas, 2001). They need to learn a shared vocabulary for expressing their needs and perspectives. Members must have skills related to reasoning and argumentation, including the ability to convince others of the cogency of their reasons, the ability to judge the cogency of others' reasons, and the ability to know whether they are having an influence. They must be able to listen respectfully and accurately to others' agenda suggestions and perspectives, manage conflict productively, and deal with communication barriers across different membership groups. Members must have certain dispositions, including the courage and determination to overcome fears of participating in public forums and the conviction to speak what they believe (Rossiter, 1996). Unfortunately, a group's location in the social hierarchy may reduce its members' chances to develop these communication capacities. For example, low-status and resource-poor immigrant groups may lack the abilities necessary to make effective use of opportunities to influence the deliberative process (Bohman, 1996, p. 110). Moreover, the larger community fails to offer these groups the education or training needed to overcome their communication deficits and to develop the capacities to fight for political influence (Bohman, 1997). Habermas and Bohman are proposing, then, that social workers assess and consider the relations among economic poverty, powerlessness, and communication incapacity when fighting for justice.

Certain political and social conditions have been identified as critical for effective participation in the ideal public sphere. These conditions include a set of civic rights. Habermas (1962/1989, 1986) recommends expansion of the **right of access**. All persons and groups affected by a public problem and the proposed policy or programmatic solutions must be able to participate in deliberations about this public problem. The effective operation of public spheres requires universal access. Additionally, group members must have the

right to speak and to influence political conversations. This should include the rights to introduce any idea or opinion into the deliberations, to question the ideas or opinions of others, and to express desires, needs, and reactions to the problem and the deliberations. Any speaker can challenge another's claims about what is real or what is best for the common good. Ideal democracies promote equality and effective political problem solving by providing all groups the **right to develop their public communication capacities**. Social workers should assess the degree to which a community honors these rights.

Habermas also advocates for laws and norms supporting publicity, so that those who attempt to exercise social power and to use their resource advantage for political domination are subject to the publicity of democratic processes (Habermas, 1962/1989). The norm of publicity means that arguments are not shielded and protected from scrutiny and that information and reasons relevant to the public debate are disclosed (Habermas, 2001).

CRITICAL PROBLEM FORMULATION AND ASSESSMENT: COMMUNICATION PROCESSES

Habermas, Bohman, and other critical theorists give attention to the features of ideal deliberation, "the give-and-take of reasons in a collective process of practical judgment" (Bohman, 1997, p. 325). Much public communication involves **systematic distortion**. Certain speakers violate the rules for successful communication-based cooperation but compel listeners to respond to their opinions anyway (Bohman, 2000). The powerful exclude some groups from participating in public deliberations because of their lack of power, wealth, status, expertise, or connections. Yet the powerful groups claim that they have a mandate for their policies. AIDS activists, such as members of Act-Up, were not allowed to participate in relevant forums for defining, discussing, and dealing with AIDS during the administration of President Reagan (Bohman, 1999a). A powerful group controlling a legislative assembly might not allow the airing of conflict or dissent during deliberations about matters of central importance to the state. Yet this powerful group claims that it represents the people's interests. An executive director provides client groups no opportunity to place items on the agendas for board meetings, yet claims he starts where the clients are. Women are repeatedly blocked in their efforts to chair a community task force, but the male leaders still assert that deliberations are inclusive and fair. Politicians engage in empty public speech and promises that never result in the pledged or predicted actions (Bohman, 2000).

Critical theorists label ideal communication as *nondistorted, authentic, inclusive, dialogical,* or *rational*. The public conversation is free from any use of coercion, control, or manipulation. Participants are honest and sincere in their assertions. People across many social groups or even across societies are invited to participate in deliberations. The claims, interpretations, and arguments of these diverse groups are heard and honored. Forum members attempt to promote dialogue characterized by mutual respect and mutual perspective taking. Deliberations have a back-and-forth quality and do not become monologues. Ideal speech situations are rational. The best arguments prevail. The ideal speech situation is like the perfect town meeting. All community groups listen to one another and together try to determine how best to understand the public problem, agreeing to find a remedy that is reasonable and acceptable to all. Social workers should collect information and make judgments about the degree to which communication is distorted or authentic.

CRITICAL PROBLEM FORMULATION AND ASSESSMENT: PUBLIC PROBLEM SOLVING

Critical theorists like Habermas were influenced by the American pragmatists. Deliberations must lead to practical judgments and solve public problems (Bohman, 1997). Habermas theorized about the ideal structural arrangements, capacities, conditions, and communication processes to contribute to the advancement of democracy. He posited that full or deep democracy is achieved only when public groups participate in deliberations about politics, policies, and problem solutions and when the forums for deliberation provide opportunities to achieve consensus. The concept of **consensus** refers to mutual and cooperative agreement to a decision considered reasonable by all. Referring to Figure 13.2, we can summarize this model of justice work by the proposition that societies that develop equitable structural arrangements, foster the development of the communication capacities of all citizens, create conditions ensuring the rights to participate and be heard, and regulate deliberations so that they are dialogical and reasonable will more often arrive at legitimate and effective political solutions than societies lacking these qualities and commitments.

Proposed solutions are considered legitimate in ideal speech situations because all participants recognize that the final decisions take into account the concerns and reasons of all groups with a stake in the outcome of the deliberations (Bohman, 1996). Solutions are considered legitimate also because participants appreciate that the rules governing the public forum were fair and not tyrannical. Participants are held accountable to each other for their arguments and have offered good reasons (Habermas, 2001). Solutions arrived at through ideal communication tend to be effective. Members develop commitments during deliberations to the careful implementation of the agreed-upon solution. Decision making benefits also from the integration of multiple perspectives on the problematic situation into a common perspective. Communication under conditions of ideal speech results in uncorrupted and rational interpretations of the public problem (what is so rather than what the institutional dominators claim is so) and thus facilitates emancipatory problem solving (Feagin & Vera, 2001).

Without the legitimacy obtained by genuine democratic agreements (Bohman, 1996), groups may reluctantly comply with the political decisions of the powerful because they see no viable alternatives or they cannot afford to ignore the regime's will. However, such compliance hardly motivates committed and effective problem solving. Some groups engage in systematic resistance to the public problem solving and challenge decisions and policies appraised as illegitimate because they do not meet standards of political equality or rationality. Repeated attempts to bypass democratic deliberations often result in serious doubts about the legitimacy of the governing body and a withdrawal from civic engagement that is dangerous to democracy and its citizens (Habermas, 2001).

CRITICAL INTERVENTION: FOSTERING DEMOCRACY

The model of justice work pioneered by Jurgen Habermas has many implications for social work practice. Only a few can be discussed here. Habermas calls for social workers to become involved in politics, and to work specifically to improve the processes of public communication and problem solving.

The assessment should focus on areas of breakdown and failure in public deliberations. The characteristics of ideal speech can be used as a tool to gauge the gap between reality and what is possible. Such an assessment might be used with governmental institutions, social work agencies, and smaller deliberative bodies such as the family and peer group.

Critical theory–oriented justice intervention requires that social workers learn to use institutions, the law, and politics to improve the procedural and distributive conditions necessary to political equality and effective and responsive political problem solving. Logical projects might include voting rights legislation, campaign rights reform, and efforts to regulate public affairs discourse (Bohman, 1996). Social workers should build the communicative capacities, resources, spaces, and opportunities of the voiceless or silenced client groups they serve. Specifically, social workers might lend support to social and educational movements that build communicative capacities, fight for public attention to the voiceless and for adding the concerns of excluded groups to policy-making agendas, help fund efforts to form alternative public spheres, support collective challenges to the dominant group's interpretations, and work to make grievances public and to expand the arenas and forums for communal deliberation.

LEARNING ACTIVITIES

1. Exercise your sociological imagination. Identify two or three important personal experiences, and trace how these experiences were influenced by historical processes, public policies, or large social structures and organizations (for example, economic cycles, demographic changes, wars, migration, or widespread disease).

2. Place yourself in your society's social stratification system using membership categories such as social class, race, ethnicity, sexual orientation, gender, and religion. Now imagine several specific ways your life chances would change if you were cast into less privileged membership groups (from middle class to lower class or from Caucasian to African American, for example).

3. Compare and contrast the challenges faced by working-class, middle-class, and upper-class students at your college or university.

4. Try this way of conceptualizing power: Power is the ability to command someone to do something that he or she would prefer not to do. Reflect on how powerful you are. Who can command you? What are your reactions to taking orders? Whom do you command? How often do you consider the other person's feelings when giving orders? What lessons might you generalize to the daily experiences of powerless clients?

5. Inequality can be found in small-scale social systems as well as in societies and social institutions. Recall daily life with your family when you were young. Identify the major activities or chores necessary to your family's survival and growth. How was this work typically divided? Reflect on any inequalities in the household management of labor, and relate these to differences in family members' gender, social status, role, or age.

6. What price would you place on social privilege and advantage? Compare briefly the life chances and opportunities of the members of different groups in society's stratification system. How much money would you require to accept arrangements for your grandchild to be born to a low-status family in a neighborhood with deteriorating schools, high crime rates, and few high-paying jobs as opposed to a high-status family in a safe, exclusive, and resource-rich community? What would be fair compensation? What does this exercise tell you about inequality?

7. Reflect on how gender matters. Think about your family, your school, your community, and your society. Across the life span, how are females treated differently than males? How is differential treatment manifest at the large-scale level of social structure (political or economic) and culture? How is differential treatment manifest at the small-scale level of face-to-face interaction? What are some consequences for this differential treatment at the level of personality and individual behavior? What advantages do men experience at each level? How are men disadvantaged by a social system organized to perpetuate gender inequality?

8. Discuss with several students what you each mean by the concept of *citizenship*. Consider how each of you might become a more active and engaged citizen. How might you help clients realize their rights and obligations as citizens? Report on your insights here.

9. Construct a utopian or ideal society. Describe how your society or community deals with stewardship of resources, the organization of work, the exchange of goods and services, governance, biological reproduction, socialization, social control, and the creation and use of cultural meanings. Summarize how your design minimizes the problems associated with inequality, social difference, and power imbalances common to most contemporary societies.

ADDITIONAL RESOURCES

Additional resources are available on the book companion website at **www.thomsonedu.com/ social_work/forte**. Resources include key terms, tutorial quizzes, links to related websites, and lists of additional resources for furthering your research.

AFTERWORD

CHAPTER 14

Multitheory Practice and Routes to Integration

Hallmark Institute/IndexStock

The social work profession has a vast knowledge base. It includes reports by social workers on research, practice, and policy accumulated over more than 100 years. It includes information from books, studies, policy analyses, and recorded oral histories collected by social workers and borrowed from dozens of other disciplines. If we think of the knowledge base as the profession's library, the library is huge. For instance, each social worker can access knowledge about dozens of different theoretical frameworks for understanding human behavior and the environment. Social workers also can check out library holdings on a multitude of practice theories for helping client systems and for improving environmental contexts. Unfortunately, the profession's knowledge base is not located in one actual library. Unlike patrons of public libraries, social work knowledge users must search widely to find librarians with expertise on the profession's entire collection, and few refined and tested tools are available for selecting and integrating the knowledge needed to meet contemporary practice challenges.

In this final chapter, I will try to help you map a route through the Human Behavior and the Social Environment wing of the profession's virtual library. I will review some of the relevant strategies for knowledge assembly developed by social workers and therapists from allied professions, and expand on my own dialogical communication approach. I will remind you of the tools for knowledge translation that I have introduced and used in the previous 13 chapters of the book. I will conclude with some suggestions for the use of knowledge from multiple theories when collaborating with team members, helping clients, and deliberating about practice challenges. When possible, this chapter's discussion will use my recommended tools for knowledge building—role models, conceptual models, metaphors, and maps—to clarify the presentation of ideas.

THE CONCEPT OF KNOWLEDGE INTEGRATION

In this section, I will introduce you to a new way of thinking about the term **integration.** The verb *integrate* has many synonyms, including *incorporate, assemble, combine, coordinate, join, consolidate, desegregate, mix, assimilate, blend, unify,* and *converge.* Its antonyms, or opposites, include *segregate, differentiate,* and *diverge.* You may have used some of these synonyms or antonyms for *integrate* in your everyday conversations, and you have probably learned some of the different meanings of the noun *integration* in your social work classes.

In your practice classes, you may have read about *personality integration,* a concept referring to a goal of some counselors and clients. Personality integration involves bringing together and organizing all aspects of the personality, including thoughts, feelings, desires, and behavioral tendencies, into a harmonious whole. The related concept of *systems integration* is taught in courses on family and organizational practice. It refers to the goal of bringing together the different parts of a family or social work agency so that they are coordinated as elements in a well-functioning system.

In your policy and policy practice classes, you may have covered processes of globalization and policies that facilitate or hinder international cooperation. Here you may have discussed the concept of *economic integration*. This term refers to the reduction of barriers between nations and to the harmonization of policies, standards, and regulations so that each nation's economy is included in a global system of trade. In your policy class, you probably learned about varied political ideologies, too, and the notion of *political integration* central to democracies. Each citizen can contribute something useful to the whole, and successful democracies incorporate or integrate all members and build on their different strengths. Unsuccessful governments, often because of their extreme political ideologies, leave societal members divided, alienated, or estranged from one another.

Your research teachers may have been less explicit in their use of the term *integration*. Nevertheless, you have learned to systematically integrate data into your analysis of a research topic or your evaluation of worker effectiveness. Your statistics instructor may have even introduced you to notions of *mathematical integration*.

A major theme of all social work field internships is integration. I am certain that you have heard this term used by your field coordinator, by your field supervisors, and by your practice teachers. In this usage, *integration* refers to linking what you learned in your academic classes with what you are learning day to day from direct experience with clients, and bringing back your field experiences to enrich the lessons at your school. In your classes covering content on human diversity, you have learned about *social integration,* the process of incorporating groups with different backgrounds (ethnic, racial, social class, sexual orientation, or religious, for example) into a neighborhood, community, or society as equal and collaborating partners. You have also learned about the history of discrimination and segregation and about the contemporary political, economic, and social barriers to the integration of very different social groups into peaceful and respect-giving collectives.

In the next sections, I will offer a new and very important variation on the concept of integration, a variation critical to human behavior and the social environment (HBSE) classes and to the application of HBSE knowledge in practice: **theoretical integration.** Let me conclude this section, however, with several quotations about integration. Schacht (1984) provides the following concise summary of the general meaning of the term: "Integration is both etymologically and conceptually related to ideas of oneness. It implies a reduction of multiplicity into a unitary form. All efforts to integrate . . . signify attempts, however piecemeal, to transform currently perceived multiplicities into a unified perspective" (p. 123). Bernstein, Goodman, and Epstein (1997) relate the term to knowledge application and suggest "competent social workers do not merely apply a single theory in their practice. Instead, they reflectively integrate multiple theories and values with each of their actions in different, complex, changing contexts" (p. 140).

THE CHALLENGE OF THEORETICAL PLURALISM

Let's next discuss why theoretical integration has become a necessity for contemporary social work practitioners. I began the chapter with a comparison of the social work knowledge base to a vast library. The theory or HBSE wing is large, disorganized, and filled with dark corners and hard-to-reach shelves. Contemporary scientists and social philosophers use the term **theoretical pluralism** to characterize the current scene.

PLURALISTIC SOCIETIES AND MULTITHEORY PRACTICE ARENAS

This is an extension of the concept of cultural pluralism. In sociology and anthropology, societies are often characterized by the degree of uniformity among their member groups. In pluralistic societies, many different groups, such as religious organizations, professional associations, or ethnic minorities, demand some degree of autonomy and protection for their traditions. Advocates of pluralism believe that societies benefit from the acceptance of such differences. Pragmatist and symbolic interactionist theorists, for example, often argue that reality is multiperspectival. Regarding the social realm, William James (1907/1958) asserted "the universe is many" (p. 92). Different spheres of reality are associated with different human enterprises: art, science, religion, dream states, sexuality, ritual, play, commerce, and so on. Each sphere has a distinctive language of symbols, and thus distinctive experiences are generated for members of each symbolic world. George Herbert Mead agreed with this view and argued that, consequently, knowledge is enhanced by appreciation of plural perspectives. As indicated in the Chapter 10 discussion of the interactionist appreciation for diversity and international-mindedness, Mead's position applauds efforts to gain familiarity with minority groups, with powerless peoples, and with various social worlds that present alternatives to any dominant versions of reality. Andersen (1991) advanced the pluralistic theme articulated by James and Mead. He encourages us to replace our notion of *universe*, which comes from the Latin and means "turn into one," with the idea of a *multiverse*.

The complexity of the intellectual life and the professional work of scientists and applied scientists is like the complexity of social participation in a contemporary pluralistic society. Social work requires communication across disciplines and the use of multiple theories. One paradigm cannot adequately illuminate all facets of the pluralistic social and theoretical universe. Social work requires that practitioners get along with neighbors with different backgrounds and traditions. Theoretical pluralists believe that the social work knowledge base is enriched by the contributions of diverse and different theoretical communities.

The metaphors familiar to students of cultural pluralism can help us understand theoretical pluralism. Pluralistic societies are like giant stew pots. Different groups are added to the stew, lending their own flavor yet ultimately producing a complex but unified broth. Theoretical pluralism holds that the masterful social work chef gathers many different theoretical perspectives when shopping. The chef prepares a final stew (knowledge for use) that incorporates the distinct flavors of each theoretical ingredient.

Pluralistic societies are polyvocal. Many speakers join the call and response of democratic deliberations in the crowded public forum: men and women, young and old, Protestant and Muslim, conservative and liberal, straight and gay. Responsible leaders listen to all these voices before making decisions. Theoretical pluralism holds that the contemporary practice scene includes many voices, the voices of traditional theorists and the voices of new or alternative theorists. Each theorist has a different story to tell about human behavior and the social environment (Cronen, Chen, & Pearce, 1988). Participants in wise deliberations about practice challenges and public problems listen to as many of these theoretical voices as possible.

Pluralistic societies are like a multiethnic and multilanguage community where the members of different neighborhoods accept and find ways to communicate with one another. Theoretical pluralism holds that social work is like a professional community within the larger community of all applied scientists. The community includes other disciplinary groups and professions with many different theoretical languages. Yet despite differences, community members can coexist as peaceful neighbors. They can learn to interact with others respectfully, and even to work together to solve problems of importance to the set of neighborhoods. Some theory users may even become multilingual and learn to speak in the theoretical languages of those from distant homelands.

When I went to graduate school, I learned an ego psychological approach to helping in each of my theory and practice courses. I only heard about two or three other theoretical approaches, but was not taught to speak these languages. The social work professional library has grown rapidly since the 1970s. In Chapter 1, I documented the proliferation of theoretical frameworks. Current HBSE textbooks introduce more than 40 different theoretical approaches. Social work practitioners surveyed about their theoretical preferences in the last several decades identified more than 18 different theoretical frameworks guiding their practice. Prochaska and Norcross (1999), experts on theoretical diversity, estimated that there were more than 400 theoretical approaches available to therapists. Professional helpers (social workers, psychologists, nurses, applied sociologists, and others) constitute an interconnected discursive community but one with multiple theoretical traditions and languages.

The Potential Benefits of Theoretical Pluralism

There are many good reasons to appreciate this theoretical pluralism. The complexity of the social work job and the multidimensionality of human transactions with the environment necessitate the development and accumulation of multiple theories (Corey, 2001). Any effort to understand a multicultural society demands a grasp of multiple languages and of various cultural traditions. Likewise, no one theoretical approach provides adequate knowledge for all the jobs faced by generalist social workers. Safran and Messer (1997/2003) suggest "the pluralistic perspective holds that all theories are necessarily limited and that the best way of approaching the truth is through the ongoing confrontation of multiple, competing theories with data and with each other" (p. 7).

Social workers also appreciate increasingly that human behavior must be understood as situated in a particular time and a particular place (Phillips, 1993). Social systems change over time, and different theoretical perspectives vary in their ability to describe aspects of these systems at different points in their history. Human and social systems act differently in different places. Multiple theories provide the tools necessary to appreciate these ecology-based differences.

Social workers assume a holistic orientation. Human behavior is influenced by the interplay of bodily processes and structures, mental processes and structures, social processes and structures, and cultural meaning systems. Many in the profession recognize that "any theoretical system is a tentative and partial explanation of the person" (Lecomte, Castonquay, Cyr, & Sabourin, 1993, p. 491). The use of multiple theories will help us better attend to the biological, psychological, social, and spiritual dimensions and their interrelationships.

The process of theoretical diversification is an indication of the quality of a professional group's library, too (Slunecko, 1999). The size and diversity of a book collection, for instance, tells us much about a professional's commitment to knowledge-based practice. A professional knowledge base with size, depth, and range provides more possibilities for understanding and for helping solve member and community problems than does a small and narrow base.

New developments in the philosophy of science support the contention that the profession's knowledge should be pluralistic. Stanley Messer (1987, 1992/ 2003) provided an early statement in support of theoretical pluralism. Reality does not exist independent of its interpretation, he argued. Our interpretation or perspective on reality depends on our position or vantage point in the larger social context. Migrant workers on the Eastern shore of the United States have very different notions about economic realities and their fairness than stockbrokers working on Wall Street, New York City. Since there are many strata and subcultures in any society, there are multiple perspectives on reality. This is good. Multiple interpretations of reality are legitimate and desirable. Contact between groups with different versions of reality can spur the creation of new knowledge, and this increases the resources available for practical problem solving.

The scientific community and the community of applied scientists also construct multiple theoretical interpretations of reality. Knowledge is socially constructed by groups of theory creators who interact in particular circumstances. The variability in historical era and environmental context in which knowledge is developed results in multiple versions of reality. Some are useful. Some are not useful. Nazi scientists working in labor camps conducted research based on their beliefs in an abhorrent theory of a German master race. This theory has been widely repudiated since. Tucker, Garvin, and Sarri

(1997) give the example of the recent emergence of Afrocentric theories and "queer" theories. These theories were created from a vantage point in the United States where the oppression of African Americans and of people with alternative sexual orientations was blindingly visible. Social workers are making frequent use of Afrocentric and queer theories.

The postpositivists, successors to the logical positivist philosophers of science who grounded science in sensory observations and embraced the ideal of seeking the one truth, acknowledge that there are many different viewpoints on reality (Reid, 1997). They accept the value of theoretical pluralism. Alternative paradigms and theoretical perspectives can become important additions to the profession's toolbox. Postpositivists offer one caveat. Useful knowledge is knowledge backed by evidence, and the gatekeepers for progressive knowledge building (entry into the profession's master library) must subject new theoretical candidates to evaluation by high standards.

In earlier chapters, I have referred to the multitheory practice universe and to a conception of science as the coordination of efforts by scientists from many different communities, each speaking a different theoretical language. Clinicians and researchers have shown an increased appreciation for these ideas of theoretical pluralism (Kurtines & Silverman, 1999). They recognize, for instance, that effective practitioners are not limited to a single theoretical reference system, but integrate various theoretical systems into their knowledge base and helping repertoire (Lewis & Kelemen, 2002). Theoretical pluralism is the alternative to **theoretical parochialism.** Parochial theory users are like neighbors with a restricted and intolerant outlook. They avoid and hate contact with foreigners or members of other theoretical factions. Different theoretical lifestyles are condemned, not encouraged. The primary allegiance of parochial theory users is to their neighborhood clique, and they will seek power for this in-group no matter what the cost to rival factions and to other neighborhood theory groups. They make weak excuses or blame others when their monolithic theory does not produce the desired results.

Theoretical pluralists reject parochialism and seek the more comprehensive understanding that multiple theories provide. They avoid nonproductive or destructive conflict with adherents to different theoretical traditions (Fischer, 1986). Critical and comparative examination of different theoretical approaches is valued. Such inquiry is like talking across the table to a fellow citizen who has very different ideas about solving public problems but is committed to working for the common good. Multitheory users like their access to new ways of thinking and the stimulation of creative action that follows cross-boundary exchanges (Netting & O'Connor, 2003). Theoretical pluralists will not force all clients, problems, and events into one theoretical framework even when the fit is poor. Theoretical pluralists want to learn new theoretical languages (Cronen, 1995), and they resist the inhibition of thought associated with the uniformity and conformity of the parochial view.

Social workers have long had an appreciation for cultural diversity, and our profession prides itself on its commitment to affirm the cultural orientations of diverse groups. Theoretical pluralism challenges social workers to replicate their appreciation for cultural diversity with an appreciation for theoretical diversity.

ALTERNATIVE MAPS FOR THEORETICAL INTEGRATION IN A PLURALISTIC WORLD

Theoretical pluralism can be dealt with in numerous ways. Each is like a map for traversing a landscape with many paths and some obstacles (Lampropoulos, 2000). Mahoney (1993) compared these approaches to land maps. He reported on psychological research into how subjects in experiments choose paths on a map and extended several findings to theoretical integrationists. First, subjects resisted changing their originally chosen paths even when these paths no longer guided them toward their originally chosen goals. Practitioners too must be wary of clinging to a practice theory or a way of integrating various theories that loses its utility for pathfinding. Second, study participants preferred maps that increased rather than decreased the number of routes that were available for future travel. Practitioners likewise can learn to value the various maps for theoretical integration because these maps increase the number of routes to our problem formulation, assessment, and intervention destinations. In this section, I will review the major strategies for theoretical integration, provide examples of each, and report on some identified limitations.

THE NO THEORY OR ONE THEORY MAP

One approach to theoretical pluralism is to ignore it. The no theory and the one theory stances were reviewed in Chapter 1. Here, I will briefly write about the one theory approach to theoretical integration.

The one theory practitioners are like language purists (Norcross & Newman, 1992/2003). Jeeves the Butler exemplifies this approach. He is committed to and trained in the use of proper English and frowns at those who speak inferior languages or mongrel dialects of English. For the one theory practitioner, only their orientation or theoretical perspective is right (Downing, 2004). This theoretical language is assumed to be adequate for all clients and all problems regardless of different client needs or different client membership backgrounds.

The one theory practitioner needs a simple map for navigating the pluralistic world. The local terrain is mapped by the one theory cartographer, but he or she need not explore further. The one theory practitioner simply refuses to venture into foreign lands or other neighborhoods. Many university sociologists that I know, for example, confine themselves to their own departments, indifferent to the knowledge developments in adjacent departments such as social work or psychology. Users of only one theory are insular and proud of their pure lineage. They believe that theoretical schools should be kept distinct because they are like different species, such as dogs and birds, or different breeds. Mating is impossible. Hybrids cannot be grown. If cross-fertilization does occur, only monsters result. Different theoretical perspectives are "fundamentally incompatible and disparate" (Schacht, 1984, p. 115), and there is no route to integration.

The metaphor of the Iron Curtain can be extended to one theory practitioners (Mahoney, 1993). This "curtain" was a geographic and social barrier erected by the Soviet Union after World War II to separate communist and noncommunist nations. All travel and communication across the border was controlled. It sealed off Soviet-dependent Eastern European countries from open contact with the West and other noncommunist areas. Leaders of the Soviet Union asserted and backed up with violence their principle regarding theoretical integration: the communist way was the only acceptable way of life. Leaders of one theory practice campaigns seek similar control over social work travel.

MAPS FOR MULTITHEORY INTEGRATION

Much of this section builds on the intellectual work of the psychotherapy integration movement. This is a social movement of professionals that began officially with the formation of the **Society for the Exploration of Psychotherapy Integration (SEPI)** in 1983. SEPI is now an international association of mostly psychotherapists (Corey, 2001). The movement has roots in studies of psychotherapy in the 1930s and 1940s "concerned with the translation of concepts and methods from one psychological or psychotherapeutic system into the language and procedures of another" (Gold, 1993, p.4). The society has focused on issues related to the selection and blending of elements of various theoretical orientations. Society members share the conviction that the spirit of theoretical integration better helps clients than the spirit of segregation and theory isolation. SEPI members have endeavored to expand the range of concepts, strategies, techniques, and theories available to practitioners by encouraging cross-theory communication. Arkowitz (1992) characterizes the society's labor as "various attempts to move beyond the confines of single-school approaches in order to see what can be learned from other perspectives. It is characterized by an openness to various ways of integrating diverse theories and techniques"(p. 262).

Social work has a less vigorous but still important tradition of theoretical integration. Phillips (1993), for example, argued that "integrationists challenge us to choose from a variety of theories and treatment alternatives . . . to be much more creative and flexible in our work" (p. 255). Social work contributions to theoretical integration will be noted in the next sections also.

Four maps for theoretical integration will be presented. All the mapmakers share a belief in theoretical integration and urge theory users to range widely in the libraries of many different professions, disciplines, and theoretical perspectives (Mahrer, 1989).

INTEGRATION VIA COMMONALITIES: THE COMMON FACTORS MAP   The common factors approach starts with a process of desegregation. The unique contributions of each theoretical approach to practice are separated from the **common factors**, those elements that contribute to the positive outcomes of the helping process whatever the theoretical perspective. Then a process of reintegration begins, and theoretical approaches are aligned on the basis of their possession of these common factors (Mahoney, 1993). The process can be compared to that of a community organizer who attempts to understand the unique cultural orientations of different groups in a multiethnic community, but then identifies the common and shared human qualities of the members of all the groups. The organizer understands differences but accentuates commonalities—what is shared by all, not what differentiates people—as the groups participate in collaborative community-building projects.

Common factors unite diverse approaches to healing across historical periods, cultural groups, social institutions, and theoretical perspectives. Integrationists who have studied theoretical approaches to practice have generated several lists of common factors. Rosenzweig (1936/2002), the first theorist to identify common factors, included catharsis, the worker's personality, consistency of the rationale for helping and of the conceptual framework, and provision of alternative formulations of the biopsychosocial events troubling the client system on his list. Weinberger (1993) reported more recently that practice theories share an emphasis on a positive helping relationship or working alliance, an appreciation for certain helper qualities such as empathy and nonjudgmental acceptance, a structuring of the planned change process into phases, expectations for positive change, and support.

When we compare theories to languages, the search for common factors in helping theories is like the search for conceptual universals by linguists. Common or shared concepts that transcend various local vocabularies are identified and inventoried (Lampropoulos, 2001). Here are two relevant examples. At the annual student advocacy day in Maryland, the National Association of Social Workers provided a name tag to each participating student. Each tag included words for the concept "I greet you," but the words were in dozens of different languages—*bonjour* for French, *ciao* for Italian, *aloha* for Hawaiian, and so on. The greeting was universal, but the spelling and pronunciation of the greeting word varied. Think of this second example. For theory users, the concept *empathy* would be a universal with a shared meaning for all speakers of a helping language but different shades of meanings depending on theoretical orientation. Each theory, like each dialect of English, would attach additional and diverse specific meanings to the universal concept.

The **transtheoretical approach** exemplifies the use of the common factors map. Its developers discovered that all leading practice theorists recommend similar "processes of change"—"covert and overt activities that people engage in to alter affect, thinking, behavior, or relationships related to a particular problem or more general pattern of living" (Prochaska & Norcross, 1999, p. 11). Each theoretical approach gives preference, however, to a different process. Critical theorists favor consciousness-raising processes, whereas psychodynamic theorists prefer cathartic processes and corrective emotional experiences. All practice theorists also apply these change processes to common "stages of change" or points in the helping process (precontemplation, contemplation, preparation, action, and maintenance). Advocates of different theoretical approaches, however, may conceptualize the stages and stage-specific intervention tasks in somewhat different ways. Prochaska (2000) studied 184 family service agencies to test the universality of this common factors approach at the macro level of practice. She provided empirical support demonstrating that the transtheoretical model of stages accurately described many organizations' change to time-limited counseling services in response to the demands of managed health care providers.

The common factors map for theoretical integration has its critics. Commonalities may exist at a very abstract level (helpful practitioners make interpretations). In practical situations, great differences are apparent in the way the common factors are operationalized by different theory users. The psychodynamic, behavioral, and humanistic approaches to interpretation of patterns, for example, are more unlike than like each other. Additionally, what seems like a factor unifying varying theories may not be as common as assumed (Lampropoulos, 2001). For example, when working with applied behaviorists at a school for emotionally disturbed children, I listened and observed carefully. The concept *positive relationship* may have been endorsed, but there was no evidence in day-to-day practice that this concept was a significant part of the behaviorists' helping work. Finally, there is no empirical evidence that any list of common factors contributes harmoniously to the unique features of each theoretical approach that social workers use (Sheldon, 1978). For example, conflict or critical theory–based approaches to public advocacy are probably less effective when practitioners empathize with oppressors.

The common factors map is still a helpful tool for navigating across a multitheory landscape. This map directs us to assemble and integrate common therapeutic factors, such as humanistic worker qualities and facilitative relationship processes, into our professional toolboxes. As we travel through the multitheory practice world, we can ask repeatedly: What do I have in common with those who speak different theoretical languages? This map still permits us to reserve certain compartments of our toolboxes for those helping factors specific to our favorite theoretical perspectives. My toolbox includes a caring and accepting stance for all my work but also a section for symbolic interactionist theories and helping procedures. The common factors map also indicates that a good route to breaking down barriers differentiating language speakers from various theory communities is to focus on our similarities (we all aim to lend clients a hopeful vision of the future) more than our differences (we conceptualize problematic client–environment transactions in dissimilar ways).

INTEGRATION OF TECHNIQUES: THE ECLECTIC MAP The **eclectic approach** to navigating across a terrain including many different theoretical communities directs us to look everywhere for specific techniques to help clients. It requires a commitment to assembling from a variety of theories the techniques, and the concepts and theories supporting these techniques, that work best (Norcross, 1986). Those who use the eclectic approach vary in how systematic, planned, conscious, and critical they are in the assembling and use of techniques and procedures (Feixas & Botella, 2004).

Intuitive eclectics select helping strategies and techniques from various theories based on life experiences, practice style, practice preferences, and hunches. They closely monitor their use of helping interventions, and if clients do not respond to one technique, then the worker selects a different one from the toolbox.

Guided eclectics accumulate techniques from different approaches based on the guidelines from each theory. Recommendations from behaviorists for when and how to use systematic desensitization are carefully followed, for example.

Technical eclectics add techniques to their toolboxes based on established efficacy. Most frequently they choose techniques from different theoretical approaches, and less often they assemble the theoretical metaphors and assumptions of different frameworks. Selection is based on empirical evidence for the effectiveness of the selected techniques. The technical eclectic questions whether a given technique has proven utility before adding it to her or his toolbox. Fischer (1986) reports that technical eclectics make "a commitment to being guided in practice by what works, a commitment that takes precedence over devotion to any theoretical orientation" (p. 325). Technical eclectics are sometimes atheoretical, therefore, and focused more on collecting validated helping tools than on grappling with theoretical diversity (Norcross & Newman, 1992/2003) or synthesizing a set of helping theories (Coady & Lehmann, 2001b).

Systematic eclectics integrate techniques chosen because of an explicit logic or framework indicating which techniques to use with which client, with which particular problems, for what desired outcome, under what set of specific circumstances (Lampropoulos, 2001). Systematic eclectics make "use of a wide range of theories and techniques that are selected on the basis of their relevance to each unique client situation" (Coady & Lehmann, 2001a, p. 8). The logic for matching techniques to situations may consider any or all of the following variables: stage of the helping process, characteristics of the client system problem, the client's psychiatric diagnosis, the personality characteristics of the client, the qualities of the practitioner, and the characteristics of the environment and the setting in which helping services are provided (Lampropoulos, 2000; Patterson, 1989). Assessment of the client–worker–environment configuration precedes the selection of the best strategy for aiding the client (Mahrer, 1989). Systematic eclectics may also match clients with a theoretical approach. These theory users are "geared towards an overall framework that provides for effective and responsible assigning of a particular client with a particular symptom to a certain therapist of a specific therapeutic school" (Slunecko, 1999, p. 132).

Returning to my metaphor of applied science as a multicultural society, the eclectic map directs workers to identify tools from many different nations without concern about the culture or language of the toolmakers. An American's personal collection might include a Swiss watch, a German car, a cell phone designed and made in Japan, and a computer with software from the United States. Each tool will be helpful in different circumstances. An eclectic theory user might incorporate techniques including a sweat ceremony derived from a Native American spiritual healing tradition; a role-playing technique created by Jacob Moreno, the great role theorist; and a dream analysis procedure from the Freudian literature.

Critics of the eclectic map for dealing with theoretical pluralism have several complaints. Eclectics are prone to the undisciplined and sloppy selection of techniques (Robbins, Chatterjee, & Canda, 1998; Simons & Aigner, 1985). Concepts and techniques from different theoretical traditions and practice models are often mixed and matched with minimal self-awareness; with insufficient attention to the evidence supporting or failing to support the elements added; and with too little sensitivity to client variables, including the client's goals, perspectives, and situational constraints. Eclectics who talk about their tool collection may sound as though they are speaking gobbledygook: a bizarre mixture of words that make little sense to the listener. They are like parents who start speaking the jargon of their teenage child with minimal understanding of the local slang. Finally, intervention techniques and procedures are not like watches, cars, or cell phones. They are not material products that can be removed from their cultures of origin without affecting their essence. Techniques and procedures are theory-specific; each theory provides its own way of explaining reality, assessing and framing client problems, and generating methods to solve problems (Mahrer, 1989). A sweat lodge makes no sense when separated from its matrix of theoretical assumptions, concepts, propositions, and generalizations. Messer argues, therefore, against eclecticism by observing "a psychological procedure can not be administered like a pill, but will be shaped by the language and framework in which it is couched. When we move from the biological sphere to the arena of social science, we enter the realm of human meanings" (Lazarus & Messer, 1991, p. 156).

The eclectic map for theoretical integration directs the practitioner to add many techniques to his or her toolbox and to use the techniques that work for the particular helping job whatever the original theoretical language of the technique. Workers with a toolbox with many techniques will have a large range of intervention choices, and they are more likely than workers with only a few tools to find helping strategies acceptable to client systems. The eclectic map directs us to relate to and converse with theory users from different theoretical communities by asking for demonstrations of their problem-solving strategies and techniques. When there is evidence of effectiveness, we ask for the permission and knowledge necessary to make the technique our own.

INTEGRATION OF THEORETICAL APPROACHES: THE ASSIMILATIVE MAP The **assimilative integration** of theoretical approaches requires the creation of a new superordinate or overarching conceptual framework into which other theories will fit (Norcross & Newman, 1992/2003). The umbrella conceptualization integrates and organizes many theories and capitalizes on the strengths of all the theoretical elements assimilated into the larger framework (Safran & Messer,

1997/2003). The umbrella framework may integrate certain theoretical traditions or attempt to incorporate all existing therapy schools (Lemmens, de Ridder, & van Lieshout, 1994). Developers of the umbrella framework, for example, might assemble and integrate various disciplinary approaches under one disciplinary leader like the theorists who assert that psychology, sociology, and even social work should be ordered under the master discipline of biology.

The assimilative approach has parallels to the process of socialization of immigrants into a new country. The United States is a nation but also a concept. Those arriving at our shore have the opportunity to adopt the structure of language, values, beliefs, laws, and customs that characterize our society. With time and effort, they understand the core concepts of this nation and earn the status of citizen. They add an appreciation of the American way of life to their memories of their native culture. Concurrently, elements of the immigrant group's language, traditions, and practices become part of this great American experiment in democracy.

The assimilative approach is also like a master code of discourse and conduct that synthesizes different communities. My university provides a policy and procedural framework that integrates diverse groups on campus. I will address the issue of language only. English is our university's primary language, but it is supplemented by sign language at cultural and community events for general audiences such as the graduation ceremony. The school's procedural guidelines ensure the provision also of translation for events directed toward speech subcommunities such as Hispanic Americans. The code also prohibits hate speech directed against minorities because of a minority member's race, sexual orientation, gender, or religion. Assimilated university members relate to and converse with others by operating within this larger framework for language use and community behavior.

Finally, the assimilative approach is like the process of **syncretism** studied by language experts. This refers to the fusion of different inflected forms of speech into a more homogeneous language characterized by reduced use of inflections. In other words, there is a tendency of language users over time to reduce their use of inflections (stress and intonation, the rise and fall of voice pitch in word usage, for example) as they are assimilated into the dominant language. My great grandmother who lived in Italy most of her life spoke very few English words and did so with a singing quality similar to that of spoken Italian. My grandmother, Italian born but a U.S resident from early adolescence, spoke mostly English but with a clearly Italian sound. My father spoke a clear and standard version English with occasional hints of Italian word usage and intonation, and I speak English with a flattened and fairly indistinguishable American style. The assimilative approach to theoretical integration focuses on the juxtaposing, joining, and eventual merging of different theoretical language communities into one community characterized by fewer distinctions.

Social work provides many examples of the assimilative approach. Ecological theories and systems theories, for example, have been integrated into a larger ecosystems paradigm that most social workers learn. Ecosystems theorists argue that other theoretical traditions can be assimilated into this superordinate conceptual framework. Advocates of this grand and comprehensive conceptual system want it to serve as a way to incorporate all the knowledge available for social work use. Many HBSE textbooks use a holistic framework and integrate knowledge according to its contribution to assimilating knowledge about the biological, the psychological, the social, and the spiritual dimensions of human functioning (see Robbins et al., 1998, for example). Rigazio-Digilio, Goncalves, and Ivey (1996) specifically recommend a holistic framework for integrating theory, one that assimilates knowledge of the feeling self from the humanistic approaches, the thinking self from cognitive approaches, the behaving self from behavioral and social learning approaches, and the interpersonal self from interactional and systems theoretical approaches.

Simons and Aigner (1985) use an interactionist–role theory umbrella to integrate knowledge about seven common client problems. Practice theories and helping roles are organized according to their differential contribution to solving each problem area. Critical theory and social action practice models, for example, best illuminate the use of the advocate role with clients who lack opportunities. Communication or symbolic interactionist theory best informs the use of the mediator role to help resolve conflicting role expectations. Rational-emotive cognitive theory can guide social workers when enacting the confronter role to challenge a client's unrealistic role expectations. Each theoretical perspective is assimilated into their larger synthesis.

Slunecko (1999) elaborates on the attempt to establish a superordinate discipline, in which authority is delegated to a leading academic discipline and other disciplinary perspectives are subordinated to the leading science. For example, psychology, sociology, and social work knowledge are subordinated to the discipline of medicine. Helping professionals bring their disciplinary and theoretical perspectives to support and assist the higher-status medical professionals. Social workers are auxiliaries assimilated into the dominant medical culture. Knowledge claims are examined against the prioritized neurophysiological explanation of human behavior problems and integrated into a comprehensive biological paradigm.

Assimilative integration involves an additive learning process (Lampropoulos, 2001; Messer, 1992/2003). Theory users learn and maintain allegiance to a first or native theoretical language. Concepts and techniques from other theoretical traditions are incorporated after their meanings are transformed in accord with the dictates of the primary language. Both the imported theoretical language element and the primary theoretical language change as a result of the assimilation. The process involves a selective assimilation of theories, concepts, techniques, and attitudes after transforming the new elements into one's evolving theoretical approach to practice while adding some of the value of the elements' original theoretical meaning (Lazarus & Messer, 1991). In this textbook, I have acknowledged that most social work students learn the language of the ecosystems framework. New languages such as behaviorism are assimilated later into the primary ecosystems language. Assimilation is possible only when the meanings of imported concepts or techniques are compatible with the core assumptions and root metaphors of the primary language (the language's constitutive rules). The contemporary ecosystems framework, for example, assumes the interrelatedness of person and environment. Theoretical concepts based on a conception of persons as independent of, and separate from, social and physical contexts cannot be successfully incorporated without damaging the integrity and identity of the primary social work language.

The premise of this assimilative map to theoretical integration is that theory users "always encounter new theories and practices from an existing base in one theory" (Fraenkel & Pinsof, 2001, p. 60). There is a theoretical imprinting, and the first language forever influences our perceptions and our helping work. My work in theories for practice (Forte, 2001) started from my primary theoretical language of symbolic interactionism and then examined ten other theoretical frameworks. Selected concepts from each theory were translated into the language of interactionism and assimilated into a broader, expanded synthesis, a richer applied symbolic interactionism. The concept *ego defenses*, for example, was redefined in line with interactionism's emphasis on social relationships and communication. Ego defenses were transformed conceptually into strategies for developing verbal accounts of one's conduct that allow one to live with oneself and others despite being self-condemned and socially condemned for deviant impulses and actions.

There are potential landmines, detours, and obstacles that practitioners must avoid when using the assimilative map. Integrating theories into a larger framework substantially modifies and usually reduces the meaning and value of the integrated theoretical element. Many theory-specific concepts assimilated into the ecosystems framework become pale shadows of their former selves. The critical theory notion of oppression, for example, has a much richer meaning than the concept taught as part of ecosystems thinking. Some theories come from different language communities and do not mingle easily with those from other language communities (Mahrer, 1989). Critics assert, for example, that humanistic client-centered approaches are incompatible with behavioral approaches and a holistic umbrella theory merges these rival theories at peril. Nor can an umbrella framework do justice to all of the elements (explanation of client system problems, classification systems of problems and systems, conception of helping goals, and intervention methods) of each of the applied theoretical approaches incorporated into the larger whole (Lemmens et al., 1994). There is also the educational problem. Students who are taught integration through assimilation may become fluent in one language and borrow terms from other languages, but critics doubt that they become fluent in multiple theoretical languages. Finally, Lampropoulos (2001) warns that the creation of umbrella frameworks represents the creation of additional theories and contributes to the problem of theory proliferation.

The assimilative map directs the worker to seek a clever and useful way to organize his or her theoretical toolbox. In your travels as a social work professional, you can collect and integrate various theories into a super and carefully arranged toolbox starting from your primary language. This language is assigned to the choice sections of the toolbox, and elements of other theoretical languages are added across your career as they can be fit into the other sections.

So far, I have reviewed three maps that can guide your efforts to cross a multitheory continent. I have described and illustrated each, and pointed out limitations. The three maps highlight different destinations. The common factors map directs the traveler to assemble and integrate into his or her toolbox a set of therapeutic or curative factors shared across theories. The eclectic map directs the social work traveler to assemble and integrate a large set of different techniques, and the assimilative map directs the explorer to learn a primary helping language and integrate additional theories as possible.

These maps for integration have several problems. First, the mapmakers for each approach focus mostly on the final product of knowledge integration, not the intellectual and social process of integrating theories. Second, therapists and theorists of therapy have done most of the map development work. They assume that knowledge is used to guide one-to-one helping work rather than practice with all sizes of social systems. They emphasize the role of therapist rather than performance in various social work roles, including administrator, policy analyst, advocate, and researcher. Maps for integration must be useful for multirole social workers, too (Thomas, 1997). Finally, the mapmakers tend to assume that there is one best route for navigating theoretical pluralism.

In the next subsection, I will present a process-oriented map for knowledge integration that will be useful to generalist social workers. My focus will be not on the destination but on the journey, not on a final integrative product but on **episodes of integration.**

INTEGRATION BY COMMUNICATION: THE DIALOGICAL MAP I have discussed the challenges of dealing with theoretical pluralism and documented that social workers and other helping professionals now use many theoretical languages and vocabularies. I have also discussed how social workers learn a generalist foundation for practice and are expected to help people in many different settings with many different client systems and many kinds of problems. Social workers will need to cooperate with allies from numerous other professions and many disciplinary backgrounds. Social workers will help clients who speak many different natural languages and who believe in assorted everyday theories. The dialogical map for theoretical integration assumes that the major obstacle facing practitioners in a multitheory world will be language differences. The dialogical map offers a set of path-finding tools and strategies designed to promote understanding among interactants who speak differently (Mahrer, 1989; Sheldon, 1978).

The dialogical or "linguistic" map directs the practitioner to look for opportunities for integration. Advocates of this approach are not looking ahead to a final or complete theoretical integration, but are focused primarily on improving the communication between the members of different theoretical schools. Episodes of integration for practical purposes might be followed by theoretical integration using the common factors, eclectic, or assimilative methods (Lemmens et al., 1994, p. 247).

The root metaphor for the dialogical approach is translation. The problem of translation across theoretical languages is like the problem of translating across cultures (Cronen, 1995). Applied science is conceptualized as a set of semiotic or symbol systems. Members of the same theoretical language community share a vocabulary and a way of talking that are central to how they approach practice situations. But applied science is a pluralistic society that includes many different language communities. Contemporary social work practice might be compared to work at the United Nations, the international organization of the world's countries dedicated to addressing problems of global peace and security. United Nations diplomats must be flexible, as they may interact with people from dozens of different speech communities. Language fluency and the ability to work with partners from diverse backgrounds are essential skills. When mutual understanding is blocked by language differences, diplomats make use of expert translators. A diplomat's job also has a high degree of unpredictability, uncertainty, and ambiguity. Diplomats may not be able to draft long-term plans for achieving their goals under such circumstances, but they can learn to seize opportunities as they emerge.

The dialogical map, then, directs social work practitioners to increase their mastery of diverse theoretical languages and of translation tools. The map prepares workers to respond creatively to emergent contingencies. Clarkson (1992) at the Metanoia Psychotherapy Training Institute, for instance, reports on how the center uses a communication approach and teaches "multilingualism so that a trainee will be able to converse about a particular client or patient in a number of psychotherapeutic languages" (p. 274). The center also shows trainees how to "employ effective translators" (p. 275) to make collaborations with different theory users possible and productive. Fraenkel and Pinsof (2001), who teach family counseling, aim to help their students become multilingual and to use the concepts and techniques from various family theory languages.

Travels using the dialogical map, like travels in a foreign land, are not easy. Multilanguage mastery takes time. Practitioners must take the risk of moving from their secure primary language base to learn a new language. Grasping new languages and their associated cultures requires a willingness to deal with great complexity.

Before explaining my own map for dialogical integration, I will report on the **common language strategy** pioneered by the psychotherapy integrationists. This was an effort to find a common integrative vocabulary for therapists of all persuasions (Mahrer, 1989). The common language would replace the specialized languages that had fragmented applied psychology. The language would become a new common tongue, and concepts would be translated from various theoretical perspectives into this shared common vocabulary.

The common language approach has many potential benefits. It can help practitioners trying to communicate with each other. It can help the researchers who test various theories. It offers an alternative to the theoretical jargon of each school and can lessen the negative reactions to each theoretical orientation's buzzwords (Norcross & Newman, 1992/2003). It can make foreign terms familiar for novice helpers, and it might offer a comprehensive vocabulary for practice (Messer, 1987).

The common language strategy is an attempt to create a new **Esperanto** for the helping professions. Esperanto was an attempt to create an artificial language that would unify the nations of Europe, a language based as far as possible on words common to all the European languages (Lemmens et al., 1994). Several rules have been suggested for this Esperanto for practitioners. The common language should be based on informal spoken English. The translation of theories into common English helps demystify the theories and facilitates dialogue among those who speak different theoretical languages (Coady & Lehmann, 2001b). The common language should define terms following the research conventions of variable operationalization. The common language should create a vocabulary that does not favor any one specific theoretical school.

Unfortunately, critics of the common language strategy have prevailed, and this attempt at integration has stalled. Critics argue that there are no agreed-upon criteria for selecting the best concepts for a common language from various theoretical vocabularies and little indication that theory users from different orientations could agree on the best terms to share (Messer, 1987). Critics such as Messer also assert that the use of terms from ordinary language is problematic. Some concepts, such as *resistance,* already have multiple meanings (resistance fighters in World War II, children resisting the directives of their parents, a person resisting an infectious cold, and so on). Selecting the core meaning for a common language translation would not be easy. Moreover, candidates for the common language vocabulary are not theory neutral. Some everyday terms, such as *reward* and *punishment,* are compatible with one theoretical orientation but not with others. Critics complain, too, that a theoretical word gains meaning though its relationships to a network of other theoretical concepts (*habituation* in the behavioral vocabulary, for example). A concept can be pulled from its theoretical network and translated, but much of its significance and value are lost (Lemmens et al., 1994). Finally, Messer (1988) suggests that everyday words are not rich enough to convey the full complex meaning of the concepts enmeshed in a formal theoretical language. The concept *resistance* has a multilayered, complex meaning to psychodynamic theorists that far exceeds the dictionary definition. It loses too much meaning when translated (Messer, 1988).

Perhaps social workers have a greater degree of unity than psychotherapists, and maybe the ambitions of the original common language integrationists were too great. If these premises are true, then the common language strategy has unrealized potential. I have suggested so in this book, using the ecosystems vocabulary as a common social work language.

The dialogical map provides practical directions for the process of theoretical integration. Learn how to talk and cooperate with colleagues and clients who use different theoretical languages. Take advantage of opportunities for integration during your journeys. With the help of colleagues, team members, and clients, assemble into your toolbox different theories, concepts, and techniques as these contribute to the particular job at hand in the specific cultural and environmental setting with distinctive client systems of certain membership characteristics. In your dialogues with speakers of other theoretical languages, use the other maps for integration—common factors, eclecticism, and assimilation—as these increase your versatility and effectiveness in the multitheory arenas you enter. In the next section, I will expand on the dialogical map and suggest a set of translation tools designed primarily for facilitating cross-theory conversations rather than for creating a common language.

THE DIALOGICAL APPROACH TO INTEGRATION AND TRANSLATION TOOLS: A REVIEW

This book is organized on the foundation of a **metatheory**. In your science classes, you learned how to read and understand a research study, a report on the investigation of a hypothesis or research question. You may have even learned about meta-analysis, the process of studying a whole set of research studies and identifying common themes and findings. In your practice class, you have learned about metacommunication, the higher meaning identified in a series of communications or elements of communication. In this book, I have introduced the idea of theory and presented information about ten different theoretical frameworks. A metatheory is a theory about theories and about the use of theories (Ritzer, 1991a, 1991b). My metatheory compares theories to languages and theory use to translating symbol systems for practical purposes.

Table 14.1 summarizes the necessary components of multitheory integration. They are organized from the most abstract (metatheory) at top to the most specific (theory application) at the bottom.

At the Tower of Babel in biblical times, builders aimed too high. They built toward heaven, and God punished them by transforming their shared language into a multitude of tongues. Workers could no longer understand one another, and cooperation became impossible. The proliferation of theoretical perspectives and practice models can have a Tower of Babel effect on contemporary practitioners. Tools that help reconceptualize or translate from one theoretical language to the language of social work (Safran & Messer, 1997/2003) and strategies for fostering dialogue between contending theoretical and professional camps are needed (Albeniz & Holmes, 1996).

My county's department of social service provides translation tools that facilitate helpful interactions between English-speaking social workers and clients who speak Spanish, Korean, Japanese, and many other languages. My university provides a "writing across the curriculum" seminar that helps new professors learn how to teach writing by comparing the language systems and communication needs of many disciplines, including math, business, legal studies, social work, and mass media studies. Practitioners need tools to communicate with team members who speak different formal theoretical languages and with clients who use different everyday theoretical languages.

TABLE 14.1
MULTITHEORY
INTEGRATION:
FROM
METATHEORY
TO APPLICATION

Metatheory (a theory about theories)

- Constructionist and pragmatist assumptions about knowledge
- Science as symbol system
- Contemporary science as many languages
- Applied science as coordinating activities among diverse language speakers

Formal theoretical languages or perspectives

Theoretical language translation tools

- Exemplary role models or articulate spokespersons
- Architectonics and theoretical mapping
  - Root metaphor
  - Assumptions
  - Concepts
  - Propositions
  - Middle-range theories
- Central root metaphors
  - Person
  - Environment
  - Social worker
- Theory-specific maps of person, systems, and the environment
- Conversion of theory-specific vocabulary into ecosystems language
- Conceptual models

Theory application: Appraisal by universal social work standards

Theory application: The use of theory-based practice models

- Preferred goals
- Problem formulation
- Assessment factors and data-gathering methods
- Interventions (strategies and techniques)
- Effectiveness evaluation approach

This HBSE book provides such tools. I have presented an approach to cross-theoretical translation and a set of translation tools in Chapters 1 through 3. In Chapters 4 through 13, I have demonstrated the use of these tools in the translation of ten major theoretical frameworks. I have proposed that these metatheoretical tools can help you learn new theoretical languages and integrate many theories, concepts, and techniques into your professional toolbox.

THEORETICAL DIALOGUE ABOUT EXEMPLARY MODELS

Table 14.2 summarizes the book's presentation of exemplary models. Every theoretical community has its founding fathers and mothers, its most articulate spokespersons, and for applied theories, its scholarly practitioners. Dialogical conversations might compare and contrast the lessons and insights provided by

TABLE 14.2 | MODELS: USEFUL THEORISTS AND SCHOLARLY PRACTITIONERS

Theoretical Perspective	Useful Theorists	Scholarly Practitioners
Ecological	Robert Park, Rachel Carson	Carel Germain
Systems	Ludwig von Bertalanffy, Talcott Parsons	Gordon Hearn
Biological	Charles Darwin, Gregor Mendel	Harriette Johnson
Cognitive	Jean Piaget, Aaron Beck	Albert Ellis, Sharon Berlin, Paula Nurius
Psychodynamic	Sigmund Freud, Erik Erikson	Florence Hollis
Behavioral	Ivan Pavlov, John Watson, B. F. Skinner	Albert Bandura, Bruce Thyer
Interactionist	John Dewey, George Herbert Mead	Jane Addams, Hans Falck
Social role	Robert Linton, George Herbert Mead, Erving Goffman	Jacob Moreno, Helen Harris Perlman
Economic	Adam Smith, John Maynard Keynes	Jane Addams, Harry Lloyd Hopkins
Critical	Jurgen Habermas, C. Wright Mills	Bertha Capen Reynolds

useful theorists and scholarly practitioners from diverse traditions. For example, a practitioner might ask a colleague: How does your practice reflect the influence of your role model, Erik Erikson? or How does your style of work reject the dictates of B. F. Skinner?

THEORETICAL DIALOGUE BY METAPHORS

Dialogical conversations will be enhanced by attention to root metaphors. In conversations with colleagues from social work and allied professions, listen for the metaphors that they use to understand the client and to explain the patterned ways in which the client relates to the environment. When you hear that the client "seems like a _____," or the client "reminds me of a _____," you are hearing some clues to the root metaphors that guide the practitioner's work.

You may also be able to predict the likelihood of working well with other workers based on how similar or dissimilar their root metaphors are from your root metaphors. The worker who compares clients to members may have a hard time cooperating with the worker who prefers the imagery and symbolism of the client as a machine. Conversations about the metaphorical bases for conceptualizing the environment and the role of the social worker may also be fruitful. Table 14.3 summarizes my attempt to identify the root metaphors of ten different theoretical languages.

TABLE 14.3 | ROOT METAPHORS FOR TEN THEORETICAL LANGUAGES

Theoretical Perspective	Environment	Person	Social Worker
Ecological	Field or garden	Living organism	Gardener
Systems	Machine, body, species	A part	Mechanic, systems analyst
Biological	Jungle, health system	Animal, patient	Unnecessary, auxiliary
Cognitive	Computer network	Computer	Technician
Psychodynamic	Circus, mountain	Beast, climber	Tamer, guide
Behavioral	Laboratory	Monkey, pigeon	Behavioral engineer
Interactionist	Clubhouse	Member	Club group worker
Social role	Theater	Actor	Director
Economic	Marketplace	Buyer/seller	Business consultant
Critical	Factory, public forum	Combatant, debater	Revolutionary, critic

THEORETICAL DIALOGUE BY ECO-MAPS

All social work students are familiar with the eco-map. This is a tool that we can use as a universal translator. I encourage you to learn the theory-specific eco-maps in this book, to learn how to make maps of new theoretical perspectives that you discover, to fill in the details of a theory-specific map as you use theory to work with a particular client system, and to experiment with mapping the client system–environment configuration in the terms and symbols of different theory-specific maps.

Dialogical conversations will be enhanced if you ask other team members to develop maps, if you learn how to read their maps and how they use these maps to guide their helping work, if they learn how to read social work ecosystem maps, and if you and your collaborators (your clients, your colleagues, and your supervisors) compare and contrast maps based on various theoretical languages.

Ecosystems terminology is deemed the primary or common language for social workers. It can serve as a common language or "interlanguage" to facilitate cooperative exchanges and problem solving among practitioners from varied theoretical language communities (Duncker, 2001). In addition to theory-based eco-maps, each theory chapter in this book includes my translation of the concepts and language of the theoretical perspective into ecosystems terminology. So, for example, where ecosystems theorists use the term *connections*, ecological theorists prefer the concept *transactions*. I have tried to avoid distorting the meaning of the original theoretical concept but recognize the risks of translation. Theoretical meanings are specific to their historical origin and the social context of their use, and meanings change over time and differ across subgroups of theory users (Schacht, 1984). As you learn more about each theory, test my translations against your own and those of theory experts.

Psychotherapy integrationists select from a narrow set of theoretical approaches focusing on individual behavior (psychodynamic, behavioral, and cognitive are the most common). Social workers need a broader array, so I have translated theories with links to psychology, biology, sociology, social psychology, political science, and economics. Table 14.4 summarizes my translation of concepts from ten languages into the ecosystems vocabulary of *connections, qualities, environment, resources,* and *change*. These terms are common to social workers and are generally familiar, everyday, ordinary vernacular words. Following Mahrer's (1989) advice about the limits of the common language approach to theory integration, I share this not as an effort to develop a single, comprehensive shared language for social work but to identify a small set of terms on whose meanings theorists from different theory communities can agree.

TABLE 14.4 | TRANSLATION OF TEN THEORIES INTO ECOSYSTEMS LANGUAGE

Theoretical Perspective	Connections	Qualities	Environment	Resources	Change
Ecological	Transactions	Good–bad fit	Natural and built world	Renewable Nonrenewable	Natural life process
Systems	Information transfer	On- or Off-course feedback	Totality of systems	Natural Formal Social	Reverberation
Biological	Life adjustments	Adaptive Maladaptive	Body's inner & outer	Knowledge Tools	Adaptation
Cognitive	Information processing	Accurate Distorted	Conceptualized environment	Know how Know about	Cognitive development
Psychodynamic	Attachments	Loving Hateful	Social reality Psychic reality	Ego support Nurturance	Ego strengthening
Behavioral	Rewards and punishments	Desirable Undesirable	Stimulus collage	Models Learning labs	Behavior modification
Interactionist	Communication	Coherent Incoherent	Symbolic web	Cultural meanings	Sense making
Social role	Expectations	Consensus Dissensus	Role network	Attributes Vitality	Performance improvement
Economic	Exchanges	Equitable Inequitable	A set of markets	Money Goods Services	Profit accumulation
Critical	Public deliberations	Symmetry Asymmetry	Public & private spheres	Power Status Wealth	Furthering democracy

THEORETICAL DIALOGUE BY ARCHITECTONICS: MAPPING THE BUILDING BLOCKS

Theory mastery requires the formal study and discussion of "the components and structures of theories" (Mahrer, 1989, p. 181). Dialogical conversations among theory users from different theory groups can be enhanced by discussions about the building blocks of each theory (assumptions, root metaphors, key concepts, propositions, middle-range theories, and so) and about how these building blocks compare. Systems theorists and feminist-oriented critical theorists have struggled to communicate cordially about their approaches to wife battering. Their radically different theoretical assumptions about the relationship of power imbalances to family change processes contribute to the impasse.

In many practice situations, social work practitioners and their colleagues do not explicitly reference their theoretical orientation. More commonly, workers refer to the concepts used without identifying the theoretical edifice in which the concepts are located (Fook, Ryan, & Hawkins, 1997). Familiarity with the interrelated set of theoretical building blocks for many theoretical languages will help you connect the concepts to the appropriate theoretical orientation. Such familiarity will also help you speculate and inquire intelligently about the likely theoretical assumptions and root metaphors that inform the concept user's approach.

Participants in dialogical conversations might ask questions such as the following: If we use this practice model, what are the foundation theoretical assumptions, and how do these assumptions influence our perceptions and actions during all phases of the planned change process (Downing, 2004)? Here are some other useful questions: What assumptions form the foundation for different theoretical languages relevant to this case? Which theoretical assumptions accord best with the cultural factors, values, needs, social class, gender, sexual orientation, and other membership characteristics of members of the client system? Questions comparing root metaphors, key concepts, and middle-range theories might pinpoint sources of misunderstanding and also facilitate collaborative exchanges.

Let me discuss my first social work job again. I worked at a center for emotionally disturbed teenagers. The psychologist used a behavior modification approach in his work with both the developmentally disabled and troubled adolescents in the center. He assumed that the students had little capacity for self-direction and directed us to focus on modifying simple classroom behaviors such as "sitting quietly in a seat for an extended period of time." My earlier training as a volunteer in a humanistic and client-centered helping model disposed me to challenge this approach. I assumed that the troubled teens from a poor New Jersey city had a capacity for self-direction but needed help understanding and making choices. Active listening, especially to these boys' feelings and values, might release potentials for self-governance. I wanted to do more than say "good sitting." The assumptive base of my preferred interventions conflicted with that of the behavioral psychologist. Dialogical conversations would have increased our ability to work together.

THEORETICAL DIALOGUE BY CONCEPTUAL MODEL

Students take courses on Human Behavior and the Social Environment, in which they learn about theoretical schools and about general ideas for their application. Practitioners, however, more often make contact with theory at a lower level of abstraction, as a practice theory or as a conceptual model that guides work with a particular client group facing a specific life challenge. Practice models are constituted from certain common components, whether the models direct micro-level work with individuals and couples; mezzo-level work with extended families, large groups, and social networks; or macro-level practice aiding communities and organizations, changing policy, or advocating for social justice. Useful books and articles about a practice model describe its conceptualization of problem formulation, of the assessment process, and of the selection and implementation of an intervention. In this textbook, I have selected a set of theoretical models associated with each of ten theoretical languages. I have described each model, its practice focus, and its conception of the problem, the assessment process, and the preferred intervention strategy. Table 14.5 summarizes this work.

TABLE 14.5 | TEN CONCEPTUAL MODELS OF THE PLANNED CHANGE PROCESS

Theoretical Model Focus	Problem	Assessment	Intervention Strategy
Ecology of homelessness	Contested territory	Geography of meanings	Mediate sociospatial dispute
Military family systems	Adaptability and cohesion	System functionality	Manage change and reorganize
Biology of alcoholism	Changed biochemistry	Brain circuitry	Administer drugs
Neglectful mother's cognitions	Damaged self-concepts	Working and future self	Restructure cognitive patterns
Loss dynamics and grief work	Severed attachments	Coping responses	Provide corrective emotional experience
Behavior treatment of substance abuse	Stimulus–response chains	Abuse triggers	Extinguish undesirable links
Making sense of chronic depression	Ambiguous meanings	Symbolizations	Collective reinterpretation
Promoting the volunteer role	Minimal expectations	Role identities	Socialization for a new role
The economics of computer-based advocacy	Low-value SW program	Cost–benefit calculations	Increase costs of elimination
Critical approach to political participation	Inequality	Resource control	Fight for responsive political problem solving

Theory users from different theory groups may improve communication and their capacities for mutual understanding if they identify the theory-based conceptual models that they bring to a practice situation. Discussion questions can center on cross-model comparisons: What concepts and linkages do you use to explain the client system troubles? What information about the person, the relevant social systems, and the environment does your model prioritize for the assessment process? How does your model conceive of the person–environment change, and what interventions can activate such change?

THEORETICAL DIALOGUE BASED ON UNIVERSAL STANDARDS

Social workers cannot responsibly endorse the convictions of some pluralists (McNamee & Gergen, 1999) that theoretical languages are equivalent and that no theoretical language (or theory application) should be privileged over another. We are bound by our professional code to compare theories in terms of their suitability for ethical practice. We are usually working for social agencies or private organizations that demand accountability. Our clients have real and damaging troubles and deserve positive results.

Not all worldviews, everyday theories, or formal theories are equal. Hate groups have coherent perspectives on societal ills. Astrologists have a system for predicting the consequences of alternative courses of action. Pharmaceutical companies would be pleased if all human problems were blamed on chemical imbalances and deficiencies. Yet social workers should firmly challenge the suitability of all these perspectives.

Yes, social workers should consider multiple theoretical perspectives on a problem, and professionals will benefit from considering alternative ways of understanding and helping any client system. However, in many circumstances we must make tough decisions about which theory or which combinations of theories to use. Therefore, social workers are obligated to enter into dialogical conversations that evaluate theoretical frameworks, the elements of these frameworks, and the use of theory in practice.

Social workers should endorse a policy regarding theory use that gives preference to theoretical perspectives and their related practice models that are appraised as most responsive to high and universal standards (Sheldon, 1978). Good theories, and useful theory integrations, will be judged favorably against general scientific standards of theory construction and against specific social work standards. Chapter 3 discusses this topic in greater detail. Here, I will suggest that theory users from different theoretical communities need to question each other about a theoretical candidate for inclusion in the social work library of knowledge. Is the theory testable? Is the theory parsimonious, stated as simply as possible? Does the theory have the power to explain a great deal of the topic or challenge considered by the social work theory user? Does the theory help us make accurate predictions? Does the theory have a large scope and help us understand many important public problems and social work topics? Have the theorists aligned with the theory taken a cumulative approach and revised the theory whenever new evidence is discovered? Has the theory been developed formally and precisely; that is, have assumptions, concepts, nominal definitions, operational definitions, propositions, and the linkages between propositions been explicitly articulated? Does the theory have heuristic value and generate ideas for social work practice and research?

Social workers must also ask tough questions specific to our tradition. Is the language of the theoretical candidate compatible with central social work value commitments? Does the theory share the profession's emphasis on health, human possibility, and personal strengths? Will the theory help social workers to understand and change oppressive community practices and policies and to work well with diverse client groups? Does the theory guide practice in accord with ethical standards related to the client's rights to dignity, respect, privacy, and self-determination? Does the theoretical candidate contribute to a holistic stance in our work with clients? Is the theory under review—whether an entire theoretical tradition, a midrange theory, a conceptual model, or a practice model—scientifically sound?

THEORETICAL DIALOGUE BY MEMBERSHIP

I have discussed Falck's (1988) membership approach to social work only briefly in this book. For example, I offered it as an important practice perspective based on symbolic interactionism. I want to mention it here as an umbrella or superordinate theoretical framework. It might serve well as an alternative to ecoystems theory because of its use of everyday language, its focus on the indivisibility of members and membership groups, and its link to the essence of social work as articulated by Jane Addams, the Hull House social workers, and the early group workers (Forte, 1989, 1991). Dialogical conversations between social workers and theory users from diverse traditions might be enhanced if talk were organized around membership, membership behavior, membership organizations, and membership problems. Table 14.6 presents my attempt to show what ten different theoretical languages contribute to the understanding of human membership.

TABLE 14.6 TEN THEORETICAL LANGUAGES UNDER A MEMBERSHIP UMBRELLA	Theoretical Language	Contribution to Understanding Membership
	Ecological	Environment as context and medium for membership action
	Systems	Structuring of membership processes
	Biological	The living force of ancestral memberships
	Cognitive	Progress toward intelligent membership
	Psychodynamic	Internalized memberships
	Behaviorism	Learned membership behavior
	Interactionist	The meanings of membership
	Social role	Performances in various social membership organizations
	Economic	Negotiating costs and benefits among members
	Critical	Privileged members' domination of other members

ON THE ROUTE TO INTEGRATION: TRAVEL STRATEGIES FOR DIALOGICAL CONVERSATIONS

In this book, I have been using the terms *theoretical language* and *theoretical perspective* as interchangeable concepts referring to a comprehensive and abstract theoretical orientation or system. Let me make a simple distinction referring to the human senses. **Theoretical language** refers to the orientation as spoken and as heard. The tongue, mouth, and ears are the relevant sense organs. You will often hear the language of behaviorism, especially the vocabulary of punishment, reward, and behavior modification, spoken by workers in homes for delinquents, for example. **Theoretical perspective** refers to the orientation as a basic point of view about human behavior and the social environment (Weerasekera, 1996), a way of seeing some aspect of reality. The eyes are the relevant sense organs. Language and perspective are inseparable. For example, the American language is rich with concepts and imagery appropriate to a consumer-oriented economy, and the American perspective sharply focuses on surface appearances of objects as commodities, calculations of value, and acquisition.

The previous section reviewed a set of translation tools useful during dialogical conversations. Next, I intend to introduce a set of interaction strategies that may also contribute to your efforts at knowledge integration. Let's begin with the assumption that **perspectival knowing** is inevitable (Downing, 2000; Neimeyer, 1993). Human beings understand every aspect of social life through their cultural perspectives and social membership perspectives. Women see and experience their marriages differently than their husbands. Gender is a membership lens that brings certain aspects of intimate relationships into focus while others are blurry. Persons with power see and experience organizational life differently than their subordinates. One's place in a hierarchy is another membership perspective that, like a camera lens, powerfully influences one's picture of reality.

Social work practitioners and other theory users understand human behavior in the environment from a particular theoretical perspective. Technically defined, a **perspective** is a mental framework or system of perceptions, cognitions, and emotions for making sense of a client–environment configuration (Schwalbe, 1988b). Theoretical perspectives are formalized and tested frameworks for sense making. Contemporary practice occurs in a multiperspective universe. Cooperative and effective inquiry about the meaning of client problems requires us to take the perspective of clients, colleagues, supervisors, and the collaterals of our clients. Various formal and informal perspectives may make a contribution, if only a partial contribution, to clarifying the case dynamics (Fraenkel & Pinsof, 2001).

I will rule out perspective dominating as a strategy for dealing with theoretical diversity. This may be the preferred approach of theoretical monists and gladiators, but it has limited utility and will not result in dialogical conversations. Instead, I will describe strategies that can improve our theoretical fluency and the quality of theory-oriented exchanges.

PERSPECTIVE ADDING

In this strategy, the worker identifies an area of inquiry (relationship difficulties between husband and wife, for example) and successively adds the contributions of various theoretical perspectives to create a more comprehensive understanding. This strategy requires judging whether the new perspective is compatible with the original. Are the building blocks of each perspective, especially the root metaphors and basic assumptions, similar enough to allow the additive process? Or are elements of the new perspective incompatible and contradictory? Root metaphors, assumptions, and language styles may diverge so greatly that addition does disservice to the original perspective (Cronen, Chen, & Pearce, 1988).

Rank and LeCroy (1983) provide an example of successful perspective adding. They offer a framework for assessing intimacy problems reported by a husband and wife by considering the quality of communication (the interactionist perspective), the equity of the social exchanges (the economic perspective), and the degree of relationship conflict or oppression (the critical theory perspective). Their additive process became the basis for a multidimensional assessment that suggested a coordinated set of helping interventions. Delon and Wenston (1989) began with Erikson's psychosocial development theory and added social role theory to create an enriched framework for assessing and helping depressed elderly clients.

Agencies and other professional workplaces might stimulate perspective adding. Organizational leaders should model and teach practitioners the importance of adding new theoretical perspectives "for their potential to inform each other toward more encompassing theories" (Lewis & Kelemen, 2002, p. 270). Vinokur-Kaplan (1997) suggests specifically that organizational administrators provide adequate time and suitable places for dialogical conversations among agency team members from different disciplines and with different theoretical orientations. Each can then learn the other's theoretical perspectives and add them to their overall understanding of the client and of the best treatment plan for the client.

Perspective adding is also an important strategy for workers on the path toward **theoretical multilingualism.** It is central to the educational process of increasing reasonable fluency in more than one theoretical language (Messer, 1987).

PERSPECTIVE CHALLENGING

Perspective challenging is a more assertive and confrontational approach to dialogical conversations. For this strategy, collaborating practitioners with different theoretical allegiances identify area of inquiry. They then present their competing perspectives as tentative proposals for understanding and helping action. Collaborators weigh the relative strength of each perspective using arguments based on evidence, values, logic, or client interests. Arguments might be resolved, for example, only after a practical verification of the claims of adherents to different perspectives has been presented (Bohman, 2001). Perspectives may be challenged at times in terms of their past consequences and predicted future consequences for the agency, for the lives of clients, or for the efforts of the helping team (Cronen, 1995). The use of force or intimidation is not allowed during perspective challenges. Contenders must persuade others of the greater utility of their position on its merit (Downing, 2000). The process of deliberation and debate continues until the most useful perspective, or combination of theoretical perspectives, emerges.

Downing (2000) prefers a dialectic approach to the debate style of perspective challenging. This involves the use of dialogue between adherents of oppositional theoretical perspectives and the juxtaposition of seemingly conflicting or contradictory concepts and middle-range theories. One position is the thesis. The other position is the antithesis. Dialectical exchanges lead to a higher-level synthesis incorporating the best ideas from two different perspectives.

Some theoretical perspectives escape critical scrutiny for too long (Lewis & Kelemen, 2002). Social workers might use perspective challenging to take on a dominant and unquestioned theoretical perspective (for example, the biological model as an explanation of many school-related conduct problems). Such workers can call on the status quo theory to compete with a social justice–oriented alternative (for example, a critical theory perspective that highlights large class size, deteriorating school buildings, poorly trained and paid teachers, and inadequate community supports as central to conduct problems).

Perspective challenging might occur in public forums or in the private forum of the worker's mind. During private deliberations, theoretical perspectives can be examined mentally like "debating voices, presenting their views, reacting to others, elaborating disagreements, and possibly finding shared ground" (Lewis & Kelemen, 2002, p. 266).

Several theoretical integrationists have pointed to the value of perspective challenging. Messer (1987) declares that "progress in any field is achieved precisely through the generation and clash of new ideas each expressed by means of their own linguistic metaphor" (p. 196). Sheldon (1978) recommends that "competing explanations must be made to compete, in practice, in supervision, at case conferences, in tutorials, seminars, and lectures, wherever social workers discuss the theoretical basis of what they are trying to achieve" (p. 12). Fraenkel and Pinsof (2001) tout the creative benefits of respectful and reciprocal theoretical challenges. Slunecko (1999) believes that even encounters between different or contradictory theoretical perspectives stimulate worker creativity.

Participation in perspective-challenging conversations increases interactants' awareness of the assumptions and limitations of their own perspectives while eliciting a heightened sense of the value for competing approaches. Cronen, Chen, and Pearce (1988) see value not only in the mutual understanding that emerges during perspective-challenging sessions but also in the misunderstandings, confusions, ambiguities, and uncertainties. These communication setbacks often motivate efforts toward greater clarity and understanding.

PERSPECTIVE COMPARING

In this strategy for dialogical conversations, participants identify an area of inquiry and then compare different theoretical perspectives on this area of inquiry, searching for similarities and differences in the perspectives. Interactants focus the discussion by deciding what to compare and how to make the comparisons. For example, Netting and O'Connor (2003) provide an extensive comparison of four theoretical paradigms that social workers can use to facilitate organizational change. They compared these perspectives on their conceptualization of organizational goals; the language used to characterize the planned organizational change process; and the paradigms' different depictions of assessment, problem identification, change, desired results, and social work leaders.

Perspective comparing might take place in private. Immerse yourself in your preferred theoretical perspective, for example, and then hold it on the side as you consider how a comparative perspective might provide answers to the same practice questions (Bernstein et al., 1997). This will help you better appreciate the strengths and limitations of your own perspective (Lewis & Kelemen, 2002).

There is a sizable literature on the methodology of perspective comparing. One approach uses **reflecting teams.** These are teams of helpers reflecting on a particular case and talking to each other and to the clients about their observations and ideas. The novel element is that these teams engage in conversations in front of and with the clients during actual helping sessions (Lax, 1995). Koopmans (1995) involved field interns in weekly reflecting teams and gave them opportunities to observe family therapists using and talking about various theoretical perspectives. Koopmans also invited guests to reflecting team meetings (other clients, field liaisons, and special experts) to share and compare their distinctive perspectives during the reflection session. Thomlison (1995) required students to develop a multiperspective case analysis. She helped by exposing students on the reflecting team to students from other disciplines. One team included three MSW social work students, a master's-level nursing student, an educational psychology student, and a doctoral-level psychology student. Students had opportunities to see each other practice and to hear the discipline-specific concerns and issues generated during multidisciplinary dialogues. Social work educators might supplement this approach with process records. Students might be required to include the different theoretical perspectives and social science knowledge that they used during the helping work (Forte, 1994) and to make comparisons regarding the utility of various perspectives.

Walder (1993) developed an approach called **integrative case seminars** in his Institute for Integrated Training in Psychotherapy. These seminars included students and two faculty members representing divergent theoretical approaches. Walder moderated the discussion of case materials and proposed a set of discussion questions to promote comparative inquiry.

The **clinical exchange** is a similar approach to perspective comparing developed for the *Journal of Psychotherapy Integration* to foster cooperative, open inquiry and cross-theoretical dialogue in terms of actual psychotherapy cases (Allen, 2005). Experts in various theoretical orientations are invited to examine the same case. They present in writing and in everyday language their perspective on problem formulation, the optimal therapeutic relationship, intervention methods, and the likely progression of the helping process. The journal also allows for a discussion of the points of similarity and difference between the different theory users. Readers can easily compare the perspectives and their implications for helping work.

Theoretical integrationists encourage novice practitioners to seek training and practice environments that encourage the comparison and eventual integration of multiple perspectives (Schacht, 1984). You might try perspective comparing in collaboration with your clients, your supervisors, and your helping team members before deciding on your preferred practice models and techniques (Coady & Lehmann, 2001a). Perspective comparing may also increase appreciation for and ease with practitioners who hold theoretical perspectives constructed from different building blocks (Downing, 2004).

PERSPECTIVE MATCHING

Perspective matching is a conversational strategy similar to the systematic eclectic approach to theoretical integration. Participants in a dialogue about theories identify an area of inquiry and the social context for this inquiry. They search together for the theoretical perspective or perspectives best matched to the specifics of the helping situation (Bohman, 2001). They may make their matching judgments based on both empirical evidence and practice wisdom (Weerasekera, 1996). They tailor their choice also to the particular circumstances of a particular client with a particular difficulty or need (Coady, 1995).

PERSPECTIVE REVERSING

Perspective reversing is like the role-play and interpersonal mediation strategy of reversing positions with an opponent. This strategy begins, as the others do, with the identification of an area of inquiry and a theoretical perspective different from one's preferred perspective (Lax, 1995). Then, the theory integrator attempts to reverse roles and take the perspective of the person from a different theory group. How does the exchange theorist, for example, understand and appraise my use of family systems theory in this case? How might I best answer questions from the point of view of the exchange theorist about my conception of client problems and about ideal working alliances?

What would the exchange theorist consider blinders in my theoretical perspective?

Slunecko (1999) refers to this as a process of "strangification." The practitioner treats her own approach as if she were a stranger to it. Slunecko compares perspective reversing to the work of anthropologists who attempt to understand their own culture by taking the perspective of foreigners. Interactional difficulties during contact with those with different perspectives can help us increase awareness of our biases and preferences. When crowded and jostled by dozens of Irish pub drinkers in Dublin, for example, I became fully aware of my socialized American preference for physical distance from nonintimates. The perspective-reversing theory user will return home with enriched understanding and new theoretical flexibility.

Moments of successful translation by members of different theoretical language communities satisfy and foster cooperation. The "points of unsuccessful translation" can also provide promising opportunities for theoretical integration (Slunecko, 1999). They challenge us to reverse positions and to work harder at grasping what our assumptions, concepts, propositions, and helping procedures might mean to those who do not know our theoretical language. Persisting and reversing perspectives to clear up communication problems can help us reflect critically on our perspective and our taken-for-granted theoretical beliefs and value premises, and thus increase our capacities for reflective practice.

PERSPECTIVE SEQUENCING

Theoretical perspectives might be presented during a dialogical conversation in a presequenced order. In this strategy, theory users identify an area of inquiry and then decide on the best sequence for introducing or using different theoretical perspectives on this case. For example, the issue of stigma and stigma management lends itself to perspective sequencing. Many social work clients are stigmatized because of their HIV infection, mental disorder, state of homelessness, or criminal record. Gramling (1990) argues that client–worker partners might tackle this problem in an orderly fashion. The team might first use the exchange perspective to appraise the personal gains and costs of the stigmatized condition and to plan to bargain for tolerance. Then, the team might use the interactionist perspective and choose and implement a preferred interactional strategy: deny the condition, conceal the condition, or excuse the stigma. Finally, the team might try a critical-constructionist perspective that challenges the norms oppressive to stigmatized groups and that recommends fighting for a social order ensuring respectful public encounters.

This theoretical integration strategy has been used in field education. Thomlison (1995) developed a system of rotational supervision for her team of student interns. Agency staff members with different theoretical perspectives rotated responsibility for leadership and supervision of the student team. The students had opportunities to learn about multiple treatment approaches and styles. Unfortunately, Thomlison did not clarify her sequence preference or the logic of this ordering of perspectives. Walder (1993) has also outlined a sequential model for teaching multiple theories. Students first become fluent in one theoretical language and then learn additional theoretical languages. His curriculum introduced students to the psychodynamic perspective in their first year, cognitive and behavioral perspectives in the second year, and integration concepts and strategies the third year. However, he observed that students were likely to become biased in favor of the first language. They commonly reverted to the first theoretical language or "mother tongue," abandoning later languages when dealing with stressful helping situations.

Perspective sequencing is relevant to practice also. Weerasekera (1996) recommended that a worker select a set of particular practice theories and implement them in sequence in relationship to "process markers." These are predetermined behavioral, cognitive, intrapsychic, or system indicators of the need to shift from one theoretical perspective to the next. For example, as the worker uses a behavioral approach with a client struggling with anxiety disorders, the client begins to discuss underlying developmental issues. The social worker follows the behavioral work with psychodynamic ego psychology and begins the use of life review processes. This approach assumes that one helper can become knowledgeable and skilled enough to use one and then another perspective in a logical sequence.

Several other methods can be used for perspective sequencing. Schacht (1984) proposes that agencies consider systematically sequencing therapists working with the same case. Each helper takes responsibility for the phase of the helping process in which his or her theoretical perspective is most relevant. Lewis and Kelemen (2002) suggest that a worker consider the expected phases in the helping process with an organization, family, group, or client and identify which theoretical perspective best contributes to phase-specific work. Long-term helping work might also be sequenced by formality of the theory. A helping team starts with the perspective of the client, the naïve theory, supports the beginning-level worker's use of a primary theoretical perspective, supplements this with the supervisor's contribution of a deeper theoretical comprehension of the primary perspective and of supplemental theoretical perspectives, and then refines the helping work with the guidance of a consultant expert on a set of advanced theories.

PERSPECTIVE SYNTHESIZING

This strategy requires collectively or individually identifying an area of inquiry, locating theoretical perspectives that usefully illuminate the area, and engaging in a conversational interplay (public or private) that leads to a new viewpoint. Dialogical conversations are geared toward generating new ways of conceptualizing client system challenges or helping dynamics that synthesize two or more perspectives (Lax, 1995). Albeniz and Holmes (1996) suggest that the "creative conflict between different models will lead to new integrative syntheses, further differentiation" (p. 569), and Schacht (1984) believes that new ideas for understanding a case and new ideas for therapeutic techniques often emerge following the interrelationship of two or more theoretical perspectives. Mahoney (1993) calls this a "dialectical/developmental" strategy because "differences between theoretical perspectives are examined, useful comparisons are made, and novel integrations are welcome" (p. 7).

Weerasekera (1996) has refined a formal process of **multiperspective case formulation** for perspective synthesis. Helpers from different disciplines are invited to collaborate in developing a new blend of theoretical perspectives by identifying how their various perspectives contribute to the completion of a case grid. The grid describes individual factors (biological, behavioral, cognitive, and psychodynamic) and social systems factors (couple, family, occupation, school, and social supports) that explain the particular client problem and that identify alternative coping responses and possible treatment strategies. After filling in the grid, participants identify new and creative theoretical combinations for particular client problems.

Coady (1995) presents a novel approach to perspective synthesis. He proposes that practitioners generate their own theories of a particular case by assembling inductively all their relevant observations and hunches. The worker becomes, then, a producer of theories rather than a consumer of theories. The opportunity for integrative synthesis occurs when the worker talks with the client about the client's naïve or informal theory of his or her troubles. The client's naïve theory and the worker's grounded theory are synthesized to improve their mutual ability to make sense of the case specifics.

MULTITHEORY DIALOGICAL INTEGRATION: GOALS, RULES, AND FORUMS

Dialogue, open and respectful communication, cooperative inquiry, and mutual perspective taking are critical concepts in my approach to using knowledge about human behavior and the social environment. In this section, I will expand on my earlier discussions of the dialogical map for journeying toward theoretical integration.

PHILOSOPHY OF SCIENCE INFLUENCES

If I were to map the architectonics of this approach starting with its philosophical assumptions, I would name several influences. Social constructionists lend the assumption that reality is interpreted and our knowledge about reality is created socially (Lazarus & Messer, 1991; Slunecko, 1999). Constructivists share a kinship with social constructionists and lend the assumption that theory users and clients alike understand reality by means of a personalized set of constructs (Neimeyer, 1993). Postmodernists assume that there are multiple realities, that powerful groups are more often able to persuade or force others to accept their versions of reality, and that no versions of reality should be privileged (Safran & Messer, 1997/2003). My approach builds on the first two assumptions of postmodernists but casts doubt on their third assumption. Pragmatists and neopragmatists (Downing, 2000; Forte, 2002a) lend the assumption that knowledge should be useful and, consequently, theory users should select the knowledge that best enhances the quality of human memberships. This is not the place to expand on these assumptions or to trace the assumptions to the concepts, propositions, and linkages forming the edifice of my metatheory. Table 14.1 outlined the elements, however.

Participants in Dialogical Conversations

Dialogue among theory users speaking different languages can be characterized as "sense-making conversations" (Calton & Payne, 2003). A collective of stakeholders organize inquiry around the following question: How do different theoretical perspectives help us make sense of the case and of the planned change process? Conversational members share an openness to multiple theoretical voices, a commitment to selecting and attributing the most useful meanings to the case, and a resolve to act on the basis of these preferred meanings. Dialogical or sense-making conversations may occur between theorists and practitioners, theorists and researchers, theorists and educators, theorists aligned with different theoretical schools, practitioners aligned with different theoretical schools, members of different professions, members of different disciplines, or practitioners and clients. Dialogical conversations may take place in the mind of an individual practitioner. They may use spoken words or written words. Dialogical conversations may even consider the perspectives of dead, physically absent, or imagined useful theorists and scholarly practitioners.

Uses of Dialogical Conversations

Dialogical conversations have many potential uses. They can help theory users consider alternative ways of making sense and talking about reality (McNamee & Gergen, 1999). These conversations can make intelligible complex or mysterious client–environment configurations by using the metaphors, concepts, models, and narratives from multiple theories as resources for enhancing understanding and increasing action options. They can furnish a sense of direction for helping work.

Dialogical conversations can unite communities of practitioners who speak the same theoretical language. They can remove barriers to cooperation and facilitate the coordination of the work of practitioners who speak different theoretical languages but agree to engage in cross-theory translation.

Dialogical communication can advance the profession's development of a knowledge base by creating "a context of constructive dialogue and collaboration among scientists and practitioners of diverse viewpoints" and by initiating a process "open to future developments that cannot be either foreseen or strategically engineered" (Mahoney, 1993, p. 8). This approach to theoretical integration provides a framework for communication that replaces dissension among diverse social work knowledge builders with cooperation (Feixas & Botella, 2004).

Dialogical conversations have other benefits for the practitioner. They can increase our appreciation for theoretical diversity within our professional unity. They can help us master different theoretical languages, and they can enrich professional learning by fostering the discovery of new and different solutions to practice problems and the improvement of our current approaches to helping (Feixas & Botella, 2004).

GROUND RULES AND APTITUDES FOR DIALOGICAL CONVERSATIONS

Dialogical conversations are structured like democratic deliberations about public problems among the citizenry. Certain conditions must be ensured for optimal problem solving. All participants are equals, and the contributions of each, whatever the speaker's profession, theoretical language, or degree of expertise, deserve a hearing. There is an agreement that no one's perspective can trump the others, and no one can insist that "his or her most cherished conceptual framework is the only one in which the salient aspects of the problem at hand can be expressed" (Depew, 2000, p. 46). Such veto power and theoretical dominance would constrain communication and weaken the deliberative and decision-making process.

Exchanges are free and open; members are invited to share their thoughts, feelings, hunches, and reservations. The exchange is reciprocal. Dialogue involves "seeking to listen to and understand what the other is saying, and a willingness to test our opinions through such encounters" (Safran & Messer, 1997/2003, p. 11). Monologues are discouraged, and conversational monopolizing must be limited (Strong, 2002).

The exploration of differences is important during multitheory conversations as it is during democratic deliberations. Unique or minority perspectives enrich rather than detract from the conversation. All members are respected (Lewis & Kelemen, 2002), but the suggestions regarding problem formulation, assessment, and intervention are examined critically. Participants compare and contrast, judge the usefulness, and weigh the evidence supporting or challenging each theory-based claim.

Dialogical discussions are not abstract and detached. Participants offer contributions in relation to the specific case circumstances: the client system's problem or challenge, characteristics of the client system, characteristics of the social worker, and characteristics of the context. Deliberations are organized as a search for the perspective or perspectives that best fit these particulars (Norcross, 1986). Discussants also work toward creative synthesis, the ability to see and make connections among different and seemingly unconnected theoretical perspectives (Kurtines & Silverman, 1999).

Children must be taught the rules and procedures for participatory and democratic decision making. They also learn the aptitudes and capacities necessary for civic engagement. Theory users, too, must learn and cultivate a set of aptitudes to maximize their contributions to dialogical conversations.

Intellectual flexibility is important. This includes a "spirit of adventure, relentless curiosity, and openness to new perspectives" (Fraenkel & Pinsof, 2001, p. 82) and the acceptance "that an event can be viewed, defined, or perceived in more than one manner, through several focal points" (Wicklund, 1999, p. 667). Perspective-taking dispositions and skills are important (Schwalbe, 1988b). These include **perspective-taking accuracy,** the motivation and ability to understand the theoretical viewpoints that others are taking; **perspective-taking depth,** the motivation and ability to understand fully the building blocks of another person's theoretical orientation; and **perspective-taking range,** the motivation and ability to discern and understand a variety of theoretical viewpoints. Dialogical conversations begin from the starting point of theoretical pluralism. Participants must find a way to tolerate the uncertainty and ambiguity that follows when the theory use principle of one and only one correct theoretical approach is rejected. Dialogical conversationalists must balance their search for confidence and conviction in the use of knowledge with acceptance of the humility and doubt that are part of daily helping work in multitheory practice arenas (Downing, 2004).

FORUMS FOR DIALOGICAL CONVERSATIONS

Where might we convene dialogical conversations with the aim of multitheory use or theoretical integration? A social work practitioner can take time from direct service and initiate a private and subvocal forum within his or her mind. The forums for dialogue might also be public. Members of a helping relationship—client, worker, and even the family, friends, and other client collaterals—can meet for a dialogical exchange. A helping team may include diverse members—practitioners from different professions, academic consultants from various disciplines, supervisors, and administrators, for example. These members can assemble and discuss cases in agency, university, or community settings.

All dialogical forums consider multiple perspectives: the first-person perspective of the primary worker or team leader; the second-person perspective of the client whom the worker or team helps; and the third-person perspective of the general public, the social work profession, and the standards and conventions of science (Bohman, 2001).

THE PRIVATE FORUM: MULTITHEORY DIALOGUES AND PROFESSIONAL SELFING In Chapter 2, I discussed the worker's use of the private forum, the realm of internalized conversations with imagined others. These others are internalized and significant role models. Table 14.2 summarized my coverage of exemplary models. Inner dialogues with internalized useful theorists and scholarly practitioners can help us find new ways to deal with practice challenges. This conceptualization proposes an interactionist theoretical perspective on the use of the professional self during the helping process. It acknowledges a long tradition in the helping professions, one that recognizes the impact of the worker's personality on effectiveness (Baldwin, 2000) and asserts that self-aware and "reflective practitioners" will be more effective than practitioners who refrain from private dialogues (Hamilton, 1954; Harrison, 1987; Kondrat, 1999; Papell & Skolnik, 1992).

The interactionist perspective offers a semiotic or communication model for conceptualizing the activation of personality processes for the sake of the helping work. It suggests that the key to self-awareness and the effective use of the worker's personality is self-talk. Social workers can learn to increase the quantity and quality of their self-talk, to monitor this self-talk better, and to manage inner conversations so that they contribute to rather than hinder performance (Nutt-Williams & Hill, 1996). The particular focus of this book has been HBSE and the cultivation of the internalized voices of theory experts. My conceptualization of multitheory self-talk invites workers to seek help during private conversations from their imagined allies. You might turn to an imaginary ally for support. Jane Addams will applaud your attempts to help vulnerable groups and to fight indifferent politicians. You might use the insights of imaginary allies to avoid mistakes and lines of action that might not be effective. George Herbert Mead will remind you that clients must be understood as members of their society. Lawrence Kohlberg will urge you to use your moral reasoning abilities to escape ethical traps. You might turn to imaginary allies for alternative interpretations of client problems. B. F. Skinner, Gordon Hearn, and Harry Hopkins will provide different but stimulating ways to look at poverty, for instance. You might converse with imaginary allies about what it means to be a social worker in a country unfriendly to social work. Or you might ask and answer questions internally about the perspective of different imagined theory experts on all phases of the helping process: the selection of theoretical knowledge to guide the work, problem explanation, goal formulation and the articulation of desired futures, the assessment information needed and the best tools and procedures to obtain this information, alternative interventions and their rationales, and the way to approach practice evaluation. Chapters 4 through 13 summarize my ideas about how different theorists would answer these questions.

During these private dialogical conversations, listen as different voices offer their answers to each of the questions above and their arguments regarding the superior usefulness of their conceptualization. Remember that you must play the role of discussion leader and mediate, referee, challenge, summarize, or change the topic of discussion as the conversation requires. With a set of smart internalized forum guests and your discussion leadership skills, these inner conversations will sharpen your knowledge, capacities, and aptitudes for theory application.

THE PUBLIC FORUM: MULTITHEORY DIALOGUES AND THE HELPING RELATIONSHIP   Clients can and should be invited to participate in multitheory dialogues. The forum for such dialogues is the helping dyad, group, or larger system. The forum members include the client or clients and the social worker. Persons significant to the client system might join in dialogical conversations as needed. In this subsection, I will illustrate the use of multitheory dialogues by one worker and one client.

This dialogical or social constructionist perspective on helping work requires the worker to immerse herself or himself in the client's culture and language, including the everyday theoretical languages that the client uses to make sense of transactions with others. The worker tunes in to the client–problem–agency configuration by exploring many different positions on the case: the client's everyday natural and theoretical language, the agency language, the profession's ecosystems language, and relevant theory-specific languages. The worker assumes a critical and reflective stance toward each language and asks how each opens possibilities or constrains and limits client choice and development. The worker and client give preference to the meanings that will best help the client. Formal theoretical perspectives are conceptualized as conversational resources, and the worker explains that worker and client will use these resources as alternative and potentially liberating "lenses on reality" that free the client from "reality tunnels" (Strong, 2002).

Kelly's personal construct theory offers a useful slant on client problems. Clients most often seek help or are referred because their everyday theories or perspectives are not achieving the outcomes they desire or that relevant others desire for them (Downing, 2000). Client–environment difficulties are viewed as blockages in the interactional and narrative processes necessary for generating meanings to deal effectively with challenging experiences. The client's theories of substance abuse, relationship conflict, workplace setbacks, or depression are not working. The client cannot see a way to use the theories to formulate more viable hypotheses or to use experience and evidence to improve or replace these theories. Workers help clients reconstruct their inadequate perspectives by posing alternative ways to investigate and respond to biopsychosocial challenges. Workers offer the languages and perspectives of applied science to facilitate the exploring and testing of new ways to solve problems.

Dialogical conversations between the worker and the client are directed to the creation of new narrative meanings, meanings that transform positively the client system's construction of reality and capacity for action in relation to this reality (Feixas & Botella, 2004). The worker attempts to understand fully the natural language and everyday theories that the client and his or her significant others use by gathering information from these speakers about "how they articulate and hear meanings" (Strong, 2002, p. 220). The worker attempts to learn about the private and public conversations that are central to the client's efforts to improve his or her biopsychosocial functioning. Together the worker and the client identify the client's narratives and theories. The worker conveys respect for the client's everyday theories and does not argue that formal theories are superior or privileged sense-making tools. During the assessment process, the worker might shift across theoretical perspectives and try out alternative modes of observing the client, listening to the client, and conversing with the client (Mahrer, 1989).

The worker and client focus on the co-construction of new meanings during collaborative dialogues (Lax, 1995; Strong, 2002). Therapeutic multitheory dialogue is bidirectional, and the worker promises the client that the words in their dialogue will be "half mine and half yours" (Strong, 2002, p. 222). The client shares memories, assumptions, ideas, dreams, and strengths during the dialogical conversations, and the worker contributes life experiences, practice experiences, and theoretical knowledge.

The formal theories and professional language that the worker contributes, and the new symbol system created by the worker and client during their helping conversations, with the accompanying generation of new meaning systems, make possible more effective, responsible, and satisfying lines of action. The worker might conduct a multitheory literature review, for example, to identify diverse viewpoints on the client system challenges and then engage the client in considering the relative usefulness of these different theoretical resources (Lewis & Kelemen, 2002). For some of the helping work, the practitioner may facilitate the client's attempts to coordinate his or her theories and other meaning systems with those of relevant and important others in the environment (Andersen, 1991).

In collaborative conversation, the worker and the client merge or integrate everyday languages and formal theoretical languages into a new symbol system for grasping the particularities of the situation. A client's report of "being stuck in" and "frustrated by" repetitive patterns regarding food use, alcohol consumption, or sexual activity, for example, might be integrated with behavioral theory concepts of habit, habit formation, habit maintenance, and habit change. A client who is deeply anxious after surviving an earthquake and who says things like "I don't feel like I am on solid ground anymore" and "My basic foundation has been shattered" can learn to conceptualize these adjustment difficulties in cognitive theory terms as threatened self-schemas, threatened relationship schemas, and catastrophic event schemas and to use this new theory-based narrative to begin to construct a coherent construct system that incorporates the reality of disaster.

Theoretical languages provide the tools and resources for describing and dealing with challenging experiences. During dialogical multitheory conversations, the worker helps the client discover new words for conceptualizing his or her problem, and then helps the client transform these words into restorative or growth-enhancing actions (Downing, 2000).

THE PUBLIC FORUM: MULTITHEORY DIALOGUES AND TEAM WORK   Social workers might convene or participate in various public forums with colleagues from diverse theory groups. These include meetings for multidisciplinary and multiprofessional projects, common referral meetings, interdisciplinary case conferences, group supervision, reflecting teams, and planning and processing meetings with cotherapists or coleaders (Andersen, 1991; Calton & Payne, 2003; Duncker, 2001). Such meetings need good translators. Gambrill (1997) asserts, for instance, "Different disciplines and professions have different content as well as different ways of approaching topics of concern. They have different languages. These differences may seem foreign, even jarring, to those in other disciplines and professions, and they may encourage misunderstandings that get in the way of exploring possible contributions" (p. 25). I have discussed teamwork extensively in earlier chapters. Here I will add only a few points.

Multitheory dialogues lessen divisiveness, disagreements, and misinterpretations. Light (1996, 1997), for example, drew on his experiences with the environmental movement to highlight the dangers of within-family theoretical hostilities. Such battles are not uncommon in the social work practice community. The current conflict between social work constructionists and positivists illustrates his point. Such battles, unfortunately, hinder efforts to build knowledge for use and to apply this knowledge. Light offered a pragmatic alternative. He proposed that mutual communication with and tolerance of those from competing theoretical traditions and schools be guided by the spirit of **compatibilism.** Theoretical dialogue is preferable to public divisiveness, rivalry, and disdain. Nasty competition undermines collective aid to distressed client groups. Theoreticians may speak different languages, but they should commit to constructive discourse. They need not ignore the distinct intellectual commitments of each tradition or silence any claims about the quality and best application of their frameworks. These frameworks contribute differentially to particular practice interests as selected by a team: promoting democratic practices and freedoms, ensuring the material and social prerequisites for system survival, deepening self-understanding, or extending human dignity and respect (Brown, 1992).

Contentious conversations should be conducted, according to Light (1996), in relatively private forums such as specialized journals and conference sections. Battles in public forums weaken the ameliorative powers of a profession, just as battles between extreme partisans of opposing political parties lessen public faith in legislators. A period of contest and controversy also distracts practitioners from practical and unified public activity toward professional goals. Pragmatists advise that theorists and practitioners can best serve their constituencies if they resist institutional and personal inclinations toward parading in- and out-group distinctions. Social workers and our theoretical partners, whatever their theoretical orientation, need to instead voice agreed-upon and high-priority moral, policy, and social change goals and then dedicate our theoretical and intervention resources toward cooperatively achieving these mutual goals.

Multitheoretical dialogues can serve as bridges between supervisors or mentors from various theoretical perspectives and novice social workers; between theoreticians, researchers, and practitioners; between members of helping teams, giving all participants, including clients, the opportunity to experience the multiple options for meaning making in the helping work (Strong, 2002); and between social workers specializing in work with social systems of different sizes—individual, family, group, community, organization, polity, or associations of nations (Rigazio-Digilio et al., 1996).

SUMMARY OF DISCUSSION AND FUTURE CONVERSATIONS

To finance my college education, I worked with my cousin during several summers as a carpenter's helper. He taught me the use of many different carpentry tools, the importance of selecting the right tool for each job, and the utility of a large and well-organized toolbox. These lessons have helped me as a social work practitioner and social work educator.

Knowledge is one of our most important tools. In this chapter, I have examined the challenge of theoretical pluralism. Using the metaphor of a library, I compared the social work knowledge base to a huge, ever growing library with hundreds of rooms, some dark corners, and a few poorly marked passages. How might we make sense of and integrate the knowledge from this library that we need to do our social work job? In this chapter, I have reviewed a set of well-developed maps for finding our way through the library: the eclectic map, the common factors map, and the theoretical assimilation map. I have also introduced some new ideas about a dialogical map, a guide to convivial, constructive, and collaborative conversations with library users who speak diverse theoretical languages. I reviewed a set of translation tools—role models, root metaphors, theoretical models, theoretical mapping, and theory-specific eco-mapping—that can facilitate cross-disciplinary, cross-profession, and cross-role (worker, client, and collateral, for example) communication. Through the use of these translation devices along with strategies for mutual perspective taking (perspective adding, challenging, comparing, matching, reversing, sequencing, and synthesizing), we can communicate with fellow explorers and add continuously to our toolbox of theoretical languages. My hope is that you have started to add many of these tools and strategies to your own intellectual toolbox and that these tools and strategies will help you on your professional journeys.

LEARNING ACTIVITIES

1. Interview several agency directors or workers in the personnel department. What are the agency's populations and public problems of concern? What theoretical perspectives and theory-based concepts would best prepare you to help in that agency?

2. Form a student panel. Invite each student to study a particular useful theorist or scholarly practitioner and imagine how he or she would approach an agreed-upon practice situation (group work with battered women, individual counseling for at-risk high school students, family services to a recently evicted family).

Each panelist will briefly present a summary of his or her approach, the panel members will debate the relative merits of the different approaches, and the panel members will respond to questions from the other students.

3. Reflect on the various routes to theoretical integration examined in this chapter. Which map appeals to you most: the eclectic map, the common factors map, the assimilation map, or the dialogical map? Why? How might you prepare for travels in your multi-theory practice community using your preferred map?

4. Practice perspective shifting in a simple way. Think about a client who is difficult to help. Consider multiple perspectives on the difficulty. What is the client's perspective? How do family members and significant others view the client's troublesome pattern? What would be the viewpoint of neighbors and other community members? How do your administrator and supervisor think about this client? What is your perspective? Try to alternate perspectives and reconcile them into some more complex and deep understanding of the client.

5. Observe an interdisciplinary team meeting. What different theoretical perspectives do team members represent? How well do team members take each other's perspectives? What were some missed opportunities for cross-theory dialogue?

6. In what ways is a client like a scientific theory user? How is a client different from a scientific theory user? Consider how the metaphor of client and practitioner as theory users might change your use of the planned change process.

ADDITIONAL RESOURCES

Additional resources are available on the book companion website at **www.thomsonedu.com/ social_work/forte.** Resources include key terms, tutorial quizzes, links to related websites, and lists of additional resources for furthering your research.

REFERENCES

Aaron Beck Homepage. (200?). A biography of Aaron T. Beck, MD. Retrieved December 31, 2002, from http://mail.med/penn.edu/~abeck/index.html

Abbot, C. W., Brown, C. R., & Crosbie, P. V. (1973). Exchange as symbolic interaction: For what? *American Sociological Review, 38*(4), 504–506.

Abercombie, N., Hill, S., & Turner, B. S. (1994). *The Penguin dictionary of sociology* (3rd ed.). London: Penguin Books.

Aboulafia, M. (1995). George Herbert Mead and the many voices of universality. In L. Langsdorf & A. R. Smith (Eds.), *Recovering pragmatism's voice: The classical tradition, Rorty, and the philosophy of communication* (pp. 179–194). Albany: State University of New York Press.

Addams, J. (1920). *Democracy and social ethics.* New York: Macmillan. (Original work published 1902)

Addams, J. (1990). *Twenty years at Hull-House with autobiographical notes.* Urbana: University of Illinois Press. (Original work published 1910)

Addams, J. (2002). The settlement as a factor in the labor movement. In J. B. Elshtain (Ed.), *The Jane Addams reader* (pp. 46–61). New York: Basic Books. (Original work published 1895)

Adoption History Project. (2005). Arnold Gesell (1880–1961). Retrieved July 9, 2005, from http://darkwing.voregon.edu/~adoption/people/gesell.html

Ainsworth, M. D. S. (1991). Attachments and other affectional bonds across the life cycle. In C. M. Parkes, J. Stevenson-Hinde, & P. Marris (Eds.), *Attachment across the life cycle* (pp. 33–51). London: Tavistock-Routledge.

Ainsworth, M. D. S., Blehar, M., Waters, E., & Wall, S. (1978). *Patterns of attachment: Assessed in the strange situation and at home.* Hillsdale, NJ: Erlbaum.

Akers, R. L. (1977). *Deviant behavior: A social learning approach* (2nd ed.). Belmont, CA: Wadsworth.

Akers, R. L. (1996). Is differential association/social learning cultural deviance theory? *Criminology, 34*(2), 229–247.

Akers, R. L., Krohn, M. D., Lanza-Kaduce, L., & Radosevich, M. (1979). Social learning and deviant behavior: A specific test of a general theory. *American Sociological Review, 44,* 636–655.

Albas, C., & Albas, D. (1989). Aligning actions: The case of subcultural proxemics. *Canadian Ethnic Studies, 21*(2), 74–82.

Albeniz, A., & Holmes, J. (1996). Psychotherapy integration: Its implications for psychiatry. *British Journal of Psychiatry, 169*(5), 563–570.

Aldous, J. (1978). *Family careers: Developmental changes in families.* New York: Wiley.

Allen, D. M. (2005). The clinical exchange. *Journal of Psychotherapy Integration, 15*(1), 67–68.

Allen, V. L., & van de Vliert, E. (1984). A role theoretical perspective on transitional processes. In V. L. Allen & E. van de Vliert (Eds.), *Role transitions: Explorations and explanations* (pp. 1–18). New York: Plenum Press.

Allen-Meares, P., Hudgins, C. A., Engberg, M. E., & Lessnau, B. (2005). Using a collaboratory model to translate social work research into practice and policy. *Research on Social Work Practice, 15*(1), 29–40.

Ames, L. B. (1989). *Arnold Gesell: Themes of his work.* New York: Human Science Press.

Andersen, T. (1991). *The reflecting team: Dialogues and dialogues about the dialogues.* New York: Norton.

Anderson, C. M. (1979). Family communication: Words, messages and meanings. *Smith College Studies in Social Work, 49*(2), 91–110.

Anderson, R. E., & Carter, I. (1990). *Human behavior in the social environment: A social systems approach* (4th ed.). New York: Aldine de Gruyter.

Anderson, S. M., & Glassman, N. S. (1996). Responding to significant others when they are not there: Effects on interpersonal inference, motivation, and affect. In R. M. Sorrentino & E. T. Higgins (Eds.), *Handbook of motivation and cognition: Vol. 3. The interpersonal context* (pp. 262–321). New York: Guilford Press.

Andreasen, A. R. (1995). *Marketing social change.* San Francisco: Jossey-Bass.

Aneshensel, C. S. (2002). *Theory-based data analysis for the social sciences.* Thousand Oaks, CA: Sage.

Angell, R. C. (1968). Introduction. In A. J. Reiss Jr. (Ed.), *Cooley and sociological analysis* (pp. 1–12). Ann Arbor: University of Michigan Press.

Arkowitz, H. (1992). Integrative theories of therapy. In D. K. Freedheim (Ed.), *History of psychotherapy: A century of change* (pp. 261–303). Washington, DC: American Psychological Association.

Aronoff, N. L., & Bailey, D. (2003). Social work practice guidelines in an interprofessional world: Honoring new ties that bind. In A. Rosen & E. K. Proctor (Eds.), *Developing practice guidelines for social work practice: Issues, methods, and research agenda* (pp. 253–267). New York: Columbia University Press.

Artinian, B. M. (1997). Overview of the intersystem model. In B. M. Artinian & M. M. Conger (Eds.), *The intersystem model: Integrating theory and practice* (pp. 1–17). Thousand Oaks, CA: Sage.

Ashford, J. B., LeCroy, C. W., & Lortie, C. W. (2001). The biophysical dimension for assessing social functioning. In *Human behavior in the social environment: A multidimensional perspective* (2nd ed., chap. 2, pp. 38–68). Pacific Grove, CA: Brooks/Cole.

Ashforth, B. E. (2000). *Role transitions in organizational life: An identity-based perspective.* Mahwah, NJ: Erlbaum.

Athens, L. (1994). The self as a soliloquy. *Sociological Quarterly, 35*(3), 521–532.

Averill, J. R. (1990). Inner feelings, works of the flesh, the beast within, diseases of the mind, driving force, and putting on a show: Six metaphors of emotion and their theoretical extensions. In D. E. Leary (Ed.), *Metaphors in the history of psychology* (pp. 104–132). Cambridge, UK: Cambridge University Press.

Baker, R. (1976). The multirole practitioner in the generic orientation to social work practice. *British Journal of Social Work, 6*(3), 327–352.

Baldwin, J. D. (1988). Mead and Skinner: Agency and determinism. *Behaviorism, 16*(2), 109–127.

Baldwin, J. D., & Baldwin, J. I. (1998). *Behavior principles in everyday life* (3rd ed.). Upper Saddle River, NJ: Prentice Hall.

Baldwin, M. (2000). *The use of self in therapy* (2nd ed.). New York: Haworth Press.

Bandura, A. (1967). Behavioral psychotherapy. *Scientific American, 216*, 78–86.

Bandura, A. (1977a). Self-efficacy: Toward a unifying theory of behavioral change. *Psychological Review, 84*, 191–215.

Bandura, A. (1977b). *Social learning theory.* Englewood Cliffs, NJ: Prentice-Hall.

Bandura, A. (1983). The self and mechanisms of agency. In J. M. Suls & A. G. Greenwald (Eds.), *Psychological perspectives on the self* (Vol. 2, pp. 3–39). Hillsdale, NJ: Erlbaum.

Bandura, A. (1986). *Social foundations of thought and action: A social cognitive theory.* Englewood Cliffs, NJ: Prentice-Hall.

Bandura, A. (1999). Social cognitive theory: An agent perspective. *Asian Journal of Social Psychology, 2*, 21–41.

Barker, C. (2000). *Cultural studies: Theory and practice.* London: Sage.

Barker, R. L. (2003). *The social work dictionary.* Washington, DC: NASW Press.

Barley, S. R. (1989). Careers, identities, and institutions: The legacy of the Chicago school of sociology. In M. B. Arthur, D. T. Hall, & B. S. Lawrence (Eds.), *Handbook of career theory* (pp. 41–65). New York: Cambridge University Press.

Barriteau, V. E. (2000). Feminist theory and development: Implications for policy, research, and action. In J. L. Parpart, M. P. Connelly, & V. E. Barriteau (Eds.), *Theoretical perspectives on gender and development* (pp. 161–202). Ottawa: International Development Research Centre.

Bartlett, R. L. (1996). Discovering diversity in introductory economics. *Journal of Economic Perspectives, 10*(2), 141–154.

Bartlett, S. (2000). Discursive democracy and a democratic way of life. In L. E. Hahn (Ed.), *Perspectives on Habermas* (pp. 367–386). Chicago: Open Court.

Baumgartner, T., Buckley, W., Burns, T. R., & Schuster, P. (1976). Meta-power and the structuring of social hierarchies. In T. R. Burns & W. Buckley (Eds.), *Power and control: Social structures and transformations* (pp. 215–288). London: Sage.

Beck, A. T. (1976). *Cognitive therapy and the emotional disorders.* New York: New American Library.

Becker, H. S. (1994). Professional sociology: The case of C. Wright Mills. In R. C. Rist (Ed.), *The democratic imagination: Dialogues on the work of Irving Louis Horowitz* (pp. 175–187). New Brunswick, NJ: Transaction.

Beckett, J. O., & Coley, S. M. (1987). Ecological intervention with the elderly: A case example. *Journal of Gerontological Social Work,* 11(1/2), 137–157.

Becvar, D. S., & Becvar, R. J. (1996). *Family therapy: A systemic integration* (3rd ed.). Boston: Allyn & Bacon.

Begley, S. (1995, February 13). Three is not enough. Surprising new lessons from the controversial science of race. *Newsweek,* 67–69. Belmont, CA: Wadsworth.

Benson, P. (1991). Autonomy and oppressive socialization. *Social Theory and Practice,* 17(3), 385–408.

Bentz, V., & Shapiro, J. J. (1998). *Mindful inquiry in social research.* Thousand Oaks, CA: Sage.

Berg, J. H., Piner, K. E., & Frank, S. M. (1993). Resource theory and close relationships. In U. G. Foa, J. Converse Jr., K. Y. Tornblom, & E. B. Foa (Eds.), *Resource theory: Explorations and applications* (pp. 169–195). San Diego, CA: Academic Press.

Berger, R. M. (1986). Social work practice models: A better recipe. *Social Casework,* 67(1), 45–54.

Berger, R. M., & Kelly, J. J. (1993). Social work in the ecological crisis. *Social Work,* 38(5), 521–525.

Berlin, S. B. (1996). Constructivism and the environment: A cognitive-integrative perspective for social work practice. *Families in Society,* 77(6), 326–335.

Berlin, S. B. (2001). *Clinical social work practice: A cognitive-integrative perspective.* New York: Oxford University Press.

Bernhardt, B., & Rausch, J. B. (1993). Genetic family histories: An aid to social work assessment. In J. B. Rausch (Ed.), *Assessment: A sourcebook for social work practice* (pp. 279–293). Milwaukee, WI: Families International.

Bernstein, S., Goodman, H., & Epstein, I. (1997). Grounded theory: A methodology for integrating social work and social science theory. In D. J. Tucker, C. Garvin, & R. Sarri (Eds.), *Integrating knowledge and practice: The case of social work and social science* (pp. 139–148). Westport, CT: Praeger.

Bertalanffy, L. von. (1952). *Problems of life.* New York: Harper.

Bertalanffy, L. von. (1962). *Modern theories of development: An introduction to theoretical biology.*

New York: Harper. (Original work published 1928)

Bertalanffy, L. von. (1969). *General systems theory.* New York: Braziller.

Biddle, B. J. (1979). *Role theory: Expectations, identities, and behaviors.* New York: Academic Press.

Biddle, B. J., & Thomas, E. J. (Eds.). (1966). *Role theory: Concepts and research.* New York: Wiley.

Black, M. (1962). *Models and metaphors: Studies in language and philosophy.* Ithaca, NY: Cornell University Press.

Blatner, A. (1996). *Acting-in: Practical applications of psychodramatic methods* (3rd ed.). New York: Springer.

Blatner, A., & Blatner, A. (1988). *Foundations of psychodrama: History, theory, and practice* (3rd ed.). New York: Springer.

Bloom, B. S. (Ed.), & Krathwohl, D. R. (1956). *Taxonomy of educational objectives: Handbook 1. Cognitive domain.* New York: David McKay.

Bloom, M. (1975). *The paradox of helping: Introduction to the philosophy of scientific practice.* New York: Wiley.

Bloom, M. (1992). A conversation with Carel Germain on human development in the ecological context. In M. Bloom (Ed.), *Changing lives: Studies in human development and professional helping* (pp. 406–409). Columbia: University of South Carolina Press.

Bloom, M., Wood, K., & Chambon, A. (1991). The six languages of social work. *Social Work,* 36(6), 530–534.

Blumer, H. (1969). *Symbolic interactionism.* Berkeley: University of California Press.

Blumer, H. (1990). *Industrialization as an agent of social change: A critical analysis.* Hawthorne, NY: Aldine de Gruyter.

Bohman, J. (1996). *Public deliberation: Pluralism, complexity, and democracy.* Cambridge, MA: MIT Press.

Bohman, J. (1997). Deliberative democracy and effective social freedom: Capabilities, resources, and opportunities. In J. Bohman & W. Rehg (Eds.), *Deliberative democracy: Essays on reason and politics* (pp. 321–348). Cambridge, MA: MIT Press.

Bohman, J. (1999a). Democracy as inquiry, inquiry as democratic: Pragmatism, social science, and the cognitive division of labor. *American Journal of Political Science,* (43)2, 590–607.

Bohman, J. (1999b). Theories, practices, and pluralism: A pragmatic interpretation of critical social science. *Philosophy of the Social Sciences,* 29(4), 459–480.

Bohman, J. (2000). Distorted communication: Formal pragmatics as a critical theory. In L. E. Hahn (Ed.), *Perspectives on Habermas* (pp. 3–20). Chicago: Open Court.

Bohman, J. (2001). Participants, observers, and critics: Practical knowledge, social perspectives, and critical pluralism. In W. Rehg & J. Bohman (Eds.), *Pluralism and the pragmatic turn: The transformation of critical theory* (pp. 88–113). Cambridge, MA: MIT Press.

Boisen, L., & Syers, M. (2004). The integrative case analysis model for linking theory and practice. *Journal of Education for Social Work,* 40(2), 205–217.

Boulding, K. E. (1983). Introduction. In M. Davidson, *Uncommon sense: The life and thought of Ludwig von Bertalanffy, father of general systems theory* (pp. 17–19). Los Angeles: Tarcher.

Bowlby, J. (1988). *A secure base: Parent-child attachment and healthy human development.* New York: Basic Books.

Brace, C. L. (1995). Race and political correctness. *American Psychologist,* 50(8), 725–726.

Brace, C. L. (2005). *"Race" is a four-letter word.* New York: Oxford University Press.

Brauckmann, S. (2004). Ludwig von Bertalanffy. Retrieved December 4, 2004, from http://www.isss.org/lumLVB.htm

Breakwell, G. M. (1982). Models in action: The use of theories by practitioners. In P. Stringer (Ed.), *Confronting social issues: Applications of social psychology* (Vol. 1, pp. 51–69). London: Academic Press.

Bretherton, I. (1992). The origins of attachment theory: John Bowlby and Mary Ainsworth. *Developmental Psychology,* 28, 759–775.

Bretherton, I. (1997). Bowlby's legacy to developmental psychology. *Child Psychiatry and Human Development, 28*(1), 33–43.

Brinquier, J. C. (1980). *Conversations with Jean Piaget.* Chicago: University of Chicago Press.

Britt, D. (1997). *A conceptual introduction to modeling: Qualitative and quantitative perspectives.* Mahwah, NJ: Erlbaum.

Bronfenbrenner, U. (1979). *The ecology of human development: Experiments by nature and design.* Cambridge, MA: Harvard University Press.

Bronfenbrenner, U. (1986). Ecology of the family as a context for human development: Research perspectives. *Developmental Psychology, 22*(6), 723–742.

Bronfenbrenner, U. (1990). Discovering what families do. In D. Blankenhorn, S. Bayme, & J. B. Elshtain (Eds.), *Rebuilding the nest* (pp. 27–38). Milwaukee, WI: Family Service America.

Bronfenbrenner, U. (1992). Ecological systems theory. In R. Vasta (Ed.), *Annals of child development: Six theories of child development: Revised formulations and current issues* (pp. 187–250). London: Jessica Kingsley.

Bronfenbrenner, U. (1999). Environments in developmental perspective: Theoretical and operational models. In S. L. Friedman & T. D. Wachs (Eds.), *Measuring environments across the life span: Emerging methods and concepts* (pp. 3–28). Washington, DC: American Psychological Association.

Bronfenbrenner, U., & Evans, G. W. (2000). Developmental science in the 21st century: Emerging questions, theoretical models, research designs and empirical findings. *Social Development, 9*(1), 115–125.

Brooks, W. K. (1986). Human behavior/social environment: Past and present, future or folly? *Journal of Social Work Education, 1,* 18–23.

Brower, A. M. (1988). Can the ecological model guide social work practice? *Social Service Review, 62*(3), 411–429.

Brower, A. M., & Nurius, P. S. (1993). *Social cognition and individual change: Current theory and counseling guidelines.* Newbury Park, CA: Sage.

Brown, R. H. (1992). Science and society as discourse: Toward a sociology of civic competence. In S. Seidman & D. G. Wagner (Eds.), *Postmodernism and social theory: The debate over general theory* (pp. 223–243). Cambridge, MA: Basil Blackwell.

Bruyn, S. T. (1977). *The social economy: People transforming business.* New York: Wiley.

Bruyn, S. T. (1991). *A future of the American economy: The social market.* Stanford, CA: Stanford University Press.

Buckley, W. (1967). *Sociology and modern systems theory.* Englewood Cliffs, NJ: Prentice-Hall.

Buckley, W. (1968). Society as a complex adaptive system. In W. Buckley (Ed.), *Modern systems research for the behavioral scientist: A sourcebook* (pp. 490–513). Chicago: Aldine.

Buckley, W. (1998). *Society—A complex adaptive system: Essays in social theory.* London: Routledge.

Bulmer, M. (1984). *The Chicago school of sociology: Institutionalization, diversity, and the rise of sociological research.* Chicago: University of Chicago Press.

Burns, D. D. (1980). *Feeling good: The new mood therapy.* New York: Signet.

Burr, W. R. (1973). *Theory construction and the sociology of the family.* New York: Wiley.

Burr, W. R. (1995). Using theories in family science. In R. D. Day, K. R. Gilbert, B. H. Settles, & W. R. Burr (Eds.), *Research and theory in family science* (pp. 73–90). Pacific Grove, CA: Brooks/Cole.

Burr, W. R., & the Editors. (1979). Metatheory and diagramming conventions. In W. R. Burr, R. Hill, F. I. Nye, & I. L. Reiss (Eds.), *Contemporary theories about the family: Research-based theories* (Vol. 1, pp. 3–24). New York: Free Press.

Burr, W. R., Klein, S. R., & Associates (1994). *Reexamining family stress: New theory and research.* Thousand Oaks, CA: Sage.

Burr, W. R., Leigh, G. K., Day, R. D., & Constantine, J. (1979). Symbolic interaction and the family. In W. R. Burr, R. Hill, F. I. Nye, & I. L. Reiss (Eds.), *Contemporary theories about the family: General theories/theoretical orientations* (pp. 42–111). New York: Free Press.

Cahill, S. E. (1980). Directions for an interactionist study of gender development. *Symbolic Interaction, 3*(1), 123–138.

Cahill, S. E. (1983). Reexamining the acquisition of sex roles: A social interactionist approach. *Sex Roles, 9*(1), 1–15.

Cahill, S. E. (1986a). Childhood socialization as a recruitment process: Some lessons from the study of child development. *Sociological Studies of Child Development, 1,* 163–186.

Cahill, S. E. (1986b). Language practices and self definition: The case of gender identity acquisition. *Sociological Quarterly, 27*(3), 295–311.

Cahill, S. E. (1989). Fashioning males and females: Appearance management and the social reproduction of gender. *Symbolic Interaction, 12*(2), 281–298.

Cahill, S. E. (1994). And a child shall lead us? Children, gender and perspectives by incongruity. In N. J. Herman & L. T. Reynolds (Eds.), *An introduction to social psychology* (pp. 459–469). Dix Hills, NJ: General Hall.

Cairns, R. B., & Cairns, B. D. (1995). Social ecology over time and space. In P. Moen, G. H. Elder Jr., & K. Luscher (Eds.), *Examining lives in context: Perspectives on the ecology of human development* (pp. 397–422). Washington, DC: American Psychological Association.

Callero, P. L. (1985–1986). Putting the social in prosocial behavior: An interactionist approach to altruism. *Humboldt Journal of Social Relations, 13*(1–2), 15–32.

Callero, P. L. (1986). Toward a Meadian conceptualization of role. *Sociological Quarterly, 27*(3), 343–358.

Callero, P. L. (1994). From role-playing to role-using: Understanding role as resource. *Social Psychology Quarterly, 57*(3), 228–243.

Calton, J. M., & Payne, S. L. (2003). Coping with paradox: Multistakeholder learning dialogue as a pluralistic sense-making process for addressing messy problems. *Business and Society, 42*(1), 7–42.

Camic, C., & Joas, H. (2004). The dialogical turn. In C. Camic & H. Joas (Eds.), *The dialogical turn: New roles for sociology in the postdisciplinary age* (p. 1–19). Lanham, MD: Rowman and Littlefield.

Campbell, J. (1992). *The community reconstructs: The meaning of pragmatic social thought.* Urbana: University of Illinois Press.

Carel Bailey Germain Papers, 1922–1998. (2004). Sophia Smith Collection, Smith College. Retrieved June 4, 2004, from http://asteria. fivecolleges.edu/findaids/ sophiasmith/mnsss24.html

Carey, J. T. (1975). *Sociology and public affairs: The Chicago school.* Beverly Hills, CA: Sage.

Carruthers, B. G., & Babb, S. L. (2000). *Economy/society: Markets, meanings, and social structure.* Thousand Oaks, CA: Pine Forge Press.

Carson, R. (1961). *The sea around us.* New York: Signet. (Original work published 1951)

Carson, R. (1962). *Silent spring.* New York: Houghton Mifflin.

Carson, R. (1998). The edge of the sea. In L. Lear (Ed.), *Lost woods: The discovered writing of Rachel Carson* (pp. 133–146). Boston: Beacon Press. (Original work published 1953)

Carter, B., & McGoldrick, M. (1999). Overview: The expanded family life cycle: Individual, family, and social perspectives. In B. Carter & M. McGoldrick (Eds.), *The expanded family life cycle: Individual, family, and social perspectives* (pp. 1–26). Needham Heights, MA: Allyn & Bacon.

Catton, W. R., Jr. (1992). Separation versus unification in sociological human ecology. *Advances in Human Ecology, 1,* 65–99.

Caughey, J. L. (1984). *Imaginary social worlds.* Lincoln: University of Nebraska Press.

Chafetz, J. S. (1978). *A primer on the construction and testing of theories in sociology.* Itasca, IL: Peacock.

Chaiklin, H. (1975). Social work, sociology, and social diagnosis.

Journal of Sociology and Social Welfare, 2, 102–107.

Chang, J. H-Y. (2000). Symbolic interaction and the transformation of class structure: The case of China. *Symbolic Interaction, 23*(3), 223–251.

Chetkow-Yanoov, B. (1992). *Social work practice: A systems approach.* New York: Haworth Press.

Chodorow, N. J. (1990). What is the relation between psychoanalytic feminism and the psychoanalytic psychology of women? In D. L. Rhode (Ed.), *Theoretical perspectives on sexual difference* (pp. 114–130). New Haven, CT: Yale University Press.

Choldin, H. M. (1978). Social life and the physical environment. In D. Street & Associates (Eds.), *Handbook of contemporary urban life* (pp. 352–384). San Francisco: Jossey-Bass.

Churchman, C. W. (1968). *The systems approach.* New York: Dell.

Cicourel, A. V. (1981). The role of cognitive-linguistic concepts in understanding everyday social interactions. *Annual Review of Sociology, 7,* 87–106.

Clark, C. (1987). Sympathy biography and sympathy margin. *American Journal of Sociology, 93*(2), 291–321.

Clark, C. (1997). *Misery and company: Sympathy in everyday life.* Chicago: University of Chicago Press.

Clarke, E. (2001). *Aging and caregiving in Canada.* Lewiston, NY: Edward Mellon Press.

Clarkson, P. (1992). Systemic integrative psychotherapy training. In W. Dryden (Ed.), *Integrative and eclectic psychotherapy: A handbook* (pp. 269–295). Buckingham, UK: Open University Press.

Clausen, J. A. (1986). *The life course: A sociological perspective.* Englewood Cliffs, NJ: Prentice-Hall.

Cloward, R. A., & Piven, F. F. (1975). Notes toward a radical social work. In R. Bailey & M. Brake (Eds.), *Radical social work* (pp. vi–xlviii). New York: Pantheon.

Coady, N. (1995). A reflective/inductive model of practice: Emphasizing theory-building for unique cases versus applying theory to

practice. In G. Rogers (Ed.), *Social work field education: Views and visions* (pp. 139–151). Dubuque, IA: Kendall/Hunt.

Coady, N., & Lehmann, P. (2001a). An overview of and rationale for a generalist-eclectic approach to direct social work practice. In P. Lehmann & N. Coady (Eds.), *Theoretical perspectives for direct social work practice: A generalist-eclectic approach* (pp. 3–26). New York: Springer.

Coady, N., & Lehmann, P. (2001b). Revisiting the generalist-eclectic approach. In P. Lehmann & N. Coady (Eds.), *Theoretical perspectives for direct social work practice: A generalist-eclectic approach* (pp. 405–420). New York: Springer.

Cocozelli, C. L. (1987). *Social workers' theoretical orientations.* Lanham, MD: University Press of America.

Collins, R. (1993). Emotional energy as the common denominator of rational action. *Rationality and Society, 5*(2), 203–230.

Colomy, P. (1991). Metatheorizing in a postpositivist frame. *Sociological Perspectives, 34*(3), 269–286.

Colomy, P., & Brown, J. D. (1995). Elaboration, revision, polemic, and progress in the second Chicago School. In G. A. Fine (Ed.), *A second Chicago School? The development of a postwar American sociology* (pp. 17–81). Chicago: University of Chicago Press.

Comstock, D. (2005). Women's development. In D. Comstock (Ed.), *Diversity and development: Critical contexts that shape our lives and relationships* (pp. 111–132).

Connelly, M. P., Li, T. M., MacDonald, M., & Parpart, J. L. (2000). Feminism and development: Theoretical perspectives. In J. L. Parpart, M. P. Connelly, & V. E. Barriteau (Eds.), *Theoretical perspectives on gender and development* (pp. 51–159). Ottawa: International Development Research Centre.

Conrad, P., & Schneider, J. W. (1992). *Deviance and medicalization: From badness to sickness.* Philadelphia: Temple University Press.

Cook, K. S., & Whitmeyer, J. (2000). Richard M. Emerson. In G. Ritzer (Ed.), *The Blackwell companion to major social theorists* (pp. 486–512). Malden, MA: Blackwell.

Cooley, C. H. (1930). *Sociological theory and research: Selected papers of Charles Horton Cooley.* New York: Henry Holt.

Coon, D. (1989). *Introduction to psychology: Exploration and application.* St. Paul, MN: West.

Corey, G. (2001). *Theory and process of counseling and psychotherapy* (6th ed.). Belmont, CA: Wadsworth.

Cornett, C. W., & Hudson, R. A. (1987). Middle adulthood and the theories of Erikson, Gould, and Vaillant: Where does the gay man fit? *Journal of Gerontological Social Work, 10*(3/4), 61–73.

Corning, A. F. (2000). Assessing perceived social inequity: A relative deprivation framework. *Journal of Personality and Social Psychology, 78*(3), 463–477.

Couch, C. J. (1979). Bargaining, economic exchange, and civilization. In N. K. Denzin (Ed.), *Studies in symbolic interaction* (Vol. 2, pp. 377–398). Greenwich, CT: JAI Press.

Couch, C. J. (1989). *Social processes and relationships: A formal approach.* Dix Hills, NY: General Hall.

Council on Social Work Education (2001). *Educational policy and accreditation standards.* Retrieved January 12, 2005, from http://www.cswe.org

Cournoyer, B., Powers, G. T., Johnson, J., & Bennett, R. (2000). Economic modeling in social work. *Advances in Social Work, (1) 2,* 161–175.

Craib, I. (1998). Sigmund Freud. In R. Stones (Ed.), *Key sociological thinkers* (pp. 59–70). New York: New York University Press.

Craig, W. C. (1980). *Theories of development: Concepts and applications.* Englewood Cliffs, NJ: Prentice-Hall.

Crawford, C. (1998). Environments and adaptations: Then and now. In C. Crawford & D. L. Krebs (Eds.), *Handbook of evolutionary psychology: Ideas, issues, and applications* (pp. 277–302). Mahwah, NJ: Erlbaum.

Cronen, V. E. (1995). Practical theory and the tasks ahead for social approaches to communication. In W. Leeds-Hurwitz (Ed.), *Social approaches to communication* (pp. 217–242). New York: Guilford Press.

Cronen, V. E., Chen, V., & Pearce, W. B. (1988). Coordinated management of meaning: A critical theory. In Y. Y. Kim & W. B. Gudykunst (Eds.), *Theories in intercultural communication* (pp. 66–98). Newbury Park, CA: Sage.

Csikszentmihalyi, M., & Rochberg, Halton, E. (1981). *The meaning of things: Domestic symbols and the self.* Cambridge, UK: Cambridge University Press.

Cullen, Y. (1980). A maverick mind: Bertha Capen Reynolds and social work, 1885–1978. *Australian Social Work, 33*(2), 25–31.

Cuzzort, R. P., & King, E. E. (1989). *Twentieth-century social thought* (4th ed.). Fort Worth, TX: Holt, Rinehart and Winston.

Dankoski, M., Penn, C., Carlson, T., & Hecker, L. (1998). What's in a name? A study of family therapists' use and acceptance of the feminist perspective. *American Journal of Family Therapy, 26*(1), 95–104.

Danto, E. A. (2005). *Freud's free clinics: Psychoanalysis and social justice, 1918–1938.* New York: Columbia University Press.

Darwin, C. (1996). *The origin of the species.* Oxford, UK: Oxford University Press. (Original work published 1859)

Darwin, F. (1958). *The autobiography of Charles Darwin and selected letters.* New York: Dover. (Original work published 1892)

Davidson, M. (1983). *Uncommon sense: The life and thought of Ludwig von Bertalanffy.* Los Angeles: Tarcher.

Davis, A. (1967). *Spearheads for reform: The social settlements and the progressive movement 1890–1914.* New York: Oxford University Press.

Davis, L. V. (1986). Role theory. In F. J. Turner (Ed.), *Social work treatment: Interlocking theoretical approaches* (3rd ed., pp. 541–563). New York: Free Press.

Deegan, M. J. (1988). *Jane Addams and the men of the Chicago School, 1892–1918.* New Brunswick, NJ: Transaction Books.

Deegan, M. J. (1989). Sociology and conviviality: A conversation with Ellenhorn on convivial sociology. *Humanity and Society, 13*(1), 85–88.

Deegan, M. J. (1992). The genesis of the international self: Working hypotheses emerging from the Chicago experience (1892–1918). In L. Tomasi (Ed.), *Non-European youth and the process of integration* (pp. 339–353). Trento, Italy: University of Trento.

Deegan, M. J. (1994). "The marginal man" as a gendered concept: A feminist analysis of Robert E. Park's epistemology. In R. Gubert & L. Tomasi (Eds.), *Robert E. Park and the "melting pot" theory* (pp. 55–71). Trento, Italy: University of Trento.

Deflem, M. (1999). Teaching theory for sociology students: Junior notes. *Perspectives, 21*(2), 7–8.

Delon, M., & Wenston, S. R. (1989). An integrated theoretical guide to intervention with depressed elderly clients. *Journal of Gerontological Social Work, 13*(3–4), 131–146.

Delshadi, L. (1998). The development of therapists' clinical orientations (Doctoral dissertation, University of Toronto, 1998). *Dissertation Abstracts International: Section B. The Sciences and Engineering, 59,* 12-B, 6485.

Denzin, N. K. (1992). *Symbolic interactionism and cultural studies.* Cambridge, MA: Blackwell.

Denzin, N. K. (1994). Postpragmatism: Beyond Dewey and Mead. *Symbolic Interaction, 17*(4), 453–463.

Depew, D. J. (2000). Between pragmatism and realism: Richard McKeon's philosophical semantics. In E. Garver & R. Buchanan (Eds.), *Pluralism in theory and practice: Richard McKeon and American philosophy* (pp. 29–53). Nashville, TN: Vanderbilt University Press.

Derezotes, D. S. (2000). *Advanced generalist social work practice.* Thousand Oaks, CA: Sage.

Dewey, J. (1951). The biography of John Dewey. In P. A. Schilpp (Ed.), *The philosophy of John Dewey* (pp. 3–45). La Salle, IL: Open Court.

Dewey, J. (1990). *The school and society and the child and the curriculum.* Chicago: University of Chicago Press. (Original work published 1902)

Dewey, J., & Bentley, A. F. (1949). *Knowing and the known.* Boston: Beacon Hill.

Dodge, K. A. (2004). The nature-nurture debate and public policy. *Merrill-Palmer Quarterly, 50*(4), 418–427.

Downing, J. N. (2000). *Between conviction and uncertainty: Philosophical guidelines for the practicing psychotherapist.* Albany: State University of New York Press.

Downing, J. N. (2004). Psychotherapy practice in a pluralistic world: Philosophical and moral dilemmas. *Journal of Psychotherapy Integration, 14*(2), 123–148.

Duncker, E. (2001). Symbolic communication in multidisciplinary cooperations. *Science, Technology, and Human Values, 26*(3), 349–386.

Dunlap, R. E. (1997). The evolution of environmental sociology: A brief history and assessment of the American experience. In M. Redclift & G. Woodgate (Eds.), *The international handbook of environmental sociology* (pp. 21–39). Cheltenham, UK: Edward Elgar.

Dunlap, R. E. (2002). Paradigms, theories, and environmental sociology. In R. Dunlap, F. H. Buttell, P. Dickens, & A. Gijswijt (Eds.), *Sociological theory and the environment: Classical foundations and contemporary insights* (pp. 329–350). Lanham, MD: Rowman and Littlefield.

Dunn, L. C. (2002). Gregor Mendel. *Encyclopedia Britannica 2002.* Macintosh Software. SelectSoft Publishing and Encyclopedia Britannica (http:www.support.selectsoft.com).

Duvall, E. M. (1962). *Family development* (2nd ed.). Philadelphia: Lippincott.

Duvall, E. M. (1977). *Marriage and family development* (5th ed.) New York: Harper & Row.

Dykhuizen, G. (1973). *The life and mind of John Dewey.* Carbondale: Southern Illinois University Press.

Eagle, M. N. (1984). *Recent developments in psychoanalysis: A critical evaluation.* New York: McGraw-Hill.

Egan, G. (1979). *People in systems: A model for development in the human-service professions and education.* Monterey, CA: Brooks/Cole.

Ellis, A. (1973). *Humanistic psychotherapy.* New York: McGraw-Hill.

Ellis, A. (2005). Rational emotive behavior therapy. In R. J. Corsini & D. Wedding (Eds.), *Current psychotherapies* (7th ed., pp. 166–201). Belmont, CA: Wadsworth.

Ellis, A., & Harper, R.A. (1975). *A new guide to rational living.* North Hollywood, CA: Wilshire.

Emerson, R. M. (1962). Power-dependence relations. *American Sociological Review, 27,* 31–41.

Emirbayer, M. (1997). Manifesto for a relational sociology. *American Journal of Sociology, 2,* 281–317.

Encyclopedia Britannica. (2002). Keynes, John Maynard. *Encyclopedia Britannica Standard Edition CD.* http://www.selectsoftware.usa

Endleman, R. (1981). *Psyche and society: Explorations in psychoanalytic society.* New York: Columbia University Press.

England, P., & Browne, I. (1992). Internalization and constraint in women's subordination. *Current Perspectives in Social Theory, 12,* 97–123.

Ephross Saltman, J. E., & Greene, R. R. (1993). Social workers' perceived knowledge and use of human behavior theory. *Journal of Social Work Education, 29*(1), 88–98.

Erikson, E. H. (1963). *Childhood and society* (2nd ed.). New York: Norton.

Erikson, E. H. (1968a). *Identity: Youth and crisis.* New York: Norton.

Erikson, E. H. (1968b). Identity, psychosocial. In D. L. Sills (Ed.), *The international encyclopedia of the social sciences* (pp. 60–65). New York: Crowell Collier Macmillan.

Erikson, E. H. (1975). *Life history and the historical moment: Diverse presentations.* New York: Norton.

Erikson, E. H. (1980). *Identity and the life cycle.* New York: Norton. (Original work published 1959)

Erikson, E. H., & Newton, H. P. (1973). *In search of common ground: Conversations with Erik H. Erikson and Huey P. Newton.* New York: Norton.

Evans, R. (1973). *Jean Piaget: The man and his ideas.* New York: Dutton.

Evans, R. I. (1989). *Albert Bandura: The man and his ideas—A dialogue.* New York: Praeger.

Facing History. (2005). Carol Gilligan. Retrieved October 9, 2005, from http://www.facinghistory.org/facing/fhao2.nsf/scholars/Carol & Gilligan?opendocument

Falck, H. S. (1988). *Social work: The membership perspective.* New York: Springer.

Falicov, C. J. (1988). Family sociology and family therapy contributions to the family development framework: A comparative analysis and thoughts on future trends. In C. J. Falicov (Ed.), *Family transitions: Continuity and change over the life cycle* (pp. 3–51). New York: Guilford Press.

Fararo, T. J. (1989). The spirit of unification in sociological theory. *Sociological Theory, 7*(2), 175–190.

Faris, R. E. L. (1967). *Chicago sociology: 1920–1932.* Chicago: University of Chicago Press.

Farris, B., & Marsh, J. (1982). Social work as a foreign body in late capitalism. *Journal of Applied Behavioral Science, 18*(1), 87–94.

Fawcett, J., & Downs, F. S. (1986). *The relationship of theory and research.* Norwalk, CT: Appleton-Century-Crofts.

Feagin, J. R., & Vera, H. (2001). *Liberation sociology.* Boulder, CO: Westview Press.

Feffer, A. (1993). *The Chicago pragmatists and American progressivism.* Ithaca, NY: Cornell University Press.

Feixas, G., & Botella, L. (2004). Psychotherapy integration: Reflections and contributions from a constructivist epistemology. *Journal of Psychotherapy Integration, 14*(2), 192–222.

Fenstermaker, S., West, C., & Zimmerman, D. H. (1991). Gender inequality: New conceptual terrain. In R. L. Blumberg (Ed.), *Gender, family, and economy: The triple overlap* (pp. 289–307). Newbury Park, CA: Sage.

Ferguson, K. E. (1980). *Self, society and womankind: The dialectic of liberation.* Westport, CT: Greenwood Press.

Fine, G. A. (1998). *Morel tales: The culture of mushrooming.* Cambridge, MA: Harvard University Press.

Fine, G. A., & Manning, P. (2000). Erving Goffman. In G. Ritzer (Ed.), *The Blackwell companion to major social theorists* (pp. 457–485). Malden, MA: Blackwell.

Finfgeld, D. L. (2003). Metasynthesis: The state of the art—so far. *Qualitative Health Research, 13*(7), 893–904.

Fischer, J. (1986). Eclectic casework. In J. G. Norcross (Ed.), *Handbook of eclectic psychotherapy* (pp. 320–352). New York: Brunner/Mazel.

Fishman, D. B. (1999). *The case for pragmatic psychology.* New York: New York University Press.

Fitzpatrick, J. J. (1997). Nursing theory and metatheory. In I. M. King & J. Fawcett (Eds.), *The language of nursing theory and metatheory* (pp. 27–29). Indianapolis, IN: Sigma Theta Tau International.

Flavell, J. H. (1985). *Cognitive development* (2nd ed.). Englewood Cliffs, NJ: Prentice-Hall.

Foa, U. G. (1973). Interpersonal and economic resources. *Science, 171,* 345–351.

Fonagy, P. (1999). Psychoanalytic theory from the viewpoint of attachment theory and research. In J. Cassidy & P. E. Shaver (Ed.), *Handbook of attachment: Theory, research, and clinical applications* (pp. 595–624). New York: Guilford Press.

Fook, J. (2002). Theorizing from practice: Towards an inclusive approach for social work research. *Qualitative Social Work, 1*(1), 79–95.

Fook, J., Ryan, M., & Hawkins, L. (1997). Towards a theory of social work expertise. *British Journal of Social Work, 27,* 399–417.

Foote, N. N. (1957). Concept and method in the study of human development. In M. Sherif & M. C. Wilson (Eds.), *Emerging problems in social psychology* (pp. 29–40). Norman: University of Oklahoma Press.

Forte, J. A. (1988). Group services for the hard to reach in a new age settlement house. In M. Liederman, M. Birnbaum, & B. Dazzo (Eds.), *Roots and new frontiers in social group work* (pp. 13–26). New York: Haworth Press.

Forte, J. A. (1989). Restoring positive membership: Group counseling in community based corrections. In J. Lindsay & J. Landriault (Eds.), *Proceedings of the 11th Annual Symposium of the Association for the Advancement of Social Work with Groups* (pp. 661–681). Montreal: Coordinating Committee of the 11th Annual Symposium of Social Work with Groups.

Forte, J. A. (1990). *Men's personal, dyadic, and family well-being across the family life cycle.* Unpublished doctoral dissertation, Virginia Commonwealth University, Richmond.

Forte, J. A. (1991). Operating a member-employing therapeutic business as part of an alternative mental health center. *Health and Social Work, 16*(3), 213–223.

Forte, J. A. (1994). The teaching record: A framework for teaching group process. *Journal of Social Work Education, 30*(1), 116–128.

Forte, J. A. (1997). Calling students to serve the homeless: A project to promote altruism and community service. *Journal of Social Work Education, 33*(1), 151–166.

Forte, J. A. (1999). Calling students to serve the homeless: The reflective research story. *Reflections, 5*(3), 23–32.

Forte, J. A. (2001). *Theories for practice: Symbolic interactionist translations.* Lanham, MD: University Press of America.

Forte, J. A. (2002a). Mead, contemporary metatheory, and twenty-first-century interdisciplinary team work. *Sociological Practice: A Journal of Clinical and Applied Sociology, 4*(4), 315–334.

Forte, J. A. (2002b). Not in my social world: A cultural analysis of media representations, contested spaces, and sympathy for the homeless. *Journal of Sociology and Social Welfare, 29*(4), 131–157.

Forte, J. A. (2003). Applied symbolic interactionism: Meanings, memberships, and social work. In L. T. Reynolds & N. J. Herman (Eds.), *Handbook of symbolic interactionism* (pp. 915–936). Walnut Creek, CA: Altamira Press.

Forte, J. A. (2004a). Symbolic interactionism and social work: A forgotten legacy, Part 1. *Families in Society, 85*(3), 391–400.

Forte, J. A. (2004b). Symbolic interactionism and social work: A forgotten legacy, Part 2. *Families in Society, 85*(4), 521–530.

Forte, J. A. (2005). E-mail as the modern SOS: Enlisting cyber allies in a "Save Our Undergraduate Program" campaign. *Reflections, 11*(2), 32–46.

Forte, J. A., Barrett, A. V., & Campbell, M. H. (1996). Patterns of social connectedness and shared grief work: A symbolic interactionist perspective. *Social Work with Groups, 19*(1), 29–52.

Forte, J. A., Franks, D. D., Forte, J., & Rigsby, D. (1996). Oppressive social situations and asymmetrical role-taking: Comparing battered and non-battered women. *Social Work, 41*(1), 59–73.

Fraenkel, P., & Pinsof, W. M. (2001). Teaching family therapy–centered integration: Assimilation and beyond. *Journal of Psychotherapy Integration, 11*(1), 59–85.

Franklin, C. W., II. (1982). *Theoretical perspectives in social psychology.* Boston: Little, Brown.

Franklin, C. W., II. (1988). *Men and society.* Chicago: Nelson-Hall.

Franklin, C., & Jordan, C. (1999). *Family practice: Brief systems methods for social work.* Pacific Grove, CA: Brooks/Cole.

Franklin, C., & Warren, K. (1999). Advances in systems theory. In C. Franklin & C. Jordan (Eds.), *Family practice: Brief systems methods for social work* (pp. 397–425). Pacific Grove, CA: Brooks/Cole.

Freese, L. (1997). *Environmental connections.* Greenwich, CT: JAI Press.

Freud Loewenstein, S. (1978). Preparing social work students for life-transition counseling within the human behavior sequence. *Journal of Education for Social Work, 14*(2), 66–73.

Freud Loewenstein, S. (1985). Freud's metapsychology revisited. *Social Work, 66*(3), 139–151.

Freud Museum. (2005). Freud and religion. Retrieved July 27, 2005, from http://www.Freud.org.uk

Freud, Sophie. (1992). Psychodynamic theories: A frame for development. In M. Bloom (Ed.), *Changing lives: Studies in human development and professional helping* (pp. 419–427). Columbia: University of South Carolina Press.

Freud, Sophie. (2005). Freud goes up in smoke. *Toronto Star*, November 16, 2003. Retrieved July 26, 2005, from http://www.ahrp.org/infomail/03/11/16.php

Fuller, B. (1983). Foreword. In M. Davidson, *Uncommon sense: The life and thought of Ludwig von Bertalanffy, father of general systems theory* (pp. 13–15). Los Angeles: Tarcher.

Galper, J. H. (1975). *The politics of social service*. Englewood Cliffs, NJ: Prentice-Hall.

Gambrill, E. D. (1994). Concepts and methods of behavioral treatment. In D. K. Granvold (Ed.), *Cognitive and behavioral treatment: Methods and applications* (pp. 32–62). Pacific Grove, CA: Brooks/Cole.

Gambrill, E. D. (1997). Making decisions about integration. In D. J. Tucker, C. Garvin, & R. Sarri (Eds.), *Integrating knowledge and practice: The case of social work and social science* (pp. 25–37). Westport, CT: Praeger.

Gandhi, R. S. (1978). Socialization and personality. In J. S. Roucek (Ed.), *Social control for the 1980s* (pp. 63–75).Westport, CT: Greenwood Press.

Gardner, M. (2000). Little Red Riding Hood. *Skeptical Inquirer, 24*(5), 14–16.

Garvin, C. D. (1997). *Contemporary group work* (3rd ed.). Boston: Allyn & Bacon.

Gaziano, E. (1996). Ecological metaphors as scientific boundary work: Innovation and authority in interwar sociology and biology. *American Journal of Sociology, 101*(4), 874–907.

Gecas, C., Calonico, J. M., & Thomas, D. L. (1974). The development of self-concept in the child: Mirror theory versus model theory. *Journal of Social Psychology, 92*, 67–76.

Gecas, V. (1989). The social psychology of self-efficacy. *Annual Review of Sociology, 15*, 291–316.

George, L. K. (1983). Socialization, roles and identity in later life. In A. Kerckhoff, N. Krishnan, R. Corwin, & A. Pallas (Eds.), *Research in sociology of education and socialization* (Vol. 4, pp. 233–263). Greenwich, CT: JAI Press.

George, L. K. (1993). Sociological perspectives on life transitions. *Annual Review of Sociology, 19*, 353–373.

Gergen, K. J. (1982). *Toward transformation in social knowledge*. New York: Springer- Verlag.

Gergen, K. J. (1990). Metaphor, metatheory, and the social world. In D. E. Leary (Ed.), *Metaphors in the history of psychology* (pp. 267–299). Cambridge, UK: Cambridge University Press.

Germain, C. B. (1973). An ecological perspective in casework practice. *Social Casework, 54*, 323–330.

Germain, C. B. (1978). Space: An ecological variable in social work practice. *Social Casework, 59*(9), 515–522.

Germain, C. B. (1979). Ecology and social work. In C. B. Germain (Ed.), *Social work practice: People and environments* (pp. 1–22). New York: Columbia University Press.

Germain, C. B. (1987). Human development in contemporary environments. *Social Service Review, 61*, 565–580.

Germain, C. B. (1990). Life forces and the anatomy of practice. *Smith College Studies in Social Work, 60*(2), 138–152.

Germain, C. B. (1991). *Human behavior in the social environment: An ecological view*. New York: Columbia University Press.

Germain, C. B. (1997). Should HBSE be taught from a stage perspective? In M. Bloom & W. C. Klein (Eds.), *Controversial issues in human behavior in the social environment* (pp. 33–48). Boston: Allyn & Bacon.

Germain, C. B., & Gitterman, A. (1996). *The life model of social work practice: Advances in theory and practice* (2nd ed.). New York: Columbia University Press.

Gesell, A., Ilg, F. L., Ames, L. B., & Bullis, G. E. (1977). *The child from five to ten*. New York: Harper & Row.

Gesell Institute. (2005). Developmental screening. Retrieved July 8, 2005, from www.gesellinstitute.org

Giacalone, R. A., & Beard, J. W. (1994). Impression management, diversity, and international management. *American Behavioral Scientist, 37*(5), 621–636.

Gibbs, P. (1986). HBSE in the undergraduate curriculum: A survey. *Journal of Social Work Education, 2*, 46–52.

Gil, D. G. (1998). *Confronting injustice and oppression: Concepts and strategies for social workers*. New York: Columbia University Press.

Gilgun, J. F. (1996). Human development and adversity in ecological perspective: Part 1. A conceptual framework. *Families in Society, 77*(7), 395–402.

Gilligan, C. (1982). *In a different voice: Psychological theory and women's development*. Cambridge, MA: Harvard University Press.

Gilligan, C. (1987). Moral orientation and moral development. In E. F. Kittay & D. T. Meyers (Eds.), *Women and moral theory* (pp. 19–33). Totowa, NJ: Rowman and Littlefield.

Gilson, S. F. (1999). The biological person. In E. D. Hutchison, *Dimensions of human behavior: Person and environment* (pp. 81–108). Thousand Oaks, CA: Pine Forge.

Gilson, S. F., Depoy, E., & MacDuffie, H. (2002). Disability and social work education: A multitheoretical approach. In S. F. Gilson (Ed.), *Integrating disability content in social work education: A curriculum resource* (pp. 1–8).

Alexandria, VA: Council on Social Work Education.

Ginsburg, H., & Opper, S. (1969). *Piaget's theory of intellectual development: An introduction.* Englewood Cliffs, NJ: Prentice-Hall.

Gitlin, T. (2004). C. Wright Mills: Free radical. Retrieved March 25, 2004, from http://www .uni-muenster.de/Pealon/dgs-mills/ mills-textte/GitlinMills.htm

Gitterman, A. (1988). Teaching students to connect theory and practice. *Social Work with Groups,* 11(1/2), 33–41.

Goffman, E. (1959). *The presentation of self in everyday life.* New York: Doubleday, Anchor Books.

Goffman, E. (1963). *Stigma: Notes on the management of spoiled identity.* Englewood Cliffs, NJ: Prentice-Hall.

Goffman, E. (1974). *Frame analysis: An essay on the organization of experience.* Cambridge, MA: Harvard University Press.

Golan, N. (1981). *Passing through transitions: A guide for practitioners.* New York: Free Press.

Gold, J. R. (1993). The sociohistorical context of psychotherapy integration. In G. Stricker & J. K. Gold (Eds.), *Comprehensive handbook of psychotherapy integration* (pp. 3–8). New York: Plenum Press.

Goldfarb, R. S., & Griffith, W. B. (1991). The "theory as map" analogy and changes in assumption sets in economics. In A. Etzioni & P. R. Lawrence (Eds.), *Socioeconomics: Toward a new synthesis* (pp. 105–129). Armonk, NY: M. E. Sharpe.

Goldhaber, D. E. (2000). *Theories of human development: Integrative perspectives.* Mountain View, CA: Mayfield.

Goldstein, E. G. (1984). *Ego psychology and social work practice.* New York: Free Press.

Goldstein, E. G. (2001). *Object relations theory and self psychology in social work practice.* New York: Free Press.

Goodman, A. H. (2000). Why genes don't count (for racial differences in health). *American Journal of Public Health, 90,* 1699–1702.

Goodman, N. (1985). Socialization II: A developmental view. In H. A. Farberman & R. S. Perinbanayagam (Eds.), *Foundations of interpretive sociology: Original essays in symbolic interaction* (pp. 95–116). Greenwich, CT: JAI Press.

Gordon, W. E. (1969). Basic constructs for an integrative and generative conception of social work. In G. Hearn (Ed.), *The general systems approach: Contributions toward an holistic conception of social work* (pp. 5–11). New York: Council on Social Work Education.

Gore, A. (2002). Introduction. Rachel Carson's *Silent spring.* Boston: Houghton Mifflin.

Gosnell, D. (1974). Some similarities and dissimilarities between the psychodramaturgical approaches of J. L. Moreno and Erving Goffman. In I. A. Greenberg (Ed.), *Psychodrama: Theory and therapy* (pp. 395–411). New York: Behavioral Publications.

Graham, J. R., & Barter, K. (1999). Collaboration: A social work method. *Families in Environment, 80*(1), 6–13.

Gramling, R. (1990). A multiple perspective approach to using micro theory. *Sociological Inquiry, 60*(1), 87–96.

Green, R. G., & Harris, R. N., Jr. (1989). *Survey of the Virginia Army National Guard: Preliminary results of the member survey.* Richmond: Virginia National Guard Family Research and Service Program.

Green, R. G., Harris, R. N., Jr., Forte, J. A., & Robinson, M. (1991). The wives data and FACES IV: Making things appear simple. *Family Process, 30*(1), 79–83.

Greene, R. R. (1991). Eriksonian theory: A developmental approach to ego mastery. In R. R. Greene & P. H. Ephross (Eds.), *Human behavior theory and social work practice* (pp. 79–104). New York: Aldine de Gruyter.

Greene, R. R. (1994). *Human behavior theory: A diversity framework.* New York: Aldine de Gruyter.

Greene, R. R. (1999). *Human behavior theory and social work practice* (2nd ed.). New York: Aldine de Gruyter.

Greene, R. R., & Ephross, P. H. (1991). *Human behavior theory and social work practice.* New York: Aldine de Gruyter.

Gregg, G. (2002). A sketch of Albert Ellis. Albert Ellis Institute, Retrieved December 31, 2002, from http://www.rebt.org

Grieder, T., & Garkovich, L. (1994). Landscapes: The social construction of nature and the environment. *Rural Sociology I 59*(1), 1–24.

Grief, G. L. (1986). The ecosystems perspective "meets the press." *Social Work, 31*(3), 225–226.

Grolier Encyclopedia. (1999). Smith, Adam. *Grolier Multimedia Encyclopedia, OEM Version 11.0.* Danbury, CT: Grolier Interactive. http://gi.grolier.com

Gubrium, J. F., & Holstein, J. A. (1997). *The new language of qualitative method.* New York: Oxford University Press.

Guest, A. M. (1984). Robert Park and the natural area: A sentimental review. *Sociology and Social Research, 69*(1), 1–21.

Gutheil, A. (1992). Considering the physical environment: An essential component of good practice. *Social Work, 37*(5), 391–397.

Habermas, J. (1984). *The theory of communicative action: Vol. 1. Reason and the rationalization of society.* Boston: Beacon Press. (Original work published 1981)

Habermas, J. (1985). Questions and counterquestions. In R. J. Bernstein (Ed.), *Habermas and modernity* (pp. 192–216). Cambridge, MA: MIT Press.

Habermas, J. (1986). *Between facts and norms.* Cambridge, MA: MIT Press.

Habermas, J. (1989a). *The structural transformation of the public sphere.* Cambridge, MA: MIT Press. (Original work published 1962)

Habermas, J. (1989b). *The theory of communicative action: Vol. 2. Lifeworld and system: A critique of functionalist reason.* Boston: Beacon Press. (Original work published 1981)

Habermas, J. (1992). Further reflections on the public sphere. In C. Calhoun (Ed.), *Habermas and the public sphere* (pp. 421–461). Cambridge, MA: MIT Press.

Habermas, J. (1997). Popular sovereignty as procedure. In J. Bohman & W. Rehg (Eds.), *Deliberative democracy: Essays on reason and politics* (pp. 35–65). Cambridge, MA: MIT Press.

Habermas, J. (2001). From Kant's ideas of pure reason to the idealizing presuppositions of communicative action: Reflections on the detranscendentalized use of reason. In W. Rehg & J. Bohman (Eds.), *Pluralism and the pragmatic turn: The transformation of critical theory* (pp. 11–40). Cambridge, MA: MIT Press.

Hage, J., & Powell, C. H. (1992). *Post-industrial lives: Roles and relationships in the 21st century.* Newbury Park, CA: Sage.

Haley, J. (1969). *The power tactics of Jesus Christ and other essays.* New York: Avon.

Hamilton, G. (1954). Self-awareness in professional education. *Social Casework, 35*(9), 371–379.

Hampden, Turner, C. (1981). *Maps of the mind.* London: Mitchell Beazley.

Handelman, D. (1976). Bureaucratic transactions: The development of official client relationships in Israel. In B. Kapferer (Ed.), *Transaction and meaning: Directions in the anthropology of exchange and symbolic behavior* (pp. 233–275). Philadelphia: Institute for the Study of Human Issues.

Hansen, D. A. (1976). *An invitation to critical sociology: Involvement, criticism, exploration.* New York: Free Press.

Hansen, D. A. (1988). Schooling, stress, and family development: Rethinking the social role metaphor. In J. Aldous & D. Klein (Eds.), *Social stress and family development* (pp. 44–78). New York: Guilford Press.

Hanson, B. G. (1995). *General systems theory beginning with wholes.* Washington, DC: Taylor and Francis.

Hardiker, P., & Barker, M. (1991). Towards social theory for social work. In J. Lishman (Ed.), *Handbook of theory for practice teachers in social work* (pp. 87–101). London: Jessica Kingsley.

Hardy, M. E., & Conway, M. E. (1988). *Role theory: Perspectives for health professionals* (2nd ed.). Norwalk, CT: Appleton and Lange.

Hare, A. P. (1985). *Social interaction as drama: Applications from conflict resolution.* Beverly Hills, CA: Sage.

Hare, A. P., & Blumberg, H. H. (1988). *Dramaturgical analysis of social interaction.* New York: Praeger.

Hare, A. P., Blumberg, H. H., & Kressel, G. M. (2001). Social interaction as drama. In A. P. Hare & G. M. Kressel (Eds.), *Israel as center stage* (pp. 1–11). Westport, CT: Bergin and Garvey.

Harre, R. (1978). Architectonic man: On the structuring of lived experience. In R. H. Brown & S. M. Lyman (Eds.), *Structure, consciousness, and history* (pp. 139–172). Cambridge, UK: Cambridge University Press.

Harre, R., & Lamb, R. (1986). *The dictionary of personality and social psychology.* Cambridge, MA: MIT Press.

Harrison, W. D. (1987). Reflective practice in social care. *Social Service Review, 61,* 393–404.

Hartman, A. (1978). Diagrammatic assessment of family relationships. *Social Casework, 59*(8), 465–476.

Hartman, A. (1986). The life and work of Bertha Reynolds: Implications for education and practice today. *Smith College Studies in Social Work, 56*(2), 79–94.

Hartman, A., & Laird, J. (1983). *Family-centered social work practice.* New York: Free Press.

Hawley, A. H. (1986). *Human ecology: A theoretical essay.* Chicago: University of Chicago Press.

Hazan, C., Gur-Yaish, N., & Campa, M. (2004). What does it mean to be attached? In W. S. Rholes & J. A. Simpson (Eds.), *Adult attachment: Theory, research, and clinical implications* (pp. 55–85). New York: Guilford Press.

Healy, M. E. (1972). *Society and social change in the writings of Thomas, Ward, Sumner, and Cooley.* Westport, CT: Greenwood Press.

Hearn, G. (1958). *Theory building in social work.* Toronto: University of Toronto Press.

Hearn, G. (Ed.). (1969a). *The general systems approach: Contributions toward an holistic conception of social work.* New York: Council on Social Work Education.

Hearn, G. (1969b). Introduction. In G. Hearn (Ed.), *The general systems approach: Contributions toward a holistic conception of social work* (pp. 1–4). New York: Council on Social Work Education.

Hearn, G. (1974). General systems theory and social work. In F. J. Turner (Ed.), *Social work treatment: Interlocking theoretical approaches* (pp. 343–371). New York: Free Press.

Hearn, G. (1979). General systems theory and social work. In F. J. Turner (Ed.), *Social work treatment: Interlocking theoretical approaches* (2nd ed., pp. 333–359). New York: Free Press.

Heimer, K. (1995). Gender, race, and the pathways to delinquency: An interactionist explanation. In J. Hagan & R. D. Peterson (Eds.), *Crime and inequality* (pp. 140–173). Stanford, CA: Stanford University Press.

Heimer, K. (1996). Gender, interaction, and delinquency: Testing a theory of differential social control. *Social Psychology Quarterly, 59*(1), 39–61.

Heimer, K., & Matsueda, R. L. (1994). Role-taking, role commitment, and delinquency: A theory of differential social control. *American Sociological Review, 59,* 365–390.

Hektner, J. M., & Csikszentmihalyi, M. (2002). The experience sampling method: Measuring the context and content of lives. In R. B. Bechtel & A. Churchman (Eds.), *Handbook of environmental psychology* (pp. 233–243). New York: Wiley.

Hill, R., & Mattessich, P. (1979). Family developmental theory and life span development. In P. Baltes & O. Brim (Eds.), *Life span development and behavior* (Vol. 3, pp. 161–204). New York: Academic Press.

Hinkle, R. C. (1967). Charles Horton Cooley's general sociological orientation. *Sociological Quarterly, 8*(1), 5–20.

Hiranandani, V. S. (2005). Rethinking disability in social work: Interdisciplinary perspectives. In G. E.

May & M. B. Raske (Eds.), *Ending disability discrimination: Strategies for social workers* (pp. 71–81). Boston: Pearson Education.

Hochschild, A. R. (1983). *The managed heart: Commercialization of human feeling.* Berkeley: University of California Press.

Hodge, D. R. (2005). Spiritual life-maps: A client-centered pictorial instrument for spiritual assessment, planning, and intervention. *Social Work, 50*(1), 77–87.

Hoff, M. D. (1998). Sustainable community development: Origins and essential elements of a new approach. In M. D. Hoff (Ed.), *Sustainable community development: Studies in economic, environmental, and cultural revitalization* (pp. 5–21). Boca Raton, FL: Lewis.

Hoff, M. D., & McNutt, J. G. (1994). Introduction. In M. D. Hoff & J. G. McNutt (Eds.), *The global environmental crisis: Implications for social welfare and social work* (pp. 1–11). Aldershot, UK: Avebury.

Hoff, M. D., & Polack, R. J. (1993). Social dimensions of the environmental crisis: Challenges for social work. *Social Work, 38*(2), 204–209.

Hoff, M. D., & Rogge, M. E. (1996). Everything that rises must converge: Developing a social work response to environmental injustice. *Journal of Progressive Human Services, 7*(1), 41–57.

Hoffman, L. W. (1985). The changing genetics/socialization balance. *Journal of Social Issues, 41*(1), 127–148.

Hoffman, R. R., Cochran, E. L., & Nead, J. M. (1990). Cognitive metaphors in experimental psychology. In D. E. Leary (Ed.), *Metaphors in the history of psychology* (pp. 173–229). Cambridge, UK: Cambridge University Press.

Hofstadter, R. (1963). *Social Darwinism in American thought.* Boston: Beacon Press.

Hogan, R. (1976). *Personality theory: The personological tradition.* Englewood Cliffs, NJ: Prentice-Hall.

Hogan, R., & Smither, R. (2001). *Personality: Theories and appli-cations.* Boulder, CO: Westview Press.

Hollingsworth, L. D. (1999). Symbolic interactionism, African American families, and the transracial adoption controversy. *Social Work, 44,* 443–453.

Hollis, F., & Woods, M. E. (1981). *Casework: A psychosocial therapy* (3rd ed.). New York: Random House.

Holmes, J. (1993). *John Bowlby and attachment theory.* London: Routledge.

Holton, R. (1998). Talcott Parsons. In R. Stones (Ed.), *Key sociological thinkers* (pp. 96–107). New York: New York University Press.

Honeycutt, J. M., Zagacki, K. S., & Edwards, R. (1989). Intrapersonal communication, social cognition, and imagined interactions. In C. V. Roberts, K. W. Watson, & L. L. Barker (Eds.), *Intrapersonal communication processes: Original essays* (pp. 166–184). New Orleans: Spectra.

hooks, b. (1984). *Feminist theory: From margin to center.* Boston: South End Press.

Horowitz, I. L. (1983). *C. Wright Mills: An American utopian.* New York: Free Press.

Horster, D. (1992). *Habermas: An introduction.* Philadelphia: Pennbridge Books.

Howard, J. A. (1995). Social cognition. In K. S. Cook, G. A. Fine, & J. A. House (Eds.), *Sociological perspectives on social psychology* (pp. 90–116). Boston: Allyn & Bacon.

Howe, D. (1997). Relating theory to practice. In M. Davies (Ed.), *The Blackwell companion to social work* (pp. 170–176). Oxford, UK: Blackwell.

Hudgins, C. A., & Allen-Meares, P. (2000). Translation research: A new solution to an old problem. *Journal of Social Work Education, 36*(1), 2–5.

Hughes, E. C. (1984). *The sociological eye: Selected papers* (2nd ed.). New Brunswick, NJ: Transaction Books.

Humphreys, P. (1998). Sociological models. In A. Sica (Ed.), *What is social theory? The philosophical debates* (pp. 253–264). Malden, MA; Blackwell.

Ilg, F. I., & Ames, L. B. (1955). *Child behavior: From birth to ten.* New York: Harper & Row.

Ivey, A. E. (1986). *Developmental therapy: Theory into practice.* San Francisco: Jossey-Bass.

Ivey, A. E. (1991). *Developmental strategies for helpers: Individual, family, and network interventions.* Pacific Grove, CA: Brooks/Cole.

Ivey, A. E., Ivey, M. B., Myers, J. E., & Sweeney, T. J. (2005). *Developmental counseling and therapy: Promoting wellness over the lifespan.* Boston: Lahaska Press/Houghton Mifflin.

Jackson, P., & Smith, S. J. (1984). *Exploring social geography.* London: Allen and Unwin.

James, W. (1958). *Pragmatism.* New York: Meridian Books. (Original work published 1907)

Jayaratne, S. (1980–1981). Characteristics and theoretical orientations of clinical social workers: A national survey. *Journal of Social Service Research, 4*(2), 17–30.

Jensen, J. P., Bergin, A. E., & Greaves, D. W. (1990). The meaning of eclecticism: New survey and analysis of components. *Professional Psychology: Research and Practice, 21*(2), 124–130.

Johnson, H. C. (1980). *Human behavior and social environment: New perspectives: Vol. 1. Behavior, psychopathology, and the brain.* New York: Curriculum Concepts.

Johnson, H. C. (1999). *Psyche, synapse, and substance: The role of neurobiology in emotions, behavior, thinking, and addiction for non-scientists.* Greenfield, MA: Deerfield Valley.

Johnson, H. C., Atkins, S. P., Battle, S. F., Hernandez-Arata, L., Hesselbrock, M., Libassi, M. F., & Parish, M. S. (1990). Strengthening the "bio" in the biopsychosocial paradigm. *Journal of Social Work Education, 26*(2), 109–123.

Johnson, L. C., & Yanca, S. J. (2001). *Social work practice: A generalist approach.* Needham Heights, MA: Allyn & Bacon.

Jones, E. (1955). *The life and work of Sigmund Freud* (Vol. 1). New York: Basic Books.

Kagan, J. (2003). Biology, context, and developmental inquiry. *Annual Review of Psychology, 54*, 1–23.

Kantor, D., & Lehr, W. (1975). *Inside the family: Toward a theory of family process.* San Francisco: Jossey-Bass.

Kapferer, B. (1976). Introduction: Transaction models reconsidered. In B. Kapferer (Ed.), *Transaction and meaning: Directions in the anthropology of exchange and symbolic behavior* (pp. 1–22). Philadelphia: Institute for the Study of Human Issues.

Kaplan, C. P. (2002). An early example of brief strengths-based practice: Bertha Reynolds at the National Maritime Union, 1943–1947. *Smith Studies in Social Work, 72*(3), 403–416.

Karp, D. A. (1996). *Speaking of sadness: Depression, disconnection, and the meanings of illness.* New York: Oxford University Press.

Karp, D. A., Stone, G. P., & Yoels, W. C. (1991). *Being urban: A sociology of city life* (2nd ed.). New York: Praeger.

Katovich, M. A. (1987). A radical critique of behaviorism: Mead versus Skinner. In N. K. Denzin (Ed.), *Studies in symbolic interaction* (Vol. 8, pp. 69–90). Greenwich, CT: JAI Press.

Kellner, D. (2000). Habermas, the public sphere, and democracy: A critical intervention. In L. E. Hahn (Ed.), *Perspectives on Habermas* (pp. 259–287). Chicago: Open Court.

Kerson, T. S. (1978). The social work relationship: A form of gift exchange. *Social Work, 23*(4), 326–327.

Kessler, R. C., House, J. S., Aspach, R. R., & Williams, D. R. (1995). Social psychology and health. In K. S. Cook, G. A. Fine, & J. S. House (Eds.), *Sociological perspectives on social psychology* (pp. 548–570). Boston: Allyn & Bacon.

Keynes, J. M. (1936). *The general theory of employment, interest, and money.* New York: Harcourt Brace Jovanovich.

Khalil, E. L. (1990). Beyond self-interest and altruism: A reconstruction of Adam Smith's theory of human conduct. *Economics and Philosophy, 6*, 255–273.

Kiecolt, K. J. (1994). Stress and the decision to change oneself: A theoretical model. *Social Psychology Quarterly, 57*(1), 49–63.

Kiecolt, K. J. (2000). Self-change in social movements. In S. Stryker, T. J. Owens, & R. W. White (Eds.), *Self, identity, and social movements* (pp. 110–131). Minneapolis: University of Minnesota Press.

King, I. M., & Fawcett, J. (1997). *The language of nursing theory and metatheory.* Indianapolis, IN: Sigma Theta Tau International.

Kirst-Ashman, K., & Hull, G. H, Jr. (1999). *Understanding generalist practice* (2nd ed.). Belmont, CA: Wadsworth.

Kirst-Ashman, K., & Hull, G. H, Jr. (2001). *Generalist practice with organizations and communities* (2nd ed.). Belmont, CA: Wadsworth.

Klein, D. M., & White, J. M. (1996). *Family theories: An introduction.* Thousand Oaks, CA: Sage.

Knight, J., & Johnson, J. (1999). Inquiry into democracy: What might a pragmatist make of rational choice theories? *American Journal of Political Science, 43*(2), 566–589.

Kollock, P. (1996). The logic and practice of generosity. *American Sociological Review, 61*(2), 341–346.

Kollock, P. (1998a). Design principles for online communities. *PC Update, 15*(5), 58–60.

Kollock, P. (1998b). Social dilemmas: The anatomy of cooperation. *Annual Review of Sociology, 24*, 183–214.

Kollock, P. (1999). The economies of online cooperation: Gifts and public goods in cyberspace. In M. A. Smith & P. Kollock (Eds.), *Communities in cyberspace* (pp. 220–239). London: Routledge.

Kollock, P., & O'Brien, J. (1994). *The production of reality: Essays and readings in social psychology.* Thousand Oaks, CA: Pine Forge Press.

Kollock, P., & Smith, M. (1996). Managing the virtual commons: Cooperation and conflict in computer communities. In S. C. Herring (Ed.), *Computer-mediated communication: Linguistic, social and cross-cultural perspectives* (pp. 109–128). Amsterdam: John Benjamins.

Kondrat, M. E. (1999). Who is the "self" in self-aware: Professional self-awareness from a critical theory perspective. *Social Service Review, 73*(4), 451–477.

Koopmans, J. (1995). The use of the reflecting team to enhance student learning. In G. Rogers (Ed.), *Social work field education: Views and visions* (pp. 229–233). Dubuque, IA: Kendall/Hunt.

Kramer, M. K. (1997). Terminology in theory: Definitions and comments. In I. M. King & J. Fawcett (Eds.), *The language of nursing theory and metatheory* (pp. 51–61). Indianapolis, IN: Sigma Theta Tau International.

Kuhn, T. S. (1970). *The structure of scientific revolutions* (2nd ed.). Chicago: University of Chicago Press.

Kunda, Z. (2000). *Social cognition: Making sense of people.* Cambridge, MA: MIT Press.

Kurtines, W. M., & Silverman, W. K. (1999). Emerging views of the role of theory. *Journal of Clinical Child Psychology, 28*(4), 558–562.

Lakoff, G., & Johnson, M. (1980). *Metaphors we live by.* Chicago: University of Chicago Press.

Lal, B. B. (1995). Symbolic interaction theories. *American Behavioral Scientist, 38*(3), 421–441.

Lalljee, M. (1996). The interpreting self: An experimentalist perspective. In R. Stevens (Ed.), *Understanding the self* (pp.89–146). London: Sage.

Lampropoulos, G. K. (2000). Evolving psychotherapy integration: Eclectic selection and prescriptive applications of common factors in therapy. *Psychotherapy, 37*(4), 285–297.

Lampropoulos, G. K. (2001). Bridging technical eclectism and theoretical integration: Assimilative integration. *Journal of Psychotherapy Integration, 11*(1), 5–19.

Land, K. C. (2001). Models and indicators. *Social Forces, 80*(2), 381–410.

Landon, P. S. (1995). Generalist and advanced generalist practice. In *Encyclopedia of social work* (19th ed., pp. 1101–1107). Washington, DC: National Association of Social Workers.

Langan, M., & Lee, P. (1989). Whatever happened to radical social work? In M. Langan & P. Lee (Eds.), *Radical social work today* (pp. 1–18). London: Unwin Hyman.

Larson, D. (1980). Therapeutic schools, styles, and schoolism: A national survey. *Journal of Humanistic Psychology, 20*(3), 3–20.

Lathrope, D. E. (1969). The general systems approach in social work practice. In G. Hearn (Ed.), *The general systems approach: Contributions toward an holistic conception of social work* (pp. 45–62). New York: Council on Social Work Education.

Lauzun, G. (1965). *Sigmund Freud: The man and his theories.* New York: Fawcett World Library.

Lawrence, R. J. (2002). Healthy residential environments. In R. B. Bechtel & A. Churchman (Eds.), *Handbook of environmental psychology* (pp. 394–412). New York: Wiley.

Lax, W. D. (1995). Offering reflections: Some theoretical and practical considerations. In S. Friedman (Ed.), *The reflecting team in action: Collaborative practice in family therapy* (pp. 145–166). New York: Guilford Press.

Lazarus, A. A., & Messer, S. B. (1991). Does chaos prevail? An exchange on technical eclecticism and assimilative integration. *Journal of Psychotherapy Integration, 1*(2), 143–157.

Lear, L. (1997). *Rachel Carson: Witness for nature.* New York: Holt.

Lear, L. (Ed.). (1998). *Lost woods: The discovered writing of Rachel Carson.* Boston: Beacon Press.

Leary, D. E. (1990). Psyche's muse: The role of metaphor in the history of psychology. In D. E. Leary (Ed.), *Metaphors in the history of psychology* (pp. 1–78). Cambridge, UK: Cambridge University Press.

Lecomte, C., Castonguay, L. G., Cyr, M., & Sabourin, S. (1993). Supervision and instruction in doctoral psychotherapy integration. In G. Stricker & J. K. Gold (Eds.), *Comprehensive handbook of psychotherapy integration* (pp. 483–497). New York: Plenum Press.

Lee, J. A. B., & Swanson, C. R. (1986). The concept of mutual aid. In A. Gitterman & L. Shulman (Eds.), *Mutual aid groups and the life cycle* (pp. 361–380). Itasca, IL: Peacock.

Leighninger, L. (1986). Bertha Reynolds and Edith Abbott: Contrasting images of professionalism in social work. *Smith College Studies in Social Work, 56*(2), 111–121.

Lemmens, F., de Ridder, D., & van Lieshout, P. (1994). The integration of psychotherapy: Goal or utopia? *Journal of Contemporary Psychotherapy, 24*(4), 245–257.

Lengermann, P. M., & Wallace, R. A. (1981). Making theory meaningful: The student as active participant. *Teaching Sociology, 8*(2), 197–212.

Leonard, P. (1975). Towards a paradigm for radical practice. In R. Bailey & M. Brake (Eds.), *Radical social work* (pp. 46–61). New York: Pantheon.

Lerner, R. M. (2005). Urie Bronfenbrenner: Career contributions of the consummate developmental scientist. In U. Bronfenbrenner (Ed.), *Making human beings human: Bioecological perspectives on human development* (pp. ix–xxix). Thousand Oaks, CA: Sage.

Lewis, M. A., & Widerquist, K. (2001). *Economics for social workers: The application of economic theory to social policy and the human services.* New York: Columbia University Press.

Lewis, M. W., & Kelemen, M. L. (2002). Multiparadigm inquiry: Exploring organizational pluralism and paradox. *Human Relations, 55*(2), 251–275.

Lidz, V. (2000). Talcott Parsons. In G. Ritzer (Ed.), *The Blackwell companion to major social theorists* (pp. 388–431). Malden, MA: Blackwell.

Lie, J. (1997). Sociology of markets. *Annual Review of Sociology, 23,* 341–360.

Light, A. (1996). Compatibilism in political ecology. In A. Light & E. Katz (Eds.), *Environmental pragmatism* (pp. 161–184). London: Routledge.

Light, A. (1997). Materialists, ontologists, and environmental pragmatists. In R. S. Gottlieb (Ed.), *The ecological community: Environmental challenges for philosophy, politics, and morality* (pp. 255–269). New York: Routledge.

Littlefield, A., Lieberman, L., & Reynolds, L. T. (1982). Redefining race: The potential demise of a concept in physical anthropology. *Current Anthropology, 23*(6), 641–655.

Locke, B. (1998). *Generalist social work practice: Context, story, and partnerships* Pacific Grove, CA: Brooks/Cole.

Lofland, J. (1984). Erving Goffman's sociological legacies. *Urban Life, 13*(1), 7–34.

Lofland, L. (1980). Reminiscences of classic Chicago: The Blumer-Hughes talk. *Urban Life, 9*(3), 251–281.

Lofland, L. H. (1982). Loss and human connection: An exploration into the nature of social bonds. In W. Ickes & E. S. Knowles (Eds.), *Personality, roles and social behavior* (pp. 219–242). New York: Springer-Verlag.

Lofland, L. H. (1985). The social shaping of emotion: The case of grief. *Symbolic Interaction, 8*(2), 171–190.

Longres, J. F. (1995). Hearn, Gordon. In R. L. Edwards (Ed.), *Encyclopedia of social work* (19th ed., pp. 2590–2591). Washington, DC: NASW Press.

Lopata, H. Z. (1994). *Circles and settings: Role changes of American women.* Albany: State University of New York Press.

Lovell, M. L., & Johnson, D. L. (1994). The environmental crisis and direct social work practice. In M. D. Hoff & J. G. McNutt (Eds.), *The global environmental crisis: Implications for social welfare and social work* (pp. 199–218). Aldershot, UK: Avebury.

Lowery, C. T., & Mattaini, M. A. (1999). The science of sharing power: Native American thought and behavior analysis. *Behavior and Social Issues, 9,* 3–23.

Lundblad, K. S. (1995). Jane Addams and social reform: A role model for the 1990s. *Social Work, 40,* 661–669.

Lyman, S. M. (1995). Interstate relations and the sociological imagination revisited: From social distance to territoriality. *Sociological Inquiry, 65*(2), 125–142.

Lyman, S. M. (1997). *Postmodernism and a sociology of the absurd and other essays on the "Nouvelle Vague" in American social science.* Fayetteville: University of Arkansas Press.

Lyman, S. M. (2002). Restoring the self as subject: Addressing the question of race. In J. A. Kotarba & J. M. Johnson (Eds.), *Postmodern existential sociology* (pp. 15–40). Walnut Creek, CA: Altamira Press.

Lyman, S. M., & Scott, M. B. (1967). Territoriality: A neglected sociological dimension. *Social Problems, 15*(2), 236–248.

Lyng, S. (2002). Gideon Sjoberg and the countersystem method. In N. K. Denzin (Ed.), *Studies in symbolic interaction* (Vol. 25, pp. 91–107). Oxford, UK: Elsevier Science.

Mackey, R., Burek, M., & Charkoudian, S. (1987). The relationship of theory to clinical practice. *Clinical Social Work Journal, 15*(4), 368–383.

Mackie, M. (1987). *Constructing women and men: Gender socialization.* Toronto: Holt, Rinehart and Winston of Canada.

Mahoney, M. J. (1993). Diversity and the dynamics of development in psychotherapy integration. *Journal of Psychotherapy Integration, 3*(1), 1–13.

Mahrer, A. R. (1989). *The integration of psychotherapies: A guide for practicing therapists.* New York: Human Sciences Press.

Maier, H. W. (1978). *Three theories of child development.* New York: Harper & Row.

Maines, D. R., Bridger, J. C., & Ulmer, J. T. (1996). Mythic facts and Park's pragmatism: On predecessor-selection and theorizing in human ecology. *Sociological Quarterly, 37*(3), 521–549.

Malkinson, R. (2002). Cognitive behavioral grief therapy: Shifting

theory, new approaches. *Social Work Today, 2*(21), 17–19.

Marks, S. R., & Leslie, L. A. (2000). Family diversity and intersecting categories: Toward a richer approach to multiple roles. In D. H. Demo & K. R. Allen (Eds.), *Handbook of family diversity* (pp. 402–423). New York: Oxford University Press.

Marris, P. (1982). Attachment and society. In C. M. Parkes & J. Stevenson-Hinde (Eds.), *The place of attachment in human behavior* (pp. 185–201). New York: Basic Books.

Marris, P. (1991). The social construction of uncertainty. In C. M. Parkes, J. Stevenson-Hinde, & P. Marris (Eds.), *Attachment across the life cycle* (pp. 77–90). London: Routledge.

Marris, P. (1996). *The politics of uncertainty: Attachment in private and public life.* London: Routledge.

Marshall, G. (Ed.). (1994). *The concise Oxford dictionary of sociology.* Oxford, UK: Oxford University Press.

Marshall, T. (1989). *The whole world guide to language learning: How to live and learn any foreign language.* Yarmouth, ME: Intercultural Press.

Marson, S. M. (2004). Ecological perspective: Carel B. Germain and Alex Gitterman. Retrieved June 4, 2004, from http://www.uncp.edu/home/marson/348-ecological.html

Martin, P. Y., & O'Connor, G. G. (1989). *The social environment: Open systems applications.* White Plains, NY: Longman.

Martindale, D. (1975). *Prominent sociologists since World War II.* Columbus, OH: Merrill.

Marx, G. T. (1984). Role models and role distance. *Theory and Society, 13*(5), 649–662.

Matsueda, R. L. (1988). The current state of differential association theory. *Crime and Delinquency, 34*(3), 277–306.

Matsuoka, J. K., & McGregor, D. P. (1994). Endangered culture: Hawaiians, nature, and economic development. In M. D. Hoff & J. G. McNutt (Eds.), *The global environmental crisis: Implica-*

tions for social welfare and social work* (pp. 100–116). Aldershot, UK: Avebury.

Mattaini, M. A. (1990). Contextual behavior analysis in the assessment process. *Families in Society, 71*(4), 236–245.

Mattaini, M. A. (1993). *More than a thousand words: Graphics for clinical practice.* Washington, DC: NASW.

McCall, G. J. (1988). The organizational life cycle of relationships. In S. W. Duck (Ed.). *Handbook of personal relationships* (pp. 467–484). Chichester, UK: Wiley.

McCall, G. J., & Simmons, J. L. (1982). *Social psychology: A sociological approach.* New York: Free Press.

McClean, M. (2000). Alternative approaches to women and development. In J. L. Parpart, M. P. Connelly, & V. E. Barriteau (Eds.), *Theoretical perspectives on gender and development* (pp. 180–202). Ottawa: International Development Research Centre.

McKenzie, R. D. (1924). The ecological approach to the study of the human community. *American Journal of Sociology, 30,* 287–301.

McMillen, J. C. (1992). Attachment theory and clinical social work. *Clinical Social Work Journal, 20*(2), 205–218.

McNamee, S., & Gergen, K. J. (1999). *Relational responsibility: Resources for sustainable dialogue.* Thousand Oaks, CA: Sage.

McPhail, C. (1991). *The myth of the madding crowd.* New York: Aldine de Gruyter.

McReynolds, P. (1990). Motives and metaphors: A study in scientific creativity. In D. E. Leary (Ed.), *Metaphors in the history of psychology* (pp. 133–172). Cambridge, UK: Cambridge University Press.

Mead, G. H. (1907). The newer ideals of peace [Review]. *American Journal of Sociology, 13,* 121–128.

Mead, G. H. (1907–1908). The social settlement: Its basis and function. *University of Chicago Record, 12,* 108–110. Retrieved October 3, 2000, from http://paradigm.soci.brocku.ca/~lward/pubs/MEAD_084.html

Mead, G. H. (1918). Social work, standards of living and the war. *Proceedings of the National Conference of Social Work, 637–644.* Retrieved October 3, 2000, from http://paradigm.soci.brocku.ca/ ~lward/pubs/ MEAD_082.html

Mead, G. H. (1934). *Mind, self and society.* Chicago: University of Chicago Press.

Mead, G. H. (1964). National-mindedness and international-mindedness. In A. J. Reck (Ed.), *George Herbert Mead: Selected writings* (pp. 355–370). Chicago: University of Chicago Press. (Original work published 1929)

Mead, G. H. (1968). The working hypothesis in social reform. In J. W. Petras (Ed.), *George Herbert Mead: Essays on his social philosophy* (pp. 125–129). Indianapolis, IN: Bobbs-Merrill. (Original work published 1899)

Meddin, J. (1982). Cognitive therapy and symbolic interactionism: Expanding clinical potential. *Cognitive Therapy and Research, 6(2),* 151–165.

Meier, S. T. (1999). Training the practitioner-scientist: Bridging case conceptualization, assessment, and intervention. *Counseling Psychologist, 27(6),* 846–849.

Meleis, A. I. (1988). The sick role. In M. E. Hardy & M. E. Conway (Eds.), *Role theory: Perspectives for health professionals* (2nd ed., pp. 365–374). Norwalk, CT: Appleton and Lange.

Meleis, A. I. (1997). Theoretical nursing: Definitions and interpretations. In I. M. King & J. Fawcett (Eds.), *The language of nursing theory and metatheory* (pp. 31–39). Indianapolis, IN: Sigma Theta Tau International.

Merrick, E. N. (1995). Adolescent childbearing as career "choice": Perspective from an ecological context. *Journal of Counseling and Development, 73(3),* 288–295.

Merton, R. K. (1949). *Social theory and social structure: Toward the codification of theory and research.* Glencoe, IL: Free Press.

Merton, R. K. (1975). Structural analysis in sociology. In P. M. Blau (Ed.), *Approaches to the study of social structure* (pp. 21–52). New York: Free Press.

Messer, S. (2000). A psychodynamic clinician responds to Fishman's case study proposal. *Prevention and Treatment, 3,* Retrieved September 16, 2002, from http:// gateway1.ovid.com:80/ovidweb .cgi

Messer, S. B. (1987). Can the Tower of Babel be completed? A critique of the common language proposal. *Journal of Integrative and Eclectic Psychotherapy, 6(2),* 195–199.

Messer, S. B. (1988). The case of multiple languages. *Journal of Integrative and Eclectic Psychotherapy, 7(3),* 246–248.

Messer, S. B. (2003). A critical examination of belief structures in integrative and eclectic psychotherapy. In J. G. Norcross & M. R. Goldfried (Eds.), *Handbook of psychotherapy integration* (pp. 130–165). New York: Oxford University Press. (Original work published 1992)

Meyer, C. H. (1976). *Social work practice: The changing landscape* (2nd ed.). New York: Free Press.

Miley, K. K., O'Melia, M., & DuBois, B. (2001). *Generalist social work practice: An empowering approach.* Needham Heights, MA: Allyn & Bacon.

Miller, D. L. (1973). *George Herbert Mead: Self, language and the world.* Austin: University of Texas Press.

Miller, G. (1997). *Becoming miracle workers: Language and meaning in brief therapy.* New York: Aldine de Gruyter.

Miller, P. H. (2002). *Theories of developmental psychology* (4th ed.). New York: Worth.

Miller, W. L. (1980). Casework and the medical metaphor. *Social Work, 25(4),* 281–285.

Milligan, M. J. (2003). Loss of site: Organizational site moves as organizational deaths. *International Journal of Sociology and Social Policy, 23(6/7),* 115–152.

Mills, C. W. (1956). *The power elite.* New York: Oxford University Press.

Mills, C. W. (1959). *The sociological imagination.* New York: Oxford University Press.

Minuchin, S., & Montalvo, B. (1967). Techniques for working with disorganized low socioeconomic families. *American Journal of Orthopsychiatry, 37,* 880–887.

Mithaug, D. E. (2000). *Learning to theorize: A four-step strategy.* Thousand Oaks, CA: Sage.

Mizrahi, T. (2001). The agency as embodiment and reflection of social policies: An ecological analysis. In Jansson, B. (Ed.), *Instructor's manual for "The Reluctant Welfare State"* (pp. 57–59). Pacific Grove, CA: Brooks/ Cole.

Monane, J. H. (1967). *A sociology of human systems.* New York: Appleton-Century-Crofts.

Moran, E. F. (1990). Ecosystem ecology in biology and anthropology: A critical assessment. In E. F. Moran (Ed.), *The ecosystem approach in anthropology: From concept to practice* (pp. 3–40). Ann Arbor: University of Michigan Press.

Morgaine, C. A. (1992). Alternative paradigms for helping families change themselves. *Family Relations, 41(1),* 12–17.

Mullahy, B. (1997). *Structural social work: Ideology, theory, and practice* (2nd ed.). Don Mills, Ontario: Oxford University Press.

Mullen, E. J. (1983). Personal practice models. In A. Rosenblatt & D. Waldfogel (Eds.), *Handbook of clinical social work* (pp. 623–649). New York: Wiley.

Munson, M. A., & Schmitt, R. L. (1996). Triggering and interpreting past drug-related frames: An insider's view of a treatment modality at an adolescent drug treatment facility. In N. K. Denzin (Ed.), *Studies in symbolic interaction* (Vol. 20, pp. 39–72). Greenwich, CT: JAI Press.

Musolf, G. R. (1995). Symbolic interactionism and the state: From reform to radical reconstruction. *Michigan Sociological Review, 9,* 19–40.

National Association of Social Workers. (2003). Environmental policy. In *Social work speaks: National Association of Social Workers policy statements* (pp. 116–123). Washington, DC: NASW Press.

Neimeyer, R. A. (1993). Constructivism and the problem of psychotherapy integration. *Journal of Psychotherapy Integration, 3*(2), 133–157.

Netting, F. E., & O'Connor, M. K. (2003). *Organization practice: A social worker's guide to understanding human services.* Boston: Allyn & Bacon.

Neugeboren, B. (1996). *Environmental practice in the human services: Integration of micro and macro roles, skills, and contexts.* New York: Haworth Press.

Neuhaus, J. W. (1996). *Toward a biocritical sociology.* New York: Peter Lang.

Nobelprize.org. (2005). Ivan Pavlov— Biography. In *Nobel Lectures, Physiology or Medicine 1901– 1921.* Amsterdam: Elsevier. Retrieved August 6, 2005, from http://nobelprize.org/medicine/laureates/1904/pavlov-bio-html

Norcross, J. C. (1986). Eclectic psychotherapy: An introduction and overview. In J. G. Norcross (Ed.), *Handbook of eclectic psychotherapy* (p. 3–24). New York: Brunner/Mazel.

Norcross, J. C., & Newman, C. F. (2003). Psychotherapy integration: Setting the context. In J. G. Norcross & M. R. Goldfried (Eds.), *Handbook of psychotherapy integration* (pp. 3–45). New York: Oxford University Press. (Original work published 1992)

Norcross, J. G., & Thomas, B. L. (1988). What's stopping us now? Obstacles to psychotherapy integration. *Journal of Integrative and Eclectic Psychotherapy, 7*(1), 74–80.

Norlin, J. M., Chess, W. A., Dale, O., & Smith, R. (2003). *Human behavior and the social environment: Social systems theory* (4th ed.). Boston: Allyn & Bacon.

Norris-Shortle, C., & Cohen, R. R. (1987). Home visits revisited. *Social Casework, 68*(1), 54–58.

Nurius, P. S. (1989). The self-concept: A social-cognitive update. *Social Casework, 70*(5), 285–294.

Nurius, P. S. (1994). Assessing and changing self-concept: Guidelines from the memory system. *Social Work, 39*(2), 285–294.

Nurius, P. S., Lovell, M., & Edgar, M. (1988). Self-appraisals of abusive parents: A contextual approach to study and treatment. *Journal of Interpersonal Violence, 3*(4), 458–467.

Nutt-Williams, E., & Hill, C. E. (1996). The relationship between self-talk and therapy process variables for novice therapists. *Journal of Counseling Psychology, 43*(2), 170–177.

O'Brien, J. (1998). Introduction: Differences and inequalities. In J. O'Brien & J. A. Howard (Eds.), *Everyday inequalities: Critical inquiries* (pp. 1–39). Malden, MA: Blackwell.

Olson, D. H. (1988). Family types, family stress, and family satisfaction: A family developmental perspective. In C. J. Falicov (Ed.), *Family transitions: Continuity and change over the life cycle* (pp. 55–79). New York: Guilford Press.

Olson, D. H. (1989). Circumplex model of family systems VIII: Family assessment and intervention. In D. H. Olson, C. S. Russell, & D. H. Sprenkle (Eds.), *Circumplex model: Systematic assessment and treatment of families* (pp. 7–49). New York: Haworth Press.

Olson, D. H. (1995). Family systems: Understanding your roots. In R. D. Day, K. R. Gilbert, B. H. Settles, & W. R. Burr (Eds.), *Research and theory in family science* (pp. 131–153). Pacific Grove, CA: Brooks/Cole.

Olson, D. H., Russell, C. S., & Sprenkle, D. H. (1983). Circumplex model of marital and family systems VI: Theoretical update. *Family Process, 22,* 69–83.

Olson, D. H., Sprenkle, D. H., & Russell, C. S. (1979). Circumplex models of marital and family systems I. *Family Process, 18,* 3–15.

O'Neill, J. (2001). Psychoanalysis and sociology: From freudo-marxism to freudo-feminism. In G. Ritzer & B. Smart (Eds.), *Handbook of social theory* (pp. 112–124). London: Sage.

Opp, K.-D. (1997). Can identity theory better explain the rescue of Jews in Nazi Europe than rational actor theory? *Research in Social Movements, Conflict, and Change, 20,* 223–253.

Orel, V. (1984). *Mendel.* Oxford, UK: Oxford University Press.

Outhwaite, W. (1994). *Habermas: A critical introduction.* Stanford, CA: Stanford University Press.

Outhwaite, W. (1998). Jurgen Habermas. In R. Stones (Ed.), *Key sociological thinkers* (pp. 205– 214). New York: New York University Press.

Outhwaite, W. (2000). Jurgen Habermas. In G. Ritzer (Ed.), *The Blackwell companion to major social theorists* (pp. 651–669). Malden, MA: Blackwell.

Ozer, E. M., & Bandura, A. (1990). Mechanisms governing empowerment effects: A self efficacy analysis. *Journal of Personality and Social Psychology, 58*(3), 472–486.

Papell, C. P., & Skolnik, L. (1992). The reflective practitioner: A contemporary paradigm's relevance for social work education. *Journal of Social Work Education, 28*(1), 18–26.

Park, R. E. (1967). The urban community as a spatial pattern and a moral order. In R. H. Turner (Ed.), *Robert E. Park: On social control and collective behavior* (pp. 55–68). Chicago: University of Chicago Press. (Original work published 1926)

Park, R. E. (1972a). Reflections on communication and culture. In H. Elsner Jr. (Ed.), *Robert E. Park: The crowd and the public and other essays* (pp. 98–116). Chicago: University of Chicago Press. (Original work published 1938)

Park, R. E. (1972b). Symbiosis and socialization: A frame of reference for the study of society. In H. Elsner Jr. (Ed.), *Robert E. Park: The crowd and the public and other essays* (pp. 117–142). Chicago: University of Chicago Press. (Original work published 1939)

Park, R. E. (1979). Human ecology. In R. H. Turner (Ed.), *Robert E. Park: On social control and collective behavior* (pp. 69–84). Chicago: University of Chicago Press. (Original work published 1936)

Park, R. E., & Burgess, E. W. (1921). *An introduction to the science of sociology.* Chicago: University of Chicago Press.

Parpart, J. L., Connelly, M. P., & Barriteau, V. E. (Eds.). (2000). *Theoretical perspectives on gender and development.* Ottawa: International Development Research Centre.

Parsons, T. (1952). *The social system.* New York: Free Press.

Parsons, T. (1967). *Sociological theory and modern society.* New York: Free Press.

Parsons, T. (1968). Cooley and the problem of internalization. In A. J. Reiss, Jr. (Ed.), *Cooley and sociological analysis* (pp. 48–67). Ann Arbor: University of Michigan Press.

Parsons, T. (1969). *Politics and social structure.* New York: Free Press.

Parsons, T. (1973). *Working papers in the theory of action.* New York: Free Press.

Parsons, T., & Bales, R. F. (1955). *Family, socialization and interaction process.* New York: Free Press.

Patterson, C. H. (1989). Eclecticism in psychotherapy: Is integration possible? *Psychotherapy, 26,* 157–161.

Payne, M. (1997). *Modern social work theory* (2nd ed.). Chicago: Lyceum.

Payne, M. (2002a). The politics of systems theory within social work. *Journal of Social Work, 2*(3), 269–292.

Payne, M. (2002b). Social work theories and reflective practice. In R. Adams, L. Dominelli, & M. Payne (Eds.), *Social work: Themes, issues, and critical debates* (2nd ed., pp. 123–138). Houndmills, UK: Palgrave.

Pearman, J. R. (1973). *Social science and social work: Applications of social science in the helping professions.* Metuchen, NJ: Scarecrow Press.

Pearson, G., Treseder, J., & Yelloly, M. (1988). Introduction: Social work and the legacy of Freud. In G. Pearson, J. Treseder, & M. Yelloly (Eds.), *Social work and the legacy of Freud: Psychoanalysis and its uses* (p. 1–57). Houndmills, UK: Macmillan Education.

Pease, B., Allan, J., & Briskman, L. (2003). Introducing critical theories in social work. In J. Allan, B. Pease, & L. Briskman (Eds.), *Critical social work: An introduction to theories and practices* (pp. 1–14). Jaipur, India: Rawat.

Peet, R. (1999). *Theories of development.* New York: Guilford Press.

Pepper, S. C. (1942). *World hypotheses: A study in evidence.* Berkeley: University of California Press.

Perinbanayagam, R. S. (2000). *The presence of self.* Lanham, MD: Rowman and Littlefield.

Perlman, H. H. (1968). *Persona: Social role and personality.* Chicago: University of Chicago Press.

Perlstadt, H. (1998). Comment on Turner. *Sociological Perspectives, 41*(2), 268–271.

Petras, J. (1968a). John Dewey and the rise of interactionism in American social theory. *Journal of the History of the Behavioral Sciences, 4,* 18–27.

Petras, J. (1968b). Social-psychological theory as a basis for a theory of ethics and value: The case of Charles Horton Cooley. *Journal of Value Inquiry, 2,* 9–21.

Pfeiffer, D. (2005). The conceptualization of disability. In G. E. May & M. B. Raske (Eds.), *Ending disability discrimination: Strategies for social workers* (pp. 25–41). Boston: Pearson Education.

Phillips, D. C. (1976). *Holistic thought in social science.* Stanford, CA: Stanford University Press.

Phillips, D. G. (1993). Integration and alternatives: Some current issues in psychoanalytic theory. *Clinical Social Work Journal, 21*(3), 247–256.

Piliavin, J. A., & LePore, P. C. (1995). Biology and social psychology: Beyond nature versus nurture. In K. S. Cook, G. A. Fine, & J. S. House (Eds.), *Sociological perspectives on social psychology* (pp. 9–40). Boston: Allyn & Bacon.

Pincus, A., & Minahan, A. (1973). *Social work practice: Model and method.* Itasca, IL: Peacock.

Pol, E. (2002). Environmental management: A perspective from environmental psychology. In R. B. Bechtel & A. Churchman (Eds.), *Handbook of environmental psy-chology* (pp. 55–84). New York: Wiley.

Postel, S. (1994, March/April). Carrying capacity: Earth's bottom line. *Challenge,* pp. 4–12.

Pottick, K. J. (1988). Jane Addams revisited: Practice theory and social economics. *Social Work with Groups, 11*(4), 11–26.

Powers, C. H. (2004). *Making sense of social theory: A practical introduction.* Lanham, MD: Rowman and Littlefield.

Pribram, K. H. (1990). From metaphors to models: The use of analogy in neuropsychology. In D. E. Leary (Ed.), *Metaphors in the history of psychology* (pp. 79–103). Cambridge, UK: Cambridge University Press.

Price, R. H. (1997). Mechanism, conflict, and cultural symbol: Three views of the relationship between social insight and social transformation. In D. J. Tucker, C. Garvin, & R. Sarri (Eds.), *Integrating knowledge and practice: The case of social work and social science* (pp. 38–45). Westport, CT: Praeger.

Prigoff, A. (2000). *Economics for social workers: Social outcomes of economic globalization with strategies for community action.* Belmont, CA: Wadsworth.

Prilleltensky, I., & Gonick, L. S. (1994). The discourse of oppression in the social sciences: Past, present, and future. In E. J. Trickett, R. J. Watts, & D. Berman (Eds.), *Human diversity: Perspectives on people in context* (pp. 145–177). San Francisco: Jossey-Bass.

Prochaska, J. M. (2000). A transtheoretical model for assessing organizational change: A study of family-service agencies' movement to time-limited therapy. *Families in Society, 81*(1), 76–84.

Prochaska, J. O., & Norcross, J. C. (1999). *Systems of psychotherapy: A transtheoretical analysis* (4th ed.). Pacific Grove, CA: Brooks/Cole.

Psi, Café. (2005). Thesis on classical conditioning. Retrieved August 6, 2005, from http://www.psy.pdx.edu/PsiCafe/Just4Fun/Jokes/ClassCondThesis.htm

Pugh, S. L., Hicks, J. W., Davis, M., & Venstra, T. (1992). *Bridging: A teacher's guide to metaphorical thinking*. Urbana, IL: National Council of Teachers of English.

Qin, D., & Comstock, D. L. (2005). Traditional models of development: Appreciating context and relationship. In D. Comstock (Ed.), *Diversity and development: Critical contexts that shape our lives and relationships* (pp. 1–24). Belmont, CA: Wadsworth.

Quinn, J. A. (1934). Ecological versus social interaction. *Sociology and Social Research, 18*(6), 565–570.

Rank, M. R., & LeCroy, C. W. (1983). Toward a multiple perspective in family theory and practice: The case of social exchange theory, symbolic interactionism, and conflict theory. *Family Relations, 32,* 441–448.

Reddock, R. (2000). Why gender? Why development? In J. L. Parpart, M. P. Connelly, & V. E. Barriteau (Eds.), *Theoretical perspectives on gender and development* (pp. 23–50). Ottawa: International Development Research Centre.

Reese, W. A., II (1997). Alienation: Extending an interactionist conceptualization. In D. E. Miller, M. A. Katovich, & S. L. Saxton (Eds.), *Studies in symbolic interaction: Constructing complexity: Suppl. 3. Symbolic interaction and social forms* (pp. 59–84). Greenwich, CT: JAI Press.

Reid, W. J. (1979). The model development dissertation. *Journal of Social Service Research, 3*(2), 215–225.

Reid, W. J. (1992). *Task strategies: An empirical approach to clinical social work*. New York: Columbia University Press.

Reid, W. J. (1997). Is neo-positivism a suitable epistemological framework of HBSE courses? In M. Bloom & W. C. Klein (Eds.), *Controversial issues in human behavior in the social environment* (pp. 1–15). Needham Heights, MA: Allyn & Bacon.

Reid, W. J. (1998). The paradigms and long-term trends in clinical social work. In R. A. Dorfman (Ed.), *Paradigms of clinical social work* (Vol. 2, pp. 337–351). New York: Brunner/Mazel.

Reid, W. J. (2001). The role of science in social work: The perennial debate. *Journal of Social Work, 1*(3), 273–293.

Reinharz, S. (1994). Toward an ethnography of "voice" and "silence." In E. J. Trickett, R. J. Watts, & D. Berman (Eds.), *Human diversity: Perspectives on people in context* (pp. 178–200). San Francisco: Jossey-Bass.

Reisch, M., & Andrews, J. (2001). *The road not taken: A history of radical social work in the United States*. New York: Brunner-Routledge.

Reitzes, D. C., & Reitzes, D. C. (1993). The social psychology of Robert E. Park: Human nature, self, personality, and social structure. *Symbolic Interaction, 16*(1), 39–63.

Residents of Hull House. (1970). *Hull House maps and papers: A presentation of nationalities and wages in a congested district of Chicago*. New York: Arno. (Original work published 1895)

Resnick, H., & Jaffee, B. (1982). The physical environment and social welfare. *Social Casework, 63*(6), 354–362.

Reynolds, B. C. (1951). *Social work and social living: Explorations in philosophy and practice*. Washington, DC: NASW.

Reynolds, B. C. (1963). *An uncharted journey: Fifty years of growth in social work*. New York: Citadel Press.

Reynolds, B. C. (1992). Re-thinking social case work. *Journal of Progressive Human Services, 3*(1), 73–84. (Original work published 1938)

Richmond, P. G. (1970). *An introduction to Piaget*. New York: Basic Books.

Rifkin, J. (1991). *Biosphere politics: A cultural odyssey from the middle ages to the new age*. San Francisco: HarperCollins.

Rigazio-DiGilio, S. A., Goncalves, O. F., & Ivery, A. E. (1996). From cultural to existential diversity: The impossibility of psychotherapy integration within a traditional framework. *Applied and Preventive Psychology, 5,* 235–247.

Rigney, D. (2001). *The metaphorical society: An invitation to social theory*. Lanham, MD: Rowman and Littlefield.

Riley, J. G. (1991). Genetics, environment, and development. In R. R. Greene & P. H. Ephross (Eds.), *Human behavior theory and social work practice* (pp. 297–319). New York: Aldine de Gruyter.

Ritzer, G. (1975). *Sociology: A multiple paradigm science*. Boston: Allyn & Bacon.

Ritzer, G. (1991a). *Metatheorizing in sociology*. Lexington, MA: Lexington Books.

Ritzer, G. (1991b). The recent history and the emerging reality of American sociological theory: A metatheoretical interpretation. *Sociological Forum, 6*(2), 269–287.

Ritzer, G. (1996). *Classic sociological theory* (2nd ed.). New York: McGraw-Hill.

Ritzer, G., & Smart, B. (2001). Introduction: Theorists, theories and theorizing. In G. Ritzer & B. Smart (Eds.), *Handbook of social theory* (pp. 1–9). London: Sage.

Roazen, P. (1976). *Erik H. Erikson: The power and limits of a vision*. New York: Free Press.

Robbins, S. P., Chatterjee, P., & Canda, E. R. (1998). *Contemporary human behavior theory: A critical perspective for social work*. Boston: Allyn & Bacon.

Rochberg-Halton, E. (1984). Object relations, role models, and cultivation of the self. *Environment and Behavior, 16*(3), 335–368.

Rock, P. (1979). *The making of symbolic interactionism*. London: MacMillan Press.

Rogge, M. E. (1993). Social work, disenfranchised communities, and the natural environment: Field education opportunities. *Journal of Social Work Education, 29*(1), 111–120.

Rogge, M. E. (1994). Environmental injustice: Social welfare and toxic waste. In M. D. Hoff & J. G. McNutt (Eds.), *The global environmental crisis: Implications for social welfare and social work* (pp. 53–74). Aldershot, UK: Avebury.

Romaine, S (2000). *Language in environment: An introduction to sociolinguistics.* Oxford, UK: Oxford University Press.

Rosen, H. (1985). *Piagetian dimensions of clinical relevance.* New York: Columbia University Press.

Rosen, H. (1988a). The constructivist-developmental paradigm. In R. A. Dorfman (Ed.), *Paradigms of clinical social work* (pp. 317–355). New York: Brunner/Mazel.

Rosen, H. (1988b). Evolving a personal philosophy of practice: Towards eclecticism. In R. A. Dorfman (Ed.), *Paradigms of clinical social work* (pp. 388–412). New York: Brunner/Mazel.

Rosenblatt, P. C. (1994). *Metaphors of family systems theory: Toward new constructions.* New York: Guilford Press

Rosenfeld, P., Giacalone, R. A., & Riordan, C. A. (1994). Impression management theory and diversity: Lessons for organizational behavior. *American Behavioral Scientist, 37*(5), 601–604.

Rosenzweig, S. (2002). Some implicit common factors in diverse methods of psychotherapy. *Journal of Psychotherapy Integration, 12*(1), 5–9. (Original work published 1936)

Ross, D. (1998). Gendered social knowledge: Domestic discourse, Jane Addams, and the possibilities of social science. In H. Silverbert (Ed.), *Gender and American social science: The formative years* (pp. 235–264). Princeton, NJ: Princeton University Press.

Rosser, S. V., & Miller, P. H. (2000). Feminist theories: Implications for developmental psychology. In P. H. Miller & E. K. Scholnick (Eds.), *Toward a developmental psychology* (pp. 11–28). New York: Routledge.

Rossiter, A. B. (1996). A perspective on critical social work. *Journal of Progressive Human Services, 7*(2), 23–41.

Rule, J. B. (1997). *Theory and progress in social science.* Cambridge, UK: Cambridge University Press.

Sable, P. (1995). Pets, attachment, and well-being across the life cycle. *Social Work, 40*(3), 334–342.

Sable, P. (1997). Disorders of adult attachment. *Psychotherapy: Theory, Research, Practice, Training, 34*(3), 286–296.

Safran, J. D., & Messer, S. B. (1997). Psychotherapy integration: A postmodern critique. *Clinical Psychology: Science and Practice, 4*(2), 140–152.

Safran, J. D., & Messer, S. B. (2003). Psychotherapy integration: A postmodern critique. Retrieved February 27, 2003, from http://www.cyberpsych.sept/safran.html [Original work published 1997 in *Clinical Psychology: Science and Practice, 4*(2), 140–152]

Saleeby, D. (1985). In clinical social work, is the body politic? *Social Service Review, 59*(4), 578–591.

Saleeby, D. (1992). Biology's challenge to social work: Embodying the person-in-environment perspective. *Social Work, 37*(2), 112–117.

Salkind, N. J. (1985). *Theories of human development* (2nd ed.). New York: Wiley.

Saltman, J. E., & Greene, R. R. (1993). Social workers' perceived knowledge and use of human behavior theory. *Journal of Social Work Education, 29*(1), 88–98.

Sammons, M., & Gravitz, M. (1990). Theoretical orientations of professional psychologists and their former professors. *Professional Psychology: Research and Practice, 21*(2), 131–134.

Sanderson, S. K., & Ellis, L. (1992). Theoretical and political perspectives of American sociologists in the 1990s. *American Sociologist, 23*(2), 26–42.

Sarbin, T. R. (1984). Role transition as social drama. In V. L. Allen & E. van de Vliert (Eds.), *Role transitions as social drama* (pp. 21–37). New York: Plenum Press.

Sarbin, T. R., & Allen, V. L. (1968). Role theory. In G. Lindzey & E. Aronson (Eds.), *Handbook of social psychology* (2nd ed., Vol. 1, pp. 488–567). Cambridge, MA: Addison-Wesley.

Sarukkai, S. (2002). *Translating the world: Science and language.* Lanham, MD: University Press of America.

Schacht, T. E. (1984). The varieties of integrative experience. In H. Arkowitz & S. B. Messer (Eds.), *Psychoanalytic therapy and behavior therapy: Is integration possible?* (pp. 107–138). New York: Plenum Press.

Schaffer, J. B. P., & Galinsky, M. D. (1974). *Models of group therapy and sensitivity training.* Englewood Cliffs, NJ: Prentice-Hall.

Schatz, M., Jenkins, L., & Sheafor, B. (1990). Milford redefined: A model of initial and advanced generalist. *Journal of Social Work Education, 26*(3), 217–231.

Scheff, T. J. (1985). Universal expressive needs: A critique and a theory. *Symbolic Interaction, 8*(2), 241–262.

Scheff, T. J. (1987). Creativity and repetition: A theory of the coarse emotions. In J. Rabow, G. M. Platt, & M. S. Goldman (Eds.), *Advances in psychoanalytic sociology* (pp. 70–100). Malabar, FL: Robert E. Krieger.

Scheff, T. J. (1995). Academic gangs. *Crime, Law, and Social Change, 23*, 157–162.

Scholnik, E. K., & Miller, P. H. (2000). Engendering development–developing feminism: Defining the partnership. In P. H. Miller & E. K. Scholnick (Eds.), *Toward a developmental psychology* (pp. 241–254). New York: Routledge.

Schriver, J. M. (1998). *Human behavior and the social environment: Shifting paradigms for essential knowledge in social work practice* (2nd ed.). Boston: Allyn & Bacon.

Schudson, M. (1989). How culture works: Perspectives from media studies on the efficacy of symbols. *Theory and Society, 18*(2), 153–189.

Schwalbe, M. L. (1988a). Meadian ethical theory and the moral contradictions of capitalism. *Philosophy and Social Criticism, 1*(4), 25–51.

Schwalbe, M. L. (1988b). Role-taking reconsidered: Linking competence and performance to social structure. *Journal for the Theory of Social Behaviour, 18*(4), 409–436.

Schwalbe, M. L. (1992). Male supremacy and the narrowing of the moral self. *Berkeley Journal of Sociology, 37*, 29–54.

Schwalbe, M. L. (1996). *Unlocking the iron cage: The men's movement, gender politics, and American culture*. New York: Oxford University Press.

Schwartz, W. (1969). Private troubles and public issues: One social work job or two? In National Conference on Social Welfare Staff (Eds.), *Social welfare forum* (pp. 22–43). New York: Columbia University Press.

Seidman, S. (1996). Pragmatism and sociology: A response to Clough, Denzin and Richardson. *Sociological Quarterly, 37*(4), 753–759.

Seigfried, C. H. (1993). Shared communities of interest: Feminism and pragmatism. *Hypatia, 8*(2), 1–14.

Seigfried, C. H. (1996). *Pragmatism and feminism: Reweaving the social fabric*. Chicago: University of Chicago Press.

Seigfried, C. H. (1998). John Dewey's pragmatist feminism. In L. A. Hickman (Ed.), *Reading Dewey: Interpretations for a postmodern generation* (pp. 187–216). Bloomington: Indiana University Press.

Shalin, D. (1986). Pragmatism and social interactionism. *American Sociological Review, 51*, 9–29.

Shalin, D. (1990). Jane Addams and the men of the Chicago School, 1892–1918 [Review]. *Theory and Society, 19*, 127–132.

Shalin, D. (2000). George Herbert Mead. In G. Ritzer (Ed.), *The Blackwell companion to major social theorists* (pp. 302–344). Malden, MA: Blackwell.

Sheldon, B. (1978). Theory and practice in social work: A reexamination of a tenuous relationship. *British Journal of Social Work, 8*(1), 1–22.

Sherman, E. (1987). Reminiscence groups for community elderly. *Gerontologist, 27*(5), 569–572.

Shoemaker, P. J., Tankard, J. W., Jr., & Lasorsa, D. L. (2004). *How to build social science theories*. Thousand Oaks, CA: Sage.

Shove, E., & Warde, A. (2002). Inconspicuous consumption: The sociology of consumption, lifestyles, and the environment. In R. Dunlap, F. H. Buttell, P. Dickens, & A. Gijswijt (Eds.), *Sociological theory and the environment: Classical foundations and contemporary insights* (pp. 230–251). Lanham, MD: Rowman and Littlefield.

Simons, R. L., & Aigner, S. M. (1985). *Practice principles: A problem-solving approach to social work*. New York: Macmillan.

Simpson, J. C. (2000, April). It's all in the upbringing. *Johns Hopkins Magazine*. Retrieved August 7, 2005, from http://www.jhu.edu/~jhumag/0400web/35.html

Sinclair, M. S. (2001, December 18). Brave New World revisited. *Style Weekly*, 22–28.

Siporin, M. (1989). Metamodels, models, and basics: An essay review. *Social Service Review, 63*(3), 474–480.

Sjoberg, G. (1996). The human rights challenge to communitarianism: Formal organizations and race and ethnicity. In D. Sciulli (Ed.), *Macro socio-economics: From theory to activism* (pp. 273–297). Armonk, NY: Sharpe.

Sjoberg, G., & Vaughan, T. R. (1993). The ethical foundations of sociology and the necessity for a human rights alternative. In T. R. Vaughan, G. Sjoberg, & L. T. Reynolds (Eds.), *A critique of contemporary American sociology* (pp. 114–159). Dix Hills, NY: General Hall.

Skidmore, W. (1975). *Theoretical thinking in sociology* [2nd. ed.]. Cambridge, UK: Cambridge University Press.

Skidmore, W. (1979). *Theoretical thinking in sociology*. Cambridge, UK: Cambridge University Press.

Skinner, B. F. (1948). *Walden two*. New York: Macmillan.

Skinner, B. F. (1967). B. F. Skinner: An autobiography. In E. G. Boring & G. Lindzey (Eds.), *A history of psychology in autobiography* (Vol. 5, pp. 387–413). New York: Appleton-Century-Crofts.

Skinner, B. F. (1971). *Beyond freedom and dignity*. New York: Knopf.

Skvoretz, J. (1998). Theoretical models: Sociology's missing links. In A. Sica (Ed.), *What is social theory? The philosophical debates* (pp. 238–252). Malden, MA: Blackwell.

Slunecko, T. (1999). On harvesting diversities into a dynamic directedness. *International Journal of Psychotherapy, 4*(2), 127–144.

Smelser, N. J. (1996). Erik Erikson as social scientist. *Psychoanalysis and Contemporary Thought, 19*(2), 207–224.

Smelser, N. J. (2004). Interdisciplinarity in theory and practice. In C. Camic & H. Joas (Eds.), *The dialogical turn: New roles for sociology in the postdisciplinary age* (pp. 43–64). Lanham, MD: Rowman and Littlefield.

Smelser, N. J., & Swedberg, R. (1994). The sociological perspective on the economy. In N. J. Smelser & R. Swedberg (Eds.), *The handbook of economic sociology* (pp. 3–26). Princeton, NJ: Princeton University Press.

Smith, A. (1776). *An inquiry into the nature and causes of the wealth of nations*. London: McCulloch.

Smith, D. E. (1974). Women's perspective as a radical critique of sociology. *Sociological Inquiry, 44*(1), 7–13.

Smith, D. E. (1996). Telling the truth after postmodernism. *Symbolic Interaction, 19*(3), 171–202.

Smith, D. M. (1977). *Human geography: A welfare approach*. New York: St. Martin's Press.

Smith, L. D. (1990). Metaphors of knowledge and behavior in the behaviorist tradition. In D. E. Leary (Ed.), *Metaphors in the history of psychology* (pp. 239–266). Cambridge, UK: Cambridge University Press.

Smith, T. V. (1931). Social philosophy of George Herbert Mead. *American Journal of Sociology, 37*, 368–385.

Sontag, J. (1996). Toward a comprehensive theoretical framework for disability research: Bronfenbrenner revisited. *Journal of Special Education, 30*(3), 319–345.

Soullier, D., Britt, D. W., Maines, D. R. (2001). Conceptual modeling as a toolbox for grounded theorists. *Sociological Quarterly, 42*(2), 253–269.

Specht, H. (1977). Theory as a guide to practice. In H. Specht & A. Vickery (Eds.), *Integrating social work methods* (pp. 28–35). London: Allen and Unwin.

Specht, H. (1988). *New directions for social work practice.* Englewood Cliffs, NJ: Prentice Hall.

St. Clair, M. (1994). *Human relationships and the experience of God. Object relations and religion.* Mahwah, NJ: Paulist.

Stalker, C. A. (2001). Attachment theory. In P. Lehmann & N. Coady (Eds.), *Theoretical perspectives for direct social work practice: A generalist-eclectic approach* (pp. 109–127). New York: Springer.

Stein, I. (1974). *Systems theory, science, and social work.* Metuchen, NJ: Scarecrow Press.

Stein, M. C., & McCall, G. J. (1994). Home range and daily rounds: Uncovering community among urban nomads. *Research in Community Sociology, 4*(Suppl. 1), 77–94.

Stephens, M. (1994, October 23). Jurgen Habermas: The theologian of talk. *Los Angeles Times Magazine.* Retrieved October 8, 2005, from http://www.nyu.edu/classes/stephens/Habermas%20 page.htm

Stewart, R. L., & Reynolds, L. T. (1985). The biologizing of the individual and the naturalization of the social. *Humanity and Society, 9*(2), 159–167.

Stoesz, D., Guzzetta, C., & Lusk, M. (1999). *International development.* Boston: Allyn & Bacon.

Stolte, J. F. (1987). The formation of justice norms. *American Sociological Review, 52,* 774–784.

Strauss, A. L. (1977). Sociological theories of personality. In R. J. Corsini (Ed.), *Current personality theories* (pp. 277–302). Itasca, IL: Peacock.

Strauss, A. L. (1987). *Qualitative analysis for social scientists.* Cambridge, UK: Cambridge University Press.

Strauss, A. L., & Corbin, J. (1994). Grounded theory methodology: An overview. In N. Denzin & Y. Lincoln (Eds.), *Handbook of qualitative research* (pp. 273–285). Thousand Oaks, CA: Sage.

Strong, T. (2002). Collaborative "expertise" after the discursive turn. *Journal of Psychotherapy Integration, 12*(2), 218–232.

Stryker, S., & Statham, A. (1985). Symbolic interactionism and role

theory. In G. Lindzey & E. Aronson (Eds.), *Handbook of social psychology* (Vol. 1, pp. 311–378). New York: Random House.

Stuhr, J. J. (1997). *Genealogical pragmatism: Philosophy, experience, and community.* Albany: State University of New York Press.

Stuhr, J. J. (1998). Dewey's social and political philosophy. In L. A. Hickman (Ed.), *Reading Dewey: Interpretations for a postmodern generation* (pp. 82–99). Bloomington: Indiana University Press.

Sundel, M., & Sundel, S. S. (1999). *Behavior change in the human services: An introduction to principles and applications.* Thousand Oaks, CA: Sage.

Susman, E. J. (2001). Mind-body interaction and development: Biology, behavior and context. *European Psychologist, 6*(3), 163–171.

Swanson, G. E. (1985). The powers and capabilities of selves: Social and collective approaches. *Journal for the Theory of Social Behaviour, 15*(3), 331–354.

Swanson, G. E. (1988). *Ego defenses and the legitimation of behavior.* New York: Cambridge University Press.

Takahashi, L. M. (1997). The sociospatial stigmatization of homelessness and HIV/AIDS: Toward an explanation of the NIMBY syndrome. *Social Science Medicine, 45*(6), 903–914.

Thomas, E. J. (1997). Themes and perspectives on integration and related models. In D. J. Tucker, C. Garvin, & R. Sarri (Eds.), *Integrating knowledge and practice: The case of social work and social science* (pp. 256–272). Westport, CT: Praeger.

Thomas, E. J., & Biddle, B. J. (1966). The nature and history of role theory. In B. J. Biddle & E. J. Thomas (Eds.), *Role theory: Concepts and research* (pp. 3–19). New York: Wiley.

Thomas, J. (1993). *Doing critical ethnography.* Newbury Park, CA: Sage.

Thomas, R. R. (1999). *Human development theories: Windows on culture.* Thousand Oaks, CA: Sage.

Thomas, R. R. (2001). *Recent theories of human development.* Thousand Oaks, CA: Sage.

Thomlison, B. (1995). Student perceptions of reflective team supervision. In G. Rogers (Ed.), *Social work field education: Views and visions* (pp. 234–244). Dubuque, IA: Kendall/Hunt.

Thompson, N. (2000). *Theory and practice in human services.* Buckingham, PA: Open University Press.

Throssell, H. (Ed.). (1975). *Social work: Radical essays.* St. Lucia, Queensland, Australia: University of Queensland Press.

Thyer, B. A. (1988). Radical behaviorism and clinical social work. In R. A. Dorfman (Ed.), *Paradigms of clinical social work* (pp. 123–148). New York: Brunner/Mazel.

Thyer, B. A. (1992). A behavioral perspective on human development. In M. Bloom (Ed.), *Changing lives* (pp. 410–418). Columbia: University of South Carolina Press.

Thyer, B. A. (1994). Social learning theory: Empirical applications to culturally diverse practice. In R. R. Greene (Ed.), *Human behavior theory: A diversity framework* (pp. 133–146). New York: Aldine de Gruyter.

Tibbetts, P. (1981). The transactional theory of human knowledge and action: Notes toward a "behavioral ecology." *Man–Environment Studies, 2*(1), 37–59.

Tilman, R. (1984). *C. Wright Mills: A native radical and his American intellectual roots.* University Park: Pennsylvania State University Press.

Tilman, R. (2004). *Thorstein Veblen, John Dewey, C. Wright Mills and the generic ends of life.* Lanham, MD: Rowman and Littlefield.

Toates, F. (2000). The embodied self: A biological perspective. In R. Stevens (Ed.), *Understanding the self* (pp. 37–88). London: Sage.

Tolman, R. M., & Molidor, C. E. (1994). A decade of social group work research: Trends in methodology, theory, and program development. *Research on Social Work Practice, 4*(2), 142–159.

Tolson, E. R., Reid, W. J., & Garvin, C. D. (1994). *Generalist practice: A task-centered approach.* New York: Columbia University Press.

Tomey, A. M. (1998). Introduction to analysis of nursing theories. In A. M. Tomey & M. R. Alligood (Eds.), *Nursing theorists and their work* (4th ed., pp. 3–15). St. Louis, MO: Mosby.

Tomison, A. M., & Wise, S. (1999). Community-based approaches in preventing child maltreatment. *Issues in Child Abuse Prevention, 11.* Retrieved June 28, 2005, from http://www.aifs.gov.au/nch/issues11.html

Toulmin, S. (1953). *The philosophy of science: An introduction.* New York: Harper & Row.

Townsend, C. R., Harper, J. L., & Begon, M. (2000). *Essentials of ecology.* Malden, MA: Blackwell Science.

Tracy, E. M., & Whittaker, J. K. (1993). The social network map: Assessing social support in clinical practice. In J. B. Rauch (Ed.), *Assessment: A sourcebook for social work practice* (pp. 295–308). Milwaukee, WI: Families International.

Treesong. (2004). Social ecology. Retrieved August 1, 2004, from http://treesong.org/philosophy

Tucker, D. J., Garvin, C., & Sarri, R. (1997). Introduction: Evolution and change in the relationship between social work and social science. In D. J. Tucker, C. Garvin, & R. Sarri (Eds.), *Integrating knowledge and practice: The case of social work and social science* (pp. 1–20). Westport, CT: Praeger.

Turner, C. H. (1981). *Maps of the mind.* London: Mitchell Beazley.

Turner, F. J. (1983). Directions for social work education: The challenge of developing a comprehensive, coherent and flexible integrating network of theories. In L. S. Bandler (Ed.), *Education for clinical social work practice* (pp. 125–141). Oxford, UK: Pergamon Press.

Turner, F. J. (1996a). An interlocking perspective for treatment. In F. J. Turner (Ed.), *Social work treatment: Interlocking theoretical approaches* (4th ed., pp. 699–711). New York: Free Press.

Turner, F. J. (Ed.). (1996b). *Social work treatment: Interlocking theo-*

retical approaches (4th ed.). New York: Free Press.

Turner, F. J. (1999). Theories of practice with vulnerable populations. In D. E. Biegel & A. Blum (Eds.), *Innovations in practice and service delivery across the lifespan* (pp. 13–31). New York: Oxford University Press.

Turner, J. (2000). Herbert Spencer. In G. Ritzer (Ed.), *The Blackwell companion to major social theorists* (pp. 81–103). Malden, MA: Blackwell.

Turner, J. H. (1986). Analytical theorizing. In A. Giddens & J. H. Turner (Eds.), *Social theory today* (pp. 156–193). Padstow, UK: Polity Press.

Turner, J. H. (1998). *The structure of sociological theory* (6th ed.). Belmont, CA: Wadsworth.

Turner, J. H. (2002). *Face to face: Toward a sociological theory of interpersonal behavior.* Stanford, CA: Stanford University Press.

Turner, R. (1991). The use and misuse of rational models in collective behavior and social psychology. *Archives Européennes de sociologie, 32,* 84–108.

Turner, R. H. (1978). The role and the person. *American Journal of Sociology, 84*(1), 1–23.

Turner, S. P. (1980). *Sociological explanation as translation.* Cambridge, UK: Cambridge University Press.

Turner, S. P. (2004). The maturity of social theory. In C. Camic & H. Joas (Eds.), *The dialogic turn: New roles for sociology in the postdisciplinary age* (pp. 141–170). Lanham, MD: Rowman and Littlefield.

Udry, J. R. (1995). Sociology and biology: What biology do sociologists need to know? *Social Forces, 73*(4), 1267–1278. UK: Oxford University Press.

Ungar, M. (2002). A deeper, more social ecological social work practice. *Social Service Review, 76*(3), 480–497.

Vaillant, G. E., & Milofsky, E. (1980). Natural history of male psychological health: IX. Empirical evidence for Erikson's model of the life cycle. *American Journal of Psychiatry, 137*(11), 1348–1359.

van de Vliert, E., & Allen, V. L. (1984). Managing transitional strain: Strategies and intervention techniques. In V. L. Allen & E. van de Vliert (Eds.), *Role transitions as social drama* (pp. 345–355). New York: Plenum Press.

Vargas, J. S. (2005). Brief biography of B. F. Skinner. Retrieved August 7, 2005, from http://www.bfskinner.org/bio.asp

Verhoeven, J. C. (1993). An interview with Erving Goffman, 1980. *Research on Language and Social Interaction, 26*(3), 317–348.

Vinokur-Kaplan, D. (1997). Integrating work team effectiveness with social work practice: An ecological approach. In D. J. Tucker, C. Garvin, & R. Sarri (Eds.), *Integrating knowledge and practice: The case of social work and social science* (pp. 196–208). Westport, CT: Praeger.

Visano, L. (1988). Generic and generative dimensions of interactionism: Towards the unfolding of critical directions. *International Journal of Comparative Sociology, 29*(3–4), 230–244.

Wagner, A. (1997). Social work and the global economy: Opportunities and challenges. In M. C. Hokenstad & J. Midgley (Eds.), *Issues in international social work: Global challenges for a new century* (pp. 45–56). Washington, DC: NASW Press.

Wagner-Pacific, R., & Bershady, H. (1993). Portents or confessions: Authoritative readings of a dream text. *Symbolic Interaction, 16*(2), 129–143.

Wakefield, J. C. (1996). Does social work need the eco-systems perspective? Part 1. Is the perspective clinically useful? *Social Service Review, 70*(1), 1–32.

Walder, E. H. (1993). Supervision and instruction in postgraduate psychotherapy. In G. Stricker & J. K. Gold (Eds.), *Comprehensive handbook of psychotherapy integration* (pp. 499–512). New York: Plenum Press.

Walker, P. (1995). Community based is not community: The social geography of disability. In S. J. Taylor, R. Bogdan, & Z. M. Lutfiyya (Eds.), *The variety of community experience: Qualitative studies of family* and community life (pp. 175–192). Baltimore: Paul H. Brookes.

Walrond-Skinner, S. (1976). *Family therapy: The treatment of natural systems*. London: Routledge and Kegan Paul.

Walster, E., Walster, G. W., & Berscheid, E. (1978). *Equity: Theory and research*. Boston: Allyn & Bacon.

Watson, J. B. (1970). *Behaviorism*. New York: Norton. (Original work published 1924)

Watson, W. (1985). *The architectonics of meaning: Foundations of the new pluralism*. Albany: State University of New York Press.

Weerasekera, P. (1996). *Multiperspective case formulation: A step towards treatment integration*. Malabar, FL: Krieger.

Weigert, A. J. (1995). A sociological imagination informing social psychologies. *Humanity and Society, 19*(2), 3–24.

Weigert, A. J. (1997). *Self, interaction, and natural environment*. Albany: State University of New York Press.

Weigert, A. J., & Gecas, V. (1995). Multiplicity and dialogue in social psychology: An essay in metatheorizing. *Journal for the Theory of Social Behaviour, 25*(2), 141–174.

Weinberger, J. (1993). Common factors in psychotherapy. In G. Stricker & J. K. Gold (Eds.), *Comprehensive handbook of psychotherapy integration* (pp. 43–56). New York: Plenum Press.

Weinstein, F., & Platt, G. M. (1973). *Psychoanalytic sociology: An essay on the interpretation of historical data and the phenomena of collective behavior*. Baltimore: Johns Hopkins University Press.

Wells, L. E., & Stryker, S. (1992). Stability and change in self over the life course. In D. L. Featherman, R. M. Lerner, & M. Perlumutter (Eds.), *Life span development and behavior* (pp. 191–229). New York: Academic Press.

Wentworth, W. M., & Yardley, D. (1994). Deep sociality: A bioevolutionary perspective on the sociology of emotions. In W. M. Wentworth & J. Ryan (Eds.), *Social perspectives on emotion*

(Vol. 2, pp. 21–55). Greenwich, CT: JAI Press.

Werner, H. (1965). *A rational approach to social casework*. New York: Association Press.

West, C. (1996). Goffman in feminist perspective. *Sociological Perspectives, 39*(3), 353–369.

West, C., & Fenstermaker, S. (1993). Power, inequality, and the accomplishment of gender: An ethnomethodological view. In P. England (Ed.), *Theory on gender / Feminism on theory* (pp. 151–174). New York: Aldine de Gruyter.

West, C., & Fenstermaker, S. (1995). Doing difference. *Gender and Society, 9*(1), 8–37.

West, C., & Zimmerman, D. H. (1987). Doing gender. *Gender and Society, 1*, 125–151.

White, J. M. (2005). *Advanced family theories*. Thousand Oaks, CA: Sage.

White, J. M. (2005). *Advanced family theories*. Thousand Oaks, CA: Sage.

White, M., & Epston, D. (1990). *Narrative means to therapeutic ends*. New York: Norton.

Wicker, A. W. (2002). Ecological psychology: Historical contexts, current conception, prospective directions. In R. B. Bechtel & A. Churchman (Eds.), *Handbook of environmental psychology* (pp. 114–126). New York: Wiley.

Wicklund, R. A. (1999). Multiple perspectives in person perception and theorizing. *Theory and Psychology, 9*(5), 667–678.

Wickman, S. M., Daniels, H., White, L. J., & Fesmire, S. (1999). A "primer" in conceptual metaphor for counselors. *Journal of Counseling and Development, 77*, 389–394.

Wiley, N. (1994). *The semiotic self*. Chicago: University of Chicago Press.

Wierzbicka, A. (1997). *Understanding cultures through their key words: English, Russian, Polish, German, and Japanese*. New York: Oxford University Press.

Wiley, N. (1994). *The semiotic self*. Chicago: University of Chicago Press.

Wilson, W. J. (1995). Jobless ghettos and the social outcomes of

youngsters. In P. Moen, G. H. Elder Jr., & K. Luscher (Eds.), *Examining lives in context: Perspectives on the ecology of human development* (pp. 527–543). Washington, DC: American Psychological Association.

Wolfe, A. (1993). *The human difference: Animals, computers, and the necessity of social science*. Berkeley: University of California Press.

Wood, J. T. (1994). Engendered identities: Shaping voice and mind through gender. In D. R. Vocate (Ed.), *Intrapersonal communication: Different voices, different minds* (pp. 145–167). Hillsdale, NJ: Erlbaum.

Woods, M. E. (2000). Tribute to Florence Hollis: January 30, 1907–July 3, 1987. In M. E. Woods & F. Hollis, *Casework: A psychosocial therapy* (5th ed., pp. xxv–xxviii). Boston: McGraw-Hill.

Woods, M. E., & Hollis, F. (2000). *Casework: A psychosocial therapy* (5th ed.). Boston: McGraw-Hill.

World Book. (1999). Hopkins, Harry Lloyd. *World Book Multimedia Encyclopedia*. Chicago: World Book.

World Book. (2001). Freud, Sigmund. *World Book Multimedia Encyclopedia*. Chicago: World Book.

Yoels, W. C., & Karp, D. A. (1978). A social psychological critique of "oversocialization": Dennis Wrong revisited. *Sociological Symposium, 24*, 27–39.

Young, G. L. (1998). Holism: Writ and riposte in ecology and human ecology. In L. Freese (Ed.), *Advances in human ecology* (Vol. 7, pp. 313–366). Greenwich, CT: JAI Press.

Young, I. M. (1997). Difference as a resource for democratic communication. In J. Bohman & W. Rehg (Eds.), *Deliberative democracy: Essays on reason and politics* (pp. 383–406). Cambridge, MA: MIT Press.

Zelizer, V. A. (1999). Multiple markets, multiple cultures. In N. J. Smelser & J. C. Alexander (Eds.), *Diversity and its discontents: Cultural conflict and common ground in contemporary society* (pp. 193–212). Princeton, NJ: Princeton University Press.

Zeruvabel, E. (1999). *Social mindscapes: An invitation to cognitive sociology.* Cambridge, MA: Harvard University Press.

Zhao, S. (2001). Metatheorizing in sociology. In G. Ritzer & B. Smart (Eds.), *Handbook of social theory* (pp. 386–394). London: Sage.

Zlotnik, J. L., McCroskey, J., Gardner, S., Gil de Gibaja, M., Taylor, H. P., George, J., et al. (1999). *Myths and opportunities: An examination of the impact of discipline-specific accreditation on interprofessional education.* Alexandria, VA: Council on Social Work Education.

Name Index

SUBJECT INDEX